D1752601

THAILAND AND WORLD WAR II

DIREK JAYANAMA

Revised English Edition

Edited by

JANE KEYES

Sathirakoses-Nagapradipa Foundation

SILKWORM BOOKS

This book is respectfully dedicated
to my father and mother
Phraya and Khunying Uphaiphiphaksa
(Kluean and Chan Jayanama),
my first and most benevolent teachers.

This publication was made possible by a grant from
The James H. W. Thompson Foundation.

Original Thai text © 1967 by Direk Jayanama
English text © 2008 by Jane Keyes

All rights reserved. No part of this publication may be reproduced,
stored in a retrieval system, or transmitted, in any form or by any means,
electronic, mechanical, photocopying, recording or otherwise,
without the prior permission in writing of the publisher.

ISBN 978-974-9511-33-6

This edition is published in 2008 by
Silkworm Books
6 Sukkasem Road, T. Suthep, Chiang Mai 50200, Thailand
E-mail: info@silkwormbooks.com
http://www.silkwormbooks.com

The three photographs (figs. 3, 4, and 5) were kindly contributed by Mrs. Nilrat Jayanama.
Set in 11 pt. Adobe Janson Pro by Silk Type

Printed in Thailand by O.S. Printing House, Bangkok

6 5 4 3 2 1

CONTENTS

List of photographs vii
Acknowledgments ix
Preface to the first Thai edition xi
Preface to the second Thai edition xiv
Editor's introduction to the first English edition xv
Editor's introduction to the revised English edition xviii
Biography of the author xxi

Part I: From the Beginning of the War in Europe to the Beginning of the War in Asia

Chronology of World War II: 1 September 1939 to 8 December 1941   2
1   Background 3
2   Non-aggression pacts between Thailand and France, England and Japan, 1940 7
3   Border dispute and Peace Agreement between Thailand and French Indochina 23
4   Thailand in the midst of economic warfare 49
5   Japan declares war 61

Part II: During the War

Chronology of World War II: 7 December 1941 to 2 September 1945   82
6   To Japan 85
7   In Japan, from January 1942 to September 1943 89
8   Return to the Ministry of Foreign Affairs in Bangkok 117
9   Final year of the war and involvement in the Free Thai movement   123

Additional facts on the situation in Thailand during World War II
    Thawi Bunyaket 133
Temporary soldier
    Puey Ungphakorn 157

Activities in Kandy, New Delhi and the United States during and after the war: A brief report
Phra Phisansukhumwit (Prasop Sukhum) 183

Part III: After the War: Between August 1945 and June 1948

10 Negotiations between Thailand and Britain, and Exchange Agreement between Thailand and Australia 205
11 Relations between Thailand and China 227
12 Thailand's financial situation 237
13 Foreign affairs 253
14 Negotiations with France 265
15 Cancellation of the Heads of Agreement with England [and treaty terminating the state of war with Australia] 291
16 Thailand's application for membership in the United Nations ... 299
17 Negotiations with England regarding the Formal Agreement ... 315

Appendixes

List of appendixes 343
Editor's note regarding the appendixes 344

1 Pacte de Non-Agression entre la République Française et la Thaïlande 345
2 Treaty of Non-Aggression between Great Britain and Northern Ireland and Thailand 351
3 Treaty between Thailand and Japan concerning the continuance of friendly relations between the two countries and the mutual respect of each other's territorial integrity 354
4 Convention de Paix entre la France et la Thaïlande 356
5 Formal Agreement for the termination of the state of war between Siam and Great Britain and India, and exchange of notes between the Siamese government and Australia with a view to terminating the state of war 373
6 Communiqué, Heads of Agreement and Annex [attached to the Formal Agreement] 387
7 Treaty of Amity between the Kingdom of Siam and the Republic of China 395
8 Final Peace Agreement between the Government of Siam and the Government of Australia 400
9 Agreement to end the conflict between Siam and France ... 411
10 Rapport de la Commission de Conciliation Franco-Siamoise ... 426

11 Report of findings and opinion of the Committee to Investigate the Expenditures out of National Revenue by the Free Thai movement both within and outside the kingdom 506

Notes 515
Index 553

Fig. 1. H.M. King Ananda Mahidol receiving the salute from the Allied forces, with Lord Louis Mountbatten by his side.

LIST OF PHOTOGRAPHS

1	H.M. King Ananda Mahidol receiving the salute from the Allied Armed forces, Lord Louis Mountbatten by his side.	vi
2	The author.	xx
3	Nai Direk Jayanama, when he was Ambassador to Japan, 1942.	xxii
4	Nai Direk with his wife, M.L. Pui, when he was Ambassador to Germany, 1962.	xxii
5	Nai Direk and M.L. Pui Jayanama, with their four sons at home, taken shortly before Nai Direk's death in 1967.	xxii
6	The Council of Ministers of Colonel Luang Phibun Songkhram, December 1938.	4
7	The Council of Ministers of Major-General Luang Phibun Songkhram, 1939.	4
8	The signing of the Non-Aggression Pact between Thailand and France at Suan Kulap Palace on 12 June 1940.	20
9	The signing of the Non-Aggression Pact between Thailand and Great Britain at Suan Kulap Palace on 12 June 1940.	20
10	The Royal Thai Embassy staff, Tokyo, 1942.	90
11	A special group of diplomats led by Phraya Phahonphonphayuhasena and the Thai Ambassador meeting with the Prime Minister of Japan at the Prime Minister's office in Tokyo to celebrate the conclusion of the alliance between Thailand and Japan.	92
12	The signing of the Cultural Pact between Mr. Tani, the Japanese Minister of Foreign Affairs, and Nai Direk Jayanama, the Thai Ambassador, on 20 October 1942, in Tokyo.	103
13	A group of British military officers visiting the author's house at Soi Santisuk, Sukhumwit Road, on 30 August 1945, following the declaration of peace.	124
14	General Nakamura and his wife visiting the author and his wife in 1954.	132
15	Nai Pridi Banomyong ("Ruth"), the leader of the Free Thai in the country.	146

16 A lunch given in honor of Admiral Lord Louis Mountbatten at the Prime Minister's office. 151
17 A group of American officers visiting the author at his house in Soi Santisuk, Sukhumwit Road, on 30 August 1945, following the declaration of peace. 153
18 Members of the Royal Thai Embassy and their wives, London, July 1947. 316
19 A dinner given at the Savoy Hotel by the British government in honor of the author before he left England. 338

ACKNOWLEDGMENTS

Soon after the first Thai edition of *Thailand and World War II* by Direk Jayanama was published in 1966, the author told me that he would love to see it translated into English. I then contacted my very good friend, Jane Keyes, who was willing to prepare and edit an English language edition *gratis*. Although unfortunately the author passed away in 1967, work on the English language edition continued during the editor's subsequent visits to Thailand. In 1976 she became very ill, but Mme. Pui Jayanama, the author's widow, and her family, the author's former colleagues and students, and his admirers were grateful to the editor for the work she had already done, even though it remained in unfinished form due to her health, and the first English language edition appeared in 1978. I was also instrumental in having an abridged German edition of this book published by Erdman Verlag in the Federal Republic of Germany and Switzerland.

Jane Keyes had told me she would appreciate an opportunity to revise and complete the English version if a new edition was brought out. Bearing in mind that Khun Direk's centenary would be in 2005, I contacted Khun Jane and asked her to undertake this, which she kindly agreed to do—again gratis. When the manuscript was ready I asked the Faculty of Political Science, Thammasat University, to be the publisher since the author had been its first dean. The present dean accepted the manuscript and did nothing until the centenary was over. The dean then informed me that neither the faculty nor the university had any budget to undertake the publishing of the new English edition.

In fact, this was the same faculty that submitted Khun Direk's name to UNESCO via the Ministry of Education so that on his centenary he would be recognized internationally as an exemplar in the field of education, culture, and science. Yet the nomination did not quite fit UNESCO's criteria, and it asked the Thai government to resubmit his name within three months. But the Thai government failed to do so, which is understandable since Khun Direk's caliber and virtues plus his moral courage and gentleness in refusing to serve dictatorial regimes since 1947 are difficult to grasp by those in power at the governmental as well as the university levels.

As for the English version of *Thailand and World War II*, I had no alternative but to ask for the return of the manuscript. As the Sathirakoses-Nagapradipa Foundation and the Foundation for Children had in the past collaborated in producing books in honor of worthy Thai scholars like Bhikkhu Buddhadasa (*Radical Conservatism: Buddhism in the Contemporary World*, 1990), Bhikkhu Payutto (*Socially Engaged Buddhism for the New Millennium*, 1999) and Dr. Puey Ungphakorn (*Santi Pracha Dhamma*, 2001), our two foundations therefore pooled our financial resources to publish the new English edition. However, the translator suggested that I contact Khun Trasvin Jittidecharak of Silkworm Books, who would be able to do a better job producing a scholarly publication and distributing it internationally. I am so glad that Khun Trasvin agreed to publish this new edition of *Thailand and World War II* and that Khun Nilrat Jayanama, holder of the translation rights of the book, kindly gave her permission for the new publication. She has also authorized a new Thai edition of *Thailand and World War II*, which has recently been published.

On behalf of our two foundations I wish to thank everyone, especially the editor and the publisher, as well as the in-house editor, Susan Offner, all of whom deserve the gratitude of those who want to learn from *Thailand and World War II*.

> Sulak Sivaraksa,
> on behalf of the
> Sathirakoses-Nagapradipa Foundation
> and Foundation for Children
> 18 January 2007

PREFACE TO THE FIRST THAI EDITION

During the Second World War which broke out twenty-seven years ago Thailand was forced by circumstances to commit itself [i.e. to ally itself with one side during the conflict, thereby departing from its traditional policy of neutrality]. The events which drew our country into that war may be of interest to readers, if not for any specific reason then simply for the sake of information. I feel that while I still have the energy and the gift of memory I should, before being overtaken by old age, set down the facts of these events for the benefit of my fellow-citizens, particularly as many events tend to be forgotten with time. I believe that the young people of today who were either very young or as yet unborn at the time these events took place should be given a chance to learn about them to some extent, for they too will one day have an opportunity to serve their country to the best of their abilities. Even fellow-citizens of my own generation may benefit somewhat from this book, for the lessons of the past should be learned for the sake of the future.

I happened to be involved to a certain extent with our foreign policy, not only during the pre-war period, but also during the war itself and after the war came to an end. During this time I kept a record of events, sometimes jotting down notes about them in my diary. This now helps me greatly as an aide-mémoire. As well as drawing on recollections of my own personal experiences, I have also used information gathered from a number of different people or acquired from a great variety of documents, both Thai and foreign. The United States government published the documents and letters sent between its State Department and American diplomatic representatives abroad, and its account of the United States' intricate diplomatic relations with Siam runs to almost four hundred pages. Others have also written about [Thailand's role in] the Second World War [and immediate post-war period]. They include Sir Josiah Crosby, British Minister to Bangkok from 1934 up till the time the Japanese invaded Thailand; Admiral Jean Decoux, French Governor-General of Indochina during the period of the French conflict with Thailand; Mr. [Mamoru] Shigemitsu, former Minister of Foreign Affairs for Japan; Mr. Cordell Hull, former United States Secretary of State; and Mr. Anthony Eden (now Lord Avon), the British Foreign

Minister during the war. All have written in detail of their war experiences, while British and American ambassadors sent to Thailand soon after the war have also written accounts of their respective countries' relations with Thailand.

As I was connected somewhat with the events described in this book, it is inevitable that you will find myself mentioned throughout, a point which I hope the reader will be good enough to bear with. Throughout the book I have adhered strictly to the principle of describing only those events which I had first-hand knowledge of or evidence about. Incidents about which I had no direct knowledge or with which I was not personally involved have not been mentioned. There may be a few minor inaccuracies here and there, but this is unavoidable. I would, however, like to make it clear here that I have no intention of disparaging any nation or person what or whomsoever.

The book is divided into three parts. The first covers the period from the outbreak of war in Europe to the beginning of the war in Asia. The second part deals with events during the war in Asia and goes up to the end of the Second World War, while the third part covers the [immediate] post-war situation.

One event which delighted us Thai greatly was the gracious return of King Ananda Mahidol (King Rama VIII) to Bangkok once the war ended. Allied forces had already entered Thailand by this time. Recognizing that he was the leader of our nation, and the symbol of Thailand's sovereignty and unity of its people, they expressed a wish to give a parade for his inspection. This is worthy of note, as certain of the Allied nations had taken up our declaration of war against them and numbered us among the enemy. During this parade, Admiral Lord Louis Mountbatten, Supreme Commander of the Allied forces in Southeast Asia, stood by His Majesty's side.

I should like to record my gratitude here to my many colleagues who helped me both while I was in the government and while I was temporarily in retirement during the war. All of them contributed to the service of the nation. Although I cannot mention all of them by name, there is one person to whom I should like to express my special appreciation. This is H.R.H. Prince Narathip-phongpraphan, now Deputy Prime Minister. Throughout the time I worked with him, he was most kind to me, generously giving me his advice on the many occasions on which I sought it. He is widely recognized as having been of great service to his nation.

I should also like to express my deep gratitude to three others who helped make this book more complete by supplying me with certain information which I did not have access to. They are Nai Thawi Bunyaket, formerly Prime Minister and my close friend; Dr. Puey Ungphakorn, Chairman of the Bank of Thailand and Dean of the Faculty of Economics at Thammasat University, and Phra Phisansukhumwit (Prasop Sukhum), formerly Director-General of the Highway Department, Advisor to the Office of the Prime Minister and Under-Secretary of State for the Ministry of Industry. These last two men are acquaintances of mine and men whom I have long respected. Nai Thawi Bunyaket filled an important role during the war by helping the Allies from within Thailand, while Dr. Puey Ungphakorn helped get a message from Admiral Lord Louis Mountbatten, [then the] Supreme Allied Commander of South-East Asia Command, to the Thai Regent. He later acted as an important liaison officer between our country and the Allies during his [subsequent] stay in England. Phra Phisansukhumwit also played an important role by slipping out of the country and contacting the Allies in the United States, where he stayed for eight months. I asked these three men to describe their different experiences, which they did willingly. I would also like to thank them for having been so kind as to have reviewed the draft of this book before it was sent to the printers. I should stress, however, that any shortcomings in this book are my sole responsibility.

I am also indebted to Nai Sala Sivaraksa, Second Secretary at the Royal Thai Embassy in Bonn, who helped make photocopies of the draft of this book; to Nai Thongtoem Komonsuk (L.L.B.), Third Secretary at the Ministry of Foreign Affairs, who tirelessly typed this entire book from my handwriting; to Nai Sulak Sivaraksa, Barrister-at-Law from England and B.A. (University of Wales), who helped proof-read and research the references mentioned at the end of the book; to the Phrae Phitthaya Press and Nai Chit Phraephanit for having been most helpful and for having assigned Nai Yot Watcharasathian to carry out detailed supervision of the publication of this work; and last but not least to Nai Sanit Charoenrat, a former Member of Parliament and a man who has long been my close friend. He helped me tirelessly throughout, acting on my behalf in regard to the publishing of this book. I will always recall the kindness of all these people with deep gratitude.

Throughout my government career and the preparation of this book, my wife has given me constant encouragement. I shall always remember this with gratitude and with deep affection.

If this book serves in any way to encourage my fellow citizens in their various duties so that our beloved country and way of life flourishes forever, then I shall be more than pleased.

                                        Direk Jayanama
                                        7 October 1966
                                        25 Soi Santisuk
                                        Sukhumwit Road
                                        Bangkok

PREFACE TO THE SECOND THAI EDITION

Phrae Phitthaya press has told me that it wishes to reprint *Thailand and World War II*, as the first edition has been sold out. I am happy to grant permission for a second printing, and have taken the opportunity to make a few minor revisions to the book. However, no major alterations have been made to it.

I am very glad that this book has been widely accepted. High-ranking persons both within and outside the government, as well as teachers, students and people in news and other communication media have shown great interest in the work. I would like to thank them most sincerely for their interest.

Again, I should like to emphasize that my main object in writing this book is educational. In order to make sure that it can be used as a reference work, I have described only incidents of which I had first hand experience. I am convinced that when, and only when, a number of such works are in print will future historians be able to detail and analyze all the events described in this book correctly.

Direk Jayanama
15 February 1967
25 Soi Santisuk
Sukhumwit Road

EDITOR'S INTRODUCTION TO THE FIRST ENGLISH EDITION

Some while back I was asked by Mr. Sulak Sivaraksa, the well-known Thai writer and publisher, if I would be willing to edit an English edition of *Thailand and World War II* by the late Professor Direk Jayanama. Professor Direk, a leading figure in Thai foreign affairs for many years, first joined the foreign service in 1933. Between 1938 and 1941 he became first Deputy and then Foreign Minister of Thailand. In 1942 he was sent as Thai Ambassador to Tokyo, and after his return to Thailand at the end of 1943 served once again as Foreign Minister until August 1944, when he retired from public life in order to devote his energies to the Free Thai resistance movement. During the post-war years Professor Direk served successively as Thailand's Finance Minister, Foreign Minister, Deputy Prime Minister, Ambassador to England and later Ambassador to West Germany and to Finland. He also became a law lecturer and later Dean of the Faculty of Political Science at Thammasat University, where he was well known for his writings on public affairs.

Professor Direk died in 1967. Although I never had an opportunity to meet him, nor, therefore, to consult him on the questions that arose during the course of editing the English-language edition of his memoirs, I was fortunate in having the help of his widow, Khunying Pui, together with that of one of his sons, Mr. Voraphuthi Jayanama, himself a member of the Thai foreign service. Both showed me great kindness, and gave me access to documents and materials in Professor Direk's personal library. I would also like to thank Mr. Sulak Sivaraksa for the help he has given me in checking and verifying various points in the text.

When I first received the memoirs they had already been roughly translated into English by a number of different people. I worked from these various unfinished translations, checking them against the original Thai and rendering them into correct English. I also added editor's footnotes to explain any material that might be unclear to readers unfamiliar with Thai history or politics.

It has been my aim to keep as closely as possible to the original text. However, there are some differences between the Thai original and the English edition of the book presented here. The Jayanama family specifically asked that an effort be made to reduce the length of the book in the English edition. Passages that were felt to be repetitious, together with background material on world history that the editor regarded as widely known to Western readers, have therefore been omitted. The longest single omission consists of part 2, chapter 2, which has been omitted in its entirety. This dealt with political conditions in pre-war Japan, and was considered by the editor to be tangential to the main themes of the book. Whenever alterations have been made to the original text either by removing material or by inserting editorial comments, this is shown in square brackets so as to immediately distinguish these changes from the basic text.

A few other points remain to be mentioned. The first concerns the use of the terms "Siam" and "Thailand." During the period covered by these memoirs the country was known first as Siam, and then, during World War II, as Thailand. After the war the name was changed back to Siam, and it was not until Field Marshal Pibul Songkhram returned to power in 1949 that the country became known as Thailand again. It was felt that using the terms interchangeably according to the period under discussion would be confusing. Moreover Professor Direk himself was said to have preferred the use of the term "Siam." To avoid confusion and in deference to his wishes and those of his family, I have therefore elected to use the terms "Siam" and "Siamese." The only exceptions are to be found in official documents, where the editor has adopted whatever form is given in the original texts, and in the use of "Free Thai" rather than "Free Siamese movement," since the former is the way the resistance organization is usually referred to in English-language publications.

In regard to the system followed for transliterating Thai personal and place names, the system of transcription devised by the Royal Thai Institute has been employed except in cases where there is a well-established and preferred alternative rendering of the name in English. Such cases include the name of the author himself. Other names that have not been rendered in accordance with the Royal Institute system include: Chakri dynasty, King Chulalongkorn, King Ananda Mahidol, King Bhumibol Adulyadej, Queen Rambhai Barni, Prince Chula Chakrabongse, Prince Damrong Rajanubhab, M.C. Subha Svasti, Field Marshal Pibul Songkhram, Mr. Thanat Khoman, Dr. Puey Ungphakorn, Mr. Sulak Sivaraksa, Mr. Sala Sivaraksa and Ms. Amara Bhumiratana.

Finally, I should like to thank the Jayanama family for having entrusted me with preparing the English edition of Professor Direk's memoirs. As I worked on them, I came to share the deep admiration in which Professor Direk is held by his fellow-countrymen. He was respected not only for his integrity, but as a man who gave himself whole-heartedly to the service of his country. I can only hope that had he still been living, he would have been content with the English edition of his memoirs.

But for my husband, Charles F. Keyes, I would not have been able to undertake this project. I would like to thank him here for the kindness, help and encouragement he has given me in the preparation of this text.

Jane Keyes

EDITOR'S INTRODUCTION TO THE REVISED ENGLISH EDITION

In 1976, while I was working on an English edition of Professor Direk Jayanama's *Thailand and World War II*, I became very ill and was given only a few months to live. Although my manuscript was then only in the draft stage, as an act of kindness in view of my health it was nonetheless rushed to the publishers and appeared in print in 1978.

After I recovered some months later, I regretted that the manuscript had appeared in an unfinished form; by then, however, it had already gone to press. When, therefore, I was approached by Mr. Sulak Sivaraksa, the well-known writer and public figure, and asked if I would be interested in preparing a revised English edition of Professor Direk's book for what would be the 100th year celebration of his birth, I jumped at the opportunity.

As in the 1978 version, in keeping with the Jayanama family's wishes that the book be reduced in length in the English edition, certain passages that appear in the Thai text have been omitted here. They include sections that are either repetitious, lend themselves to being condensed without any loss of information, (as, for example, with lengthy speeches), or that bear only tangentially on the main themes of the book. As with the first English edition, the single largest omission in the revised edition is that of part 2, chapter 2, dealing with political conditions in pre-war Japan. Wherever omissions or changes of any kind have been made or comments added by the editor, these appear in square brackets so that the reader can immediately distinguish these changes from the author's own words.

One change that has been made in the revised English edition concerns the use of "Thailand" and "Thai" for "Siam" and "Siamese." Although the Jayanama family had originally expressed a preference for the latter, over the years "Siam" and "Siamese" have increasingly come to be associated with historical materials while "Thailand" and "Thai" have become the standard ways in which to refer to the country and its people today. Moreover, although there was a brief reversion to using the term "Siam" after World War II, for much of the period covered by Professor Direk's memoirs (December 1938 to July 1948) the term "Thailand" was in use as the official English-language name for the country. I have, therefore, used "Thailand" everywhere except in historical passages in which the term "Siam" was commonly employed by Westerners, or in treaties with Britain or with other countries that followed British usage, since the British continued to use the term "Siam" until the late 1940s.

As in the first English edition, the Royal Institute system of transliteration has been employed except in those cases where there is a well-established standard alternative rendering of the name in English. Such cases include the name of the author himself, as well as the names of several members of the Royal family and others whose names are commonly transliterated into English using Sanskritized forms. In addition to the names shown in the Editor's Introduction to the First English Edition the following names are exceptions in the revised edition: King Prajadhipok, Prince Devawongse Varoprakarn, Prince Chumbhot Boriphat, Prince Phisadet Ratchani, M.C. Subha Svasti, Seni Pramoj, and the Banomyong, Bunnag, and Svasti family names, while "Pibul Songkhram" is rendered as "Phibun Songkhram." Also, although "Nai" ("Mr.") as a term of address has been retained here, in keeping with the Thai original, the term is more formal than would be commonly used today.

As I worked for a second time on Professor Direk's memoirs, I came to share again the deep admiration and respect in which he is held by his fellow-countrymen, as a man who gave himself whole-heartedly to the service of his country. *Thailand and World War II* not only provides us with a unique firsthand account of politics during a turbulent period in Thai history; it adds greatly to our understanding of the relations between Thailand and Japan during the war. I can only hope that this revised English-language edition of Professor Direk's memoirs brings them to the attention of English readers to the extent they deserve.

Lastly, in 2006 as in 1978, but for my husband, Charles F. Keyes, I would not have been able to undertake this work. Again I would like to thank him for the support he has given me in the preparation of this text.

Jane Keyes

Fig. 2. The author.

BIOGRAPHY OF THE AUTHOR

Professor Direk Jayanama was born on 18 January 1905 in Phitsanulok, north central Thailand, to Phraya and Khunying Uphaiphiphaksa (Kluean and Chan Jayanama). At the time of Professor Direk's birth, his father was in the judicial branch of the government civil service, later rising to become a leading judge of the Supreme Court.

Professor Direk was not the only one of his brothers and sisters to later attain prominent positions in public life. His younger brother, Phairot Jayanama, later became Deputy Secretary for Foreign Affairs. Another younger brother, Narandon Jayanama, became the Governor of Chiang Mai province. Yet another, Usa Jayanama, became Air Force General Staff College Commandant Air Vice-Marshal. His brother Ophat Jayanama rose to the position of Second Secretary in the Foreign Ministry, while one of his sisters married a prominent official in the Ministry of Interior.

In 1914 Professor Direk entered secondary school (which at that time began with the fifth grade) at Assumption College in Bangkok. There he specialized in the study of English. In 1921 he entered King's College, where he stayed for two years. In 1925 he entered the Law School of the Ministry of Justice, and was called to the Bar in 1928. Professor Direk's knowledge of English was so good that in 1924, when he was only nineteen years of age and little more than a junior college graduate, he was hired by the Justice Ministry as a legal interpreter. He kept this job during his first year in law school, and served as interpreter to the Professor of Law at the Ministry of Justice Law School from 1926–32.

The year 1932 was an important one in Professor Direk's career. In that year, at the age of twenty-seven, he was not only appointed head of the Legal Division of the Foreign Ministry but became a civilian member of the Promoters, a group of men which in 1932 staged a coup that transformed Thailand from an absolute to a constitutional monarchy. It was during this year that Professor Direk also became an M.P. for the first time, serving the Bangkok fifth district—a position he continued to hold until after the end of World War II.

Following a brief period as Secretary to the Minister of Foreign Affairs from 1933–34, Professor Direk became Assistant to the Secretary of the Council of

Fig. 3. Nai Direk Jayanama, when he was Ambassador to Japan, 1942.

Fig. 4. Nai Direk with his wife, M.L. Pui, when he was Ambassador to Germany, 1962.

Fig. 5. Nai Direk and M.L. Pui Jayanama, with their four sons at home, taken shortly before Nai Direk's death in 1967.

Ministers in 1935. A year later he was moved up to become Secretary to the Council, and continuing until 1940 to hold this appointment concurrently with his subsequent appointments as Acting Director-General of Public Relations (1938) and Acting Secretary of the Legislative Reduction Department.

In December 1938, the date at which this book opens, Professor Direk received his first Cabinet appointment as a Minister without portfolio in the Finance Ministry, moving to a similar appointment in the Ministry of Foreign Affairs shortly thereafter. In 1939 he was appointed Deputy Minister of Foreign Affairs, and in August 1941 became Thailand's Foreign Minister.

On 8 December 1941, within a few months of Professor Direk's appointment, Japan invaded Thailand. Concerned that his country had abandoned its traditional policy of neutrality, Professor Direk tendered his resignation as Foreign Minister. However, he was pressed by the Prime Minister, Field Marshal Luang Phibun Songkhram, into reluctantly accepting the post of Thai Ambassador to Tokyo, a position he held from January 1942 until September 1943. Although poor health forced his return to Bangkok at that time, the Prime Minister insisted on Professor Direk returning to public life, and from the end of 1943 until July 1944 the author served once again as Minister of Foreign Affairs. Following a vote of no-confidence in the government in July 1944, Professor Direk resigned along with the entire Cabinet. For the remainder of the war he devoted himself to taking part in the Free Thai, or underground resistance movement that opposed Japan and cooperated with the Allies during the latter part of the war.

Immediately after the war Professor Direk was elected to the Senate, and became Minister of Justice and concurrently Minister of Finance in the Thawi Bunyaket government, which held office briefly from 1 September to 17 September 1945. During the subsequent Cabinet of M.R. Seni Pramoj from 17 September 1945 to 31 January 1946 Professor Direk held the position of Minister of Finance. He was made Minister of Foreign Affairs during the Pridi Banomyong regime that held power from 24 March 1946 to 22 August 1946, and held the positions of Deputy Prime Minister and Minister of Foreign Affairs during the following government of Rear Admiral Thawan Thamrongnawasawat. Throughout this immediate post-war period Professor Direk devoted his attention to seeing Thailand restored to its pre-war status in the eyes of the world, and was successful in securing Thailand's admittance to the United Nations on 15 December 1946.

Two months later, in February 1947 Professor Direk, concerned at the way public affairs were being handled by the government, resigned as Minister of Foreign Affairs, although he continued to remain as M.P. for the Bangkok fifth district. Rear Admiral Thawan, the Prime Minister, persuaded him, however, to take up a new position as Ambssador to London, and in July 1947 Professor Direk became the Thai Ambassador to the Court of St. James.

The following November a coup took place in Thailand, ousting the Thawan government and eventually bringing Field Marshal Phibun Songkhram back to power. Professor Direk resigned his position in London and returned to Thailand, where he resumed his life as an academic. He had held a position as lecturer in comparative law at Thammasat University between 1934 to 1941, and in 1947, after he came back from England, the university appointed him its first Dean of the Political Science Faculty, a position he held until 1952. In 1954 Thammasat awarded him an honorary doctorate in Diplomacy.

Between 1953 and 1959 Professor Direk traveled widely, lecturing at universities in the United States, England, Pakistan and the Philippines at the invitation of the United States State Department, the British Council and the South East Asia Treaty Organisation. Professor Direk, who was a devout Buddhist, also served as Thai representative at the Fifth Conference of the World Fellowship of Buddhism held in Bangkok in 1958. In 1959 he was appointed Ambassador to Germany, and in 1962 made Ambassador to Finland concurrently.

In 1965 Professor Direk finally retired fully from government office after a lifetime of service to the Thai nation. Sadly, he had only a short while to live. In 1967 he died of stomach cancer, leaving behind him a wife and four sons. In addition to serving in a great variety of capacities in public life, Professor Direk was also the author of many articles and lectures. His best known works include *Kanthut* (Diplomacy), first published as a textbook for Thammasat University students in 1947. The author subsequently published a second edition of the first part of this work in 1959. He later revised this and reissued it under the title *Khwamsamphan rawang prathet* (International Relations), published by the Social Science Association Press of Thailand in 1966. This was the same year that Professor Direk's other major work, namely the Thai edition of this book, *Thai kap songkhram lok khrang thi song* (Thailand and World War II) was published.

Professor Direk's record of service is an exemplary one embodying the highest ideals of service to the nation. His wide-ranging experience in law, foreign affairs and finance and his skill at diplomacy enabled him not only to serve his country during World War II while retaining his opposition to the Japanese occupation, but enabled him to guide the country through the dangerous postwar shoals of restoring Thailand to its rightful place among the nations of the world immediately after the war.

PART I

FROM THE BEGINNING OF THE WAR IN EUROPE TO THE BEGINNING OF THE WAR IN ASIA

CHRONOLOGY OF WORLD WAR II
1 September 1939 to 8 December 1941*

1939		
1 September		Germany invades Poland. That same day both England and France send Germany an ultimatum demanding that it vacate Poland at the risk of both countries declaring war on Germany.
3 September		England and France declare war on Germany.
27 September		Poland defeated.
29 September		Germany and the U.S.S.R. agree to the partition of Poland.
30 November		U.S.S.R. invades Finland.
1940		
12 March		U.S.S.R. and Finland sign peace treaty.
9 April		Germany invades Denmark and Norway.
12 May		Germany invades France.
15 May		The Netherlands defeated.
28 May		King Leopold of Belgium surrenders.
28 May–3 June		Evacuation of British forces from Dunkirk.
12 June		Thailand signs non-aggression treaties with France. Britain and Japan.
14 June		Paris seized by German forces.
22 June		France signs peace treaty with Germany at Compiègne.
27 September		Germany. Italy and Japan sign the Triple Alliance.
28 October		Italy invades Greece.
1941		
13 April		Soviet-Japanese neutrality pact signed.
14 June		Although it had not yet declared war on the Axis powers, the United States orders all Axis assets deposited in the U.S.A. to be frozen.
22 June		Germany invades the U.S.S.R. despite the non-aggression treaty signed between the two countries in August 1939.
16 October		General Tojo appointed Prime Minister of Japan.
7 December		Japan attacks Pearl Harbor and declares war on England and the U.S.A.
8 December		Japanese troops invade Thailand and Malaya. England and the U.S.A. declare war against Japan in return.

*[This chronology has been taken from the middle of chapter 1 in the Thai original and placed here to provide a parallel to the similar chronology which comes before part 2, and to enable the reader to locate this information more easily.]

I
Background

Much of my government career was spent as an official in the Ministry of Foreign Affairs—a field which had long been of special interest to me. I began my government career, however, not in the Foreign Ministry but in the Ministry of Finance. In December 1938, when Colonel Luang Phibun Songkhram[1] was first appointed Prime Minister of His Majesty's government, I was made a Minister without portfolio in the Finance Ministry, which was then headed by Luang Praditmanutham.[2] I had only been attached to the Ministry for a few months, however, when Chaophraya Sithammathibet, the Minister of Foreign Affairs and a man I had long known and respected, proposed to the Council of Ministers that I be transferred to the Ministry of Foreign Affairs. I accepted this change readily, as I was already interested in this branch of work. Even after I had been transferred Colonel Luang Phibun Songkhram had me continue, however, to fill the position of Secretary to the Council of Ministers—a position I had held since 1936.[3]

MEMBERS OF THE COUNCIL OF MINISTERS UNDER COLONEL LUANG PHIBUN SONGKHRAM
(20 December 1938 to 7 March 1942)[4]

1. Colonel Luang Phibun Songkhram — Prime Minister
2. Colonel Luang Phibun Songkhram — Minister of Defense
3. Luang Praditmanutham — Minister of Finance
4. Chaophraya Sithammathibet[5] — Minister of Foreign Affairs
5. Group Captain Phra Wetchayanrangsarit — Minister of Agriculture
6. Captain Luang Sinsongkhramchai, R.N. — Minister of Education
7. Luang Kowit-aphaiwong — Deputy Minister of Education
8. Colonel Luang Phibun Songkhram — Minister of the Interior
9. Police-Colonel Luang Adun Adundetcharat — Deputy Minister of the Interior

Fig. 6. The Council of Ministers of Colonel Luang Phibun Songkhram, December 1938.

Fig. 7. The Council of Ministers of Major-General Luang Phibun Songkhram, 1939.

10.	Captain Luang Thamrongnawasawat, R.N.	Minister of Justice
11.	Colonel Phra Boriphanyutthakit	Minister of Economics
12.	Group Captain Luang Katsongkhram	Minister without portfolio
13.	Luang Chamnannitikaset	Minister without portfolio
14.	Major Luang Chawengsaksongkhram[6]	Minister without portfolio
15.	Nai Direk Jayanama	Minister without portfolio
16.	Luang Detsahakon	Minister without portfolio
17.	Nai Tua Laphanukrom	Minister without portfolio
18.	Luang Naruebetmanit[7]	Minister without portfolio
19.	Commander Luang Nawawichit	Minister without portfolio
20.	Lieutenant-Colonel Prayun Phamonmontri	Minister without portfolio
21.	Colonel Luang Phromyothi[8]	Minister without portfolio
22.	Luang Wichitwathakan[9]	Minister without portfolio
23.	Colonel Luang Sarityutthasin	Minister without portfolio
24.	Khun Samahanhitakhadi	Minister without portfolio
25.	Commander Luang Sangwonyutthakit, R.N.	Minister without portfolio
26.	Colonel Luang Seriroengrit	Minister without portfolio

A few months after I was transferred to the Ministry of Foreign Affairs, Chaophraya Sithammathibet resigned for health reasons. Major-General Luang Phibun Songkhram, the Prime Minister, took on the position of Minister of Foreign Affairs in his stead, while I was promoted to Deputy Minister of Foreign Affairs.[10] Some two years later, on 22 August 1941, the Prime Minister resigned from his concurrent position as Minister of Foreign Affairs, as well as from that as Minister of the Interior, and I was elevated to the vacant post of Minister of Foreign Affairs.[11]

Although Japan did not declare war on England and the United States until 7 December 1941,[12] formally opening the war on the Asian front, the war in Europe was already well advanced by that time. On 1 September 1939 Germany invaded Poland. On the third of that month England and France declared war on Germany, and by the end of September Poland had fallen. The U.S.S.R. invaded Finland at the end of November 1939; Norway and Denmark fell to Germany the following April, and Holland and Belgium in May. On 10 June 1940, shortly before the fall of France, Italy declared war on England and France, and on 22 June 1940 France surrendered to Germany and signed the peace treaty of Compiègne.

At first glance it might seem that Thailand would be little involved in these events in Europe, but in fact the war on the European front, and in particular the fate of France, played a considerable role in Thailand's destiny. As the collapse of France became imminent, Japan began increasing its pressure and encroachment on Indochina—policies that were eventually to impinge on Thai territory. Even before 12 June 1940, the date of the signing of the non-aggression pacts between Thailand and France, England and Japan respectively that form the opening point of these memoirs, Japan was beginning to extend its influence southwards into Indochina. In an effort to completely isolate the Chungking government, Japan had seized Canton in October 1938, Hainan in February 1939, and the Spratley Islands the following month. By early 1939 Japan had also made it clear that it was determined to cut off all war supplies being shipped in to the Chungking government via the Haiphong-Kunming railway, and began to put pressure on Indochina to ensure this outcome.

During the early years of the war, when Luang Phibun Songkhram was both Prime Minister and Foreign Minister, it was frequently my duty as Deputy Foreign Minister to stand in for him at meetings with heads of diplomatic missions, for the Prime Minister was often engaged on other business. After I became Foreign Minister in August 1941, as the likelihood of Japanese invasion drew ever closer between September and 8 December 1941, I began to receive numerous calls on my own account from diplomatic representatives, particularly from the British and American Ministers. The Japanese Minister, however, insisted on communicating with the Prime Minister either directly or through one of the representatives assigned by the Prime Minister specifically for that purpose.

When I took over as Minister of Foreign Affairs, the overall policy of the Thai government was one of friendship towards all nations. Furthermore the government observed with the utmost integrity any treaty obligations Thailand had incurred with foreign powers. Once the Japanese invaded Thailand on 8 December 1941, however, I felt that this policy of neutrality had been irrevocably compromised, and tendered my resignation accordingly. Field Marshal Phibun Songkhram took over the position of Foreign Minister as well as that of the Ministry of the Interior once again. He refused to allow me to resign entirely, however, insisting that I remain as Deputy Foreign Minister, while Lieutenant General Mangkon Phromyothi was reappointed as Deputy Minister of the Interior. Not long afterwards, on 5 January 1942, I was relieved of my position yet again. This time I was sent to Tokyo to take up a new position as Thai Ambassador to Japan—an appointment which is discussed later, in part 2 of this book.

2
Non-Aggression Pacts Between Thailand and France, England and Japan, 1940

Before going into details of the non-aggression pacts which Thailand drew up with France and England, and the treaty signed by Thailand with Japan for the mutual recognition of one another's sovereignty, the reader first needs to be familiarized with the historical background of our relationship with these three countries. Only then will he or she be in a position to understand both the reasons for and nature of the treaties described in this chapter, and the relationships between Thailand and other countries mentioned later in this book.[1]

HISTORICAL BACKGROUND TO THAILAND'S RELATIONS WITH FRANCE, ENGLAND AND JAPAN

Relations Between Thailand and France[2]

French Jesuits first came to what was then known to foreigners as Siam to spread the word of Christianity in 1662, during the reign of King Narai [1657–1688].[3] As a Buddhist country showing tolerance towards all faiths, the Thai placed no hindrance in the path of the French missionaries, even assisting them in a number of ways. King Narai gave them land so that the missionaries could build churches and schools. In trade, as in religion, our country also opened its doors to all nations alike. The king took into his service a Greek national named [Constantine] Phaulkon who obtained royal favor for his efficiency and was subsequently raised to the rank of Chaophraya Wichayen.[4] Phaulkon, a Catholic, was in close contact with French bishops at the court of Louis XIV, and in 1680 King Narai sent a diplomatic mission to establish friendly relations with France. Unfortunately the ship carrying members of the mission was wrecked, and never reached French shores.

King Narai [persisted in his efforts, however, and] sent a second mission in 1684. The following year, in response to the king's attempts to establish Franco-Thai relations, France sent an envoy, the Chevalier de Chaumont, to open trade negotiations with our country. He was welcomed by the Thai, and

France was granted a number of special privileges. These included a monopoly over tin mining in Phuket,[5] and jurisdiction over its own company employees who committed crimes of robbery while in Siam. Around 1686, Siam sent a third diplomatic mission to France, led by Kosapan [Phraya Wisut]. The following year it drew up another pact with France granting the latter yet further economic and judicial concessions.

It was not long, however, before the French missionaries became very unpopular with Thai officials for their overly zealous attempts to convert the Thai to Christianity.[6] At the death of King Narai in 1688 Phra Phetracha [1688–1703], who had successfully usurped the throne, got rid of Chaophraya Wichayen and cut off our relations with France, although still permitting French bishops and European merchants to carry on their customary business at Ayutthaya.[7]

Formal relations between Thailand and France were not re-established for more than one and a half centuries. In 1855, during the reign of King Mongkut (Rama IV) [1851–68], Siam signed what was known as the Bowring treaty with Britain. This gave the British extraterritorial and other rights in Siam, placing our country in a disadvantageous position. Seeing the benefits that England had received,[8] the French also started pressing for the same rights, and in 1858 we were obliged to sign a similar treaty with France. A year later France began occupying Cochin-China and claiming it as her colony, and in 1863, Cambodia was squeezed out of Thailand's jurisdiction. Four years later Siam was forced to recognize both Cambodia[9] and the Khong Island [in the Mekong River] as French territories. In 1888 our country was further obliged to cede the Sipsong Chu Thai[10] area to France, and in 1893 all lands lying on the left bank of the river Mekong. In 1904 the French took over additional Thai territories lying on the right bank of the Mekong facing Luang Prabang and Pakse, and finally, in 1907, France seized Battambang, Siemreap and Sisophon.[11]

During the First World War Siam fought on the side of France and England. At the end of the war we therefore started negotiating for the revision of the treaties we had previously been forced to sign with those and several other countries that had also obliged us to grant them extraterritorial rights. Our demands met with considerable opposition, as these countries fiercely opposed giving up their privileges. We were fortunate, however, in having an upright man in the service of the Thai nation at that time—Dr. Francis Bowes Sayre (Phraya Kalayanamaitri),[12] son-in-law of President Woodrow Wilson and Advisor to the Ministry of Foreign Affairs in the reign of King Rama VI. Thanks in large part to his efforts, treaties were signed with thirteen countries, including France in 1924 and England in 1925 that reduced the judicial and fiscal restrictions that had been placed on our country.

Although these treaties went a considerable way toward meeting our demands, we still remained subject to certain foreign restrictions. Among these was the stipulation that the consular courts would be dissolved and foreign nationals made subject to Thai law only if and when Siam promulgated a full legal code. Even then, for five years after that time, if members of the consulate or the consul himself saw fit to remove a case in which their own nationals were involved and have the case re-tried in the consular court, they were to be allowed to do so, except when the case had already been presented to the Supreme Court. We also still remained subject to certain tax restrictions, in particular those concerning the extent of the duties we were permitted to levy on certain classes of products imported from England. Thus Siam still did not enjoy absolute sovereignty. We continued to suffer from unilateral obligations that limited our ability to control our national affairs, and were not free to levy taxes fully for the benefit of our country in the way that nations with full sovereignty over their affairs had the right to do.[13]

To overcome the legal restrictions on our country, during the reign of King Rama VI [1881–1925] the government hastened to compile a legal code. The first, second and third books of the Civil Law Code were published in 1925, and the fourth and fifth books followed in 1931. The following year our country underwent a bloodless revolution whereby the absolute monarchy was replaced by a constitutional one. In 1935 the new government finished compiling the Criminal Court procedures, while Civil Court procedures and the constitution of the Court were also drawn up.

Thus armed with the complete legal code required by foreign nations, our government reopened negotiations with a number of countries, including England and France, pointing out that the circumstances under which the treaties had originally been drawn up had now changed considerably. In the 1920s Western nations had been concerned that Siam did not have an up-to-date body of law by which to judge its own or foreign nationals. Now we had a complete legal code drawn up on the same basis as those of other countries governed by the rule of law, and one that moreover had been compiled by both Thai and foreign legal experts jointly. We therefore hoped for cooperation and sympathy in requesting those countries to grant us full and equal rights based on the principles of reciprocity and mutual benefit which all countries duly accepted.

In 1937 new treaties were signed between Siam and thirteen other countries, including England, France and Japan whereby we regained our complete judicial independence. Foreigners and Thai alike now had to submit to the jurisdiction of Thai courts. We were also left free to levy taxes and to grant citizenship to persons born in our land, as well as obtaining absolute freedom to reserve unsettled land for the use of Thai subjects. In short, our nation regained full sovereignty over its territory.[14]

No discussion of Thailand's historical relations with France would be complete without an examination of the Mekong boundary question.[15] Many people still find it difficult to understand why Thailand should have placed such importance on having the Mekong as a frontier-line. I will therefore give a brief account here of the origin of this question to demonstrate its importance to Thailand strategically, economically and politically. The first can be readily appreciated. With the river Mekong forming the boundary line, invasion of Thailand from the left bank of the river would at least be discouraged, if only temporarily, whereas a land frontier placed us in a more vulnerable position and left us an easy prey to hostile infiltration.

Once Cambodia was squeezed out of our protection in 1863, as described earlier, and France's territories thereby came to border ours, the Mekong became an international boundary, flowing through lands under both Thai and French jurisdiction. The real basis of the Mekong problem could, however, be said to have started in 1893,[16] when Thailand was forced to cede to France not only all lands on the left bank of the Mekong as previously described, but also the shallow islands lying in the river. Because of ambiguities in the treaty that the French translated for their own benefit, numerous problems began to arise. Thailand was obliged to suffer this state of affairs until 1926, when a special agreement was signed with French Indochina fixing the frontier line and establishing demilitarized zones between the two countries. Agreements were also made at that time on commercial navigation, fishing rights, maintenance or regulation of the Mekong as a navigable waterway, police-patrolling, and finally on the establishment of a joint Franco-Thai committee responsible for overseeing the execution of these arrangements and for settling border conflicts.

Although this treaty helped ease some of the problems, it still ran counter to international law by stating that whereas in those parts of its course where the Mekong flowed clear, rather than being divided into several branches by islands, the navigation channel of the river should form the boundary line. Where the Mekong flowed in several channels because of islands, however, then the frontier line would be fixed at the channel nearest the Thai bank instead of the deepest channel navigable throughout the year.

Further difficulties arose as a result of the 1904 treaty whereby France seized certain Thai territories on the right bank of the Mekong opposite Luang Prabang in the north and Pakse further south as described earlier. From that time on the river Mekong no longer formed the entire frontier line between Thailand and Indochina. There were two areas, namely from Chiang Khan to the mouth of the Thai [sic] river, where the Mekong flowed through French territory, in the north, and from the sea to the confluence of the Mun[17] River with the Mekong in the south that were contested. In disregard of international law, the French treated the Mekong as a French river where it flowed through these two areas, and made large profits by levying taxes on foreign boats that passed through these sections of the river. This greatly hampered our use of the Mekong, as was clearly demonstrated by a case in 1935 in which a Thai national called Intha Banchongchit had to give up floating his timber down river from Chiang Rai to Saigon because of France's harsh regulations. The incident well illustrated the way in which France used the Mekong for its sole benefit.

THAILAND'S EARLY RELATIONS WITH ENGLAND

According to history, the first Englishmen to come to Siam were traders who landed at Ayutthaya in 1612 during the reign of King Song Tham [1610–1628], bringing with them a letter from King James I of England. The Thai monarch allowed the English to open a trading house in the country, but on suffering trade losses, they closed down the business in 1632 [1622?],[18] much to the delight of Dutch merchants, who now no longer faced any foreign competition.[19] The Thai feared a Dutch trade monopoly, however, and tried, unsuccessfully, to persuade individual English traders to reopen their trading house. Instead, the British East India Company started pressing for conditions such as monopolies over certain products that would have benefited the company, but not private English traders. Despite these restrictions some individual English traders still managed to carry on business under the protection of Constantine Phaulkon, who became very unpopular with the East India Company for supporting this competition, particularly when he appointed an Englishman named Samuel White as Governor of Mergui,[20] thereby giving White the virtual monopoly over trade in that town. When White got into a business quarrel with the East India Company, the Company sent a warship to seize Mergui and arrest him, resulting in the kingdom of Siam declaring war against England in 1687. Although no battle was actually fought, relations between the two countries were broken off. It should be noted that our first conflict with England was thus caused by trade competition between an individual English subject and an English company supported by the English government. A Thai official (Phaulkon) was also involved in the commerce, resulting in a conflict of interest.[21]

During the reign of King Rama II [1809–1824] our relations with foreign countries, including England, were resumed. England began to raise a number of objections to our trading procedures, in particular those whereby Thai government officials, on boarding ships arriving at Thai ports, selected those products the government wanted to buy, prohibited their sale to other buyers, and fixed their price. The British also objected to the government holding monopolies over certain goods, and to the variable rate of customs duties, which rose and fell according to the demands of customs officials. In 1821, England sent an envoy, John Crawfurd, to open negotiations with Siam over these questions, but the mission met with no success. Five years later, during the reign of King Rama III [1824–1851], another envoy, Henry Burney, was sent to Siam and eventually a trade pact was signed between Siam and England whereby English traders received certain trading facilities and many of the obstacles formerly facing them were removed. British subjects in Siam remained, however, subject to Thai law like any ordinary Thai citizen. This was the first agreement made by us with a foreign country since we cut off contact with the West in the reign of Phra Phetracha as noted above.

In 1855, during the reign of King Rama IV (1851–1868), England sent Sir John Bowring, then its governor in Hong Kong, to open new negotiations with us. This led to the signing of an agreement that same year, followed by a supplementary one between the two countries in 1856. The Bowring treaty was the first of a number of subsequent treaties between Thailand and foreign countries under which we suffered unilateral disadvantages. The treaty, which could not be ended except with the consent of England, laid down that the duty payable on goods imported by the British would be limited to 3 percent *ad valorem*, while export duties were to be paid according to fixed rates. Further, any privileges granted to other countries must likewise be extended to England. In addition British subjects who found themselves at variance with the law were to be tried by British consular courts.[22] No arrest of any British subject could be made without the prior authorization of the British Consul, nor were British subjects liable for any taxes other than customs revenue, unless these had first been approved by the Consul. (This last condition was not in fact written into the treaty, but was interpreted as such by England, and Thailand was obliged to consent to it.)

The Thai government was well aware of the disadvantages it was placed under by the Bowring treaty, and recognized that it amounted to a partial loss of our sovereignty. King Rama IV considered it wiser, however, to cede partial rights to Britain rather than risk losing our total independence given that a number of Western powers were advancing into Asia at that period, and that England had already annexed Arakan, Martaban and Tenasserim in neighboring Burma in 1826,[23] and had claimed Lower Burma in 1852.

Other countries soon began demanding rights comparable to those granted to England. Thailand was obliged to sign treaties containing similar clauses with fourteen other countries, including France and the United States in 1856,

Denmark in 1858, Portugal in 1859, the Netherlands in 1860, Germany in 1862, Sweden, Norway, Belgium and Italy in 1868, Austria-Hungary in 1869, Spain in 1870, Japan in 1898 and Russia in 1899.

I would like to add some points regarding these extraterritorial treaties under which our country suffered unilateral disadvantages. In all fairness one has to admit that our judicial system at that time was not as up-to-date as European judicial systems. Although having to grant foreign countries consular jurisdiction over their own nationals was a blow to our absolute sovereignty, foreign demands in this regard could not be judged unreasonable. However, forcing us to levy customs duties at fixed rates was grossly unfair, and an extremely oppressive measure.

We all know that this was a period of Western colonial expansion. Countries which had sought to oppose England, such as India and Burma, had been defeated and seen much of their territory annexed as a result, while in 1842, only thirteen years prior to the Bowring treaty, England had extracted concessions from China following the Opium War.[24] H.R.H. Prince Damrong Rajanubhab[25] has remarked in regard to this war that many Thai at the time did not feel China had been defeated, but rather that it had agreed to these arrangements in order to put an end to a troublesome nuisance. Only three high-ranking Thai recognized that China had definitely been overpowered and realized that powerful Western influences were fast approaching in the East. They were King Rama IV (King Mongkut), who at the time of the signing of the 1855 treaty was still in the monkhood; Phra Pinklao, his royal brother; and Somdet Chaophraya, who was later appointed Regent during the reign of King Rama V [1868–1910]. They all saw the need for acquiring a Western education in order to be able to defend our country through diplomatic means.[26] It was known that England was not entirely satisfied with the Bowring treaty, and that it had made preparations to coerce us by sending gunboats, as it had already done against China, should we refuse its demands.

In 1909, we signed a further agreement with England ceding parts of the Malayan peninsula to it. They included Kelantan, Trengganu, Kedah, Perlis and several islands adjacent to British territory. In return England agreed to allow its subjects, both English and Asian registered as British subjects, to be tried in the Thai courts once our country came up with a complete legal code. In the meantime, they were to remain subject to the jurisdiction of the consular court.

Finally, between 1925 and 1937, as has already been described, all the above measures restricting our economic and judicial rights were eliminated and replaced by new agreements under which Thailand recovered its full sovereign rights.

CHAPTER 2

RELATIONS BETWEEN THAILAND AND JAPAN

There is no concrete evidence to show exactly when the first Japanese came to Siam, but historical annals mention five hundred Japanese soldiers being enlisted in the Thai army in 1593 during the reign of King Naresuan the Great [1590–1605]. This would suggest that Japanese must have come to Siam earlier than that date. The Japanese in Siam at that time came from all walks of life. They included sailors who came to trade, and soldiers who enlisted in the Thai army. The Shoguns of Japan had direct contact with Thai monarchs from 1606 on. In the reign of King Ekathotsarot [1605–1610] the Shogun wrote to the King praising our expertise in building firearms and requesting gifts of these guns, which were duly sent to Japan. Diplomatic missions were sent to Japan three times during the reign of King Song Tham, the first in 1621, the second in 1623 and the third in 1626. Many letters still exist to show the close relationship that existed between Siam and Japan at that time, and there is evidence that numerous gifts were exchanged between the two countries. King Song Tham even set up a Japanese Division of Volunteers and appointed a Japanese named Yamada Nagamasa as head of the Division.

In 1636, during the reign of King Prasat Thong [1630–1656], the Shogun of Japan became distrustful of foreigners, however, particularly of the Portuguese missionaries who were in his country spreading Catholic doctrines. He therefore forbade any Japanese from leaving Japan and from having any contact whatsoever with an alien, on pain of death. Japan closed its doors against outsiders, refusing to admit foreigners into the country, and its relationship with Siam thus came to a standstill.

This self-imposed isolation on the part of Japan lasted until 1853, when Commodore Perry, Commander of the Far East Squadron of the American Navy, sailed his gunboat into Japanese waters and forced Japan not only to admit American traders into its country but also to sign a treaty with the United States the following year. England followed suit that same year, and Japan later had to sign similar treaties with Russia and the Netherlands.

On the death of Emperor Komei in 1867, Crown Prince Mutsuhito [1852–1912] succeeded to the throne. The shogunate was overthrown, and the new Emperor came into his full imperial powers. From this time onwards Japan began to play an active role on the international scene, although it too had to accept the imposition of unilateral obligations by foreign powers similar to those which Thailand had been forced to accept between 1855 and 1899.

In 1897, H.R.H. Prince Devawongse Varoprakarn, the Thai Minister of Foreign Affairs, went to Japan and signed a joint communiqué with Mr. Aoki, the Japanese Deputy Minister of Foreign Affairs, agreeing to exchange legations and promote trade and shipping between the two countries. A year later Japan sent a Minister to Siam, and a treaty was signed with us on the 25 February 1898. This bore clauses and contained conditions similar to those we had agreed to with England in 1855, that is to say that we had to agree to grant the Japanese consular court judicial power over its own nationals. Japan was also placed on the same footing as other nations that had been granted special tax privileges, so that if we agreed to charge no more than 3 percent tax on imports from England or France, then the same rate had to apply to Japanese imports. There was a slight difference from the treaties we had concluded with other nations, however, in that it was specially agreed in the treaty with Japan that once a complete legal code had been drawn up by our country, the Japanese consular court would automatically be dissolved. It should be noted, moreover, that in the same year in which this treaty was signed Japan was in turn made to grant similar rights to other nations regarding their nationals in Japanese territory. These stipulations were abrogated in 1899, when Japan completed the compilation of its legal code, at which time all foreign consular courts in Japan were dissolved.

In 1923, three years after the United States revised its Trade and Shipping Act with us, Japan also agreed to revise its treaty with us in the same way that France and England had done, and after the 1932 revolution, when the absolute monarchy in Thailand was replaced by a constitutional monarchy and we opened talks for the revision of our treaties with all nations, Japan, along with those other nations, signed new treaties with us in 1937 restoring full sovereignty to our country.

Our two countries were brought even closer by an incident that took place in 1933. In February of that year, a committee of nineteen nations reported to the League of Nations that the Manchukuo government, established by the Japanese in Manchuria, was merely a puppet regime, and should not be recognized by League members. I happen to remember the incident clearly, as it took place during the early days of my career. Phraya Siwisanwacha, then Minister of Foreign Affairs, consulted the Council of Ministers, which decided that Thailand should abstain from voting on the issue for the sake of our friendship with Japan. Luang Phattharawathi[27] later reported that Thailand was the only country that abstained from voting, and that before the Japanese delegate2[28] walked out of the conference to protest the overall vote, he had come up and shaken hands with the Thai delegate and expressed his gratitude to him, declaring that should Thailand ever find itself attacked by foreign powers, Japan would definitely come to its aid. Our abstention from voting clearly displeased many Western countries, however, particularly as Japan [used the occasion to] declare that we had given it moral support.[29] One month after the incident, in March 1933, Japan withdrew from the League of Nations.

CHAPTER 2

NEGOTIATIONS LEADING TO THE SIGNING OF NON-AGGRESSION PACTS BETWEEN THAILAND AND FRANCE, ENGLAND AND JAPAN IN 1940

As negotiations between Thailand and these three countries were held at the same time, I will deal with them all together instead of giving a separate account of each treaty. In August 1939, a few days before the Second World War broke out in Europe–or to be more exact, at the time that tension in Europe was reaching its peak with Hitler's threats towards Poland—the French Minister to Thailand, Monsieur Paul Lépissier, approached Major-General Luang Phibun Songkhram in the latter's capacity as Minister of Foreign Affairs with a request that Thailand sign a non-aggression treaty with France. Luang Phibun consulted the Council of Ministers, which consented to the proposal. In October the Ministry of Foreign Affairs sent a reply memorandum on behalf of the government to the French Minister stating that we were quite willing to enter into such a treaty, but pointing out at the same time that there were a number of outstanding problems concerning the Mekong boundary line that we would like to see settled according to the *Thalweg* principle[30] supported by international law. We maintained that this was not currently being observed by France, which was treating the river as its own. The French government agreed to consider the matter in principle.

Given the French request for a non-aggression treaty, the Thai government felt that as England also held territories adjacent to ours, namely in Burma and the then Federation of Malaya, we should hold [similar] talks with England. [Events meanwhile, however, began to overtake us.] In September 1939 war broke out in Europe. England and France entered into an alliance with one another on the one side, while Japan, although not yet at war, entered into treaty obligations with Germany and Italy on the other. In order to dispel any suspicions Japan might have over our holding such talks, the government felt it would be reasonable to invite Japan to also take part in them, even though its territories were not contiguous with ours. The Foreign Ministry therefore handed memoranda to the British Minister to Bangkok, Sir Josiah Crosby, and to Mr. Murai, his Japanese counterpart, announcing our approaching negotiations for the conclusion of a non-aggression treaty with France, and stating that we would be willing to negotiate similar non-aggression treaties with their countries if they were interested. Prince Wanwaithayakon, who at that time was Advisor to the Office of the Prime Minister and to the Ministry of Foreign Affairs, was charged by the government with drafting the agreement with the representatives of the three countries.

NON-AGGRESSION PACTS BETWEEN THAILAND AND FRANCE, ENGLAND AND JAPAN, 1940

By April 1940, France and England had consented to the signing of non-aggression pacts, but Japan had not yet shown any sign of interest in our proposal. On 11 April 1940 I therefore invited the Japanese Minister over and asked if he could give any indication of Japan's attitude on the subject now that both France and England had given us their replies, as the treaties with them would be signed in a matter of two or three weeks. The Japanese Minister told me informally that Japan was not particularly concerned with the treaties one way or the other, as it had no territories bordering ours. It was concerned, though, that if Japan were to sign such a treaty it might be misinterpreted by Germany and Italy. The Minister said that he would nonetheless take up the matter with his government right away.

After I had reported on these negotiations, the Prime Minister instructed me to inform the Ministers of Germany, Italy and the United States of our position, and to sound out their reactions. I therefore invited the three respective Ministers over on 13 April, and told them that the Prime Minister/Minister of Foreign Affairs wished me to give them a confidential report on our negotiations with France, England and Japan so that they could pass this information on to their respective governments. To demonstrate our goodwill and to show that we were not conducting these negotiations in secret, the Prime Minister authorized me to present the three Ministers with copies of the memoranda we had sent to the French, English and Japanese Ministers, as well as with drafts of the non-aggression treaties.

The German Minister, Mr. Wilhelm Thomas, thanked me, and commented that he saw nothing about the negotiations that could be taken amiss by his country. The actions taken by the Thai government thus far were, in his opinion, reasonable, and proof of our sincere wish to remain neutral. The Italian Minister, Mr. Crolla, expressed similar views. The American Minister, Mr. Neville, also expressed thanks for our goodwill, and said he would send the information on to Washington, where he believed his government would well understand the matter.

On 22 April 1940, eleven days after I had asked the Japanese Minister about Japan's reaction to our proposal, he came to tell me that his government now agreed in principle to the signing of a non-aggression treaty. Japan had delayed coming to this decision because it feared being misunderstood, especially by its allies, and also because it had not had any experience of this type of agreement before. The Minister said he would be discussing details with Thai officials within five to six days, once the Japanese Parliament and Privy Council had given their formal agreement to the measure. The Minister mentioned that he also needed to let our Prime Minister know that if England was the first of the three countries to sign the treaty, the Japanese public might misinterpret our intentions and become displeased with the Thai government for what would be considered an act of favoritism towards England. He therefore felt it would be wiser to wait for another three or four weeks before signing the treaty with England, as Japan would like to be the first to sign, or at least to sign on the same day as England.

I told the Minister that it would in fact be a matter of another three weeks or more before the drafting, re-checking and publication of the treaty would be completed, and that moreover France was not yet ready to sign, but was still studying the draft. France, I told him, was also concerned that we should not sign with England first, so the Minister had no cause for concern. It would be best if all signed on the same day. Later the Japanese Minister suggested certain changes to the draft we had drawn up, explaining that Japan would like to avoid having the same clauses in its treaty as in those of France and England. Following discussions in the Council of Ministers it was decided that as long as the main proposal of declaring mutual respect for one another's territory was contained in the treaty, we would be comfortable with the outcome. I personally disliked the use of certain phrases that Japan suggested including, such as a clause arranging for the exchange of information and news and for discussion on matters of mutual interest, for these seemed to imply special notes of friendship. However, on the insistence of Japan, which was not opposed by the Thai Council of Ministers, on the grounds that these phrases were not compromising in any way, I did not pursue the matter further.

On 10 May 1940, the Japanese Minister came to see me again, this time to say that his government found our clause regarding the expression of mutual respect for one another's political regimes unacceptable. Japan fully understood that we had only put this in so that our treaty with Japan would contain wording similar to that in our treaties with England and France. However, Japan did not want such similarity, and regretted that it must therefore reject this clause. He said that a clause bearing on mutual respect for one another's boundaries would be sufficient. The Minister told me that there were a number of strange ideas in his country, and that even he himself could not understand some of them as he had been living abroad for a long time. He himself saw no objection to the pledging of mutual respect for one another's political regimes, but his government had instructed him to let me know that such a clause would be taken in Japan to refer to the Emperor, and that it would be regarded as an insult against the monarchy if the Emperor was referred to in this way. He told me of an incident five years previously, when a Professor Mitobe of the Imperial University had given a talk on the constitution in which he had referred to the Emperor as an arm of the state. The professor had been fired from the government and all his writings confiscated as a result, as such a statement was taken to be highly defamatory to the Emperor. Given such arguments, the Thai Council of Ministers consented to the proposed revision.

Three days later, the German Minister came to tell me that his government thanked us for our consideration in keeping it informed, and fully understood the issues involved. On the same day the Italian Minister also came to see me with a statement similar to that of the German Minister.

Eventually it was agreed that the treaties should be signed at Government House, then situated at Suan Kulap Palace, on 12 June 1940 between Major-General Luang Phibun Songkhram, our Minister of Foreign Affairs, and the French, British and Japanese Ministers, in order of the respective approaches made to these countries.

However, on 23 May 1940, the Japanese Minister came to see me, apologizing for thus troubling me repeatedly, but stating he had now received further instructions from his government expressing the wish that Japan sign the treaty a day or two before England or France. Japan's explanation was that as the Japanese government had declared its non-intervention in the war in Europe, signing a treaty with us on the same day as France and England could be misinterpreted by some countries as meaning that Japan was giving France and England cooperation in Asia. I replied that it would be more suitable for the three to sign on the same day, and that no country would misinterpret this action as both the German and Italian governments had already informed us of their full understanding of the matter. Besides, if the arrangements were changed now, what reasons could I give to the French and English Ministers? I told the Japanese Minister that his request would nevertheless be forwarded to the Prime Minister/Foreign Minister.

The following day I told the Prime Minister/Foreign Minister about the Japanese request. I expressed the opinion that we should not agree to Japan's proposal, not only because it would be considered bad etiquette by France and England, but also because we would be accused of being too subservient to Japanese demands, to the extent of disregarding internationally accepted practices. The Prime Minister expressed agreement with my views.

On 27 May 1940 I therefore invited the Japanese Minister over to inform him that the Prime Minister had considered his request with sympathy, but felt we would be placed in an extremely embarrassing position if we agreed to it, both in terms of the precedence of talks held with the three nations, or even if we were just to go by alphabetical order. England and France had already agreed to all three countries signing on the same day, so that if the Thai government was to go back on its word and allow Japan to sign before the other two nations, we should be put in an extremely bad light in the eyes of the first two countries. We hoped that Japan would understand our situation and view it sympathetically. The Minister replied that he fully recognized that for us to accept the Japanese

Fig 8. The signing of the Non-Aggression Pact between Thailand and France at Suan Kulap Palace on 12 June 1940. *From left:* the author, Captain Phra Riam Wiratchaphak [Director-General of the Protocol Department], Major-General Luang Phibun Songkhram and the French Minister [M. Paul Lépissier].

Fig. 9. The signing of the Non-Aggression Pact between Thailand and Great Britain at Suan Kulap Palace on 12 June 1940. *From left:* the author, Captain Phra Riam Wiratchaphak [Director-General of the Protocol Department], Major-General Luang Phibun Songkhram and the British Minister [Sir Josiah Crosby].

demand would amount to diplomatic discourtesy to the English and French governments, but that he had been forced to make the request on the instructions of his government. However, on my having clarified the matter he would immediately report on it to his government. Later he came to see me yet again to say that his government was now willing to sign the treaty on the same day as France and England, but would prefer to sign it in Tokyo. We agreed to this arrangement.

The non-aggression pacts were finally signed with France and England on 12 June 1940 at Suan Kulab Palace, and in Tokyo on the same day between Mr. Hachiro Arita, the Japanese Minister of Foreign Affairs, and Phraya Sisena, the Thai Minister to Japan.[31] The essential clauses in the treaties signed with France and England laid down that parties to the agreement would not declare war on one another and would not use force to invade one another's territory, either on their own or by siding with other powers, nor would they give help to any country that had declared war on the other party to the agreement. In addition, the two countries pledged mutual respect for one another's territorial integrity. The agreement with Japan stated that both powers agreed to respect one another's territories, and would withhold aid to any country attacking the other party to this agreement. It also contained a clause agreeing to maintain friendly contacts in order to exchange information and discuss any matters of mutual interest that might arise.

The treaties between Thailand and England and Thailand and Japan were later ratified by their respective governments, thus rendering them effective and enforceable. Our treaty with France, however, remained unratified by the Thai government, for reasons which will be taken up in part 1, chapter 3 of this volume.

Looking at the three treaties we can see that our treaties with France and England were similar in almost every detail, although the French treaty contained an additional clause stating that the boundaries between Thailand and French Indochina along the Mekong would have to be adjusted along certain lines that had already been proposed.[32] Our treaty with Japan was, however, different in terms from the other two, as Japan did not wish to have its treaty drawn up on the same lines as those of England and France. The main difference lay in the second clause, which stated that Japan and Thailand agreed to maintain friendly contacts in order to exchange information and to consult one another on any matters of common interest. The British Minister asked me if this could be taken as a pledge of alliance, but I replied in the negative, explaining that the words had been inserted at the insistence of Japan, which wanted to avoid having similar clauses and wordings to those of our treaties with England and France, and that we had only agreed to the changes because they did not place us under any military obligations towards Japan.

3
Border Dispute and Peace Agreement Between Thailand and French Indochina[1]

A few days after the non-aggression treaties had been signed between Thailand and France, England and Japan, international events began to change very rapidly. On 14 June 1940 German troops entered Paris without encountering any real opposition, and on 22 June France surrendered at Compiègne. Our non-aggression treaty with France was therefore received with great joy by the French populace. On the night of 12 June 1940, in spite of the heavy gloom surrounding the possible defeat of France, Radio Saigon broadcast its praises of Thailand's goodwill. This gesture of friendship on our part, it was maintained, would not be forgotten in a hurry. Sounds of cheerful music accompanied the broadcast.

On 24 June 1940, which at that time was our National Day, Major-General Luang Phibun Songkhram, the Prime Minister, delivered a broadcast to the nation. In it he referred to relations between Thailand and France, stating that "…in view of recent events I have received many enquiries from those of you who take an interest in our neighbor, Indochina. I beg you, my dear brother-citizens, to forget the past and think of it as only a bad dream.[2] In this way you will be able to sympathize with the fate of France, our friend, and extend her your understanding…." On that same day Saigon again broadcast its appreciation and gratitude for our manifestations of goodwill.

Meanwhile tension in Indochina steadily increased. Five days after Paris had been occupied by the German army the Japanese government sent an ultimatum to Indochina demanding the temporary closure of the Chinese frontier and the right to send Japanese officials to ensure that no help was being funneled from the Allies to the Chiang Kai-shek government at Chungking.[3] The French replied that the Chinese frontier had already been closed since 17 June, and that trucks and gasoline shipments had been forbidden entry into Chinese territory. Forbidding the transport of other provisions was also being envisaged. The French further acquiesced to Japan's demands by permitting it to send a group of inspectors to supervise the carrying out of these arrangements. The agreement was protested by the Chinese government, but France made no attempt to reply. Twelve days later Japan sent a military mission to Hanoi. It was led by

General Nishihara and was sent to control the points of entry into the country at Haiphong, Ha Giang, Laokay, Chao Bang, Lang Son and Fort Bayard.[4]

In mid-July 1940 General Nishihara requested that Japan be allowed to establish air bases in French Indochina, and that right of passage for Japanese troops through Indochinese territory be granted. The Governor-General[5] tried to evade the issue by suggesting that this request be referred to the French government at Vichy. The French Ambassador to Tokyo, M. Charles Arsène Henry,[6] subsequently relayed the response from the Vichy government that such an agreement would amount to loss of French sovereignty and to its joining Japan in the war against China. [At the end of] August 1940 the Vichy government nonetheless instructed its Ambassador in Tokyo to present the Japanese Minister of Foreign Affairs, Mr. Matsuoka,[7] with a letter of exchange. In it France recognized Japan's vital political and economic interests in the Far East, and agreed to accord Japan a privileged economic position in Indochina as well as allowing it military privileges to help Japan bring the Sino-Japanese war to an end. Japan, for its part, agreed not to abuse these privileges by overreaching its military position. Further details were to be worked out between the Japanese and French military authorities. As a return gesture, Japan agreed to respect the rights and interests of France in the Far East, and in particular, French sovereignty over Indochina.[8]

According to the memoirs of Mr. Cordell Hull, the United States Secretary of State at that time, the Vichy government, following the drawing up of this agreement, had its Ambassador in Washington approach Mr. Hull to request that the United States demand a guarantee from Japan similar to that acquired by France regarding respect for French sovereignty over Indochina. Mr. Hull not only refused, but told the Vichy government it should not have made an agreement with Japan recognizing Japanese vital interests in the Far East. The United States government had repeatedly protested to Japan regarding its pressure on Indochina, but could not possibly make such a demand, nor could it provide France with military aid, for this might lead to a declaration of war.[9] (I believe the true reason underlying Mr. Hull's position was that the United States was not yet ready for war at that time).

On 4 September 1940 General Nishihara signed a military pact with General Martin, Supreme Commander of the French forces in Indochina. Evidence produced later before the Far East International Military Tribunal in Tokyo revealed that under this agreement France consented to the passage of 25,000 Japanese soldiers through Tongking.[10]

Major-General Luang Phibun Songkhram had meanwhile told me to press the French Minister for the arrival of the French delegation so that we could open negotiations over our mutual frontier problems as arranged for in the letters of exchange attached to the treaty of mutual non-aggression[11] of 12 June. The French asked, however, for the talks to be postponed for a while in light of the disruptions in France following its surrender to Germany. Two months thus passed by without the French delegation arriving to hold talks. Luang Phibun meanwhile called together a meeting of the Council of Ministers. At this he announced that since signing the pact with France the situation in Indochina had deteriorated, and it was now necessary for the Thai government to take steps to secure the return of our lost territories [referring to formerly Thai lands seized by the French.] Should these lands be handed over to Japan without our government even trying to recover them, we would be regarded as culpable in the eyes of Thailand's future generations.

On 2 August 1940 Major-General Luang Phibun asked me to invite M. Lépissier, the French Minister, to see me at the Foreign Ministry. I informed him of the concern over the adjustment of our frontiers felt not only by the Prime Minister, but by the National Assembly and indeed our entire nation. If the Minister could tell us when the French delegation would be arriving in Thailand to open negotiations, we would appreciate it very much. We were ready to conduct negotiations whenever France decided on a date, as we were anxious to reach an agreement on the adjustment of our mutual frontiers at the same time that the non-aggression pact was ratified.

The French Minister replied that he was no less concerned than us about the matter. However, he wanted to know if the treaty would be ratified by the Council of Ministers or by the National Assembly, as according to the terms of our Constitution any change in our boundaries required the approval of the National Assembly. I simply emphasized again that it was highly desirable that both matters be settled at the same time.

The Minister next claimed that the water level of the Mekong was high at the moment, making it difficult to draw up a frontier line.[12] He suggested that we therefore wait for another two months for the water to recede. I countered that we could still go ahead immediately using a topographical map. Major frontier lines could be defined first, and the details left to a sub-committee of experts. The main point was, I told him, that we do something so that there be progress to report to the nation, as several weeks had already gone by without anything having been done. Further delay would cause ill-feeling among the Thai and affect the outcome of the ratification of the non-aggression treaty. Thailand hoped, and was indeed confident, that the matter would be settled justly and successfully, for the Minister was himself on the French sub-committee. M. Lépissier expressed his understanding of the situation, and asked if we had a map detailed enough for the purposes of preliminary frontier definition. I said we had, and the Minister concluded our discussion by saying that there should be no problem in principle over the matter, and that he would send a letter to our Minister of Foreign Affairs, Major-General Luang Phibun Songkhram, as soon as possible to discuss it. M. Lépissier further expressed the belief that the adjustment of our frontiers should be completed well before November.

In July 1940, as the course of events in Indochina became increasingly subject to Japanese pressures Mr. Chapman, the American Chargé d'Affaires, came to see me to enquire about our reaction to the Japanese build-up. I referred him to the Prime Minister's broadcast of a few days earlier delivered on our National Day in which the latter had stated that the Thai government was following the situation with deep concern.

At almost the same time the British Minister, Sir Josiah Crosby, came to see me with a similar question. I replied on more or less the same lines. He then asked what our reaction would be should Japan lay claim to Indochina. I replied that as the Minister had been in Thailand for thirty years,[13] he was well acquainted with the history of relations between Thailand and Indochina and must be aware that Thailand had been forced to cede territory in Indochina to France on a number of occasions. As a result there were many areas in French Indochina that had once been under Thai jurisdiction and where the people were of Thai descent. I therefore affirmed that should it become necessary, the Thai government would have to ask for the partition of Indochina lest the whole country fall into Japanese hands. I also pointed out that our acquisition of part of Indochina would be in the interests of England, as it would place a greater distance than before between Japanese-held territory and Malaya.

The British Minister expressed agreement with these views, stating that if France had to abandon Indochina, it should certainly first consider giving us back our territories before handing Indochina over to Japan.[14] However, he believed that if Japan agreed to Thailand's partition of Indochina, it would be only in return for our acceptance of many conditions such as Thai recognition of the New Order in Asia.[15] If we were asked to accept such conditions, the Minister went on, what would Thailand's course of action be? I answered that as the nature of this New Order was still ambiguous, I was not in a position to give a definite answer on the subject. Sir Josiah thereupon concluded our discussion by saying that our government should at least bear in mind that Japan had been carrying out a policy of continuous territorial expansion. We should therefore be on our guard. He told me he would, nevertheless, recommend to the British government that in the event of France having to relinquish Indochina, Thailand should first be given back its former territories there.

Later the French Minister came to see me at the Foreign Ministry. He brought a request from his government that the non-aggression treaty between France and Thailand take effect immediately without waiting for it to be ratified by the two governments. I told him that this would be completely out of line with constitutional procedure, but that his request would nevertheless be passed on to the Prime Minister.

After consultation with the Council of Ministers, it was decided that in view of the French request, we should hold talks to discuss the French demand. However, before proceeding any further, I was instructed to sound out the opinions of the British, American, German and Italian Ministers and to try to obtain their support for our forthcoming negotiations with France. On 15 August 1940 I therefore invited the four of them to see me at the Ministry, and told them that I had been instructed by the Prime Minister/Foreign Minister to talk over the Indochinese problem with them. As they were all familiar with the matter in hand, having held various discussions on the subject with both the Prime Minister and myself in the past, I simply mentioned that as they must be aware, the situation in Indochina had deteriorated. Given that they were all well-versed in the history of our loss of territories in Indochina to France, I would not go over this again, but was bringing the matter up because the Prime Minister/Foreign Minister wished me to have them ask their respective governments what their course of action would be should the occasion arise when the Thai government felt obliged to ask for the return of our lost territories in Indochina. We hoped for a sympathetic response from the Ministers' respective governments.

The British Minister agreed to send a cable to his government concerning our enquiry, but said he believed his government would have to consult with the American government first. He then asked if we would still persist in our demands if the Japanese government decided to maintain the *status quo* in Indochina. I replied that I had not been given any instructions on the subject, but that in my personal opinion, should Japan decide to maintain the *status quo*, there would be no reason for us to make such a demand and that this would be put forward only in the event of Indochina falling completely into Japanese hands. The British Minister then told me he believed that in fact both his government and the government of the United States would insist on the maintenance of the *status quo* in Indochina. Should Japan decide to the contrary, however, and we persisted in our demands, he believed that England would be on our side. Sir Josiah also asked me to pass on the following information to the Prime Minister, namely that he had received reports from reliable sources that Japan was planning to set up a monarchy in Vietnam and Cambodia in the same way as it had done in Manchukuo. We were to get back Laos on condition that we accepted the New Order in Asia. This, the British Minister pointed out, would more or less amount to placing Thailand in the same category as Manchukuo. In addition we would have to recognize any other countries Japan might set up in the future, as well as allow the Japanese special economic privileges in Thailand and grant it the right to supervise these arrangements. Sir Josiah therefore warned us to be wary. Though we might well get back our territories, he claimed that doing so would be like cutting our own throats, for they would be returned to us only at the cost of our absolute sovereignty over our own affairs.

The American Minister[16] asked if we intended to use force to carry out our demands. I told him no, saying that the Thai government planned to employ only diplomatic means in pressing for its rights. The Minister expressed his approval of this and went on to ask if we would continue with our demands if Japan agreed to maintain the *status quo* in Indochina. I told him that I had not received any instructions on this, but that I personally believed we would see no reason in making further demands if Japan agreed to the *status quo* arrangement.

Both the German and Italian Ministers said they believed their respective governments would support us in our demands as they already had sympathetic feelings towards us.

I did not approach the Japanese Minister myself, as the Prime Minister told me he had already instructed other persons to keep in contact with him. I was therefore greatly surprised to receive a call from the Japanese Chargé d'Affaires, Mr. Asada, at my office at the Ministry on 21 August 1940. He asked if the American Minister had been to see me with a reply from his government, but I told him we had not received a reply yet. The Japanese Chargé then became very reproachful, saying that Thailand should never have sought the opinion of England and the United States in the beginning. I retorted that we had only done so to demonstrate our honest intentions, since we saw no reason to keep the matter secret.

On 27 August 1940 the American Minister called on me to deliver his government's reply to our discussions. He reminded me that on 16 July 1937, at the outset of the Sino-Japanese conflict, the United States government had made an announcement, a [written] copy of which had been handed to Luang Praditmanutham [Nai Pridi Banomyong], then our Minister of Foreign Affairs. The Minister was now giving me a further copy of this document. It ran to the effect that at that time the entire world was facing grave problems that on the surface appeared to affect only countries bordering the troubled areas, but which on closer study affected nations throughout the world. No matter where the fighting was going on, every nation would be involved and its rights and interests affected. For this reason, then, Mr. Cordell Hull, the United States Secretary of State, as spokesman for the government of the United States, asked that every nation exercise self-restraint and try to avoid the use of force in carrying out its policies. All countries should refrain from intervention in the internal affairs of other nations and try to solve international problems through peaceful negotiations. Bearing the above communiqué in mind, the American Minister gave it as his personal opinion that it would be much better for us to wait until the war was over before putting forward our demands in regard to Indochina.

I felt like telling him that Thailand had already learned its lesson in this regard from the First World War. The Allies had persuaded us to enter the war on their side, yet when the war was over not a single country, with the sole exception of the United States, was willing to revise its unequal treaties with us, and even in the case of the United States we had run into great difficulties and secured revision of the treaties only through the help of Dr. Sayre, who happened to be the son-in-law of President Wilson.[17] However, out loud I merely mentioned that there were two questions involved here. The first was who would win and who lose the war? The second was, supposing that the Allies were victorious, could the Minister assure us that the United States would support us in our future demands? He replied that this lay in the future, and that he was not in a position to answer this. All that he had expressed so far was merely his personal opinion.

England took its time before responding to our discussions. Almost six weeks passed from the day I brought the matter up with the four Ministers on 15 August 1940 to the day when the British Minister came to see me on 26 September with a reply memorandum from his government. This stated that although the government of His Majesty the King of England stood by the principle of maintaining the *status quo* in Indochina for as long as possible, it nonetheless recognized that in the event of the dissolution of Indochina or of a change of jurisdiction over the area Thailand would like to get back certain regions in Indochina over which it claimed its rights. However, His Majesty's government beseeched Thailand to consider carefully whether it would not be more in its interest to have Indochina remain under French jurisdiction than let it be ruled by Japan, which would then have lands contiguous with Thai territory. It was the right of Thailand to determine its own policy, but in the opinion of the British government it was strongly desirable that Thailand think carefully before taking any steps it might later regret. The British government had reason to believe that an agreement between Japan and France would cover Japan's guarantee of the *status quo* in Indochina, in which case there would be no question of Thailand's demanding the return of such extensive territories. As to Thailand's limited territorial demands connected with the ratifying of the non-aggression treaty,[18] the British government had no objection to these, and believed that such an adjustment of the frontiers could be negotiated between the governments of Thailand and France at any time. As Thailand and England had been friendly with one another for a long time, the British government would always appreciate being told in advance of the Thai government's intentions and plans in these regards.

On 20 August 1940 the Prime Minister/Foreign Minister asked me to see the French Minister to ask him once again when the French delegation would be arriving, as we wanted to complete preliminary talks on our border issues. M. Lépissier replied that the Indochinese government had constantly sought postponement of the discussions, as it was currently preoccupied with coping with Japanese pressures. I told him that it seemed that the Indochinese government did not clearly appreciate the Thai position, or was even refusing to understand it. A number of recent actions on the part of French Indochina pointed to such a supposition, I charged, for example the fact that the Indochinese government had allowed its military planes to violate Thai territory on several occasions. The French Minister apologized for these actions, bringing to our attention that Indochina was currently in a very desperate situation, as it had just received an ultimatum from Japan calling for the passage of Japanese troops and the establishment of Japanese naval bases in Indochina.

On 10 September 1940 we finally received an official letter from the French listing the six delegates they had nominated as members of the committee to conduct negotiations with us on the demarcation of the Mekong boundary line. We asked when this delegation would be arriving, and were told by the French Minister that it should be here forthwith. Ten days later Thailand accordingly announced the formation of a ten man committee, which included the author among its members, to present the Thai viewpoint at the discussions.[19]

Meanwhile, also on 10 September 1940, our Minister at Vichy, Phra Phahitthanukon,[20] cabled us to say that the French Foreign Minister had expressed the wish that we ratify the non-aggression treaty immediately without waiting on an exchange of letters of ratification between the two countries.

On receiving this request, the Prime Minister, Major-General Phibun Songkhram, ordered a memorandum to be sent to the French Minister in Bangkok stating that while the government of Thailand would be willing to agree to the French request that the non-aggression treaty take effect without having to wait on the exchange of instruments of ratification between the two governments, it would like to point out that at the time the treaty was signed on 12 June 1940, the situation in Indochina was still stable, whereas this was no longer the case. The Thai government hoped that the French government would understand that it was, therefore, only natural for the government of Thailand to be concerned about the fate of Thai nationals in Indochina. Before allowing the non-aggression treaty to come into effect the Thai government would, therefore, like to propose that definite agreement be reached over the following problems, namely that the boundary line at the river Mekong be adjusted according to principles of international law, that is by adhering to the *Thalweg* line, with administrative problems related to this being settled as outlined in the exchange of letters of

12 June 1940,[21] and secondly that the boundary should be redefined according to natural frontier lines, with the river Mekong forming the boundary line between Thailand and Indochina from the north southwards to the frontier with Cambodia. Thailand would thereby recover her territories on the right bank of the Mekong opposite Luang Prabang and Pakse; this clause was to be fully effective from the time the agreement was signed. Lastly, the government of Thailand intimated that it would be very grateful if it could be undertaken in writing that in the event of Indochina being taken out of French jurisdiction, France would return Laos and Cambodia to Thailand. In such an event, the Thai government would treat French officials in those territories favorably (meaning that they could stay on in the Civil Service if they wished to). The Thai government meantime cabled its Minister at Vichy that same day instructing him to hand a memorandum containing these same clauses to the French Foreign Minister.

While we were waiting on a reply from the French, the American Minister frequently visited me to discuss the *status quo* situation. I explained to him that our demands to France were twofold: firstly that there be an adjustment of our frontiers, and secondly that in the event of a change in the *status quo* position, France would return the territories we had formerly held to us instead of handing them over to Japan. Mr. Grant told me that the American Ambassador to Tokyo, Mr. Grew, had been to see Mr. Matsuoka, the Japanese Minister of Foreign Affairs, to enquire what the Japanese course of action in Indochina was going to be. Mr. Matsuoka had stated that Japan would maintain the *status quo* in Indochina, so that nothing would change even if Japanese troops entered Indochinese territory.

From the records of the International Military Tribunal, Far East, Tokyo, we later learned that during this same period the French Ambassador to Japan, M. Arsène Henry, had called on the Japanese Ministry of Foreign Affairs and charged that Thailand was carrying out acts of aggression. The Japanese Vice-Minister of Foreign Affairs, Mr. Chuichi Ohashi, evaded the issue, saying that it was none of Japan's business. The French Ambassador then commented that Japanese support for Thailand might slow down talks over Japan's request for establishing military bases in Indochina. Mr. Ohashi replied that if France refused this request, the use of force might have to be contemplated.[22]

On 17 September 1940 France sent a reply to our earlier memorandum through the Thai Minister at Vichy. This stated that firstly the French government had never requested that the non-aggression treaty become effective prior to the ratification thereof by the two governments. It had merely expressed the wish that the exchange of ratifications be carried out as soon as the French instrument of ratification reached Bangkok. Next, the French government did not see why the Thai government should regard the situation in Indochina as abnormal. It therefore saw no reason for the Thai government to be concerned over certain groups of people living in territories under French jurisdiction. Thirdly, the French government was ready to send a delegation to carry out negotiations for settling differences relating to the Mekong at the same time that the non-aggression treaty was ratified; and lastly, the French government was firmly resolved to resist any demand or attack, whatever its origin, designed to alter the political status or territorial integrity of Indochina. It therefore rejected our demand for territories on the right bank of the Mekong. As for our demands concerning the possible return of Laos and Cambodia, they were regarded as groundless.

Our Minister at Vichy reported that he had already explained to the French Director-General of the Far East Department who had handed him this memorandum that its first clause was incorrect. The French Foreign Minister had indeed made such a request, as could be proved by existing evidence. However, Phra Phahitthanukon was told that in any event the first clause was of minor concern, and it was the third clause that France considered to be the important one.

It can be seen from the French reply that France was simply trying to evade the issue. Its insistence, for example, that the situation in Indochina was normal, was patently contradicted by the fact that Japan had already been allowed to set up military bases in Indochina—a situation that could not be regarded as normal under any circumstances. France further denied that it had asked for the non-aggression treaty to become effective immediately without having to wait on the exchange of ratifications by the two governments, claiming it had merely asked that ratification take place as soon as the French letter of ratification arrived in Bangkok. This was merely another way of saying the same thing. France wanted to see the treaty ratified before it agreed to a readjustment of our frontiers; only after the treaty was ratified was it willing to have its delegation conduct negotiations on the Mekong boundary dispute. Why else would France have continued to put off sending its delegation to Thailand?

On 25 September 1940 the Thai government replied to the French government that it was pleased to learn that the French government was still willing to conduct negotiations to settle the problems concerning the Mekong frontier line. Our proposal that the Mekong be taken as the frontier line between Thailand and Indochina all the way from the north southwards to the Cambodian frontier had not, however, been fully understood. It had no connection whatsoever with the present international crisis, nor was Thailand seizing on France's present predicament to put forward this request.[23] Rather it had been presented for the French government's consideration and sympathy in order that good relations between Thailand and France might be maintained. The frontier question had long been a subject of study by the Thai government. It had arisen as a result of the long historical relationship between our two countries, during the course of which Thailand had ceded extensive areas of territory to France, including land on the right bank of the Mekong. France had already admitted that this section of Indochina was ours, and had advocated the use of friendly negotiations as a means to settle frontier disputes, so Thailand was merely abiding by this principle in putting forward its proposal. In fact, if the Thai government's proposal was viewed in the light of international goodwill, it could be seen to be preeminently reasonable. The river Mekong formed a natural frontier between our two countries, and accepting it as such would not result in any great loss of territory to France. On the contrary, acceptance of such an arrangement would serve to show that France had shown fairness in its dealings with Thailand, and would help to enhance the good relations already existing between our two countries. Thailand had long considered and discussed the settlement of these remaining problems with France, and was only putting forward this proposal officially as she felt that the forthcoming negotiations over the Mekong boundary line would be a good opportunity to discuss other matters as well. The presence of foreign troops in Indochina did demonstrate, however, that the situation in Indochina could not in any way be described as normal. This made it all the more necessary that we should abide by a joint natural frontier. The Thai government therefore called on the French government to consider the matter impartially and in the spirit of justice, and to bear in mind the need for friendly understanding and good relations between neighboring countries. The Thai government further hoped that the subject of Laos and Cambodia would also be taken up at the meeting for revision of the Mekong boundary. However, this could be taken up for discussion later if and when the necessity arose should there be a change of circumstances in Indochina. Lastly, the Thai government wished to emphasize once again that it was ready to ratify the non-aggression treaty, and hoped that the French representatives from Indochina would arrive in Bangkok shortly.[24]

[Meanwhile border violations by the French increased.] On 28 September 1940, Major-General Luang Phibun Songkhram, the Prime Minister, instructed me to protest about the situation to the French Minister.[25] Our first grounds for complaint concerned the continuing violation of our territory by French planes. Planes of the Royal Thai Air Force had been sent up to try to get the French pilots to bring their planes down, but these signals had been totally ignored and the French planes had been allowed to escape back to the French side of the border. That very afternoon planes of the Royal Thai Air Force making an observation flight over the Mekong frontier had been fired on by the French.

Fortunately, no damage was done. However, I handed the French Minister a letter of protest as a matter of record.

Further grounds for complaint concerned reports received by the Thai government that on 26 September 1940 a Thai national named Chantha Sintharako had been shot to death by the French police in Vientiane because he carried no entry permit. We held that he should have been detained, and legal proceedings brought against him, but that he should not have been shot. The Minister expressed his regrets over this affair, and asked the Thai Foreign Ministry to send a letter confirming the incident. This we did the following day. Later, on 4 and 7 October 1940 we received two letters from the French Minister. The first stated that he had asked both the Vichy and Hanoi governments to find the person responsible for the incident, while he himself was willing to confer with the Thai over any possible reparations for this tragic affair. The second letter, dated 7 October 1940, announced that the French were ready to have Thai officials take part in a post-mortem examination of the dead man, who had been buried by that time.[26]

I also took up with the French Minister the question of our reply to the French government's memorandum of 17 September described earlier. I gave him a copy of our reply memorandum, and added that we regretted the apparent misunderstanding of the matter by the Vichy government. We had in no way wished to challenge France, nor were we contemplating the use of force under any circumstances. Our proposal had been put forward in the interest of mutual benefit, and on the grounds of justice and fairness. As the French Minister was well aware, the present demarcation of the frontier line was not acceptable to us, and our proposal that the Mekong be treated as a natural frontier in its entire stretch from Luang Prabang to Pakse so that lands on its right bank came under Thai jurisdiction was in every respect reasonable.

The French Minister expressed his agreement with the above, and stated that he would send in a report supporting our proposal, for which I expressed my gratitude. I added that in fact our proposal for the readjustment of the frontier would only involve France's ceding one-eighth of her territory in Indochina. The Minister thereupon asked me to take a look at the map in the reception room with him, and asked me to tell him in all sincerity the extent of the territory we wanted, and whether this would be all, or whether we would continue to make further demands. I told him that we were not keeping anything secret, but only wanted back the lands we had been forced to cede to France in 1904, or in other words, those lands on the right bank of the Mekong opposite Luang Prabang and Pakse, as we wished to have a natural frontier for purposes of self-defense. As for other territories ceded to France, we only asked for the right to carry out negotiations concerning them should the situation in Indochina change.

On 5 October 1940 the French government replied through our Minister at Vichy. It stated that the French government was pleased to learn that Thailand was still willing to ratify the non-aggression treaty, and saw that the Thai government had taken note of the French position regarding Laos and Cambodia. The French government wished to see the treaty ratified as soon as the French letter of ratification arrived in Bangkok. To accommodate the Thai request for a joint conference to be held by a joint French and Thai delegation to consider the question of the Mekong boundary line and to ratify the non-aggression treaty, the French government had gathered together a team of experts on Indochinese affairs who were ready to travel to Thailand as soon as a date for the conference had been fixed. The French government could not, however, yield to the Thai government's wish that this same committee confer over the question of lands on the right bank of the Mekong, as the French government did not in any way accept the principle of returning these territories to Thailand. On the contrary, the French government considered the present frontier arrangements as final, and wished to refer to the clause in the treaty of 23 March 1907 whereby both parties undertook to refrain from making any future territorial claims. The French government agreed last June to give special consideration to the question of ownership of islands in the Mekong only upon receipt of an undertaking that no further territorial demands would be made upon it. Given recent developments, the French government found it necessary, moreover, to uphold its political status and its sovereignty in Indochina against all claims and attacks regardless of their origins.[27]

It should be noted that while our arguments had always been presented with courtesy, the French government's reply was defiant and provocative. France referred to the treaty of 23 March 1907, which contained a clause stating that the frontier agreement made therein was final. It therefore claimed Thailand had no right to make any further territorial demands. France also alleged that the word "final" had been inserted at the insistence of Thailand, and that the agreement was therefore not open to any changes. I have no evidence of the truth or falsity of this allegation, but even supposing that the Thai government of that time (1907) really did insist on the insertion of this word, surely this was not done with the intention of tying Thailand's hands in the future so that we would be prevented for ever after from making demands for the return of our territories? Surely the word "final" was inserted merely to indicate that this would be the last agreement Thailand would make ceding territory to France, so that France could not make any further territorial demands on us in the future? It would have been most unlikely that the Thai government of that time would have inserted the word "final" for the benefit of France.

As to France's other allegation, namely that [at the time the non-aggression treaty was signed] we had given an undertaking not to make any further territorial claims, I can find no evidence of such an undertaking in the records of the negotiations I have already outlined in detail in chapter 2. On the contrary, the letter from our Prime Minister, Major-General Luang Phibun Songkhram, to the French Minister clearly states the frontier should be revised according to the principles of international law.[28]

On 20 October 1940, in a speech to the nation,[29] the Prime Minister went over the whole course of our negotiations with France for the readjustment of our mutual boundaries. In his speech, the Prime Minister recalled the goodwill Thailand had shown toward France. He pointed out that Thailand had suggested that discussions be held regarding adjustment of the frontier as far back as 1936, when negotiations were held for a Franco-Thai trade and shipping agreement. At that time France had asked, however, that any discussions about the boundary line be postponed until such time as talks were held on Indochina. In order to maintain good relations between our two nations, the Thai government had agreed to wait.

Some time before the outbreak of the Second World War, however, France had approached the Prime Minister and requested that Thailand sign a treaty of non-aggression with her. The Prime Minister had not seen any necessity for this at the time. Later France had requested such a treaty again, but the Prime Minister had refused to take this up lest other nations misunderstand Thailand's motives. However, shortly before war broke out in Europe, France had approached Thailand yet a third time asking that a treaty of non-aggression be drawn up between the two countries. This time, the Prime Minister continued, realizing that the outbreak of war was imminent, and because we wanted to show France that Thailand was well intended towards it, we agreed to such negotiations. However, we first wanted to see our frontiers adjusted according to principles of international law. France agreed to adjust our mutual frontiers to the extent of adhering to the deep water channel of the Mekong, and it was understood that at the same time negotiations were held to put this agreement into effect, the question of adjustment of our frontiers in general would be taken up.

The Prime Minister pointed out that Thailand's agreement to sign the [non-aggression] treaty, and her demands for boundary adjustment had been motivated solely by a love of peace and a desire to establish Thailand's borders on a permanent and stable basis. They were in no way to be construed as aggressive in intent. Moreover, the signing of a non-aggression treaty with France had provided France with an opening to atone for her acts of injustice towards Thailand in the past so that no further ill-feeling need exist to mar the friendship between the two countries in the future. Unfortunately, however, France had misconstrued Thailand's good intentions. Following our signing of the treaty of non-aggression on 12 June 1940, it had agreed to go only as far as ratifying the treaty and considering giving us the islands in the river Mekong.

The Thai government felt this was unjust, and that unless France was prepared to show good faith [by considering the whole range of issues involved], then it would be pointless to ratify the non-aggression treaty, as any such mutual non-aggression pact implies that the two nations concerned pledged sincere and lasting friendship with one another, and friendship can only be based on the principle of fair treatment of each other. The Thai government therefore felt it should delay ratifying the non-aggression treaty for the time being.

In regard to Thailand's lost territories, the Prime Minister claimed he was confident that Thailand would recover these, for its demands were supported by a considerable body of documentation. To begin with, the records showed beyond any doubt that France had taken these lands from Thailand by force, and this was widely recognized by other nations. The Thai people, moreover, firmly supported the government in its demands for restitution of these territories, as demonstrated by the support being offered by volunteers who had declared their willingness to give their lives for their country, or as witness the many donations and demonstrations that had taken place in support of the government's position. These reactions had not been artificially engendered, the Prime Minister claimed, but were completely spontaneous outbursts on the part of the Thai people. The Prime Minister wished to express his profound gratitude for this support. There was also support for the government's demands from Thailand's brothers in Laos and Cambodia who were now suffering under French rule, as well as from the Vietnamese community and even from French citizens living in Thailand.

The Prime Minister stressed that everybody should remain calm and coolheaded. They should resort to arms only as a last resort, and even then see that the least possible blood was spilled. In the event of war, the populace would be divided into three groups. The first would be made up of able-bodied men who would be sent to the front. The size of this group would depend on the quantity of arms available for them. A ceiling on the numbers of this group had already been set by the Ministry of Defense. The second group would consist of supply and medical officers who would work behind the lines. The Ministry of Defense had also made preparations for the formation of this group, but would need to ask for additional volunteers should the requisite time come. The third group would comprise the general mass of the population. This group should work to increase national production and be as frugal as possible in order to ensure that the entire nation was well supplied with food and other necessities. The

Prime Minister also asked that those in this last category try to stay in their normal places of work and living, and not move to other districts in response to war scares.

As far as Thailand's attitude towards other countries was concerned, the Prime Minister continued, it was one of goodwill to all nations in keeping with our national policy, excepting, naturally, towards those nations that treated us unjustly. Many people are mistaken, he went on, in believing that our Thai brothers in Cambodia and Laos are Khmer or Lao and therefore of different nationality than ourselves. The people of Cambodia and Laos, he stressed, are people of Thai descent who were deprived of their independence when they fell under French jurisdiction. Many similarities in religion, customs and traditions existed between the peoples of Thailand and those of Cambodia and Laos. However, the Prime Minister explained, the citizens of Thailand benefited from the freedoms and liberties of a constitutional monarchy. They differed in this way from Thailand's brothers in Cambodia and Laos, who had fallen under French rule. The Prime Minister called on Admiral Decoux, the Governor-General of Indochina, to grant these brothers of Thailand the same rights and freedoms as their French counterparts in Indochina and their Thai counterparts in Thailand.

There was no chance of any improvement in France's position in Indochina, the Prime Minister declared. Once the French had been rendered powerless [by the Japanese], Thailand's brothers in Laos and Cambodia as well as the citizens of Vietnam would receive their freedom and have self-government restored to them. There was no doubt but that Thailand's brothers in these lands would be returned to the jurisdiction of the government and restored to the protection of the Thai monarchy.

Finally, the Prime Minister called on all Thai to remember their heritage. They should try to follow the advice of the government, which would undoubtedly succeed in obtaining the adjustment of the frontier line that was in the forefront of every Thai person's hopes.[30]

Meanwhile tension over the frontier increased as French planes continued to violate our territory either in the course of observation flights or by flying across the border and intimidating local inhabitants. Several times our fighter planes had to take off to chase them back over the border. In the meantime M. Lépissier, the French Minister, was recalled on charges that he was too soft in his dealings with us. Monsieur Roger Garreau[31] was sent to take charge of the legation in his place. However, the latter did not hold an official position in our eyes, as his appointment was not officially announced to the Thai government either via our Minister at Vichy or through our Ministry of Foreign Affairs. I think this matter deserves to be touched on in a little more detail, as it involved diplomatic procedures.

On 13 December 1940 Mr. Grant, the American Minister, came to see me. He mentioned that M. Garreau had told him he had been unsuccessful in arranging any contacts with the Thai government, as no Thai officials would agree to see him. M. Garreau had tried to initiate talks with us, but the letter he had sent to the Prime Minister in the latter's capacity as Foreign Minister two days earlier had not even been answered. In other words, M. Garreau had insinuated to Mr. Grant that French attempts to initiate negotiations with us had not met with any signs of cooperation on the part of the Thai government. M. Garreau also claimed he had been unable to get in touch with either Vichy or Indochina as all the cable lines had been tampered with.

I told the American Minister that as M. Garreau was merely in charge of the legation he had no authority to open talks on political issues. Sir Josiah Crosby, the British Minister, told me that M. Garreau had been to see him as well with similar complaints. However, Sir Josiah had expressed the opinion that the Thai government was correct in its treatment of him, as M. Garreau was not officially the French Chargé d'Affaires. The British Minister had even suggested that if M. Garreau wanted to be treated as a Chargé d'Affaires, he had only to ask his government to announce his official appointment immediately through the Thai Minister at Vichy. As far as the charge that the cable lines had been tampered with was concerned, I told the American Minister I knew nothing about this. However, I said I would like to point out to him that communications between the Thai Consul in Saigon and the Foreign Ministry in Bangkok had also been disrupted as a result of the French switching the cable lines.

The American Minister retorted that we should, nevertheless, pay attention to M. Garreau's remarks. If we did not do so, France might tell other governments that it had sought to open negotiations with us, but had been prevented from doing so by the Thai government. Mr. Grant emphasized that this was merely an expression of his own personal opinion and not in any way an official statement. I could see, however, that Mr. Grant was not interested in seeing our point of view, so I changed the topic of conversation. Later I reported on this conversation to Field Marshal Phibun Songkhram in the latter's capacity as Minister of Foreign Affairs. He told me that I should in turn take up with the American Minister the question of our not having received the planes we had ordered from the United States even though we had paid in full for them.[32] He instructed me to ask Mr. Grant what the United States intended to do about the fact that we had neither received the planes nor had our money returned to us.

Throughout November 1940, French planes continued to bombard our territory. They violated the frontier around the district of Mukdahan, and raided the border along the provinces of Nong Khai and Nakhon Phanom [all areas in northeast Thailand bordering the Mekong River.] We duly retaliated by sending our air force to bombard French territory.

On 28 November 1940 a critical point was reached. On that day the Prime Minister, in his capacity as Commander-in-Chief of the Armed Forces, received a cable from the governor of Nakhon Phanom. This reported that at 08.00 hours that day five French planes had flown over Nakhon Phanom with dubious intent. Our fighter planes had been sent up to defend the town. The French planes had thereupon bombed it, injuring six civilians. On receipt of this news, the Prime Minister instructed me to inform the Ministers of Britain, the United States, Germany and Italy and the Japanese Chargé d'Affaires of the incident. The Thai Air Force bombarded French military barracks in Indochina on the same day as a return measure.

From that time on there were frequent clashes between our two countries. On 5 January 1941, French troops launched an attack on Aranyaprathet.[33] Our troops entered Cambodia in retaliation. Twenty-two days of fighting followed. During that time we took over much ground.[34] On the eastern front, Thai forces attacked Poipet, a frontier post across the border from Aranyaprathet, seized the highway from the frontier to the city of Sisophon, and then fanned out along the border for approximately forty kilometers from the area opposite Buri Ram and Surin down towards Chanthaburi, later taking some villages near Ban Phailin. On the northeastern front, the Thai Northeastern Army pushed westwards from Ubon to join forces with the Eastern Army across the frontier from Buri Ram and Surin, seizing about ninety kilometers of land around Siemreap and Angkor Wat. It also moved eastwards into the triangular area of land on the right side of the Mekong opposite Pakse and Champassac. The Thai government had been seeking the return of this area as part of its claims for readjusting of the frontier. Thai forces occupied it by 22 January. Lastly, the Northern Army occupied the entire Luang Prabang region on the right side of the Mekong—the other piece of territory sought by Thailand in its memorandum to the French government asking to have the river Mekong form the natural boundary between the two countries.

JAPANESE MEDIATION

Some people have said that Thailand sought the return of her territories at the instigation of Japan, and that Japan hoped to gain certain benefits by helping us in this way. I do not know for sure if this was true or not, as Major-General Phibun Songkhram never alluded to the matter in front of me. However, records of the International Military Tribunal at Tokyo obtained through documents of the Japanese Ministry of Foreign Affairs do not show the slightest evidence of Japanese instigation or support for Thailand's claims. On the contrary, it would seem that our demands were actually embarrassing to Japan, as it was in the process of negotiating for military bases in Indochina at the time, as mentioned earlier.[35]

I have already mentioned that in the course of my various discussions with the British Minister, the latter had expressed the view that should Indochina be ceded to Japan, it would be best to let Thailand have the two portions of land on the right side of the Mekong that we had been seeking. England considered it worthwhile retaining the gratitude of our country, and even went so far as to suggest that Britain, rather than Japan, act as the mediator in our dispute with French Indochina. This was revealed in an *aide-mémoire* from the British legation to the United States Department of State dated 6 January 1941, which stated that Admiral Decoux, the Governor-General of Indochina, had sent his *aide de camp*, Captain Jouan, to Singapore to discuss the question of economic cooperation between Indochina and Singapore and of resistance against Japanese encroachments with the British. During the course of the discussions, the question of the conflict between Thailand and Indochina was raised, and Captain Jouan indicated that Indochina would be willing to have the United States, or the United States jointly with England, act as mediators in the dispute. He also claimed that Indochina could produce evidence to show that Japan had been providing Thailand with planes and ammunition despite the latter's claim to neutrality in the conflict.

The *aide-mémoire* went on to state that the British Minister in Bangkok had heard that Germany had also expressed sympathy for Thailand's territorial claims. The British government felt that the conflict must be resolved peacefully and as soon as possible, and that Japan, with or without the support of Germany, should not be allowed to act as mediator. The British government was concerned that neither Thailand nor France become indebted to Japan, and believed that bringing the conflict to an end would help France offer stronger resistance against Japan. France and Thailand should therefore either enter into direct negotiations with one another to settle the dispute, or the United States or England should act as mediators.

The British government recognized that negotiations would be successful only if both parties were willing to make concessions. France would have to cede the two portions of territory on the right side of the Mekong claimed by Thailand, together with certain islands in the Mekong, while Thailand would have to be satisfied with these concessions and provide an undertaking that it would not make any further territorial demands.

CHAPTER 3

The British government was aware that Mr. [Sumner] Welles, the United States Under-Secretary of State, believed that if France agreed to cede even a small amount of territory to Thailand at this time, it would amount to her allowing Thailand to succeed in an act of blackmail, and that this could possibly produce repercussions with other nations. The British government recognized the force of this argument, but if France was unwilling to agree to any territorial changes as a means of bringing the fighting to an end, then the British government did not wish to offer its mediation in the dispute. However, the *aide-mémoire* continued, this did not appear to be the case. The United States should take into account Captain Jouan's sense that France would be willing to negotiate, and should consider the following arguments.

The longer the fighting went on, the more both parties laid themselves open to Japanese intervention or attack. Japan was busily supplying Thailand with arms in an effort to prolong the war, as by prolonging it both the Thai and the French would be weakened. Should Japan become the mediator in the dispute, it would use its position to obtain numerous strategic advantages from both Thailand and France that would assist the Japanese in their plans to advance further south (towards Malaya). Thus, if the fighting continued or Japan was allowed to intervene in the situation, it would strengthen Japan's position in Southeast Asia, thereby threatening not only Indochina and Thailand, but also the Netherlands East Indies and British possessions in the Far East, and thus ultimately Great Britain and the United States themselves.

Given these circumstances the British government wished to know right away if the United States government considered British mediation could be of use. If so, it should be offered without delay. The United States or England would not in any event be able to act openly as mediators, as Germany and Japan would undoubtedly raise objections to this. Instead, France and Thailand would have to hold direct negotiations, with England and the United States exercising influence in the background.[36]

On 10 January 1941 the United States State Department sent an *aide-mémoire* in reply stating that while the United States government agreed with Britain that fighting between Thailand and Indochina must be brought to an end peacefully and without delay, it considered both countries to be in a precarious situation. In both countries there was a division of opinion and attitudes among their leaders. An inescapable aspect of the background situation in Indochina was France's defeat by Germany; in Thailand it was that Japan had embarked on a course of aggression in the Far East. It was therefore doubtful that a permanent and guaranteed settlement could be reached in the near future.

The government of the United States agreed with the British government that an open offer of mediation would be unsuccessful. It could not therefore see that offering to act as mediator would serve any useful purpose at this time. However, if Thailand and French Indochina agreed to enter into negotiations directly or otherwise, and if the circumstances were such that the two parties felt they could benefit from the friendly advice of the United States, then the government of the United States would of course be willing to offer its assistance.[37]

In the meantime, the Japanese government learned that Admiral Decoux had sent his representative to Singapore. Mr. Matsuoka, the Japanese Minister of Foreign Affairs, therefore called on M. Arsène Henry, the French Ambassador to Japan, to deliver a protest, claiming that France had thereby violated the bonds of friendship with Japan. At the same time he let the French Ambassador know that he had heard that the British Minister in Bangkok had offered to mediate in the conflict.[38]

I meanwhile tried on a number of occasions to persuade M. Garreau that we should come to terms with one another lest others reap the profits of our dispute. During my last such attempt, made on 13 January 1941, the French Chargé d'Affaires told me he had sent a report on the subject to his government at Vichy, but that evidently the latter did not agree with his suggestions.

As for Japan acting as mediator in the conflict, so far as I can remember Major-General Luang Phibun Songkhram, the Prime Minister/Foreign Minister, never once intimated to me that Japan had approached Thailand offering itself as mediator. However, on 21 January 1941, the Japanese government put the following proposition to the Vichy government. According to the reports of the French Ambassador in Tokyo, Mr. Matsuoka, the Japanese Foreign Minister, invited the former over on 19 and 20 January to tell him that he had been authorized by the Emperor to insist on offering Japan's mediation in this conflict.[39] Japan could not allow England to intervene in the affairs of Thailand at the expense of Japanese interests, and Japan's offer of mediation was being made solely for the sake of peace in the region. The same offer was also being put forward to the Thai government. It was hoped, therefore, that the French government would see fit to accept it. Mr. Matsuoka pointed out that the offer was made within the framework of Japan's agreement with Indochina of August 1940.[40] Japan wished to point out to Indochina that acceptance of England's offer of mediation would, therefore, be in violation of that agreement. If Japanese mediation was accepted, an immediate cease-fire would be called for. The French government thereupon accepted the Japanese proposals.[41]

On 22 January 1941 Mr. Matsuoka, the Japanese Minister of Foreign Affairs, announced that the Thai were presently demanding the return of certain territories from French Indochina. Thai troops were facing French forces along the Indochina border, and frequent clashes had taken place between them. Japan, as leader of Asia, could not feign indifference to this conflict, and hoped, therefore, that the fighting would stop at the first opportunity. This was the first time the Japanese government openly announced its desire to mediate the conflict; until then it had taken a position of non-intervention.

Two days later, on 24 January 1941, Radio Tokyo broadcast that the governments of both France and Thailand had accepted Japan's mediation offer. On the same day, Major-General Luang Phibun Songkhram called a meeting of the Council of Ministers and announced that Japan had made this offer, and that we had no choice but to accept it.[42]

I had in fact been told by the Prime Minister/Foreign Minister of the Japanese offer at the last minute, about a day before Japan made the above broadcast. However, I had been told to keep the matter totally secret. When the American Minister questioned me as to when Japan had put forward this offer, I was, therefore, truthful in telling him that I really did not know.[43]

At 10.00 hours Bangkok time on 28 January 1941 a ceasefire was declared on all fronts.[44] Japan proposed that a fifteen day truce be declared by the two combatant countries, starting from the above time.

On 29 January 1941 a Thai delegation of civilian and military officials[45] under Group Captain Phra Sinlapasatstrakhom, chief of the delegation, left for Saigon to negotiate the truce agreement with the Japanese and French delegations. This was signed off Saigon aboard the Japanese *natori*[46] cruiser on 31 January 1941. The delegation returned to Bangkok on 1 February.

By the terms of the cease-fire each side was to withdraw its troops ten kilometers from their positions as at 10.00 hours on 28 January 1941, so that clashes between the two could be avoided before an absolute settlement of the dispute had been negotiated. At sea a demarcation line was drawn. Warships of the countries concerned were not to cross this, while in the air similar lines were drawn that planes of the nations concerned might not violate. Withdrawal of troops by both sides was to be completed within seventy-two hours of the signing of the cease-fire. The period of cease-fire agreed to was fifteen days. During this time the governments of the countries concerned were to send delegations to Tokyo to negotiate a final peace agreement. If no agreement was reached, then the cease-fire could be extended at the mutual consent of Thailand, Japan and France.

On 4 February 1941 the Thai government sent a second delegation made up of civilian and military officials and led by Prince Wanwaithayakon to Tokyo to conduct peace talks and carry out negotiations for an adjustment of our frontiers.[47] Talks opened in Tokyo on 7 February 1941, but as the discussions took longer than expected, the cease-fire was extended twice, from 12 to 25 February, and again from 25 February to 7 March 1941.

Finally a preliminary agreement between Thailand and France was initialed on 11 March 1941 at 14.00 hours Bangkok time. Details were broadcast to the Thai people over Radio Tokyo by Prince Wanwaithayakon that evening. In his message he stated that under the agreement Thailand had regained all its lands on the right bank of the Mekong together with those territories in Cambodia that had been ceded to France by the treaties of 1904 and 1907, although Siemreap and Angkor Wat were to remain under French jurisdiction. Thailand had also gained territory in Cambodia from Angkor Wat north to the Mekong just below Stung Treng. In addition, the deep water channel, or thalweg, had been accepted as the frontier line in the Mekong, with islands to the right of this line to be regarded as Thai property. In return, Thailand had agreed to treat French nationals living within the territories now returned to Thai jurisdiction on terms of equality with the Thai. The lands now returned were to be treated as demilitarized zones, with the French drawing their own demilitarized zones parallel to ours.[48]

Following the broadcast of Prince Wanwaithayakon's speech, Nai Thawi Tawethikun, [the secretary of the delegation], broadcast an official joint communiqué between Thailand and France. This reiterated the points already covered in Prince Wan's speech. It also included additional points covered by the agreement concerning the Thai government being willing to respect the Mausoleum of the Luang Prabang Royal House, and the question of jurisdiction over the Khong and Khone islands in the Mekong. These last were to be placed under Thai sovereignty, but administered jointly by Thailand and France.[49]

The joint communiqué further announced that letters had been exchanged between Japan, and France and Thailand respectively, to the effect that Japan guaranteed the definitive nature of the agreement. Agreements were to be made later regarding the maintenance of peace in the Far East and the establishment and promotion of special relations between Japan and France and Japan and Thailand.[50]

The final peace agreement was signed [in Tokyo] on 9 May 1941, together with accompanying documents.[51] On 9 June 1941 the Prime Minister gave a speech to the nation in which he went over the entire course of relations between Thailand and France from 1936 through to the signing of the 9 May 1941 peace treaty. At the end of it he asked people to think over the actions that had been taken by the government and if they were in favor of these then to vote in favor of ratifying the treaty.[52]

Finally, I should like to add just a little more about the conflict between Thailand and France. Although clashes between our two armies took place, there was never a declaration of war nor were diplomatic relations broken off between us. I therefore continued to see both the French Minister and Chargé d'Affaires throughout the conflict in an attempt to find a peaceful solution to the dispute. However, this was to no avail. In truth I did not have much influence nor was my opinion of much weight in my position as Deputy Minister of Foreign Affairs. At a time when the French were extremely unpopular in our country I tried, nonetheless, throughout the period to negotiate with their representatives and show them genuine courtesy. In this way they were able to see that even though we might be at variance with France, we nevertheless still respected and abided strictly by international diplomatic etiquette. In this regard, M. Garreau, the French Chargé d'Affaires, wrote to me saying that he was glad to see that the Saigon press, reporting on my speech to the Bangkok Rotary Club of 29 May 1941, in which I had given a brief account of the negotiations leading up to the recent peace treaty signed in Tokyo, had shown recognition of my correct and courteous attitude. He enclosed a clipping of the article of 6 June 1941 from *L'Opinion* praising my impartial attitude and statesmanlike qualities.[53]

JAPAN RAISES ITS LEGATION IN THAILAND TO EMBASSY STATUS

During discussions over the frontier dispute, the Japanese Minister informed the Prime Minister, Major-General Luang Phibun Songkhram, that Japan was thinking of raising the status of its legation in Thailand to that of an embassy, and hoped that Thailand would consider effecting a similar raise with its legation in Japan. The Prime Minister raised no objections to this idea, which the Japanese Minister told him was merely being contemplated at this stage by his government. Once an official decision on the matter had been reached, he would notify us.

When the Prime Minister told me about this matter, I expressed the opinion that should Japan formally put forward such a proposal, then we should give both England and the United States the opportunity to effect a similar raise in order to demonstrate our neutrality and impartiality in such matters. I had learned that by proposing to raise the status of her legation to that of an embassy Japan sought to make itself leader of the diplomatic community, or in other words Dean of the Diplomatic Corps, since at that time diplomatic representation of foreign countries in Thailand existed only at legation level. The Prime Minister agreed with my suggestion.

In November 1940 the British Minister came to tell me he had received a cable from Sir Robert Craigie, the British Ambassador to Tokyo, mentioning that Japan intended to raise the status of its legation in Bangkok to that of an embassy, and that the Japanese government had already received an increase in the 1941 budget to carry this out. The British Minister wished to know if this report was true, for if so he would like to know in advance the date such an arrangement was to be carried out so that England would have an equal opportunity with Japan [to raise its legation to an embassy]. Without such an opportunity Japan would receive an [unfair] advantage. I told the Minister I had already discussed this matter with him earlier at the time the Japanese Minister had originally approached the Prime Minister on the subject, and that to date Japan had not presented any official proposal in this regard. The British Minister seemed satisfied with this answer.

In July 1941 we received a formal request from Japan to raise the status of its legation in Thailand to that of an embassy. The Council of Ministers saw no objection to this, but agreed with my suggestion that we should also invite Britain and the United States to do likewise lest we be accused of partiality. I therefore invited the British and American Ministers over to let them know that we wanted to give them an equal opportunity to raise their legations if they so wished. Otherwise, they might think us unfair. Not only that, but the British Minister had already requested this of me. If their respective governments agreed to effect such a raise, I suggested that this should be carried out at the same time as that with Japan. The British Minister thanked me and said he would report on the matter to his government without delay, but that in his personal opinion (I understood that the Minister had already received instructions on the matter from his government before this discussion was held) he did not believe his government would follow in Japan's footsteps, but would let Japan raise its legation on its own.

The American Minister, Mr. Grant, for his part admonished us at length, saying that the Thai government should not have been so weak, and that we should never have agreed to Japan's proposal. We could always have claimed, he said, that with Thailand being a small country we did not see the need for an embassy, and that to establish one would be nothing but a waste of money. I told the American Minister that our government had, however, already given its consent to Japan, and that in fact we had only let the United States know of the arrangement to demonstrate our impartiality. I pointed out to him that the Thai government was under no obligation to inform the Minister about it. Finally Mr. Grant agreed to report on the matter to his government and to make the United States aware of the goodwill thus being shown them by our country.

Our Foreign Ministry also sent a cable to our Minister in Washington, M.R. Seni Pramoj, telling him to pass on the same information to Mr. Hull, the United States Secretary of State. M.R. Seni later reported that he had been to see Mr. Hull as instructed. He then went on to report that no sooner had he entered the room than the Secretary of State had handed him the *curriculum vitae* of a Mr. Peck.[54] Mr. Hull had then proposed that Mr. Peck replace Mr. Grant, who would be recalled as American Minister to Thailand; this, he added, was to be kept completely confidential. At the same time Mr. Hull had explained that the appointment of Mr. Peck would not interfere with the United States' considering the suggestion of the Thai government regarding the establishment of an American embassy in Thailand. He added that such an establishment was unlikely, however, as a number of small countries had made similar requests.

Two to three weeks later, both the British and American Ministers informed me that their respective governments thanked the Thai government for its gesture of friendship, but that the two governments were not yet ready to raise the status of their legations.

Japan, however, agreed to exchange ambassadors with us in October 1941. Mr. Tsubokami was appointed as Japanese Ambassador to Thailand, while we raised Phraya Sisena, our Minister in Tokyo, to the rank of Ambassador.

4
Thailand in the Midst of Economic Warfare

It is generally agreed that World War II was not restricted solely to the battlefields and trenches, but was what is known as a total war in that the inhabitants of the combatant countries were also involved. Economic warfare as well as military battles played an important role in the conflict, for without a strong economic base no country could hold out no matter how powerful. The combatant nations therefore tried every means of annihilating their opponents not only through force, but by applying economic pressure. Between September 1940 and 8 December 1941 even Thailand, despite its status as an avowedly neutral country, found itself subjected to intense pressure as the opposing sides sought to gain economic advantages for themselves and their allies.

During this period England, together with several other countries, formed an allied front on the one side, while Germany and Italy established the Axis coalition on the other. In June 1941, when the U.S.S.R. was attacked by Germany, the Soviet Union joined the Allies. Meanwhile, in the Pacific, Japan continued to pursue its war against China. Although it had not yet entered the Second World War, it entered into an alliance with Germany and Italy. [The relationship proved uneasy, however.] Japan was very displeased when Germany signed a non-aggression treaty with the U.S.S.R. in August, 1940[1] [should be 1939—Ed.], for Hitler neither consulted Japan as its ally nor informed it in advance of Germany's intentions.

During the time that Japan was engaged in war with China, it also began speeding up its preparations for a southwards advance. As Japan did not wish to depend on Germany for economic support, it looked to a number of Commonwealth countries for raw materials such as iron, rubber, tin, oil, cotton and fur that it needed to produce certain industrial goods and ammunition, and to the United States for copper, petroleum and metal scrap.

Before the war Germany had relied for much of its raw materials on certain Asian countries, including what were then known as the Dutch East Indies, as well as China, Japan, Malaya, Thailand and Manchuria. When war broke out, the Allies saw no need to make special arrangements to ensure that those countries restrict the sale of these products to Germany, as they knew that the materials would have to be transported by sea, which greatly facilitated their control and check. Only Japan was singled out by England and asked to restrict the export of certain goods to Germany; unless it did so, England threatened, Britain in turn would be forced to restrict the supply of essential commodities exported to Japan from Commonwealth countries.

Once France fell to Germany in June 1940 the economic situation in the Far East began to change rapidly, however. England could no longer allow Japan to buy raw materials from Commonwealth countries for fear that these would be passed on to Germany or Italy either in their existing form or as finished products. As Japan became increasingly aggressive, the United States also started to place economic pressure on Japan. Although it never imposed absolute trade sanctions, the United States began restricting the sale of certain goods to Japan on the grounds that they were needed in the United States for the production of armaments.

[The situation also began to change in the Dutch East Indies.] Initially the Netherlands allowed its East Indies colony to conduct trade as usual with Japan, given that the latter was not a combatant opponent. Once Germany launched its attack on the Netherlands [in May 1940], however, Holland joined England in an effort to impose trade controls. Japan attempted to draw up a contract with the Dutch East Indies calling for the annual sale to Japan of 3,000 tons of tin, 20,000 tons of rubber, 1,000,000 tons of mineral oil, 3,750,000 tons of oil, 200,000 tons of bauxite, 100,000 tons of metal scrap, as well as nickel, manganese, wolfram, chrome, salt and many other materials. The quantity demanded for some of these materials was so great that it exceeded the amount that the colony was capable of producing. After consultations with the United States and England the Dutch government rejected the Japanese contract proposal, but as a gesture to appease Japan's annoyance stated it would be willing to sell Japan 1,956,000 tons of petroleum, or part of the amount requested. This arrangement was entered into only after the American government calculated in July 1940 that the Japanese navy had approximately 69 million tons of petroleum in stock, giving it roughly a year's supply in time of war. It was felt that a total oil embargo on Japan would only push it towards a declaration of war. The United States was not yet ready to cope with this. Neither was England, which was currently facing difficulties in Europe. Not until May 1941, by which time the United States was starting to build up its forces, and only after Japan continued to ignore all protests regarding its aggressive advance southwards did the United States seriously tighten controls over the sale of strategic products to Japan.

By the end of June 1941 the Allies had definite evidence that Japan was planning to take over Indochina, and in mid-July Japanese troops began occupying bases there. The United States government immediately ordered the freezing of all Japanese assets. England followed suit the next day. Over the ensuing months negotiations were held between the government of Japan and that of the United States on economic problems and on the question of aggressive action on the part of Japan. However, these negotiations met with no success. On 7 December 1941 Japan declared war on Britain and the United States. On 8 December Japanese troops entered Thailand, the details of which are taken up in the next chapter of this book.

As events in the Pacific arena began to move toward war, England and the United States found themselves competing directly with Japan for Thailand's rubber and tin supplies, since possession of these raw materials was extremely important to their respective war efforts. According to statistics, 1940 world rubber production amounted to 1,410,276 tons, of which 30,024 tons came from Thailand and 547,532 tons from Malaya. Japan bought about 12 percent of that year's production, and 50 percent of the following year's slightly increased production, the remaining 50 percent of the 1941 production being purchased by the Allies.

Statistics for 1940 also show that Thailand produced 6,300 tons of tin ore during that year. Two-thirds of the mines in Thailand were in the hands of British or Australian mine-owners. Two-thirds of that year's production was therefore claimed by England and the United States, while the remaining one third was sold on the open market.

As has already been stated, it was in 1941 that World War II extended to the Asian front, and was thus the period when economic warfare between the two opposing sides became increasingly fierce. Japan tried to exert as much pressure as possible on Field Marshal Phibun Songkhram, our Prime Minister, to obtain our entire tin and rubber production. His attention was drawn to Japan's mediation of the Indochina dispute, and promises were made to provide us with fuel [if Thailand complied with Japan's demands]. The United States and England strove for the same ends. Although they did not request our entire [tin and rubber] production, they asked that these be sold on a roughly fifty-fifty basis. The argument they put forward in support of their request was that since Thailand had declared its neutrality in the war, it should therefore give the two opposing sides equal opportunities for purchasing such goods. The United States and Britain also promised to help supply us with fuel as best they could [again, if Thailand went along with their requests]. England also threatened that if we showed favoritism towards Japan, then India would have to place controls over the export of jute sacks. This would have meant that we would have had no sacks for our rice exports, for at that time Thailand was not yet able to manufacture its own sacks, and therefore had to rely on India for its supply of these.

Meantime, officials sent by the Prime Minister to negotiate with the Japanese authorities signed a contract agreeing to sell our entire rubber and tin production for the year 1941 to Japan. They submitted this contract to the Prime Minister, who gave me a copy to study. Police-General Adun Adundetcharat, the Deputy Prime Minister, and I were of the opinion that the signatories of this contract had no authority to sign such an agreement, as this was a matter which fell under the authority of the Ministry of Foreign Affairs. Moreover, we felt that agreeing to such a contract would have disastrous results, as both Britain and the United States would regard it as unjustifiable and place even greater pressures on us in consequence.

The United States already suspected us of being dominated by Japan[2] because Japan had acted as mediator in our territorial dispute and in light of certain other matters. Indeed, the United States had even gone so far as to order the delaying of delivery of planes we had ordered and paid for, and which had been transported as far as the Philippines.[3] In the end the contract [i.e. the contract awarding Japan 100 percent of Thailand's rubber and tin for 1941] was declared null and void. Japan was extremely displeased, and accused the Thai Ministry of Foreign Affairs of having stood in its way. The Thai government eventually let both sides compete with one another in the open market for the purchase of our rubber and tin.

Another matter which weighed heavily on us during this period was the question of Japan placing pressure on the Prime Minister to make loans of Baht currency to Japan. The reason Japan gave for this need was that Japanese assets had been frozen by the United States and British governments.[4] The Yokohama Specie Bank[5] in Bangkok needed Baht currency, for it had run short of pounds sterling to exchange into Thai currency and Japan was therefore unable to pay for Thai products.

England tried to prevent us from helping Japan in this way, for it feared that the Japanese would then have the means to purchase war materials such as rubber and other products. The Council of Ministers assigned the Ministry of Finance[6] to study the problem. The report of the Minister of Finance was in agreement with the views expressed by the Prime Minister, namely that if we did not compromise with Japan, it might provoke a fierce outburst on Japan's part, or produce a situation where Japan would accuse us of showing favoritism towards the United States and England.

It was therefore decided that a 10 million Baht loan should be made to this Japanese bank by a group of three Thai banks known as the Bank Federation, comprising the Siam Commercial Bank, the Siam City Bank and the Bank of Asia. Japan could then purchase our products within the amount of this loan. The Thai government insisted that the loan be repaid in gold bullion, in spite of Japan's request that it be repaid in Yen, as we were unable to find a country to exchange Yen currency with at this time. Japan finally agreed, therefore, to repay the loan in gold bullion.

Despite this arrangement, Japan exhausted the 10 million Baht loan within a matter of months. In the middle of August 1941, the Japanese Minister, Mr. Futami, made a request for another loan to the Ministry of Foreign Affairs and the Prime Minister. Japan proposed that an additional loan of 25 million Baht be made on guarantee of repayment in gold, but that such gold be left with the Bank of Japan. The conditions surrounding the arrangement were so rigid that we would have had no way of transferring the gold to Thailand. The Council of Ministers again consulted the Minister of Finance, and authorized him to negotiate with Mr. Ono, former Japanese Deputy Minister of Finance and now Financial Advisor to the Japanese Ministry of Finance, who was currently in Thailand. The Thai Finance Minister, [Nai Pridi Banomyong], agreed to make the loan on condition that the gold bullion was delivered in Bangkok. The negotiations were conducted with such acrimony that Japan complained to the Prime Minister that the Thai Minister of Finance was an obstructionist and had insulted Japan. He asked why Thailand should trust England and the United States with custody of her gold, yet not do the same with Japan? Despite these exchanges, however, in the end Japan accepted our conditions.[7]

Another matter that concerned us at that time was that Thailand was short of fuel and military equipment, and particularly of planes and armaments necessary for our national self-defense. We had hoped for support from the United States in this regard. However, the latter suspected us of being in alliance with Japan, and our demands for territory in French Indochina had made the United States even more displeased with us. However, the American attitude changed to one of cooperation once Mr. Grant, the American Minister, was recalled and replaced by Mr. Peck.[8] England wanted to help us, but was unable to do so given its limited fuel supplies. All it could do was to try to persuade the United States to give us aid. England realized that if it helped us out it would earn the gratitude of our country, for Japan, which was then selling us planes and fuel, was squeezing every possible economic advantage out of us in return. I will be discussing the details of this further on in this book.[9]

From the beginning of 1941 on, I took the opportunity to suggest to Sir Josiah Crosby, the British Minister, and Mr. Grant, the American Minister, that England and the United States issue announcements stating that if Japan continued in its aggressive advance southwards, those two nations would deem such acts to be acts of aggression against their own territories. The British Minister agreed with my proposal, and made a detailed report on this request to his government. However, the American Minister disagreed with the British

Minister, for from the time of our border dispute with French Indochina and Japan's mediation of it, he had regarded us as totally subservient to Japan. The American Minister's view was not only a regrettable misunderstanding, but also mistaken, as can be seen from our refusal to sign the contract granting Japan the monopoly of our rubber and tin production [for 1941] and instead allowing all parties to purchase these vital raw materials on the open market as mentioned earlier.

England felt that it should help Thailand both politically and economically, and provide us with military equipment, for it feared that unless it did so we would be made the instrument of Japan, which would be a great disadvantage to the Allies. However, it felt that Thailand would first have to give an undertaking that we would not help Japan in any way that would undermine the security of British territory, and that we would not sell any military equipment directly or otherwise to the Axis. Moreover England felt that any proposals it might make alone would not carry much weight, as England was currently in a difficult position and could not provide us with any [significant amount of] military or economic aid. For this reason England invited the United States to join the negotiations with Thailand, and also asked Australia to try to persuade the United States [of the importance of providing Thailand with economic aid]. However, Mr. Cordell Hull, the United States Secretary of State, replied that providing such support would not result in a satisfactory outcome, as Thailand was already dominated by Japan.[10]

On 8 May 1941, Mr. Grant, the American Minister, sent a cable to the American government stating that plans were being made to persuade the United States to supply Thailand with fuel, not only for domestic purposes and for the iron and steel industry, but also for the use of the military and for manufacturing planes and other military equipment. Schemes were also under way to ask for a loan, he added. The United States should be on guard against any such maneuvers, Mr. Grant warned. As grounds for making such requests Thailand would be dwelling on the long-standing friendly relations between the two countries, and would claim that Thailand was seeking help because it wanted to resist Japan and align itself with the democracies. American aid, it would assert, would enable Thailand to resist Japanese aggression such as, say, a request for setting up air bases in Thailand. Mr. Grant warned that Thailand would use the British Minister [Sir Josiah Crosby] in their schemes by having him explain and clarify matters with London and Washington.

The cable continued that the American Minister had talked with the British Minister, who had told him he had received confirmation from the Thai Prime Minister that every effort would be made to resist Japanese aggression in the same way that Greece and Yugoslavia had resisted the German invasions. To carry this through, however, Thailand needed strong well-equipped forces. The British Minister had therefore been asked to help out by supplying Thailand with fighter-planes, military equipment and financial loans. The Thai Prime Minister had made it known that if the democracies could not help Thailand in these regards, then he would have to turn to Japan. Mr. Grant pointed out that similar arguments had been put forward when the United States held up the delivery of the airplanes [which it had sold to Thailand] in October 1940.[11]

Mr. Grant went on to say that the arguments put forward by the Thai Prime Minister seemed to have fooled not only the British but also American businessmen in Bangkok. The latter turned a blind eye to everything except matters affecting their immediate profits, the American Minister continued. The Minister himself believed that the Thai government had planned this policy so that it could cooperate with Japan while at the same time receiving American equipment. As for himself, he did not believe for one moment that Thailand would offer any resistance should Japan invade its territory. Indeed, all the signs pointed the other way. The cable ended by warning the American government to watch its step, therefore, lest it fall into Thailand's trap.[12]

What the British Minister told the American Minister was in fact exactly what I had been told by Field Marshal[13] Phibun Songkhram, the Prime Minister. It also accorded with my own opinion, which I had often expressed to both the British and American Ministers, namely that the more aid given to Thailand by the democracies, the greater the chance we stood of withstanding Japanese intervention. The British Minister agreed with this view. However, the American Minister, in his report of 8 May [i.e. the above-described report of 8 May 1941], on the eve of our signing the peace agreement with France in Tokyo,[14] maintained that if such aid was given to Thailand it would amount to United States government recognition of Thailand's right to recover its territories [in Indochina] through the aid of Japan.

The British government instructed its Minister to consult the State Department Advisor on Political Relations, a senior official in the State Department, about the United States' attitude on the subject. The British Minister thereupon asked why the United States was unwilling to support Thailand, commenting that it would be desirable to retain Thailand's friendship, whereas America's attitude could only produce the opposite result. The American official confirmed the British Minister's belief that the United States had grave doubts about Thailand's direction, and when pressed further for the reasons for such views replied that England had contributed to a considerable extent to the unsatisfactory state of affairs in regard to Thailand.

When Thailand had first sounded out the opinion of foreign governments regarding its request for the return of territories from the French, the British

Minister in Bangkok had initially advised the governments of both England and the United States to show an indifferent attitude while advising Thailand to refrain from initiating the conflict. Later on, however, [Sir Josiah] had supported Thailand's pressure on the French. The United States government, in contrast, had proposed from the outset that the Thai government refrain from taking any course of action that might extend the conflict, and had exhorted it to wait until a suitable time arrived for peaceful negotiations to be held over the boundary question. The American Advisor claimed that although this had been the policy of the United States throughout, Thailand had been able to make gains at the expense of France due to the encouragement of England and with the help of Japan. As a result, in the opinion of the United States, Thailand had fallen greatly under the influence of Japan.

The use of force was now the chief influencing factor left in the situation. At the present time Thailand could hope for little help from England or the United States, and in turn stood in little fear of these two countries. Japan, on the other hand, not only had much to offer Thailand, but was in a position to carry out effective punitive action against Thailand as well. The American Advisor argued that Thailand did not wish to fall under the control of Japan in the least; indeed, it did not want to be dominated by any country. Japan was nevertheless in a position to demonstrate to Thailand that the latter could gain many advantages by relying on Japan, and that it would be more realistic for it to fear Japan than to rely on or fear the United States or England.

The British Minister claimed that hopes for Thailand were not altogether lost, however, as Thailand might still be restrained through her economic needs. The American Advisor retorted that if in face of the evidence of Japan's steady encroachment and of the facts that its nationals were pouring money into Thailand in increasingly larger quantities and that an extravagantly large sum of money was being used by Japan for propaganda purposes England still thought it could hold Thailand back by supplying her with funds and commodities, then the United States would not place any obstacles in the way of British policy. However, England could not count on the cooperation of the United States, as the latter totally disagreed with this policy. The American Advisor continued that as England had some oil available, and that as the amount of money being called for by Thailand was not large, England might therefore wish to take the risk [of supplying Thailand with oil and funds]. If it decided to do so, it would, however, have to face the consequences on its own. The United States was not interested in taking such a risk itself, as it believed that any equipment given to Thailand would probably be confiscated and used by Japan for its own benefit.[15]

As far as I can remember about our fuel shortage situation, this dated back to the pre-war period, when an English oil company, Royal Dutch Shell, and an American firm, the Standard Vacuum Oil Company, were the two oil distributors in Thailand. Later, as a result of the Defense Ministry's policy of seeking complete freedom in regard to national fuel distribution, and of freeing the nation from dependence on these two oil companies in case of emergency, a Fuel Department was established, giving the nation a fuel stock of its own. Negotiations were conducted[16] whereby the two companies would be allowed to have in stock a sufficient amount of oil to last for a limited period, believed to be one year, but the Fuel Department would hold the right to sell the fuel to the nation.

The two companies agreed to the proposal of giving the Department rights to distribute fuel, but could not agree about the quantities or the price of the oil to be sold to the Department. The main factor which could not be settled on between the parties was the amount of oil that the Department proposed should be maintained as a constant quantity throughout. The two companies put forward a number of reasons as to why they could not accept the figures put forward (although it was understood that they must in fact have received instructions from the governments of Britain and the United States to give replies based on the deteriorating situation in Europe and their consequent concern to avoid a large amount of oil falling into the hands of the enemy), and ultimately threatened to withdraw their interests and businesses if forced to comply with the new arrangements. The Council of Ministers consulted the Fuel Department, which stated that even if the two companies closed down their businesses the Fuel Department still had enough oil to keep the fuel supply running in the country.

Several meetings of the Cabinet were held to discuss the matter. A number of Ministers felt that as Britain and the United States controlled considerable oil supplies, it would be best if we were to exercise a prudent and accommodating policy towards them. However, the Fuel Department stated that Japan had promised to help us [over our fuel shortage situation]. The Prime Minister, who was also the Minister of Defense, encouraged this offer for military and strategic reasons. The Council therefore decided that as the two companies would not carry on their business on our terms, the Fuel Department should therefore take over the business in their stead. If I remember rightly, this decision was made in July 1940. A few months later, however, the Ministry of Defense reported to the Council that the Fuel Department did not in fact have enough oil in stock for essential domestic consumption. Meanwhile Japan kept reminding us that it had had to use a great deal of fuel in its war against China, and that furthermore it was suffering from pressure on the part of Britain and the United States, which had placed restrictions on Japan's purchase of oil from the Dutch East Indies. The Council of Ministers recommended that the Ministry of Foreign Affairs negotiate directly with England and the United States for help over the crisis, but these negotiations met with no success.

Between February and March 1941 the Fuel Department reported that we were about to run out of domestic fuel, namely diesel oil, natural gas, fuel oil, aviation gasoline, motor gasoline and kerosene. The Council of Ministers decided to open negotiations with Japan. Japan straightaway started raising conditions and objections, such as asking us to agree to give Japan a monopoly over our rubber and tin supplies in return for fuel, and pointing out that Japan could not send us the full amount of fuel we were asking for as she was then in the process of making preparations [to advance southwards].

The Prime Minister thereupon instructed me to conduct negotiations with the British and American Ministers, and with the Dutch Chargé d'Affaires, M. Touissaint. The British Minister was willing to help us, but told us that England did not have enough oil for its own needs. He therefore offered to try to persuade the United States to help us. The American Minister, however, was unwilling to help, although he agreed to send a report on the matter to his government. The Dutch Chargé expressed his sympathies, but explained that as the Netherlands had now been occupied by Germany, his government had been forced to go into exile in London. The Dutch therefore had to follow British and United States government policy over such matters. However, certain documents have shown that the Dutch government suggested to the United States government that help be given to Thailand through an arrangement between the oil companies in the Dutch East Indies and the Thai government whereby a certain quantity of oil, limited to the lowest necessary amount, would be sold to the Thai government by the month. The United States government, meanwhile, consulted with the Standard Vacuum Oil Company. It recommended that the two companies [Royal Dutch Shell and the Standard Vacuum Oil Company] reopen their businesses provided they were granted the rights [they had enjoyed prior to July 1940]. However, the American government insisted that such an arrangement would be sure to meet with Japanese opposition.[17]

Early in May 1941, the British Minister paid a call on the Prime Minister in the latter's capacity as Minister of Foreign Affairs and informed him that the British government would be pleased to help us over our problem if we could let it know the type of oil we needed the most urgently. The Prime Minister replied that we particularly needed diesel oil and motor gasoline. A few days[18] later, England sent 1,400 tons by two carriers from Singapore. England showed its decency by not making this delivery subject to any conditions, although it did ask that future allocations of rubber and tin be open to negotiations. We were also informed that our selling rubber and tin to England would amount to the same as our selling these to the United States. In other words we did not need to fear that separate demands would be made on us in this regard by the United States, as England and the United States had come to an agreement whereby the latter would not object if England acted as the sole negotiator with Thailand.

Field Marshal Phibun Songkhram let the British Minister know that we had already promised to sell Japan 30,000 tons of rubber, and that we would therefore only be able to sell England about 18,000 tons.[19] In fact, as I knew, the Prime Minister had only come to a verbal agreement with Japan about this, and had not actually signed any written contract in this regard. England was not particularly interested in tin, as it already had supplies of this, since the majority of the tin mines in Thailand were owned or managed by British or Australian firms.

Mr. Grant, the American Minister, was extremely angry with the United States for allowing England to negotiate with Thailand separately in this way. He sent a cable to the State Department protesting that the American government was being led by the nose by England. He recalled that he had already recommended that the United States exercise caution in regard to Thai requests for help, as he felt that the intentions of the Thai government were still suspect.[20]

[On 12 July 1941], the State Department explained to Mr. Grant that the United States was prepared to supply Thailand with oil so as to prevent a Thai trade alliance with Japan, and to counteract any attempts that might be made to undermine Thai sovereignty. The United States had agreed to follow the British proposals for two reasons: firstly, to support England's attempt to keep Thailand from the above dangers and to obtain good feelings towards England on the part of Thailand during the present crisis; and secondly, to secure as much Thai rubber and tin as possible for the United States.

The American Minister was therefore instructed to approach the Thai government to find out its capacity for supplying the United States with rubber and tin, while at the same time enquiring about Thailand's needs so that a list of the required products could be sent to the United States. Negotiations for the granting of [export] licenses by the American government would need to be worked out between the two countries in Washington, as the State Department would have to consult the many branches of the government concerned. As an inducement for the Thai government to act promptly, the Minister was to indicate that the more rubber and tin Thailand was able to provide, the more economic aid would be forthcoming from the United States.[21]

The United States State Department Advisor on International Economic Affairs did not agree with the United States allowing England to negotiate for her with Thailand, for he did not believe Thailand would be able to offer any effective resistance if Japan should invade Thai territory. He therefore saw no reason for providing aid to Thailand, and felt that at the most help should be given in proportion to the amount of rubber and tin Thailand agreed to sell to the United States. He also expressed the opinion that this matter should have been handled a long time ago. The United States should not have allowed England to negotiate on its behalf, for England could not supply Thailand with anything of much value beyond a small quantity of oil, so that Thailand would be turning to the United States to supply the remainder [of the goods it needed].

In the meantime, Japan, England and the United States were all clamoring for the purchase of rubber and tin on the open market. Once Japan heard that the British and Americans had been conducting negotiations for the purchase of rubber, the Japanese Minister, Mr. Futami, was instructed to protest to our Prime Minister and to add that although Japan was still ready to provide Thailand with oil supplies, the amount of rubber per year promised by the Prime Minister would have to be increased from 30,000 to 35,000 tons.[22] The Prime Minister replied that he would have to think this matter over, and asked me for my opinion. I replied that the wisest course of action would be to continue our policy of selling such raw materials on the open market. If we did not do so we would be placed in an embarrassing position, with England levying complaints of injustice and favoritism against us. The Prime Minister told me he agreed with this view and would inform Japan about it later.

I informed both the British and the American Ministers of this, and they expressed their approval.

5
Japan Declares War

From July 1941 up to the day that Japan declared war on 8 December 1941, I repeatedly told the British and American Ministers that I had heard definite reports that Japan would occupy Thailand and use our country to conduct its advance against England and the United States. I told them many times that as a small country Thailand did not wish to be involved with either side in the conflict, and pressed the British and American governments to declare that if Japan invaded Thailand it would be regarded as an act of aggression against Britain and the United States themselves. I also told Mr. Futami, the Japanese Minister, that if Japan found itself forced to declare war on England and the United States, it still had no need to occupy Thailand. Japan would benefit from the situation in any event. As a neutral power, we would be able to carry on trade with countries other than Japan or her allies.

England agreed with my views. At the end of August 1941 the British government sent a note to the United States government through its Chargé d'Affaires in Washington stating that His Majesty's government had noted that on 17 August President Roosevelt had handed an official note on the subject to the Japanese Ambassador. This had discussed the United States' concern at Japanese military activities in Indochina, and had outlined the steps which the United States government would be forced to take if Japan persisted in a policy of aggression against its neighbors. His Majesty's government, the draft memorandum continued, shared the same concern as that of the United States, and could not remain indifferent to the clear threats to the security of British territories constituted by Japan's aggressive policies. Thus His Majesty's government, while itself fostering no aggressive intention towards any country bordering British territories (meaning Thailand and China), or against Japan itself, felt obliged to inform the Japanese government in the interests of peace that should Japan encroach further into the southwest Pacific region, His Majesty's government would be compelled to take return measures, even if such measures were to lead to war between Great Britain and Japan.[1]

Mr. Hull, the United States Secretary of State, felt that this draft memorandum took an unnecessarily strong stance, and that it might be construed as a challenge by the Japanese military, particularly as the United States had already sent a warning to Japan in its note of 17 August as just mentioned. He therefore suggested that England tone down its note before sending it to Japan.

Earlier in the month, around 10 August 1941, the British Minister had been to see me to tell me that Mr. Anthony Eden[2] had announced in the House of Commons that any action that constituted a threat to the stability and sovereignty of Thailand would be regarded by the British government as an act immediately affecting the interests of England. [The United States had a different attitude, however. Previously], on 28 July 1941, Mr. Grant, the American Minister, had sent a cable to the United States Secretary of State strongly recommending that if the Department should decide to make a public announcement of support for the Thai government, then a clear demarcation line should be drawn between the territorial dispute between Thailand and Indochina on the one hand, and problems with Japan on the other. This was because the Thai government, which was now requesting American support, had, Mr. Grant alleged, at one time purposely disregarded United States' advice regarding the maintenance of the *status quo* in Indochina, and had mounted a very successful act of aggression against Indochina in collaboration with Japan. Thailand was very clever, the cable had continued, and had not laid all its cards on the table, with the result that the United States could be maneuvered into ostensibly supporting Thailand's recent territorial acquisitions in Indochina.[3] Despite Mr. Grant's way of thinking, however, the American government's reply sent through Mr. Grant, or through our Minister in Washington, M.R. Seni Pramoj, stated that if Thailand was absolutely determined to resist Japanese aggression, then the United States would help Thailand fully in the same way that it was already helping China.

On 4 August 1941 the Thai government received a cable from its Minister in Washington informing us that the United States government was requesting our approval to appoint Mr. Willys R. Peck, an official in the Far Eastern Division of the State Department, as its new Minister to Thailand on the recall of Mr. Grant. Mr. Peck was over fifty years of age, and had lived for several years in China. He was a civil servant and a diplomat, not a politician, and was a man well versed in Eastern cultures and traditions. The Thai government immediately consented to the United States proposal. I believe that Mr. Grant was recalled for a number of reasons. He was not a diplomat but a Democratic Party politician and political appointee. Even members of the American legation staff found many of his ideas hard to take. Some of them would come to my home to complain that they could no longer stand working for the Minister and would prefer to resign or be recalled to the United States. I had to restrain them, pointing out that other members of the diplomatic corps were unhappy with Mr.

Grant too. The British Minister [Sir Josiah Crosby] often said to me that Mr. Grant was a difficult man to understand, particularly in regard to his refusal to cooperate in resisting Japanese political and economic aggression. Members of the American business community in this country also did not care for Mr. Grant and had several disputes with him that I do not think necessary to relate here. [Matters reached such a pitch that] according to certain documents the British government eventually told its representative in Washington to inform the United States State Department about various incidents concerning Mr. Grant. As for myself, in spite of difficulties I encountered with Mr. Grant, I never once told our Minister in Washington to report these to the American government. I understand that the final step in recalling Mr. Grant was the result of numerous complaints being lodged by members of the American diplomatic community themselves. Even when he was recalled by his government Mr. Grant expressed displeasure at the procedure adopted for appointing his replacement. He told me it was incorrect for the new Minister to have been appointed through our Minister in Washington, and that the Thai government should have insisted that this be handled through Mr. Grant himself. I replied that such questions of procedure were the concern of the United States and had nothing to do with us.

It was most welcome when the United States replaced Mr. Grant by Mr. Peck as its new Minister to Thailand, for the latter cooperated whole-heartedly with us. Unfortunately he only arrived to take up his duties in Bangkok slightly less than two months before war was declared on the Asian front.[4] Many people expressed regrets that Mr. Peck had not been sent as a representative to this country a year or two earlier, for the new Minister was a man of deep understanding and sympathetic leanings towards Thailand whose attitude could well have altered the ultimate political outcome between Thailand, the United States and the Axis powers respectively.[5]

On 22 August 1941 Major-General Phibun Songkhram resigned from his posts as Minister of the Interior and Minister of Foreign Affairs. Colonel Luang Chawengsaksongkhram[6] was appointed Minister of the Interior and I was made Minister of Foreign Affairs in his stead. One remarkable feature about these appointments was that I only learned of them six hours before they were announced, when Mr. Thawi Tawethikun[7] came to tell me that he had heard about the appointments from Major Phao Siyanon,[8] an aide to Major-General Phibun Songkhram.

From what I gathered, Germany and Italy were indifferent to my appointment, although I received letters of congratulation from the German and Italian Ministers, and also from the Japanese Chargé d'Affaires, as was the correct procedure. England and the United States, however, expressed great pleasure, and I received the warmest letters from Sir Josiah Crosby and Mr. Chapman, the British and United States Chargés d'Affaires respectively, congratulating me on my new appointment.[9]

In his report of 2 September 1941, [in his first interview held with the author since the latter was elevated to the rank of Minister of Foreign Affairs] the American Chargé d'Affaires, [Mr. Chapman], recorded that during his conversation with me that day, I expressed satisfaction over the report received from the Thai Minister in Washington, M.R. Seni Pramoj. This had indicated that United States' authorities were sympathetic towards granting export permits for certain products sought by Thailand. I stated, the Chargé reported, that the Thai government needed, in order of priority, first military equipment, next materials required by certain governmental departments, and lastly goods to support the civilian population. Referring to a recent unequivocal statement on the part of the Thai government that Thailand would resist any aggression, the Chargé d'Affaires reported that I had stated that a great amount of military equipment would be needed, however, in order to render such resistance effective. I had said with a smile, Mr. Chapman continued, that in the past Washington may have felt uncertain about supplying Thailand with arms lest these fall into the hands of Japan. I hoped, however, that such suspicions had now been dispelled. The Chargé further noted that arrangements were being made for Mr. Peck, the new American Minister-designate, to present his credentials to His Majesty the King as soon as the former arrived in Thailand.

As the legation had reported previously on 20 August, the report from the American Chargé d'Affaires continued, some anxiety had been felt, [given their known pro-Japanese leanings,] at the appointment[10] of Colonel Prayun Phamonmontri[11] and Luang Wichitwathakan[12] as Ministers without Portfolio acting for the Ministry of Foreign Affairs. The promotion of Nai Direk Jayanama to the office of Minister of Foreign Affairs, and certain other changes to the Council of Ministers had, however, been interpreted by a number of well-informed observers in Bangkok as a sign that the group in the Council that supported the Allies and opposed the Axis had strengthened its position. This "reflects a realistic appreciation on the part of both government officials and the public of the Japanese menace to Thailand following the occupation of southern Indochina," Mr. Chapman concluded.[13]

As soon as Mr. Peck, the new American Minister, arrived in Bangkok in the middle of September 1941 he came straightway to see me. We took up many topics in the course of our discussions. These included the questions of Thailand's relations with the Axis powers and with England and the United States, as well as that of the predicament Thailand found itself in as a small nation under pressure from both sides, neither self-sufficient economically nor possessed of large supplies of military equipment. I told the Minister that Thailand admired the United States as a country that showed goodwill to all nations and aggressive intentions towards none. As far as Japan was concerned, we admired the ability it had shown in rising to the position of a great power, but at the same time we also feared her policy of territorial expansion.

Before his arrival in Bangkok, Mr. Peck had been a senior official in the Far Eastern Division of the State Department. He had held an influential position there, with power to sway government opinion, yet as material in *Foreign Relations of the United States*, Diplomatic Papers, 1941 already referred to in this book reveals, he had shown little support for our country. It was all the more rewarding, then, that only three weeks after he arrived in Bangkok, he recommended to his government that the United States give Thailand all possible support in warding off the Japanese advance. In his report Mr. Peck referred to Thailand as a politically independent country and a center of Buddhism and of Asian culture. He suggested that if certain products and materials were sold to us on credit, this would deter us from becoming involved with Japan. Support of this kind would not place the United States under any obligation and could, moreover, be called off at any time should the United States become displeased with the results. He therefore recommended that economic support be given to Thailand to encourage it in its resistance against Japan, and that no political undertakings should be called for in return by the American government, nor requests placed on Thailand for the sale of its rubber or tin. The Minister maintained that the United States' government should support Thailand, in keeping with its policy of international impartiality. This would help Thailand uphold its neutrality.[14]

About the middle of October 1941, Prime Minister Phibun Songkhram told me he had received reports that Japan would declare war within the next two weeks. He therefore instructed me to tell the British Minister that if necessary the Thai government might have to declare Bangkok an open city to forestall any Japanese claims, for otherwise Bangkok might be destroyed. Thailand urgently needed fighter planes and other military equipment before it was too late. There would be no use in England helping us once we had been attacked. Moreover, if we were forced to make a quick surrender once Japan invaded our territory, we could not be held responsible if the Allies suffered damaging consequences. The Prime Minister asked that Britain therefore let us know immediately what England's course of action would be to safeguard its own interests in the event of a Japanese invasion of Thailand, and secondly, what England was able to offer Thailand in the way of aid?

I accordingly invited the British Minister to see me and raised these points with him. He agreed to report on the matter at once to his government. When it came to the question of military equipment, however, he started making excuses, saying that England really did not have any equipment to give us. However, he agreed to speak to the American Minister on the subject.

That same day I invited the American Minister, Mr. Peck, to see me and told him our Ministry of Defense urgently needed to purchase twenty-four fighter-planes, as we had received reports from reliable sources that Japan planned to invade Thailand shortly. I also mentioned that Phraya Sisena,[15] our Minister in Tokyo, had reported that Japanese newspapers were all claiming that England was conducting a strongly anti-Japanese policy in Thailand, and that Thai sentiment was firmly in favor of England and the United States. The newspapers also alleged that England was using the Thai Ministry of Foreign Affairs (meaning myself) to pursue this policy.

Whatever Japan may have chosen to say in this regard, I had in fact received instructions from Field Marshal Phibun Songkhram to confirm before all the legations that we would resist any aggression towards our country, regardless of origin, and that we would strictly uphold our policy of neutrality. This I duly did. I commented [to the American Minister], however, that we would need military equipment for self defense purposes to enable us to maintain such neutrality. Mr. Peck said he would report this to his government at once.

During the course of subsequent meetings, the British and American Ministers told me their governments were discussing ways of helping our country. England offered to send us guns and ammunition from Singapore, but said it would have to consult the American government first about planes. On 20 November the British Minister asked to see the Prime Minister, and told him that the British government was ready to give us howitzers, mortars and ammunition. These would be transported from Malaya. It was also willing to give us any unofficial advice it could on matters of general defense, and was ready to appoint three more assistant military attachés to Bangkok for that purpose. After he had received this information from Sir Josiah Crosby, the Prime Minister told me to take a look at England's offer of mortars and howitzers. He said he had told Sir Josiah that as Thailand had next to no military equipment we would have to avoid war with Japan if at all possible, and fight only if we had to.

After his meeting with the Prime Minister, the British Minister came to see me and told me of their conversation. This the Prime Minister had already described to me as mentioned above. I told Sir Josiah that the defeat of a number of small countries in Europe one after the other had diminished the confidence of our government in Britain's promises. I pointed out that these countries were closer than Thailand to the Allied powers [geographically speaking, yet this had not saved them from disaster].

On 23 November 1941 the American Minister told me his government had instructed him to inform us that the State Department had already explained to our Minister in Washington (M.R. Seni Pramoj) several times America's policy in regard to giving aid to foreign countries resisting aggression. In Thailand's case, if we were invaded and had to resist in self defense, the United States government would consider us as being in the same position as China, and would help us in the same way as it had that country. The American and British governments had also consulted with one another about Thailand's request for planes. England could not spare us any in view of her own urgent needs. The United States government had therefore tried to find us planes elsewhere, but without success. The American Minister told me that the United States might, however, be able to help us out over our oil shortage problem. It had already entered into consultations with the British government about this, and expected these to be concluded successfully shortly.

I thanked Mr. Peck for trying to help us, even though his efforts had not been successful, but pointed out that our situation was very different to that of China. China was a vast country with a large supply of manpower. Japan had not been able to conquer China even after several years of fighting. Thailand, on the other hand, would be easy to invade in time of war and our forces were limited in number. If we should be forced to fight we would be doing so only to show that we were indomitable in spirit.

On 24 November 1941 Mr. Futami,[16] the Japanese Minister, came to see me. During our discussion of the Far Eastern crisis, he gave me an undertaking to convey to the Thai government that if it should become really necessary for Japan to seize British territory, it would only demand the passage of Japanese troops through Thailand, but would not invade our country. We did not believe this, however, for according to news reports a declaration of war by Japan was imminent, and it was already clear that Japan would use Thailand to attack British territories in Malaya.

On 3 December 1941 the American Minister reported having learned from me that even though Japanese attitudes had softened somewhat lately, the Thai government nevertheless fully expected that Japan was planning an invasion of Thailand and that Thailand would have to fight Japan. The Thai Foreign Minister [i.e. the author], the American Minister continued, had thanked the United States government for informing the Thai Minister in Washington that it would help Thailand in the same way as it was helping China, but had mentioned at the same time that the Prime Minister had been displeased with the small amount of aid offered by England. The Thai government and people, he claimed, nonetheless remained fully confident that if Thailand resisted Japanese aggression, the United States and England would come to its aid. Nai Mun and

Nai Kong, spokesmen for the Public Relations Department, had even given a radio broadcast in which they stated that Thailand need not fear being invaded, for it had friends who would come to Thailand's help. The American Minister felt, therefore, that if Japan should invade Thailand and Thailand not receive any help, the Thai people would feel considerable resentment towards the United States and England, and that Japan and certain pro-Japanese groups within Thailand would seize upon this to foment anti-United States and anti-British sentiment. The Minister therefore suggested most earnestly that the governments of both England and the United States inform the Thai government as soon as possible what immediate and long-term aid they would be able to give Thailand in the event of that country being invaded by Japan. This would enable the Thai government to plan its resistance. The Thai still believed in England and the United States despite their inability to provide us with [significant amounts of] military equipment. The Minister believed it would only be fair for the United States government to let Thailand know how it intended to help her. The Minister concluded his comments by noting that the British Minister also planned to send a report to his government relaying these same views.[17]

The following day the American Minister cabled his government again to say that the Minister of Foreign Affairs, Nai Direk Jayanama, had asked him to let the State Department know right away that the Thai government was expecting the British and American governments to make a declaration soon to the effect that if Japan should invade Thailand, it would be counted among the enemies of the United States and England. Such a declaration would greatly help Thailand resist Japanese aggression. The Thai Foreign Minister, Mr. Peck reported, had told him that the American and British declarations of the previous August had not been forceful enough. The Thai government therefore felt that a new communiqué, employing stronger terms, should be issued. This would both deter Japan, as it was known that Japan had already made its decision [to advance into Thailand], and boost the morale of those few groups of Thai that were still wavering in their allegiance because they did not really believe the United States and Britain would come to the aid of Thailand once trouble broke out. The Foreign Minister had reported that those factions had considerable political influence, and that they were beginning to be swayed by the Japanese argument that England encouraged small nations to fight, only to let them down later, as witness the nations that had been conquered by Germany. Nai Direk had confirmed that Thailand would resist aggression even if it did not receive outside aid, but said that a declaration of support from the American and British governments would be of tremendous help to the country.[18]

The following record of my discussion with the American Minister on 4 December 1941, which I handed to the Prime Minister, sheds further light on the subject. During our conversation the American Minister told me that American public opinion at that time favored the United States giving a stern warning and declaration in the event of Japan attacking Thailand. This was indeed good news, I told him. I also took the opportunity to reiterate what I had already expressed to the British Minister that same day, namely that I believed the American press was right in expressing such a view, for many Thai believed that the United States would not really help us in the event of invasion, but would, rather, leave us to our fate. It was not enough to give us help on the same lines as that being given to China, for as the Minister well knew, our situations were not the same. As long as the United States and England would not declare that they would fight should Japan invade Thailand, it was difficult to hope for peace. Such a declaration by England and the United States would also prove those nations' integrity in the eyes of the world, I continued. I told Mr. Peck that I believed that if such a declaration were made, Japan would call off its invasion of Thailand.

I reminded Mr. Peck that in August Mr. Eden, the British Foreign Minister, and his American counterpart, Mr. Hull, had issued a declaration stating only that should Japan invade Thailand, England and the United States would view this with great concern. Japan had laughed off this phrase, I told the American Minister, saying it was what might be expected, and had pointed out that this was the same phrase Britain and the United States had uttered about Europe, yet this had not prevented one small country after another from falling [to Germany]. I asked the Minister to forgive me if I was being overly frank in telling him this.

Mr. Peck replied that on the contrary, such frank talk helped a great deal, and that he was glad I had told him this in such a straightforward manner. He said he would have to try and make his government comprehend this point. The American public was beginning to come round to our views, he felt. As for himself, he believed that the American government should declare its support for Thailand. He then asked me if I felt the Thai would lose heart in their resistance against Japan if the American government did not make such a declaration.

I told him that on the contrary the Thai people were as one with their government, and would rally immediately to the call to arms. From what I had heard, our government would, moreover, definitely be making such a call. The Minister had only to reflect on the speeches that were being made exhorting our people to rise to the defense of their nation in the event of a Japanese invasion to recognize that this was the case. I told him that a declaration by America and Britain would, however, help matters in a number of ways, by making Japan stop to reflect [on its planned course of action], by boosting the morale of the

Thai, and by showing the world that small countries which sought to resist aggression would receive support.

On 5 December 1941 the American Minister reported that he had visited me regarding the question of oil transportation. I stated, the report said, that Mr. Tsubokami, the Japanese Ambassador, had just left me a while ago. The latter had declared that Japan definitely would not employ its troops in Indochina to invade Thailand, but would use them rather to concentrate Japanese forces on the road to Burma. Thailand therefore had no cause for alarm. The Foreign Minister [i.e. Nai Direk] informed me, Mr. Peck continued, that despite this undertaking the Thai government nevertheless felt seriously concerned, for it had received reports from various quarters that Japan would launch both land and air attacks within a day or two. The Foreign Minister was reluctant to tell him the source of such information, Mr. Peck reported, but was checking on the matter with the British Minister, (Sir Josiah Crosby), who had not yet heard these reports so far as he knew. Mr. Peck reported that the Thai Foreign Minister had again asked with deep concern whether he had informed the American government that the Thai government was hoping for a declaration of support for Thailand from Britain and the United States in the event of a Japanese invasion.[19]

Three days later, on 8 December 1941, Japan declared war on the United States and England. In the cable that the American Minister, Mr. Peck, sent to the Secretary of State on that date, the former reported that the Minister for Foreign Affairs, Nai Direk Jayanama, had summoned him and other diplomatic representatives in succession that afternoon. The Foreign Minister informed me, Mr. Peck reported, with, I believe, sincere grief, that his government had yielded to overwhelming Japanese force and had today signed an agreement permitting passage of Japanese troops through Thailand. They would proceed by way of Bangkok on their way to attack Burma and Malaya. In return Japan had guaranteed the sovereignty, independence and honor of Thailand and had given an assurance that the country would not be disarmed. The Japanese had also offered to restore all Thailand's lost territories to her. This the Thai government had refused, as it wanted the world to know that it had yielded only to force and not for the sake of gain. I inquired, the American Minister went on, how this arrangement affected the status of the American legation and American citizens in Thailand. The Foreign Minister replied that these points had not yet been discussed. Since Thailand was still an independent country he believed, however, that the position of Americans would not be affected. He also said that in reply to a question from the British Minister he had assured the latter that if British forces were to enter Thailand in order to oppose Japan they would not be resisted. (The Prime Minister also confirmed this over the telephone to the British Minister.)

Events now proceeded as follows, Mr. Peck reported. At eleven o'clock on the night of 7 December the Japanese Ambassador and his staff had attempted to call on the Thai Prime Minister. However, the latter was away near the frontier at Aranyaprathet [on the Cambodian border]. The Japanese were finally received by the Foreign Minister, [Nai Direk Jayanama]. The latter was told that Japan was fighting for its life against Great Britain and the United States and intended to make widespread attacks on their territory at one o'clock in the morning of 8 December. Some of these would be carried out through Thailand. Japan therefore demanded that passage of troops be allowed through Thai territory. Japan offered Thailand the following possible courses of action, the first of which was that it could join Japan in the war against the United States and Great Britain. In this case Japan would not only guarantee the sovereignty, independence and honor of Thailand but would restore all the territories Thailand had previously lost to foreign powers. Alternatively Thailand could join the Triple Alliance in addition to permitting the passage of Japanese troops through its territory. Under such a modified arrangement there would be no promise of restoration of territory. The Thai had refused to join the alliance, the American Minister reported, and the agreement finally settled on was that which has already been described. The Thai delegation had said that in the absence of the Prime Minister/the Commander-in-Chief no (final) reply could be given to the Japanese, nor could orders be issued to the Thai troops. They therefore asked that the deadline for invading Thailand at one o'clock be postponed. The Japanese replied, however, that no changes could be made in the scheduling of the planned attack.

Fighting broke out during the night and the following morning at Songkhla, Pattani and Prachuap Khirikhan on the south coast, and at Watthana and Aranyaprathet on the eastern frontier. The Thai lost about a battalion of troops at Pattani. Mr. Peck reported that the Thai Foreign Minister had been deeply moved by the course of events. The latter had recalled the efforts by his country to obtain arms for just such a contingency, and had expressed gratitude for the friendliness that had been shown by the United States. He said that the hearts of the Thai were with the United States and Great Britain. The American Minister added that he could not but be struck by the sincerity of Thailand's effort to resist Japan and the overwhelming force to which it finally yielded. It is my intention and that of the British Minister, he added, to continue our normal duties as far as possible. Although it was almost impossible for American nationals to leave the country under existing circumstances, they had been offered quarters in the legation if they wished to use them. The legation had meanwhile telegraphed American citizens in northern Thailand, advising them to consider leaving for Burma. In conclusion Mr. Peck reported that the city [i.e. Bangkok] seemed as peaceful as usual.[20]

Before giving an account of the events that took place on the night of 7 December, when the Japanese Ambassador and his staff came and called on us, I should first like to refer back to our request that England and the United States announce that if Japan invaded Thailand, Britain and America would regard this as an act of aggression against their own nations. As already mentioned, England greatly approved of this suggestion. However, the United States refused to go along with it. Mr. Hull, the United States Secretary of State, instead merely warned the Japanese Ambassador repeatedly that if Japan were to advance from Indochina into Thailand, America would view the matter with grave concern. Given the United States position, all that England could do was to make a declaration in the House of Commons.

From evidence revealed after the war it would seem that during the drawing up of the Atlantic Charter in August 1941, Sir Winston Churchill, the British Prime Minister, proposed that a joint declaration be presented to Japan. He believed that fear of Britain and the United States declaring war on her would deter Japan from invading Thailand. Churchill even put forward a proposed draft of such a declaration. However, the American Secretary of State felt that the words used were too forceful, and might be interpreted as a challenge by Japan, leading to an outbreak of war for which the United States was not yet ready.[21] I myself believe that Mr. Hull knew the United States was not yet fully prepared for war, and felt that if Japan occupied Thailand in the same way as it had occupied Indochina, in other words without actually declaring war, then such a situation would simply have to be endured until the United States was ready for direct action.

The second phase opened on 30 November 1941. As a result of our persistent and emphatic requests to the British and American Ministers on the subject, Churchill again proposed to President Roosevelt that the two countries issue a warning to Japan that the United States and England would not put up with further acts of aggression on the part of Japan.[22] On the same day the British government informed the State Department of reports regarding approaching Japanese attacks, adding that Japan intended to seize the Kra Isthmus. England had plans to seize the isthmus before the Japanese occupied it in order to lay a base for the defense of Malaya, and therefore wished to know the reaction of the American government to this state of affairs.[23] The Secretary of State (Mr. Hull) replied that he would put the matter before the President once the latter returned from his vacation.[24]

General [Hideki] Tojo, the wartime Prime Minister of Japan, subsequently revealed in evidence before the International Military Tribunal in Tokyo that the Japanese government had decided [as early as] 23 November 1941 that in the event of war Japan would have to obtain prior permission from Thailand for the passage of her troops through Thai territory. However, Japan was hoping that England would move its troops into Thailand before any declaration of war had been made. This would have given Japan the opportunity to declare that it had been forced to enter Thailand in order to resist British aggression.[25]

On 29 November 1941, the American government intercepted a confidential cable from the Japanese Ambassador in Bangkok to the Japanese government in Tokyo stating that to carry out this policy successfully Japan should make every effort to postpone landing its troops in Thailand, and should land at nearby Kota Bharu[26] in British territory instead. This would force the British troops to enter Thai territory via Padang Besar.[27] As President Roosevelt failed to reply to Churchill's query [concerning America's reaction if Britain were to seize the Kra Isthmus], the British government did not dare take any action. The British Minister in Bangkok heard reports, however, that England was planning to send troops into Thailand, and cabled his government begging England to refrain from such a policy. He was afraid it might lead Thailand to side with Japan, as the Thai government would then consider that England had been the first to invade Thai territory.[28]

Churchill then drew up another draft warning Japan [against moving its troops into Thailand]. He sent this to President Roosevelt for the latter's approval, adding that if the United States agreed to it, he would ask every country in the British Commonwealth to join in putting forward this declaration. President Roosevelt received this draft on 7 December 1941.[29] He was placed in a delicate position, for although in his heart he supported the terms of the draft, he was not sure whether he would receive Senate support should a situation arise whereby the United States would have to be the first to open hostilities against Japan. In addition he feared that the Senate might accuse him of seeking to protect the colonies of Europe. Twenty-four hours later, however, Japan helped Roosevelt get around the problem by launching an attack on Pearl Harbor.

As to the details of our negotiations with the Japanese on 7 December 1941, they were as follows. On the evening of 7 December 1941, sometime before 19.00 hours, the British Minister, Sir Josiah Crosby, came to see me at my house at Soi Santisuk, Phra Khanong. He told me that during the course of their flights British patrol planes had noticed Japanese warships coming from the Indochinese peninsula towards the Gulf of Thailand. I thanked him, and said that I would report this immediately to the government. We went on to discuss the course of action to be taken in the event of Japanese troops landing in Thailand. The British Minister told me that if Thailand offered any resistance, it would receive the maximum support England could possibly provide.

CHAPTER 5

I told him that Thailand would definitely put up a fight, but for how long I really did not know. Ours was a small country and in comparison with Japan, which was like an elephant on the warpath, we were like but a five or six year old child. The British Minister said that he appreciated our position, and took his leave at about 19.00 hours. Police-General Adun Adundetcharat, Director-General of the Police Department and Deputy Prime Minister, came to see me that evening, as I had already invited him to dinner. I told him about the British Minister's visit. We both felt that Japan was definitely declaring war. Police-General Adun complained about the Prime Minister, Field Marshal Phibun Songkhram, being out of the capital at such a time of crisis. A few moments later, General Phra Boriphanyutthakit, the Minister of Economics, called Police-General Adun on the telephone. I do not know what he said, but Police-General Adun left my house right away without eating his dinner after telling me briefly that the situation was critical. About half an hour later a telephone call came through for me from Suan Kulab Palace, which was then the Office of the Prime Minister, telling me to go there without delay. On my arrival at the palace I saw that Mr. Tsubokami, the Japanese Ambassador, and his party were already there. With him were the assistant military attaché, the assistant naval attaché, the embassy adviser and an interpreter. I took the back door upstairs to see Police-General Adun, who told me that the Japanese delegation had come to see the Prime Minister. Since the Prime Minister was away they had asked to see him instead as the Deputy Prime Minister. Police-General Adun told me that he was, however, most reluctant to see the members of the Japanese delegation, and asked that I go and receive them in his stead.

I therefore went down into the reception room to meet the members of the delegation. The Director-General of the Department of Commerce, Mr. Wanit Pananon,[30] was already there in the room. After the usual exchange of greetings Mr. Tsubokami, the Japanese Ambassador, said that he had asked to see the Prime Minister, as today the most crucial event in Japanese history had taken place. He regretted that he could not see either the Prime Minister or the Deputy Prime Minister. I explained to him that the Prime Minister was absent, I believed on an observation tour of the border, and that we had already sent a radio message to recall him to the capital. As for the Deputy Prime Minister, I explained that he felt that since the matters before us concerned foreign policy, I should receive the members of the Japanese delegation in his stead.

The Japanese Ambassador thereupon continued that all of us must be aware by now that the United States and England had constantly been putting pressure on Japan. Japan had decided that it could tolerate this no longer. Japan was now rising up in self defense, and had today declared war on the United States and Britain. The Ambassador had received instructions from his government to inform the Thai Prime Minister that the Japanese Army must therefore request the right to send its troops through our country on its way to attack two countries[31] that had now become Japan's enemies. Since the Prime Minister was away and the Deputy Prime Minister indisposed, he had therefore to make this official request to me. I replied that Thailand, as he well realized, had already declared itself a neutral country. Our policy was therefore one of withholding support for either side in the conflict. The Japanese Ambassador replied that this was, however, a matter of life and death for Japan. It was vital and absolutely imperative that it receive our permission to move its troops through our territory by land, sea and air.[32] I explained that I had no authority to either grant or refuse his request, for as he well knew I was only the Minister of Foreign Affairs, and it was the Prime Minister alone, as Commander-in-Chief of the Thai forces, who had the authority to order the army to withhold its resistance. Besides, I pointed out, as the Ambassador was aware, the Commander-in-Chief of the Army, on behalf of the government, had already passed a standing order commanding the Thai army to offer full resistance against aggression by any forces invading our territory.[33] The only person who could, then, revoke this order was the Commander-in-Chief himself.

At this Colonel Tamura, the assistant military attaché, spoke out and said that I should be aware that any delay would lead to bloodshed, as Japanese troops were about to land at various places in Thailand. I told him that as I had already explained, I had no authority in such matters. However, I would report the matter immediately to the Deputy Prime Minister so that he could straightaway call a meeting of the Council of Ministers. I would then let the members of the delegation know what the Council had decided. They agreed to this proposal and waited in the reception room.

As soon as I returned and reported on the position to Police-General Adun Adundetcharat he agreed to call a meeting of the Council of Ministers at once. Most of the Ministers were already waiting there. The meeting began at about 23.00 hours. Police-General Adun instructed me to tell the members of the Council about my discussion with the Japanese delegation. After they had consulted and discussed the matter with one another, it was concluded that we could do nothing except await the return of the Prime Minister. The Council then chose Nai Pridi Banomyong, the Minister of Finance, H.R.H. Prince Wanwaithayakon, Advisor to the Office of the Prime Minister, and myself to meet with the Japanese delegates and suggest to them that they either return to their residences, in which case we would invite them to see the Prime Minister as soon as he got back, although we had no idea when this might be, or stay on and wait.

The Japanese Ambassador chose to wait. In the meantime, members of the Council of Ministers sat waiting for the Prime Minister, while Police-General

Adun asked me to accompany him to the Posts and Telegraphs Department to contact the Prime Minister. I did not learn where the Prime Minister was, as Police-General Adun did not tell me, but found out that he would be back for the meeting of the Council of Ministers around dawn. Police-General Adun and I then went back and informed the Council of this, and I went to tell the members of the Japanese delegation that they should return home, which they did, and come back to the Office of the Prime Minister again at about 05.00 hours.

At about 07.00 hours the Prime Minister arrived for the meeting. Police-General Adun asked me to repeat the above course of events again. Before I could even finish the report, however, the Prime Minister asked what we should decide to do. Nai Pridi Banomyong, the Finance Minister, proposed that before coming to any definite decision, we should first consider the pros and cons of the situation. We should reflect on what the results might be if we were to give in to or refuse the Japanese request, lest we suffer world criticism, for this, he claimed, was a historic decision. The Prime Minister replied that we had no time to hold discussions on the matter, as the Japanese had already landed on our territory. All he wanted, then, was an expression of opinion as to whether we should yield or fight.

He turned to ask certain Ministers responsible for military affairs whether we had enough forces to resist, and was told we did not. Police-General Adun Adundetcharat felt we had no chance if we resisted, and concluded that the Allies would not come to our aid. The Prime Minister thereupon asked the opinion of a few more Ministers, all of whom replied that they saw no way of our putting up an effective resistance. The Prime Minister thereupon finally declared that it would be futile to resist as we had insufficient forces to do so, and that England and the United States had more or less admitted that they could not help us when pressed for effective aid by the Minister of Foreign Affairs. The Prime Minister then rose to go and meet the members of the Japanese delegation. I do not know the details of their discussions, as I did not follow him out of the meeting of the Council of Ministers, but about half an hour later the Prime Minister sent Nai Wanit Pananon back to report Japan's proposals to the Council. Nai Wanit explained that the Japanese delegation had proposed three possible plans for cooperation on the part of Thailand. The first asked merely for the passage of troops, the second that Thailand and Japan sign an alliance for the defense of Thailand, and the third that Thailand and Japan become allies in the war against Britain and the United States, in which case Japan was ready to give us back all the territories we had lost to France and England.

Opinions were divided on the subject in the Council. One group chose the third plan on the grounds that as we had to allow the passage of Japanese troops anyway, we might as well derive the greatest possible benefit from the situation. Another group made no comment at all. As Minister of Foreign Affairs, I recommended that as we had to give in to Japan's request since we were not strong enough to resist it, we should at least give in only to the extent of allowing the passage of Japanese troops. If we were to choose one of the other plans, I argued, we would definitely be criticized by the world and have it said that our erstwhile strict declarations of neutrality had been made merely to disguise our cooperation with Japan, since we were not only giving in to Japan, but also joining her as an ally. Police-General Adun Adundetcharat and Nai Pridi Banomyong supported my recommendation, and in the end the Council voted to accept only the first plan. Nai Wanit Pananon was sent back to deliver the message to the Japanese delegates. About an hour later an agreement was signed between the Japanese Ambassador and myself in which Thailand agreed to grant Japan the right to send troops through our territory.

After the meeting of the Council ended, I was instructed to relay the details of the new situation to all foreign diplomatic representatives in Bangkok. I told the British and American Ministers every detail about what had taken place. The essential features of these reports are given in *Foreign Relations of the United States*, 1941, referred to earlier in this book, and tally with my account given here.

On the same day the government announced that on 8 December 1941, from 02.00 hours onwards, Japanese troops had been landing in Thailand at Songkhla, Pattani, Prachuap Khirikhan, Nakhon Si Thammarat, Surat Thani and Bang Phu,[34] and had penetrated inland to the provinces of Phatthalung[35] and Samut Songkhram.[36] The Thai army and police forces, the announcement continued, had put up fierce resistance almost everywhere. In addition, the announcement continued, we had also heard news from abroad that the Japanese navy had launched attacks on Hawaii and the Philippines, and that it had landed troops at Kota Bharu in Malaya and heavily bombarded Singapore. At 22.30 hours on 7 December 1941, the announcement continued, the Japanese Ambassador had come to the Office of the Prime Minister and informed the Minister of Foreign Affairs that Japan had declared war on Britain and the United States. Although Japan did not regard Thailand as an enemy, it must therefore ask for the right of passage through Thai territory. The government of His Majesty the King had given careful consideration to the matter, the communiqué continued. It felt that our situation was indefensible. In spite of all our efforts, continued resistance on our part would only result in a futile loss of Thai lives. It had therefore decided to grant the Japanese army the right of passage through our territory on receiving an undertaking in writing that Japan would respect the independence, sovereignty and honor of Thailand. The Thai government had then granted Japanese troops rights of passage, and fighting between Japan and Thailand had ceased. The government called for the Thai people to remain calm and to carry on their normal everyday duties, the communiqué concluded. It would try to keep the situation under control as best it could, and asked that the Thai people carry out the instructions of the government.

I feel I must mention here that until such time as the Commander-in-Chief ordered a cease-fire, our soldiers fought bravely on all fronts to defend Thai territory. This was particularly true in the south, where the blood of patriotic Thai soldiers was shed for our country. We Thai will never forget the heroic deeds of all those who played a part in defending our country at that time. It has now been demonstrated that when it comes to the defense of the nation, our people are ready to sacrifice everything, even to giving up their lives. May the souls of these men rest in peace. Their heroic deeds proved to the world that Thailand gave of its best, even though we were finally forced to bow to the superior force of Japan and submit to a cease-fire.

After the events of 8 December 1941, I asked to have nothing further to do with Japan. The Prime Minister assigned Luang Wichitwathakan, the Deputy Minister of Foreign Affairs, to carry on these duties in my stead.

A few days later I asked Police-General Adun Adundetcharat to tell the Prime Minister that now that our foreign policy had changed, or in other words now that Thailand no longer upheld the policy of neutrality that I had always supported, a new Minister of Foreign Affairs should be appointed. This would be in accordance with normal international procedures. However, my proposal was rejected. The Prime Minister even said in a meeting of the Council of Ministers that we should not abandon one another at a time of crisis. This made it difficult for me to argue my position. A few days later, some minor changes were made to the Council. General Mangkon Phromyothi, the Minister of Defense, and I were reappointed to our former positions as Deputy Minister of Defense and Deputy Minister of Foreign Affairs respectively, while the Prime Minister took over the leadership of the two ministries. On 21 December of that same year the Prime Minister signed a military agreement with the Japanese Ambassador at Wat Phrasiratanasatsadaram.[37] I had nothing to do with this, and was not informed about the details of the agreement.

I have no wish to revive hard feelings or to instigate hatred for Japan by relating the above account in such detail. However, these are important historical facts. The majority of Japanese were, in fact, good men. Only a few of them were responsible for the outbreak of war—a subject which I discuss further in part 2.

In evidence given before the International Military Tribunal at Tokyo concerning the events of 8 December 1941 Mr. Tsubokami, the Japanese

Ambassador, said that he received instructions from his government on 1 December 1941 to stand ready to request the Thai government to allow Japanese troops to pass through Thai territory on their way to attack Malaya and Burma. On 7 December of that year he received definite orders to carry out this request from General Terauchi, the Japanese Commander-in-Chief of the Southern Region. On that evening the Prime Minister, Field Marshal Phibun Songkhram, was not in Bangkok, and members of his Council of Ministers did not show willingness to agree with the proposal of the Japanese Ambassador in spite of warnings that Japanese troops would be landing in Thai territory the following morning, as later proved the case.

When Field Marshal Phibun Songkhram arrived back in Bangkok the following morning, a cease-fire was ordered calling off all resistance, and an agreement was signed with the Japanese Ambassador permitting Japanese troops to enter Thailand without encountering any opposition. Field Marshal Phibun Songkhram decided to share in the fate of Japan, and later talks were held concerning military cooperation with Japan. On 21 December an agreement was signed whereby both parties agreed to respect the mutual independence and sovereignty of the other and to give one another the fullest political, military and economic support in the event of conflict of either country with a third party. Both countries agreed not to sign an individual peace treaty or to declare a truce on their own accord. The agreement had a secret clause that was not published stating that Japan would help Thailand get back her territories from England, while Thailand would help Japan in the war between her and the Allies.[38] This agreement rendered the former agreement of 8 December 1941 permitting only the passage of Japanese troops null and void.

PART 2
DURING THE WAR

CHRONOLOGY OF WORLD WAR II
7 December 1941 to 2 September 1945

1941	
7 December	Japan attacks Pearl Harbor and declares war on the United States and England.
8 December	Japanese troops land in Thailand and Malaya. England and the United States declare war on Japan.
10 December	H.M.S. "Prince of Wales" and H.M.S. "Repulse" sunk by the Japanese off the coast of Malaya.
10 December	Germany and Italy declare war on the United States. The United States retaliates by declaring war on those two countries.
22 December	Japan attacks the Philippines.
25 December	Hong Kong surrenders.

1942	
10–11 January	Japan attacks the Netherlands East Indies (now known as Indonesia).
15 February	Singapore surrenders.
18 April	The United States Air Force's first air raids on Tokyo.
4 June on	Battle of Midway Island. Japanese dispersed with heavy losses. First defeat for Japan and turning point of the war in Asia.
August on	Long battle for the Solomon Islands.
12 August	First Moscow Conference.

1943	
2 February	German forces capitulate at Stalingrad. Germany on the defensive from then on.
18 Apri	Death of Admiral Yamamoto, Commander-in-Chief of the Japanese fleet in a plane accident, shot down by the Americans.
19–10 July	Allied landings on Sicily.
19 July	First Allied air raids on Rome.
25 July	Mussolini deposed and replaced by Marshal Badoglio as Prime Minister.
8 September	Italy surrenders to the Allies.
10 September	The German Army occupies Rome.
13 October	Italy declares war on Germany, its former ally.
18 October– 1 November	Meetings of the United States Secretary of State, the British Foreign Secretary and the Russian Foreign Minister at the [Second] Moscow Conference.
22–26 November	First Cairo Conference, attended by Roosevelt, Churchill and Stalin.

CHRONOLOGY OF WORLD WAR II: 7 DECEMBER 1941 TO 2 SEPTEMBER 1945

1944

4 June	The British and American Armies seize Rome.
6 June	Allied landings at Normandy: D-Day.
15 June	Super Fortresses sent in by the American Air Force for the first time to bomb Tokyo
June–7 July	[Marianas invaded by United States forces.] Saipan fell, [followed by Guam.}
18 July	Resignation of General Tojo.
20 July	Plot on Hitler's life.
August	Germany sends V-2 rockets over London.
21 August–29 September	Allied conference at Dumbarton Oaks.
25 August	Paris liberated by the Allies.
October	Allies take Athens.
9 October	Third Moscow Conference.
End of 1944	Major sea battle between the United States and Japan in the Bay of Leyte. United States emerges victorious.

1945

January	United States' forces land on Luzon.
3 February	The American Army enters Manila.
4–12 February	Yalta Conference.
19 February–17 March	Battle of Iwo Jima. Japanese defeated.
April	Soviet forces enter Vienna.
12 April	Death of President Roosevelt.
25 April	San Francisco Conference.
28 April	Mussolini shot to death.
April–21 June	United States Army takes over Okinawa in the Ryukyus. American planes begin to bombard Japanese towns almost every day from May 1945 onwards.
30 April	Hitler commits suicide in a bomb shelter in Berlin.
2 May	The Russian army seizes Berlin.
7 May	Unconditional surrender of Germany to the Allies.
17 July–2 August	Potsdam Conference.
6 August	United States drops first atomic bomb on Japan at Hiroshima.
8 August	U.S.S.R. declares war on Japan.
9 August	United States drops second atomic bomb on Japan at Nagasaki.
14 August	Japan's unconditional surrender.
2 September	Japan signs Allied instrument of unconditional surrender aboard the American warship "Missouri" in the Bay of Tokyo.

6
To Japan

As already mentioned in the fifth chapter of part 1, once Japan declared war on the United States and England and landed its troops in Thailand I made an unsuccessful attempt to resign from the Council of Ministers. A few days later the Prime Minister was re-appointed to his two former positions as Minister of Defense and Minister of Foreign Affairs, while General Mangkon Phromyothi was re-appointed Deputy Minister of Defense and I was made Deputy Minister of Foreign Affairs.

Around 2 December [12 December—Ed.] 1941 the Prime Minister sent Police-General Adun Adundetcharat, Deputy Prime Minister and Deputy Minister of the Interior, to sound me out on the Prime Minister's view that as Thai policy toward Japan had now changed considerably, to the extent of our having formed an alliance with Japan, we should also change our ambassador to Tokyo. The Prime Minister wished me to be that new ambassador. I asked Police-General Adun how I could represent my country in Japan when my attitude towards Japan remained the same as it had always been. I told him I did not think I could carry out my duties effectively, as Japan would distrust me, and that I could not therefore see that such an appointment would be in the national interest.

Police-General Adun replied that this had already been discussed, and it had been concluded that on the contrary, such an appointment would be particularly effective, as Japan would have more confidence in us on seeing that the Thai government had sent as its representative a man who had not been popular with Japan in the past. Besides, he continued, I was a man of some political influence; it was believed that Japan would therefore heed my opinion somewhat. I persisted in my refusal, however. Two to three days later Field Marshal Phibun Songkhram called me over to Government House and we had a discussion together with Police-General Adun Adundetcharat. Field Marshal Phibun Songkhram insisted that I take up the appointment for the sake of the nation, stating that he believed Japan would trust Thailand if I agreed to do so.[1] I persisted with my arguments, however, giving the same reasons against my appointment as those I had given Police-General Adun and insisting that this was not a question of patriotism. The Prime Minister retorted that in any event he had already requested and received official approval of my appointment from Japan.[2] I still continued to refuse. The Prime Minister then became angry with me and left the room saying that if I refused to go to Japan he would go himself. At this Police-General Adun and I left Government House.

That afternoon I went to visit the Regent, Nai Pridi Banomyong,[3] and told him of my embarrassing predicament. Nai Pridi expressed the view that if the matter had gone as far as Japan's approval having been sought officially, then it was very difficult. However, he felt that if I went I might in fact be able do some good, for he believed that the Allies would emerge the victors in the war, and that a wrong move by Thailand might later cost our country its independence. He therefore felt that given the circumstances, I had better comply, but should try to use the opportunity to study the situation and see whether contacts could be made with the Government of Chiang Kai-shek so that the Allies could see that we were trying to help them in every way. He also advised taking trustworthy people along with me to be the members of my embassy staff.

That evening Police-General Adun Adundetcharat came to see me again, and we held a further discussion. In the end I accepted the appointment [as Ambassador to Tokyo], but only on the condition that the government inform the Japanese government that it had entrusted me to negotiate on all matters, so that my words would have some weight. At the same time I asked that the Thai government[4] agree to consider my suggestions favorably, or in other words that it would pay some attention to my opinions. I also requested the right to choose the members of the new embassy staff myself, for my appointment as Ambassador to Tokyo at this time was not in the course of an ordinary ambassadorial transfer. Police-General Adun told me that these conditions could certainly be arranged and that if any important matters should come up, I could contact him personally at any time.

We then went to see Field Marshal Phibun Songkhram once again to give him my consent. I asked the Prime Minister what policy he wished me to take in the course of my duties in Tokyo. He replied that I could take any course of action I considered to be in the interests of our country. I thought over these general instructions, and decided that if I could not contact the government of Chiang Kai-shek, then I would at least carry out a policy of resisting all Japanese attempts to treat Thailand as a colony. I would do this by having Japan see that it would be to its advantage to treat us fairly, and by pointing out that as Japan derived no small benefit from Thailand economically, financially and strategically, it should help Thailand in every way it could. In other words I would point out that though a small country, we were still in a position to afford Japan many facilities. Japan should not, therefore, exploit us unilaterally any more than we would take advantage of Japan.

I have to thank Field Marshal Phibun Songkhram and Police-General Adun Adundetcharat, the Deputy Prime Minister, for having allowed me to choose officials for my embassy staff whom I believed could carry out their duties satisfactorily. I chose Mr. Thawi Tawethikun[5] to be Advisor to the Royal Thai Embassy and to be Thai Chargé d'Affaires; Nai Thanat Khoman[6] as Second Secretary to the embassy; Nai Konthi Suphamongkhon[7] as Second Secretary; Nai Chan Samittawet[8] as Third Secretary; Nai Thiam Ladanon[9] as chief clerk and Nai Sala Sivaraksa[10] as clerk. The first three knew my real purpose in going to Japan. My legation and I flew to Tokyo on 5 January 1942.

7
In Japan, from January 1942 to September 1943[1]

I served in Japan for altogether twenty months. During that time I came back to Bangkok once on duty at the end of 1942, when I stayed there for about a month. What I will be discussing here, then, are relations between Thailand and Japan during this period [between the beginning of 1942 and September 1943.]

I met many ministers and important people on my arrival, but those I particularly recall were General [Hideki] Tojo, the Prime Minister; Admiral Shimada,[2] the Minister of the Navy; Mr. Shigenori Togo,[3] the Minister of Foreign Affairs; Mr. Tani, who later succeeded Mr. Togo as Minister of Foreign Affairs; Mr. [Mamoru] Shigemitsu, Foreign Minister subsequently to Mr. Tani; Mr. [Kazuo] Aoki, Minister of Greater East Asia Affairs; General Sugiyama,[4] Chief of Staff of the Army; Admiral of the Fleet Nagano,[5] Chief of Staff of the Navy; Mr. Kaya,[6] Minister of Finance; Prince [Fumimaro] Konoye,[7] former Prime Minister; Mr. [Koki] Hirota,[8] also a former Prime Minister; and Mr. Ikeda,[9] former Finance Minister. Since the first person a new diplomatic representative should meet is the Minister of Foreign Affairs, I first paid a call on Mr. Shigenori Togo, the Japanese Foreign Minister. He had been Foreign Minister at the time Japan had declared war on Britain and the United States, and had a German wife. His attitude and manner were reserved. We discussed the question of cooperation between our two countries following the pact that had been signed between us as described earlier.[10]

I presented my Letters of Credential to the Emperor on 19 January 1943. Those who accompanied me in my party that day were Nai Thawi Tawethikun, Chargé d'Affaires and Advisor to the Embassy; Major-General Phraya Sorakitphisan, Military Attaché; Rear-Admiral Luang Sombunyutthawicha,[11] Naval Attaché; Luang Ratanathip,[12] First Secretary; Nai Thanat Khoman,[13] Second Secretary; Nai Konthi Suphamongkhon,[14] Second Secretary; and Nai Chan Samittawet,[15] Third Secretary.[16]

At the appropriate time I was received in audience by the Emperor and read my Letters of Credential to him in Thai. The essential clauses of this stated that it was a great honor to be assigned to his Court, and that every attempt would be made to promote friendly relations between our two countries. The Emperor

CHAPTER 7

Fig. 10. The Royal Thai Embassy staff, Tokyo, 1942.

made a reply speech in Japanese, after which we had a discussion through the aid of interpreters. At an appropriate time I asked Royal permission to present the members of my party. After calling out their names one by one, and after they had taken leave of the Emperor, I also took leave and went to be granted an audience by the Empress. I should mention that both the Emperor and Empress extended us a warm welcome and enquired kindly and with real sincerity about Thailand. I then paid calls on other members of the Royal family, and on the Ministers of various ministries as well as on my diplomatic colleagues.

During my term of office in Japan, the Japanese press in general wrote favorably concerning the alliance with Thailand, and praised Thailand in a number of ways. We were warmly received by the people we met with in both government and private circles, and the Japanese Ministry of Education even sent out form letters to Japanese schools asking that particular help be given to any Thai students who might be in difficulties.

After I had arrived in Japan and summed up the situation, I could see that it would be impossible to contact the government of Marshal Chiang Kai-shek. The Japanese government kept strict watch on everybody's movements, and made no exception for the representative of one of its allies.

During the subsequent twenty months, a number of major problems arose requiring consultation with the Japanese government that are worthy of mention here. These included Thailand's seeking to join the Axis alliance; its recognition of the Wang Ching-wei regime in China; the establishment of the Japanese Greater East Asia Ministry; Japan's handing over to us certain territories that had been seized from Britain; and certain other general problems arising between our two countries.[17]

THAILAND DECLARES WAR ON THE ALLIES

Sometime around 26 January 1942, I received a cable from the Prime Minister in his capacity as Minister of Foreign Affairs stating that as the United States and Britain had taken aggressive action against Thailand by sending planes to bomb our territory,[18] our government had therefore declared war on those two countries on 25 January 1942.

This news produced a great feeling of uneasiness in me and in the other officials at the Thai Embassy, as we felt we had already committed ourselves deeply enough in our alliance with Japan without having had to make such a declaration.

I tried to sound out the opinion of the Japanese Minister of Foreign Affairs as well as of others in official circles [regarding our declaration of war]. Japanese opinion on the subject was divided among those who approved of and were pleased about our declaration, and those who disapproved of it. Possibly the latter group felt that if Thailand had not declared war on the United States and England, Japan would have been able to derive greater benefits from Thailand, as the Allies would not then have dared to take firm action against our country. Now that Thailand had declared war, the Allies would treat it as a full enemy.

THAILAND SEEKS TO JOIN THE AXIS POWERS[19]

Sometime in early February 1942 Luang Wichitwathakan, who was then Deputy Minister of Foreign Affairs, sent me an official letter stating that Field Marshal Phibun Songkhram, the Prime Minister and Foreign Minister, felt that although we had become an ally of Japan through having declared war on England and the United States, we had not yet been admitted as members of the Triple Alliance, that is the alliance between Germany, Italy and Japan. He therefore felt that if the Axis powers should win the war, Thailand would find itself at a disadvantage, and that we might be treated as a small country without any rights or influence. I was therefore instructed to try to negotiate with the Japanese government to get Thailand admitted as a member of the Axis alliance so that our voice would at least be heard at the peace conference.

When I received these instructions, I started thinking about what course of action I should take. I had long disliked the Axis powers for their aggressive

CHAPTER 7

Fig. 11. A special group of diplomats led by Phraya Phahonphonphayuhasena and the Thai Ambassador meeting with the Prime Minister of Japan at the Prime Minister's office in Tokyo to celebrate the conclusion of the alliance between Thailand and Japan.

policies. Moreover, I had always been convinced that they would lose the war. If that proved so, what would be the point of having entered into such negotiations? Furthermore, we had always declared before the world that we had no desire to ally with either side, and had already received world sympathy for having been dragged into the war by force as we had been too weak to keep up our resistance. Given that position we would still be able to negotiate at the end of the war [if the Allies were to win]. If we of our own accord, however, without having had pressure placed on us, were to offer to join the Axis, we would have no arguments to put forward in our defense at the end of the war.

I consulted various embassy officials including Nai Thawi Tawethikun, Nai Thanat Khoman and Nai Konthi Suphamongkhon on the matter. They agreed with me, but we could do nothing, as we had received official instructions that we had to obey. A further problem was that we had no way of telling beforehand what the Japanese reaction to the proposal that Thailand join the Axis might be. If they favored the idea, there would be no problem, but should they be opposed to it, they might become suspicious and even imagine that Thailand was planning to move away from Japan and looking toward Germany and Italy as shields in its resistance against Japan.

I therefore decided to take a risk and put forward the proposal as if it was my own personal suggestion, so that if the Japanese should suspect our actions, their suspicions would fall on me rather than on the Thai government. Before entering into official discussions with Japan, I did, however, solicit reactions from both official and unofficial Japanese sources regarding Japan's attitude to our joining the Axis, and found that most Japanese were indifferent to the idea, and showed neither enthusiasm for nor opposition to it.

One group of Japanese felt that as Thailand had already committed itself thus far, it might as well join the Axis, while the other group felt that in practice Thailand was already considered as a member of the Alliance and that there was therefore no need to confirm this position formally. I also learned from certain Japanese that there were some groups within Thailand that were opposed to our joining the Axis on the grounds that if we were to become their ally, Germany and Italy might then make extensive demands on us for economic and military aid.

On 20 February 1942 I went to see Mr. Togo, the Japanese Foreign Minister. After some personal conversation, I started in by saying that so far Thailand had been cooperating to the full with Japan, but the fact that we were not members of the Axis alliance made our partnership seem to fall somewhat short of completion. In my personal opinion, I therefore felt that Thailand should be admitted to the Axis alliance, although I was still not sure what additional benefits our respective countries might gain from such a move. I was therefore coming to enquire if Mr. Togo, as Japanese Minister of Foreign Affairs, and thus in a position to be well versed as to the advantages and disadvantages of such an arrangement, as well as being in a position to receive the expression of a range of opinions, agreed with the idea or not. According to whether he approved or disapproved of the proposal I could make further recommendations to the Thai government, or drop the idea from the start.

Mr. Togo was silent for a while, and then replied that at present Japan and Thailand were already cooperating satisfactorily with one another both economically and politically, so he saw no necessity for us to depend on others [implying Germany and Italy.] It would be better, he argued, if we Asians stuck together. I readily agreed with his opinion, as it confirmed my own.

Extremely pleased, I returned to the Embassy at once and sent a brief confidential report to the Thai government via a Thai official who was about to leave for Bangkok, requesting that the government keep this report a matter of the utmost secrecy and not let Japan have any inkling of it. In it I stated that given the Japanese position, the government would be advised to halt its plans.

I received a reply from my government expressing accord with my report, and telling me that there were in fact a number of reasons why Japan might not wish us to join the Axis alliance. Possibly it feared we might later change our policy direction and turn to cooperate with Hitler. Japan did not wish to see this happen, as it would go against its goal of building up a co-prosperity sphere in Greater East Asia.[20]

Field Marshal Phibun Songkhram instructed Luang Wichitwathakan to thank me and let me know he approved of the course of action I had taken. Some officials who read my report wrote and told me personally that the Prime Minister placed orders against it that it be kept absolutely secret. If its contents were revealed by anyone, the informer would be executed immediately. When I returned to my duties at the Ministry of Foreign Affairs [in Bangkok at the end of 1943] I took a look at the report of this incident, and saw written on my report exactly those orders calling for the utmost secrecy.

Another major reason why Japan was not anxious to have us join the Axis alliance was that although they were allies, relations between Japan and Germany had not been running smoothly. I had no opportunity to know this at the time, but learned of it later from evidence produced at the trials before the International Military Tribunal in Tokyo.

In addition to the Triple Alliance [of 27 September 1940], Germany, Italy and Japan had also signed a further agreement on 11 December 1941, following Japan's declaration of war on the United States and England on 8 December 1941. The essential conditions of this new agreement were that the three countries would help one another in their fight against the United States and England by uniting all their forces in an effort to obtain victory. They agreed not to sign any individual truce or peace treaty with their opponents unless otherwise agreed to by each party to the new agreement. Once they had won the war, the three countries would cooperate closely with one another in building up a new world order based on the principles of the Triple Alliance of 27 September 1940 already mentioned.

On 18 January 1942 military representatives of the three nations signed an agreement in Berlin dividing up the fighting zones and clearly defining the spheres of operation of each member. Japan was given general responsibility for Asia, although it was to help out with its naval forces in the Atlantic if Germany or Italy found themselves cornered there. Japan also agreed to exchange military information and to cooperate economically in furtherance of the war effort.

In practice, however, Germany and Japan did not consult one another much over plans, and each country pursued its own ultimate interests in working towards a victorious conclusion to the war. Both carried out policies without concern for the needs of the other, and even the joint German-Japanese [military] commissions in Berlin and Tokyo [set up under the 18 January 1942 agreement] hardly ever met for consultations, for there was mutual distrust between the two parties.

This went back to before the Second World War. When Japan attacked China in 1937, Germany sold weapons to the Chinese, and most of the military advisors to Marshal Chiang Kai-shek were German officers. Japan protested that these constituted unfriendly actions, and eventually Germany agreed to stop sending arms to China and recalled all its military advisors. Later, [in August 1940], when the Germans signed a non-aggression treaty with the U.S.S.R., they kept this a secret from the Japanese. Further, they failed to inform Japan when they decided to attack Russia [in June 1941]. Germany, for its part, was dissatisfied that Japan first attempted to negotiate with the United States before declaring war. In addition to these examples of lack of cooperation between the two nations, evidence from various documents shows that Hitler only befriended Japan out of expediency, while Japan in turn feared that if Germany won the war it would turn and menace Japan. Thus there were a number of grounds for distrust between the two powers.

RECOGNITION OF THE WANG CHING-WEI GOVERNMENT OF CHINA

During the war the government of Japan requested that Thailand recognize the Wang Ching-wei government. Before proceeding any further with the details of this, the reader should first be informed of the origins of the Wang Ching-wei regime.[21]

Wang Ching-wei was a close disciple of the former Sun Yat-sen, the leader of the Chinese revolution. In 1910 he was arrested for attempting to throw a bomb at the Manchu Prince Regent. [At the first National Congress of the Kuomintang in January 1924] Wang was elected second-ranking member of the Central Executive Committee, second only to Sun Yat-sen himself, so that at that time he was higher even than Chiang Kai-shek in terms of political seniority. When Sun Yat-sen died in 1925, it was Wang Ching-wei who drew up the former's final will and testament.

Wang Ching-wei was a man of great intelligence who studied and traveled in Japan, France and other European countries [as well as in Southeast Asia]. His views on foreign policy were similar to those held by Japan, namely, he believed that Asia should be for Asians, and wished to see it freed from Western influence and from Westerners who carved a living from the region. His views on economics inclined towards the left, although later he fiercely opposed China being turned into a Communist country.

[In 1932, Wang accepted an appointment as president of the Executive Yuan in the national government under Chiang Kai-shek, and from March 1933 on he also served as its acting Foreign Minister. However, his collaboration with Chiang was a very uneasy one, and became increasingly difficult as Japan advanced further into China.]

Students of Chinese history know already that the government of Marshal Chiang Kai-shek was at war with Japan from 1937 on.[22] In December, 1938, Prince Konoye,[23] the Japanese Prime Minister, declared that Japan was ready to make peace with China if the latter would agree to recognize Manchukuo[24], sign an anti-Comintern alliance with Japan on similar lines as those already made by Germany and Italy,[25] allow Japan to station troops in parts of China, grant Japan rights to trade throughout the Chinese empire, and allow Japan ownership of natural resources in regions of northern China and Inner Mongolia. If all these conditions were accepted by China, Japan would promise not to annex any Chinese territory nor demand compensation for war damages. On the contrary it would respect China's territorial sovereignty and agree to consider giving up its extraterritorial rights as well as canceling the settlement concession in Shanghai which Japan had obtained after the Boxer War.

Wang Ching-wei urged Chiang Kai-shek to accept these proposals, as he saw that continued fighting with Japan could only lead to the gradual destruction of China, while in addition he wished to cooperate with Japan in its fight against Communism. Many have said that Wang Ching-wei was, moreover, sure the Axis would win the war, and that if Germany really emerged victorious, it would not let Japan treat China as it wished. His arguments were not heeded by Chiang Kai-shek, however, who claimed that to accept the Japanese proposals would amount to agreeing to be their slaves.

In December of the same year Wang Ching-wei, together with some of his friends, fled from China to Hanoi. Four months later, in April 1939, he returned to Shanghai, which had already been occupied by Japanese troops. There he opened negotiations with Japan, asking that the proposals Japan had already put forward to Chiang Kai-shek be used as a starting point for discussions.

In June of that year Wang Ching-wei made a trip to Japan, where he met with Baron Hiranuma, the Japanese Prime Minister,[26] and General Itagaki,[27] the Japanese War Minister, to arrange for the establishment of a new Chinese government. The negotiations lasted roughly a year. In March 1940 Japan agreed to recognize Wang Ching-wei as President of Nationalist China with headquarters in Nanking, while Wang Ching-wei agreed to accept the government of Manchukuo with the former Emperor Pu-yi of China as its Emperor. In January 1943 Wang Ching-wei, in the name of the Chinese government at Nanking, declared war on England and the United States.

To return now to the facts leading up to Thailand being requested to recognize the government of Wang Ching-wei, on 22 May 1942 Mr. Shigenori Togo,[28] the

Japanese Minister of Foreign Affairs, invited me over to the Ministry. After a general conversation, he mentioned that as Thailand and Japan had already formed an understanding over Thai troops entering Burma,[29] he believed that our troops would soon clash with those of the Chungking government of Marshal Chiang Kai-shek.[30] When that occurred, it would become necessary, he pointed out, for the Thai government to declare its position in regard to the Chungking government. The Japanese government felt that rather than our declaring war on the Chungking government, which would amount to our tacit recognition of the Chungking regime, it would be better if we took the opportunity to announce our recognition of the new Nationalist China (meaning the government of Wang Ching-wei).

Mr. Togo added that he would also like me to report to the Thai government that Japan's policy insofar as China and Greater East Asia was concerned was to accord legal recognition to the Wang Ching-wei government. Germany and Italy had already recognized the latter government [as the government of China], so that when Chiang Kai-shek had declared war on the two Axis powers, they had not made any return declaration of war. If Thailand was to carry on a policy that differed from that of Japan and its allies, many would feel this to be odd, and it might cause an awkward situation between nations of the same alliance. The Japanese government would like the Thai government to fully recognize the importance of Asian countries cooperating with one another in building up a co-prosperity sphere in Greater East Asia, in adhering to the common policy towards China adopted by Japan and its allies, and in leading the war to a successful conclusion. The Japanese government was therefore asking that the Thai government take this opportunity to recognize the Wang Ching-wei government as Japan's other allies had already done, without concerning itself about past relations between Thailand and China. Togo concluded by adding that it would be rather surprising, seeing that the Thai government had been willing to recognize the Manchukuo regime, if it should now hesitate over the case of China.

I replied that the question of Manchukuo differed somewhat from that of China. We had large numbers of Chinese in Thailand. This caused us certain problems, and the Thai government would have to consider the matter with caution. I told him that I would, however, report on our conversation to the Thai government. That same afternoon I sent a brief cable to our Ministry of Foreign Affairs, following this up the next day with a detailed report recommending that the government consider the matter with great care, as the Chinese problem was a very complex one.[31]

On the afternoon of 18 June, or twenty-seven days after I had been to see Mr. Togo, the secretary to the Minister of Foreign Affairs telephoned me to say that

CHAPTER 7

Mr. Togo had called to speak to me, but as I had been away from the embassy at the time, the Thai Secretary had been instructed to pass on a message to me. This was to say that the Foreign Minister had received a cable from the Japanese Embassy in Bangkok stating that Luang Wichitwathakan, the Deputy Minister of Foreign Affairs, had told the Japanese Ambassador to Bangkok that the Thai government, after consulting with members of the Council of Ministers, had agreed to recognize the Wang Ching-wei regime. The Japanese Minister of Foreign Affairs wanted to know why, seeing that he had made the request through me, I had not been to see him to deliver the official answer myself.

From the time that I had reported on the matter to the Thai government, I had not received any views or instructions in response. I was therefore greatly surprised, as the message left by the secretary to the Japanese Minister of Foreign Affairs was the first I had heard of the matter. I told the Minister's secretary that the reason I had not been to see the Minister was that I had not been informed of my government's decision. I said that I would, however, send a cable to Bangkok enquiring further, and would contact the Minister as soon as I received any message.

That same evening I sent a cable to the Thai Ministry of Foreign Affairs giving details of the Japanese Foreign Minister's protest. The next day I received a cable from the Thai Ministry of Foreign Affairs, which crossed with mine, stating that the Thai government had agreed to recognize the Wang Ching-wei government, and that I should inform the Japanese Minister of Foreign Affairs of this. The cable added that the Japanese Ambassador in Thailand had already been informed of this decision.

I asked to see Mr. Togo at once, and passed on the contents of the cable to him. Mr. Togo expressed his thanks, but asked that I protest to the Thai government that since he had originally made the proposal to the Thai government through me, the first person who should have been informed of the answer was himself, not the Japanese Ambassador in Bangkok. (I learned later that Mr. Togo had not told the Japanese Ambassador in Bangkok when he sent the proposal via me, and so was highly annoyed when the Thai government answered through the Japanese Ambassador in Bangkok). I tried to cover up the incident by saying that the Thai government had only informed the Japanese Ambassador in Bangkok out of a wish to speed up matters and to satisfy the Japanese government. I then sent a detailed report of this conversation to our government. On 7 July 1942 the Thai government officially announced its recognition of the Wang Ching-wei government.

The government of Chiang Kai-shek was furious at the Thai government's recognition of the Wang Ching-wei regime. At the end of the war, the *Ta Kung Pao*, a Chungking newspaper, published an article in which it even demanded that Thailand face the same surrender procedures as other hostile powers, and that senior government officials such as Field Marshal Phibun Songkhram be tried as war criminals.[32] Fortunately for us, however, during the war Thailand secretly cooperated with the Allies, particularly with the United States and England; post-war treatment of Thailand was therefore somewhat lightened, as will be discussed later in part 3, chapter 1 [now chapter 10].

On 7 July 1942, the day that our government announced its recognition of the Wang Ching-wei government, the Ambassador to Japan of the Wang Ching-wei regime, Mr. Sui Liang, came to see me. He asked me to convey his thanks to the Thai government for our goodwill gesture. As far as the question of establishing diplomatic relations between our two countries was concerned, as it was wartime, the Chinese Ambassador stressed that cutting costs should be given weighty consideration. He therefore suggested recommending to his government that it appoint him Ambassador or Minister to Thailand concurrently with his present position [as Ambassador to Japan], and if I was agreeable that I should make a similar recommendation to the Thai government that it appoint me Ambassador or Minister to Nanking [in addition to my present post]. The Chinese Ambassador stated that he had already discussed this idea with Mr. Togo, the Japanese Foreign Minister, and that the latter had raised no objections. I replied that I would send a report on the subject to the Thai government.

Regarding our recognition of the Wang Ching-wei regime, I had advised the Thai government to consider the question very carefully, as it had always been our policy to avoid making any agreements with China in view of the large Chinese population in Thailand. Even though the government went ahead anyway and decided, out of favor towards Japan, to recognize the Wang Ching-wei government, I did not see that we need go so far as to agree to exchange ambassadors between the two countries. I was obliged to report to my government on the proposals made by the Chinese Ambassador, but I also expressed my own opinions on the subject.

On 20 August 1942 the Chinese Ambassador came to see me again to tell me that his government had agreed to his proposal, and had instructed him to inform me that his government was ready to appoint him as its diplomatic representative to Thailand in addition to his post as Ambassador to Tokyo. His government well recognized Thailand's concern regarding its large Chinese population, and would therefore like to provide an undertaking that it would not interfere in matters relating to them. On the contrary, it would encourage the Chinese to obey and abide by Thai law in every way, and to support the Thai government in its war effort.

I told the Chinese Ambassador that although I had sent a report on our conversation to the Thai government, I had not yet received a reply. I assured him that I would, in any event, send a further report to my government outlining today's conversation. The Ambassador thereupon commented that as Japan had helped in the negotiations leading to Thailand recognizing the Wang Ching-wei government, he thought he would also call on Mr. Togo, the Japanese Minister of Foreign Affairs, to inform him of our arrangements to date and to sound out his opinion thereon. He would come back afterwards and tell me the outcome of this conversation.

I raised no objections, and the following day the Chinese Ambassador came to see me once again. He stated that the Japanese Foreign Minister had informed him that the Chinese government believed Thailand might not like the idea of an exchange of Ministers. It would therefore like to have Mr. Togo's opinion on whether Thailand was ready to effect such an exchange yet, or whether simply having the Chinese government send a special delegation to thank the Thai government for having recognized the Wang Ching-wei regime would be sufficient.

Mr. Togo had replied that he did not think sending a special delegation would be at all suitable in the present circumstances, as it would incur unnecessary and extravagant expense. He thought it would be better to exchange diplomatic representatives. When asked whether he thought the exchange of diplomatic representatives should be made at ministerial or ambassadorial level, the Japanese Foreign Minister had replied that if an exchange was made at ambassadorial level, then the case of Manchukuo would have to be reconsidered, for there the Thai representative was only at ministerial level. He therefore saw no need for the Wang Ching-wei government and Thailand to exchange diplomatic representatives at the level of ambassador.

On 24 August 1942 I was instructed to sound out the opinion of the Chinese Ambassador as to whether he thought it would be suitable if we were to appoint our Minister in Manchukuo, Major-General Luang Wirayotha[33] to also be our Minister to Nanking. The Chinese Ambassador asked if seeing that Luang Wirayotha's rank was merely that of Minister this would involve his being promoted to the rank of ambassador or not. I told Mr. Sui Liang that he himself had mentioned that Japan was not particularly enthusiastic about having diplomatic representatives exchanged at the level of ambassadors. Would our suggestion therefore be suitable? Although the Chinese Ambassador made no objections, it was clear that he himself would have preferred to have our two countries exchange embassies.

On 29 August 1942 Luang Wichitwathakan, who by that time had been promoted to Minister of Foreign Affairs, talked with me over the radio about the matter. The Thai government had decided to have a separate Minister stationed in Nanking, or in other words plans to have Luang Wirayotha serve as Minister to both Manchukuo and Nanking had now been changed. I told him that from what the Chinese Ambassador had gathered from the Japanese Minister of Foreign Affairs, the position would only be a temporary one anyway. Luang Wichit told me I was to try to make the position a permanent one. I replied that I would try to do so.

On 31 August 1942 I went to see Mr. Togo, the Japanese Minister of Foreign Affairs, regarding Japan sending the draft of a cultural pact to Thailand for our consideration.[34] I took the opportunity to also sound out his views on the exchange of diplomatic representatives as I had been instructed to do by Luang Wichit, and was told that the establishment of permanent legations would be a sheer waste of money. It would be quite sufficient for the respective Ministers to present their Letters of Credential, after which they could return.

Later I was instructed to inform the Chinese Ambassador that the Thai government was willing to appoint a representative to Nanking in a permanent position at the level of an ambassador. As the Chinese Ambassador had himself mentioned that his government would guarantee not to interfere in the affairs of the Chinese in Thailand, the Thai government would, however, like to have this undertaking in writing. The Chinese Ambassador replied that there should be no problem about this, but would I object if he told the Japanese Minister of Foreign Affairs about it? I told him that it was not up to me to express approval or objection to this, as this was a matter that rested solely between Japan and China. Eventually the Chinese Ambassador told me that the reason Japan did not want us to exchange permanent legations was probably a fear that the Chinese Minister would encourage the Chinese in Thailand to unite and support China in certain of her policies.

In the middle of September 1942 I met the Chinese Ambassador again during the tenth anniversary celebrations of the establishment of the Manchukuo government. Mr. Sui Liang whispered to me that the establishment of embassies between our two countries did not appear to be feasible seeing that the Japanese government wanted the appointments to be only at ministerial level. I replied that in that case we had a problem, seeing that the Chinese representative in Manchukuo was of ambassadorial rank. The Chinese Ambassador said he agreed with me in every way, but the Wang Ching-wei government did not know as yet which course of action to take.

Later certain events took place that took care of the situation, which was a great relief to me. On 24 December 1942 President Wang Ching-wei, President of the Chinese government at Nanking, and Mr. Chu Min-gi, its Minister of Foreign Affairs, paid an official visit to Japan. The latter came to see me at my residence, and after a general conversation on the subject of the Chinese and Thai being brothers, as well as allusions to many important and high-ranking Thai officials of Chinese descent, Mr. Chu Min-gi informed me that following discussions between President Wang Ching-wei, General Tojo, the Prime Minister of Japan, Mr. Tani, the Japanese Minister of Foreign Affairs,[35] and Mr. Aoki, the Japanese Minister for Greater East Asian Affairs, it had been decided that as the Nanking government was not yet familiar with the situation in Thailand, the two countries being yet fresh to their newly formed relationship, it would be better to study the general situation and exchange a special delegation to begin with. It had been decided that Mr. Chu Min-gi would himself head up a Chinese delegation and pay a visit to Thailand. General Tojo would be discussing this with me further, the Chinese Foreign Minister informed me.

On the following day I went to take leave of the Prime Minister, as I was returning to Thailand on duty for a brief visit. We had a general discussion which lasted almost an hour, but the subject of the Wang Ching-wei government was never once raised by General Tojo. Thus it was that the question of recognition of the Wang Ching-wei regime and matters connected with it came to an end in so far as I was concerned.

CULTURAL PACT BETWEEN THAILAND AND JAPAN

During my term of office in Japan another important agreement which our country signed with Japan was the Cultural Pact of October 1942.

On 25 or 26 of August 1942, the Japanese Minister of Foreign Affairs, Mr. Togo, invited me over to the Ministry, where he presented me with the draft of a cultural agreement between Thailand and Japan which he asked to be sent on to the Thai government as the basis for drawing up a permanent agreement between us.

Our embassy in Tokyo had received no information at all on this matter, so we only acted as mail man in conveying the letter to our Foreign Ministry in Bangkok. Afterwards I gave Luang Wichitwathakan, who had by then been promoted to Thai Foreign Minister as mentioned earlier, a long distance call telling him I was sending on this proposal from Japan, but that our embassy had had no inkling or knowledge about the affair before we had suddenly been handed this draft.

Luang Wichitwathakan explained that sometime around 20 August 1942 Mr. Koichi, Advisor to the Japanese Embassy in Bangkok, had come to see him to tell him that the Japanese government wished to see a cultural agreement drawn up with Thailand. It had been agreed that Luang Wichit would draft this agreement himself. However, it was good to learn that the Japanese government had done so instead, as reported in my cable. Luang Wichit had therefore told

Fig. 12. The signing of the Cultural Pact between Mr. Tani, the Japanese Minister of Foreign Affairs, and Nai Direk Jayanama, the Thai Ambassador, on 20 October 1942, in Tokyo.

Mr. Koichi that this being so he, Luang Wichit, would study the draft when he received it from the Thai embassy in Tokyo.

Sometime in October I received instructions that the Thai government had now studied this draft, and after slight revisions, was sending me a letter authorizing me to sign a pact with Japan. This cultural pact was finally signed on 20 October 1942 at the Japanese Foreign Ministry, with Mr. Tani, the Japanese Foreign Minister, signing for Japan.

The main conditions of the agreement were that the governments of the two countries would cooperate in facilitating the exchange of cultural institutions between them and in carrying out publicity by means of radio broadcasts. The exchange of student textbooks, films, and language courses, etc. would also be promoted. These activities were in line with Japan's policy of building up the Greater East Asia Co-Prosperity Sphere.

I realized, of course, that the policy of the Japanese government was to get other Asians to understand and admire Japanese culture. While it is true that there are many aspects of Japanese culture that are worthy of study, we need to remember that there are also many good points about our own Thai culture that are equally worthy of being promoted. I learned that Japan had put out about forty to fifty booklets giving information and details on the Japanese way of life, Japanese traditions and customs, Japan's history, Japanese drama such as the Noh plays and Kabuki, and so on. I contacted Viscount Okabe, Vice-President of the Japan-Thailand Association, and Count Kuroda of the Association for International Cultural Relations, both of whom sent me many books on Japanese culture which I hastened to send on to our Ministry of Foreign Affairs. The Foreign Affairs Ministry expressed its thanks and stated it would arrange for the publication of similar booklets on our own culture.

I should like to add some further points on the subject of Japan's interest in spreading and promoting its culture. During my term of office in Japan, mass media, whether through the press, radio, or books generally stressed cultural subjects.[36] The basic aims behind this were first to instruct Japanese citizens themselves in their highly complex culture and art forms, and secondly to attain certain political ends. By stressing the characteristics of Japanese culture through the schools, the government instilled a sense of loyalty and admiration in its students. The Ministry of Greater East Asian Affairs, which is discussed subsequently, even established a Division for Cultural Affairs to attend to the establishment of schools, cultural centers and clinics throughout many countries in Asia. Japan had always borne in mind that if Western missionaries had been successful in a number of Asian countries, then the Japanese, as Asians and thus able to mix more easily with other Asians, should be able to carry out their own mission more easily and rapidly than missionaries from a different European culture.

JAPAN SETS UP THE GREATER EAST ASIA MINISTRY

Japan's establishment of the Greater East Asia Ministry was a major issue, as it affected a number of different nations and produced varying reactions from the governments of different countries in Asia.

As soon as I heard of the establishment of this Ministry I sent a report on the matter to the Thai government right away stating that on 1 September 1942 the Japanese Department of Public Relations had announced the resignation of Mr. Shigenori Togo, Minister of Foreign Affairs, for personal reasons. At the same time newspapers throughout Japan were reporting that a Greater East Asia Ministry would be set up and that General Tojo, the Prime Minister, would be appointed Minister of Foreign Affairs in place of Mr. Togo.

Speculation on the cause of Mr. Togo's resignation centered on the question of the reorganization of the Ministry of Foreign Affairs being carried out in connection with the establishment of the Greater East Asia Ministry. The South Seas Bureau, the East Asia Bureau and other departments connected with Manchukuo and China were all to be transferred to the new Ministry. All

Japanese ambassadors, chargé d'affaires and officials in Japanese embassies and legations abroad were also to be placed under its control.

Under such circumstances it was impossible for the Foreign Minister to remain in his post, since much of his authority would be eliminated. A day before the announcement concerning the resignation of Mr. Togo was announced, the Department of Public Relations issued a statement saying that the Prime Minister and the Foreign Minister had held a long discussion after which the Foreign Minister had held a conference with the Deputy Minister[37] and the Advisor to the Minister of Foreign Affairs. This possibly indicated that the Minister of Foreign Affairs was not totally in agreement with the new arrangement. He had then resigned together with the Deputy Minister. The reason given in official circles for the establishment of the Greater East Asia Ministry was that this would contribute greatly to Japan's foreign policy in the region. Its main purpose was to bring countries within the eastern region of Asia into closer contact with one another, by providing a center where plans and preparations could be made instead of these having to be worked out within different ministries. Such a centralization of administrative procedures would prove very useful in the immediate future, aiding in the efficient assembly of forces to continue the war, as Japan had to depend greatly on a number of Asian countries for raw materials and military equipment as well as for military bases. Furthermore Japan felt that if it emerged the victor in the war then these countries would again be of value to Japan economically, as they provided markets for Japanese products while at the same time serving as sources of agricultural produce to feed the Japanese population.

Japan felt that as a first step in building up the Greater East Asia Co-Prosperity Sphere, it was essential that this new ministry be established to supervise and closely control countries within the region. It was stressed officially that any negotiations and dealings between Japan and these countries on purely diplomatic matters would still be carried out through the Ministry of Foreign Affairs. Despite this insistence it was recognized that the establishment of the new Ministry would, however, in effect place these countries in East Asia in a position of subservience to Japan, either directly or indirectly. It is true that Japan claimed that these countries remained free and independent according to the internationally accepted meaning of the terms. However, countries within the Co-Prosperity Sphere would be required to cooperate with Japan in promoting the success of this sphere under Japanese leadership. In theory, then, we might conclude that Japan would treat China, Indochina, Thailand etc. as it would any independent country. In practice, however, it might treat them as it had treated Manchukuo, which had to cooperate with Japan in pursuance of the latter's war effort and by building up the Co-Prosperity Sphere in East Asia.

CHAPTER 7

With the establishment of the Greater East Asia Ministry Japan's foreign policy thus changed greatly. Establishment of the Ministry was just a first step in expanding Japan's influence and authority in this part of the world, and it was now clear that Japan's object in building up the Greater East Asia Co-Prosperity Sphere was none other than to bring this region under its "protectorship" and "leadership".

Such were the thoughts in all diplomatic circles in Japan. They were felt even by [Mr. Sui Liang], the representative of the Wang Ching-wei government. There was no doubt as to the opinion of the representative of Manchukuo, a region known by all for a long time to have merely a puppet government. Even the Japanese press was somewhat afraid that the countries of greater East Asia might take a rather critical view of Japan on the matter. It therefore admonished the Japanese government to explain clearly the issues involved to the representatives of the various countries in the region.

The Japanese government had already prepared a variety of arguments to cope with such a reaction. On the legal side the Japanese government alleged, for instance, that these reforms and the establishment of the new Ministry had been carried out solely in the interest of Japan's internal administrative procedures. However, Japan had in fact already dissolved its Overseas Ministry and transferred the scope of duties of this Ministry to the new Greater East Asia Ministry, giving rise to suspicions that the sphere of duties of the new Ministry would be not far off those of a Ministry for Colonies, or an Overseas Ministry set up under a new guise.

On the ethical front, the Japanese government claimed it had placed the handling of matters connected with the countries of Greater East Asia within the scope of this new Ministry as it felt this would be like grouping all members of the same family together, and that it would make for a close relationship between them. These countries should therefore regard such an arrangement as an honor, particularly as it had been carried out in a friendly and relaxed manner instead of being laden with red tape and all the other regulations that would normally be required for carrying out such an arrangement among countries of other races. Although these sentiments were put forward by the press, it was clear that they actually represented the views of the government.

Only two days after the announcement of the establishment of the new Ministry, a Japanese whom I knew well and who was an unofficial representative of government circles, came to see me to say that he knew Thailand would have received news of the establishment of the Greater East Asia Ministry by now, and that deep down we might not be at all pleased about this. He therefore wanted to let me know that Japan had no wish to insult Thailand by this gesture, or to treat it as if it was not independent. The Ministry had only been set up to accelerate the handling of affairs, as the Ministry of Foreign Affairs had formerly had to heed military opinion all the time and had not had much real power. The new Ministry, on the other hand, would have absolute and effective power, he told me, as the military had agreed to help run it.

I thanked him, but pointed out that according to the announcement, while we could approach the Japanese Ministry of Foreign Affairs directly on purely diplomatic matters, all questions of a political, economic or cultural nature would now, however, have to be taken up with the Greater East Asia Ministry. This, I claimed, amounted to placing Thailand in the same position as Indochina, and indeed the announcement had stated that the affairs of Manchukuo, China, islands in the South Seas under Japanese jurisdiction, Indochina and Thailand all fell within the sphere of this new Ministry. I told him international principle and practice dictated that a representative of a government of an independent country could not approach any Ministry either on purely diplomatic matters or on a matter of any other nature unless he had been authorized by his Ministry of Foreign Affairs to do so. Japan could not compare us with lands it had occupied that had long been colonies of England or the United States, for we had been independent for a long time and had never been colonized by any nation. I pointed out that Thailand had been a good friend to Japan, and that we had also become its military ally. If Japan persisted in these actions, the United States and Britain would definitely take the opportunity to announce that Japan was treating us as a colony, which would not serve Japan's interests in any way. My Japanese informant denied most emphatically, however, that Japan had ever entertained such thoughts in coming to this arrangement.

I had already sent a cable reporting on the establishment of the Greater East Asia Ministry to the Thai government, and had requested the latter's instructions on the matter. As I never received such instructions, I therefore decided to take sole responsibility in letting the Japanese government know we were displeased at the establishment of the new Ministry.

About four to five days after the announcement was made, I tried to see Mr. Yamamoto, [former] Director-General of the American Bureau of the Foreign Affairs Ministry, who had been assigned as acting Deputy Minister of Foreign Affairs when Mr. Nishi, the former Deputy Minister, resigned together with Mr. Togo as described earlier. I told him that I had come to pay a courtesy call on him in his capacity as acting Deputy Minister, and was taking the opportunity to discuss the establishment of the new Ministry. To lay the way for future negotiations between our embassy and the Japanese Foreign Ministry, I was asking Mr. Yamamoto to clarify the situation for us.

Mr. Yamamoto explained that contacts between our nations would be made in the same manner as before. When I mentioned that the announcement had stated that such contacts would be limited to matters of a purely diplomatic nature Mr. Yamamoto was, however, unable to elaborate further. I let him know that I would therefore like to pay a courtesy call on General Tojo, who had now also temporarily taken over the position of Minister of Foreign Affairs [following the resignation of Mr. Togo][38], and was told that I would have an opportunity to do so soon, as the Prime Minister was about to receive foreign diplomatic representatives in the usual manner.[39]

About two to three days later General Tojo, the Prime Minister, received calls from diplomats in order of seniority. I thanked him for receiving me, to which the Prime Minister replied quickly that I was welcome. He told me I need not stand on ceremony with him, as we Asians should stand together in building up the Greater East Asia Co-Prosperity Sphere in every way. I took the opportunity to reply that I was willing to cooperate with him in every way, but that at the same time I was still not clear what the correct procedure for contacts between our embassy and the Ministry of Foreign Affairs was now that the new Greater East Asia Ministry had been established, even though Mr. Yamamoto had explained this to me somewhat.

General Tojo gave me a lengthy clarification, saying he would explain this to me as he would to his own brother. The foreign affairs of Japan were divided into two branches, he told me, one covering Europe and America, countries with which Japan did not consider itself affiliated with in any way, and the other covering countries in Asia, which Japan considered its brothers, particularly Thailand, which had similar traditions and cultural features to Japan, and whose people had similar physical characteristics. As Japan considered Thailand its brother, it was not therefore necessary to stand on ceremony with one another, and there was no need to pay attention to the correctness of this or that procedure. This very day, he pointed out, he was receiving me as his brother, and we were having a friendly chat in a casual atmosphere, while only a few moments earlier he had been receiving European diplomats in a formal diplomatic way. He asked me to reflect deep down in my heart whether as brothers Thailand and Japan should not stand together for better or for worse. He felt that it would, then, be better for us to contact the new Ministry so that affairs could be handled more rapidly, again stressing that our relations should be as between kin.

General Tojo asked that I convey this to the Thai government so that the peoples of Thailand and Japan would understand one another. I told him that I was willing to report the matter in detail to my government but that what gave me cause for concern was that in the eyes of others the situation would look somewhat odd. The following day I met Mr. Sui Liang, the Chinese Ambassador to Tokyo of the Wang Ching-wei government. He told me he had also been to see General Tojo the previous day, and had received exactly the same explanations as those I have related here.

About two or three days later I went to see an important person close to Mr. Togo, the former Minister of Foreign Affairs. He told me that Mr. Togo had resigned because he did not agree with the policy of establishing a new Greater East Asia Ministry. He felt it would cause suspicion among the countries of Asia, and that its establishment was planned by military men who wished to place the affairs of Thailand, China, Manchukuo and Indochina all within the same hands. The former Foreign Minister had raised objections all the way along, for he feared that the countries concerned would consider that this in essence rendered them colonies of Japan. The matter had dragged on until recently it had reached a point at which Mr. Togo had felt obliged to resign. The most that the Foreign Ministry had been willing to agree to was to give the new Ministry power over Japanese occupied territories, but General Tojo had remained adamant in his stand, and had even declared that either Mr. Togo resign, or the whole Cabinet resign. Mr. Togo had asked for time to think over the issue, and two hours later, at 18.00 hours [on 1 September 1942] had returned and handed General Tojo his resignation.

From evidence obtained after the war before the International Military Tribunal in Tokyo, the same facts were found as those I have described above, namely, that General Tojo had decided to create a special organization to supervise and coordinate policies in furtherance of his aim of inducing a special relationship between Japan and its occupied territories. His first step towards the later establishment of a Greater East Asia Ministry was the formation of a committee to study the Greater East Asia question in March 1942. Mr. Togo, the Minister of Foreign Affairs, first learned of this project from Mr. Michio Yuzawa, the Home Minister. The former put up fierce opposition, as the powers of the Ministry of Foreign Affairs had been cut down several times before, for example by new regulations that had stated that any matter connected with Manchukuo must henceforth pass through the China Affairs Board. Once it had been decided that the powers of the Foreign Ministry were to be reduced solely to matters of pure diplomacy, which, according to Mr. Togo's statement to the International Military Tribunal were explained to him by Mr. Hoshono, President of the Planning Board, as meaning the handling of diplomatic procedures such as the reception of foreign diplomats, the signing of treaties, etc., Mr. Togo decided to fight these measures to the end. He was determined not to resign over the issue in order to force the resignation of the whole Tojo government. It turned out, however, that General Tojo was also obstinate in his purpose, while the Army and the Navy sent their representatives to inform Mr. Togo that the two forces were in agreement with the new arrangement. When

Mr. Togo tried to get the support of civilian ministers, no one was willing to pledge him their support.

On 1 September 1942 the Cabinet held an emergency meeting at which General Tojo proposed the establishment of the new Ministry. He claimed that as countries within the region of Greater East Asia had a special relationship similar to that of kin within the same clan, he therefore thought it necessary to establish this Ministry to uphold and further these good relations. The Foreign Minister, Mr. Togo, argued that these countries would undoubtedly resent the setting up of this new Ministry, for they would feel they had been treated with contempt as subordinates of Japan. Besides, he pointed out, if the duties of this new Ministry were to be anything like those of the China Affairs Board, he saw no possible benefit to be derived from such an organization, as that Board had done nothing but arouse the continuing antagonism of China. Two organizations for diplomatic affairs would, moreover, only result in confusion as well as cause division in the government's foreign policy. The Foreign Minister further pointed out to the Cabinet that Japan had not yet won the war, so all thoughts should be concentrated on this question first, and that of Japan's relationship with the occupied territories left for the time being. General Tojo, however, persisted in his arguments, and when Mr. Togo saw that his objections were not going to produce any results, nor was his attempt to bring down the whole government going to be successful, he finally tendered his resignation.

The Cabinet thereupon consented to the formation of the new Ministry. However, when the matter was brought before the Investigation Committee of the Privy Council, which had been formed to study the draft proposed by the government, fierce opposition was raised by certain members of the committee, including Dr. Hara, the President of the Committee, himself. The reasons for this opposition were similar to those raised by Mr. Togo, namely that the establishment of another ministry involved with diplomatic affairs would only create confusion, and that many countries affected by the new arrangement would be dissatisfied with it.

General Tojo, however, went himself to explain to the Committee that it was absolutely necessary to set up this new Ministry in order to give free rein to the policy of co-prosperity in Greater East Asia. When asked as to the extent of the powers to be exercised by this Ministry, General Tojo explained that the Ministry would not have any authority over regions under Japanese military administration, but that the military authorities there would, however, cede to civilian power as soon as the opportunity presented itself.

One member of the Committee posed a pertinent question by saying that the administrative personnel on the island of Formosa [now Taiwan][40] were nearly all Japanese, but how would it be possible to find the staff for all the newly occupied territories? General Tojo explained that attempts would gradually be made to bring in local people to join in the administration of their territories. Most of the members of the Committee of the Privy Council were nonetheless dissatisfied with General Tojo's explanations and with the statements made in his support by Mr. Tani, the new Minister of Foreign Affairs. However, in the end General Tojo scored a victory over the Committee, and the Emperor signed a decree announcing the establishment of the Greater East Asia Ministry in October 1942. The Ministry was [formally] opened the following month [on 1 November 1942].

At this point I should like to say a little about the phrase "Greater East Asia" used by Japan. The Japanese referred to the war as the "Greater East Asia" War, or "Dai Toa Senso" in Japanese, and believed that the war had among its aims the creation of a Greater East Asia Co-Prosperity Sphere, or what was called the "Dai Toa Kyoeiken". This last had economic, political and cultural aspects. On 30 November 1942, the day designated for celebrating the friendship treaty between Japan, China and the Manchukuo government, General Tojo, the Prime Minister, and Mr. Aoki, the Greater East Asia Minister, made speeches in which they claimed that the building of the Greater East Asia Co-Prosperity Sphere was based on principles of justice and righteousness. It had as its aims not only the building of a new economic system, but also of helping the people of the region receive the full advantages and rightful status to which they were entitled as a result of being born in this part of the world. The Japanese position therefore differed in purpose from the colonialism of the Western powers. Japan's purposes and aims in Asia were, rather, similar to those of her allies in Europe (meaning Germany and Italy). The war was being fought not primarily to acquire natural resources, but to build a new order in which every nation would derive its share of the profits, and to ensure a permanent peace. The successful establishment of a Greater East Asia Co-Prosperity Sphere would not only bring about a situation in which Japan could become a self-sufficient empire, but would also make it the leader of the culture and civilization of Asia. In other words, Japan would become the Light of Asia. In view of Japan's wish to help other Asian nations, the countries concerned should cooperate in bringing about the success of the Co-Prosperity Sphere. Any resistance would be considered an act of treachery against Japan punishable by death. (This had already been demonstrated in the Philippines, where citizens pledged loyalty to the United States and joined hands in helping the United States resist Japan everywhere). The Japanese Prime Minister and the Minister for Greater East Asia therefore called on the nations of the region to be patient and endure hardships without complaining too much until such time as they should taste the sweetness of success. They called on these nations to make sacrifices for the sake of the common community, claiming that in the course of the war Japan had had to make greater sacrifices than any nation in Asia.

In regard to the cultural aspects of the Greater East Asia Co-Prosperity Sphere, Japan sought to wipe out all traces of Western influence and to uphold the cultures of the various nations [under its aegis], as, for example, in China and Manchukuo, where Japan sought to uphold the doctrines of Confucius. It was also Japanese policy to support the religions of the countries of the area. As Thailand was a firm adherent of Buddhism, Japan gave full support to Buddhism, even to sending Japanese monks to Thailand. In Malaya and the Dutch East Indies (today Indonesia) Japan gave full support to Islam, and in the Philippines to Roman Catholicism.

Once the war was over, the Allies found drafts of projects which Japan had planned to carry out in the territories it conquered. One draft was dated 14 December 1941. When the Allies produced this evidence before the International Military Tribunal in Tokyo Mr. Togo, the Minister of Foreign Affairs at that period, denied having seen or heard of such a draft or even having contemplated such a project, and it is possible that it may have been drawn up by junior officials. It included many plans, such as placing British North Borneo and Sarawak under Japanese suzerainty, ruled by a Japanese Governor-General operating from Singapore. The Dutch East Indies (now Indonesia) were to be grouped together as the Federation of Indonesia, with Dutch New Guinea, Dutch Borneo and Dutch Timor being placed under Japanese supervision within the Federation. The Philippines, on the other hand, were to be given their independence, although Japan would have maintained certain military and economic rights there. Hong Kong was to be claimed as Japanese territory, although consideration would have been given to returning it to China once the government of Chiang Kai-shek had been overthrown.

The Allies held the view that if Japan had emerged the victor in the war it would immediately have claimed as its own lands of strategic importance such as Hong Kong, Singapore, Borneo, New Guinea, and Dutch Timor. States such as Malaya, Sumatra, Java, Madoya [Madura?—Ed.], and the Celebes would have been ruled by Japan initially and then allowed to rule themselves within certain guidelines. As for Manchukuo, China, the Philippines, Indochina, Thailand and Burma, these countries would either have been given their independence, or continued respect would have been shown for their sovereignty. However, Japan would have made certain claims for special privileges [in these territories], especially in regard to military bases, together possibly with insisting on agreements for military and political aid. Economically, countries within the Greater East Asia Co-Prosperity Sphere would have been prosperous and self-sufficient, producing the maximum from their resources, but would have had to agree to buy products they could not produce themselves from other countries within the Co-Prosperity Sphere.

JAPAN'S HANDING OVER TO THAILAND CERTAIN TERRITORIES FORMERLY UNDER BRITISH JURISDICTION

I believe that Japan's handing over of the four states of Perlis, Kedah, Kelantan, and Trengganu in northern Malaya, together with the two provinces of Kengtung and Mueang Pan in the Shan States [of Burma] to Thailand must have been the result of the meeting between Japan's Prime Minister, General Tojo, and Thailand's Prime Minister, Field Marshal Phibun Songkhram, in Bangkok on 4 July 1943.

General Tojo had already twice expressed a wish to go to Thailand. The first time was just after the war on the Asian front had broken out. He was advised against going then because of the insecurity of air travel. The second time was after the return from Bangkok of Mr. Aoki, the Greater East Asia Minister [in April 1943]. Again General Tojo was advised not to go since Mr. Aoki had only just visited there.

A little later, however, General Tojo decided to go to Singapore, and felt that as he was going there already, he might as well see Field Marshal Phibun Songkhram too. Instructions were therefore given to the Japanese Ambassador in Bangkok to discuss the possibility of Field Marshal Phibun Songkhram meeting the Japanese Prime Minister in Singapore. The Thai government accepted this proposal, and I received instructions to inform the Greater East Asia Minister of the proposed visit, which I accordingly did on 26 June 1943.

Mr. Aoki expressed his delight and told me that the exact date of the meeting would be fixed later for security reasons. He added that General Tojo would be taking the opportunity to discuss the improvement of the present good relations between Japan and Thailand with Field Marshal Phibun, as well as the subject of aid given by Japan. In addition, continued consultations would be held over Thailand's wishes (regarding the return of certain territories to Thailand), the subject of which had already been hinted at in the General's speech to the Japanese Diet of 16 June 1943. I went to listen to General Tojo's speech given at the meeting of the Japanese Diet. In it he stated that he wished to announce once again that Japan recognized the age-old aspirations of the Thai people, and hoped for continual progress and renewed co-operation with our country. The speech was translated for me by General Ott, the German Ambassador, who was seated next to me.[41]

CHAPTER 7

On 2 July 1943 I received a personal letter from Mr. Aoki, the Greater East Asia Minister, saying that General Tojo had decided to go to Bangkok, but that as his trip was to be kept a matter of the greatest secrecy for security reasons Mr. Aoki regretted to have to tell me that direct contacts would be made through the Japanese embassy in Bangkok. I was greatly surprised by the letter, as it had been agreed formerly that the two Prime Ministers would be meeting in Singapore, so I made an appointment to see Mr. Aoki the following day, on 3 July 1943, in order to have a correct understanding of the matter.

Mr. Aoki told me that General Tojo had been thinking that he might as well go to Bangkok for the meeting with our Prime Minister; the (Japanese) Ambassador in Bangkok had therefore been instructed to inform Field Marshal Phibun Songkhram of this change. On 5 July 1943 Mr. Aoki invited me over to the Ministry and said he was pleased to be able to inform me that General Tojo had already arrived in Bangkok. He had reached there on the afternoon of 3 July, and had seen Field Marshal Phibun Songkhram the following day, when a two-hour discussion had been held between the two men in a cordial atmosphere. These talks had led to Japan handing over to us territories in the Shan States (of Burma) as well as four states in Malaya. A joint communiqué had been issued, a copy of which Mr. Aoki now gave me, stating that the two Prime Ministers had exchanged opinions on the general world situation, on the relationship between Thailand and Japan, and on their plans to build up the stability and unity of Greater East Asia and combine their efforts to bring the war to a successful conclusion. The two countries had agreed to respect one another's sovereignty, and to let the states of Perlis, Kedah, Kelantan, and Trengganu in Malaya, together with the two provinces of Kengtung and Muang Pan in the Shan States, be annexed by Thailand.

I thanked him out of general courtesy and said that this gesture would make the people aware of the good intentions Japan had towards them. Three to four days later my government sent me the same information as that which Mr. Aoki had already relayed to me.[42]

MY RETURN TO THAILAND

In July 1943 I became ill and had to return home on sick leave in September of that year as will be mentioned in the next chapter.

During my twenty months of office in Japan I have to say that I received every bodily comfort, but my heart always felt heavy because the news from Thailand regarding our relations with Japan was not good. The Thai government faced constant demands by the Japanese military in Bangkok, several creating problems that were transferred to Tokyo for me to handle. During the period I was away from Thailand major floods also left many of my fellow citizens homeless or caused them hardship. In addition their towns were bombed at regular intervals, while the cost of living had risen to such an incredible point that the government had to issue more bank notes.

What gave me most concern, though, was the question of what Thailand's position would be when the war ended. If Japan won the war, even though we might be independent we would still be in a position of having to obey Japan, or again might be classed in a category similar to that of the Manchukuo regime. If, on the other hand, the United States and England won the war, and Thailand had neither taken part in fighting for the defense of the Thai nation nor cooperated with the Allies, or in other words if we had played no part in the sacrifices involved [in such a victory], then the United States and Britain might treat us as little better than a colony, or cause us to suffer severe reprisals. I recalled clearly the words of an English statesman, possibly Sir Winston Churchill, who said during the war that any country that had not sacrificed lives and blood for the defense of the nation did not deserve to be allowed its independence.

As far as the people of Japan in general and senior Japanese officials both in and outside of government circles were concerned, I must say that the majority, or even 99 percent of them, showed sincere friendship towards Thailand. When Thailand passed through a difficult period during the floods of 1942, the Japanese government was most kind in sending clothing and medical provisions to the Thai people.

As Thai Ambassador to Japan, I received a warm welcome from the Emperor and Empress. I felt deeply honored by this. The Japanese royal family was most gracious to my wife and me throughout the period of our stay in Japan. Before I left Japan the Emperor and Empress kindly gave a dinner reception for us both and instructed the Lord Chamberlain to bring portraits of them to give me at the Thai Embassy.

As for the Thai embassy officials, they all cooperated with me and were united in their efforts to serve our nation during a time of crisis. I should like to express my deep gratitude to all of them here for this.

8
Return to the Ministry of Foreign Affairs in Bangkok
(November 1943–July 1944)

During my term of office in Japan, sometime in the middle of July 1943, I was stricken with phlebitis, or a hardening of the arteries of the leg, caused in my case by a careless hard collision with a table. I had to remain at home and rest for over a month on my doctor's advice, and even after I got better I could not walk properly. Because of this, and because I wanted to help my country, I sent a letter to Field Marshal Phibun Songkhram stating that I wished to resign from my position for reasons of health.

Field Marshal Phibun replied that I could return to Thailand and that we could discuss the matter once I arrived in Bangkok. At the end of September 1943 I therefore returned to Thailand after one year and eight months of office in Japan. The Thai government sent Luang Wichitwathakan, the Minister of Foreign Affairs, to replace me as Thai Ambassador to Japan. When I arrived in Bangkok sometime in early November, I went to see Field Marshal Phibun Songkhram together with Police-General Adun Adundetcharat, the Deputy Prime Minister. The Prime Minister asked me to return to the Ministry of Foreign Affairs, but upon my insisting that I resign, he did not say any more. I therefore went on vacation to Hua Hin.

One evening, as I recall it was on 20 October 1943, a radio broadcast announced that I had been appointed Minister of Foreign Affairs by Royal Decree. I was taken by surprise, as I never dreamed that Field Marshal Phibun Songkhram would appoint me to the position without having first received my consent. I therefore sent a telegram to Colonel Chai Prathipasen,[1] Secretary to the Council of Ministers, asking him to inform the Prime Minister that I did not wish to take up the position. Colonel Chai did not reply, but delegated Police-General Adun Adundetcharat to respond in his stead asking me to return to Bangkok for further discussions.

I returned at once. Police-General Adun came to see me and explained that Field Marshal Phibun had only made the announcement because he feared that if he waited to consult me, I would not accept the position. He called on my sympathy, saying that with our country under Japanese occupation, we all needed to help one another. I told him that I did not want to accept the position as I had already learned my lesson. Before the Japanese invaded our country I had been Minister of Foreign Affairs, yet the Prime Minister had never made me a party to his true policies. Police-General Adun gave me his word that this would not happen again, saying that the Prime Minister had agreed to heed my views with good grace. In the end I was forced to become Minister of Foreign Affairs once again.

I remained in this post until July 1944, when the National Assembly rejected a bill for the establishment of Phetchabun as the capital of Thailand and another for the setting up of a holy Buddhist city at Saraburi.[2] Following this demonstration of non-confidence in the government, its members resigned *en masse*, and I resigned from my position as Minister of Foreign Affairs along with everyone else.

During my nine months at the Ministry of Foreign Affairs this time my work was concerned mainly with relations with Japan, but also to a lesser degree with those with other countries such as Germany and France. Questions regarding military cooperation with Japan were dealt with by the Coordination Department,[3] headed by Colonel Chai Prathipasen, Secretary to the Council of Ministers. When political issues arose, the Japanese Ambassador would refer these either to the Ministry of Foreign Affairs or to the Prime Minister directly.

FINANCIAL RELATIONS WITH JAPAN[4]

Throughout this period Japan's primary concern was to win the war. It therefore believed that Thailand should set aside its own interests, or in other words that we should be patient and put up with present hardships in the hope of ultimate victory. To aid in the war effort, Japan believed Thailand should lend it as much Baht currency as possible so as to enable Japan to purchase the military equipment it needed.[5]

Our financial aid to the Japanese military took shape through arrangements whereby the Japanese received Baht currency for their expenditures in Thailand. When the Japanese first entered our country, this was arranged through loans under the terms of which the Yokohama Specie Bank of Bangkok would draw money from the Bank of Siam at 4 percent annual interest, and agreed to repay the capital in gold bullion at 3.06 Baht per gram of gold.

Later, between the middle of 1942[6] and the end of 1943, this loan system was replaced by the granting of mutual credit. Under this arrangement, the Yokohama Specie Bank in Bangkok would send instructions to the National Bank of Japan to credit the account of the Bank of Siam opened with the National Bank of Japan in Tokyo with a certain sum in Yen, whereupon the Bank of Siam would credit an equivalent amount to the account of the Yokohama Specie Bank in Bangkok. Initially the Japanese government allowed us to use about 50 percent of these Yen credits to buy gold in Japan, but later, during the middle of 1943, it reduced the proportion of Yen credits that could be used to buy gold to 21 percent and raised the price of gold to 4.80 Baht per gram.

This mutual credit system was maintained throughout the first six months of 1944, or up till a month before the Field Marshal Phibun Songkhram government resigned. During this same period, Japan announced it would need another 275 million Baht from us, but that it could now only allow us to use 18 percent of the Yen credits received in return to buy gold, or in other words the percentage of Yen credits available to buy gold was reduced yet further. At the same time the price of gold was increased again, this time to 5.78 Baht per gram.

Meanwhile the expenditures of the Japanese military from the time that Japanese forces first landed in Thailand up to the end of 1943 rose to 216,701,083 Baht, and by June 1944 Japan had received an overall sum of 491,701,083 Baht, from us, or an average of 196,700,000 Baht per annum. This far exceeded the expenditure of the Thai government in any one year. To cope with this situation, our government was forced to increase the number of its bank notes in circulation. Coupled with the fact that our exports had been running low due to our inability to trade with other nations, the market price of goods began to rise to a frightening level.

M.L. Det Sanitwong, the Minister of Commerce, gave me the following statistics on the increased cost of living in Bangkok so that I could press Thailand's case with Japan:

Cost of Living Index		
1938	100.00	
1941	132.00	
1942	176.99	
1943	291.56	
1944	January	301.12
	February	327.56
	March	409.07

Sometime in the middle of June 1944 I received instructions to explain this situation to the Japanese in detail, in an attempt to obtain their sympathy for our plight. I was to indicate that we were willing to continue to provide Japan with Baht currency for the expenditure of its troops in our country, but that we would appreciate the sum requested being limited to that which the Thai government was capable of supplying. At the same time I was also to ask Japan to send us certain goods and products, such as railway engines, automobiles and spare parts, tires, oil and clothing that were in short supply in our country.

I accordingly invited Mr. Koichi, the Japanese Chargé d'Affaires, to see me, and went over the situation with him. He replied that as this was a matter of great importance, he would immediately report on it to his government. However, I never learned about the outcome of our discussions, as a month later I resigned from the Ministry of Foreign Affairs.

Whenever negotiations on financial matters, including Baht loans to Japan, were conducted with the Japanese delegation headed by the Japanese Ambassador and including military and civilian attachés, we would hold conferences beforehand to work out the arguments we would present during the course of these negotiations. Among those who attended these conferences and who put forward excellent ideas for presenting these were General Phra Boriphanyutthakit, Minister of Finance; M.L. Det Sanitwong, Minister of Commerce; H.R.H. Prince Wanwaithayakon,[7] Advisor to the Ministry of Foreign Affairs; M.C. Wiwatthanachai Chaiyan,[8] Advisor to the Ministry of Finance; and Colonel Chai Prathipasen.

THE RESIGNATIONS OF GENERAL TOJO AND FIELD MARSHAL PHIBUN SONGKHRAM

July 1944 was marked by two major events, namely the resignation of the Japanese government of General Tojo and that of the Thai government of Field Marshal Phibun Songkhram.

From the beginning of 1944 onwards, in particular during June and July of that year, Japan suffered several military defeats. The Japanese people became disheartened by this news, and even the Japanese Cabinet started becoming concerned. General Tojo, as Minister of War and Commander-in-Chief of the Army as well as Prime Minister, was held largely responsible for the course the war was taking, [and pressures were brought to bear on him to resign].

The most forceful pressure came from a group of former Prime Ministers known as the Jushin. This group held a meeting to consider the situation, and despite General Tojo's extreme reluctance to do so finally forced him to step down. On 18 July 1944 General Tojo handed the Emperor his resignation as Prime Minister, Minister of War, and as Commander-in-Chief of the Army.

On 21 July 1944 I invited Mr. Koichi, the Japanese Chargé d'Affaires, to see me, and expressed regret in the names of Field Marshal Phibun Songkhram, the Prime Minister, and myself that General Tojo had been obliged to resign, as he had been Prime Minister of Japan, an ally of Thailand's. I asked the Chargé the reasons for General Tojo's resignation, and was told they were mainly in the interests of greater solidarity in the Cabinet, and because of the need to improve on the results of the war effort. He added that a number of major industrialists had become dissatisfied with General Tojo's policy, and felt he had not mobilized all possible forces towards the war effort in the way he should have.

Sometime on either the 21 or 22 of July Field Marshal Phibun Songkhram handed in his resignation to the Thai Council of Ministers following the National Assembly's rejection of a bill calling for the creation of a Buddhist Territory and another for the establishment of Phetchabun as Thailand's capital.[9] Rejection of these bills amounted to an expression of non-confidence in his government. The resignation of the government had to wait on the formal acceptance of the Council of Ministers, however, before it could be considered absolute.

The Japanese Chargé d'Affaires came to see me on 24 July to ask whether it was true that the government had resigned. I told him it was seeking to do so. The next day he came to see me again, asking again if the news was true, as it had been circulated all over Bangkok that Field Marshal Phibun Songkhram, the Prime Minister, had resigned. I told him that it was true, although it had not yet been announced officially. His resignation was not connected with the conduct of foreign affairs in any way, but rather related to the rejection of two bills, failure to pass which was regarded as a motion of non-confidence in the government.

Nai Khuang Aphaiwong subsequently replaced Field Marshal Phibun Songkhram as Prime Minister. He asked me to stay on in my post as Minister of Foreign Affairs, but I declined to do so, so that I might have the opportunity to help my country in other ways.[10]

The members of the Council of Ministers of Nai Khuang Aphaiwong, who was appointed Prime Minister on 2 August 1944, were as follows:[11]

1. Major Khuang Aphaiwong — Prime Minister
2. Vice-Admiral Sin Kamonnawin — Minister of Defense
3. Major Khuang Aphaiwong — Minister of Finance
4. Nai Leng Sisomwong — Deputy Minister of Finance
5. Nai Sisena Sombatsiri — Minister of Foreign Affairs
6. Nai Chit Sithammathibet (Chaophraya Sithammathibet) — Minister of Health
7. Rear-Admiral Phan Nawawichit — Minister of Industry
8. M.L. Udom Sanitwong — Deputy Minister of Industry
9. Vice-Admiral Sin Kamonnawin — Minister of Agriculture
10. Major Khuang Aphaiwong — Minister of Communications

11.	Nai Saphrang Thephatsadin Na Ayutthaya	Deputy Minister of Communications
12.	Captain Bung Suphachalasai, R.N.	Minister of the Interior
13.	M.L. Det Sanitwong	Minister of Commerce
14.	Nai Thawi Bunyaket	Minister of Education
15.	Nai Chit Sithammathibet	Minister of Justice
16.	Nai Duean Bunnag	Deputy Minister of Education
17.	Nai Sithammarat Kanchanachot	Minister without portfolio
18.	Major-General Phin Amonwisaisoradet	Minister without portfolio
19.	Captain Thahan Khamhiran, R.N.	Minister without portfolio
20.	Captain Chalit Kunkamthon	Minister without portfolio
21.	Lieutenant-General Chit Mansin Sinatyotharak	Minister without portfolio
22.	Nai Pora Samahan	Minister without portfolio
23.	General Phot Phahonyothin (Phraya Phahonphonphayuhasena)	Minister without portfolio

The Khuang Aphaiwong government lasted for thirteen months, until 31 August 1946, or about two weeks after Japan's surrender, when the entire government resigned. Throughout the premiership of Nai Khuang Aphaiwong my relationship with Japanese officials continued as before. In particular I held Lieutenant-General Nakamura, Commander of the Japanese Army [in Bangkok] in high esteem. Even after the war we continued to maintain contact, and still exchange greeting cards every New Year. Every time he and his wife came to Bangkok they would drop by and see me frequently. We both understood well the duties of one another towards our own nation.

THAILAND'S RELATIONS WITH GERMANY AND ITALY

During my nine months' term of office at the Foreign Ministry, our relations with Germany and Italy continued as usual. Dr. Wendler,[12] the German Minister at that time, maintained good relations with me. Our conversations usually centered on the war situation. As to our relations with Italy, because Mussolini had recently been deposed[13] and the Fascist regime had fallen, Dr. Crolla, the Italian Minister, could not decide which side he should take.[14] Japan and Germany told us that the Italian Minister should therefore be regarded as having an indefinite status for the time being.[15]

9

Final Year of the War and Involvement in the Free Thai Movement[1]

From the time that I resigned from the Ministry of Foreign Affairs together with other members of the Field Marshal Phibun Songkhram government in July 1944 until August 1945, the month in which Japan surrendered, I spent all my time, along with many other Thai citizens, cooperating with the Allies in Thailand in what was known as the Free Thai movement,[2] led by the Regent, Nai Pridi Banomyong.[3]

General Net Khemayothin,[4] in a book that he wrote later about the movement, quotes a speech by Nai Pridi in which the latter described the aims of the movement and the way it first came into being. It was established not as a political party or special interest group, he explained, but rather represented the united efforts of all those who wished to see our nation restored to the *status quo ante* of the period prior to 8 December 1941. M.R. Seni Pramoj, who was then serving our country abroad [as Thai Minister to Washington], and who was widely known, decided to call both the movement and its members "Free Thai", in contradistinction to the members of our nation who were under Japanese domination at the time. The Free Thai thus consisted of those Thai who did not accept the rule of Japan. The resistance movement in Thailand had in fact, according to Nai Pridi, begun right from 8 December 1941, but was not given a name at first. However, once the activities of the Free Thai overseas began to be recognized by other countries, and as contacts were established between underground groups within Thailand and those abroad, he began to receive letters from foreign officials referring to Thai resistance activities within and outside the kingdom as "the Free Thai movement." He therefore adopted the name, and started using it in correspondence with foreign nations.

Nai Pridi went on to point out that unlike a political party, the Free Thai movement had a limited time span. Once the war was over, its members no longer had work to do, and the movement was therefore disbanded. It should be noted, however, he said, that throughout the years it was operative, Free Thai members carried out their missions purely out of service to the nation. Although it was true that many were government officials, it needed to be made clear that those individuals carried out whatever duties their respective positions made possible,

Fig. 13. A group of British military officers visiting the author's house at Soi Santisuk, Sukhumwit Road, on 30 August 1945, following the declaration of peace.

and did not work for the movement with an eye to obtaining high ranking jobs or other rewards once the war was over.

By the same token members of the Free Thai did not regard themselves as the liberators of Thailand, for they had merely been serving their country. The liberation of the country was brought about by the entire Thai population of some 17 million citizens. Even though many were not directly connected with the Free Thai organization, they helped make it possible for those who were members to carry out their tasks without encountering opposition. Thus all citizens who aided the resistance helped work for the liberation of our country. Although admittedly there had been a few who had obstructed the work of those serving the nation, either in word, deed or spirit, they were Thai who were not worthy of the name.

Finally the Regent took the occasion to give special thanks to M.R. Seni Pramoj and to all Thai nationals in the United States, the United Kingdom and China who had helped the work of the Free Thai movement overseas. As for those who had provided assistance within the kingdom, he wished to pay special tribute to certain senior officials in the Thai administration, including Nai Thawi Bunyaket, Police-General Adun Adundetcharat, Rear Admiral Sangwon Suwanchip, Nai Direk Jayanama, Lieutenant-General Chit Mansin Sinatyotharak, and Captain Luang Suphachalasai, R.N., all of whom, he concluded by saying, had helped greatly in directing the resistance.[5]

I also feel that the entire Thai population played a part in the resistance movement. As for the members of the Free Thai themselves, they came from all walks of life. They included members of the Royal family such as M.C. Subha Svasti[6] and M.C. Karawik Chakraphan, as well as officers of the army, navy and air force, civilian officials, members of the National Assembly, merchants, businessmen, and members of the population at large.[7]

[After the war] certain groups charged that some members of the Free Thai had used their positions to enrich themselves personally. [These charges were circulated so widely that] the National Assembly had to set up a committee to investigate the claims.[8] In his book General Net Khemayothin points out that because a great many people joined the Free Thai movement, inevitably there were both good and bad individuals and both honest citizens and opportunists among them. Once the war was over, a number of individuals who had served in the Free Thai movement did in fact become unusually rich, and several received official appointments. It was equally true, however, that many others continued in their former positions with no rise in rank, and that the circumstances of their lives were not affected in any way. Yet other former members of the movement were ignored and their services forgotten. Unfortunately these same men were now discriminated against by certain groups of people. Instead of emphasizing the fact that former members of the Free Thai movement had all made real sacrifices in the service of the nation, they were now charged with being followers of Nai Pridi Banomyong. Regrettably this distrust and suspicion created jealousy and petty rivalries that later led to the emergence of factions and conflicts between those who had been members of the Free Thai movement and those who had not.[9]

During the final months of the war close cooperation was maintained between Thailand and the governments of Britain and the United States. Representatives of the respective governments were smuggled in and out of Thailand to keep the underground network going. The Japanese were well aware that such activities were going on, but they did not take any action against us, as the tide of war was now turning against them. Moreover they recognized that if they were to take harsh action against Thailand not only could it lead the Thai to rise up in open opposition to Japan, but it would arouse world opinion against it. If Japan treated us harshly, it would also appear to contradict its assertions that it was seeking to free Asia from oppression. And lastly, Japan happened to have a military Commander-in-Chief in Thailand at that time, General Nakamura,[10] [Commander of Japan's 39th Army, Bangkok], who was a man of great foresight and wisdom [and who helped keep down the growing tensions between Japan and our people].

Even so, tension increased daily. Fearing that Japan might use our country to defend itself [from the advancing Allied forces], the Thai army began to build small defensive positions and machine-gun bases on streets throughout Bangkok. When the Japanese questioned us about these, we replied that we were merely preparing in case we should be invaded by the Allies. These answers did not fool the Japanese. We owe thanks here to Nai Khuang Aphaiwong for enabling us to keep up this farce.

Sometime in December 1944 the Supreme Allied Commander South-East Asia Command, Lord Louis Mountbatten, sent us a letter from [what was then known as] Ceylon. In it he called for closer cooperation between the Allies and ourselves, urging us to allow the Allies to set up a radio station to broadcast news about Japanese movements and activities, and in turn requesting that we help by sending out news and intelligence information [from within Thailand]. He also wanted to know the extent of the cooperation we could give the United Nations [a term often used then for nations that were opposed to Germany and Japan], and requested that we send a military delegation to Ceylon to meet secretly with the Allies to discuss these matters. An amphibious plane would be sent to pick up members of the mission.

The Regent thereupon called together a number of officials who were members of the Free Thai movement. At the meeting it was decided that if our delegation were to discuss only military affairs it would not be of much value to our country, and would benefit only the Allies. We therefore replied in code through Major Puey Ungphakorn[11] that we wanted to send a delegation that had both military and political authority.

Lord Louis Mountbatten insisted that Ceylon did not have the authority at that time to discuss political issues. He requested that we therefore send only a military delegation. Following consultations we concluded that if we did not follow through on Lord Mountbatten's request, we might be accused of being too fearful to avail ourselves of this opportunity and have it alleged that while members of the Free Thai were willing to serve their nation, they did not want to take any risks. We therefore finally accepted the proposal.

After further consultations the Regent appointed me head of the delegation. Its members also included Lieutenant-General Luang Chatnakrop,[12] then Chief of the Army General Staff. I was permitted to choose the other members and the secretary of the delegation from such men as I felt I could trust. I asked Nai Thanat Khoman if he would be willing to serve his country once again as he had done earlier in Japan. He accepted readily. Meanwhile Nai Konthi Suphamongkhon[13] had already been sent to the United States to make further contacts there.[14] Our delegation was given the code name "Violet" by the Allies, while I was known as "Omar." We were given 2,000 Baht for our expenses, to cover a limited period of not more than fourteen days. I handed this to Nai Thanat Khoman, as he was in charge of the delegation's expenditures. We spent altogether 750 Baht for provisions and the boatman's fee, and returned 1250 Baht to headquarters.

Our party, which also included two students sent out from England, Nai Chun Kheng[15] and Nai Praphruet na Nakhon,[16] left Bangkok on a date that I cannot remember exactly, and stopped for six hours at the house of a Nai Chengchue Lueprasoet's father at Samut Sakhon[17] before boarding a motor boat which took us to Tarutao[18] Island about eighteen hours later. We spent the night there, and were picked up the following night by an amphibious plane sent in by the British as previously arranged.

We then flew to Calcutta, and from there continued on to Trincomalee in Ceylon, where we were driven to a house in a rubber plantation called Riverdale Estate in Kandy. There we met the head of Force 136, Major-General Mackenzie, and other Englishmen who had been working in Bangkok. During the seven days we were in Kandy meetings were held every day in which Mr. [Maberly] Dening,[19] [the Political Advisor to Lord Louis Mountbatten], took part. We returned to Bangkok at the end of February 1945.

I later[20] made a statement to the National Assembly concerning our mission to Ceylon and the reasons why Lord Louis Mountbatten, the Supreme Allied

Commander Southeast Asia Command, did not meet with us himself, sending Major-General Mackenzie and Mr. Dening in his place. The latter had explained that as Thailand was at war with England, a meeting with Lord Mountbatten would technically constitute a formal confrontation. Major-General Mackenzie and Mr. Dening were therefore sent in his stead to discuss military matters with members of our delegation. The British wanted to know the strength of our forces as well as those of Japan, and how much military support we could give them. We told them what we knew, and let them know that we were ready to help them in every way to the best of our ability. As they did not want to hold political discussions, we did not touch on political subjects.

However, one day Mr. Dening, the Political Advisor to Lord Louis Mountbatten, told our delegation that he would like to have an informal chat with us on political issues. During the course of this talk he asked us what Thailand's stand would be after the war. We told him that the true feelings of the Thai people as expressed through the National Assembly were ones of reluctance at ever having had to join the war on the side of Japan. As Japan had approached ever nearer, given that we were a small country, Thailand had had no chance, however, but to succumb. Our position was thus one that called for sympathy. The members of our delegation added that England would be making a wise policy move if it were to declare that England would respect the independence and sovereignty of Thailand, recognizing that we had only cooperated with Japan out of necessity and were now ready to rise against it. A policy statement along similar lines to that made by the United States[21] would be received by us with real appreciation and would encourage us greatly in our opposition to Japan.

Mr. Dening replied that he would need to take time to think about this. The British had never dreamed that Thailand would declare war on England. Furthermore, we had strongly attacked Britain verbally over the radio. He pointed out that the British had had no way of knowing what the true facts of the situation were.

Our delegates argued that we had had no choice in the matter. If we had made an outright declaration [in favor of Britain] we would have suffered reprisals at the hands of Japan. We would then have been unable to help the Allies when [a suitable] time came. We therefore thought that the best thing England could do was to quickly make a declaration along the lines we had suggested.

Mr. Dening answered that this could not be done. England was a democracy, and if the British government was to suddenly make a surprise announcement of this nature, people would take it amiss, as they had not been previously informed about the facts of the case. However, Mr. Dening continued, British and Thai delegates getting together like this was a move in the right direction. Our political discussions thus left us with no commitments on either side. Nonetheless they were a step forward in proving to England's satisfaction that we were really in earnest regarding our desire to cooperate with the Allies.

A couple of months later, around March or April 1945, our resistance movement came to the conclusion that if we did not show the world and the United Nations we were ready to make sacrifices, our efforts would have been in vain. We therefore decided to make a more radical move. The Regent sent telegrams to the leaders of the Free Thai movement overseas, including one to Washington to M.R. Seni Pramoj to be forwarded to the United States government and another to Lord Louis Mountbatten, telling them that Japan was trying to squeeze another 100 million Baht out of us. Nai Khuang Aphaiwong, the Prime Minister, had consulted the Regent on the matter, and it had been agreed that we would refuse to grant the loan. If strong pressure was brought to bear on us, then the government of Nai Khuang Aphaiwong would resign. Once a new government was formed, it would declare all agreements and policies made with Japan void, or, in other words, although Thailand would not declare war on Japan, it would call for a return to the *status quo* ante position of the period prior to 8 December 1941. Once this position was reestablished, Japanese troops would no longer have the right to remain on Thai soil.

We fully expected that Japan, as the arbiter of power in Thailand, would not allow the Thai government to carry out such measures. An open break, or declaration of war, would therefore result between us. Even though the weapons sent in by the United Nations would not be sufficient for us to carry on fighting effectively we believed, nevertheless, that with the efforts of the civilian population of Thailand as well as the military we would be able to withstand any belligerent acts on the part of the Japanese. Because making such a declaration and taking such steps would affect the interests of the United Nations, we were informing the governments of the United States and Britain as well as Lord Louis Mountbatten as Supreme Commander of the Allied Forces in Southeast Asia of our decision. On the day that we changed our government and our policy, if the governments of both the United States and Britain would make a declaration approving these steps and agreeing to respect our sovereignty and independence in every way, this would definitely raise our morale and help us offer the fullest possible resistance to Japan.

In effect we were looking for certain concessions from the United States and England. Our efforts produced results, for Mr. Grew, the United States Under Secretary of State and former Ambassador to Tokyo, sent a message to the Regent thanking the people of Thailand and pledging that at a suitable time the United States government would be willing to declare it had never regarded Thailand as an enemy nation but rather as a country that was under Japanese occupation. The United States government would therefore be prepared to declare that the sovereignty and independence of Thailand should be respected, and that it would not hold Thailand as having declared war against it. However, Mr. Grew stated, the United States government must ask us to stop short in our own plans for the moment, and continue patiently as we had done before, in the military interests of the United Nations.

England did not reply right away, but when it eventually did so, it stated that the views of the British government were similar to those of the United States. It was fortunate that we received such replies, as Allied objections to our going ahead with our plans right away prevented us from suffering unnecessary bloodshed.[22] We knew, nonetheless, that the British were dissatisfied with us for a variety of reasons.[23]

In a statement made after he became Prime Minister [in September 1945], M.R. Seni Pramoj clarified why this was so. He pointed out that members of the Thai resistance movement had been successful in escaping from Thailand and establishing contacts abroad since 1943. [The first contacts had been made with the Chiang Kai-shek government in China, resulting in that regime] declaring sometime in mid-1943 that China would respect the independence and sovereignty of Thailand.[24] The United States State Department adhered to a similar policy. M.R. Seni had therefore approached the British and asked them for a similar undertaking.

Following the Thai Peace Proclamation [of 16 August 1945],[25] United States Secretary of State Byrnes had made a worldwide declaration stating that Thailand had offered to fight Japan, but had been prevented from doing so by England and the United States. In other words, M.R. Seni Pramoj continued, the Thai were considered by the United States as having played their part on the side of the Allies even though they had not engaged in [open insurrection against the Japanese.] At the end of the speech Byrnes had made a statement of great significance for Thailand, namely that the United States had never regarded Thailand as an enemy.[26]

The British, however, had held a somewhat different view regarding their post-war relations with Thailand. On his way back there in September 1945, M.R. Seni had stopped by in London. There he had spoken with Mr. Bennett, Director General of the Far Eastern Political Division of the Foreign Office. Mr. Bennett, M.R. Seni recorded, had greeted him cordially, but told him that England had been shocked that Thailand declared war on her. While England was willing to do away with the state of war that existed between their two countries, Thailand would first have to fulfill three conditions set by [Ernest] Bevin, [Britain's Foreign Minister].[27]

As for the English being very upset at Thailand having declared war on Britain, M.R. Seni reported that he had taken the opportunity to enquire among

English people themselves on the subject. He found almost nobody who knew that Thailand had declared war on the United Kingdom; indeed, he declared, the ordinary Englishman did not even know where Thailand was.

[M.R. Seni reported that Mr. Bennett spoke for about ten minutes, after which] he asked if the former had anything to say. The latter told him he did not. Mr. Bennett seemed surprised by this, but, M.R. Seni reported, he did not know what decisions had been taken on the matter within Thailand, and was therefore unable to say anything. Instead he quickly took his leave without making promises of any kind to the British.

M.R. Seni said he was not at all concerned about the Americans. Their attitude towards Thailand was, he claimed, the very opposite to that of Britain. Americans wished to see our standard of living raised so that we could provide a market for their products. They know we are very keen to have these products, and would like us to become rich so that we could purchase them. Americans are people who say what they feel, M.R. Seni explained, whereas he could not tell what the English planned to do. He only knew that they were adhering rigidly to the war situation [or in other words insisting that as Thailand had declared war on Britain, it would be treated accordingly]. As for China, M.R. Seni ended by saying, from what he had heard Chiang Kai-shek had already stated that he had no desire to interfere with our independence.[28]

Once all the evidence demonstrated that Thailand was cooperating in earnest with the Allies, England agreed to send out a military mission under the leadership of General Jex.[29] This set up headquarters in Bangkok. Meetings were held and contacts made every day with members of our movement. Our representatives usually consisted of Nai Thanat Khoman and certain other individuals, with the people present varying according to the nature of the topic under discussion. I do not know what went on at these meetings, as they were always held in secret.

Meanwhile in Indochina Admiral Decoux, the French Governor-General, had been preparing to collaborate with the United States against Japan in the event of the United States landing troops in Indochina. The Japanese military command was well aware of such preparations, and finally decided that it could ignore the situation no longer. On 9 March 1945 Decoux was presented with an ultimatum demanding that French military, naval, air and police forces be placed under Japanese command, and that the administration become directly subject to Japanese control. Two hours were given for the acceptance of these demands. Admiral Decoux tried to bargain, but his efforts were rejected by the Japanese, and within twenty-four hours Japan had taken over administrative control of Indochina. This *coup de force* in neighboring Indochina made us in Thailand even more cautious about our resistance activities.

In June 1945 General Nakamura, the Commander of the Japanese Army in Bangkok, invited a number of senior Thai officials to dinner. Some accepted the invitation, while others had to stay at their posts. We later learned that the Japanese government had planned to arrest us at dinner, but later ordered against doing so. It was fortunate indeed that nothing of the kind took place, for had it done so there would undoubtedly have been bloodshed, and one cannot say what the outcome might have been.

Over the course of the next few months Japan lost the remaining battles of the war,[30] and on 6 August 1945 the shattering news was received that the United States government had dropped an atomic bomb on Hiroshima. This was followed on 9 August 1945 by a second atomic bomb being dropped on Nagasaki, and on 14 August 1945 Japan declared its unconditional surrender.

It was fortunate for Thailand that we had the divine protection of Phra Sayamthewathirat[31] whereby Japan sent General Nakamura as its Commander of the Japanese forces in Thailand, for otherwise fighting would have broken out in our country. General Nakamura was, however, a statesman as well as a soldier. He possessed great foresight, and was able to prevent bloodshed between the Thai people and Japanese troops.

On the day that Japan announced her surrender General Nakamura's aide, who also taught my son Japanese, came to see me and handed me the General's personal sword. When I asked why he had brought this to me, he told me that the General would rather hand it to me than to a representative of some other foreign country. To express my appreciation of the General's gesture I sent my son to give General Nakamura a Buddha statue from the Ayutthayan period. Later on, when I met General Nakamura again, he told me he always worshipped before that particular statue of the Buddha.

Fig. 14. General Nakamura and his wife visiting the author and his wife in 1954. I am sad to say that General Nakamura died on 12 September 1966.

Additional Facts on the Situation in Thailand During World War II

Thawi Bunyaket

Nai Direk Jayanama told me he had written a book called *Thailand and World War II* so as to leave a historical record of the period for the younger generation. Through it our young people could learn how Thailand was brought into the war, the part it played in this world conflict, and how we managed to avoid being thrown into turmoil and disaster following the defeat of Japan.

In presenting these historical facts, Nai Direk had to show great caution and care, professing a neutral attitude and avoiding showing bias towards either side in his presentation of the course of events. To maintain this approach he decided to describe only those events about which he himself had personal experience. However, many other events that are of considerable importance to the history of Thailand also took place during this period, and the younger generation needs to learn about these as well. [For example], during Nai Direk's almost two-year term of office as Ambassador to Tokyo, a number of important events took place [in Thailand] that need to be mentioned in order to make the record more complete. If he was to maintain the impartial approach described above Nai Direk felt, though, that he could not write about these.

He believed that one person who was well qualified to present a record of these events was myself, seeing that I had served at ministerial level in several different governments [both during and after the war], and had also played an important role in the Free Thai movement. As Nai Direk considered me to be well versed in the events of the war period, he asked me to describe those which I had personally experienced.

I feel deeply honored that Nai Direk should have asked me to do this, and share his view that a true account of Thailand's situation during the Second World War will be valuable to future generations. It is now almost twenty-two years since World War II ended, so if these events are not set down now, later generations will have no way of learning about them. Those of us who are knowledgeable about the period and had personal experience of it are getting old now. Many, indeed, have already died, so that there are only a few people left now who are in a position to give a first-hand account of the facts. There is also no longer any need to maintain secrecy about events that were regarded as secret twenty years ago.

I felt that since politicians in many other countries have produced accounts of the events affecting their respective nations during the war, someone should do likewise for Thailand. Such a record could be used not only for purposes of information, but would be of general benefit. Having reached this conclusion, I agreed to write this article. In so doing, I am abiding by the principle of writing down the truth about the events that took place, and of maintaining an impartial attitude throughout my account.

My record will not in fact add much to what Nai Direk Jayanama has already described in great detail in his book. I am, nonetheless, giving an account of those events I either know about, have evidence for, or that I personally experienced. I will not mention events I had no connection with, so that in this way what I am about to write may be of historical value.

At the time that the Japanese forces were preparing to invade Thailand in December 1941, I was Secretary to the Council of Ministers. I therefore had to attend every meeting of the Council, to prepare the agenda and record the discussions held at them.

During the government of Field Marshal Phibun Songkhram, meetings of the Council of Ministers were usually held three times a week, on Mondays, Wednesdays and Fridays. They started at about 9:30 a.m. and continued until 12:30 or 1:00 p.m. One night, however, around 20.30 or 21.00 hours, I received a telephone call from Police General Adun Adundetcharat in his capacity as Deputy Prime Minister, instructing me to get in touch with every Minister and call them to an emergency meeting at the Council of Ministers conference room, which was then situated in a building opposite Suan Kulab Palace. I had officials try to contact every Minister by telephone, but as it was then night time, it was difficult to get in touch with all of them. Some Ministers were not at home, while others were out of town. It was almost midnight before they could all be assembled, and even then, several were absent, including Admiral Sin Kamonnawin, Minister of Education and Commander-in-Chief of the Navy, who was being held by the Japanese at Khlong Dan, Samut Prakan province.[1]

I reached the conference room and waited there from 21.30 hours on for the meeting to begin. The Ministers began to arrive in response to the calls sent out to them. While waiting for their arrival we received news by cable, radio and telephone that Japanese troops had landed at several places in Thailand, and that at those places fighting had broken out between Japanese forces and Thai soldiers, police officers or boy scouts.[2]

The meeting of the Council of Ministers opened at 01.00 hours on 8 December 1941. It was chaired by Police General Adun Adundetcharat, the Deputy Prime Minister, as Field Marshal Phibun Songkhram, the Prime Minister, was away up country on what were termed official duties. (Later we learned that he had gone to inspect the defense line at Phratabong province,[3] as he had heard rumors that Japan might invade Thailand).

Once the meeting was declared open Police-General Adun informed the group that the Prime Minister had not yet returned from his inspection trip up country, but that cables had been sent requesting his prompt return. The Deputy Prime Minister then told the meeting that representatives of the Japanese government consisting of the Japanese Ambassador, the military attaché and other officials, had delivered a memorandum to the Thai government requesting the right for Japanese troops to pass through Thailand on their way to attack British territories in Malaya. The delegation had also stated that Japan had declared war on England and the United States and was attacking these countries simultaneously. Thailand was asked not to obstruct Japan in these plans. In return Japan pledged that it would respect Thailand's independence. It was seeking only the right for Japanese troops to pass through certain towns dictated by military movements. We were asked to reply by 02.00 hours of that same day.

While the meeting was under way, reports began to come in one after the other stating that Japanese troops had come into conflict with Thai military and police forces at a number of different places. At some of these the fighting was so fierce that the combatants had engaged in hand-to-hand combat. At others boy scouts had joined in the fighting the Japanese, thereby showing their patriotism and heroic valor.

The time drew nearer to 2:00 a.m., but still the Prime Minister had not returned. Members of the Council of Ministers could not decide what course of action to take, firstly because they did now know what policy the Prime Minister, as Commander-in-Chief of the Army, had decided upon for the defense of the kingdom, and secondly because a short time before the Japanese entered the country a [government] decree had been issued regarding the duties of all Thai citizens in the event of invasion. This stated that all Thai citizens should fight to the last man against any invaders. If they saw no hope of holding out any further, they should adopt a scorched earth policy and destroy all food and property so that nothing was left that could be made use of by the invaders. Given this decree the Council decided to have its representatives inform the Japanese delegates that the Prime Minister had not yet returned, and that we therefore wished to ask Japan to postpone sending its troops into Thailand so as to avoid [further] bloodshed.

The Japanese replied, however, that this request could not possibly be carried out. [Given the events that were unfolding] it was difficult to achieve rapid communication [at the moment]. Cables would first have to be sent to Japanese military headquarters in Saigon, after which orders would have to be issued to the troops from there, all of which would take a great deal of time.

Instead members of the delegation recommended that the Minister of Defense issue orders in place of the Prime Minister calling on Thai forces to cease all resistance. We told the Japanese that this was impossible, as military commands and instructions of this nature could only be issued by the Commander-in-Chief himself. As discussions continued between us, we meanwhile tried to employ diplomatic maneuvers, putting forward arguments or referring to various points of law, all in an attempt to play for time while awaiting the return of the Prime Minister. The Thai government's representatives during these negotiations were Prince Narathip-phongpraphan (then H.H. Phraongchao Wanwaithayakon), Nai Pridi Banomyong and Nai Direk Jayanama.

The Japanese delegates retorted that although they were all aware of the existence of the law stating that only the Commander-in-Chief of the Army had the authority to give military orders, they did not accept this rule, and wished to know whether the Minister of Defense or the Deputy Commander-in-Chief of the Army could give out such instructions instead. Our representatives asked them to wait just a little longer, explaining that we were trying our best to get in touch with the Prime Minister to seek his immediate return. We hoped Japan would understand our position, and postpone sending in [the full complement of] its troops for the time being.

While these talks and negotiations were taking place between our representatives and the members of the Japanese delegation, fighting was in fact raging between Thai military and police forces and Japanese troops wherever the Japanese had invaded our territory. Fighting was particularly heavy at Tha Phae in the province of Nakhon Si Thammarat and at Songkhla, Pattani and Prachuap Khiri Khan.[4] Many were killed or wounded there.

At about 6:50 a.m. on the morning of 8 December 1941 Field Marshal Phibun Songkhram, the Prime Minister, returned to Bangkok, and went straight to attend the meeting of the Council of Ministers. Police General Adun Adundetcharat reported everything that had taken place to the Prime Minister. He told him that the Japanese Ambassador, military attaché, and certain other [Japanese] embassy officials had put forward several proposals. He had told them that the correct procedure was for them to deliver these to Nai Direk Jayanama, the Minister of Foreign Affairs. Accordingly the Japanese delegates had met with the Minister of Foreign Affairs and had handed him a note stating that that day, for better or worse, the Japanese government had decided to declare war on the United States and England, as its attempts to maintain peace had not met with any success. General Tojo's announcement to the Special Council had stated that Japan was determined to cut off aid to the Chungking government, and to surround the A.B.C.D. (America/Britain/China/Dutch) line so as to cut off economic aid to these nations. The Japanese government had tried every way to attain its ends through peaceful means during talks in Washington, but had been unsuccessful. It had therefore become necessary for Japan to wage war [on the Allies]. Besides, [the Japanese delegates had pointed out], the war in Europe had already spread almost as far as Iraq and Iran, and it was feared it could spread as far as Thailand. All Asians must therefore join together to keep Asia for the Asians. Japan was now on its way to attack the enemy, not Thailand. Even though fighting had broken out between Japanese and Thai forces during the course of Japanese troops entering Thailand, Japan would never regard Thailand as its enemy. If Thailand cooperated by joining with Japan, then the term "Asia for the Asians" could become a reality, and Thailand, which was already an independent country, would be able to develop rapidly. The Japanese government was only asking Thailand to allow Japanese troops to pass through its territory because this was strategically necessary for Japan. Japan was asking that it be granted this facility so that the armies of the two countries would not have to fight with one another. Japan hoped Thailand would then cooperate with it and provide police protection for Japanese residents in Thailand.

Police General Adun added that he had also heard that Japan had sent out three naval expeditions. One, consisting of about fifteen ships, was headed for Songkhla; the second had headed eastward towards Samui island[5] in the province of Surat Thani; while the third was making its way towards Paknam[6] in the province of Samut Prakan. He had been informed that Japanese troops had already landed in Songkhla and Pattani. There they had met with resistance from Thai military and police forces. Fierce fighting had broken out at Mae Nam Noi in the province of Songkhla, and at Pattani a division of Thai youth had joined the police and seized the bridge over the river Pattani, with bitter fighting taking place.

As for events outside Thailand, he had been told that Japan had launched an attack on Pearl Harbor, and had bombed fuel supplies and cut all telegraph lines so as to prevent communication and calls for help by the United States Navy. Simultaneous attacks had also been launched on the Philippines. With regard to England, Deputy Prime Minister Adun Adundetcharat reported that he had been informed that the Japanese had attacked Kota Bharu [in Malaya] and had successfully landed in Kelantan, about fifteen miles from the Thai border, while Singapore had been bombarded from the air. The conclusion to be drawn, he pointed out, was that as Japan had launched attacks on many different places at the same time, no country would be able to come to the help of the other. Each would have to rely on itself.

Once the Prime Minister heard this report, as well as receiving further information on the fighting between Japanese troops and Thai army and police forces, he wanted to know what those present at the meeting felt should be done. He asked whether we were in favor of continuing with the fighting, or whether we should order a ceasefire. Thai citizens were dying every minute, and a whole army unit had already been wiped out at Pattani.

Police-General Adun Adundetcharat suggested that we should consider the matter very carefully, as we could not hope for help from any other countries. England was having to look after itself, and could not possibly come to our aid, while the United States was now also in the same position, and would not be able to send us troops or weapons. In short, neither England nor the United States could come to our support any more than England could help the United States or the United States England. We would have to depend on ourselves.

Meanwhile the Japanese delegation was waiting on our decision. We therefore had to make up our minds as to whether we would grant Japan certain concessions or not. If Japan did not fear England or the United States, which were major powers, they certainly had no reason to be afraid of us, Police-General Adun pointed out. It was true that we had military forces. However, if we were to continue fighting, we would be doing so alone and on the strength of the Thai army only. We should take into consideration not only the [relative] strength of the Thai and Japanese forces, he explained, but the fact that if we decided to fight we might find ourselves under a naval blockade that would cut off communications by sea. We should therefore bear in mind that we would be isolated and without hope of receiving help from the outside world; moreover, if we continued to fight but were eventually defeated, we would be conquered and made a Japanese colony.

One other alternative, if we chose to continue fighting, was that we could flee abroad and set up a government-in-exile. However, from what had been seen of other countries in Europe [that had been forced to adopt this alternative], such overseas governments did not carry much weight. Meanwhile Japan would still take over our country, and even if the governing of the country was left in Thai hands, we would still be under Japanese rule and forced to obey its demands.

After considering the various possibilities before us, Police General Adun Adundetcharat pointed out that Japan had not asked us to declare war on the United States and England, nor did we intend to make such a declaration. The United States and England should therefore be sympathetic towards our plight, particularly as they had proved unable to help us out even with military equipment. Meantime, while we awaited a final decision by the Prime Minister, our soldiers had made every effort to ward off Japanese attacks. This demonstrated that we had put up resistance and had not given way to Japan immediately without offering any effective opposition. The clashes in Pattani and Songkhla, where fierce and brave opposition to the Japanese had been put up by our soldiers, as well as the fighting going in other places from which we had not yet received reports, all clearly showed that we had done our utmost to uphold our neutrality.

What we should do as the next step, then, was to compromise and allow the passage of Japanese troops, but refuse to declare war on the United States or England. This could not be interpreted as our having cooperated with Japan, for Japan had not requested that we provide it with military support. It was true, Police General Adun admitted, that such a concession would involve a partial loss of our sovereignty. However, partial loss of our sovereignty was better than losing it completely and being turned into a Japanese colony. Should Japan lose the upper hand, on the other hand, and be defeated by England and the United States, those latter countries should still be sympathetic towards us as a small country that had done its duty trying to put up a fight against Japanese aggression.

It was apparent that the majority of the members of the Council felt the same way as Police General Adun Adundetcharat. After considerable further discussion the Prime Minister, who felt that continued fighting against the Japanese would be suicidal, ordered a ceasefire and called off all resistance. Japanese troops were granted free passage through our country as of 7:30 a.m. on 8 December 1941.

The Prime Minister then began to elaborate further, explaining that past negotiations with Japan showed that what it actually wished us to consider was whether or not we should join Japan as an ally. If we did not do so, we would be in the position of either having to fight against Japan, or we would have to feign indifference when Japanese troops passed through our territory. This matter had already been discussed in the Council once before, but no definite decision had been reached on the subject, as it had not been expected that General Tojo would move troops into Thailand so quickly.

Once a decision had been reached to order a ceasefire, the Prime Minister and Nai Direk Jayanama, the Minister of Foreign Affairs, went to meet the Japanese Ambassador and the members of his party, who had meantime been waiting outside for the government's reply. After about an hour's discussion, the Prime Minister and Minister of Foreign Affairs came back to the meeting and told the Council that Japan had put forward the following proposals for us to choose from. Firstly, we could join the Triple Alliance signed on 27 September 1940 between Germany, Italy and Japan, or what were known as the Axis powers. Secondly, we could cooperate with Japan in the military sphere by allowing the passage of Japanese troops through Thai territory and by providing all facilities for these troops in the course of their passage. In this case Thailand was also to take immediate measures to prevent any clashes between the armies of Thailand

and Japan from breaking out. Thirdly, Thailand could sign a mutual military defense pact with Japan. [In the event of the latter], Japan would undertake that the independence, sovereignty and honor of Thailand would be respected, and would help us regain our lost territories. Whatever decision the Thai government made, a ceasefire should, in any event, be proclaimed immediately. If we later decided to continue our resistance, then fighting would be resumed. Alternatively we could decide to cooperate with Japan instead. This depended on the judgment of the Council of Ministers.

Nai Pridi Banomyong asked whether the Japanese had accepted the views of Police General Adun Adundetcharat or not. If we did not wish to fight Japan, did this mean that we now, according to these new proposals, had to be on its side?

Lengthy discussions were held over the meaning of the Japanese proposals. When the Prime Minister saw that members of the Council of Ministers could not make a decision about what course of action to take, he pointed out that the primary question was whether or not we would fight against Japan.

All the members of the Council found themselves in a dilemma. On the one hand they wanted to see the fighting continued, as they were angry with Japan for having violated our sovereignty. On the other hand they fully recognized that such action would merely be suicidal, as we had no hope of withstanding the force of Japan.

In the end Nai Pridi Banomyong suggested that now that we had decided on a ceasefire and had placed the weight of our considerations on not resisting Japan, we should also make it clear that we would not fight against England and the United States either. He felt that we should follow the Danish example and allow Japan passage of troops only, but not give them any other form of help such as the military cooperation requested in the new proposals. We should draft out exactly what we were willing to grant Japan, and should make it clear that it involved permission for the passage of Japanese troops through our territory only.

After much discussion and debate, most of the Ministers concluded that the ultimate decision should be left to the Prime Minister. As both head of the government and Commander-in-Chief of the Armed Forces, he must be well informed on the general political and military situation and thus know what the best course of action would be. The majority of the members of the Council made it known, however, that they were unwilling to cooperate with Japan, but wished the fighting against the Japanese troops to be discontinued.

The Prime Minister meantime announced that we had already proven our readiness to fight for the maintenance of our neutrality. Neither the United States nor England should therefore have any cause to hold anything against us. Indeed, they ought to sympathize with us given our circumstances.

At 7:30 a.m. on 8 December 1941 the Prime Minister finally issued the order for a ceasefire, and sent H.R.H. Prince Narathip-phongpraphan [Prince Wanwaithayakon] and Nai Direk Jayanama, together with Nai Wanit Pananon, [the Director-General of the Department of Commerce] to negotiate with the Japanese delegation. The three returned to the meeting at about 10:10 a.m. with the announcement that the Japanese delegation had agreed to accept our conditions, but had added that further agreements of an economic and financial nature would also have to be concluded between us. They did not find it necessary to incorporate these into the present agreement, which was of a military nature, but would be contacting the Minister of Finance later on about these.

Nai Pridi Banomyong, the Finance Minister, thereupon stated that Japan had agreed to strictly respect our independence and sovereignty. To date we had only agreed to grant certain military concessions to the Japanese. They therefore had no business bringing up financial topics. Moreover, he wished that his view be made clearly known to the Japanese delegation. The meeting agreed with Nai Pridi's arguments, and sent the same delegation back to clarify matters with the Japanese, having them stress that the four principles we wished to see adhered to in these negotiations were firstly that our permission to allow the Japanese troops pass through our territory would not involve the disarming of the Thai army; secondly, that passage through our territory only would be strictly adhered to, and that there would be no question of residence of Japanese troops in Bangkok; thirdly that the agreement about to be made should be limited to matters of a military nature only; and lastly that this agreement would be final, with no further demands being made on us in the future. Once everything had been settled and an agreement reached, the government issued an official announcement and prepared the draft of a bill to be presented later before the National Assembly. At 11:55 a.m. the meeting ended, after an all night conference.

The account I have given here has been rather long, but I feel that 8 December 1941 was one of the most important days in our history. It was a day that every Thai had cause to regret, for it was the day on which the independence and sovereignty of our nation was tarnished. I sat in on the meeting of the Council of Ministers carrying out my duties as Secretary to the Council right from the beginning to the end, or from approximately 21:30 p.m. on 7 December 1941 until 11:55 a.m. on 8 December. Every minister in the Council, including myself, returned home after that meeting with the saddest feeling we had experienced in our entire lives.

Some while later, I cannot remember on what date exactly, but I believe it was between the 10 and 12 of December, or at least only a few days after the government signed the agreement permitting the passage of Japanese troops through Thailand, the Japanese government made its first approach to us for a loan to meet the expenses of its troops in our country.

Nai Pridi Banomyong, the Minister of Finance, told the Council of Ministers that he did not believe the Japanese government would stop at this one loan for military expenses, but would continue to make endless demands for money. If we agreed to grant these loans, we would end up having to print more Baht currency bank notes, which in turn would lead to inflation and damage the country economically. He believed it would be better if the Japanese troops were to issue their own currency notes, to be called invasion notes, for the use of their army. In this way, once the war was over, we would be able to annul the notes. The economic and financial situation of our country would not be affected once the war ended, and inflation prevented.

The Prime Minister opposed this suggestion, however, saying that even if [allowing Japan to float its own notes] was able to prevent an inflationary situation from arising, agreeing to such measures would suggest that we had already lost our independence and sovereignty. The Minister of Finance retorted by asking whether by having allowed Japanese troops into our country and giving them freedom of action in a number of ways we had not already lost our independence and sovereignty to a certain extent? Violent arguments thereupon broke out between the Prime Minister and the Minister of Finance. In the end the Prime Minister insisted on the adoption of his policy. A Baht loan was made to Japan and the requisite additional bank notes issued accordingly.

A few days later, several changes were made to the Council of Ministers. [On 17 December 1941] Nai Pridi Banomyong resigned as Finance Minister, and was appointed to the Regency Council,[7] where there was a vacancy. At almost the same time two or three other Ministers also relinquished their posts. As far as I can recall, they were the posts held by Nai Direk Jayanama, the Minister of Foreign Affairs,[8] who was appointed Ambassador to Tokyo (shortly thereafter), and Nai Wilat Osathanon.

Later we were obliged to issue yet more currency notes to cover loans for the expenditures of the Japanese troops. Originally these were guaranteed in gold bullion deposited in Japan, but later loans were covered by Yen currency. In addition the government also adjusted the rate of exchange between the Baht and the Yen making one Yen equal to one Baht,[9] although formerly there had been 1.50 Yen to the Baht. This was probably related to our providing loans to Japan, as Japan wished to repay these at a reduced rate of Yen currency.

During the early stages of the war, Japanese forces met with continual success whether they were fighting by air, sea, or land. In January 1942 (around the 23 or 24 of that month) [should in fact be 10 December 1941—Ed.] England's largest and most powerful battleships, the *Prince of Wales* and the *Repulse*, which had long been acclaimed by the British navy as unsinkable, and which German naval and air forces had been unable to destroy, were sunk by the Japanese off the coast of Malaya after having been sent there by England to protect Malaya and Singapore once war broke out in Asia. The world was shocked and taken by surprise that the Japanese navy and air force should have been able to sink these two battleships with such speed on the same day. On land Japanese troops rapidly swept through Malaya, where the British army was unable to hold them off. Hong Kong capitulated, and Singapore came under heavy air bombardment.

Germany had also made a largely victorious advance. After the *Prince of Wales* and the *Repulse* were sunk with such rapidity and ease, certain political and military groups in Thailand began suggesting to the Prime Minister that as Thailand had already committed itself to a considerable extent, and as the course of the war to date indicated that the Axis would win the war, partial cooperation with Japan on Thailand's part was insufficient. It would be of no benefit to Thailand should the Axis indeed prove victorious. They felt that Thailand should support Japan fully by declaring war on England and the United States so that we would end up on the side of the victors and obtain a share of the spoils of victory.

In my personal opinion, it was the sinking of the two British warships on the same day that prompted Luang Wichitwathakan, the Deputy Minister of Foreign Affairs, to suggest to the Council of Ministers that Thailand should declare war on the United States and England. This suggestion found support from the Prime Minister/Minister of Foreign Affairs, and it was decided that Thailand should declare war on the United States and England at noon on 25 January 1942. Once the declaration had been drafted and signed by the Prime Minister acknowledging the Royal Decree, it was sent to the members of the Regency Council for their signatures.

The correct procedure was for the King or Regent of the realm to sign a Royal Ordinance or Decree first, after which the Prime Minister would sign acknowledging his receipt of the particular edict. During the government of Field Marshal Phibun Songkhram, however, when there was a Regency Council, the Field Marshal usually signed his name acknowledging the Royal Ordinance or Decree first, and then sent it on for the members of the Regency Council to sign. The members of the Regency Council at that time were H.H. Prince Aditaya, General Chaophraya Phichayenyothin and Nai Pridi Banomyong.

On the day that we declared war [on Britain and the United States], on 25 January 1942, the Council of Ministers held a special meeting. Once the decision to declare war on England and the United States had been made by the Council, it was decided that an announcement should be made to the nation at

12:00 noon sharp. At about 11:00 hours officials reported to the Prime Minister that only two members of the Regency Council were in Bangkok, namely H.H. Prince Aditaya and General Chaophraya Phichayenyothin. The remaining Regent, Nai Pridi Banomyong, was away from Bangkok and was believed to be somewhere upcountry. Only two members of the Regency Council were thus able to sign the Royal Ordinance. They could not wait on the signature of Nai Pridi Banomyong, as the deadline set for the announcement of the declaration at 12:00 hours would otherwise have had to be postponed. The President of the Regency Council [H.H. Prince Aditaya], had the name of Nai Pridi Banomyong put down, however, even though the latter did not actually sign the ordinance, and said that he would take the responsibility for this action. Thus only two Regents of the realm actually signed the declaration, although the announcement proclaimed that all three had done so, which was not in fact the case.

Throughout 1942 Japan won one battle after another. Under the leadership of General Yamashita, who was later arrested and executed as a war criminal after Japan unconditionally surrendered to the Allies, the Japanese succeeded in seizing the whole of Malaya and Singapore. Singapore's name after its surrender was immediately changed to "Shonan" or "Shonanto".

In Europe the tide of the war began to turn in early 1943. In February of that year the German army was defeated by the U.S.S.R. at Stalingrad. [In July 1943] the Allies landed troops on Sicily, and Rome soon came under heavy bombardment. Shortly afterwards Mussolini was deposed[10] and replaced by Marshal Badoglio, his chief opponent. [In September of that year] the latter signed Italy's unconditional surrender to the Allies.

Meanwhile events in Thailand during this period were not running smoothly. The government of Field Marshal Phibun Songkhram was not very popular, for it imposed a number of laws on the public against its will, such as issuing strict orders that Thai women were to wear hats in public, prohibiting the age-old habit of chewing betel, ordering the cutting down of areca and betel trees, and so forth. Those who did not don hats in public were prohibited from entering government buildings. Thus in a number of ways the people suffered inconveniences.

The government and National Assembly also came into increasingly frequent conflict with one another. In February 1943 I resigned from my government post as Minister and as Secretary to the Council of Ministers following a difference of opinion with Field Marshal Phibun Songkhram, who had first tendered his resignation and then decided not to resign. After this I went off to Hua Hin for a vacation.

One evening, I cannot remember on what date exactly, Nai Pridi Banomyong, the Regent, sent someone to fetch me over to his residence in the Sans Souci

Palace at Hua Hin. After we were alone together in the room, Nai Pridi asked me to join the work of the Free Thai movement. He told me he had already started to make contacts with England and the United States by sending a number of people to meet with representatives of the Free Thai movement overseas. Among them was a Nai Kamchat Phalangkun [who had been sent to make contact with representatives in China].[11] Nai Kamchat had, however, fallen ill on the way and died [after reaching Chungking], for the trip had proved very arduous, involving having to beat his way through dense and treacherous jungle. Nai Pridi recommended that we establish a government-in-exile abroad in the same way that General Charles De Gaulle had done in England. The Regent said he would find ways to reason with members of the National Assembly so that they would choose me as Speaker. Once I had been elected, then Nai Pridi, as Regent of the realm, myself, as Speaker of the National Assembly, and M.L. Kri Dechatiwong, who was then a Minister in the Field Marshal Phibun Songkhram government, would leave Thailand together and form a government-in-exile abroad. With the presence of a Regent of the realm, the Speaker of the National Assembly and a Minister of the government, all of whom had been appointed in accordance with the law and the Constitution, any action or decree we might choose to make would be lawful according to legal and constitutional procedures. We discussed this idea to the satisfaction of us both, and I agreed to work with the Free Thai movement in this bid for the independence of our country.

On 26 June 1943 a meeting of the National Assembly was called in order to choose a Speaker and Deputy Speaker in accordance with normal procedure. The Assembly voted to make me Speaker and Nai Khuang Aphaiwong Deputy Speaker of the National Assembly. (I should mention here that Nai Khuang Aphaiwong had resigned from his position as Minister of Communications at the same time as I resigned from the Council of Ministers, and for the same reasons, namely ones connected with the Prime Minister having first proffered his resignation and then later denying ever having done so.) Despite the Assembly's decision, however, I did not in fact become the Speaker of the National Assembly. A Royal Decree appointing me was passed, but the Prime Minister refused to sign it. This was completely contrary to constitutional procedure.

There was a lot of confusion over this for several days. In the end the government asked the National Assembly to re-elect a Speaker and Deputy Speaker, but said that these were not to be myself or Nai Khuang Aphaiwong. The reasons given for this demand were political. It was claimed that if I was made Speaker of the Assembly this would create major problems, as it would arouse the suspicions of the Japanese seeing that both myself and Nai Khuang Aphaiwong were known to have leanings towards England and the United States. A number

Fig. 15. Nai Pridi Banomyong ("Ruth"), the leader of the Free Thai in the country.

of military reasons were also given, and in the end the National Assembly had to vote again for another Speaker[12] As I did not, then, become Speaker of the Assembly, our plans for leaving the country and establishing a government-in-exile had to be abandoned.

We therefore changed our plans and decided to establish a Free Thai movement within the country, with Nai Pridi Banomyong as head of the movement. He was given the code name "Ruth" by the American O.S.S. and the British Force 136 stationed at Kandy, India.[13] Once the Free Thai movement succeeded in making contacts with the O.S.S., led by General Donovan, and with the British Force 136, both the United States and Britain sent representatives to set up underground headquarters in Bangkok. The head of the British Force 136 was a Colonel Jex. He had his headquarters at Thammasat University. The head of the O.S.S. was a Captain Howard. His headquarters were at a building that had once been the residence of General Chaophraya Phichayenyothin, at Phra Athit Road on the river Chao Phraya.

Radio contacts with Kandy were kept up every day. At the same time we sent several Free Thai to Kandy to receive training in the use of modern weapons and radio communications. We aimed to have twenty-four divisions of Free Thai, eleven to be trained by the British, and the other thirteen by the United States. Those assigned to Britain had to contact the British Force 136 at Kandy, while those assigned to the United States had to make contacts with the O.S.S., also through Kandy. Both sectors cooperated closely with one another throughout, both at Kandy and in Bangkok.

Each division was composed of about five hundred members. The locations of the divisions so far as I can remember were at Chai Nat, Uthai Thani, Kanchanaburi, Chachoengsao, Nakhon Pathom, Chon Buri, Sukhothai and Bangkok.[14]

Transportation of these men to and from Thailand to Kandy was usually carried out in the following way. On the outgoing journey from Thailand they started off the journey by boat, and then were picked up later by a Catalina aircraft along the coast off Amphoe[15] Ban Cha-an[16] at an arranged day and time. The return trip from Kandy was made either by the same route, or by parachuting at night into the division camps or at specific pre-arranged spots. Strict patrol and vigilance were kept at each camp where a division was situated. If the camp was under American guerrilla trainers, then American officers and sergeants would be stationed there permanently to provide training on the use of weapons and in guerrilla warfare. If the camp was under British guerrilla trainers, then British officers would in turn be stationed at that camp. The Free Thai of these divisions all had new, modern weapons, including machine guns, either M35 or Sten guns, carbines, anti-tank guns or what are called bazookas, plastic explosives, hand grenades, mortars and pistols. They also had field radios and so on. However, both England and the United States made it clear to the Free Thai in our country that these weapons were solely for the use of the Free Thai, whom they considered their friends. They were not to be used by the Thai police, military or government officials, whom they considered their enemies. We had to abide by this understanding.

One factor I should like to mention here is that it had been agreed between Thailand and Japan that any American, British or Allied soldiers who were captured by the Thai police, military or official authorities were to be considered Thai prisoners-of-war and placed under the control of the Thai authorities. Japan had no right to ask for any such prisoners-of-war. If, on the other hand, such men were captured by the Japanese, then they became Japanese prisoners-of-war. The result was that the majority of prisoners-of-war were held by the Thai authorities. It was common practice for American soldiers stationed at the various [Free Thai] camps to go to Bangkok to enjoy themselves. On one such occasion, when a Free Thai naval officer from the camp at Chon Buri[17] took some American officers, fully dressed in their uniforms, in his truck to Bangkok, he had a puncture just near a Japanese camp in the fields bordering Bangkapi.[18] Showing a quick wit, the Thai naval officer walked up to the Japanese guard and gestured with his hands, giving him to understand that these were American prisoners he was taking to Bangkok for further investigations. Unfortunately they had happened to have a puncture, so he would appreciate help with repairs. The Japanese were completely taken in by the story, and called other Japanese soldiers at the camp to come and help. Once the tire was changed, the party set off again for Bangkok and assorted pleasures.

Once the Free Thai movement had been set up inside the kingdom, members of the Free Thai overseas who were connected either with England or the United States began to make regular contact with us. They arrived either by parachute, or came the first part of the way by plane, and then traveled by boat for the remainder of the trip to Bangkok. One remarkable case was that of a man whose first name I cannot exactly recall, although I remember his surname was Puripat. He was parachuted in together with four or five other Free Thai at an appointed spot in the forests of Rayong. As he jumped from the plane, the strings of his parachute got entangled with the tail or some rear part of the plane so that he was left hanging in the air. He had a cool presence of mind, however, and took out his pistol and fired a shot so that the American pilot in the plane could hear him. Once the pilot heard the shot and took a look out of the plane, he saw the man and hauled him back inside the plane to safety. Once back at Kandy, this Free Thai agent was sent to a hospital for a mental check-up. He was just fine, though, and even asked to be sent back to the same spot to join the other Free Thai who had already been parachuted in. His remarkable bravery was recorded by the American unit, and the man was awarded a special medal for courage.

The Free Thai movement within Thailand was divided into two groups. One was concerned with the camp divisions; it had as its duties training Free Thai both in the use of a variety of modern weapons and in guerrilla warfare tactics, in case they should be ordered to fight. The second group comprised the intelligence service.

The intelligence service obtained excellent cooperation from the police, as Police General Adun Adundetcharat was one of the leaders of the Free Thai movement. As a result the information obtained was satisfactory and accurate in every way. The duties of members of the intelligence branch were to spy on the movements of the Japanese army and report this information to Allied intelligence at Kandy. Its members had to provide details on matters such as where Japanese stocks of firearms were situated, the location of Japanese military camps, the destinations and times of train or automobile convoys carrying Japanese soldiers and military equipment, the various places used by the Japanese to store their provisions, and the location of their military headquarters, field offices and other such strategic locations.

If the Allies requested information on any particular matter, then our intelligence service would try to find out all the facts and would report back on its investigations. This information was extremely valuable [to the Allies]. Indeed, it was so reliable that Allied air forces were able to make use of it to score direct hits on [Japanese] targets with almost no failures. After their air strikes we were even able to report back to them on the results of their attacks. This energetic and effective cooperation [on our part] was appreciated by England and the United States, and they developed a favorable attitude towards us in consequence.

Their requests even went so far as asking us to send back their prisoners to the military base at Kandy. We were able to do this on every occasion they asked us to do so. One time the Americans made the extraordinary request that we send them a Japanese officer of the rank of general. We replied that such could be arranged, but that in that case we would have to be prepared to fight against Japan. The Americans thereupon canceled their request, as the Supreme Commander of the Allied Forces at Kandy, [Lord Louis Mountbatten], had given strict orders that every effort should be made to prevent any outbreaks of fighting in Thailand before D-Day (or the day when the Allies were ready to send in their troops to help us fight to the end for the independence of our country).

What was arranged for under a joint agreement was that on D-Day the Free Thai divisions and the Thai army and police forces within the kingdom would launch an active resistance against the Japanese forces, using guerrilla tactics such as unexpected attacks, ambushes and sabotage, while the Allies would simultaneously parachute men in at various places within Thailand, backed up by the marines. This was only a rough plan that had been broadly sketched out. Other plans were also drawn up, the details of which had not yet been agreed upon, as a suitable time [for an uprising] had not yet arrived.

During this period the Japanese forces must have heard something of our plans, or at least have been deeply suspicious of us, for they also started making preparations for their own self-defense, setting up fortifications and machine-gun bases in front of the military barracks and at other strategic points throughout Bangkok.

The Thai Army in turn began building fortifications and machine-gun bases directly opposite those being erected by the Japanese, clearly demonstrating the growing mutual distrust between us. As news of an impending clash between Thailand and Japan spread, this mutual distrust increased to the point where the Thai army and police forces were placed on a twenty-four hour alert every day. Meanwhile cooperation between the Free Thai within our country and the Thai army grew ever closer.

As head of the camp division of the Free Thai movement in Thailand, I held increasingly frequent meetings with the Chief of the Army General Staff to plan for the joining of forces between the Free Thai divisions and the Thai military. We produced a white arm band with a navy blue stripe running across it as a means of identification so that our members would know who was on the same side as them. We also identified targets that the Free Thai divisions would seek to destroy in order to deny their facilities to the Japanese troops, including bridges, places where fuel was stocked, Japanese warehouses, sites of Japanese military equipment, and so forth.

The military command at Kandy knew all about these preparations and about the growing tensions in Bangkok. They therefore sent a radio message giving strict orders that we should avoid any confrontations with the Japanese troops until D-Day, the date of which would be fixed and which they would let us know of.

I had to send instructions to various divisions telling them not to take any action that could lead to fighting. Despite this, some of our divisions, for example at Kanchanaburi and Sukhothai, did kill Japanese soldiers who trespassed into forbidden zones where Free Thai camps were situated, and then buried these soldiers in order to remove all evidence of their acts. There was also regular theft and destruction of Japanese property and military equipment such as fuel, guns, ammunition, explosives, automobiles, etc. These actions were all known to the military commanders at Kandy. In fact they became so confident and trustful of the cooperation of the Free Thai in this country that during the latter period of the war, when we ran short of medical provisions and requested these from Kandy, they brought over boxes of medicines by plane and dropped these, tied up in parachutes, right onto the Phra Men Grounds (Sanam Luang)[19] in broad daylight.

The Japanese became so infuriated and suspicious that they protested to our government. Allied air strikes during the same period were also increasingly on target and hit only Japanese bases because we sent radio messages to the Allies telling them when to come in for these air strikes, or on other occasions because they had checked with us first to see whether they could strike at a particular place.

One time the Thai Railway Department moved all its provisions to a warehouse it had set up near the Chachoengsao[20] station. Allied aircraft flying reconnaissance missions thought this was a Japanese warehouse or military base, as they could tell it had been built very recently. They therefore asked us whether they could make an air raid on the building. We immediately radioed back telling them not to do so, explaining that what they saw was our warehouse and not one belonging to the Japanese. They therefore refrained from bombing the place.

On 24 July 1944 Field Marshal Phibun Songkhram resigned following the National Assembly's rejection of a bill for the establishment of Phetchabun

Fig. 16. A lunch given in honor of Admiral Lord Louis Mountbatten at the Prime Minister's office. *From left*: the author, Nai Thawi Bunyaket, Lord Louis Mountbatten and M.R. Seni Pramoj.

as the capital of the kingdom and of another for the creation of a Buddhist Territory. Nai Khuang Aphaiwong was appointed Prime Minister of the new government, and I was made Minister of Education.

I thus gained an opportunity to work with Chulalongkorn University undergraduates. I selected a number of them and sent them to the Free Thai camp at Chon Buri for military training. This camp was located behind the Khao Bang Sai temple, and was under the supervision of Rear Admiral Sangwon Suwanchip. It proved to be one of the largest and most efficient camps we had, as its members were made up of undergraduates and naval officials, or in other words those with a high level of education.

As the war neared its end, the situation in Thailand, and particularly in Bangkok, became increasingly tense. It almost reached a breaking point, as the Japanese were sure that Thailand would turn against them. Japan declared its unconditional surrender, however, before any fighting broke out. Had Japan not done so, Thailand might well have become another battlefield.

As the Free Thai intelligence service within the country was of great service to the Allies, providing its military command in Kandy with all the information it required, and as the Free Thai both within and outside the country cooperated closely with the Allies, so the Allies, or more particularly the United States, came to develop a favorable view of Thailand.

At the end of the war we announced that the declaration of war made by the Field Marshal Phibun Songkhram government had been unconstitutional, as it had not been carried out in accordance with correct procedures. The declaration, passed at noon on 25 January 1942, had born the names of the three Regents of the realm when in fact only two had signed it. Nai Pridi Banomyong had been out of Bangkok at the time the declaration was passed, and consequently had not signed the document, even though his name was shown on it. Our declaration of war was therefore to be regarded as null and void. We also pointed out that the declaration of war had been made without the consent of the Thai people. The latter had criticized the government's action [in declaring war on Britain and the United States], as they were all opposed to the idea. This may have been partly because almost all Thai citizens at that time heartily disliked the Japanese soldiers, and by the natural laws of reaction, hatred of one side usually results in partiality towards the other.

On 16 August 1945 we issued a Peace Proclamation stating that any hostile actions carried out against the Allies had been carried out in opposition to the wishes of the Thai people, and in violation of the Constitution. The Regent,[21] [Nai Pridi Banomyong], on behalf of His Majesty the King, declared before all citizens of Thailand that our declaration of war on the United States and England was therefore to be considered as null and void.

Fif. 17. A group of American officers visiting the author at his house in Soi Santisuk, Sukhumwit Road, on 30 August 1945, following the declaration of peace.

Shortly after this, I cannot remember now exactly whether on the same day or the following day, the United States made an announcement accepting our Proclamation. It stated that the United States did not regard Thailand as an enemy and had never recognized the declaration of war made [on the United States] by the government of Field Marshal Phibun Songkhram, nor had it ever issued a return declaration of war on Thailand. As for the English, they said they would wait first and see what the attitude and reactions of the Thai government were, and to what extent we would be willing to cooperate with them.[22]

Once the Peace Proclamation had been declared, Nai Khuang Aphaiwong resigned as Prime Minister. I took over this position until such time as M.R. Seni Pramoj, the Thai Minister to Washington and leader of the Free Thai movement in the United States, arrived back in Thailand [to fill this position] as previously arranged.

A few days after I had been appointed Prime Minister, I received a draft memorandum from the British government regarding the termination of the state of war between our two countries. This ran to altogether twenty-one proposals. Many of them, such as a demand that the British supervise and control our military affairs, or that they should exercise supervision over our financial affairs, I considered unacceptable. We therefore decided that we must conduct negotiations for the revision of these terms, and to this end sent our representatives to hold talks with the British representative in Kandy.

Eventually England agreed to strike off certain clauses that were unacceptable to us, such as those relating to military control, and after a further study of those terms which we felt we could agree on to some extent, we submitted these proposals to the National Assembly.

In the midst of these negotiations, I cannot remember on exactly what date, but between 1 and 17 September 1945, I received a telephone call from Nai Pridi Banomyong inviting me to see him at his residence at Tha Chang. On my arrival he handed me a cable from M.R. Seni Pramoj enquiring as to whether Thailand could offer 1.2 or 1.5 million tons of rice to the Allies (I cannot remember the exact amount, but I am sure it was one of the two above) free of charge as a gesture of our goodwill.

I was very worried when I read this telegram, for our giving such a large amount of rice free of charge—an amount more or less equivalent to our rice exports for an entire year in peace time—virtually amounted to payment of a war indemnity. This was a very large sum of money for Thailand, amounting to the equivalent of no less than 2,000 million Baht. Besides, I did not know whether we could even provide this amount of rice, as we had been unable to sell rice on the overseas market during the war, and the Japanese had commandeered all our stocks.

I therefore told Nai Pridi Banomyong that I would have to consult other authorities on the matter before being able to give an answer. He told me, however, that we had to send a reply immediately, and that investigations and consultations such as these would take too much time. He felt that I should therefore reply saying that as M.R. Seni Pramoj was going to be returning to Thailand to take over the position of Prime Minister, he was entitled to go ahead and agree to the proposal in principle. However, he should state that the precise amount of rice we could provide would have to be settled later. I agreed with this idea and sent a cable back along these lines.

Before ending my additional notes on the situation in our country during World War II, there is one other important incident which I should relate for your information. After the war was over, American and British troops entered Thailand to disarm the Japanese forces. Rumors started going around among certain senior Allied officers, and in particular among British officers, about the military equipment that had been parachuted in to the Free Thai in our country. Doubts were expressed as to whether the numbers of Free Thai would be in proportion to the amount of equipment that had been sent in, and indeed whether such equipment was still in existence. Some suggested that we had been pulling the wool over Allied eyes. Nai Pridi Banomyong, as head of the Free Thai movement within the country, consulted me about this and suggested that to dispel these doubts and suspicions we should arrange a parade of all Free Thai in the country so that the Allies could see the number of divisions we really had, and check that the military equipment was still intact and in good order.

He asked my opinion about this idea. After considering the matter carefully, I came out strongly in favor of such a parade. We felt it would enable both England and the United States to see the preparations we had made in this country, and to appreciate the risks we had taken in training such a large number of men even while Japanese troops were still occupying our land. In this way England and the United States might be led to sympathize with us and not place too much pressure on us.

With such aims in mind, we arranged for an inspection of the troops of the Free Thai divisions by ordering every division throughout the kingdom to assemble in Bangkok, bringing with it all its military equipment except bullets and ammunition. After the day for the parade was fixed, we invited senior British and American officers to attend the parade so they could witness our actions with their own eyes. The parade started from the Phra Men Grounds (Sanam Luang) and went down Rajadamnoen Avenue past the Democracy Monument. Eight thousand members of the Free Thai divisions were in the parade, which lasted for about an hour.

Once all the Japanese troops had been disarmed, and conditions in our country had returned to normal, the Free Thai both within and outside the kingdom had no more duties to perform. Their movement and organization were therefore disbanded. All that remains now are our memories, and even these are fading somewhat as the days go by.

Thawi Bunyaket
102 Setsiri Road, Samsen Nai
Bangkok

Temporary Soldier[1]

Puey Ungphakorn[2]

ORGANIZATION OF THE FREE THAI IN ENGLAND

During World War II [and for a short period thereafter], from August 1942 until January 1946, I was a temporary soldier. The way in which I, together with my fellow Thai compatriots [who found ourselves in England when war broke out] enlisted was quite unusual. Because Britain and the United States were at war with Japan, we had to enlist in the British army. When the Japanese invaded Thailand and the Thai government agreed to ally with the Japanese, all Thai living abroad were recalled to their home country. Some, however, refused to return. They were told that if they did not do so they would be stripped of their nationality. [Ignoring these threats] they banded together, called themselves the Free Thai, and refused to accept loss of their nationality.

M.R. Seni Pramoj, the Thai Minister [to Washington], became the leader of the Free Thai movement in the United States. He asked the United States to recognize the Free Thai and permit the formation of Free Thai military units. Hence Thai soldiers in the United States were allowed to organize themselves into their own units, wear Thai military uniforms, have their own Thai commanders, and in effect remained Thai in almost every way. This was not the case in Britain, where the Free Thai were not able to organize in this way. The Minister to England was called back to Thailand, and [H.R.H.] Prince Chula Chakrabongse,[3] who was then residing in England, declined the invitation to be our leader, saying that he did not want to get involved in Thai politics, and that besides he was already in the British Home Guard. Queen Rambhai Barni[4] and her brother, M.C. Subha Svasti, were interested [in serving as leaders of the Free Thai movement in England], but it was felt that if either of them filled this role it might have created misunderstandings in internal Thai politics. Thus the Free Thai in England never had a designated leader, and was not as organized a group as that in the United States. Members of the Free Thai who enlisted [in England] had to join the British army, wear British uniform and were subject to the command of British officers. Thai who remained in England [after Thailand had declared war on Britain and the United States] were treated as enemy aliens.

Even those who enlisted in the British forces were assigned to the Pioneer Corps[5] along with Germans, Austrians, Italians and other enemy aliens.[6]

During the early years of the war, when Britain had declared war on Germany but had not yet entered the war in Asia, Thai citizens in England were treated as aliens but not as enemy aliens. They were not interned, although their movements were somewhat restricted. Legation officials were, moreover, exempted from such restrictions. After Thailand declared war on the Allies, however, the Thai in England were declared enemy aliens, and legation officials as well as members of the Thai community in general were subjected to stricter regulations. They still were not interned, but were asked not to leave their living quarters after dark. Legation officials still had some money to live on as a result of a mutual arrangement between British officials in Thailand and Thai officials in Great Britain, but Thai students found themselves cut off from financial support from home, and had to depend on their earnings in Britain for their living. Those who were on British scholarships did not suffer, but others had to work in the fields or in factories to support themselves.

At that time Thai students were scattered over a number of different places in Britain. One fairly sizeable group that included both regular students such as Nai Sanoe Tanbunyuen, Nai Sanoe Ninkamhaeng, M.L. Chirayu Nophawong, Nai Yimyon Taesuchi and M.C. Phisadet Ratchani, together with other students who moved there because of the war, including economics students from London (such as myself) and a number of medical students, settled in Cambridge. When the news was announced that Thailand, following its alliance with Japan, had declared war on Britain, Cambridge was one of the first places where members of the Thai community congregated.

As with most such groups of people, the Thai students at Cambridge came from a variety of backgrounds and positions. All, however, were concerned with the freedom and independence of their country. When the Japanese first occupied Thailand, we hoped that somehow the Japanese would subsequently withdraw from our country. Then when Thailand took the next steps first of signing a treaty with Japan and then declaring war on the United States and Britain, we were afraid of what would happen should Thailand lose the war along with the Japanese. Thailand would be in a very perilous position if all Thai nationals followed their leaders blindly. When the order came for us to return to Thailand in exchange for [Allied] prisoners-of-war,[7] we therefore had to decide whether to return home or whether we could serve our country better by remaining overseas.

Those who were most concerned about the situation were Nai Sanoe Tanbunyuen, Nai Sanoe Ninkamhaeng, and Nai Sawang Samkoset. They contacted a number of different people inviting them to become leaders of the Free Thai movement in England. Nai Sanoe was especially active as well as being very intelligent.

We often gathered in his room to hear him tell us about the course the war was taking. It was he who wrote to M.R. Seni Pramoj informing him of the situation in England, and inviting him to come over and take on the leadership of the Free Thai movement in England as well as that in the United States. M.R. Seni was very busy, however, and totally unable to leave the United States, although he agreed to send a representative in his place. Soon afterwards (although it seemed a very long time to those of us who were waiting) Nai Mani Sanasen, Seni Pramoj's representative, arrived in England. The Thai students at Cambridge delegated Nai Sanoe Tanbunyuen and me to serve as their representatives in contacting Nai Mani in London. This was in about April or May of 1942.

We had not met Nai Mani up till then, and only knew that he had worked in the League of Nations for a long time. After we became acquainted, he told us he had lived in England when he was very young, when his father had been Thai Minister to London. After completing his secondary education in England, he had received a law degree and had worked for the League of Nations from then on. When war broke out he had been told to return to Thailand to work in the Ministry of Foreign Affairs. However, on his way home via the United States he had run into certain complications due to wartime conditions. The Ministry of Foreign Affairs had therefore instructed him to remain in Washington, D.C. and to work in the legation there. Since Nai Mani was acquainted with many British officials, both military and civilian, M.R. Seni asked him to go to England to help organize the Free Thai movement there.[8]

Nai Mani set up office in Brown's Hotel in London. From there he contacted British officials, and tried to get the British government to recognize the Free Thai movement in the same way that the United States had done in America. The British government refused to grant such recognition, however, until they learned that there were more than forty Free Thai in England, none of whom intended to go back to Thailand until after the war, and all of whom had determined on working for their country by enlisting in the British army regardless of the positions and duties [that might be assigned to them]. The British government then began to accord recognition to the Free Thai in England under Nai Mani Sanasen's leadership, although they clearly indicated that this did not constitute recognition of a government-in-exile.

Nai Mani depended on us to contact other Thai. At the time that contacts were first made between M.R. Seni Pramoj and Thai students at Cambridge, Nai Sanoe Tanbunyuen circulated letters to Thai within and outside the legation informing them of the organization of the Free Thai in England and of its contacts with M.R. Seni in the United States. By the same token, when radio stations picked up news from Thailand, this was relayed to Nai Sanoe. After Nai Mani set up an office in London, Nai Sanoe and I sent out a newsletter to keep the Thai community abreast of current activities, and calling for recruits. After we were accorded recognition by the British government we made formal requests for such volunteers. Information on each volunteer was kept confidential so that those who elected to return to Thailand in exchange for prisoners-of-war could not carry any information back to Bangkok with them. In the newsletter we made it clear that we were requesting strictly volunteers, and were not attempting to place pressure on those trying to make a decision on whether to return to Thailand or to remain in England. The ship carrying Thai citizens who wished to be exchanged for prisoners-of-war was about to leave. Many of our friends who could not remain in England for personal reasons were on board. Some of them, such as Nai Mala Bunyapraphatson, later on worked for the Free Thai in Bangkok.

More than fifty applications gradually came in as more and more people decided to join the Free Thai. They ranged from former Queen Rambhai Barni and her followers to private students, many of whom we had not met previously. These last included Nai Bunphop Phamonsing (see *Sinlapa Thai nai Yurop* [Thai Artists in Europe], Niphon Co., 1952). They also included a number of legation officials, some of as high a rank as First Secretary or its equivalent.

The Free Thai in England were officially called upon to join the British armed forces on 7 August 1942. A physical examination was called for in accordance with British law. Certain of the volunteers were found to be unfit and were exempted from military service. Others were exempted for other reasons. For the benefit of future generations I am here copying down the list of Free Thai who were in England at this period, dividing them into those who had civilian duties, and those who enlisted in the army.

Free Thai Who Were Not Enlisted in the Army

1. Queen Rambhai Barni
2. M.C. Phongphatsamani Svasti (Chakraphan)
3. Nai Mani Sanasen
4. Nai Sanoe Tanbunyuen
5. Luang Chamnongditthakan
6. Nai Yim Phoengphrakhun
7. Nai Sombun Palasathian
8. Nai Phrom Watcharakhup
9. Nai Kasem Phalachiwa
10. Nai Teklim Khunwisan
11. Nai Chamnong Sumsawat
12. Nai Saman Mantraphon
13. Nai Kasem Lamsam

14. Nai Wari Wirangkun
15. Miss Suphap Raktaprachit (Yotsunthon)
16. Miss Buppha Taesuchi
17. Miss Anong Taesuchi

Nos. 5–7 were officials at the legation in London.
No. 15 was later sent to India to help with broadcasting work.

Free Thai Who Were Enlisted as Soldiers

1. Luang At-phisankit
2. Luang Phattharawathi
3. Nai Klin Thephatsadin Na Ayutthaya
4. Nai Prasoet Pathummanon ("Pao")
5. M.C. Karawik Chakraphan ("Rasami")
6. M.C. Kokasat Svasti
7. M.C. Phisadet Ratchani ("Man")
8. M.C. Chiridanai Kitiyakon ("Ri")
9. M.R. Kitinadda Kitiyakon
10. M.C. Chirayu Nophawong
11. Nai Sawat Sisuk ("Raven")
12. Nai Chunkheng (Phatphong) Rinthakun ("Phong")
13. Nai Prathan Premkamon ("Daeng")
14. Nai Puey Ungphakorn ("Khem")
15. Nai Prem Buri ("Di")
16. Nai Rachit Buri ("Kham")
17. Nai Samran Wannaphruek ("Kheng")
18. Nai Thana Posayanon ("Kon")
19. Nai Krit Tosayanon ("Khong")
20. Nai Sanoe Ninkamhaeng ("Chio")
21. Nai Praphot Paorohit ("Nun")
22. Nai Thep Semathit ("Nu")
23. Nai Kamhaeng Phalangkun ("Lo")
24. Nai Arun Sarathet ("Kai Fa")
25. Nai Yimyon Taesuchi
26. Nai Bunphop Phamonsing
27. Nai Bunloet Kasemsuwan
28. Nai To Bunnag
29. Nai Pat Patthamasathan ("Na")
30. Nai Bunsong Phuengsunthon ("Chai")

31. Nai Thot Phanthumsen ("Bun")
32. Nai Watthana Chitwari ("Thuam")
33. Nai Praphrit Na Nakhon ("Lek")
34. Nai Prachit Kangsanon (Yotsunthon) ("Kae")
35. Nai Wiwat Na Pomphet
36. Nai Sawang Samkoset
37. M.C. Subha Svasti ("Arun")

Nos. 1–4 were officials of the legation in London.

No. 8 joined the army after the date of 7 August 1942.

No. 37 was accepted by the British government as a soldier under a separate arrangement.

OVERALL GOALS OF THE FREE THAI IN ENGLAND

Those who volunteered to join the Free Thai did so for a number of reasons. Some said they did so because of their desire to free their country; some joined out of a desire for freedom and a sense of humanity. Others had no particular aim, but joined from a sense of duty. Many parents had sent their sons to study in England so that their children could avoid the draft and the hardships connected with military life, yet these same men volunteered and met with hardships far more severe than those they might have undergone in the Thai army. The overall principles governing our group might best be summarized as follows:

a. We enlisted in the British army not to help the British but in order to serve our country through the help of Britain.

b. We had no intention of becoming involved in the internal politics of Thailand and did not wish to be used by any party. We planned to join up with the Free Thai in Thailand who were opposed to the Japanese, and our group would disband at the end of the war.

c. The Free Thai would not use the situation to seek recognition or personal benefits.

d. From the time that the Free Thai movement was first organized in England we made it clear to the British government that whatever we did during the war would be carried out under military auspices, and that we would wear military uniforms and bear military titles, even as privates. Any intelligence work we carried out would be conducted while we were in military uniform, or in other words we would not serve as spies or secret agents.

In practice, members of the Free Thai movement joined the army as privates on 7 August [1942]. By October 1943, after having trained and worked in India, most had become second lieutenants. Our group was unusual in that we were recognized as being of higher status than others in the Pioneer Corps. Of the thirty-six of us (not including M.C. Subha, who did not join our group till later), there were thirty who had degrees or certificates of higher education or who were in their final year of education. Our British officers therefore allowed us to direct ourselves. Under British regulations this meant that we were permitted to elect our own leaders and representatives, and that when we moved to a new camp, our new British commanding officer would officially accept those we had chosen. Although we might only be privates, our leaders were officially entitled "Local, temporary, unpaid Lance-Corporals"—a long title of little [apparent] importance, but in fact of considerable significance in that it denoted a favorable attitude towards us on the part of the British forces.

I suspect that the British put us in the Pioneer Corps in order to test our dedication and reliability, since the unit was one of low prestige. Most men in this unit were either enemy aliens or unskilled British laborers of low rank.[9] The motto of the unit was *Labor omnia vincit*. The British themselves were assigned in such a way that engineers joined engineering corps, doctors joined military medical units, and men of other skills went into the artillery, tank corps or joined the Guards, and so on. The duties of the Pioneer Corps, however, were not specific. They included such tasks as digging potatoes, cleaning latrines, mess halls and living quarters, guard duty and other such jobs. All of us Free Thai did all these kinds of jobs even though some of us were government officials, heads of departments, diplomats, or persons of royal rank or importance. We composed a poem in memory of this period. To quote a portion:

We must part from our homely tents to live in strange buildings.[10]
We must abandon our familiar ground to sleep on beds like ladies.
We preferred cold water, which did not remove the grease from dirty dishes
    but which freshened us up, to heated warm water to wash our faces.
Rust on plates added flavor to the food we had to eat.
Now no one cares if we finish up our food.
Fortunately "fatigues" taught us ways to avoid our supervisors.
Corporal Mills, the engineer with a broom in his hand, orders us janitors
To scrub the floor, clean the latrines,
Wash the tables and carry out guard duties.
Now every day we learn how to wipe the tables.
Night guards use guns and bayonets, while day guards use clubs.
We go outside to dig up potatoes and complain and sing.
While our supervisors, unaware, are happy with us.

The Free Thai underwent training in England from 7 August 1942 until the middle of January 1943, when we were sent to India from England by way of Africa. We arrived in Bombay at the end of April 1943. From then on the thirty-six of us were dispersed according to the duties assigned us by the British. A description of our lives in the military up to this period has been recorded in some detail by Khun Bunphop Phamponsing in chapters 7–12 of his *Thai Artists in Europe* mentioned earlier.

Once we reached India we were separated as follows: one group was sent to Delhi to work on radio communications and mapping; one group went to Karachi (Khun Bunphop's group, as he records in his book); and another group was sent to work on espionage. The largest group, which included myself, was sent to a camp outside Poona [today Pune] to work on guerrilla tactics. We were called "White Elephants", and were located near a lake in a sub-district the name of which translates as "Love Nest." Later on we learned that we were in the division of "Force 136 of the Special Operations Executive" (S.O.E.) in the Ministry of Economic Warfare.

THE FIRST RADIO STATION IN THAILAND TO COMMUNICATE WITH THE UNITED NATIONS[11]

In order to reach the point where I can talk about the work of the Free Thai in Thailand in detail, I will keep the discussion of my training brief, and present our training schedule briefly and without elaboration.

May 1943–September 1943	Trained at Rang Rak ("Love Nest") near Poona [Pune].
October 1943	Trainees became Second Lieutenants.
October 1943–November 1943	Nai Samran Wannaphruek ("Kheng") and I received training in espionage at Calcutta.
November 1943	Nai Samran Wanaphruek, Nai Prathan Prem-kamon ("Daeng") and I boarded a submarine from Ceylon to Phangnga, Takua Pa, but were unable to land because we did not receive a signal from our men.
December 1943	The three of us rested at Nilgiri in southern India.
January 1944	Joined with a larger group for training in hiking at the Singha mountain range in the Poona [Pune] area.
February 1944	Trained in parachuting at Rawalpindi in the Punjab with Nai Prathan Premkamon, Nai Samran Wannaphruek, Nai Prem Buri ("Di"), Nai Rachit Buri ("Kham"), and Nai Thana Posayanon ("Kon").
March 1944	Parachuted into Thailand to perform our duty.

The following is an account of events leading up to the establishment of the first radio station in Thailand to communicate with the Allies while the Japanese still occupied our country.

By incorporating the Free Thai into their forces, the Allies hoped to use us to aid United Nations [Allied] troops behind Japanese lines militarily, politically and in communication work. The Thai joined the Allies for the sake of Thailand without any conditions, but at the same time we also planned on trying to contact members of the underground movement within Thailand so that we could explain what was going on to them.

By mid–1943 it had been confirmed that an underground resistance movement existed in Thailand. It was also known that some of its members had been sent to Chungking[12] to contact United Nations' representatives there. Most of the Free Thai from England, known as "White Elephants", were being trained in guerrilla warfare tactics outside Poona (Pune) in India when we first learned that M.C. Subha Svasti had been sent to Chungking to link up with Nai Kamchat Phalangkun, who had escaped from Thailand secretly [and made his way to China to contact the Allies]. Later we learned that M.C. Subha had been authorized by the British to organize a group to enter Thailand from Yunnan. Messages were sent by the British forces via this group requesting "Ruth", i.e. Nai Pridi Banomyong, the Regent and leader of the Free Thai in Thailand, to receive the first group of "White Elephants" who would be coming in by submarine and who were expected to land on the shores of western Thailand in December 1943. They would be bringing in equipment so that a radio station could be set up in Thailand and contact made with British forces in India.

I received orders from my commanding officer that I was to be one of the people boarding the submarine, and that the name of my unit was to be "Pritchard". Our unit included Nai Prathan Premkamon ("Daeng"), the radio man, Nai Samran Wannaphruek ("Kheng"), and me. "Daeng" was sent to Meerut [in northern India] for further education in radio systems, while "Kheng" and I were sent to a school outside Calcutta for special training.

After "Daeng" joined us in Calcutta in November, we were trained to land from a submarine by day or by night. Our training station was Trincomalee in Ceylon. We boarded the submarine at Colombo. Two naval officers and one sergeant were sent to help us land.

We reached the designated location and remained about four to five miles off shore for about one week, staying under water during the day and coming up above water at night to receive any signals which might have been sent to us. However, we waited in vain. Later we learned that the Chinese group from Yunnan did not reach Bangkok until June 1944.

The submarine trip was not without incident, however. There was considerable excitement when we located a large ship floating above water quite near to the place where we were submerged. It could have been either a Japanese or a Thai ship. Since we were unable to tell whether we had been detected or not, we had to remain very quiet for safety reasons. I almost did not dare breathe, as I felt that the sound of our breath made an unbelievably loud noise. However, we were not torpedoed. The last day we remained in station the British sergeant decided to go on shore in a small boat. (We Thai did not go as we had been given orders not to land under any circumstances unless we saw people coming for us). Our British friend had never been to Thailand. He went to spy out the land, but reported that he saw nobody on shore and claimed it would be useless to wait any longer. We therefore headed back to Ceylon. One night, on the return journey, we saw a small fishing boat and decided to surface. We knew this would frighten all the Chinese who were on board. However, we needed money and documents [faked identity cards], for which we produced Thai money and food in return.

I should not take up too much space describing our life in the submarine. Suffice it to say that it was hot and boring. There was nothing to do except eat, sleep, and play dice. We slept during the day and got up at night when the submarine came to the surface. At night we could go on deck; this was the only time when we were allowed to smoke. I can still remember the time when I gazed at our beloved country through a pair of binoculars. The white shore line, the fishermens' huts, and the tall trees stood out vividly. The village at which we were supposed to land was quite deserted. Although I had never been to that particular village, I identified with it as part of the country I loved so well and where our people were living.

We returned to Colombo in time for Christmas. Once we got close to Ceylon, we came up above water and traveled at full speed. It was quite an uncomfortable experience, as traveling by submarine above water makes one seasick and produced other discomforts.

We rested for a short period in the beautiful Nilgiri hills [in southwest India], and then went up to Meerut at the beginning of January 1944. From there we returned to Poona (Pune), where other "White Elephants" were receiving further training.

This reunion made it possible for us to discuss our future plans together for the last time. We gathered together on top of the Singha mountain to clarify our duties and obligations. For some of us, me included, the thought of parachuting and going in a submarine were matters of dread. For others, such thoughts were exciting. I cannot remember all the topics we discussed that day. I only remember that we agreed that we loved one another and that we were working for a good cause. I suggested that we try not to harm or kill any Thai once we all reached Thailand, even if this meant sacrificing our own lives. We should not let the Japanese capture us alive, but should fight to the end. I introduced this last proposal gradually, trying not to force anyone into doing what he felt to be against his instincts, namely in regard to fighting rather than being captured alive. However, most of the "White Elephants" agreed with my proposal.

Afterwards the plan of entry into Thailand was drawn up. Two or three of the "White Elephants" were to parachute into the country with radio equipment. They were to be dropped blind into forested areas in north central Thailand, between Sukhothai and Sawankhalok,[13] one night during the early waxing or waning of the moon in March and April. There were to be two groups of three men each, called "Appreciation I" and "Appreciation II" respectively. The members of "Appreciation I" were to land in March, hide in the forest, radio back to the station, and make plans to receive "Appreciation II" during the period of the next full moon. If the station did not hear back from "Appreciation I", "Appreciation II" would then make another blind drop in an adjacent province in a manner similar to that of "Appreciation I." Our duties were to keep ourselves safe, to radio back to the commanding station, to receive the next group of parachutists, and if possible to contact the underground.

The men in these two units were not the same as in the "Pritchard" group, as we needed radio experts and doctors now that we were going to be entirely on our own. The two new groups included Nai Prem Buri ("Di"), Nai Rachit Buri ("Kham"), and Nai Thana Posayanon ("Kon") as additional members. "Appreciation I" included myself, "Daeng" and "Di"; "Appreciation II" was composed of "Kheng", "Kham," and "Kon", and was led by "Kheng".

The six of us were separated from the rest of the unit in February to practice parachuting at Rawalpindi. Each of us made five trial jumps, the first four during the day and the last at night. The first drop was made from a Hudson and the other four from a Liberator. The jumps were made after we had practiced and undergone physical training for a number of days. Although we came to realize that parachuting was not a very dangerous act, we still did not like it. I myself cannot say in all sincerity that I was not afraid. Nevertheless, we tried to hide our fear. On the trip to the airport every morning we passed through a cemetery, and would tell one another that sooner or later our bodies would end up there. Whatever else, we all benefited from the training in physical fitness and from the fresh air of the Punjab, and felt very healthy after being in Rawalpindi for a week.

While waiting for "reality" in Calcutta, where we had gone from Rawalpindi, we indulged in urban enjoyments such as seeing a movie in an air-conditioned theater, eating ice cream sodas and dining in a restaurant for the last time. Finally the day arrived. "Appreciation I" was to start work on 6 March, three days before my birthday. I jokingly asked my commanding officer to send me a birthday present in the jungle. That morning we flew northeastward from Calcutta to a place the name of which I cannot remember, although the scenery remains vividly in my mind. It had a large runway with neither vegetation nor fresh water; there were only planes and pitiful huts around. For lunch we had dry canned meat, dried-out bread, and water that smelt of chlorine. It was definitely a mistake to have sent us to such a discouraging place.

That evening we boarded a Liberator for our destination. Bombers were sent off to adjacent areas on the same night to help protect us. We also noticed another Liberator taking off from the same runway a few minutes before us. We later learned that four Chinese were on board, bound for Nakhon Pathom on a mission similar to our own. We spent most of the time on the plane sleeping. It was uncomfortable and the weather was bad. I felt a little sick. During the trip we could not really eat. Although it was the night of the waxing of the moon, it was quite dark and we did not know our whereabouts. Someone told us to get ready at 22:30 hours, and by 23:00 hours we were waiting at the exit ready to slide down it. The exit was near the engine, and was large enough for a person to slide down with the equipment on his back. When the order "Go" came, we were to jump into the fateful darkness. One hour at the exit seemed like a whole year of sitting at the top of a cliff. Only the wind blowing into the exit told us that what lay below us was not hell, for we felt cold air not hot flames. The plane circled around but no orders came to jump. Finally someone tapped my shoulder and told us that we were returning to Calcutta. The pilot could not find our landing place, the map was bad, and the area was dark.

We did not stay in Calcutta long since we were all anxious to go on with our work. A week after the first attempt, the British informed us that they were ready to try again. The procedure and plan were exactly the same as on the first trip except that we left about four to five hours later since the moon was now waning. We were told when we reached our designated area. The plane circled the area very close to the ground. Numerous lights on the ground made us wonder if we were at the right location. However, there was no time to ponder. The order to jump came, and we jumped.

The three of us landed close to one another on the ground. I was the most unlucky, as I sprained my ankle. When I came down one leg landed on a dike[14] while the other did not. After we hurriedly consulted the map we realized that we were about twenty-five to thirty kilometers away from our destination, and too close to a village for our purposes. Seven parachutes containing a month's supply of food and other equipment had also been sent with us, but we only found six in the field. The seventh was later spotted in the middle of the village, which was separated from the field where we landed by only a few bushes. We therefore decided to leave the area immediately.

It was about 4:00 a.m.; we had about one hour before dawn. We could not move very quickly because of our supplies, yet we were too close to the village to try to bury them. With no time to make a careful decision, we saw five or six farmers approaching us. They saw us.

The farmers proved to be charcoal-burners from another village who had gone into the forest to cut wood and who were now on their way home. They had camped the night before outside Muban[15] Wang Nam Khao (the name of the village where we had landed); it was in Chai Nat[16] province. We had planned to land northwest between Tak[17] and Nakhon Sawan).[18] The charcoal-burners had seen our parachutes coming down, although some had mistaken them for smoke, as the parachutes were white. They were surprised to find that we were Thai and not Europeans coming in to bomb our country.

They knew that we had not jumped from either a Thai or a Japanese plane, because the plane had had four propellers. Despite our attempts to persuade them that the plane was a new model supplied to the Thai Air Force by the Japanese for training purposes, they did not believe us, although only one man expressed his disbelief verbally.

Having encountered an unexpected problem, we had to think up a way out of it. We pretended that we were planning to go to the village in the morning, and asked the men to help carry our supplies there. They gave us a hand willingly, and left us at the outskirts of the village, where we said we were to meet our friends. We thanked them.

By then it was about 5:00 a.m. Since we had no time to waste we took only the radio equipment, some food and some clothing. The rest of the supplies we either hid in the bushes or buried in the ground. In any event it was almost useless to try to hide things since one whole parachute full of supplies had landed right in the village straight in front of the temple. We did what we could and walked back westward into the forest. My sprained ankle retarded our trip. After four to five hours' walking, we were in quite deep forest and decided to rest. Actually it was not a safe place, but we wanted to contact the station in India to say that we had landed outside the designated area, and that where we were was not safe. We planned to bury the radio equipment and then move northwestward, where we would wait and meet up with the members of "Appreciation II" the following month. In the radio message we would warn them to be extra careful and not to make the same mistake as we had done, as the villagers here now knew of us.

While we were waiting for the proper time to send our message, we dug holes so that once our message had been sent we could bury the radio equipment and any other unnecessary supplies so that we could travel with the least possible weight on us. We then settled ourselves in an area of thick forest some away from the place where the radio equipment was to be buried. Although there was a path about four to five meters from our camp, passers-by would have been unable to see us.

The day was hot and the forest quiet except for the sound of birds and monkeys. My ankle ached and was swollen, and we were tired after walking in the warm weather for half a day. Moreover we had not expected the incident that had occurred early that morning, and were upset at having been seen and that we had lost one parachute in the center of the village. According to our original plans we had also been supposed to land near a stream; now we had only three bottles of water. At least we were not hungry, so we did not have to worry about food.

Daeng and Di attempted to radio India at the appropriate time. After I had watched the area for about half an hour, they reported they could not get the message through. They could only hear the voice from the commanding station faintly, and the commanding station could not hear them at all. In addition, the station had not waited for them long enough, and the signal to stop the message had come much sooner than had been agreed upon. We thought that possibly the commanding station had not expected us to radio them so soon after landing.

We decided that the most important thing was to try to radio the message, and that this must be sent as soon as possible. It would be impossible to go very far with the radio equipment due to its weight and my swollen foot. Besides, the place where we were camped was a reasonably good location. Daeng suggested that an antenna might help, and that we should try to send the message again the next day. As leader of the team, I agreed with this and took responsibility for the decision. While waiting till the following day we decided to try and find water to store in our bottles. We also agreed we would leave as soon as we had managed to get the message through.

Daeng and Di went off to look for water while I waited back at the camp. Although they eventually found a pond of dirty water at the edge of the forest, it took them many hours to do so, as it was not until 3.00 a.m. that the moonlight became sufficiently strong for them to travel by. Meanwhile I waited, listened to the sounds of the forest, and enjoyed the sight of the moonlight playing on various objects. I was not afraid of the wild animals at all, but I was glad to see my friends when they returned the following morning.

Our second attempt to get a radio message through to headquarters was even less successful than the first one. We could not hear from the commanding station at all. We began to get worried now, as Di felt that if we did not move on, the villagers would have time to catch up with us. At the same time, though, we were concerned that the members of "Appreciation II" might run into difficulties when they landed if we were not able to get a message through to them warning them of our circumstances. I made the decision to try to get through to headquarters one more time the following morning. We would move on after that in any case. That afternoon, while Di and I were hunting around and looking for water, we ran into some villagers. They stayed overnight with us without any suspicions as to whom we might be.

The next morning, at about 10:00 a.m., when Di and Daeng went to send the message, I was alone at the camp. Five minutes after they had left I saw a few people pass by at a distance. I thought they had not seen me, but a few minutes later our camp was surrounded from all sides. The villagers were all armed. This was the end of our game, or of my game at least. I could do nothing except yell out loudly: "I surrender. You may take me away," hoping that the other two members of our team would hear me and get away.

It seems almost unbelievable, but within that one second many thoughts came into my head. From the time I realized I was surrounded until I was captured the thoughts came so fast I cannot remember their sequence. I remembered my sweetheart in London; the last words which Khun Mani Sanasen had said to me before we left England; my friends who were still in India; my two friends in the nearby bushes; my relatives and friends in Bangkok; the message in my pocket from my commander[19] to "Ruth"; and lastly the poison in my shirt pocket. My last thought was whether I should swallow the poison and die or whether I should be captured alive. If I decided to die it would be because I had too many secrets to keep, and to be captured alive would mean that I might have to tell these secrets and so betray my friends. If I decided to be captured alive, on the other hand, it would be because being alive I would have some way of protecting the evidence I had on my body, which I would not otherwise be able to do. Life was beautiful. One could still have hope if one was alive. Certainly I would rather have died than have been tortured by the Japanese, but there were no Japanese in sight. I therefore decided to stay alive and suffer the consequences.

When I look back on these events now I always laugh, for when I was captured, the man in front of me, who was dressed in a police uniform and carried a pistol, jumped on me in the exact same way in which it is done in the *like*,[20] uttering unintelligible words the while. Many people were hidden in the surrounding bushes, but they did not come out until I surrendered and showed that I was not armed. At first there were only about five to six people, but a minute after I surrendered, about thirty people appeared. They tied my hands behind my back with a *phakhaoma*.[21] From then on I could not make sense of what the people were saying, because all of them seemed to be talking simultaneously. The man nearest to me directed many vulgar speeches at me. Another man, after making sure that I was defenseless, hit me and talked away at me. I did not say anything in return. Actually I was dazed and excited and wondering about my two friends. I was relieved, however, when I saw that even though some of the villagers had found the radio equipment, my two friends had not been captured, nor did I hear any shots.

I later learned that Daeng and Di heard the noise when I was being taken prisoner, and fled before they had been seen. They hid in another part of the forest until night time, and then went to the place where we had agreed to meet in case any of us got lost. They were hoping that I would go there if I could get away. When I did not arrive they headed northwards and were captured in Uthai Thani[22] while they were eating in a market-place without any hats on.[23]

Among those who captured me were the assistant district headman, two policemen and other farmers who seemed friendly and cheerful. They took me from the forest to Wang Nam Khao. By the time we had reached the village, many other people were claiming to have taken part in my capture. The district (named Wat Sing) headman, who was the only man on horseback, was one of those who made this claim. There were about two or three hundred people who tried to take charge of me, including the charcoal burners we had run into the first day we landed. After the charcoal burners left us they had reported us to the district office. Villagers had therefore been drafted to search for us. Since they understood that there had been four of us, inquiries were made about the other three.

Having been brought before the district headman, I was taken to a temple and chained by the ankle to a post. Since I did not try to escape, I was exempted from being chained at the wrists. From what I could overhear the policemen were debating about me. One group was convinced I was a very important and dangerous prisoner, a traitor who was trying to destroy our nation and people. Another group, which equaled the first in number, showed kindly feelings towards me. They believed me when I said, without giving my name, that I was a student on a government scholarship who had been sent to England. Many questions were asked about how the war was going. A polite assistant district headman was among this latter group. In contrast, another assistant district headman was quite coarse. He scolded the villagers who gathered around me and ordered them not to come near me. The reason for this treatment was that he believed I was a revolutionary. I felt that the villagers in general were very kind, not because they knew about politics or what the war was about, but just because of the innate kindness and sincerity of their natures. There were yet others who did not care one way or the other, and who were curious about me but not unpleasant. I noticed that both the police officers and the villagers were impressed that I had jumped by parachute from a four-propeller bomber.

I drew them a picture of the plane, stating that it was about the size of the *bot*[24] but not as large.

The villagers brought a delicious lunch and dinner for the officers and me. I ate with an appetite even though my mind was not fully on what I was doing. That afternoon many people from other villages came and sat around me in the *sala*.[25] Though they were interested in me as a parachutist, they could not come very close, as those officers who disliked me forbade them to do so. Late that afternoon, however, several officers took a nap, giving the villagers a chance to move closer and ask questions. Among these was an old lady who sat by me for about two hours without moving. When not many people were left she told me that I resembled her son. Upon being asked, she told me that her son had been drafted and she did not know where he was. Her sincerity captured my heart, and I felt the love of a mother for her child.

That night, being tired, I slept soundly. The next morning at dawn a cart was made ready to take me to Wat Sing district office. I was chained to the cart. Two policemen sat with me as guards, and about twelve villagers walked alongside. Our supplies and radio equipment had been sent along earlier in another cart. The policemen were friendly and agreeable. At about 7:00 a.m. we stopped at a village for breakfast, which had been prepared by the villagers prior to our arrival. They probably knew I was coming. Everyone in the village came to take a look at me. The two policemen teased the girls, asking if they were not somewhat attracted to the parachutist, but they denied it and went off and prepared some excellent food, including a curry, vegetables and hot sauce. The policemen invited me to drink the whisky which was brought out by the villagers, as I might not have an opportunity to do so again for a long time. I enjoyed myself, even though I felt that 7:00 a.m. was much too early to drink. The villagers surrounded my cart and enquired about planes, the bombing and the war. They seemed glad to hear that the Japanese were losing the war. None of the villagers had any feelings against me, and many were surprised that I was a Thai. They called out "Chaiyo!" ["Hurray!"] as our caravan started to move off.

We received similar treatment when we stopped at another village for lunch. I answered similar questions with more expertise. Before I left a villager approached me and handed me a piece of *wan*[26] when nobody was watching. He whispered that I should keep it for good luck as protection against harm. However, [he said, I need have no fears, as] my forehead showed that I would succeed in whatever I undertook.

The next village was larger than the other two we had stopped at earlier. We reached this village at 4:00 p.m. The villagers were more knowledgeable, and included monks, teachers, and people who had been to Bangkok.

We reached Wat Sing district in the evening, and I was sent to the police station. Before entering the district center the two policemen who had been my guards gathered up a contribution of twelve Baht. They suggested that this money might be useful to me over the next few days. The next day these same two policemen brought me hard-boiled eggs in jail, as the jail food was insufficient.

My status as a prisoner became formal once we reached the district center. I was taken to a jail similar to those to be seen all over the country. The cell was ten feet in width and length, with bars on all sides except for the floor. There was one inmate in there already. He looked like a strong, healthy, happy farmer, even though he had been charged with murder. At a party he had got drunk, quarreled with another man, hit him, and stomped on him as he lay on the ground. The man had died. Having learned previously of my expected arrival, this inmate was delighted with the opportunity of observing the parachutist. We chatted. Three hours later a third man, charged with spying, came to join us. He had gone to Wat Sing three or four days previously to look for minerals in the area of Wang Nam Khao where our parachutists had landed. While he was trying to get workmen and carts together for his journey, he was arrested because the police suspected that he had connections with the parachutists. He had denied this, but in vain. Only I knew he was innocent. Four months later I ran into this same man at the police department in Bangkok. He had been denied the opportunity to go home even though there was no evidence against him.

The villagers of Wat Sing came to visit me in jail. Although the guards tried to keep them away at first, they finally got a look at the "queer" figure. The guards wanted their relatives and their friends' relatives to have the chance to see a parachutist once in their lifetimes, too, so the entire police station was occupied by villagers. They made comments about parachutists, some of them mean, others kind. The man with a murder charge against him enjoyed himself, but the miner was very unhappy, since he was innocent. The villagers could not decide which of the three was the parachutist, and would ask. We joked and tried to confuse them. The miner, however, would not join in; he sat sadly in a corner. However, he became friendlier the next day. Being a palm reader, he read my hand and told me I would not die yet. My good lines were still quite distinct. His own fortune, he said, was not so good.

The governor of Chai Nat province arrived the next afternoon with his family, the provincial chief of police and a judge. An hour later the three of us [prisoners] left with these government officials for Chai Nat. On our way from the police station to the boat, we were chained together. The miner felt very ashamed. Feeling awkward at having to chain me, a government student who had been sent abroad, the governor made me a personal apology. On our way to the boat people gathered on both sides to see the inmates, especially the parachutist. I recognized some law students whom I had met a few days ago. We waved.

In Chai Nat I was separated from the other inmates and sent to the governor's office, where I spent many hours. I asked for permission to bathe. This was granted on my promising that I would not try to escape. I shaved with my "Roll razor" shaver, which, when it was being sharpened, made noises similar to those of fireworks. The bathroom door swung open, the sound of the shaver having been mistaken for that of a machine gun. After bathing and dining, the provincial chief of police and the provincial public prosecutor arrived for preliminary investigations. I gave them my name and the real goal of our project. However, I did not tell them the number of my Thai friends in the British forces or any other secrets. The first set of enquiries was put forward politely, but the politeness seemed to disappear when I refused to answer important questions. The investigation ended at about 10:00 p.m., when I was sent back to jail for the night.

There were about twelve people in the jail, many of whom seemed to be younger than twenty years of age. There was just enough room for the twelve of them. When I arrived someone had to sleep on the top bunk. I volunteered, but was refused, and a boy was nominated instead. I later came to realize that this boy had a skin problem and was avoided by everybody. I slept in his place and he slept on the bunk on top of me. He scratched all night, and the falling skin dropped down on my body. I could not sleep that night because of the scratching noise, mosquitoes and other insects, although I clothed myself from head to foot.

I was transferred to the provincial jail at Chai Nat the next morning. This jail housed a doctor who had a murder charge against him and who served as the jail doctor. Originally he was to have been imprisoned for life, but on one of the special occasions (the King's birthday, New Year's, etc.) [on which prisoners sometimes had their sentences commuted], the King had reduced his sentence. The doctor had now almost completed his reduced sentence, and with his medical knowledge and good conduct record, he had been put in charge of the jail hospital—although with no medicines it could hardly have been called a hospital. The patients had to sleep on the floor. The doctor was very well liked by everybody, but could not do much without facilities. Most of the people had malaria, but had to wait for nature to take its course. New inmates with severe charges against them were normally chained at the ankles. If they showed good conduct, restrictions on them would be lessened. Many inmates had permission to work outside the jail, and the best were exempted from work and were permitted to go to town during the day, returning [to the jail] at night.

Reading, writing and handcrafts were taught in jail. One building was reserved especially for women, and I was told that many of the married couples had met their partners while in jail. All the inmates ate red rice and vegetables for their two meals a day. Some of them had permission to go out and fish and could cook for themselves in addition to receiving the food already provided. The red rice was much too dry for new inmates like me; I needed much more soup than the others. At this point the twelve Baht I had been given came in handy for buying extra food. The guard was also kind enough to send me white rice, eggs and soup every meal. I shared the food with the doctor and the other inmates who were his assistants.

I cannot remember the length of my stay in that jail exactly, but it was probably between three and seven days. I was called to the police station one morning, and left for Bangkok by boat at 11:00 a.m. that day. The provincial chief of police was my guard. Another man who was chained to me had fled from a mental hospital and killed a monk afterwards. He told me, and as far as I could see with my eyes, he had no mental problems. I often wondered what happened to him afterwards.

The chief of police who was my guard very much liked to show me off to his friends. On the way to Bangkok I was taken to another police station. Interesting as the stories of my inmates were, unfortunately I cannot relate them all here since it would take up too much space. [One time when we stopped], I had breakfast with the governor of Ang Thong.[27] He commented that we were like actors in a Chinese play that fought with one another, and then dined together after the fight. The last night of the trip I slept at the police station in Nonthaburi,[28] and headed for Bangkok the following morning.

From the time I had first landed up till now every passerby had stopped to look at the parachutist. Once I reached Bangkok, however, nobody paid any attention to the small police boat on which I was boarded. When I landed at Tha Chang[29] near Thammasat University I could see no familiar faces. After two hours of waiting, a police car came to take me to the [central] police department. There I met Daeng and Di, who had arrived earlier. We had lunch together and chatted.

Before long the number of "war criminals" increased rapidly. Before the arrival of the three of us, two Thai-speaking Chinese who were supposed to have landed at Nakhon Pathom[30] (part of the group I mentioned earlier: the third man was killed and the other fled) were taken into custody. At the time of the full moon the following month, the members of "Appreciation II" (Kheng, Kham and Kon) arrived safely but were also taken into custody. In a similar manner two out of five Chinese who had boarded a submarine and landed in the southern part of Thailand were also captured. From then on Free Thai from the United States were taken in a few at a time, first two people, then one, and then five people respectively. Some of the Free Thai from the United States had traveled on foot from Yunnan; others had flown in by hydroplane from Colombo; two more were killed after being captured in the northeast.[31] All six of us "White Elephants" were thankful to be alive. Due to the increasing number of prisoners, we were transferred from the Police Department jail to police living quarters in the compound of the Police Department. Two of the Free Thai from England, Nai Sawat Sisuk ("Raven") and Nai Chunkeng Rinthakun ("Phong"), came to live with us even though they had not been captured. We were allowed to walk around the compound. Our allowance was also increased so that we were able to buy food, and we became regular customers of the merchants and peddlers in the compound. (At this time Japanese officers came to investigate us. We were guarded by Thai officers. The details of the investigation appeared in *Ukotsan* 1952, under the title "Musawatha weramani"[32] and will not be discussed here.)

During this period we were able to contact the commanding station in India by radio with the help of Free Thai of both high and low rank within the country. Some even gave up their houses so that they could be used as radio stations. We observed the normal activities of prisoners by day, and slipped out to send off radio messages at night. At first it was difficult to make contact, as the commanding station in India thought we had been captured when we had not contacted them as agreed upon. We tried and tried to make contact for many months, but without success. It was not until September [1944] that we finally succeeded, when a messenger sent overland to Chungking contacted the British forces there with news of us, while at the same time an informal anecdote using our code names was broadcast through the station of the Thai Public Relations Department on the other. After we finally made contact we were so excited that we could not sleep.

With the aid of many high officials in Thailand, the work of the Free Thai went smoothly and safely from then on. We had the support of the police, and later of the army, navy and air force. Military officials, from generals to privates, and civilians from Ministers to common citizens enthusiastically gave us a hand. Around May 1945, when the Free Thai movement was well under way, I received permission to take a vacation in India and England. I boarded a Catalina from Hua Hin, and returned on a Dakota, landing at a Thai Air Force runway in the northeast.[33] The "White Elephants" and the Free Thai from the United States, who were more numerous and more efficient than us, had been landing in Thailand since November 1944. Now that many more radio stations were able to contact India, the importance of the "Appreciation" groups gradually decreased. We finally decided to separate and start earning our livings. Phong and Raven had already left to go to work. In April 1945 Kon and Kham went to Yala,[34] while

Di and Kheng later left for another southern province. Daeng and I remained in Bangkok not doing much for the remaining few months of the war.

FINAL NOTES AND EXPLANATIONS

The description in the last section was written a long time ago. At the time I tried to write clearly and concisely, but I feel that further explanation is due at this point, even though the story still will not be complete. Since this article is to be part of a work by Professor Direk Jayanama, I would like, however, to make some further comments in connection with his book.

First, as for why I was chosen to be the first person to contact the Free Thai inside our country, a short answer is that the British knew that the Free Thai in Thailand were led by Nai Pridi Banomyong, and that he was connected with Thammasat University. I was a graduate of that university, and had worked there for many months. Although I did not know the Rector, Nai Pridi, personally, the following connection existed between us.

I graduated from Thammasat in June 1936 in the first class to graduate from that university since its establishment two years earlier. As one of its first graduates, I had the opportunity to become acquainted with some of the professors there. After I received a Bachelor's degree in Economics with first class honors from London University, Professor Wichit Lulitanon, who was then on the faculty at Thammasat, hearing of my good record, passed on my name to the Rector (i.e. Nai Pridi Banomyong). He in turn sent me a telegram not only as Rector, but also in the name of the Ministry of Finance, which had awarded me my scholarship, congratulating me. It was therefore felt that I would be a good person to try to make secret contact with the leader of the Free Thai movement, for there would be no need for me to verify my credentials with him.

When I was captured and sent to the Police Department in Bangkok, I was guarded by a Police Captain Phayom Chantharakkha (now a full Colonel), who was also a Thammasat university graduate. Well before the Chief of Police (General Adun Adundetcharat)[35] granted us permission to set up a radio station to contact India, Khun Phayom had already taken the risk of taking the radio equipment and trying it out at home. He also contacted Professor Wichit Lulitanon (then Secretary General of Thammasat University), who in turn contacted Professor Pridi. Khun Phayom took me to meet Professor Pridi for the first time at Professor Wichit's house in Bang Khen.[36] It was there that I relayed to Nai Pridi the message from the Supreme Commander of the Allied Forces (Lord Louis Mountbatten) to the leader of the Free Thai. By that time my friends and I had been busy sending radio messages to India. We had also been able to receive Khun Prasoet Pathummanon and Khun Krit Tosayanon, who had come in by parachute at Hua Hin, and who had made contact with other Free Thai leaders such as Professor Direk Jayanama.

Our meetings with Free Thai leaders were held at night (except for the meeting at Professor Wichit's house in Bang Khen). I would usually disappear from my quarters at the Police Department, pretending to be taking a walk along Sanam Ma Street. When Khun Phayom drove by, all of us prisoners-of-war would get into the car when no one appeared to be looking. Khun Phayom would then drive to the designated place and we would transfer from the car. We met Professor Direk for the first time in this way. We would later return by the same car to our quarters. On the nights of these secret meetings we usually went to bed at early dawn or during alarms signaling an air attack. Later on the Chief of the Police Department would arrange for us to meet him after midnight each time; sometimes we would meet at 3:00 a.m. We walked and talked in the vicinity of the plaza containing the equestrian statue of King Rama V, or in the area around the Democracy Monument. We had already been sending out radio messages when permission to do so was granted to us, so he knew we were quite efficient.

The first group of parachutists to be received formally at Phu Kradueng comprised Nai Sanoe Ninkamhaeng, Nai Praphot Paorohit and Nai Thep Semathit. Later units [i.e. those that arrived after the Chief of Police had placed his full support behind the Free Thai] were received much more conveniently, for by then there was no longer any need to keep such matters secret from not only the Japanese but the Police Department. Police cooperation made our tasks much easier, particularly as there were police units all over the country. If a Japanese soldier saw us with Europeans and policemen, the explanation would be that the Europeans had been captured as war criminals.

I would also like to explain why I was allowed to take a vacation in India and England. Permission to leave Bangkok was granted to me in June 1945 because the British command wanted to see me personally and also because I requested leave to go to England. Since the main work [of establishing contacts between the Free Thai in Thailand and the Allies] had been successfully accomplished, the commanding unit gave me permission to take a vacation in England to see my girl friend.

While in England, I undertook both economic and political tasks for Professor Pridi. He charged me with asking the British government to recognize the Free Thai as the legal government of Thailand [once the war ended], in the same way as the United States had been asked to do. He also told me to ask the British government to release the frozen Thai currency reserves being held in England,[37] working through Mr. Anthony Eden, then the Secretary of State for

Foreign Affairs. I told Professor Pridi that I did not know Mr. Eden, and that with only a few days in England it would be quite impossible for me to make such a contact. I said that I would, however, try my best to contact somebody else with whom to discuss the matter.

By this time the war in Europe had come to an end. General elections were planned for England, and from conversations I overheard among British army officers I anticipated that the Labour Party would win the elections. The leader of the party at that time was Professor [Harold] Laski of London University. Although I did not know him personally, he had been head of the Political Science Department when I was an economics student at the University, and I had attended his lectures. I realized that the likelihood of being able to meet him was much greater than that of meeting Mr. Eden, and that if the Labour Party won the elections, then meeting with Mr. Eden would be of no use anyway. I therefore made an appointment to meet Professor Laski, who agreed to see me at his home. I wore my British military uniform to show that I had pledged my life for the cause by joining the British Army. I do not know whether my attempts to impress Professor Laski worked, but after I had talked to him about the requests of the Free Thai he promised to help us, but only on one condition. He took more than an hour to explain this condition. In summary it amounted to his being willing to help the common people of Thailand but not the powerful or its rich landowners.

The meeting with Professor Laski was not as successful as might have been hoped, for the British government continued to treat our country as having enemy status. However, Professor Laski did follow through on his words, and wrote to Mr. [Ernest] Bevin, the Foreign Secretary [in the new Labour Cabinet of 26 July 1945], a number of times about our situation. My friends in the Foreign Office told me that Professor Laski's notes to Bevin were fully examined, and although they did not produce any real results Professor Laski did try to help Thailand as best as he could.

Another topic I should like to mention concerns the negotiations in Kandy after the surrender of the Japanese. I was sent with other Thai representatives to Kandy twice after the Japanese surrendered. Both times I was told to wear British uniform without fail. The talks with the British were extremely important to us, as the British did not show themselves as well disposed towards us as the United States.

The first mission was led by General Luang Senanarong as our military representative. He had the reputation of having fought very hard against the Japanese when they first landed and attacked Thailand on 8 December 1941]. His unit had won its battle. He was an outstanding soldier, honest, patriotic and brave. There were no real discussions at this first meeting; Thailand was, rather, just showing the flag and letting it be known to the British and to news reporters in general that it had not only fought the Japanese [at the beginning of the war], but had been willing to carry out an uprising against them at the end if it had not been dissuaded from doing so by the Allies.

The second mission to Kandy was led by M.C. Wiwatthanachai Chaiyan. Since the details of the discussions that took place on this occasion have already been given in Professor Direk's book,[38] there is no need for further elaboration on them here. Moreover I was called back to England to continue my studies before the negotiations ended.

Lastly, before concluding my article, I want to mention the importance of Luang Suranarong and Mr. Martin. When we first arrived in India they gave us a great deal of moral support. We Free Thai were afraid and depressed after many months of intensive traveling, particularly as we did not know what the future held for us. However, there we met a number of Englishmen who had worked in Thailand, spoke Thai, and were members of our commanding unit. They included Messrs. Pointon, Micholoyn, Bryce, Smith, Hobbs and Hopkins, all of whom gave us help and moral support. The other people who boosted our morale were General Luang Suranarong and Mr. Martin. General Luang Suranarong had come to India from Singapore, where he had been sent on military duties.[39] When the Japanese invaded Singapore, he had fled to India rather than surrender to the Japanese. We young men gained much spirit from his example. The other man was an elderly Englishman named Mr. Martin, the father of a Thai doctor, Dr. Bunsom Martin. He had left Thailand for India on foot rather than be taken prisoner by the Japanese. We knew his son and regarded him as a Thai. The example of "Uncle Martin" also gave us much moral support.

Activities in Kandy, New Delhi and the United States During and After the War: A Brief Report

Phra Phisansukhumwit (Prasop Sukhum)

Khun Direk Jayanama, the author of *Thailand and World War II*, asked me to write an article to be incorporated in his book concerning my duties and activities as a member of the Thai resistance movement in Kandy, New Delhi and the United States during and immediately after World War II.

It is a pleasure for me to fulfill this request for a man whom I respect and admire, and to have the honor of contributing to some small extent to a book which will be of great value to historians and students of World War II. The Second World War was a period of great historical importance, and Khun Direk Jayanama was a senior figure during that period, serving as a member of the Council of Ministers and as Ambassador to Japan during the war and to Britain after the war. [Through these positions] he was able to establish direct contacts with representatives of the nations involved, and acquired a detailed knowledge of the events of the period.

As an article in a book, this account must necessarily be kept brief; certain details have therefore been omitted.

ASSIGNMENT OF DUTIES

In November 1944 my brother, Luang Sukhumnaipradit (Pradit Sukhum) and I were asked to meet with the Regent, Nai Pridi Banomyong, at Tha Chang Wang Na [Tha Chang Palace] at about 21:00 hours. As the leader of the underground movement in Thailand, Nai Pridi asked us to work on a secret mission for the sake of our country. In agreeing to carry out this mission, and without knowing its nature, we must swear that we would keep every detail secret, even from our families. We were told of the resistance work that was being carried out against the Japanese, and were asked to slip out of the country and make our way to the United States. Without even knowing about our escape route, we agreed to work for the underground, and were told to await further orders.

On Saturday, 19 May 1945, the leader of the underground, [Nai Pridi], asked if we could be ready to leave in two days, or in other words on the following Monday,

21 May. After we had got ready, we were given details about our journey. We were to leave Bangkok at night and board a hydroplane at a designated place.

Our main duty was to try and persuade the United States to reduce the demands it might make on Thailand as the result of the position we had taken during the war.[1] We were to try to demonstrate to the people of the United States that Thailand was on the side of the Allies, and that our signing a treaty with Japan and declaration of war against the United States, Great Britain and Australia had been the action of a few people, not of the majority. We were also to try to arrange for measures to help relieve and rehabilitate [the economy] of our country after the war. We were therefore asked to contact organizations that provided help to countries in distress and sought to improve their condition.

IN COLOMBO, KANDY AND NEW DELHI

On Monday night, 21 May 1945, we left Bangkok in a small motor boat about nine meters long. After traveling for two days and two nights we boarded a plane which the United States had sent to pick us up in the Gulf of Thailand. We spent one night in Madras on our way to Colombo, and from there went to Kandy, which was the headquarters of the Supreme Commander of the Allied Forces in South-East Asia, Admiral Lord Louis Mountbatten. It was also the headquarters of Colonel Coughlin, who was in charge of all O.S.S. activities in the region.

During the two to three days we were in Kandy, I was occupied with duties all the time. We held many discussions with Colonel Coughlin and other officers. The O.S.S. made a practice of questioning all nationals who had escaped from countries under Japanese occupation so as to obtain detailed reports of their [home] situations from them. Being a high-ranking official[2] I was expected to be able to supply extensive and important information, and in addition to the questions I was asked, I also had to explain certain matters which were not clear to the O.S.S. For example, I was asked to study the secret biographies of important Thai leaders that the O.S.S. had drawn up, and to correct or add to these where necessary according to my knowledge of the facts. I thus got an opportunity to learn about the positions these individuals held in the eyes of the United States government. I also asked about the Allies' plans, and asked them to send arms to the Free Thai movement in Thailand.

The most significant items of information that Colonel Coughlin conveyed to me were as follows:

    a. He was very concerned lest the Japanese take over in Thailand too soon.[3] If this should occur, then the Allies would be unable to help us in time.

The Supreme Allied Commander, Lord Louis Mountbatten, was trying to enter Thailand right away, but he had to make arrangements and wait for arms and equipment first.

b. The governments of the United States and Britain accepted that "Ruth" (code name for Nai Pridi Banomyong) was the leader of the Thai people.

c. The geographical region [in which Thailand lay] would fall under the command of the British, not the Americans [once Japan was defeated].

d. If Thailand should happen to incur the displeasure of either the United States, Britain or China, it would be best for her if that country were the United States [in other words, of the three countries the United States was the most favorably disposed towards Thailand].

e. Colonel Coughlin wanted Major-General (William J.) Donovan, Director of the O.S.S., to meet "Ruth," and Major-General Donovan himself wanted to go to Thailand to talk to him. However, any such action was prohibited by the United States for high-ranking officers, since an officer of as high a rank as Donovan knew too many secrets for the enemy to forego trying to capture him.

f. Thailand was on the outer perimeter of the war zone, and it was therefore not very easy for it to secure arms and equipment [from the United States], as Washington preferred to supply combatants in the Pacific area first. A request had recently been made for a fleet of planes to supply arms to Thailand, but no one could tell if this request would be granted. All such requests had to be passed on by Washington first before they could be filled.

g. Supplies to China had to be sent in by air because this was much faster than sending them by land. However, the weather was a real enemy in such missions. The planes had to fly over high mountain ranges, with the result that the wings and other parts of the planes got covered with ice. This had led to a number of crashes during the last months. One plane, (Colonel Coughlin mentioned), could carry up to 15,000 lbs. (6,818 kilograms).

h. The United States had set aside a budget of one billion five hundred thousand dollars to build a nuclear device which, when completed, would be used to attack the islands of Japan.

i. The United States wanted to see the war brought to an end as quickly as possible so as to reduce expenditure. They were therefore annoyed by the slow tactics of the British.

j. At first there had been concern that there were too many leaders of the Free Thai. However, once the United States and Britain learned that

"Ruth" and "Betty" (code name for Police General Adun Adundetcharat) were working together, they were relieved.

k. In October the O.S.S. would be setting up a headquarters in Rangoon.

In the course of contacts with other officers I was asked routine questions, as is the way of organizations such as the O.S.S. This information was for the use of the American forces. While in Kandy I was regarded as the expert in residence on Thai geography. Whenever the O.S.S. received a report that a patrol plane had seen movements on a particular highway, in a village or in the jungle, I was asked about the geography of these places.

While I was in Kandy I took the opportunity to request that Allied planes refrain from bombing religious buildings, palaces and other [monuments that were a part of our] cultural heritage. I was assured that the Allies always sought to avoid bombing such places. However, it was admitted that unintentional mistakes had sometimes been made. I returned to Colombo on Thursday, 31 May to prepare for the trip first to New Delhi and then to the United States, and on Thursday, 7 June I left for New Delhi after spending a week in Colombo.

The United States' forces in New Delhi were made up mainly of supply units, Air Transport Command and O.S.S. units, to which I was attached. Lieutenant-General [Daniel I.] Sultan[4] was the commander of the O.S.S. in New Delhi, but at the time I arrived he was away, and Lieutenant-General [Frank] Merrill[5] was in command. I asked General Merrill for supplies of arms for the Free Thai movement in Thailand, and was told that everything was ready except for the order from the Supreme Commander of the Allied Forces in South-East Asia [Lord Louis Mountbatten].

On Wednesday, 13 June I left New Delhi for the United States.

MISSION TO INFORM THE UNITED STATES OF THAILAND'S POSITION DURING THE WAR

[From New Delhi] we went to Karachi, and from there flew over North Africa and the Atlantic Ocean, reaching New York on Sunday, 17 June 1945. After spending one night in New York, we went on to Washington. D.C.

Our plan was to inform the American people about Thailand and its position in the war, and to seek their understanding, explaining that Thailand was friendly to the United States, but had been swayed by a few people to join the Japanese. In talking to numerous Americans, it became clear that except for a few people who were directly involved in the war they did not know anything about Thailand or her part in the war. I felt that we should talk with some

Congressmen. We therefore looked for someone among our friends who might be able to introduce us into such circles. The man who helped us was Herman F. Scholtz, a good friend of mine who had been a businessman in Thailand and who knew many prominent people in the United States. We had known one another since 1923, when we both arrived in Thailand at the same time, he as a contractor who was going to build the railroad track to Aranyaprathet,[6] and I on my return from the United States.[7] Mr. Scholtz later set up the International Engineering Company. When the Japanese attacked Thailand, he was living in Bangkok, and was captured and interned at Thammasat University together with other prisoners-of-war. When they were [later] exchanged for Thai citizens who wished to return to Thailand from abroad,[8] he returned to the United States and began working for the O.S.S. He was subsequently posted to India and worked [for the O.S.S.] there, later resigning and returning to the United States. After I talked with him about our aims, he agreed to help us.

At the appointed time on the morning of 11 July 1945, Mr. Scholtz took Luang Sukhum and me to meet Mr. Emmet O'Neal. Mr. O'Neal was a Congressional representative from Kentucky and a member of the Budget Committee. Not only did he have a voice in Congress, but he also knew many influential people. Mr. Scholtz and Mr. O'Neal had been good friends since childhood, both coming from Kentucky. After we had been introduced and had discussed general matters, Mr. Scholtz informed Mr. O'Neal of the Thai situation based on what we had told him and what he knew from his own experience. We stated that the majority of the people of Thailand had not wanted to ally with the Japanese and fight the Allies, but that we had been swayed by a few people to do so. [Our underlying opposition to the Japanese had been demonstrated], however, by the growth of the [Free Thai] resistance movement, which was continuing to expand. We were ready to rise against the Japanese at any time if we could get supplies of arms from the United States [to help make this possible].[9] Mr. O'Neal was also informed about pre-war political and economic conditions [in Thailand], when there had been considerable British influence there. We also pointed out that we produced certain raw materials that the United States needed, such as wolfram, rubber and teak. We were here to let United States' Congressmen know about Thailand's position in order to avoid possible misunderstandings which might have been generated by a few people.

Mr. O'Neal was very interested and suggested that since most Congressmen did not know about Thailand's position, we should meet with a number of Senators and Congressmen. He arranged for us to have lunch with them in the Congressional dining room. I was very pleased that our determination and our acquaintance with one or two people had made it possible for us to meet with a number of people who were influential in American political circles. Given an opportunity to inform Congress about Thailand's situation we should be able to disentangle any misunderstandings that might exist and supply people with the facts.

At noon Mr. Scholtz, Luang Sukhum and I met Mr. O'Neal and had lunch in the Congressional dining room. While dining we talked with a number of Congressmen. Mr. O'Neal told us that he had talked to Mr. Sol Bloom, Chairman of the Foreign Affairs Committee of the House of Representatives, who had decided to call a special meeting the following day, 12 July, at 11:00 a.m. in order to give us an opportunity to inform the members of the Committee about our country. This meeting was to be secret. We were quite surprised to hear Mr. O'Neal's words, as we had not expected such an opportunity. However, seeing the chance before us, even though it was at such short notice, we determined to do our best for our country. Once the Foreign Affairs Committee of the House of Representatives learned about our country, our enemies would not be able to lie to Congress about us. Many people were already blaming Thailand [for having allied with Japan during the war]. In addition our information should make it easier for the United States government to make tactical plans over matters where the United States and Thailand were involved jointly.

After lunch we went to see the Thai Minister [to Washington], (M.R. Seni Pramoj), to inform him of the forthcoming meeting and asking for suggestions on what we should tell the Committee. The Minister expressed the view that this opportunity to talk to the Foreign Affairs Committee of the House of Representatives should be very useful to us.

The next day, Thursday 12 July 1945, Luang Sukhum and I met Mr. Scholtz at the House at 10:45 a.m. to attend the meeting at 11:00 a.m. The meeting was chaired by Mr. Sol Bloom, and about twenty people attended it. Mr. O'Neal began by introducing Mr. Scholtz to the Committee, saying that they were good friends and that Mr. Scholtz had lived in Thailand for twenty years, including during the period when the Japanese had attacked Thailand. He had been interned and later exchanged for other prisoners-of-war under the arrangement covering these exchanges.[10] Mr. Scholtz was thus well informed about Thailand and its people, and about the overall situation there.

Mr. Scholtz then took over and repeated that he had lived in Thailand for over twenty years. Originally he had been a railway engineer, but had later opened an import/export company. He knew the Thai people intimately, and felt they were good friends of America, as Americans did not try to influence Thailand politically, but had given it aid in the form of schools and hospitals. He had employed one hundred Thai in his company, all of whom had proved honest. He had himself shown fairness to his employees, and he had been shown hospitality by the Thai people throughout the twenty years he had spent there.

After he left Thailand he had volunteered to work for Thailand (through the O.S.S.) in India. However, he had now resigned, and had bought himself some property in Virginia. He would like to reciprocate the kindness and hospitality that he had received from the Thai people by informing the Committee of the events and conditions he had experienced while he was in Thailand. He had brought with him two Thai friends from the Free Thai movement who had left Thailand two months ago, and who would be informing the Committee [about the current situation in Thailand] themselves.

Mr. Scholtz went on to state that four to five years before the war the Japanese had sent a "fifth column" into Thailand, and had tried to persuade the Thai to rise and demand the return of their territories in Indochina, even giving out money for this purpose. The Japanese had hired people to march in demonstrations for this cause. Mr. Scholtz said he knew this because his driver was one of those who had been hired. This inciting of the people to demand lands that had been taken from them by the French had fallen on willing ears, as the Thai still felt keenly about this matter. Actually both the French and the British had seized territories formerly belonging to Thailand. However, the British had accomplished their ends through negotiation, while the French had used force. Japan had [ultimately] been successful in causing an outbreak of fighting between Thailand and France.[11] This conflict had not lasted very long before the Japanese, who had originally incited the fight, had stepped in to act as mediators in the dispute. [At the subsequent peace agreement] a decision had been reached to restore certain territories formerly owned by Thailand to Thai sovereignty.[12]

When the Japanese invaded Indochina, Mr. Scholtz continued, it had been expected that Thailand would be their next target. The Thai National Assembly had agreed that Thailand would resist any enemy invasion. Unfortunately, during the period before this decision was reached, the United States Minister to Thailand had not been able to get along with the Thai government and people. Thailand had felt it could not depend on the United States. Upon being asked who this [former United States] Minister was, he said that it was Mr. Grant. Mr. Scholtz said that he himself had helped in the negotiations between the Thai Ministry of Foreign Affairs and the British Minister [Sir Josiah Crosby], and had been informed by the Ministry of Foreign Affairs that Thailand was planning to resist any invasion, but that when it had asked for military supplies [to enable it to accomplish this], it had met with no response from the British.

On the same day that Japan attacked Pearl Harbor it had also invaded Thailand, landing troops in southern Thailand and near Bangkok. The attacks showed that the Japanese had been planning this invasion for a long time. Initially Thailand had fought the Japanese, but Prime Minister Phibun

Songkhram, the Supreme Commander of the Thai forces, had ordered an end to the resistance. Mr. Scholtz added that in his personal opinion had Thailand continued to fight, it would have been destroyed, given its lack of armaments and the fact that those it had were out of date. After the Japanese occupied Thailand, all British and American citizens had been interned. However, they were still treated with kindness by the Thai. Thai soldiers were given internal control of the camps, while the Japanese were stationed outside them. Mr. Scholtz and others had had an opportunity to do some underground work while interned, listening to the radio and copying down messages that were then torn up as soon as they had been read. His Thai friends and former co-workers had also sent him care packages. Since the Thai did not like the Japanese, an underground network was soon formed in Thailand. The first representative to be sent to contact the Allies had escaped from Thailand in 1942. Unfortunately, he disappeared in the jungles of Burma.[13] The second set of representatives, sent to China by the Thai underground, was held in custody by the Chinese, and their leader died.[14] Finally, contact was made by the third group of representatives. After Mr. Scholtz left Thailand he worked in India for the Thai underground. At the moment Thailand needed arms, and General Merrill, who was stationed in India, was ready to send such supplies, but had been waiting, and was still waiting on orders from Admiral Lord Louis Mountbatten. (This corroborated what General Merrill had told us). [Such approval was required since Allied operational] responsibility for the Southeast Asia area had been assigned to the British, under the command of Admiral Lord Louis Mountbatten, following a meeting in Quebec in August 1943.][15]

One of the members of the Committee asked why Great Britain did not want to send the supplies? Mr. Scholtz replied that Britain wanted to synchronize its actions [with those of the rest of the Allies], as it did not want to lose credit for the fight. Another point Mr. Scholtz made was that his company had been the only American company in Thailand. The rest had all belonged to Britain and various other nations. Thailand had tin, rubber and teak in great quantities, and Great Britain had sought to control Thailand by maintaining Advisors to the different Ministries.[16] One Committee member asked how such control was carried out. Mr. Scholtz replied that from his experience in Thailand he could only say that these Advisors had ways of controlling government offices.

The Chairman of the Committee asked me to speak after Mr. Scholtz. I told the Committee that I intended to provide information additional to that which had already been given by Mr. Scholtz. I said that when the Japanese invaded Indochina in August 1941, the Thai had become very suspicious, and in September 1941 the National Assembly had passed a law stating that all Thai must resist in the event of invasion. If subsequently it became apparent that such resistance stood no chance of success, then they were to destroy all their goods and property so as to deny their use to the enemy. The Thai accepted this law as an order. When the Japanese attacked Thailand, fighting therefore broke out and many people on both sides were killed. However, after a certain period of time the Prime Minister had ordered all resistance to cease, despite the opposition of a number of members of the Council of Ministers. Some among this group had actually cried; others felt that Thailand had lost its honor. Later a declaration of war against the United States and Great Britain had been put before and signed by the members of the Regency Council.[17]

From that time on, a number of Thai underground units had been established independently of one another. These had ultimately been united into one group, as was now evident. One member of the Committee asked me the approximate number of Thai who were opposed to the Japanese. I estimated this to represent almost the entire population. I then went on to say that the Free Thai movement was large enough to operate [i.e. carry out an armed uprising] now, as it had representatives all over the country, and we wanted to fight the Japanese in order to make our country independent. However, the organization needed arms from United States [if it was to fulfill this task]. We also needed United States' aid to help us buy machinery and other supplies needed to rehabilitate the country at the end of the war. I was asked if the United States and Great Britain would be able to trade freely in Thailand after the war, and replied warmly in the affirmative. Thailand needed foreign trade if it was to develop economically. We therefore welcomed foreign investment. I was further asked whom I represented. When I stated that I represented the people of Thailand, the member who had questioned me went on to say that it was a strange phenomenon that while Thailand had declared war on the United States, yet certain Thai were now coming to seek help from the United States.

At this meeting Mr. O'Neal also asked me about the distress being felt by Thai students in Japan. I told the meeting that the Thai government had sent students abroad to study in a number of different countries including the United States, Britain, France and Germany as well as Japan. Thai students in Japan were [now] reporting that the Japanese were suffering famine, and that each person had only one bowl of rice per day. The only food they had to eat with the rice was soy beans. This famine would go on as long as Allied bombing continued. The Committee wanted to know if the Japanese had been making the same complaints. I replied that this was so.

The meeting closed as the time allotted came to an end. A number of members of the Committee came forward to shake hands with Mr. Scholtz, Luang Sukhum and myself, and expressed their appreciation of our speech. I noticed that during the meeting everyone listened with interest.

Upon reflection after the meeting, and on thinking back over the impressions I had received and the general atmosphere of the meeting, I felt that our words would be quite influential. The meeting had heard from an American who had been involved in the affairs of Thailand at the beginning of the war, and from a Thai member of the Free Thai movement who had recently come out of Thailand. I understood that I was the first person who had had an opportunity to talk to the Foreign Affairs Committee of the House of Representatives, and that I might be the last.

We left the meeting at 12:30 p.m. and had lunch in the Congressional dining room. We were accompanied by some Committee members who wished to continue the discussions.

While in Washington we also became acquainted with the O'Neal family. After I went back to Thailand we still corresponded Later Mr. O'Neal was appointed Ambassador to the Philippines after it became independent.

We also learned that the Ministry of Defense wished to interview us on military matters. Luang Sukhum and I therefore made an appointment to see Colonel [Arthur] Hutchinson, the head of the intelligence branch of the O.S.S. He told us on our arrival that the Defense Department wanted to interview us about Thailand at the Pentagon that afternoon at 3 o'clock. The Navy would also be sending representatives to the meeting. Luang Sukhum and I were quite taken aback that Colonel Hutchinson had not told us ahead of time of such an important event. Whether the reason was a desire to keep the matter secret, or whether he had confidence in our ability to respond at the interview off the cuff I could not tell. In any event, the appointment had already been set up, so there was no way for us to avoid it. We therefore agreed that I would be the one to be interviewed, and that Luang Sukhum would act as my assistant. We, that is Colonel Hutchinson, Mr. Garden [an official in the Southeast Asia Division of the State Department], Luang Sukhum and I arrived at the Pentagon at 14:45 hours.

At 15:00 hours we were invited into a large rectangular room about twenty meters square with a stage on one side. I assumed it was a lecture room. On the wall of the stage side there were a number of maps hanging. Colonel Hutchinson led us onto the stage and seated us in a row, first himself, then me and then Luang Sukhum. About forty officers of different ranks together with civilian experts were already waiting for us. There were representatives from the Army, Navy, and Air Force.

Seeing that most of the people in the audience were military officers, before Colonel Hutchinson introduced Luang Sukhum and me, I asked him to state that we were civilians, not military officers, and that our knowledge of military affairs was thus limited to that of civilians. Many types of questions were asked by the officers—political, military and economic. The questions asked showed the detailed interest that the United States took in the movements of the Japanese, and included questions such as how many Japanese wooden boats there were floating in the Chao Phraya River, and what kind of wood they were made of. I tried not to give direct answers to questions asked in connection with the work of the Free Thai movement such as who the leader of the underground was. I answered most of the questions, and avoided or gave indirect answers to questions that I either could not or felt I should not answer. We were interviewed for about forty-five minutes. At the end of the interview I felt exhausted, because within these forty-five minutes I had had to answer questions prepared by forty military, naval and air force experts without a break, and without having had any prior preparation. These experts came in with big notebooks while I sat on the stage empty handed. The questions jumped from one subject to another, and would range from politics to military questions and back to politics again, depending, for example, on who had had the opportunity to raise the question. Everyone came armed with a whole set of questions, and hands were raised all the time.

A few days after we arrived in Washington, the [Thai] Minister, M.R. Seni Pramoj, took us to meet Mr. [Abbot Low] Moffat, the Chief of the Division of Southeast Asian Affairs in the State Department. I found Mr. Moffat well disposed towards Thailand and willing to help us. While in Washington I contacted him all the time, and whenever I had something I wished to put forward I went to see him. He always tried to handle my needs, and took time to talk with me.

In conclusion, the United States government knew Luang Sukhum and me to be representatives of the Thai resistance movement who had come to the United States, and officials of different departments met us when the opportunity arose.

Once Luang Sukhum and I arrived from India in Washington and met with some of the Free Thai there, we became aware of the lack of reporters in the United States broadcasting news of our activities to the American public. In fact even when American newspapers or the American populace sought information on Thailand, there was no one to inform them. When the legation felt it was necessary to answer certain questions, it responded within the limits [of its diplomatic position.] We discussed this matter many times, and on Friday, 20 July, Luang Sukhum called a meeting to set up a news station for the Free Thai. The purpose of this station was to inform the American people and American organizations about Thailand and the Free Thai. We decided that this station should be independent and not under the direction of the legation. This way it could broadcast without having to be concerned about diplomatic etiquette.

The service was to be known as the "Thai Information Service". Luang Sukhum explained its aims and functions to anyone who wanted to help. Nai Chun Praphawiwat became its director, and remained so for a number of years after the war ended.

As well as establishing contacts with American newsmen in Washington and asking them to broadcast about Thailand, we went to New York to meet with other reporters there. On 8 August 1945 we met with Mr. Darrell Berrigan (then the owner and editor of the *Bangkok World*, but now dead). Mr. Berrigan was a reporter who had been in Thailand when the Japanese attacked the country. He fled to Burma and became the news correspondent attached to General Merrill's forces behind the Japanese lines. He was currently working for the United Press (U.P.). I had known Mr. Berrigan previously, and knew him to be a brave, patient and intelligent man who was always sent to the fighting lines or to danger spots. He was a good friend of Nai Kumut Chanrueang,[18] and we felt we could depend on him to broadcast our news. We contacted not only Mr. Berrigan while in New York, but also arranged to meet with other newsmen. We invited them for drinks in the apartment of our friend. This led to meetings with many other news reporters. After a few drinks we became quite friendly with one another, and I heard many interesting items of information. Mr. Berrigan promised that he would help us send new about Thailand through the U.P. This cooperation on the part of news reporters was very useful in our work, especially as the U.P.'s network extended all over the world, so that news sent out under its aegis spread far. That night we did not end our gathering until about 2:30 a.m.

On 14 August 1945 President Truman announced over the radio at 19:00 hours that the Japanese had unconditionally surrendered. On 6 September 1945 Luang Ditthakanphakdi, our Chargé d'Affaires [in Washington], called a meeting of all legation staff and informed them that the British forces in Thailand were putting pressure on Thailand to sign an agreement which was very harsh in its terms. Its exact nature was being kept secret, and details had not been printed in the newspapers. Those attending the meeting decided to ask the United States to stop [Britain putting pressure on us to] sign this agreement. We were informed that Mr. Moffat, the Chief of the Division of Southeast Asian Affairs at the State Department, was working on the matter. We therefore decided to wait on the action of the State Department before contacting United States' Congressmen and news reporters.

On 5 October 1945 I went to see Mr. Moffat at the State Department concerning the financial aid we needed for medical and other supplies. (During the war the United States had frozen part of our currency reserves held in the United States.) Mr. Moffat promised to see that our money was released.

ACTIVITIES IN KANDY, NEW DELHI AND THE UNITED STATES DURING AND AFTER THE WAR

[Meanwhile] we waited anxiously for news of the British proposals. We searched for [a record of] them both through the legation and through the United Press, but could find nothing. Britain eventually put forward twenty-one proposals[19] for Thailand to sign, but these were not printed by an American newspaper until 5 December 1945. As was expected, the requirements contained in the proposals were such that to have accepted them would have involved placing Thailand under virtual British control.[20] We concluded that the Free Thai and our delegation in the United States were the only groups that could ask the United States to step in and see if they could bring about a modification of these demands.

Lieutenant-Colonel M.L. Khap Kunchon[21] (now Lieutenant-General), Nai Kumut Chanrueang,[22] and I (Luang Sukhum had returned to Thailand by this time) decided to ask Mr. Richard Eaton, a Washington news commentator, to discuss the matter over the air. We agreed to broadcast on the following day, namely Friday, 7 December [1945], with M.L. Khap Kunchon and Nai Chamrat Follet[23] as the Thai speakers.

At 20:05 hours Mr. Richard Eaton opened his regular program over the air. In the course of it he discussed the agreement[24] put forward by the British to the Thai representatives. He then made a number of strong statements in support of Thailand. Readers doubtless realize that a famous commentator like Mr. Richard Eaton attracted a wide audience. Moreover, his comments usually had a considerable influence on the views of his listeners. When I heard him support Thailand and attack England so strongly in the course of the program, I was very surprised that he would come out with such strong statements against Great Britain. The British probably realized that there were certain Thai behind the program, for Mr. Richard Eaton would have had to be on our side to have made such statements. M.L. Khap and Nai Chamrat followed Mr. Eaton in the discussion. Both of them were excellent speakers, and we were very pleased with the results. The broadcast undoubtedly helped Thailand greatly. Many people wrote to the papers expressing opinions similar to those contained in the program. The Thai Information Service kept all these letters.

I met Mr. Scholtz and asked him to request Mr. O'Neal to speak in the House [about Britain's demands]. Mr. O'Neal asked for factual details about the matter from Mr. Dean Acheson, the Acting Secretary of State. Mr. Acheson told Mr. O'Neal that the United States was in the process of conducting negotiations with the British to try to get them to reduce their demands. Mr. O'Neal stated that he had been, moreover, prepared to discuss the matter in the House of Representatives, but [had learned] that the agreement had been signed already. It was unfortunate that the United States learned of this too late. The news came out in the beginning of December 1945, and the agreement between Great Britain and Thailand was signed on 1 January 1946. If Thailand had released the news sooner, we would have been able to get more help from the United States.

Another man I met who proved very helpful and well disposed towards Thailand was Mr. Otto Praeger. He was a former Advisor to the Thai Post and Telegraph Department, and the former United States Assistant Postmaster General. He introduced the United States airmail system, and was a former Congressional correspondent. He was very well known among Congressmen. I myself had been acquainted with him when he was working in Thailand. Mr. Praeger promised to talk to his friend Mr. Cordell Hull, who had resigned as Secretary of State[25] and was now Advisor on Foreign Affairs to the President. He also promised to talk to a number of Senators such as Mr. Tom Connally, Chairman of the Senate Committee on Foreign Relations, and Mr. Thomas, a Senator and Chairman of the Armed Services Committee, and a member of the Foreign Affairs Committee. Mr. Thomas showed his support for Thailand by broadcasting his views over the air and by writing newspaper articles [presenting our point of view]. Later on Mr. Praeger gave me copies of his letter to Mr. Hull together with the latter's reply, as well as of his letters to Mr. Connally and Mr. Thomas. I also met many State Department officials, including Mr. John Chapman, (formerly the Chargé d'Affaires in Thailand), and Mr. Clark, formerly a Secretary attached to the United States legation in Thailand. Mr. Clark told me that the State Department was working to get the British to reduce their demands on Thailand.

Initially the State Department did not show much interest in the matter. However, after being pressed by newspapermen and congressional representatives, Dean Acheson reported on 18 December 1945 that the United States had asked both Great Britain and Thailand to postpone the signing of the agreement between them until after Washington as well as London was satisfied with the conditions of the treaty. The following day the British Embassy in Washington responded by saying that Mr. Acheson's report was out of date; the British had in fact presented a new proposal to the American Embassy in London, and since both the United States Ambassador in London and the British government were now in agreement on the matter, England and Thailand would sign the treaty at the end of December. The State Department thanked both England and Thailand for postponing the date set for the signing of the agreement. Eventually it was announced that the date had been set for 1 January 1946. Thus the efforts on the part of the United States to persuade the British to reduce their demands on Thailand were successful. The new agreement was published in a number of newspapers. It should be mentioned that at the time that the newspapers and the House of Representatives were placing pressure on the State Department over the situation in Thailand, Britain was in the midst of negotiating a loan of four million U.S. dollars. Although Mr. Truman had agreed to this request [in principle], it had not yet been passed by Congress. Certain United States' Congressmen used this issue as leverage to attack United States government policy on Thailand, taking the American government by surprise.

On 24 January 1946 I went to see Mr. Moffat at the State Department to remind him of the details of our previous discussions, to thank him for his help, and to say goodbye. Our talks lasted for over an hour. The issues we discussed were:

a. I asked Mr. Moffat to once again press the matter concerning Thailand getting help from UNRRA [United Nations Relief and Rehabilitation Administration] for post-war relief and rehabilitation of our country. This issue had been raised previously, but had been blocked by the British at a meeting in London. I suggested that though Thailand might not be eligible for such aid, the United States should still raise the issue again to show our desire and determination in having put forward the proposal in the first place. Mr. Moffat agreed to reconsider the matter, but said he could not raise it again if it seemed that it might affect relations between the United States and Britain adversely.

b. I asked Mr. Moffat to have the United States government encourage American companies and businessmen to open up trade in Thailand as soon as possible. The longer the United States waited, the more competition it would face from other nations and the fewer the opportunities would be open to it in this regard. Mr. Moffat agreed to follow through on this suggestion.

c. Mr. Moffat told me that the United States should be able to release our frozen Thai currency reserves at the beginning of the following month. However, he did not know how far the paperwork had gone on this to date.

d. Mr. Moffat agreed that American traders should buy goods such as tin, rubber and teak directly from Thailand instead of through England.

e. He suggested that Thailand should pay off the rice allocations agreed to [under the terms of the agreement with Britain][26] as soon as possible in order to maintain our honor.

f. Mr. Moffat stated that since Thailand had to work closely with Britain we should try to maintain cordial relations between our two countries.

g. Finally, Mr. Moffat informed me that the State Department had not in fact been satisfied with the terms of the agreement with Britain, but that from the time the United States had first opened negotiations with the British on the question of the wording of the agreement so as to ensure there were no cases of ambiguous wordings, a long period of time had elapsed. The British had become quite annoyed at the amount of time it was taking to conclude the agreement, and it had been necessary to compromise with them. I had already heard from Mr. Hensley of the United Press in Washington that the United States had asked Great Britain to report in secret to the United States government explaining these ambiguous clauses, so that if any questions arose concerning the agreement, the United States government could judge [the rights and wrongs of the situation]. The British fulfilled this request.

My other task had been to convince businessmen and industrialists to conduct trade with and establish industries in Thailand. Before the war trade between the United States and Thailand had been very limited, and trade in raw materials such as rubber had been carried out through London. There had been only one American company, and that of medium size (apart from the oil companies) in Thailand, whereas other nations had conducted a considerable amount of trade with us. We wanted Americans to start up industries and become more involved in the Thai economy, as this would enable Thailand to expand its commercial activities and industrialize without being exploited by less friendly countries. On 1 November 1945 Mr. Brackman of the United Press interviewed me about the Thai economy, indicating that Americans were starting to take an interest in [possible future] commercial opportunities in this field.

RELIEF AND REHABILITATION AFTER THE WAR

I had also been charged by the leader of the Free Thai movement in Thailand with trying to secure aid for the relief and rehabilitation of our country. To this end I contacted the UNRRA [United Nations Relief and Rehabilitation Organization] organization.

Not many days after my arrival in Washington, on 20 June 1945, the Thai Minister, M.R. Seni Pramoj, took me to meet Dr. Francis B. Sayre at the offices of UNRRA. Dr. Sayre had been an Advisor to the Thai Ministry of Foreign Affairs during the reign of King Rama VI. He had worked for Thailand devotedly [by helping it get rid of the extraterritorial treaties that had placed curbs on Thailand's independence], and had received the title Phraya Kalayanamaitri for his work.[27] When I went with M.R. Seni to visit him, he recognized me even though we had not met for twenty years. He shook hands with me and called me by my first name, Prasop. I was very glad to meet my friend who remembered me so well, and to find that he now happened to hold an important position in

UNRRA, namely as Diplomatic Advisor to UNRRA, as I felt that this would make my task much easier.

I told Phraya Kalayan of Thailand's desire to seek aid for relief and rehabilitation purposes from UNRRA. He informed me that Thailand was not in a category to which UNRRA could give aid, as Thailand was not one of those countries that had been destroyed by the enemy, but was a liberated country. Since Thailand had signed a treaty allying with the Japanese and had declared war on the United States, Great Britain and Australia, in order for it to receive aid a special decision would have to be come to by the combined board of UNRRA.

He explained that there were two categories of countries that were eligible to receive aid: firstly countries that did not have any foreign credits, such as Greece, which UNRRA would provide aid to free of charge, and secondly countries that had credits outside the country such as France, Holland and Belgium, which UNRRA would supply aid to at a charge. If Thailand was to receive aid, she would fall into this second category. Phraya Kalaya had also invited Mr. Ed Arnold, head of the Southeast Asia unit, to join our discussions, which were in the nature of preliminary talks. Mr. Arnold and I agreed to meet again. Phraya Kalayan, however, was about to leave for South Africa to undertake negotiations for India to receive coal. I said goodbye to him, and awaited his return.

Since Mr. Arnold was one of the members of the combined board of UNRRA, I asked him to put Thailand's request that it be accepted as a country to receive aid without charge before the board. He promised me that he would put forward this proposal. On 17 July he called a meeting in his office and told me to bring along lists and notes of what Thailand needed so that he could give this to the board. (The Thai underground had prepared such a list prior to my departure from Thailand; it filled a sizeable book).

After Dr. Sayre returned from his trip I went to see him again on 8 January 1946 and asked him about the decisions made by the UNRRA board. He promised to give me these. (Mr. Arnold had been transferred by this time).

On 11 January I went to see Phraya Kalayan as agreed upon. He informed me that at the meeting of the combined board in London, the United States had tried to propose aid for Thailand, but that the British had resisted the idea even before the proposal had been made, as they still regarded Thailand as an enemy nation. I asked Dr. Sayre what would be the best tactic for Thailand to follow. In other words should we continue to ask for aid, [seek to] join the organization [the United Nations], or not do anything at all, since it looked as if Thailand would be ineligible to receive aid? If we were to join the United Nations it would mean having to pay 1 percent of our national income to it. Phraya Kalayan did not give me an answer, but tended to favor our joining the United Nations.

In addition to the aid I had sought through UNRRA I also sought support from the Foreign Economic Administration, or FEA for short, asking to buy materials left over from the war. I contacted Colonel Reedall, the director of the organization, bringing with me a list of the materials we needed. We agreed that the materials should be stored in India so that they could be got hold of by Thailand as soon as possible after the Japanese left. I asked for his opinions as to the likelihood of our receiving aid from UNRRA. In a straightforward military manner he advised me that Thailand should try to help itself and buy the materials. I decided to check the prices and put in an order before other countries bought up the materials we needed.

Since our railway stocks had been destroyed during the bombing, I decided to concentrate on improving our railroad communications as soon as possible. I contacted the Baldwin Locomotive Company (Thailand had bought a large number of engines from this company). An official of the company devoted a whole day to taking me on a tour of the plant, which was in Chester [Pennsylvania.] I asked him about prices and the time it took to produce a train and found out that it would take too long for our immediate purposes. After I returned to Thailand, the government set up an organization in April 1946 with me as director the function of which was to obtain materials for relief and rehabilitation purposes. We ordered twenty train engines and six hundred freight cars from stocks the British had received from the United States on lend-lease to be used in India. Later on the organization was changed in structure and became like a regular trading company, with middlemen responsible for supplying government offices.

We also needed a variety of materials immediately for everyday living purposes, such as medical supplies and clothing. I tried to order these materials and looked into having them transported to us. However, nothing could be done without funds, and the United States' government was still withholding our frozen currency reserves. I contacted Mr. Moffat, the Chief of the Southeast Asian Division at the State Department, and asked him to try to help us over this. He guaranteed his help, as previously mentioned. [At this point, however], I received orders to return to Thailand, and arrived back in Bangkok on 31 January 1946.

In conclusion I should like to thank all the Americans who were so understanding and helpful towards Thailand during this critical period. I was also very pleased to see my fellow Thai in the United States at that time, all of whose names I cannot list here due to their great number. All, however, [whether mentioned by name or not], worked together for the good of our country.

Phra Phisansukhumwit,
Saladaeng House,
5 Silom Road, Bangkok.

Free Thai in the United States

1. Nai Prayun Athachinda
2. Nai Sombun Phongakson
3. Nai Chintamai Amatayakun
4. Nai Banchoet Phalangkun
5. Nai Udomsak Phasawanit
6. Nai Bunrot Binthasan
7. Nai Pradit Chiaosakun
8. Nai Sawat Chiaosakun
9. Nai Chaloem Chittinan
10. Miss Krongthong Chutima
11. Nai Sala Thotsanon
12. Nai Bunmak Thetsabut
13. Nai Chamrat Follet
14. Miss Phunsap Kraiyong
15. Nai Chuea Hunchamlong
16. Nai Malai Huwanan
17. Miss Ubon Khuwansen
18. Nai Phon Intharathat
19. Nai Ayut Itsarasena
20. Miss Inthra Intharathut
21. Nai Nithiphat Chalichan
22. M.L. Ekkachai Kamphu
23. Nai Rachan Kanchanawanit
24. Nai Somchit Kangsanon
25. Miss Chintana Nakwatchara
26. Nai Banthit Kantabut
27. Miss Prapha Tanphairot
28. Miss Saiyut Kengradomying
29. Nai Karun Kengradomying
30. Nai Ian Khamphanon
31. Nai Pao Kham-urai
32. Nai Sunthon Khanthalak
33. Nai Phunphoem Krairuek
34. Nai Charot Losuwan
35. Nai Bunyiam Misuk
36. Miss Amphon Chaiyaprani
37. Nai Anon Na Pomphet
38. Nai Bunyong Nikhrothan
39. Nai Sawat Nitiphon
40. Nai Kusa Panyarachun
41. Nai Phiset Pattaphong
42. Nai Worathep Phongphithak
43. Nai Amnuai Phunphiphat
44. Nai Chun Praphawiwat
45. Khun Prathumrokprahan
46. Nai Udom Phuphat
47. Nai Chalong Puengtrakun
48. Nai Khrui Bunyasing
49. Nai Chok Na Ranong
50. Nai Chanai Rueangsiri
51. Nai Samoechai Saiyasut
52. Nai Songsuk Sakhonbut
53. Nai Somphong Sanlayaphong
54. Nai Nirat Samatthaphan
55. Nai Bunyen Sasirat
56. Nai Sit Sawetsila
57. Nai Chun Silasuwan
58. Nai Anon Siwatthana
59. Nai Karawek Siwichan
60. Nai Phisut Suthat
61. Nai Renu Suwannasit
62. Nai Bunliang Tamthai
63. M.C. Yuthitsathian Svasti
64. Nai Chamrun Ditsayanan
65. M.R. Singkhatha Thongyai
66. Nai Charoen Watthanaphanit
67. Nai Wichian Waiwanon
68. M.C. Chettanakon Worawan
69. Nai Wimon Wiriyawit
70. M.L. Suchin Chumsaeng
71. Nai Anan Khittasangkha
72. Miss Chirawat Khittasangkha
73. Nai Kamchon Phonyothin
74. M.C. Chakraphanphensiri Chakraphan

75. Miss Phongchanthon Kengradomying
76. Mom Wipha Chakraphan
77. Nai Bian Bunyarak
78. Nai Praphai Thantharanon
79. Nai Wiphat Chutima
80. Nai Chan Charuwat
81. Miss Chanchaem Inthusophon
82. Nai Rueang Nimmanhemin
83. Nai Pluem Punnasiri
84. Nai Chinda Singhanet
85. Nai Somphon Bunyakhup
86. Nai Bunthom Waithayanuwat
87. Nai Tui Wutthikun

Note: This list was given to me by Professor Wichit Lulitanon, who was in charge of the financial affairs of the Free Thai movement during the war. He told me that this list had come from the Ministry of Foreign Affairs and had been sent from the Thai legation in Washington, D.C. to the Office of the Secretariat of the Council of Ministers. The Office of the Secretariat had sent it to the Minister of Finance, as Chairman of the Working Committee on Principles and Practices for Students and Government Officials Abroad according to formal letter number K. 6231/2489 dated 15 October 1946. The list of officials in the (United States) legation, according to Nai Anan Chintakanon, were:

1. M.R. Seni Pramoj, Minister.
2. Luang Ditthakanphakdi, Second Secretary.
3. Colonel M.L. Khap Kunchon, Military Attaché.
4. Nai Anan Chintakanon, Third Secretary.

D.[irek] J.[ayanama]

PART 3
AFTER THE WAR:
BETWEEN AUGUST 1945 AND JUNE 1948

10
Negotiations Between Thailand and Britain,[1] and Exchange Agreement Between Thailand and Australia

On 16 August 1945, two days after the Japanese surrendered to the Allies, the Regent, Nai Pridi Banomyong, issued a Peace Proclamation. This stated that the National Assembly had agreed that Thailand's declaration of war against the United States and Great Britain of 25 January 1942 was to be regarded as null and void, as it had been unconstitutional and contrary to the wishes of the Thai people. Thailand further sought to restore the friendly relations with the United Nations [the "democracies," or Allies] that had existed prior to the Japanese occupation of Thailand, and was willing to return to Great Britain and France the territories that had been transferred to Thailand by the Japanese. It would also consider repealing any laws that might be regarded as prejudicial to the United States, Great Britain or the British Commonwealth, and promised to pay a just price for any damages that might have resulted from the application of such laws. Lastly, Thailand promised to cooperate to the best of its ability with the United Nations to help maintain world stability.

A few days later Nai Khuang Aphaiwong, the Prime Minister, resigned so that a post-war government could be set up. Those present at the meeting [to discuss who should be the new Prime Minister] were Nai Pridi Banomyong, the Chairman; Nai Thawi Bunyaket; Police General Adun Adundetcharat; Captain Luang Suphachalasai; Lieutenant General Chit Mansin Sinatyotharak; Rear Admiral Sangwon Suwanchip and myself.

This committee decided that M.R. Seni Pramoj, the leader of the Free Thai movement in the United States, was the most fitting person to fill the role, as it seemed inappropriate for someone within the country to take the position.[2] While awaiting M.R. Seni's return we agreed, however, that it was necessary to form an interim caretaker government, particularly now that Allied troops had begun moving into the country.[3] The committee therefore asked the King's permission[4] to appoint Nai Thawi Bunyaket as interim Prime Minister. Nai Thawi accepted the position even though it was only to be for a short time, and was appointed Prime Minister of Thailand by the King[5] on 1 September 1945. He retained this position until 17 September 1945, when M.R. Seni Pramoj took over as Prime Minister.

CHAPTER 10

Members of the governments set up under the leadership of Nai Thawi Bunyaket and M.R. Seni Pramoj respectively were as follows:

COUNCIL OF MINISTERS OF NAI THAWI BUNYAKET[6]
(1 September 1945–17 September 1945)

Nai Thawi Bunyaket	Prime Minister
Nai Direk Jayanama	Minister of Finance
Nai Thawi Bunyaket	Minister of Foreign Affairs
Lieutenant General Chit Mansin Sinatyotharak	Minister of Defense
Rear Admiral Sangwon Suwanchip	Deputy Minister of Defense
Air Force Lieutenant General Luang Thewaritphanluek	Deputy Minister of Defense
Nai Thawi Bunyaket	Minister of Agriculture
Nai Thawi Bunyaket	Minister of Public Health
Nai Prachuap Bunnag	Deputy Minister of Public Health
Nai Saphrang Thephatsadin Na Ayutthaya	Minister of Industry
Nai Saphrang Thephatsadin Na Ayutthaya	Minister of Communications
Nai Direk Jayanama	Minister of Justice
(Naval) Captain Luang Suphachalasai	Minister of Commerce
Nai Duean Bunnag	Deputy Minister of Commerce
(Naval) Captain Luang Suphachalasai	Minister of the Interior
Police General Adun Adundetcharat	Deputy Minister of the Interior
Nai Thawi Bunyaket	Minister of Education
Nai Thawi Tawethikun	Minister without portfolio
Nai Wichit Lulitanon	Minister without portfolio
Phraya Atthakariniphon	Minister without portfolio
Phra Tironasanwitsawakam	Minister without portfolio
Nai Thong-in Phuriphat	Minister without portfolio
Nai Tiang Sirikhan	Minister without portfolio
Nai Thawin Udon	Minister without portfolio
Nai Phueng Sichan	Minister without portfolio
Nai Thong Kanthatham	Minister without portfolio
Nai Sanguan Tularak	Minister without portfolio
Luang Bannakonkowit	Minister without portfolio
Nai Chamlong Daorueang	Minister without portfolio
Nai Wutthi Suwannarak	Minister without portfolio

After only seventeen days in office the members of this Council of Ministers resigned, and a new Council of Ministers under M.R. Seni Pramoj was set up.

THE COUNCIL OF MINISTERS OF M.R. SENI PRAMOJ[7]
(17 September 1945–31 January 1946)

M.R. Seni Pramoj	Prime Minister
Police General Adun Adundetcharat	Deputy Prime Minister and Minister of Public Health
Lieutenant General Chit Mansin Sinatyotharak	Minister of Defense
Nai Direk Jayanama	Minister of Finance
M.R. Seni Pramoj	Minister of Foreign Affairs
Phraya Atthakariniphon	Minister of Agriculture
M.L. Udomsanitwong	Minister of Commerce and Industry
Nai Saphrang Thephatsadin Na Ayutthaya	Minister of Communications
Nai Thawi Bunyaket	Minister of the Interior
Phraya Nonlaratsuwat	Minister of Justice
Phra Tironasanwitsawakam	Minister of Education
Nai Prachuap Bunnag	Deputy Minister of Public Health
Nai Thawi Tawethikun	Minister without portfolio
Nai Sanguan Tularak	Minister without portfolio
Nai Wichit Lulitanon	Minister without portfolio
Nai Tiang Sirikhan	Minister without portfolio
Nai Thong Kanthatham	Minister without portfolio
Nai Phueng Sichan	Minister without portfolio
Nai Chamlong Daorueang	Minister without portfolio
Nai Charun Suepsaeng	Minister without portfolio
Phra Sutthiatnaruemon	Minister without portfolio
Chao Worathat Na Lamphun	Minister without portfolio
Nai Chit Wetprasit	Minister without portfolio

On 14 October 1945 Lieutenant General Chit Mansin Sinatyotharak resigned and Lieutenant General Chira Wichitsongkhram took over the position of Minister of Defense, while two more Ministers without portfolio were announced. They were Nai Thong-in Phuriphat and Nai Thawin Udon. This Council of Ministers was in office for three months and fourteen days.

The most immediate problems facing the governments of Thawi Bunyaket and M.R. Seni Pramoj were to adjust and improve Thailand's relations with Britain and France, and to negotiate with the Chinese.[8]

Thailand's chief difficulty lay in the adjustment of its relations with the British and French. As far as its relations with the United States were concerned, they remained cordial both within and outside the country (see also part 2, chapter 5 [now chapter 9]), for the United States did not consider Thailand an enemy country even though we had declared war on America. Right from the time we had declared war on Britain, however, it had regarded Thailand as its enemy, even though we had cooperated with the British throughout the war.[9] Britain pointed out that it had suffered considerable damages during the war [as a result of Thai actions], and that Thailand had seized certain territories that had formerly belonged to the British. Britain undoubtedly wanted to revenge itself on Thailand and teach it a lesson, as can be seen in the following account of our negotiations with that country.

FOREIGN AFFAIRS

As has already been mentioned, a few days after the Japanese surrender, the Regent, [Nai Pridi Banomyong], issued a Peace Proclamation. In the United States Mr. James Byrnes, the United States Secretary of State[10] announced on 21 August 1945 that M.R. Seni Pramoj, the Thai Minister Plenipotentiary to the United States, had brought the Regent's proclamation of August 16 before him. This had stated that Thailand's declaration of war against the United States of 25 January 1942 was to be considered void since it was unconstitutional and had been carried out against the wishes of the Thai people. The Thai government had also announced its desire to maintain the friendly relations it had formerly enjoyed with the United Nations prior to the occupation of Thailand by the Japanese. It further promised to consider repealing any laws that might be prejudicial to United States' interests, and had guaranteed to pay fair compensation for any damages resulting from the application of such laws. Furthermore Thailand had promised to cooperate with the United Nations to the best of its ability in helping to maintain world unity and peace. [Byrnes stated that] this action on the part of the Thai government [i.e. the issuing of such a declaration] was a welcome step in American-Thai relations.

The Japanese had occupied Thailand at the same time they attacked Pearl Harbor, [Byrnes continued]. Several weeks later Thailand had declared war [on the United States and Britain]. By that time the Thai government had, however, fallen fully under the control of the Japanese. The American government had always believed that the declaration of war was not the wish of the Thai people. For this reason it had never accepted the declaration of war, but had continued to recognize the Thai Minister Plenipotentiary to Washington, M.R. Seni Pramoj, as representing the Thai government, and had not accorded recognition to the Japanese-controlled government of Thailand in Bangkok.

After the Japanese seized control of Thailand, the Thai Minister in Washington had immediately organized a Free Thai movement among Thai living outside their country, and from that time on this group had helped the Allies greatly by working for the Allied cause. Not long after the Japanese occupied Thailand a group of people within the country who were opposed to the occupying regime had also emerged. The American and British governments had given considerable aid to and had received equally substantial cooperation from this group in its activities against the Japanese. Lately, [i.e. towards the end of the war], the United States had been in constant contact with this resistance group working for the independence of Thailand. For many months the group had been prepared to rise against the Japanese, but had been asked by the United States and British governments for strategic reasons to postpone carrying out a *coup*. It was solely because of this [express request on the part of the Allies] that there had not been a rising by the resistance movement in Thailand. The surrender of the Japanese had meantime rendered any such uprising unnecessary.

Prior to the war [Byrnes continued], Thailand and the United States had enjoyed a long history of close and friendly relations. The United States hoped that these friendly relations would become even closer in the future. Over the past four years America had viewed Thailand not as an enemy nation, but rather as a country to be liberated from the enemy. Now that it was free from enemy control, the United States would like to see Thailand resume its former place in the community of nations as a free, sovereign and independent country.[11]

Meanwhile in England, on 19 August 1945, Mr. Ernest Bevin, the British Foreign Secretary, announced that the British government acknowledged the help it had received from the Thai resistance movement, and would consider the Thai Peace Proclamation carefully to see if it included grounds for reconsidering the wrongful position that Thailand would normally be deemed to have placed itself in. By having allied itself with the Japanese Thailand had, however, created numerous problems that would first need to be settled, and these would have to be gone over by the British government. The attitude of the British would depend on the extent to which the Thai cooperated with the British forces now in Thailand, on its willingness to correct the faults of the [Phibun Songkhram] regime, on its agreement to pay compensation for the damage, destruction and hindrance caused by that regime to the interests of the British and the Allies, and on how far it assisted and cooperated in restoring peace and economic well-being in Southeast Asia.[12]

From the time that the Thai government issued its Peace Proclamation, and even before the United States and Great Britain had issued any statements [regarding our post-war treatment], we had been trying in every way to gain sympathy from both powers to ensure that Thailand maintained its independence. [To demonstrate our willingness to cooperate we had,] for example, provided immediate help to Allied prisoners-of-war who had been interned by the Japanese, and covered their food, clothing and medical expenses free of charge in accordance with the demands of Allied officers. In addition we had provided all facilities necessary for disarming and controlling the Japanese troops in Thailand.

The following month, that is to say in September 1945, the representative of the British forces in Thailand told the Regent to inform the Thai government that Thailand was to send delegates to negotiate and sign a military treaty with the British government. To protect the dignity of our nation, the Thai government was to announce that it was sending representatives to Kandy, Ceylon[13] to negotiate on various matters of its own accord. The Thai government agreed to this, and on 4 September 1945 sent representatives to carry out detailed negotiations on military matters, including the question of the Japanese surrender and the disarming of Japanese troops. This delegation consisted of General Luang Senanarong, Deputy Commander of the Army, as head of the delegation; First Lieutenant Chaloemsak Chuthaphong, a close friend of the head of the delegation; Nai Thawi Tawethikun, Director of the Political Department of the Ministry of Foreign Affairs; Rear Admiral Chaem Patchusanon, Deputy Chief of Staff of the Navy; Colonel Surachit Charuserani, Deputy Commander of the Army; Wing Commander Thawi Chulasap, representative from Air Force Command; and Major Puey Ungphakorn, as both delegate and secretary.

[At the meeting that ensued], the British put forward the following twenty-one proposals, namely that Thailand:

1. Abolish all military, para-military and political organizations conducting propaganda hostile to the United Nations [i.e. the Allies].
2. Hand over to the Allied authorities all United Nations' ships lying in [Thai] ports.
3. Do everything possible to relieve the distress of all Allied prisoners-of-war and internees, and provide them, free of charge, with adequate food, clothing, medical services and transportation in consultation with the Allied authorities.
4. Take responsibility for protecting, maintaining and repairing all Allied properties.
5. Cooperate with the Allied authorities in:-
    a. Disarming the Japanese in Thailand and handing them over to the Allies.

b. Confiscating and surrendering to the Allied authorities all Japanese war materiél including warships and freighters, aircraft, arms, ammunition, motor and other vehicles, and other military stores including aviation and other fuels, clothing, radio accessories, and any other properties of the Japanese troops.
6. [Agree] not to trade with enemies of the Allies.
7. Seize and submit to the Allies all properties of the Japanese (and other enemies).
8. Cooperate in charging and investigating persons accused of having been war criminals or of having afforded active assistance to Japan or of having been open enemies of the Allies.
9. Hand over to the Allies all deserters of Allied nationality.
10. Maintain and be ready to place at the disposal of Allied officers Thailand's naval, military and air forces, together with the use of its ports, airfields, communication routes, equipment, construction materials, arms and other stores as might be required from time to time for accommodation and storage purposes by Allied officers arriving to disarm the Japanese.
11. Provide the use of its ports and traffic facilities to Allied officers as demanded.
12. Arrange in accordance with the wishes of the Allied military authorities press and other censorship and control over radio and telecommunication installations or other forms of intercommunication.
13. Continue its civil administration subject to the requirements of Allied officers in the pursuance of their tasks.
14. [Agree that] in case of need for facilities in recruiting and employing local labor for the utilization in Thai territory of industrial and transport enterprises and of means of communication, [all] power stations, public utilities and other facilities, stocks of fuel or other material [must be made] available according to the requirements of the Allied authorities.
15. [Agree that] Thai freighters, whether in home or foreign waters, be subject to Allied control for use as required by the Allies.
16. [Agree to] the setting up of a military mission to be appointed by the appropriate military authority to act as consultants on the organization, training and equipping of the Thai armed forces.
17. [Agree] not to export rice, tin, rubber and teak for a period of time. The Allied authorities felt such a prohibition to be necessary because of present economic circumstances.[14] Exception might be made only at the direction of a committee of Allied representatives or similar authority that might [later] replace this committee.

18. [Note that] while the world was still in need of rice, the Combined Boards[15] or other authority acting on behalf of the Allies had determined that Thailand must increase its rice production. The resulting surpluses were to be made available to the Allied Rice Committee[16] at prices to be agreed upon by this said committee and based on the controlled price of rice in other Asian countries.
19. [Agree with] the Allied Rice Committee on the details necessary to bring about the above requirement in the most effective manner. These details were to be included in the appendices to this treaty, and were to provide for the following, namely that:-
    a. The Allies would take whatever measures might be required for the fulfillment of these obligations until the Thai government was itself, in the opinion of the Allies, in a position to ensure this; and for
    b. The continued cooperation thereafter of the Thai government with the Allied Rice Committee in order that obligations already incurred continued to be administered.
20. [Agree that] Thai monetary policy (together with the rate of exchange) be fixed according to the advice of Allied representatives, with a view to facilitating the production of the greatest possible yield of rice and other necessary food commodities, and to avoid economic problems.
21. Report as soon as possible and carry out the actions requested in the attached appendices.

Appendix A

Procedures that must be followed in order to guarantee the production of the required amount of rice yield for export:
1. Owners must declare how much milled and unmilled rice they had in their possession.
2. The amount of surplus rice in Thailand must then be estimated.
3. Such surplus rice was to be put aside, or if necessary, requisitioned.
4. This surplus rice was to be sold to the Allied Rice Committee according to Article 18 of the treaty. The price for this was not to exceed the price of rice set up in Burma.
5. Milled and unmilled rice was not to be exported except at the orders of Allied officers.
6. Export taxes on milled and unmilled rice were not to be collected except by permission of officers of the Allied Rice Committee.
7. The planting of rice was to be encouraged as much as possible.

8. All rice mills were to be licensed and the price of rice controlled and not to exceed the established price.
9. Rice mills were to be restored in every possible way including using machinery from ruined rice mills to repair those in better condition in order to ensure that there would be enough rice mills in operation.
10. Transportation adequate for the quantity of rice yield was to be provided to take the rice from the fields to the mills and from the mills to the ports.
11. Port facilities were to be repaired as soon as possible.
12. The distribution of food supplies was to be controlled in such a way as to persuade as many people as possible to go into agricultural production.
13. The controls set out above were to be in effect until the rice shortage should have come to an end.

Appendix B

An appendix B dealt with control over the news media that the Thai government must undertake. Details of this particular appendix are not given here, but their purport was that Thailand was to allow the British control over all communications in the country.

Readers can see that if all of these twenty-one proposals had been put into effect, it would have amounted to controls being placed over all of Thailand's political, military and economic affairs. Take, for example, proposal number 1 regarding the abolishing of all military organizations, or proposal number 8 concerning joining the Allies in charging war criminals. Application of these clauses would have meant that the Allies (read the British)[17] would have had a controlling hand in [Thailand's internal affairs.] Or take proposal number 13; by this the governing of the country would have been regulated in accordance with the requirement of the Allies (the British). Proposal number 16 would have placed Allied representatives in charge of the organization and equipping of Thai troops, while proposal number 17 would have placed controls over the export of Thai rice, tin, rubber and teak. Proposal number 18 involved handing over rice to the Allies, and proposal number 20 would have placed controls over Thailand's monetary and fiscal policies.

Our representatives did not sign the treaty, for they had been authorized to agree only to military arrangements. A number of the representatives were instead sent back to Thailand to confer with the Thai government.[18] A meeting was called [to consider the stipulations of the treaty], but the government was unable to reach a decision and put the matter before the National Assembly. Meanwhile the Thai delegates who were still in Ceylon and the Regent, Nai

Pridi Banomyong, immediately contacted United States' representatives[19] complaining that despite the full cooperation that Thailand had given [the Allies], they [i.e. the British] were putting pressure on Thailand as if it was not an independent country. It then came out that the United States had not in fact been consulted [by the British] over the situation. Meanwhile the National Assembly, on hearing that the Thai representatives [in Kandy] were having pressure placed on them to sign the treaty, reluctantly agreed to have them do so, but directed that the representatives should record that they had been forced to sign under pressure from the British and not of their own free will.[20] Fortunately for Thailand, the United States government immediately raised strong objections to Britain's actions. It claimed that since the proposals had been put forward in the name of the Allies, the United States government should have been consulted about them. At the same time United States representatives told us to postpone signing the agreement, as the United States government was in the process of raising objections to the British government. In the end the treaty (the "Twenty-one Proposals") was never signed.[21] In fact the United States government had cause to feel considerably annoyed with the British government, since prior to the end of the war Mr. Cordell Hull, then the United States Secretary of State,[22] had reported to the British government that the United States did not think of Thailand as an enemy even though the government of Thailand had declared war on America on 25 January 1942. The United States had not declared war in return because it had felt that the government in Bangkok was under the control of the Japanese and did not represent the real desires and wishes of the Thai people. The United States had therefore continued to accept the Thai Minister Plenipotentiary in Washington, D.C., (M.R. Seni Pramoj), as the representative of Thailand.

The United States wanted to see Thailand an independent country. However, [Mr. Hull had continued], the British government still thought of Thailand as an enemy nation that needed to work its passage to independence. Mr. Eden, the British Foreign Secretary, had promised the United States that the British wanted to see Thailand independent, but did not want to declare this publicly, as it had a direct bearing on the security of Britain. They also wanted to have Thailand promise not to dig a canal across the Kra Isthmus. As to territories that Thailand had acquired from the French through Japanese mediation, [the United States felt] that these should be returned by Thailand, but that Thailand should not lose the right to conduct negotiations later for a revision of this situation. Finally, [Mr. Hull reported], President Roosevelt had sent word to United States' ambassadors in London, Paris and The Hague stating that the United States expected to be consulted on all arrangements concerning the future of Southeast Asia, including Thailand.

[Mr. Hull went on to state that] when he left office, United States' policy in regard to Thailand was that Thailand should be an independent democratic country with a government that represented the free will of the people. The United States did not blame the Thai government [for its actions] during the war, and sympathized with the Free Thai movement that had started here (in Washington D.C.), and then sprung up in other countries. However, the United States did not want to be committed politically to this movement, as the United States wished to see the people of Thailand choose their own government.[23]

In the end the [Thai] representatives [at Kandy] signed only the following military proposals, namely that Thailand would do whatever possible to help in relieving the distress of prisoners-of-war and internees and would pay all expenses for their food; that it would cooperate with the Allied forces in disarming the Japanese, interning Japanese and German nationals and in seizing and submitting to the Allies all war materials and other belongings of the Japanese; and that it would make its naval, land and air forces available for the use of the Allied military authorities. This agreement would not affect the status of either Allied government's relations with Thailand in any way, nor would it counteract any other agreements that each individual Allied nation might make with Thailand.

As has already been mentioned, Nai Thawi Bunyaket held the position of Prime Minister temporarily from 1 September until 17 September 1945, at which time M. R. Seni Pramoj returned from the United States. Nai Thawi Bunyaket then resigned, and on 17 September 1945 the King[24] appointed M.R. Seni Pramoj Prime Minister and Minister of Foreign Affairs. I remained on as Minister of Finance during the M.R. Seni Pramoj government. This lasted until 31 January 1946, when the government resigned in accordance with the constitution following a general election.[25]

During the government of M.R. Seni Pramoj the two major issues that were settled with the Allies were the negotiating of an agreement with the British,[26] and the drawing up of a treaty of friendship between Thailand and China.[27]

NEGOTIATIONS LEADING TO THE SIGNING OF THE FORMAL AGREEMENT [WITH BRITAIN]

M.R. Seni Pramoj had only been Prime Minister and Minister of Foreign Affairs for five days when, on 22 September 1945, he received a request from the British to send a further group of representatives to Kandy, Ceylon to negotiate with the British regarding the re-establishment of normal relations between Great Britain and Thailand. The Thai government agreed to this request and sent a delegation led by M.C. Wiwatthanachai Chaiyan,[28] Advisor to the Office of the President of the Council of Ministers and to the Ministry of Finance, and including Lieutenant General Phraya Aphaisongkhram,[29] Nai Soem Winitchaiyakun,[30] Major-General M.C. Chitchanok Kridakon,[31] Commander M.C. Uthaichaloemlap Wutthichai,[32] Nai Konthi Suphamongkhon,[33] Major Puey Ungphakorn[34] and Nai Prayat Buranasiri.[35]

On 25 September 1945 the Thai representatives were presented with an outline of the agreement to be considered. It turned out that these [new] proposals would have placed an even heavier burden and inconvenienced Thailand even more greatly than the "Twenty-one Proposals" described earlier. Thailand was asked, for example, to provide one and a half million tons of rice free of charge—an amount that would have been worth at least 2,500 million Baht at the time. Further we were not only to provide for Allied prisoners-of-war, but to compensate for damage and destruction caused to [Allied] property.

When our representatives reported back to the government they were told to request changes to many of the proposals. The British agreed to forward our objections to the British government for its consideration. Particularly important to us was the issue of the one and a half million tons of rice that were being demanded. Thailand was already run down [i.e. it had been weakened by the war], and therefore asked Britain to reduce its demands. Our representatives reported that negotiations over the matter proceeded very slowly, but that if we agreed to the amount of rice which the British were demanding, agreement might be possible on certain other proposals we also wished to see changed. The government of M.R. Seni Pramoj put the matter before the National Assembly to seek its approval one way or the other. It was to be understood that the one and a half million tons of rice would include the 240,000 tons which we had already said right after the end of the war that we would give away free of charge.[36] The National Assembly agreed in principle, provided that Thailand received satisfaction over the other changes it had asked for. The negotiations still did not make any headway, however, and our representatives therefore returned to Bangkok.

In early December 1945 the British issued a new notice requesting the Thai government to send representatives to Singapore.[37] We agreed to do so, and on 9 December 1945 our representatives (the same group that had gone to Ceylon) left Bangkok for Singapore. One day before their departure, Mr. Bird,[38] the British Foreign Office representative who was attached to the Allied military forces in Bangkok, brought a letter from Mr. Dening, [Chief Political Advisor to Lord Louis Mountbatten], to M.R. Seni Pramoj, the Prime Minister and Minister of Foreign Affairs. The letter essentially stated that the British were still not satisfied about the extent of the help that Thailand had given to the anti-Japanese movement, as they felt this had been insufficient to help the Allies effectively during the war. The British admitted that Thailand had demonstrated its willingness to fight the Japanese in May 1945. However, the Supreme Commander, [Lord Louis Mountbatten], had felt that the Thai had neither sufficient training nor the arms to have been able to have carried this out without the aid of the Allies. Thailand should therefore be grateful to the Allies for having defeated the Japanese before any actual fighting took place in Thailand, for the Thai had thereby been spared the sufferings of war. The British also felt that Thailand had been dragging out the current negotiations until Mr. Dening had to leave for Java,[39] even though the latter had already told the Thai representatives in Kandy that the proposals put forward there might be changed in form but not in substance, nor as to their essential requirements. Thailand must agree to give up one and a half million tons of rice, and it was to give this freely and without any conditions attached. Furthermore it must provide this amount of rice immediately. If it did not do so those countries that were in need of rice might be very critical of Thailand when they learned what had accounted for the shortages. Britain had already proved extremely merciful towards Thailand. It had not imposed peace terms on the country, but had on the contrary been generous towards us, for example by helping arrange for the return of King Rama VIII to Thailand.[40]

On 11 December 1945 Prince Wiwatthanachai Chaiyan, the leader of the Thai delegation, reported to the Thai government that at the opening meeting [in Singapore] that day the British representative, Mr. Dening, had stated in a preaching manner that the reason the meeting had had to be called at all was because Thailand had declared war on Britain. The British recognized that Thailand had acted favorably [i.e. had helped the Allied cause] through the Free Thai movement, but felt that the sacrifices this had entailed had been insufficient [to outweigh the consequences of having declared war on Britain.] The new proposals that had been put forward could not therefore be changed. The demands they entailed were the minimum conditions [Britain would accept as a basis for ending the state of war between Britain and Thailand] and were not negotiable. The British government was ready to end the state of war existing between Thailand and Great Britain right away. This being so, was the government of Thailand ready to have its representatives sign their names to the treaty?

Prince Wiwatthanachai Chaiyan, the leader of the delegation, returned to Bangkok on 12 December to report on the situation. The Council of Ministers met the following day to consider the pros and cons of the matter and concluded it would be best to sign the treaty. It had already sought and received the approval of the National Assembly to negotiate on the latter's behalf, but now, with the negotiations in their final form, even though the government had the right to act in the name of the National Assembly, the Council of Ministers chose to make an announcement to both Houses, stating that the proposals put forward by the British were the minimum Britain would accept, and that the government would report again to the National Assembly on the matter at a later date.

On 15 December 1945 Prince Wiwatthanachai Chaiyan returned to Singapore and presented his report to the British representative that same day. Meanwhile, however, the Regent, [Nai Pridi Banomyong], invited the American representative in Thailand, [Mr. Charles Yost, the United States Political Advisor in Thailand][41] to see him and outlined the situation to him in order that the latter might report back to the United States on the matter immediately.

That same day Mr. Yost met with M.R. Seni Pramoj, the Prime Minister and Minister of Foreign Affairs, and told him that when the United States government had heard of the harsh treatment Thailand was receiving at British hands, it had complained to the British government, asking it to reduce the demands it had laid down in the treaty. The United States government had moreover asked that the British government not sign any treaty until the United States government was satisfied [with its terms.] The British government had promised to consider America's request and to reply to the United States government before the end of December 1945. As to the British government's urging Thailand to sign the treaty right away,[42] Mr. Yost said that the United States government had already raised objections about this with London. He therefore recommended that the Thai government send word to its representatives in Singapore immediately telling them not to sign the treaty, promising that if Thailand's pleading for time should lead the British to push for yet harsher terms, the United States government would take responsibility for the situation.[43] M.R. Seni Pramoj put the issue before the Council of Ministers, which straightway agreed to send word to its representatives in Singapore telling them not to sign the treaty.[44] Meanwhile all the newspapers in the United States came out with articles accusing Great Britain of oppressing Thailand.

As was expected, on 20 December 1945 Prince Wiwatthanachai Chaiyan returned [from Singapore] and reported to the Council of Ministers that he had met with the British representative, Mr. Dening, who had asked for the reply from Bangkok. Prince Wiwat had answered that since it was understood that the demands put forward were the minimum the British would accept, and that they were not subject to further negotiation, the Thai government must reluctantly accept the proposals, except for those issues that required legislative action, which must wait until the next meeting of the National Assembly. Mr. Dening said that in addition to the Heads of Agreement and Annex, Thailand would have to sign another agreement, to be known as the Formal Agreement, which the British Foreign Office was in process of drawing up. Prince Wiwatthanachai Chaiyan reported that he had asked what this might include, but that Mr. Dening had only said he was not sure yet, but suspected it would consist either of a document containing the Heads of Agreement already settled on, but in the form of an agreement, or would spell out the details of implementation of the agreement.

The Council of Ministers told Prince Wiwatthanachai Chaiyan that if this Formal Agreement was only the treaty in a new form, then the Thai delegation could conduct negotiations thereon; but that if it contained additional topics, then the representatives would have to return to Bangkok to consult with members of the National Assembly.

During the negotiations that took place between Prince Wiwat's return to Singapore [on 15 December] and 20 December our representatives only agreed to sign the proposals in due course. In the end, however, the Heads of Agreement and Annex were never ratified. Instead it was decided that an exchange of letters concerning the Heads of Agreement and Annex would take place, and that these letters would be exchanged on the same day that the representatives signed the Formal Agreement. The governments concerned would publicly announce the signing of the Formal Agreement, but not the exchange of letters concerning the Heads of Agreement and Annex.

Meantime the Thai government asked its representatives to remind the British to send a draft of the Formal Agreement so that the Thai government could examine it. However, it was told that the text of the agreement would not be forthcoming until the end of January 1946, and that now it probably would not be signed together with the Heads of Agreement and Annex.

On 21 December 1945 the Council of Ministers held a meeting with Prince Wiwatthanachai Chaiyan, the leader of the Thai delegation, at which it was agreed that Thailand could sign the Heads of Agreement before the Formal Agreement, and further that it would not insist on the inclusion of the phrase "the minimum requirement"[45] in the exchange of letters. The British did not want to have this phrase included, and refused to sign the treaty unless it was withdrawn. Thailand did not therefore insist on this, lest its inclusion should also render the United States government, which was now involved in the situation and was working to get the British to reduce their demands, dissatisfied with Thailand.[46]

On 24 December 1945 Mr. Yost, the United States Political Advisor, met with M.R. Seni Pramoj, the Prime Minister, to explain about the changes [in the terms of the treaty] that the United States had asked the British to make, and to let him know that Britain had agreed to ease its demands. The United States was satisfied with the modifications that had now been effected, and was therefore withdrawing its [former] words advising Thailand not to sign the treaty. As to the rice situation, a mixed body that would include some Americans among its members was to be set up to estimate the amount of rice which Thailand was to provide. Yost also stated that a committee would be established to estimate the damage caused to the Allies [by Thailand's cooperation with Japan during the war], and to fix the amount to be paid in compensation. It had been agreed that this should not exceed a sum that Thailand was capable of paying. This promise was a welcome guarantee for us.

On 26 December 1945 the Thai government sent a telegram to Prince Wiwatthanachai Chaiyan telling him to ask Mr. Dening why a copy of the text of the Formal Agreement had not been received from London, as this had been quite slow in coming. Prince Wiwat replied the following day that the reason for the delay was that the British Foreign Office thought the Formal Agreement could not be signed until the Thai National Assembly had called a meeting to discuss the matter. Prince Wiwat had explained that there was no need to wait on any such meeting, and the British representative had therefore asked the British government to send a draft of the Formal Agreement by telegram immediately.

During the negotiations in Singapore, the British had arranged for representatives from India and the Commonwealth of Australia to join in the negotiations with Thailand. In regard to India, it had been agreed that India would be a partner to whatever agreement the British might make with Thailand, or in other words, that in ending the existing state of war [between Britain and Thailand] the government of Thailand need not negotiate with India separately from Great Britain. As far as Australia was concerned, the Australian and Thai representatives would exchange agreements whereby the Thai would first undertake to fulfill certain obligations, and later negotiate to end the state of war existing between the two countries. These agreements were to be exchanged on the same day that the agreement with Great Britain and India was signed.

Finally, on 1 January 1946 the Thai representatives received permission from the Thai government to sign the treaty with the British representative in Singapore. It was entitled the Formal Agreement for the Termination of the State of War between Thailand and Great Britain and India,[47] and contained twenty-four articles. On the same day, before the signing of the Formal Agreement, the Thai representative exchanged letters with the British representative acknowledging receipt from the British of a copy of the Heads of Agreement and Annex setting out all the terms under which the United Kingdom and India were prepared to end the state of war with Thailand. Thailand was to reply as to whether the Thai government was ready to sign these provisions one at a time or altogether. Pending the signing of this agreement, the Thai government was to undertake to act in accordance with all the provisions thereof. This the Thai representatives agreed to do.

The British never ceased to point out how light the demands made on us under the Formal Agreement were. To us Thai, however, they seemed quite burdensome—as who should know best but ourselves. However, we hoped that the terms of the agreement might be altered in the future, and in fact this hope became a reality, as will be described in part 3, chapters 6 and 8.

The essential provisions of the Formal Agreement were as follows:[48]

1. Restoration of the *status quo ante bellum*.
2. Thailand declared void any actions that it had carried out against the British following the Japanese occupation. The *status quo ante bellum* would be restored and compensation paid for damages to British properties.
3. Thailand would take responsibility for safeguarding and restoring unimpaired British property, rights and interests in Thailand.
4. Thailand agreed that the war with Japan had demonstrated the importance of Thailand to the defense of Malaya, Burma, India and Indochina as well as the security of the Indian Ocean, and would, therefore, cooperate fully in international security arrangements to be made by the United Nations or its Security Council [regarding these countries or areas].
5. Thailand would not dig a canal across Thai territory to connect the Indian Ocean with the Gulf of Thailand (i.e. [across] the Kra Isthmus) without the consent of the United Kingdom.
6. Until a date not later than 1 September 1947 the Thai government agreed that, except at the recommendation of the Combined Boards in Washington, D.C. or any other committee that might come to replace this body, and in the case of rice except at the express order of a special organization to be set up for the purpose, it would not export rice, tin, rubber or teak. Thailand would regulate trade in and stimulate the production of these goods.
7. Thailand was to give, free of charge, one and a half million tons of rice to an organization to be specified by the government of the United Kingdom.[49] (At the time the price [of rice] was £28 sterling per ton, with 60 Baht/£1 sterling. The amount [of rice demanded was therefore] equivalent to 2,520 million Baht).
8. Until a date not later than 1 September 1947 Thailand would arrange to make available to the aforesaid rice organization all of her rice over and above that required for domestic purposes. The price to be paid for this rice would be fixed by the organization.
9. Thailand would arrange with the governments of Great Britain and India for the upkeep of war graves.
10. On the basis of the obligations that Thailand had undertaken in this agreement, the governments of Great Britain and India would support Thailand as a candidate for membership in the United Nations.

The essential issues in the Heads of Agreement[50] that the British sent to the Thai representatives and which were agreed upon [in principle] were similar to those in the Formal Agreement but were much more detailed. As a condition of agreeing to terminate the state of war between us, it was stated that the governments of the United Kingdom and India would expect that Thailand adhere to the following procedures:[51]

    a. **Measures of Repudiation.**

These were to include repudiating the declaration of war of 25 January 1945; repudiating the military alliance with the Japanese; and recognizing as null and void all acquisitions of British territory [made after 7 December 1941].

    b. **Measures of Restitution and Readjustment.**

These were to include the repealing of all laws and administrative measures regarding the purported annexation or incorporation into Thailand of British territories [carried out after 7 December 1941]; withdrawing all [Thai] military and civilian officials from these territories; returning all properties that were taken from the jurisdiction of the British and paying compensation for destruction or damage to the property, rights and interests in these areas resulting from the occupation of the Thai government; redeeming in sterling out of sterling reserves all Thai currency in these areas; and relieving and caring for all prisoners-of-war and internees in Thailand and in the said territories.

    c. **Measures for Post-war Strategic Co-operation.**

Thailand was to recognize that the war had demonstrated the importance of Thailand to the defense of Malaya, Burma, India and Indochina and the security of the Indian Ocean and the southwestern Pacific region, and to agree to cooperate fully in all international security arrangements that the United Nations or its Security Council might approve [relating to this region]. Further, Thailand was to undertake not to dig a canal connecting the Indian Ocean with the Gulf of Thailand [the Kra Isthmus] without the consent of the British.

    d. **Measures for Post-war Economic Cooperation.**

Details of this were similar to articles 8-15 of the Formal Agreement.

    e. **Regularization of Thailand's Position in regard to the Treaties with Britain.**[52]

The Annex that was submitted by the British on the day of the signing of the Formal Agreement contained the following essential points, namely that Thailand would agree to:

1. Take responsibility for safeguarding and returning in undamaged condition all property, rights and interests of the British[53] in Thailand and pay compensation for losses and damages sustained.
2. Desequestrate Allied commercial and banking concerns and allow them to resume business.
3. Hold all Japanese and other enemy property for the use of the Allies.
4. Cooperate in arresting and trying persons charged as war criminals or as having actively aided the Japanese.
5. Submit all alleged deserters of Allied nationality to the Allied military authorities.
6. Grant judicial immunity and certain other privileges to the Allied forces in Thailand [for the time being.] These privileges were to include the use of Thai ports, free traffic facilities within and over Thailand, free supplies and the use of all Thai currency that might be required by the Allied military authorities, together with additional privileges.
7. To grant control of banks and businesses, foreign exchange and commercial and financial transactions as required by the Allies for so long as might be necessary for the conclusion of matters related to military, economic and financial concern to the Allies arising out of the settlement of the war with Japan.

On the day that [the Formal Agreement] was signed, the Council of Ministers agreed to have the Prime Minister and Minister of Foreign Affairs, M.R. Seni Pramoj, publish an announcement. This communiqué, put out by the Office of the Prime Minister on 1 January 1946, stated that since the time that the Thai government had declared war on Great Britain, Britain had regarded the two nations as being at war with one another. The usual procedure adopted to terminate a state of war between two countries was for the victor to demand that the defeated power sign a peace treaty, and only when such a peace treaty had been signed was the state of war considered brought to an end. Thailand had fallen into such a situation, but since the Thai people, both within and outside the country had organized a resistance movement directed against the enemies of the Allies, and since it had shown a desire to join the United Nations, and the government responsible for bringing about the state of war had already fallen, Great Britain had generously decided on a new procedure. Instead of insisting on the conclusion of a peace treaty, it had only asked that Thailand agree to certain requirements concerning the return of various properties damaged during the war, and that it cooperate in arrangements for bringing about economic rehabilitation and ensuring international security in order to prevent war arising again in the future.

The terms which Great Britain required Thailand to accept had been agreed upon and signed by representatives of both nations in Singapore on 1 January 1946, and now that this agreement had been signed the state of war between them was considered ended. The relations that had existed between the two countries in the past and which had been disrupted were now restored.

Whatever legal measures might have to be taken in order to comply with the terms of the agreement would be submitted to the National Assembly as soon as possible. In regard to the agreement between Thailand and Great Britain, it was hoped that Great Britain would insist on Thailand carrying out only those requirements that were deemed essential, and that Britain would show understanding over the application of the agreement. England had already shown its goodwill by offering to help Thailand financially so that Thailand could rehabilitate its economy rapidly. Furthermore Great Britain had agreed that now that the state of war between the two nations was regarded as over, it would act to resume friendly relations with Thailand immediately and arrange to exchange diplomatic representatives. Britain had also undertaken to support Thailand as a candidate for membership in the United Nations. Such actions, [the communiqué concluded], were evidence of Britain's goodwill towards Thailand now and in the future.[54]

The question still remains why, when Thailand had tried its utmost to help Britain during the war, the British had still showed themselves determined to deal harshly with Thailand. If we read the book written during the war by Sir Josiah Crosby, the [former] British Minister to Thailand, we may be able to see, however, the reasoning that lay behind their policy. It is true that the [former] Minister's opinion was not an official one, and that the book reflects only his point of view, but it could be taken nevertheless as representing [the British viewpoint.]

Sir Josiah stressed that the geographical position of Thailand was of great importance to the military strategy of the British Commonwealth during the years 1940 and 1941. Thailand's western boundary bordered on Burma, its southern frontier bordered on Malaya, and its northern border adjoined the Shan states. Thailand was therefore a good location for those hostile to Great Britain to establish their forces in. The flying time from Bangkok to Malaya and Burma was only a few hours, while Singapore stood as the key to the Indian Ocean.[55]

The reasons advanced by Thailand in an official communiqué for its declaration of war on the British were of "an amazingly puerile and disingenuous nature," the former Minister wrote. Since the Japanese were using Bangkok and other cities in Thailand as bases from which to attack the British, the Thai should not have been surprised when the British in turn bombed the Japanese in Thailand, nor that bombings cannot always be on target. Field Marshal Phibun Songkhram had announced that the British bombings constituted a violation of international law. Furthermore, on declaring war on the British he had also claimed that the latter had sought to control Thailand financially through its rice, rubber, tin and teak trade. This was not true, [Sir Josiah Crosby continued]. The British had never interfered in these matters.[56]

[The former British Minister to Bangkok went on to say that] the Thai government had made a bad start. It had made a world-wide announcement stating it would fight aggression to the extent of carrying out a scorched earth policy against any power seeking to invade Thailand, in order to deny advantage to the enemy, and had even told its people to destroy all railways and electrical plants if necessary. Yet only a few hours after returning from the east [i.e. from eastern Thailand, where he had been inspecting the border while Thai troops had been battling the Japanese], Field Marshal Phibun Songkhram had ordered that Thailand [end its resistance and] surrender to the Japan. Nor had that been all; Field Marshal Phibun Songkhram had further agreed, without raising any objections, to allow the Japanese to intern all British, American and Dutch nationals, and had immediately signed an agreement to fight on the side of Japan, later declaring war on Great Britain and the United States.[57]

Sir Josiah [went on to say that he] sympathized with the fact that Thailand had been placed in a difficult position, and recognized that had Thailand continued to fight, it probably would have been taken over and disarmed, and that there would have been [further] bloodshed. It would be unjust to expect Thailand to have fought to the last man, and it should not be blamed for having surrendered to the Japanese. However, the [former] Minister wrote, he did blame Thailand for having sworn it would fight to the last man, and then having surrendered. It would have been better not to have boasted.[58] Thailand was to be criticized not for having surrendered to the Japanese but for having cooperated with them at the end.

It was his hope, the [former] Minister continued, that after the war Thailand would attain self-government and enjoy true democracy. He felt that the United Nations should help Thailand so that it would be free in the true sense of the word without mistaking chauvinism for patriotism. Thailand's post-war position would also have to be looked at from the standpoint of the military security and economic stability[59] [of this part of the world.]

After reading Sir Josiah Crosby's book it is easy to understand how the British could have later submitted the "Twenty-one Proposals" described earlier.

CHAPTER 10

EXCHANGE AGREEMENT BETWEEN THAILAND AND AUSTRALIA

On the same day that the Thai delegation signed the Formal Agreement with the United Kingdom in Singapore on 1 January 1946, it also signed an agreement with representatives of the Australian government leading to the termination of the state of war existing between our two nations. The essential issues covered under this agreement were that the Thai government would do whatever possible to completely repudiate its declaration of war with Great Britain, its alliance with Japan, and any other measures that might be detrimental to Great Britain, Australia and the Allies. The Thai government would draw up a treaty with Australia when called upon to do so, and in the meantime would take responsibility for maintaining in good condition Australian war graves in Thailand, and would comply with the directions of the Australian government regarding the well-being and interests of Australian residents detained or interned in our country. Thailand would also cooperate fully in capturing and charging those who since 8 December 1941 had been guilty of war crimes against the Australians; it would agree to pay compensation to the government and people of Australia for destruction and damage to [Australian] property caused since 8 December 1941; it would cooperate in measures of regional, political and economic cooperation consistent with the principles of the United Nations set up to ensure security in southeast Asia and the southwest Pacific, and it would abide by the terms of the Formal Agreement made with Great Britain and India.

On the same day the Council of Ministers agreed to have the Office of the Prime Minister issue a communiqué [concerning the agreement with Australia]. This stated that since the Thai government of that time had declared war on Great Britain, Australia, which was a member of the British Commonwealth, had declared war on Thailand in return. A [preliminary] agreement to terminate the state of war between Thailand and Australia had now been reached. The Thai government had undertaken to carry out the obligations agreed upon and would conclude a [final] treaty to terminate the state of war [between the two nations] in the near future.[60]

11
Relations Between Thailand and China

I have already discussed the subject of our relations with China to some extent in part 1, chapter 3, where I dealt with the recognition of the Wang Ching-wei regime by the Thai government. As far as China wanting to see a treaty [formally delineating the status and legal rights of the Chinese in Thailand] drawn up with us is concerned, the Thai government had declined to do this for many decades on the grounds that Thailand had always treated the Chinese members of its population as if they were Thai, in some ways granting them even greater privileges than those accorded the Thai themselves, as will be described later. After the war, however, the Chinese government (of Field Marshal Chiang Kai-shek) insisted that a treaty [defining the legal status of Chinese in Thailand] be drawn up with us, and the Thai government was forced to agree to this. Before discussing the terms of this treaty, however, I would first like to mention a little about the history of relations between Thailand and China. According to statistical sources, right after World War II there were about seven hundred thousand Chinese in Thailand[1] out of a total population of sixteen million people. However, I suspect that this figure should be revised, being somewhat too low, and that there were probably about one million Chinese in Thailand at that time, representing a considerable proportion of the total population.

History shows that when the Thai first moved into the Golden Peninsula[2] about seven hundred years ago, the Chinese followed close behind them. It further reveals that the Thai economy has been in the hands of the Chinese ever since. The Thai should not be held to blame for this. Patterns of ancient Thai administration denied Thai the opportunity to trade, as we shall see when we turn later to discuss the *phrai som*.[3]

If we read works on Thai history written by Europeans at different periods of time, we will find that most of them mention the very large number of Chinese in Thailand as compared with other foreign nationals. John Crawfurd, the British diplomat who arrived in 1821 to open up relations [between England and Thailand], wrote that most of the Chinese who came to Thailand were from Kwangtung and Fukien, but that there were also a considerable number from the island of Hainan and some from Chekiang and Kiangnan.[4] Some also came from Yunnan, but these had usually migrated by way of northern Laos. The Chinese immigrants usually came without their families, later married Thai wives, and became Buddhists regardless of their previous religious affiliations. They made merit at temples, and some even joined the monkhood in keeping with Thai custom. Despite this they still kept their traditional style of dress.

As far as their status in Thailand was concerned, they were treated as relatives and as if they were Thai in every way. They were entitled to trade and own land, for example, yet were exempt from the draft. Despite these privileges, during the reigns of Kings Rama VI [1910–1925] and Rama VII [1925–1935], the Chinese frequently asked that a treaty be drawn up [formalizing their position]. They did not succeed in these requests, as the Thai felt such an agreement to be unnecessary given that the Chinese in Thailand already enjoyed full rights. Prior to the promulgation of the law on citizenship,[5] Chinese settlers whose wives and children were Chinese could remain Chinese if they wished without any complications beyond that of their grandchildren being regarded as Thai. It would seem that in fact most of the Thai of Chinese descent loved the country of their adoption and were proud of being Thai. If we study the history of our country, we will find that in fact the Chinese received more extensive privileges than the Thai themselves. The only period when limitations were placed on Chinese rights was during World War II, when we had to do this for reasons which will be discussed later and which concerned the conduct of the war. Actions such as these are within the rights of any sovereign nation. Admittedly the actions [taken against the Chinese during the war] may have gone too far and have been unnecessarily severe. However, later [i.e. after the war], when conditions returned to their previous state, the rights of the Chinese in Thailand were restored to them.

In former times, from the reign of King Trailokanat[6] onwards, Thai freemen, that is those who were not nobles, monks, Brahmins or slaves, were obliged to register and place themselves under the power of a patron once they reached the age of eighteen. They were then referred to as *phrai som*.[7] Once a *phrai som* reached the age of twenty, his patron had to register his client's name in a roll book with an official registrar. The latter would then in turn assign those *phrai som* to live with certain nobles. The men thus assigned were known as *phrai luang*,[8] and remained *phrai luang* until they reached sixty years of age. La Loubère, a French diplomat who came to Thailand during the reign of King Narai [1657–1688] recorded that the *phrai luang* had to provide their services free of charge for six months of the year, and that in addition, while working, they had to provide their own food.[9]

During the Chakri dynasty King Rama IV [1851–1868] reduced the time of such service to three months. King Rama V [1868–1910], recognizing the practice of having to work without pay to be cruel and unjust, abolished the system. All Thai are grateful to him for this. It should be noted that the Chinese were exempt from this *corvée* system—a system that lasted for four hundred years. They therefore had the opportunity to go into commerce, and it is therefore hardly surprising that some of them became very wealthy. The Thai meanwhile had no opportunity to engage in trade. Thai freemen had to serve their patrons; monks had to follow the way of the Lord Buddha; Brahmans had various ceremonial functions; while slaves were the slaves of their masters all their lives. It was King Chulalongkorn who saw that true Buddhists cannot take a man and make him a slave as one might treat an animal. He recognized that this went against the rights of man, and abolished the system despite the opposition of those who benefited from it. As has already been mentioned, Chinese who came to live in Thailand received many privileges from the Thai. Seventy to eighty years ago they enjoyed even greater rights than the Thai themselves, not to mention receiving ample opportunities to carry on trade and commerce within our country. Sir John Bowring, the British emissary who negotiated a treaty with us in 1855, noted that in 1850 the Chinese controlled almost all trade in the provincial areas of Thailand, and that wherever boats could reach, even in the interior of the country, the Chinese transported goods and bartered them for other products.[10] It seems that the Thai never tried to compete with the Chinese in trade. W. A. Graham wrote with regard to the Chinese in Thai history that because the Chinese never had a formal treaty with Thailand, Chinese merchants were able to travel freely throughout the country, as they were treated like Thai.[11]

Another important factor besides the fact that most Thai were not in a position to work for themselves routinely and were not therefore in a position to compete with the Chinese, was that the Chinese succeeded in securing certain trade monopolies. Originally these monopolies were controlled by the king, but during the reign of King Rama III [1824–1851] they were gradually replaced by a system of tax farming which became dominated by the Chinese.[12]

Luang Wichitwathakan has pointed out that while tax collection directly affected the livelihood of the Thai people, the Thai government was concerned as to how best to go about it, as knowledge of tax collection systems was not widespread at the time. [By farming out tax collection to the Chinese] the government did not have to be concerned about what items should be taxed, as the Chinese tax collectors then decided on this. They surveyed the livelihood of the people, reported to the king on what items could be taxed, and appointed themselves tax collectors.[13] Once they had been granted the title of tax collector or tax farmer, they had the same rights as any citizen to travel throughout the country, and enjoyed many privileges. Tax collectors, their families and their assistants were exempted from all *corvée* or other labor requirements—a privilege that gave them tremendous power. Many people would try to place themselves under the patronage of such individuals, for then they also would be exempted from such demands. As an added benefit, tax collectors and their retainers were entitled to settle disputes among their men.[14]

Dr. Purcell of Cambridge University has stated that from 1840 on, increasing numbers of Chinese came into Thailand every year. Even though no treaty was drawn up between Thailand and China, and China had no diplomatic or consular officers in Thailand, there was no danger of the foreigners in Thailand's midst joining together to overthrow the Thai government. Most of the Chinese who came to Thailand did not bring their wives and children with them but rather married Thai women. Within three generations their descendants had become Thai, and were proud to be so.

In the early part of the twentieth century a sense of nationalism began to develop in both China and Thailand. In 1909 the Chinese government[15] passed the Chinese Nationality Act.[16] This was based on the principle of descent (*jus sanguinis*), and stated that offspring of a Chinese father were Chinese no matter where they were born. Once this law was passed, it created difficulties for children born in Thailand of Chinese parents. They now came to hold dual citizenship, for Thai law was based on *jus soli*, whereby those born in Thailand were Thai. Not long after, in 1912, the government of the Republic of China [established following the overthrow of the Ch'ing/Manchu dynasty in 1911] passed an electoral law setting aside six out of the two hundred and seventy-six seats in the Chinese House of Representatives to be elected by overseas Chinese. Moreover Chinese who came to Thailand after 1910 [1911?—Ed.], the year of the revolution[17] led by Dr. Sun Yat-sen, started bringing their wives and children with them, further intensifying the growing sense of nationalism [among the Chinese.][18]

This new policy on the part of the Chinese government made the Thai government of that time, that is to say of the reign of King Rama VI, reflect on its attitude [towards the Chinese population in its midst.] Until then the Thai had never treated the Chinese as foreigners. Indeed, many Thai officials were of Chinese descent. The Thai government had instead always sought the assimilation of the Chinese. The Thai had shown great generosity in enabling the Chinese to earn a living and take up land in Thailand, and had even let them send money to their relatives in China, never clamping down on this practice. They wished to see the Chinese marry Thai, and to have their descendants become Thai and attend Thai schools. This [desire to assimilate those of different ethnic backgrounds into the main body of the population] has been the policy of all sovereign nations that seek the progress and stability of their country.

EDUCATION

Prior to the reign of King Rama VI, the establishment of schools in Thailand was not subject to any kind of legal supervision or control. In 1919, however, the government passed the Private Schools Act. This stated that all who wished to set up schools, whether they were Thai or foreigners, must register with the Ministry of Education. Thai teachers must attain certain academic standards set by the Ministry, while all foreign teachers were to learn Thai, and Thai was to be taught at least three hours a week in foreign schools. The objective of the Thai government of the time was to solidify its control over all schools and make sure that they conformed to regulations, as is the way in many other countries. Foreign schools affected by the new regulations included Catholic and missionary schools. Although no exceptions were made for schools of any nationality, the Chinese were very bitter [at the passage of this legislation, believing it to have been directed specifically against them].

In 1921 the government passed a Compulsory Education Act which required all children between the ages of seven and fourteen to attend primary school for at least four years. The school attended might be public or private, but if the latter, then that school had to follow the curriculum established by the Ministry of Education and use text books chosen by the Ministry. In fact these regulations were never fully enforced, even in Bangkok. Nonetheless, during the reign of King Rama VII the government felt its control over foreign schools was too loose, and decided to tighten up its enforcement of the laws. Teachers who did not know Thai were forbidden to teach at all. At that time most Chinese schools imported teachers from China. Once the government started enforcing the laws more rigidly, many teachers lost their jobs because they did not know any Thai. Many Chinese schools had to close down in consequence, which created great bitterness. The Chinese demanded to know why the Thai government felt obliged to intervene in [Chinese] educational affairs. The reason, as has been explained already, was that it has always been the policy of the Thai government to press for the assimilation of those of Chinese descent. If one was to become a Thai, learn to love Thailand and understand the Thai way of life then it was necessary that one first know the Thai language and become familiar with Thai culture and ways.

In 1932 there was a change of government [in Thailand whereby absolute rule was replaced by a constitutional monarchy].[19] The new ruling group issued a six-point educational policy statement listing the improvement of education as one of its main aims, as education of the people was essential if Thailand was to progress. It had decided to start with the improvement of primary education, using as its basis the law [on compulsory education] passed earlier during the reign of King Rama VI [i.e. the 1921 Act.] The regulations set out therein would be maintained and strengthened, and its provisions would be supervised closely both in Bangkok and throughout the rural areas. The Ministry of Education would now start sending out inspectors to check whether private schools had been adhering to the regulations. Leaders of the Chinese community petitioned the government for the right to devote more teaching hours to the study of Chinese than Thai, and for greater leniency regarding the requirements placed on Chinese teachers. The government in turn insisted that if the regulations were changed, the status of education in Thailand would remain at a standstill. Statistics show that despite government insistence the number of Chinese schools nevertheless continued to increase every year.[20]

SENDING REMITTANCE MONEY OUT OF THE COUNTRY

Before the end of World War II the Thai government never supervised or placed controls over the sending of money out of the country. It transpired that the Chinese in Thailand had been sending money out of the country for hundreds of years. Through a procedure known as *phoi kuan* Chinese in Thailand who wanted to send money to their relatives or friends in China would go to an agent who would handle this for them. Remittance agencies existed all over Bangkok and throughout the main cities [of Thailand.] The sender would entrust the agent with the money and give him a note to his relative or friend saying that he was sending such and such a sum of money, and would receive a receipt for this. The remittance bureau would in turn send the letter to the specified person and the money to its branch in China, usually in Hong Kong dollars or Chinese banknotes, in turn charging for this service. Sometimes the agent would convert the Baht received into rice and then export the money to China in that form. There are no statistics of the actual sum [of remittance monies sent by the Chinese community in Thailand to China], but it was estimated around fifty years ago that some 26 million Baht had been sent [out of the country in this way.][21] (At that time the national budget amounted to about 70 million Baht.) Mr. Doll,[22] the [British] Financial Advisor,[23] reported in 1930 [1936?—Ed.][24] that the amount of money sent by the Chinese through *phoi kuan* was approximately 20 million Baht a year.[25]

DURING WORLD WAR II

It has to be admitted that there were certain groups of Chinese in Thailand that cooperated with the Japanese during the war, but only because they sought to avoid being ill-treated at Japanese hands. The Thai government protested on many occasions against the unjust treatment of the Chinese by the Japanese, as the Thai government considered the Chinese members of its population to be subject to Thai not Japanese law. During the war the Chinese suffered a number of hardships. In January 1943 the government of Luang Phibun Songkhram forbade aliens from living in certain provinces. This law was enacted for the safety of the Thai people [i.e. for military security reasons]. The provinces affected were Chiang Mai, Lamphun, Lampang, Chiang Rai, Phrae and Uttaradit.[26] As a result many Chinese who lived in these areas found themselves in a difficult position and had to move to other provinces. The government was also harsh in giving the Chinese only a very short time in which to move. In addition certain occupations were reserved for Thai only, as for example those of barber, nielloware craftsman and taxi-driver.[27] Such restrictions were carried out only because they were deemed necessary. Other countries such as England acted similarly but even more harshly [towards aliens among its population].

AFTER WORLD WAR II

A few days after the war ended, that is to say during the early part of September 1945, the Chinese, regarding themselves as among the victorious powers, started raising the Chinese flag in front of their stores, especially along Yaowarat Road.[28] However, they did not raise the Thai flag simultaneously as was required by law. The police asked the Chinese to follow the regulations, but they refused to do so. On 21 September, four days after M.R. Seni Pramoj became Prime Minister and Minister of Foreign Affairs, and while police and army inspectors were on duty, a shot was fired from a building on Yaowarat Road. Police and soldiers fired back. The government ordered the roads in the area closed, and a committee consisting of both Chinese and Thai was set up to restore law and order. Investigations revealed that the act was committed by certain Chinese, angry because they considered China to be one of the victorious powers, while at the same time they felt they had been oppressed by the Thai during the war and believed it was now their turn to show their power. The Thai, for their part, felt that the Chinese should not have behaved this way towards their host country, and that the Thai flag should have been raised in accordance with the law. Moreover it was by no means certain that Thailand would be treated as an enemy nation given the views that had been expressed on the subject by the United States and Great Britain.²⁹ [China, however, did not share these views.] Eight days later, on 29 September 1945, a Chungking newspaper, the *Ta Kung Pao*, demanded that Thailand officially surrender and that it should bring those who had cooperated with the Japanese during the war, including [former] Prime Minister Phibun Songkhram, before a court and try them as war criminals.

That same month the Chinese government sent Mr. Li Tieh-cheng,³⁰ the former Chinese Ambassador to Iran, to negotiate a treaty with M.R. Seni Pramoj, the Prime Minister, in the latter's concurrent capacity as Foreign Minister. M.R. Seni indicated to Mr. Li Tieh-cheng that actually a treaty between our two countries was not necessary, as the Chinese in Thailand were already well treated. They were treated at least as well as the nationals of [other] countries that had drawn up formal treaties with Thailand, and indeed as well as even the Thai themselves. However, Mr. Li stated that he had received orders from the Chinese government insisting [that such a treaty be drawn up.] The Thai government was therefore forced to agree to conduct negotiations on the subject.³¹

Chen Su-ching,³² writing from Kunming, stated that Thailand's guilt was too clear to be overlooked. While Thailand might retain its territorial rights, it should not be allowed to continue in the same way as it had been free to do before the Japanese invasion. "In other words" [he continued], "after the war some sort of external guidance is necessary not only in her foreign conduct but also in her internal affairs, for at least a certain length of time." As far as China's relations with Thailand were concerned, it would seem only reasonable that first of all Thailand should abolish all restrictions or discrimination aimed solely or mainly at the Chinese, and that the rights that the Chinese had enjoyed at least during the period before 1930 should be restored to them. Any wrongs that had been done to the Chinese as a result of restrictions or discrimination should be redressed. "It is needless to add," [the writer continued], "that those who have been responsible for these acts should be severely punished, for their guilt is no less than that of war criminals in Germany or Japan." Furthermore Thailand should not be allowed to refuse to exchange diplomatic representatives with China any longer. During the time Thailand was under the control of Japan, Thailand was compelled to accept the diplomatic representatives of the Wang Ching-wei government.³³ Now that the war was over, Thailand had no grounds for refusing to accept diplomatic representatives [from the Chiang Kai-shek government]. Finally, every Chinese should be left free to choose his or her own citizenship regardless of whether or not they were born in Thailand, and the Chinese in Thailand should have a voice in its political system so that at least their economic and other interests could be protected.³⁴

In the end, the government of M.R. Seni Pramoj signed a Treaty of Amity between the Kingdom of Thailand and the Republic of China[35] in Bangkok on 23 January 1946. It consisted of ten articles stating that the undersigned would exchange diplomats and have the right to set up consulates in one another's countries. Members of the partner countries might travel in and out of one another's countries under the same conditions as the nationals of any other country. Nationals of the partner countries were to be accorded full protection and security of their persons and property in one another's countries. There was to be parity of treatment for nationals of the partner countries living in the territory of the other country as regards legal proceedings and the levying of taxes. Both parties had the right to set up schools for the education of their children, and finally, both countries were entitled to end the agreement after ten years if notice of such a decision was given twelve months in advance.

In addition, on the same day [that the Treaty of Amity was signed], to show goodwill on the part of Thailand, the Minister of Foreign Affairs, M.R. Seni Pramoj, made the following announcement:

1. In regard to the right to reside and to carry on all kinds of occupations as stated in article 6 of the treaty, the Chinese had the right to engage in trade and industry and might establish residence in any part of Thailand under the same conditions as any other nationals.
2. In relation to the establishment of schools outlined in article 6, these schools would receive equal treatment to those set up by other nationals. In the primary schools, which were compulsory, all children had to learn Thai. It was the wish of the government to set aside a number of hours for teaching foreign languages in certain schools. The government did not seek to limit the teaching of foreign languages at secondary school level.
3. In regard to entry into the country, the [Thai] government would like to see the quota system followed. This would be based on the size of the population of the country [of the would-be immigrant.]
4. The charge for entry into the country would be a fee, not a tax.
5. The government would not test the level of education or standard of literacy of those seeking to enter the country.

After the signing of the treaty, Chinese schools began to spring up throughout Thailand to an extent that had never been the case before. For example, in Chiang Rai, where before the war there was only one Chinese school, four more schools were established in different districts in that area in the year 1946 alone. In 1945–46 students in most Chinese schools in rural areas were taught only in Chinese, contrary to the law on private schools. In November 1946, Mr. Li Tieh-cheng, the Chinese Ambassador who had signed the treaty, announced a plan to cater to the anticipated expansion of Chinese education and to organize [Chinese] schools in Thailand by placing them under the control of the Embassy's Cultural Officer. The Thai government protested against this, pointing out that all schools must follow the regulations laid down in the law on private schools. Many Chinese schools refused to follow these rules and protested through the Chinese embassy. Some shops even closed down and refused to open for business [as a protest measure]. In time, however, [this circumventing of the law by the Chinese community] came to an end.[36]

12
Thailand's Financial Situation

I have already mentioned that I was Minister of Finance in two successive Cabinets, namely those of Nai Thawi Bunyaket, who was in office from 1 September to 17 September 1945 and of M.R. Seni Pramoj, Prime Minister from 17 September 1945 to 31 January 1946. I was thus in the Ministry of Finance for altogether five months counting both periods together.

I had not in fact wanted to serve in the Ministry of Finance, as I had not had previous experience in this field.[1] However, when the matter was discussed it was decided that under the circumstances I should be placed in charge of our financial affairs. I took over at a critical time, when the British were keeping a sharp watch on us, and were in the process of putting forward the "Twenty-one Proposals" mentioned previously that included a proposal to control our monetary policy. As to the handling of foreign affairs, this was taken over by M.R. Seni Pramoj, the Prime Minister.

The first day I took office at the Ministry of Finance, I had a chance to meet with M.C. Wiwatthanachai Chaiyan,[2] the advisor to the Ministry of Finance at that time. I asked him to prepare a report on the condition of the treasury and our financial affairs in general so that I could report on the situation to the Cabinet. He made a special effort to gather material on our financial situation right away, and to present this accurately and clearly. I would like to thank him here very much for having done this. The report showed clearly that our financial affairs right after the war were in the worst state they had ever been. Even though this report was printed in the cremation volume Wiwatthanachai Chaiyan Anuson published in 1961, I consider it to be of such educational value that I am reprinting it again in full below. M.C. Wiwatthanachai Chaiyan said he was sorry that the picture he had to present was not a pretty one, but he believed it was, however, a true one.

CHAPTER 12

THE PRESENT CONDITION OF THE TREASURY

Preface

Our present financial situation is in the most critical state it has ever been. We can summarize the situation by saying that government revenue has not been sufficient for many years. The budget for this year is not balanced. We have many debts that must be paid off this year or next year. The value of our currency is gradually depreciating, and the efficiency and rectitude of our government officials are declining.

All of the above mentioned factors are interrelated. As long as the budget is not balanced and government expenditures are greater than its revenue, we must continue to borrow or print banknotes. This in turn produces further inflation while at the same time increasing our debts. At the same time, as long as the value of our currency continues to depreciate, it is impossible to balance the budget, yet expenses continue to increase.

The following facts and figures reveal the situation in detail:

Revenue and Expenditure, 1937–1944

Figures for revenue and expenditures for the years 1937–1944 are as follows:

Year of Budget	Revenue Baht	Expenditure Baht	Budget deficit or surplus Baht
1937	109,412,310	125,940.867	- 16,528,557
1938	118,351,387	132,913,013	- 14,561,676
April–September 1939	59,611,536	74,198,340	- 14,586,804
October 1939–September 1940	146,478,068	161,480,147	- 15,002,079
October 1940–December 1940	37,180,468	28,319,181	+ 8,761,287
1941	161,064,608	198,411,870	- 37,347,262
1942	142,154,471	198,711,420	- 56,556,949
1943	176,733,761	249,055,953	- 72,322,192
1944	267,413,378	363,731,217	- 96,317,839

Initially the budget deficit was paid from money left over from previous years which had been banked in the Treasury and from money held in reserve and set aside to pay off debts—that is, from moneys set aside between 1927 and 1931 to pay off all international debts before the due date. Once the money in both these categories had been used up, the budget deficit was met through public loans on the Bank of Thailand.

Two public loans were raised to cover expenses:

a) The National Assistance Loan, 1940	3,287,860 Baht principal 2% interest
b) The National Loan (gold bonds) [of 1942]	30,000,000 Baht principal 3% interest
Total	33,287,860 Baht

These loans from the Bank of Thailand were in the form of Treasury bonds. Under the law concerning emergency funds, when the bank received these bonds, it would credit the Ministry of Finance with the amount received from them. When the Treasury withdrew the money, and the bank needed more cash, the bank then transferred the bonds from the banking department to the bond-issuing department and distributed banknotes in exchange for these bonds. Thus the issuing of the bonds was essentially the same as issuing banknotes for the government, resulting in inflation.

On 31 December 1944 there were 167,900,000 Baht worth of bonds outstanding scheduled to be paid back in 1945 and 1946.

Revenue and Expenditure, 1945

In budget estimates for 1945 it was predicted that expenditure would exceed revenue by 138,370,155 Baht during the course of the year. In fact during the first six months of the year actual expenditures exceeded actual revenue by only 26 million Baht. However, it was expected that if expenditures were not greatly reduced immediately, expenditures for the year would still exceed revenue greatly—even by as much as had been predicted. The 1945 budget was drawn up without taking into consideration the fact that the value of our currency was depreciating. Some ministries used up their entire annual budget within a few months [of the start of the year], while others had already incurred expenses in excess of their budget allocations.

The budget deficit for 1945 was being paid through a loan from the Bank of Thailand raised by issuing Treasury bonds in the way already described, or through loans from other banks in the form of "Treasury notes." The Ministry of Finance had been considering raising yet an additional public loan when the war came to an end, the Cabinet resigned, and the matter was set aside.

Public Debt

We have three types of public debt. They consist of old debts in sterling that have not been paid off; debts resulting from the budgetary deficits already described; and debts incurred for special projects such as the establishment of cooperatives.[3]

International loans not paid off as of 30 June 1945 comprise the following:

	Principal (sterling)	Interest (sterling)
Loan of 3,000,000 sterling, 1907 A.D.	886,200-0-0	144,690-6-0
Loan of 4,630,000 sterling, 1909 A.D.	1,950,388-9-2	367,107-6-2
Loan of 2,340,000 sterling, 1936 A.D.	2,086,600-0-0	1,140,671-1-0
	4,923,188-9-2	1,652,468-13-2

Debts resulting from budgetary deficits not paid off as of 30 June 1945 are as follows:

Public loans	National Assistance Loan, 1940, to be paid in 1950	3,119,360 Baht
	National Loan, 1942, to be paid in 1951	30,000,000 Baht
Floating loans	Treasury bonds to be paid in 1945–1946	202,500,000 Baht
	"Treasury notes" (four months old)	10,000,000 Baht
		245,619,630 Baht

Loans for special undertakings not paid off as of 30 June 1945 comprise:

Loans to co-operatives	1940	19,199,900 Baht
Municipal loans	1940	16,954,800 Baht
Industrial loans	1940	19,236,000 Baht
Loans to cooperatives	1942	5,800,000 Baht
Industrial loans	1942	18,000,000 Baht
		79,190,700 Baht

In this type of loan, principal and interest are to be paid by the cooperatives, municipalities, corporations or organizations that have borrowed from the Treasury. However, if these groups cannot come up with the money [to pay off the loans], then the Treasury must raise the necessary money to reimburse the bond-holders.

Currency Rate

Inflation can be measured against the level of prices, cost of goods and cost of living. Statistics are only available through December 1944, but they are as follows:

Date	Wholesale prices	Cost of living index	
		Ministry of Commerce	Japanese Chamber of Commerce
December 1942	111	133	206
December 1943	152	219	332
December 1944	214	362	905
December 1941 = 100			

Conclusion

The restoration of normal conditions upon which our future national prosperity can be based depends upon the value of our currency. In other words, our currency situation must be stabilized if trade and business are to be able to develop steadily. If the value of our currency keeps depreciating, we cannot even administer the country effectively.

Three reasons underlie the unstable currency situation. They are, in decreasing order of importance, first, the costs of having had to pay for the expenses of the Japanese military forces; next the government budgetary deficits, and lastly the exchange rate between Baht and Yen.

The first and last points relate to issues that have been described already and which will not last very long.[4] However, the second point, concerning excessive expenditures, is a matter which the government must correct.

Written at the Advisory Office,
Ministry of Finance,
15 September 1945

CHAPTER 12

THE PRESENT FINANCIAL SITUATION

Preface

Our present financial situation is in the most critical state it has ever been. We can summarize this situation by saying that the value of our currency keeps depreciating. The reasons for this are three, listed in decreasing order of importance, namely the cost of having had to pay the expenses of the Japanese military forces; the governmental budget deficit, and the exchange rates between Baht and Yen.

The issue of excessive expenditure on the part of the government has already been outlined both in facts and figures in "The Present Condition of the Treasury." This section will therefore provide facts and figures on the costs of the Japanese military forces, the exchange rates of Baht and Yen, and the present currency situation in our country.

Costs of the Japanese Military Forces

Based on the regulations concerning relations with the Japanese, the [Thai] government agreed in principle to pay for the military expenses of the Japanese forces in Thailand. The amount of money involved was agreed for each individual six month period. The procedure followed for each half year was as follows: the Japanese government would credit the account of the Bank of Thailand with [money from] the Bank of Japan. The Bank of Thailand would then in turn credit the account of the Yokohama Specie Bank in Bangkok with the same amount. When the Yokohama Specie Bank withdrew the money and cash in the Bank of Thailand thereby decreased, the banking department of the Bank of Thailand then transferred Yen to the issuing department and distributed banknotes in exchange for the Yen.

The money which the Bank of Thailand credited to the account of the Yokohama Specie Bank for the expenses of the Japanese military from December 1941 to June 1945 amounted to a total of 1,230,701,083 Baht. Meanwhile the Japanese government allowed the Yen credits in the Bank of Thailand which had been received in exchange to be used to buy gold. The figures as of 30 June 1945 are as follows:

Baht credited for the Japanese army	Yen credit received (excluding amount used to buy gold)	Gold bought	
		Amount Grams (pure)	Price Yen
1,230,701,083	1,106,699,988	25,838,433.8	124,001,095

This arrangement to make money available for the Japanese troops forced the bank's credit to expand. The amount of banknotes in circulation also increased, as normally happens in this situation. When the money (both in the form of credit and in the form of banknotes) increased but goods and services did not increase proportionately, the value of our money went down, or to put it in other words, the price of goods went up [and inflation resulted.]

Rate of Exchange of Baht and Yen

In April 1942 the Thai government was obliged to devalue the Baht by about 36 percent in order to equate the value of the Baht with that of the Yen. This equating of Baht and Yen led to disequilibrium in the balance of payments between Thailand and Japan, as can be seen from the following figures:

Balance of Payments 1944

In payments	Baht	Out payments	Baht
1. Goods and money sent in [from Japan] for the government or for individuals	136,497,521	Goods and money sent out [of Thailand] for the [Japanese] government or individuals	63,580,106
2. Money sent in for expenses of the Japanese troops	514,000,000		
	650,497,521		

The figures in the above table show that the amount of money which the Japanese government had to pay the Thai government was more than the amount which the Thai had to pay the Japanese. Therefore the amount of Baht people wanted from the bank was greater than the amount of Baht the bank received from those who wanted Yen. When the situation concerning our balance of payments came to be like this, it was the practice to increase the rate of exchange of Baht and Yen in order to bring the balance of payments into equilibrium. However, once the agreement was made to maintain the rate of exchange at 1 Baht /1 Yen, then the exchange rate could not be altered. Furthermore, even though the Japanese government agreed to let the Thai control the exchange rate, the control over balance of payments could not be carried out freely due to other related agreements. Therefore when people wanted more Baht than had been received by the bank, the bank had to keep on exchanging Yen for banknotes. This was another cause of the depreciation in value of our currency.

The Currency Situation

On 30 November 1941 our currency situation was as follows:

	Baht		Baht
Banknotes in circulation	275,331,688	Gold	123,110,485
		Sterling security	41,065,225
		Pound sterling	106,422,238
		Baht coin	1,169,825
	275,331,688		271,767,773

The above figures show that the currency situation was stable, for there were liquid assets in gold and sterling covering about 84 percent of the banknotes in circulation.

On 31 August 1945 the currency situation was as follows:

	Baht		Baht
Banknotes in circulation	1,759,114,492	Gold in Thailand	144,901,516
Amount in banks	233,535,856	Gold in Japan	194,057,577
		Yen	1,284,429,988
		Financial bonds	252,500,000
			1,875,889,081
		Gold frozen in the United States	38,390,545
		Sterling security and pound sterling confiscated in England	265,753,896
	1,992,650,348		2,180,033,522

When the present figures and the figures for 30 November 1941 are compared, it can be seen that the amount of banknotes in circulation increased by more than 1,717 million Baht, or by about 623 percent. It is therefore hardly surprising that the value of our currency depreciated greatly. In addition, the status of our currency deteriorated. Liquid assets, consisting of gold in Thailand and

Japan, covered only about 17 percent of the banknotes in circulation. Even if the United States and Great Britain were to return all our assets which they had confiscated, total liquid assets (in gold and sterling) would still cover only about 27 percent of the banknotes in circulation.

The Value of Our Currency

I have already mentioned that when the amount of money in circulation increases but the quantity of goods and services do not increase proportionately, then the value of one's currency depreciates. The rate of depreciation of our currency can be estimated by showing the increase in wholesale prices and the cost of living during the period. They are as follows:

Date	Wholesale prices	Cost of living index	
		Ministry of Commerce	Japanese Chamber of Commerce
December 1942	111	133	206
December 1943	152	219	332
December 1944	214	362	905

(Generally speaking the Japanese Chamber of Commerce figures are likely to be the most accurate).

Conclusion

A stable currency is the foundation of national rehabilitation. Restoring the stability of our currency is therefore one of the most important concerns facing us. The three reasons why this instability has arisen have been recorded above. Time has now moved on, [however], and the conditions which produced two of the three reasons will soon be over. Only one condition remains, namely the budget deficit. This condition is within the power of the government to correct. Once this has been rectified, our currency situation can be stabilized.

Written at the Advisory Office,
Ministry of Finance.
6 September 1945

From the above report we can see that if we were to enjoy a stable currency situation, then the government must not spend more than it received—a matter of plain common sense. However, at the time we still had considerable expenses to meet. Even though we did not have to pay for the expenses of the Japanese forces any longer now that the war had ended, these costs had been replaced by other obligations. They included responsibility for providing for and cooperating with the large number of Allied soldiers who had entered Thailand to disarm the Japanese; the need to pay compensation for damages [to Allied property incurred during the war], and the requirement that we export rice to the United Kingdom free of charge. At the same time the number of banknotes in circulation was increasing, although the rate of increase was not as high as during the war. The Yen had no value and could not be used as part of our Reserve Fund any longer. There was still no way we could get back the gold we had deposited in Japan. This left only the 30.86 million grams of gold within the country that could be used as part of the Reserve Fund. Although we had 7,998 million grams of gold in the United States and assets in sterling and sterling security reserves valued at 15.4 million that had been frozen in England during the war, these sums were not released immediately. We did, however, have Treasury bonds valued at over 300 million Baht.

Our financial and monetary situation was therefore somewhat precarious, as has been described above. As far as the international political scene right after the war was concerned, our country was being closely watched by the British, particularly as regards our financial and military affairs (as can be seen from the "Twenty-one Proposals"). The Cabinet of M.R. Seni Pramoj's government decided to spend money sparingly and to behave modestly in order to gain the sympathy and understanding of other nations. All unnecessary expenses were to be eliminated. The Cabinet based its planning on M.C. Wiwatthanachai Chaiyan's financial report, the fact that we had to provide one and a half million tons of rice to the Allies free of charge, and in light of the international political situation. The budget was designed to balance revenue and expenditure, by fixing regular payments for salaries and general expenses. As far as economic rehabilitation was concerned, it was decided to carry out temporary repairs so as to restore the economy only to working condition at first. As to the improvement of the country through initiating new developments, all such projects were to be submitted first for consideration by the Council of Ministers. A special budget was to be set up for such projects, the income for which would come from loans. Meanwhile all ministries were told to exercise frugality in the use of their budget allocations. Finally, in order to prevent the British from insisting that all Thai financial planning must be based on the advice of the Allies,[5] and since we still had to depend on Great Britain in regard to many financial concerns, the Cabinet decided to ask Mr. Doll, the [former] Advisor on Financial Affairs [to the Thai government], who had had to leave Thailand because of the war, to resume his previous position.

To draw in other people to help the nation in time of crisis the Cabinet set up two committees. The first was entitled "The Committee on Revenue and Expenditure", and comprised Prince Wanwaithayakon[6] as Chairman; M.C. Sakonwannakonworawan,[7] the Adviser to the Ministry of the Interior; Mr. Leng Sisomwong;[8] Prince Chumphotphong Boriphat;[9] Mr. Wichit Lulitanon;[10] Nai Thawi Tawethikun;[11] Nai Thong-in Phuriphat;[12] Nai Tiang Sirikhan;[13] Phraya Chaiyotsombat,[14] Phraya Siwisanwacha;[15] Nai Phichan Bunyong;[16] the Advisor to the Ministry of Finance (Phraongchao Wiwatthanachai); the head of the Comptroller-General's Department; the head of the Excise Department; the head of the Revenue Department; the chairman of the Currency Inspection Commission; Nai Thongpleo Chonlaphum[17] and Nai Bunma Wongsawan,[18] Secretary.

The other committee was called "The Committee to Consider and Draft the Budget for the year 1946". This was composed of the Prime Minister, [M.R. Seni Pramoj] as Chairman; the Minister of Finance [the author]; the Deputy Minister of Finance;[19] the Advisor to the Ministry of Finance;[20] Prince Wanwaithayakon; Phraya Chaiyotsombat; Phraya Siratkosa;[21] Phraya Songsurarat;[22] Nai Thong-in Phuriphat; Nai Tiang Sirikhan, and the head of the Comptroller-General's Department[23] as a committee member and secretary. This committee was to do its best for the nation by eliminating all unnecessary expenses while at the same time giving consideration to both domestic and international politics and to overall national needs.

In an article in *Thai Mai*[24] of 23 September 1945 the Minister of Finance [the author] described the measures being taken to correct existing financial problems. He pointed out that two of the reasons underlying the currently unstable currency situation, namely that the nation had been obliged to pay for the expenses of the Japanese military forces in Thailand and had been forced to equate the Baht with the Yen during the war, had now been eliminated. However, a third factor, namely that of government expenditure exceeding revenue, still existed and would have to be corrected.

The Minister then went on to discuss a number of other financial topics affecting the livelihood of the people. He listed national assets currently being held in Japan. These consisted of 38 million grams of gold valued at 190,000 Yen, with one Baht of gold being worth 86 Baht.[25] The Minister stated that Thailand had asked the United Nations to protect this property for it. We also suffered from inflation. The Finance Minister stated that this had arisen because too many banknotes had been issued. Buying power had decreased for another reason as well, namely that there were fewer goods in circulation. He stressed that the government was trying to tackle the whole question of inflation and of balancing the budget.

The question of whether new banknotes would be issued to replace the old ones was being looked into by both the Prime Minister, M.R. Seni Pramoj, and the Finance Minister. The old notes, or in other words those currently in circulation, would remain in circulation until arrangements could be made with a printing company to print new ones to replace them. There would be no increase in the number of banknotes in circulation, nor would they be devalued in any way. As to taxation, the Minister assured the people he would try not to increase taxes, but would rather seek improvement of the [existing] tax system so that taxes were apportioned on a just and equitable basis. In reply to a question from a member of the Upper House who was unclear on the subject, the Minister also stated that from now on the Thai monetary system was to be based on gold.

Regarding the establishment of an exchange rate for the Baht, the Finance Minister stated that once wartime conditions ceased and trade resumed, it would no longer be possible to go back to pre-war conditions and assume an exchange rate of 11 Baht per £1-0-0 sterling. The situation had changed and the value of the Baht had decreased because the country now had more currency in circulation than it had security to cover this currency. At the same time the nation badly needed foreign currency to purchase imports. Many people wanted to establish an exchange rate whereby the value of the Baht would be set at about 30–40 Baht to the pound sterling, but although it would be easy to set up such a rate, the problem would be to maintain it once established. If the rate could not be maintained, it would be valueless. The maintenance of the rate depended on the stability of our currency, which meant that the rate must be a realistic or natural one based on the relative buying power of Thai and foreign currency.

To increase the nation's buying power and strengthen its currency values, it was necessary to improve and increase the production of exports as much as possible. The Minister recognized that there were, however, obstacles to this aim. The necessary spare parts to repair machinery [damaged during the war] would have to be imported before the machines could be put back into operation [and thereby produce exports for the country.] The tin mines were not currently operating; the lumber industry had closed down during the war; and the British were applying pressure to obtain one and a half million tons of rice [from Thailand] free of charge.

M.C. Wiwatthanachai Chaiyan, Mr. William Doll, the Financial Advisor and I met together many times in an attempt to deal with the problem of

Kamnan Si asks: "How's the condition of our Baht, Sir? Are you sure its value will not go down?" (Cartoon from *Sri Krung*, 1 October 1945.)

the exchange rate. The question was also discussed in the Cabinet. Since the country's monetary reserves were currently unstable, and an estimate of the buying power of the Baht against foreign currency was hard to obtain, the Cabinet decided to base the value of the Baht on gold. On 11 January 1946 the Ministry of Finance announced that this decision had been made in accordance with the international treaty on currency signed at Bretton Woods.[26] The Baht was defined as .06019 grams of pure gold, and the rate of exchange fixed at 60 Baht per £1-0-0 sterling or 100 Baht per $6.12 U.S.

It might be said, then, that after the war one of the greatest problems Thailand faced was that of stabilizing its currency and placing it on a basis that would make it dependable in the eyes of other nations. We had almost no foreign exchange reserves to draw on, as has already been mentioned. Meanwhile every government department was clamoring to buy goods to repair their facilities after having suffered from a lack of supplies for so many years. Other major problems facing us included the need to meet the requirements of the Formal Agreement, including having to provide free rice and pay compensation for damages [suffered by the Allies during the war.]

Resignation of the Cabinet of M.R. Seni Pramoj

After M.R. Seni Pramoj had held the position of Prime Minister and Foreign Minister for over four months, a general election was held. M.R. Seni resigned, making way for the formation of a new Cabinet on 31 January 1946. I resigned from my job as Minister of Finance, and did not hold office in the new Cabinet of Nai Khuang Aphaiwong. The budget proposals which M.R. Seni Pramoj's Cabinet had put forward were dropped, and the new Cabinet of Nai Khuang Aphaiwong put forward a different proposal to the National Assembly. However, the essential points of this latter proposal remained the same [as those we had originally put forward.]

CABINET OF NAI KHUANG APHAIWONG[27]
(1 February 1946–23 March 1946)

1. Major Khuang Aphaiwong — Prime Minister
2. Phraya Siwisanwacha — Minister of Finance
3. M.R. Seni Pramoj — Minister of Foreign Affairs
4. Phra Sutthiatnaruemon — Deputy Minister of Foreign Affairs
5. Lieutenant-General Chit Mansin Sinatyotharak — Minister of Defense
6. Phraya Atcharatsongsiri — Minister of Agriculture
7. Lieutenant-General Luang Kriangsakphichit — Minister of Public Health
8. Nai Prachuap Bunnag — Deputy Minister of Public Health
9. [Naval] Captain Luang Suphachalasai — Minister of Industry
10. Major Khuang Aphaiwong — Minister of Communications
11. [Air Force] Major-General Muni Mahasanthana-wetchayanrangsarit — Minister of Commerce
12. Chaophraya Sithammathibet — Minister of Justice
13. Nai Sisena Sombatsiri — Minister of the Interior
14. Phra Tironasanwitsawakam — Minister of Education
15. Nai Chom Charurat — Minister without portfolio
16. Colonel Non Ketnuti — Minister without portfolio
17. Nai Liang Chaiyakan — Minister without portfolio
18. Luang Angkhananurak — Minister without portfolio
19. Nai Suwit Phanthuset — Minister without portfolio

20. Nai Yaisawittachat   Minister without portfolio
21. Nai Fong Sitthitham   Minister without portfolio
22. Nai Buntheng Thongsawat   Minister without portfolio

13
Foreign Affairs

I have already mentioned previously that after the war ended I worked in the Ministry of Finance for a total of five months in the Cabinet of Nai Thawi Bunyaket and M.R. Seni Pramoj respectively, and that I resigned along with the other members of the M.R. Seni Pramoj Cabinet [in January 1946]. About two months later, at the end of March 1946, the Nai Khuang Aphaiwong Cabinet was defeated in the National Assembly. The opposition had proposed a reduction in the standard of living, but the Cabinet insisted it could not accept such a proposal. A new Cabinet was set up with Nai Pridi Banomyong as Prime Minister.

CABINET OF NAI PRIDI BANOMYONG [1]
(24 March 1946–9 June 1946)

Nai Pridi Banomyong	Prime Minister
Lieutenant-General Chira Wichitsongkhram	Minister of Defense
Nai Pridi Banomyong	Minister of Finance
Nai Direk Jayanama	Minister of Foreign Affairs
Nai Thawi Bunyaket	Minister of Agriculture
Phraya Sunthonphiphit	Minister of Public Health
Nai Sanguan Chuthatemi	Minister of Industry
Nai Saphrang Thephatsadin Na Ayutthaya	Minister of Communications
M.L. Kri Dechatiwong	Minister of Commerce
Colonel Chuang Chawengsaksongkhram	Minister of the Interior
Luang Chamnannitikaset	Minister of Justice
Nai Duean Bunnag	Minister of Education
Nai Wichit Lulitanon	Deputy Minister of Finance
Khun Radap Khadi	Minister without portfolio
Nai Wirot Kamonphan	Minister without portfolio
Colonel Thuan Wichaikhatthakha	Minister without portfolio
Colonel Phraya Suraphanseni	Minister without portfolio

This Cabinet resigned in accordance with the Constitution at the death of King Ananda [in June 1946,[2] since the king who had appointed Nai Pridi Prime Minister was now no longer living.] The new Cabinet that replaced it consisted mainly of the members of the previous Pridi government, however, and Nai Pridi Banomyong continued to remain as Prime Minister until 22 August 1946, or for a [total] period of almost five months. He then resigned, and a new Cabinet under Rear Admiral Thawan Thamrongnawasawat was set up.[3]

CABINET OF REAR ADMIRAL THAWAN THAMRONGNAWASAWAT
(24 August 1946–28 May 1947)[4]

Rear Admiral Thawan Thamrongnawasawat	Prime Minister and Minister of Justice
Nai Direk Jayanama	Deputy Prime Minister and Minister of Foreign Affairs
Nai Wichit Lulitanon	Minister of Finance
Lieutenant-General Chira Wichitsongkhram	Minister of Defense
Nai Duean Bunnak	Minister of Education
Nai Charun Suepsaeng	Minister of Agriculture
Colonel Chuang Chawengsaksongkhram	Minister of the Interior
Nai Thong-in Phuriphat	Minister of Industry
M.L. Kri Dechatiwong	Minister of Communications
Major Wilat Osathanon	Minister of Commerce
Phraya Sunthonphiphit	Minister of Public Health
Colonel Thuan Wichaikhatthakha	Deputy Minister of Defense
Nai Yuean Phanitwit	Minister without portfolio
Nai Wirot Kamonphan	Minister without portfolio
Nai Tiang Sirikhan	Minister without portfolio
Nai Chamlong Daorueang	Minister without portfolio
Nai Thongplaeo Chonlaphum	Minister without portfolio
M.C. Nonthiyawat Svasti	Minister without portfolio

During the Cabinet of Nai Pridi Banomyong I held the position of Minister of Foreign Affairs, while [for much of the time] during that of Rear Admiral Thawan Thamrongnawasawat I was Deputy Minister of Foreign Affairs. I will now go on to discuss the subject of our international relations during the period that I held these posts, namely from April [March?—Ed.] 1946 until 6 February 1947, the day on which I resigned.

A. NEGOTIATIONS WITH GREAT BRITAIN

1. The Rice Question

On 26 March 1946 I took over the position of Minister of Foreign Affairs from M.R. Seni Pramoj, who had held this position during the Cabinet of Nai Khuang Aphaiwong. That same day I received Mr. Geoffrey Thompson,[5] the British Minister,[6] whom I had known previously. I promised him that I would do my best to cooperate with him, as our two countries had been friends with one another for quite some time. I told him that if matters should arise which called for discussion between us, I would tell him about it so that we could discuss the issues frankly and sincerely, as open discussion was the best method of cooperation. The Minister replied that he felt the same way, and was looking forward to our cooperation in the future. Past incidents should be forgotten, and as far as future relations between Thailand and Great Britain were concerned, the Minister would work to attain mutual goals, and would be glad to meet with me whenever necessary. At the end of our meeting the Minister added that as I was no doubt already aware, the rice deliveries promised under the terms of the Formal Agreement[7] signed three months ago had not been received as agreed upon. He was therefore handing me a report on this situation.

The essential point of the report stated that the British and United States governments had agreed to nullify article no. 14 of the Formal Agreement. From now on the British government would pay for the rice instead of taking it free of charge. The Thai government was in turn to deliver one million two thousand tons of rice[8] to the designated British and American organization. The price to be paid for this rice would be settled upon later. The rice was to be delivered within twelve months from the day on which a revised Formal Agreement [i.e. one incorporating these changes in regard to the arrangements for the rice deliveries] was signed. If the Thai government was unable to produce the full one million two hundred thousand tons within the specified period, then the British government would have to ask that it provide the remainder free of charge within a period of time to be specified. The Thai government was also to enter into a tripartite agreement with Great Britain and the United States setting out all the procedures to be adopted to increase rice production in Thailand, and establishing regulations regarding the export of rice.[9]

So far as I could judge, the reason the British government presented this new proposal was that during the discussions that had been taking place since the signing of the Formal Agreement, the government in Bangkok, as well as our representatives in Singapore,[10] had made it clear that it was impossible for Thailand to come up with one and a half million tons of rice—a quantity that was worth more than two thousand million Baht. Thailand had been impoverished by the war. The Japanese had borrowed about two thousand million Baht from us. Transportation and other communication systems were still in a very bad condition. We had not yet been able to produce enough goods for export to build up reserves of foreign exchange. It would be difficult and unjust to force members of the public to sell [their rice] at low prices. In addition, the rice market was not currently controlled by the government.[11] As a result, Great Britain would not get the rice it wanted, whereas certain dishonest individuals would take the rice and sell it to other countries at the higher prices available there.[12] This is in fact exactly what happened. The British government therefore had to alter its policy and purchase the rice as described above.

I promised the Minister that I would report to the Prime Minister, Nai Pridi Banomyong, on the situation immediately, and would consult with members of the Cabinet and various experts on the matter. Furthermore, I informed Mr. Thompson that the Prime Minister had recently announced that he would try to increase productivity to the maximum, especially in regard to rice. However, the Minister should bear in mind that we had suffered greatly during the war, and could not produce an unrealistic amount. Thailand could not be compared with other nations. Owing to our small size, relatively minor damage had caused serious [economic] dislocation. I also pointed out that the government had allocated fifteen million Baht for raising different strains of rice in order to produce the highest possible rice yields. This demonstrated that government policy was directed not only at caring for the people, but at fulfilling the terms of the Formal Agreement.

On 3 May 1946 the Thai government agreed to a revised Formal Agreement. We felt this was more beneficial to us than the original Formal Agreement, as article number 14 of the latter had required us to deliver rice free of charge. It was announced simultaneously in Bangkok, London, and Washington, D.C. that the three governments had agreed that from now on Thailand would not have to provide the rice free of charge. Instead the British government would buy one million two hundred thousand tons of rice from Thailand, to be delivered within twelve months at a basic price of £12-14-0 (about 762 Baht) [per ton], plus an additional premium of £3-0-0 per ton for rice delivered between 31 May and 15 June 1946. If twelve months from the date of the agreement the amount of rice produced by the Thai government should be less than that which had been agreed upon, then the Thai government would have to make good the deficiency free of charge. After the rice had been delivered by the Thai government, the Combined Food Board would decide on where it was to be distributed.[13]

Under this agreement Britain showed us leniency for the first time. The [revised] agreement was less harsh than the [terms of the original] Formal

Agreement, for in it England agreed to pay for our rice instead of taking it free of charge. However, the price to be paid for our rice was still much lower than the price of rice on the world market. Hence even this [latter] agreement did not prove totally successful. The problems [that remained in connection with the rice deliveries] are discussed in part 3, chapter 5 [now chapter 14].

2. Thai Government Purchase of the Kanchanaburi-Burma Railway Track

Around April 1946, the British Minister sent a letter to the Ministry of Foreign Affairs stating that since the Japanese had transported materials from Burma, Malaya and the Netherlands East Indies (Indonesia) to build the Kanchanaburi-Burma railway track, the British government would have to compensate these three countries before the track could be pulled out and removed. Allied forces and Japanese prisoners-of-war were still in the country and could be used as the labor force to remove the track. The British government asked the Thai government to consider the matter.

The Thai government, and in particular the Ministry of Communications, decided that it would be best for us to buy the track, as our railway system was badly in need of supplies. We therefore asked the British government to set a price for which it would be prepared to handle the tearing up and transportation involved. At first the British set the price at £3,000,000. However, the Thai government could not afford to pay such a high price. The British government then lowered the price to £1,500,000. The Thai government established a committee that sought yet a further reduction in price. In the end the British set a final price of £1,250,000. The Thai government agreed to this in October 1946.

The Kanchanaburi-Burma railway was notorious for its unhappy connotations, to the point that it was known the world over as "the death railway." The Japanese army decided to establish a line of communication with Burma by way of Kanchanaburi, and in June 1942 investigated the possibility of building a railway track linking the two together. In November 1942 they started construction, building the line from the two ends simultaneously. From the Burmese side the track started from Thanbaiyusayat in southern Burma; from the Thai side the track started from Kanchanaburi. A few months after construction was begun, the Japanese began to suffer increasingly heavy shipping losses. They felt that if the railway could be finished, it would relieve their transportation situation greatly. An order was therefore issued to finish construction by August 1943. However, as is well known, the terrain [through which the track had to pass] is extremely rugged, mountainous and heavily forested. Moreover the weather was hot. Heavy rainfall over the area contributed to the spread of many epidemic diseases. Very little machinery was available, and Allied prisoners-of-war have stated that most of the work had to be carried out by human labor. The Japanese used prisoners-of-war of many different nationalities, and also hired Tamil, Burmese, Javanese, Vietnamese, Malayan and Chinese coolies to carry out the work. The entire labor force, whether prisoners-of-war or hired laborers, had to work extremely hard from dawn till dusk. Their food supplies were insufficient. Canvas coverings provided the only means of shelter. In heavy rain it became impossible to sleep, because the area was flooded. Many laborers fell sick, yet medicines were either insufficient or non-existent. They therefore did not receive proper medical treatment, but were abandoned to their circumstances. As a result, a great many died. However, the track was finally completed, and the railway opened on 17 October 1943. It was 415 kilometers in length. There was an opening ceremony dedicated to those who had died during the course of construction of the railway. The Japanese estimated that in building the railway 10,000 Japanese, 10,000 prisoners-of-war and 30,000 hired laborers died. However, the Allies have claimed that Japanese estimates were too low, and estimated from the number of people missing that probably 12,000 prisoners and 250,000 laborers died [in the course of constructing the track.]

We can take pride in the fact that during this period the Thai people in general, and especially those in Kanchanaburi where the railway track started from, showed kindness to and took pity on the prisoners and laborers, sneaking in food, clothing, money, cigarettes, medicine and so forth to them. In the official records of the International Military Tribunal [held in] Tokyo [after the war], Allied nationals testified to the kindness of the Thai. In actuality these acts were in keeping with our custom of showing mercy to all living beings, which follows from our Buddhist beliefs. I saw with my own eyes that while we felt sorry for and took pity on the Allied prisoners during the period of the Japanese occupation, once the Allies defeated the Japanese and the Japanese in turn were made prisoners and had to work for the Allies, then we felt sorry for the Japanese and gave them food and clothing in a similar manner.

3. British Release of Part of Our Money Frozen during the War

As has already been mentioned in Prince Wiwatthanachai's report,[14] when the Pacific War began, or when Thailand entered the war, we had gold reserves in the United States worth 38,390,545 Baht, and sterling security and pound sterling reserves in Great Britain worth 265,735,896 Baht. These reserves were frozen by the two countries throughout the war. Even after the British signed the Formal Agreement[15] with Thailand after the war, they still held on to and refused to release our gold and monetary reserves. They continued to hold these as guarantee for payment of compensation for [war] damages, the cost of which was to be determined upon by a committee. This action on Britain's part created considerable difficulty for us. After the signing of the Formal Agreement, the Cabinet tried to obtain the release of our gold and monetary reserves, but was told to wait.

In March 1946 I became Minister of Foreign Affairs. The Prime Minister, Nai Pridi Banomyong, asked me to negotiate with and plead our case before the British, asking them to show understanding in regard to Thailand's situation, and pointing out to them that Thailand had cooperated with the British all along. Finally, in June 1946, the British agreed to release part of our frozen reserves, valued at £1,000,000. The remainder was still held as insurance for payment of arrears of interest and principal on money which Thailand had borrowed from Great Britain before the war, for bonuses and pensions to former British government officials who had worked in different ministries in the Thai government, and for British war claims.

4. British Withdrawal from Thailand

The most fortunate feature of this period from the Thai point of view was the withdrawal of British troops from Thailand. As is well known, having foreign troops in one's country is something that no nation enjoys unless such troops have been invited in by the host country to protect it. The British troops came into Thailand as a consequence of the Formal Agreement, and not by invitation.[16]

Around the middle of September 1946, the British Minister, [Mr. Thompson], and Major-General [Gerald] Brunskill, the Commander of the British forces in Thailand, came to tell me that the British government had decided to withdraw its troops from Thailand by the end of October 1946. I thanked them and reported this to the National Assembly. The information was only given to me verbally, but in mid-October 1946 a written statement [corroborating this message] arrived. On 31 October 1946, the day the British withdrew, I made a formal report on behalf of the Cabinet to the National Assembly stating that last month the Cabinet had told the Assembly that the Allied troops in Thailand would be leaving by 31 October. The Cabinet was now glad to inform the Assembly that the British had reported that all British and Indian troops were now out of the country. Only about five hundred military technicians and experts remained behind to aid in railway reconstruction and other projects connected with [former] enemy property. The Japanese troops [in Thailand], who as of 22 February 1946 had numbered 115,000, had now been repatriated. There were still three hundred Dutch nationals in Thailand, mostly women and children. They were waiting for a ship which was due to arrive in two or three days [and which would be repatriating them.] Laborers of various nationalities who had been drafted by the Japanese had left the country on 22 February 1946. Out of about 23,000 laborers, only seven hundred were left, and they were now also awaiting a ship which would be arriving in two or three days and returning them to their native countries. The British had thanked the Thai for allowing them the use of their facilities and for having cooperated with them throughout their stay. The Cabinet in turn was taking this opportunity to state that while the Allied troops had been in the country to disarm the Japanese forces as agreed upon in the Formal Agreement, they had also helped the Thai in many ways, especially in repairing and providing materials for communication networks. The Thai government appreciated this assistance, the report concluded.[17] The Allied forces were, thus, in Thailand for a total of fourteen and one half months.

5. Other Matters

During the period described above, negotiations over certain other matters also took place. They included the question of our relations with the French,[18] British assistance on rail communications and the repair of the Phraram Hok Bridge,[19] the question of Thailand being accepted as a member of the United Nations,[20] and the withdrawal of the [remaining] British military personnel from Thailand. During the eleven months that I worked in the Ministry of Foreign Affairs, Sir Geoffrey Thompson[21], the British Minister, and I discussed the above matters with amicability and mutual understanding, as the British Minister has recorded in his memoirs.[22]

B. NEGOTIATIONS WITH THE UNITED STATES

I had the opportunity to receive Mr. Yost, the United States Chargé d'Affaires, on the same day I received the British Minister, that is to say on 26 March 1946. Since Mr. Yost and I had met before, we were on good terms with one another and understood each other quite well. I told the Chargé that the Thai appreciated the kindness and friendliness which the United States government and people had shown to Thailand. I therefore wished to take every opportunity to cooperate with and enhance the friendly relations and understanding between our two countries. The Chargé d'Affaires reiterated that the United States had never considered Thailand an enemy. There were therefore no outstanding problems in our relations with the United States.

1. United States' Release of Our Frozen Monetary Reserves

On the very first day I met Mr. Yost I started seeking his cooperation in regard to Thai monetary securities held in the United States, pointing out that it was already past the appropriate time for America to release these. Could he therefore please tell me as soon as possible where we stood in regard to this matter? Should the United States release the reserves, the Prime Minister, Cabinet and people of Thailand would always recall this with gratitude. The Thai government needed the funds to buy materials to rehabilitate the country and help its people. We were, therefore, making this a special request to the United States. The Chargé replied that he understood there were still some technical problems surrounding the matter. However, he would contact Washington, D.C. immediately on the subject. Nine days later, on 3 April 1946, he informed me that the United States government had agreed to release the gold belonging to Thailand which was being held in the United States, and was in the process of coming to a quick decision about Thailand's monetary reserves. The latter would be released as soon as the United States received confirmation from the Thai government that none of the individual holdings involved belonged to Japanese, German or Italian nationals. The money was released not long afterwards.

2. Appointment of a United States Minister

[In mid-1946] the [American] Chargé d'Affaires, [Mr. Yost], announced that the United States government was planning to send out a Mr. Edwin [F.] Stanton, then its Consul General in Vancouver, Canada, and formerly Assistant Chief of the [State Department] Division of Far Eastern Affairs. Mr. Stanton was a man who had worked in China for many years. The United States government was now seeking the approval of the Thai government to appoint him as Minister to Bangkok. The Thai government agreed to this right away. Mr. Stanton took up office at the end of June 1946, and later became Ambassador to Thailand.[23] He left Thailand in 1953. Mr. Stanton and his wife proved to be very kind and friendly towards Thailand and its people. Even after he retired from his position, Mr. Stanton remained a warm supporter of Thailand and promoted activities and disseminated information on our country. He became chairman of the Thailand Committee of the Asia Society in New York, and currently still holds that position.[24] On 26 June 1946 he came to see me for the first time with Mr. Yost. I knew immediately that he was kindhearted and would be a good friend to Thailand, and that we would cooperate well with one another.

Mr. Stanton has described his work [during his term of office as Minister and later Ambassador to Thailand] in his book *Brief Authority*.[25] In it he mentions the negotiations on territories [i.e. the return to France of territory restored to Thailand by the Japanese during the war], the rice problem, and Thailand's diplomatic affairs [during this period]. With regard to the first, he wrote: "Nai Direk, the Foreign Minister, with whom I had already established friendly relations, made it plain to me, in polite diplomatic language, that the Thai were not happy over the prospect of returning to the French a slice of territory in Cambodia which Thailand, in 1895, had been forced to cede to the French".[26] Mr. Stanton felt that during the war these territories had come under Thai control through the mediation of the Japanese, but I contradicted him, pointing out that the Thai felt these territories rightfully belonged to Thailand and had been lost to her through [French] force.

As Mr. Stanton rightly ascertained, the problem was a delicate one which involved the honor and patriotism of the Thai people. The Minister understood the feelings of the Thai very well. Nevertheless he felt that in the interests of peace and harmony in Southeast Asia and of proper political procedure, these territories should revert to their pre-war status, particularly as Thailand had allied with Japan to the point of declaring war on Great Britain and the United States. Thailand had already returned the small areas of Burmese territory it had taken over during the war, and had agreed in principle to return the territory involved in Indochina to the French. Mr. Stanton further pointed out that as I probably knew already, if the matter was brought before the United Nations[27] and a solution could not be reached, the French would veto Thailand's entry into the United Nations.

Mr. Stanton then went on to describe how he asked me whether Thailand had delivered the rice it owed yet. The United States government was concerned about the serious food shortages which certain countries in South and Southeast Asia such as the Philippines and China were currently suffering from. It had therefore joined with Great Britain and Thailand in a tripartite rice agreement[28] under which a rice committee[29] had been set up in Bangkok to distribute food supplies according to the allocation set by the International Emergency Food Commission. Mr. Stanton records that he told me that the figures for rice exports from Thailand were very low. Could Thailand make more rice available? I asked in return for his understanding, pointing out the many difficulties our government was facing. I pointed out that much of our rolling stock, for example, had been destroyed by the Allies during the war, although I ended by saying that no matter what our government would do its best.[30]

Mr. Stanton records that he left feeling that we had reached some point of understanding. "I had had my first experience of the skill and tact of Thai diplomats," he wrote. "I must say, I became increasingly impressed by their never-failing politeness and rare tact even when disagreeable subjects came up for discussion or negotiation. They have perfected the art of polite verbal acquiescence. However, this is not necessarily followed by action if the matter is deemed to be not in the national interest."[31] This last statement of Mr. Stanton's is true. In situations where force was employed we had no choice but to comply. However, it is only natural for human beings who love freedom to fight to be free from [unwelcome or imposed] obligations.

14
Negotiations with France

The Franco-Thai conflict of 1940 has already been discussed in the third chapter of part 1. In this it was mentioned that a peace agreement was signed between Thailand and France [on 9 May 1941], with Japan acting as mediator in the dispute. Once World War II came to a close, France, however, regarding itself as one of the victorious Allied powers, decided to claim back the territories [Thailand had regained through the agreement]. It announced that France would consider itself as remaining in a state of war with Thailand until we returned them. The French further refused to acknowledge the 9 May 1941 peace agreement, claiming that the Vichy government had been forced to agree to it under pressure from Japan.

We initiated negotiations with France over these issues very soon after the war ended, during the government of M.R. Seni Pramoj, in which I served as Minister of Finance. When I moved to the Ministry of Foreign Affairs in March 1946 the negotiations were still in process, and indeed they were not concluded until 27 June 1947, during the government of Rear Admiral Thawan Thamrongnawasawat, when the Conciliation Commission[1] established by Thailand and France announced that Thailand should return the territories it had gained through the May 1941 peace treaty to France.[2] By the time this decision was finally reached, I had been sent to take up office in England.[3]

In order for the reader to get an overall picture of the way in which events developed, I will now go on to present the details of the situation.

A few days after World War II ended, Mr. Bird, the British representative who had been sent to Bangkok,[4] told the Thai government of that time[5] that as the Allies had emphasized right from the start that they would not recognize any territorial acquisitions obtained through the influence or power of the Axis, his country was requesting that the Thai government make clear its intentions in regard to territories gained from French Indochina [during the war]. The Allies would then be able to give further consideration to Thailand's Peace Proclamation.[6]

Nai Khuang Aphaiwong, who was still holding the position of Prime Minister, as a new government had not yet been established, consulted the Regent,

[Nai Pridi Banomyong], on the matter. On 22 August 1945 a communiqué was issued through the Office of the Prime Minister stating that even though the Royal Peace Proclamation of 16 August 1945 mentioned above had not made any reference to the boundary problems between Thailand and Indochina, Thailand, always wishing to seek and abide by justice, would be willing to accept the decisions of the United Nations on the subject if such were made, and to act in accordance with the constitution and principles of that organization.

The following month, in mid-September 1945, Mr. Bird went to see the Prime Minister, M.R. Seni Pramoj,[7] and expressed the British government's wish to see Thailand and France come to an agreement. A few days later, the Commander-in-Chief of the Allied Forces in Thailand, Major-General Evans, sent a letter to the Regent announcing the arrival of a French government representative in Kandy, Ceylon to make an agreement with Thailand similar to that which would be made with England.

On that same day, 18 September 1945, Mr. Bird wrote to the Prime Minister, M.R. Seni Pramoj, stating that the letter of the Commander-in-Chief of the Allied Forces in Thailand to the Regent, by implication inviting the Thai government to send a representative to negotiate with the French delegate, had been made in the name of the Supreme Allied Commander, South-East Asia Command, Admiral Lord Louis Mountbatten, who in this situation was also considered to be the representative of France.

At the end of September 1945 the Thai government sent a delegation under Prince Wiwatthanachai to negotiate with England, as has already been mentioned earlier in this book.[8] During these negotiations the French representative, Monsieur Clarac,[9] who was then in Kandy, took the opportunity to present an official note to M.C. Wiwatthanachai with a request that this be forwarded to the Regent. The note ran to the effect that France still considered itself at war with Thailand, but was nevertheless prepared to carry out negotiations for the restoration of normal friendly relations based on a return to the *status quo ante* of the period prior to June 1940.[10] M.C. Wiwatthanachai reported that the French representative at the same time made the following demands on behalf of the French government, namely that Thailand agree to a treaty incorporating conditions similar to those of the treaty it was about to sign with England, although excluding the clauses in the Annex to that treaty;[11] that it return those territories it had seized in 1941, and that it hand over the Emerald Buddha.[12]

M.C. Wiwatthanachai replied that he had not been authorized by his government to negotiate with France, and was not therefore in a position to do so. However, he mentioned that he did not personally agree with the French point of view that Thailand and France were still at war with one another, for peace had already been made between the two countries through the Peace Treaty of 9 May 1941.[13] As for the French demand for the Emerald Buddha, he did not think any [Thai] government would agree to this.[14] The French representative must have made this demand on the instructions of his government. Later M. Clarac told the Thai delegation that France was willing to withdraw its demand for the Emerald Buddha. I well remember that when the Prime Minister[15] told the Cabinet about the matter, everyone at the meeting felt the demand must have been a joke designed to tease us.

Later the British representative in Kandy[16] told the Thai representative, M.C. Wiwatthanachai, that England was anxious to see peaceful relations between Thailand and France restored as quickly as possible. As far as the territories Thailand had regained were concerned, Mr. Dening said that the Allies felt that Thailand should go ahead and return these territories to France, but reserve the right to raise the issue again at a meeting of an [appropriate] international organization. In regard to the Emerald Buddha, the British representative had already advised the French to take back their claim for this. Mr. Dening also suggested that it would be well to initiate negotiations in Kandy, where England would be willing to act as honest broker.

On receiving this report, the Thai government instructed its delegates to tell the British and American representatives that it was very surprised by the French claim that a state of war still existed between Thailand and France. Firstly no declaration of war had ever taken place between our two nations, nor had there been any active fighting between us. In the second place the resistance movements in Thailand and France could be regarded as parallels, in that the Thai resistance movement had ultimately been recognized and [a number of its members appointed to positions in the] government of Thailand in the same way that leaders of the Free French movement had now become leaders of the French government. Both resistance movements had cooperated with the Allies in fighting the Axis. It stood to reason, then, that the two movements should deal with one another on friendly terms. Besides, in so far as Indochina was concerned, the Thai resistance movement had helped the French by providing them with intelligence information. This had been fully recognized both by British Force 136[17] and the United States O.S.S.[18] There had been many instances during the war when France had been unable to obtain information from reliable sources in Indochina and the Thai resistance movement had stepped in to help. And lastly, in spite of the fact that the French government of the time had allowed the Japanese navy to use Indochina as a base for further aggression against Thailand and Malaya, the attitude of Thailand towards French Indochina and France itself had not changed, but had continued to remain friendly, as witness the shelter and help given to French citizens [from Indochina] who took refuge in Thailand [during the war].

The Thai government was willing to negotiate with France when an opportune moment arose, as it was our sincere and determined intention to do everything we could to promote peace and friendly relations both among neighbors in this region and in other parts of the world. The moment was not yet ripe, however, for such negotiations. The situation in Indochina had not yet returned to normal. Moreover the inhabitants of those territories that had been returned to us [now] enjoyed freedom and independence [under Thai jurisdiction], and even had the right to choose their own representatives in the Thai National Assembly. If those same people were to see their rights infringed by having their territories returned to French rule, they would be bitterly resentful towards Thailand for allowing them to suffer such loss.

The position of the territories Thailand had taken back in 1941 was very different from that of French territories in Europe. [It was fitting that] Alsace-Lorraine, for example, should be returned to France, for its inhabitants were French and needed to be freed from German rule. However, in the territories Thailand had reclaimed, the inhabitants had been rendered free and independent. If they were returned to French rule, they would be deprived of these freedoms.

If it was thought suitable and in accordance with the principles of the constitution of the United Nations that the opinion of the people in these territories be taken into account, then the government of Thailand would be willing to have a commission representing four of the major Powers in the Security Council, namely the United States. England, China and Russia, administer the said regions for a reasonable period, such as six months, so that they could arrange for the holding of a plebiscite.

As to the demand for the Emerald Buddha, no self-respecting Thai government could ever accept such a demand.

On 16 October 1945 the British representative at Kandy, [Mr. Dening], wrote to the Thai delegation stating that from the very beginning of these negotiations he had informed the Thai representative [M.C. Wiwatthanachai] of the importance the British government placed on agreement being reached between Thailand and France. He now wished to let Thailand know in writing that the conditions England was laying down [i.e. the requirements Britain was insisting upon as the basis for an agreement to end the state of war between the United Kingdom and Thailand] did not include the question of the territories Thailand had gained from Indochina in 1941. Nevertheless Britain hoped that this problem would be handled between Thailand and France to the satisfaction of France during the negotiations to be carried out with the latter at the same time as negotiations were being conducted with England.

Mr. Dening also stressed that England would not recognize any territorial changes that had taken place after the outbreak of World War II which had been effected through the use of force. As France had been an ally of Great Britain, the British representative also reserved the right to bring up the question of the territorial dispute during the negotiations for an agreement between Thailand and England if necessary, and to include additional provisions in the agreement at any time up to the moment of actually signing it.[19]

On 24 October 1945 M.C. Wiwatthanachai replied to the British representative that the dispute was among the problems that the Thai government was planning to deal with. However, he saw no reason why the French could not bring the matter up at any time during the negotiations as a normal part of the proceedings.

After this, discussion on the issue seemed to die down somewhat. However, on 9 January 1946 the *London Times* reported that both the British and American governments had pledged their support for the French government's demand for the return from Thailand of the territories under dispute. M.R. Seni Pramoj, who was both Prime Minister and Minister of Foreign Affairs at the time, told members of the Cabinet that he had queried both the British and American Ministers about this, and they had admitted to him that this was the case. However, they had insisted that both England and the United States were simply confirming the policy they had already made clear of insisting on a return to the *status quo ante*, meaning that they refused to recognize any boundary changes made during the war.

No further mention was made of the matter until mid-February 1946, when, during the government of Nai Khuang Aphaiwong in which M.R. Seni Pramoj was Minister of Foreign Affairs, England requested that we send a delegation to Singapore to negotiate with the French. The Cabinet put together a delegation, but before its members could set off the government resigned. A new government was established under Nai Pridi Banomyong at the end of March 1946. In this I returned to the position of Minister of Foreign Affairs, as I have already mentioned previously.

On 26 March 1946 I received Mr. Thompson, the British Minister, and Mr. Yost, the American Chargé d'Affaires, for the first time. The British Minister stressed that the new government should hurry up and send a Thai delegation to Singapore to negotiate with the French, for if we delayed France might provoke trouble (meaning agitation along the frontier). I told him that I had, however, only taken up my duties from M.R. Seni Pramoj, the [former] Minister of Foreign Affairs, that very morning, so I needed time to think the matter over. I told him the topic had not yet been discussed in the Cabinet, but that in my opinion the sending of such a delegation to Singapore would amount to opening official talks with the French. If these did not turn out satisfactorily, the results could be unfortunate. It might be better, therefore, if we were to change our plans and send a group of private representatives to discuss matters first instead.

We knew that the British government representative in Saigon at that time was a Mr. Michael Reed, formerly a British Consul in Bangkok. He was a man who knew Thailand well, and one whom we thought might be of great help to us. If a private delegation was [initially] sent to Saigon, it could get in touch with Admiral d'Argenlieu[20] and Monsieur Clarac, and hold exploratory talks on the main views and opinions of the two sides which could then be used as a basis to work from later. As soon as these (exploratory) talks had taken place, the delegates could return and report right away to the government on their findings. Then once the government had drawn up a definite policy, official talks could be opened to work towards a solution of the situation.

Mr. Thompson replied that this seemed a very good idea. However, he would have to think it over for a few days (I believe so that he could consult his government about it first). He also emphasized that even though we might be getting in touch with Mr. Reed in Saigon, it should be understood that England did not propose to interfere in this affair. I told him that I realized this, but hoped that England would give us at least outside support, for England was not only a good friend of Thailand's, but also wanted to see the conflict settled successfully. Mr. Thompson assured me we could rely on this type of outside support.

After the British Minister had left, the American Chargé d'Affaires [Mr. Yost] came to see me. In the course of the general conversation we had with one another described earlier in this book, I told Mr. Yost about my idea [regarding holding discussions in Saigon] that I had put forward to the British Minister. Mr. Yost agreed that this could help prevent a rift being caused in the event of failure of the talks. He also expressed the view that it would be best if we gave in to France as far as the border problem was concerned. Neither England nor the United States were going to change their attitudes regarding a return to the *status quo ante*, whereas Thailand would find itself faced with constant opposition from the French in regard to its application for membership in the United Nations if it did not acquiesce to France's demands.

The British attitude regarding the territorial dispute was shown clearly in a dispatch from Mr. Dening, the British representative in Singapore, to M.C. Wiwatthanachai dated 1 January 1946. This stated in essence that the government of His Majesty the King of Great Britain would not recognize the acquisition by Thailand of any territory gained after 11 December 1940. This non-recognition covered any territory whatsoever, and therefore included those lands which the Vichy government ceded to Thailand on 9 May 1941 during the regime of Marshal Pétain.[21]

The American attitude, apart from what had been conveyed verbally by the American Chargé d'Affaires at Bangkok, was demonstrated in a report of 3 January 1946 by Luang Ditthakanphakdi,[22] the Thai Chargé d'Affaires in Washington, to M.R. Seni Pramoj, the Minister of Foreign Affairs. This ran to the effect that the government of the United States refused to accept the argument presented by the government of Thailand that the return [to Thailand in 1941] of the territories in dispute had been made with the free consent of the French government. To maintain its stated policy the United States government could not therefore recognize Thailand's territorial acquisitions, and regretted that it could not support Thailand's proposals. The return of the territories in question would not, however, affect any claims that Thailand might put forward to the United Nations should such an opportunity arise in the future.[23]

I will now go back to the subject of my proposal [concerning sending a private delegation to Saigon] regarding which the British Minister had asked for time to give the matter further consideration. Two or three days after we had talked together, Mr. Thompson came to tell me that he approved our sending a private delegation to Saigon instead of to Singapore. The Cabinet thereupon established a delegation to be led by Nai Chiat Aphaiwong, Secretary to the Cabinet, and including Luang Wisutwiratchathet,[24] with Nai Bun Charoenchai[25] as secretary.

On 10 April 1946 the delegation returned and reported to the government that it had called on the French High Commissioner for Indochina and handed him the Prime Minister's letter, and that its members had been accorded a warm welcome. However, as the French High Commissioner [Admiral d'Argenlieu] had had to leave for consultations with Vietnamese government representatives in Dalat, he had asked that the Thai delegation hold its talks and discussions with M. Clarac. During the discussions with the latter, the Thai delegation had been asked if Thailand was ready to give back the territories acquired in 1941. The Thai delegation had replied that the object of this mission was simply to exchange points of view with the French, and to try to dispel any misunderstandings [that might exist between the two parties] so as to find a basis for a direct and mutually satisfactory agreement between Thailand and France.

The French had, however, the delegates reported, handed the Thai delegation the draft of an agreement similar to the Formal Agreement Thailand had signed with England on 1 January 1946. The main clauses of this had stated that Thailand must return to France the four provinces under dispute and pay compensation for losses of property, rights and interests which France had sustained thereby. Beyond this France was willing to issue a communiqué stating that it would maintain friendly relations with Thailand and permit minor frontier adjustments to be carried out (meaning adjustments of the Mekong border along international legal lines) in order to facilitate shipping along the river Mekong and communication between the different peoples [situated along either side of the river bank.][26]

The Thai delegates stated they had replied, however, that Thailand was seeking a compromise which both parties could agree on. The Thai government would be perfectly willing to put the matter before the United Nations and to allow a plebiscite in the territories under dispute. The French representative had retorted, however, that the dispute concerned only Thailand and France, and was not the concern of any international organization. As to the proposal for a plebiscite, M. Clarac stated that although the idea was acceptable in principle, a plebiscite could only be carried out if it was conducted by French, Cambodian and Lao officials in the local areas concerned. The delegates had thereupon stated that Thailand would be willing to agree to return part of the territories to France if France in turn would agree to concede certain territories to Thailand.

Later M. Clarac told the Thai delegation that he had forwarded the Thai proposals to his government, and had been instructed to inform the Thai delegation that the French government could not accept them. He therefore urged Thailand to make an agreement promptly along the lines already proposed by France. France had, he maintained, already made several concessions to Thailand such as withdrawing its demand for the Emerald Buddha and agreeing to issue a communiqué to arrange for minor frontier adjustments.

During the course of these negotiations, on 7 May 1946, the Prime Minister told me he had received two cables from Nakhon Phanom,[27] the first of which ran as follows: "From 06:30 a.m. to 07:10 a.m. the French fired heavily from Thakhaek[28] into the municipality of Nakhon Phanom using heavy weapons such as mortars and machine guns as well as small guns. Four mortar shells hit the courthouse, one hit the police station, setting the property on fire (although the fire was extinguished right away), and three hit the municipality building. Houses of some of the inhabitants of the area were also hit. One Vietnamese died from the gunfire, and two were seriously injured." The bombardment was in retaliation for the seizure of Mueang Hinbun[29] by the Free Vietnamese and the Free Lao.[30] The French claimed that Vietnamese [from the Thai side of the border] along with Thai had crossed the border and attacked [French territory in Indochina]. In fact the work was carried out by Lao and Vietnamese refugees.[31] Once they had accomplished their mission, at about 12.00 noon on 5 May they beat a retreat, but did not cross back over the border into Thailand. The only people around were those transporting goods to and fro across as already described.[32]

The second cable from Nakhon Phanom ran as follows: "From 10.00 a.m. to 11.00 a.m. on the 7th, French soldiers at Mueang Hinbun fired heavily with machine guns into Amphoe Tha Uthen, causing damage the extent of which is not yet known. At Nakhon Phanom a boat—the *Kanchana*—has been sunk, and the boats *Watthananakhon* and *Daonakon* damaged. Have already requested police from the Police School at Sakon Nakhon to come and help, and have ordered defensive measures at every *amphoe* along the border. No signs yet that they will cross over. We did not return the fire. One dead in Nakhon Phanom, two slightly injured, making a total of six casualties together with those mentioned in the last report."

I asked the British Minister and the American Chargé d'Affaires to see me right away. I not only informed them of the details of both cables, but confirmed that we had not returned fire, as it was our policy to carry out matters by peaceful means. I told them I could not guarantee, however, that our people would not become angered when they learned of the hostile actions France had taken against Thailand.

Mr. Thompson and Mr. Yost undertook to inform their respective governments of the situation at once so that France could be prevented from taking any further such action in the future. Both men told me they had heard that France intended to invade Thai territory before the coming rainy season. The British Minister had already told Colonel Saint Preux, the French Indochinese military representative who had arrived in Bangkok that if this was really carried out, world opinion would condemn France for such action.

Both the British Minister and the American Chargé d'Affaires told me that we should not delay in entering into negotiations with France over the territorial dispute, and that we should return the territories involved to France promptly. I replied, however, that if the United Nations insisted on this, or if the British or American governments officially demanded that we give these lands back, then the Thai government would have a reason to put the matter before the National Assembly. To give back these territories without conducting negotiations on the subject would, however, be beyond the capability of any Thai government.

Soon after the British and American legations agreed to send representatives to observe the border situation at Nakhon Phanom. They were to be accompanied by Nai Bun Charoenchai, our representative from the Ministry of Foreign Affairs.

On 13 May 1946 the American Chargé d'Affaires came to see me. After a general conversation on other topics, he brought up the subject of France, and warned me that France was on the lookout to find fault with Thailand. Allegations had been made that Thailand was guilty of complicity in allowing refugees to take weapons [across the border] and thereby create trouble for France. The Chargé felt that we should therefore take prompt action to disarm any such refugees. Even though he had heard that the joint troops for the province [i.e. including troops that had been brought into Nakhon Phanom from other provinces to deal with the situation] had already been disarmed, the situation remained tense. If we could arrange for the complete disarming of the refugees, this would give us a strong basis for refuting France's allegations.

I told the American Chargé that the Prime Minister had already arranged for the Ministry of the Interior to give immediate attention to the matter. Notwithstanding this, did the French have any legal right to fire on us?, I asked the Chargé. He replied that they definitely did not.

The same day that the American Chargé d'Affaires came to see me, the British Minister also met with me to discuss the situation. He said it was not clear which party was to blame for these firing incidents, as it appeared to be a situation which was beyond the control of either of them. From what the Minister had observed so far, it seemed as if Thailand had insufficient forces to disarm the refugees effectively. The French therefore suspected that the refugees would continue to escape and perform acts of sabotage, and that they were using Thailand as a base. Meanwhile, for their part, the French appeared to be unable to restrain their subordinates.

I told the Minister that the situation was not in fact beyond control. The French should not have fired into Thailand like this, however, but should have resorted to peaceful means instead. I added that as the British Minister already knew from the reports of his representative [observing the situation at Nakhon Phanom], Thailand was willing to cooperate with France in every possible way. When French nationals had fled from the Lao and Vietnamese into Thailand four to five months earlier,[33] the Thai had shown them every hospitality. The British Minister should also recall, I continued, that he himself had said that if we did not return the territories under dispute to France promptly, he feared that France might stir up trouble for us. Mr. Thompson thereupon suggested that Thailand should increase its forces along the frontier to ensure effective disarming of the refugees, and should move the latter further back from the banks of the Mekong. I expressed doubts as to whether this would be effective, pointing out that if we sent in more troops and the French were to fire on them, then the Thai soldiers were bound to return the fire. I told Mr. Thompson that the Ministry of the Interior was, however, in the process of increasing the strength of our police forces along the border.

On 27 May 1946, [following further border violations described below], Nai Pridi Banomyong, the Prime Minister, issued a communiqué on behalf of the Thai government. This was sent by cable to a number of world leaders, including the President of the United States of America, the Prime Minister of Great Britain, the President of the U.S.S.R., the President of the Republic of China, the Secretary-General of the United Nations, Herbert C. Hoover,[34] and Lord Killearn, the Special Commissioner for South-East Asia.[35]

The cable stated that on 24, 25 and 26 May of that year French troops had crossed the river Mekong into Thai territory and employed force to seize land there—land which, moreover, they continued to occupy. These raids, the communiqué continued, constituted concerted attacks that both violated Thai sovereignty and threatened the maintenance of peace in the area. Despite these groundless attacks against it Thailand had nevertheless shown self-restraint and had pursued a peaceful policy [in dealing with France].

Inhabitants of the lands under attack and those in neighboring areas had had to leave their houses and farms and evacuate the area, the communiqué continued. Moreover these attacks were taking place at the very time that the Thai government was doing its utmost to fulfill its obligations [to the Combined Boards] regarding the production and transportation of the maximum possible amount of rice to famine stricken areas. Now, with our people being pestered by French aggression, Thai efforts to help feed those stricken by hunger were being placed in jeopardy—a state of affairs for which French aggression was solely responsible. To promote peace, and in the name of those now dying of hunger in this region, Nai Pridi concluded his communiqué by therefore calling on people to show Thailand sympathy and help it to restore peaceful relations.

In addition the government and people of Thailand issued a plea to the starving people of the world which read as follows:

> The Thai government has already made several statements regarding French military aggression against Thailand. The situation has, however, not been brought to a conclusion. On 24, 25 and 26 May French troops crossed the Mekong into Thailand and are still occupying certain parts of our territory. These acts of aggression are not like other border incidents that have previously flared up now and then. Rather they constitute concerted actions violating the sovereignty of Thailand. As such they affect the maintenance of peace in the region. The Thai government has, however, refrained from taking hostile action in return. On the contrary, despite the unjust aggression being carried out against it, the Thai government has continued to pursue a peaceful policy.
>
> As a result of the French attacks, residents of the areas directly affected as well as those in neighboring areas have been forced to leave their houses and farms. This has affected the production and export of rice. Thailand has undertaken strict obligations to send the maximum amount of rice possible to those countries that are stricken by famine, and it has endeavored to carry out these obligations to the full. However, Thailand's efforts cannot be successful as long as France continues its aggressive policies. When people have to evacuate their farms and houses, this affects not only our rice production but our communications system as well. The government and people of Thailand therefore beseech all those people in the world

who love peace and have compassion to show sympathy towards and cooperate with Thailand in its attempts to keep the peace and to feed those who are starving in this part of the world.

Two days later, on 29 May 1946, Mr. (Trygve) Lie, the Secretary General of the United Nations, announced that he had received the Thai government's plea and would bring the matter before the Security Council. He also mentioned that this was the first case in which a non-member nation had brought a dispute before the United Nations.

On 30 May the French government announced that it had not carried out any acts of military aggression against Thailand. It was true, it was admitted, that French soldiers had crossed the Mekong into Thai territory in order to pursue robbers and saboteurs who had come over and disturbed the French. At the same time the High Commissioner for Indochina issued a statement declaring that the French had been forced to cross the Thai border because Thai officials were unable to keep the Lao and Vietnamese [refugees there] under control. He further alleged that Thailand had exaggerated the incidents concerned.

On 1 June 1946 the American Chargé d'Affaires informed me that when President Truman received Nai Pridi Banomyong's letter, he had immediately instructed the United States Ambassador in Paris to discuss the matter with the French Minister of Foreign Affairs. The latter had agreed to issue immediate instructions to officials in Indochina ordering them to stop any further military action against Thailand.

[About two weeks later], on 13 June, the Secretary General of the United Nations contacted our Prime Minister to say that he had given copies of our cable complaining about France's actions towards us to members of the Security Council.

In the meantime Mr. Edwin Stanton arrived to take up his duties as American Minister [to Thailand]. He often came to see me, and expressed his views not only about United States government policy, but also about our official complaint to the United Nations regarding the situation with France.

In regard to the complaint that we lodged with the United Nations, the constitution of the United Nations states that any non-member country [bringing a dispute before that organization] must agree in advance that it will abide by and carry out the decisions made by that body to end the dispute by peaceful means. Advance agreement to accept the obligations incurred in a peaceful settlement could therefore involve us in decisions over our frontiers as well. As any changes of this nature had first to be approved by the National Assembly, the government therefore proposed to that body on 17 June 1946 that it authorize the government to guarantee to the United Nations that it would carry out its obligations for settling the dispute peacefully. The National Assembly agreed to this proposal, and empowered the government with such authority that same day.

The government formed a delegation, to be led by Prince Wanwaithayakon.[36] Nai Khuang Aphaiwong, the Leader of the Opposition Party, was made Vice-Chairman, and the delegation included representatives of other political parties as well as a number of civil servants.[37] The government chose delegates from a number of different groups because it felt that the task assigned them affected the entire nation. The delegation was charged with conducting negotiations to end the dispute with France in accordance with the authority assigned it by the National Assembly.

On 15 July 1946 the government sent a note to the Secretary General of the United Nations confirming that Thailand was willing to abide by the decisions of the United Nations in every way.

At the beginning of October 1946 the government received a report from the Thai delegation meeting in New York.[38] This stated that France had, through the United States Government, proposed a new way for settling the dispute. The delegation had studied this proposal closely and saw no way but to accept the principles laid down in it. Members of the delegation would continue, however, to try to negotiate the most advantageous outcome for Thailand, along the lines expressed in the following report.[39]

SUMMARY OF THE OPINION OF THE THAI DELEGATION ON THE TERRITORIAL DISPUTE AND RELATED PROBLEMS WITH FRANCE

1. As the trip to Paris of Nai Khuang Aphaiwong and Nai Thanat Khoman has enabled the delegation to learn of France's views and opened ways for the latter to propose that direct negotiations be conducted between France and Thailand to settle the territorial dispute presently existing between the two countries within the framework of the United Nations Organization,[40] as expressed in the report of Nai Thanat Khoman and that of Nai Khuang Aphaiwong on the latter's discussions with various officials of the French government, (which reports have been handed to the delegation); and as Prince Subha Svasti has also reported to the delegation on Britain's viewpoint and on the entire outcome of his discussions in London; and on considering the observations and remarks of the delegation during its stay in Washington regarding the position held in American governmental circles, the delegation feels that on the occasion of Nai Suchit Hiranyapruek[41] returning to Bangkok on 5 October on official duties, the Thai delegation should hold discussions so that Nai Suchit can inform the Thai government thereon.

2. To begin with, Prince Wanwaithayakon, member of the Upper House[42] and leader of the Thai delegation, raised the question for discussion so that it could be put to the vote as to what the result would be if we were to take the dispute to the Security Council in accordance with our original plan. In the event of Thailand's insisting on sending the case to the Security Council, it was thought that French reaction would be as follows: (a) France would raise objections, using its right of veto and exploiting the rules and regulations of the United Nations; (b) even if France was defeated by a majority vote it would still find ways to continually obstruct us, without further thought of a compromise solution; and (c) if the situation reached that point, it would mean that good relations between France and Thailand would be ruptured indefinitely.

3. The Thai delegation had already considered the question of whether the friendly Powers [i.e. those nations most likely to support Thailand's case in the Security Council]—*viz.* England and the United States—would be in a position to help us, for our chances of success in taking the dispute before the Security Council would depend largely on their support. The attitude of these two countries was now known clearly, namely that they wished to see Thailand come to a direct agreement with France. They would not therefore encourage us in bringing the matter before the Security Council. We could not, then, hope for any [international] support if we were to place our case before the Security Council.

4. The delegation had also considered the attitude of other countries in the Security Council that would also affect the outcome of this affair. It had concluded that in the case of the U.S.S.R., as long as the question of our diplomatic relations with Moscow had not yet been satisfactorily settled,[43] we had no hope of receiving the support of the Soviet bloc. In fact we could not even be sure that the Russian delegates would not use the opportunity to debate widely beyond the bounds [of the immediate dispute in question.]

5. In brief, the delegation had therefore agreed unanimously that to take the avenue of presenting our case before the Security Council was paved with difficulties and should be avoided given the circumstances and reasons mentioned above.

6. As to the French proposal made through the United States State Department on 4 October 1946,[44] the delegation had given careful consideration to every detail of this, and could see no way but to accept it. Although the delegation felt it would be in our best interests to accept in principle the proposals that had been put forward, it would, however, conduct further negotiations in an effort to have the details adjusted in a manner that would yield the best possible results for Thailand.]

[On receiving this report], the Cabinet called an urgent meeting to discuss the matter. Extensive discussions were held, and it was finally agreed that we had no choice but to act on the suggestions of the Thai delegation, particularly as England and the United States, which we had hoped to lean on, had shown their support for France, and were not willing to consider alternative avenues of negotiation. On 12 October 1946 Rear Admiral Thawan Thamrongnawasawat, the Prime Minister, therefore sent an urgent letter to the Speaker of the House of Representatives requesting that a session be called on 14 October to discuss certain matters that the National Assembly had, on 17 June 1946, empowered the government to take any necessary action on. The Prime Minister explained that France had now put forward a new proposal which the government would go over with those attending the meeting. As the matter called for the nullification of the Peace Treaty of 1941,[45] ratification of which would involve boundary changes, the government had first to seek the approval of the National Assembly in accordance with Article 76 of the Constitution of the Kingdom of Thailand.

So that the reader can understand the details of this matter, I will now give the text of my speech made before the National Assembly on 14 October 1946. This ran as follows: On 17 June 1946 the National Assembly approved the government's proposal that the territorial dispute between France and Thailand be brought before the United Nations Organization, and authorized the government to undertake to the United Nations that we would abide by our obligation to settle this dispute through peaceful means in accordance with the rules and principles of the constitution of that body. The government then set up a delegation to place the case before the United Nations. This was headed by H.H. Prince Wanwaithayakon, with Nai Khuang Aphaiwong as Vice-Chairman. They went, together with their party, to Washington to hold talks with United Nations' representatives and to sign an agreement on the dispute.

While the delegation was [still] preparing for its trip and holding consultations and discussions, the government received a proposal from France which the American Minister in Bangkok received from the United States Department of State and handed the then Prime Minister on 3 August 1946. The main essentials of this proposal were that the two conflicting countries should go before the World Court and let it decide whether the Peace Treaty signed in Tokyo on 9 May 1941 was legally valid, or whether Thailand should withdraw its case from the United Nations.

The American Minister, [Mr. Stanton], informed us that the State Department felt it would be to Thailand's advantage to accept the French proposal. The dispute would still be handled within the framework of the United Nations Organization as Thailand wished, and would not be merely an agreement between Thailand and France alone.

The government, as well as the delegation itself, studied the French proposal and also the opinion of the United States Department of State, and concluded that we should accept the French proposal. We felt we would still be acting within the sphere of authority granted by the National Assembly, as the World Court was part of the United Nations Organization. The government therefore gave the delegation full authority to carry out measures [in accordance with the new French proposal.] However, in so far as the French proposed that we withdraw the dispute from the United Nations, the government felt that we should delay on this for the time being as the matter had already been put before the United Nations. It therefore instructed the delegation to wait on this matter until further discussion had taken place.

Once the Thai delegation reached Washington on 12 August it opened negotiations through the State Department and sought to carry out discussions on the lines proposed by France. However, before any effective results could be reached, troubles broke out in Indochina in the province of Siemreap. France accused Thailand of having played a part in the attack on Siemreap, saying that Thai subjects had crossed the border to help the rioters, and even accusing the Thai government of having sent in trained soldiers. These allegations were not true at all, as the results of investigations later announced before the National Assembly showed. However, France ultimately informed the United States that it was withdrawing its proposal that the dispute with Thailand be brought before the World Court.

Once events took this turn, the Thai delegation got in touch with the State Department to find ways to continue the negotiations. At the same time the Thai authorities issued a communiqué denying that the Thai government had had any connection whatsoever with the events and unrest in Cambodia. The Thai delegates also explained to all parties concerned that the Thai government had not been responsible in any way for these events. They even expressed the opinion that the incident was a different matter from the territorial dispute, and should not be mixed up with it. Further, Thailand was willing to allow the situation to be investigated by neutral parties. All this was to no avail, however. When the head of the Thai delegation discussed the matter with the man acting for the United States Secretary of State, he was informed that the United States could do nothing, as France had already withdrawn its original proposal [that the dispute be brought before the World Court]. The United States further expressed its wish that Thailand and France enter into direct negotiations rather than settle the matter through other means.

France later sent a Monsieur Guillaume Georges Picot, who had been Chargé d'Affaires in Thailand and was now French Ambassador to Venezuela, to hold semi-official discussions with the Thai delegation in Washington.

The basis of M. Picot's proposals was, however, still unacceptable to us, as France insisted that Thailand cancel the Peace Treaty of 1941 without prior negotiations for any adjustments to our mutual frontier. It also refused to accept any proposals by us that differed from this requirement. To enable Thailand to understand the true attitude of the French government for itself, M. Picot suggested that the Vice-Chairman of the [Thai] delegation be sent to Paris. This met with the approval of the Thai delegation, and the Chairman of the delegation therefore asked and received permission from the [Thai] government for the Vice-Chairman, together with the Secretary of the delegation, to leave for Paris. This they did on 7 September, together with M. Picot. At the same time the government also permitted Lieutenant-Colonel Prince Subha to go to London to sound out the views of the British government on the matter and to note its attitude thereon.

These three delegates returned later to Washington, where they had reported back to the delegation. After members of the delegation had held meetings and discussions, it was decided that they should put forward the views of the delegation and give various documents to Nai Suchit Hiranyapruek, an M.P. and reserve delegate, to relay to the government.

It appears from these reports that at the discussions of the Thai delegation in Paris, the French government handed the Vice-Chairman of the Thai delegation a new proposal as the basis for a direct agreement between the governments of France and Thailand, and at the same time sent this same proposal to the United States State Department to hand on to members of the Thai delegation in Washington. When delivering this proposal, which appears below as Supplementary Document no. 1, the State Department also handed the [Thai] delegation a memorandum of the verbal statements [formerly made] by France to the Thai delegation [in Paris]. This appears below as Supplementary Document no. 2, while its own memorandum to the Thai delegation appears as Supplementary Document no. 3.

In the State Department memorandum, the American government emphasized that the United States could not acknowledge Thailand's right to French Indochinese territories which had been transferred to her in 1941, and stated that Thailand should return these territories and restore the *status quo ante*.

On 17 June 1946, when the Thai government of that time sought the decision of the National Assembly [regarding a settlement of the dispute by the United Nations], it had already informed the Assembly of the attitudes of the American and British governments on the subject of the territories Thailand had received from France. However, I will give a brief summary of these attitudes again below.

CHAPTER 14

During the negotiations held in Kandy and Singapore on 16 October 1945 to end the state of war existing between Thailand and England, the British representative stated that England refused to recognize any territorial changes brought about through the use of force during the Second World War. He again informed Thailand of this view in a note of 1 January 1946 which Mr. Dening sent to M.C. Wiwatthanachai Chaiyan. This ran as follows:

Singapore. 1st January 1946.

To the representative of Thailand:

Regarding the verbal discussions which have been held in Kandy and Singapore between the Thai delegation headed by you, and myself, I have received instructions from His Majesty's government in the United Kingdom to put on record its attitude concerning Thailand's acquisition of territory either through the manoeuvres or intervention of Japan.

His Majesty's government in the United Kingdom refuses to recognize any territorial acquisitions made by Thailand later than 11th December 1940. This non-recognition includes the entire territory that the Vichy government ceded on 9th May 1941.

I have received instructions to let you know, as the representative of the government of Thailand, of these attitudes of His Majesty's government in the United Kingdom.

Yours very faithfully,
(Signed) *M.E. Dening.*

Similarly, in the case of the United States, the Thai Chargé d'Affaires in Washington, in reporting on an interview held with the State Department, stated that the American government did not recognize Thailand's recovery of territories from France according to the Peace Treaty of 1941, but had mentioned that the return of these disputed territories would not affect any appeals Thailand might later make on the subject to the United Nations when an opportunity arose. The American legation in Bangkok had made American government policy on this subject clear to the Thai Foreign Ministry several times before.

Taking into consideration both the opinion of the delegation and the attitudes of the United States and England, the government now began to consider the new French proposals. It was felt that the main principle involved was the cancellation of the Peace Treaty of 1941. As the proposals were beyond the scope of authority assigned by the Assembly to the delegation, and as this was a matter of policy affecting the entire nation, as announced in the National Assembly on 17 June of this year, the government was therefore bringing the matter up for its consideration once again.

As to the details of this matter, I should like to present the following:

Translation:
Supplementary Document No. 1.
DRAFT OF PROPOSALS TO END THE DISPUTE
BETWEEN FRANCE AND THAILAND

The government of the Republic of France and the government of Thailand agree to end the existing dispute between the two countries on the following basis:

1. To accept as void the Peace Treaty of 9th May 1941, with the government of Thailand making an announcement canceling the effect of such agreement. The Indochinese territories which Thailand has occupied would be transferred to the French authorities, to be handed over to the governments of Cambodia and Laos respectively.

2. After this return to the *status quo ante*, which would end the state of hostility between Thailand and France, diplomatic relations would immediately be restored between the two countries. The relationship between the two countries would return to that drawn up under the treaty of 7th December 1937,[46] and that of the Commercial and Customs Agreement dated 9th December 1937.[47] Furthermore, if Thailand would withdraw her complaint lodged with the Security Council, then France would no longer bar Thailand's entry to the United Nations.

3. Immediately Thailand announces as void the agreement of 9th May 1941, France would agree, in accordance with Article 21 of the treaty between France and Thailand signed on 7th December 1937, to set up a Conciliation Commission composed of two representatives from the two parties to the agreement, together with three representatives from neutral countries, in compliance with the general rules of Geneva dated 26th September 1928 on "the ending of international disputes through peaceful means", which lays down the regulations for the formation and duties of such a commission.

4. This Commission would start work once the first article of this proposal had been complied with. The Commission would have as its duties the weighing of all arguments on ethnic, geographic and economic aspects of the agreement to revise or confirm, as the case might be, clauses of the agreement signed on 23rd March 1907 which are still exercised by Article 22 of the 7th December 1937 Agreement.

5. Once diplomatic relations had been restored, negotiations would then be opened to clear up any remaining problems between the two countries, and particularly to determine the amount of the damages which the government of Thailand would have to pay as compensation for the loss of property, rights and interests of France or Indochina on the one hand, and on the other, to fix the amount of money which would be credited to the Thai government.

Translation:
Document No. 2.
RECORD OF VERBAL STATEMENTS
[Of the French Ambassador to the Thai Delegation]

The French Ambassador made additional verbal statements on the French proposals handed in today. He said that if the government of Thailand so wished, the French government would be willing, if Thailand withdrew its complaint before the Security Council, to find ways for an arrangement to be made whereby the agreement could receive the approval of that body, thus facilitating Thailand's acceptance of such an agreement.

He added that in this event [i.e. of Thailand's accepting the French proposals], not only would France withdraw its objections against Thailand's entry to the United Nations, but it would actively encourage Thailand's application for membership.

He remarked that even though the French government might have emphasized that the Conciliation Commission would not start work until the territories in question had been returned and the *status quo ante* restored, it was nevertheless ready to set up the said Commission even before that time.

He also explained that according to the usual rules, once a compromise had been decided upon, a Conciliation Commission had to be established and its work completed within a fixed period, and that the work had to be continued until it was all done.

He guaranteed that there would be no objection to several agreements being made to incorporate all the proposals. However, for several agreements to become effective, an order of procedure would have to be followed.

The Ambassador also stated it would be necessary for a ceremony to be held to mark the return of the [disputed] territories.

Lastly he declared that the French government was grateful for the help it had received from the [United States] government in working out the details of whether to have one or several agreements so that whatever arrangement was agreed to should prove effective.

The delegation also felt confident that [United States] government help would be given similarly to the government of Thailand if it so desired.

Translation:
Document No. 3.
MEMORANDUM
[Of the United States Department of State]

Members of the Thai delegation may recall that the government of the United States has made its intentions clear several times that it will not accept any boundary changes effected by Japan, or which were carried out with the aid of Japan in the course of its aggressions. The United States government cannot therefore recognize the transfer of territories which Thailand received from Indochina in 1941, and feels that Thailand should return such territories and return to the *status quo ante*.

This government will definitely be unable to request that the French government accept any proposals which have as condition that the French cede part of such territories to Thailand, for such action would mean that the United States supported a country that was acting against international practice and that the United States was allowing that country to carry through such acts by means of bargaining to satisfy its own wishes, and that the United States was encouraging that country to refuse to set such deeds right until it had received what it wanted.

Moreover this government has also clearly shown that in spite of its firm belief that the way in which Thailand acquired these territories was not right, and that they should be returned, it will not in any way decide the rights and wrongs of the territorial conflict between Thailand and Indochina prior to 1941, for this government has no direct stake in any such adjustment of frontiers or transfer of territories. This government has called on the French government throughout to give an undertaking that once Thailand has returned the territories, an opportunity be given Thailand to find ways for frontier adjustments or transfer of territories that the government of Thailand feels should rightly be made through peaceful means.

The United States government has even expressed the opinion to the French government that if possible, for the sake of preventing any future unrest or international conflict consideration should also be given to territorial changes made before 1941, and that when considering such matters attention should be given to the ethnic, geographic, economic and other such related factors rather than to the legal and historical considerations, since the latter are controversial and took place in the past.

The French government has now asked the United States government to deliver France's proposals to end the dispute between Thailand and France to the Thai delegation, and has asked that the Thai government accept such proposals, since they are in keeping with the situation which the United States has been upholding in every way. The United States feels that the proposals are also in accordance with international law, as well as with the aims and principles of the United Nations.

The government of the United States therefore hopes with all sincerity that the government of Thailand will accept the French proposals by recognizing that this is an honorable and suitable way to end the conflict between the two countries and to restore good relations between Thailand and France.

The United States government believes that a quick ending of this dispute is very important to the establishment of peace in Southeast Asia. This in turn is important to Thailand, since this problem [i.e. the territorial dispute with France] has inevitably undermined Thailand's efforts to rehabilitate the country's war-torn economy. This government therefore hopes that such proposals will be given prompt attention, and if accepted, that the details be worked out in either one or if necessary several agreements, with a date being fixed so that an agreement can be worked out at the earliest possible opportunity.

            Department of State of the United States.
            Washington.
            4 October 1946.

The members of the National Assembly debated and discussed the matter at length. Finally, with the deepest regrets, it agreed to assign authority to the government to accept the proposals recommended by the delegation. We could see that no country was going to help us over the dispute, not even Nationalist China. We had consulted Nationalist China, but had been told that it could not help us in any way as both the United States and England were committed to a return to the *status quo ante*. On the evening of 16 October 1946 Rear Admiral Thawan Thamrongnawasawat, the Prime Minister, delivered a nationwide broadcast giving details of the situation to his Thai fellow citizens. He described the return of the [disputed] territories to France as the supreme sacrifice of the Thai nation in the interests of peace and the ideals of the United Nations, and also stated that England and the United States had pressed for acceptance of the French proposals.

On 17 November 1946 the [Thai] delegation reported that H.H. Prince Wanwaithayakon, Chairman of the delegation, and the Vice-Chairman, Nai

Khuang Aphaiwong, had signed an agreement in Washington that day to end the dispute between France and Thailand.[48] The main clauses of this agreement covered the restoration of relations between the two nations; the nullification of the Peace Treaty of 9 May 1941; and the future formation of a Conciliation Commission to consider whether the agreements of 1893,[49] 1904,[50] and 1907[51] should be revised or confirmed. In brief, the *status quo ante* was upheld in accordance with the wishes of England and the United States and to the satisfaction of France. Only a few years later, the entire situation changed yet again as the different countries comprised within Indochina regained their independence and ousted the French from their territories.

The members of the Franco-Thai Conciliation Commission, established according to the agreement to end the dispute between France and Thailand of 17 November 1946, included Monsieur Victor Andrés Bélaúnde, Ambassador to Peru and member of the International Court of Arbitration at the Hague; Mr. William Phillips, former [American] Ambassador [to Rome] and [former] United States Under-Secretary of State; and Sir Horace Seymour, formerly British Ambassador [to China]. These three men were appointed by the governments of France and Thailand. The French government also appointed a fellow national, Monsieur [Paul] Emile Naggiar, while we chose H.H. Prince Wanwaithayakon, the Thai Minister to Washington. In addition each government also appointed its representatives assigned to the Commission, with France appointing Monsieur Francois Lacoste, French Minister and Councilor at the French Embassy in Washington, and Monsieur Jean Burnay, Privy Councilor; while Thailand appointed Prince Sakonwannakonworawan, Adviser to the Minister of the Interior, and Nai Tiang Sirikhan, Member of Parliament for the province of Sakon Nakhon.

On 27 June 1947 the Commission presented a detailed report of great length,[52] the summary of its recommendations and conclusions being as follows:

SUMMARY OF RECOMMENDATIONS

The recommendations of the Commission, which follow from other reports, are summarized as follows:

1. The Commission does not support Thailand's claims concerning the territory of Lan Chang [on the right bank of Luang Prabang], and feels that the agreement signed on [13] February 1904 on the Thailand-French Indochina borders in the province of Lan Chang[53] should not be revised (part 3A, paragraph 4).[54]

2. The Commission does not support Thailand's claims regarding territory on the left bank of the Mekong.[55] Thus the treaty signed on 3 October 1893 on

this matter should not be revised (part 2, paragraph 8). However, revisions should be made regarding the riparian frontier that was fixed by various treaties, so that the frontier in the river be drawn at the thalweg (deep water channel) line? (part 3B, paragraph 6).

3. The [geographic area under the] authority of the High Commission for the Mekong should be extended, as should its functions[56] (part 3B, paragraph 7).

4. The Commission does not support Thailand's claims for territory in the province of Bassac [Champassac]. Thus no revision should be made to the agreement of 13 February 1904 on this matter[57] (part 3C, paragraph 7).

5. The Commission does not support Thailand's claim on Phratabong [Battambang]. The treaty of 23 March 1907 on this matter should not therefore be revised (part 3D, paragraph 7).

6. Regarding fishing rights in the Lake,[58] the Commission recommends that an agreement be reached between the parties in order to ensure a sufficient supply of fish to Thailand (part 3D, paragraph 8).

7. The Commission recommends that the governments of France and Thailand enter into negotiations with the aim of setting up an international advisory committee in Bangkok to discuss and study technical problems of common interest to the countries of the Indochinese peninsula (part 5).[59]

CONCLUSION

The Commission wishes to stress once again that acting within the framework of the duties assigned it, it has limited its considerations and deliberations to ethnic, geographic and economic arguments, and has avoided dealing with political and historical considerations. The evidence put before the Commission has been obtained from representatives of the two governments.

Even though the Commission judged it impossible to support Thailand's territorial claims, it nevertheless has made certain recommendations which, if approved by the two governments, should be of benefit to the peoples concerned. The Commission feels that the transfer of territory from one side to the other without the consent of the people would not be beneficial to residents of the border areas, since the true happiness and security of the people concerned must be based on their freedom to enjoy relations with their neighbors across the borders. Twenty-five kilometer zones, which already exist on each side of the river and which are now demilitarized and customs-free, should favor communal exchanges and stimulate friendly relations between the inhabitants on either side of the river basin.

Under such conditions, and with the carrying out by the two governments of these recommendations, the Commission hopes with all sincerity that goodwill and cooperation will ensue between the two parties, thus contributing to the peace and prosperity so necessary not only for the future of Thailand and Indochina, but also for that of the entire peninsula.

The various delegates [who took part in the negotiations over the territorial dispute with France] cooperated well with one another. In a lecture given by H.H. Prince Wanwaithayakon at Thammasat University on 6 February 1947, he stated:

> "...first of all, I should say that the task assigned us by the government at that time [i.e. at the time the above negotiations were carried out] was one that affected the interests of the entire nation. Members of the delegation wish to thank the government for entrusting them with such an assignment. That it was a task which affected the entire nation can be seen from the fact that the government chose as Vice-Chairman of the delegation Nai Khuang Aphaiwong, the leader of the Opposition Party, indicating that this was a national concern in which the cooperation of everyone was called for [regardless of party affiliation].
>
> ...The work of the delegation sent to Washington included attending various meetings at which we would exchange opinions and engage in free discussions and debates. On each occasion that matters were put to a vote, the members of the meeting voted unanimously. Once a unanimous decision had been reached, those of us who were assigned to see such decisions put into effect, which included the Vice-Chairman and myself, would carry out the meeting's decisions on every occasion. The Prime Minister of that time, Nai Pridi Banomyong, and the present Prime Minister[60] and Minister of Foreign Affairs,[61] all placed their trust and faith in the members of the delegation, including myself. This greatly encouraged us in our work. We sometimes had to take action on issues that should have been discussed first with the government. Sometimes, however, there was no time for this. On such occasions we had to carry out the work right away and report on the matter to the government later. The members of the delegation and I would like to thank the two governments concerned for having permitted such a procedure...."

15
Cancellation of the Heads of Agreement with England
[And Treaty Terminating the State of War with Australia]¹

CANCELLATION OF THE HEADS OF AGREEMENT WITH ENGLAND

As has already been mentioned in the first chapter of part 3 [now chapter 10], on 1 January 1946 the government² signed the Formal Agreement for the Termination of the State of War between Thailand, Great Britain and India. On the same day, before the Agreement was signed, the Thai representative, [M.C. Wiwatthanachai Chaiyan], was handed an Exchange of Notes by the British representative, [Mr. Dening], stating that England had sent us the Heads of Agreement and Annex listing the clauses and conditions under which the governments of the United Kingdom and India were ready to terminate the state of war with Thailand. The Thai representative should let the latter know without delay if the government of Thailand was ready to sign a formal agreement or agreements that would include all the clauses set forth in these Heads of Agreement and Annex, and that pending signature of such agreement, the government of Thailand would abide by these clauses. The Thai representative provided this undertaking.³

Later, [however], questions arose. How far did Thailand have to carry out the requirements of the Heads of Agreement and Annex attached to the Exchange of Notes once the Formal Agreement had been signed on 1 January 1946? England felt that even though the Formal Agreement had been signed, as it did not cover all the clauses incorporated in the Heads of Agreement and Annex, Thailand was therefore obliged to carry out the clauses in the Heads of Agreement and Annex. Thailand, on the other hand, considered that once the Formal Agreement had been signed, the Heads of Agreement and Annex should automatically lapse.

The Ministry of Foreign Affairs, led by M.R. Seni Pramoj, carried out continuous negotiations on the subject with England. When I replaced M.R. Seni Pramoj at the end of March 1946, I took on the continuation of these negotiations until the beginning of September 1946, at which time England proposed to cancel the Heads of Agreement and Annex, but with Thailand and England exchanging notes on various matters [covered by the said Heads of Agreement and Annex], and with Thailand taking certain steps such as handing England a memorandum [on the issues that were still outstanding].

On 23 September 1946, in my capacity as Minister of Foreign Affairs, I sought the Cabinet's views on the arrangements we were to make with England [on the remaining points at issue] regarding cancellation of the Heads of Agreement.

1. **Joint committee to study the payment of compensation.**

Under Articles 2 and 3 of the Formal Agreement, the Thai government agreed to take responsibility for returning and paying compensation to England for property [seized during the war], but it was not clear as to how such compensation should be determined. Long discussions were held as to who the members of the committee to study the payment of compensation should be, and it was finally agreed that the committee should be composed of a British representative, who would hold the Chair, an Indian representative, an Australian representative, and three representatives from Thailand. This was agreed to in July 1946.[4]

2. **Currency needs of the Allied military authorities.**

Article 6(b) of the Annex at the end of the Heads of Agreement stated that for as long as it might be necessary for the conclusion of all matters of military concern to the Allies arising out of the settlement of the war with Japan, Thailand would provide the Allies free of charge with supplies and services as well as with all Baht currency that might be required by the Allied military authorities in Thailand.

Initially it was agreed that the Prime Minister and Minister of Foreign Affairs, M.R. Seni Pramoj, would hand the British Chargé d'Affaires a memorandum to the effect that Thailand would provide whatever amount of money was needed. However, subsequently England delivered a memorandum to us stating that with consideration to the cooperation of Allied military officers in disarming the Japanese troops and arranging for their detention in our country, the Thai government was to provide facilities [for the former] free of charge. The Allied military officers were to receive Baht currency for their expenditures according to their needs in carrying out their tasks, or in other words, no fixed maximum amount to be made available was set.

We at the Ministry of Foreign Affairs felt that if no maximum amount was fixed, the government would face opposition in the National Assembly, for members of the Assembly were convinced that England would demand too much from us. We therefore asked that a maximum sum be fixed. This request was rejected by England on the grounds that such an amount might not be sufficient.

In the end it was agreed that we would draw up a memorandum that would not specify any amount, while England on the other hand would furnish us with a memorandum containing an understanding that the money asked for would not exceed 100 million Baht,[5] although it was to be understood that this 100 million Baht was not a maximum figure, and that England might need more in unforeseen circumstances.[6]

3. **Cooperation with the Allies.**

The Annex at the end of the Heads of Agreement attached to the Exchange of Notes which the representative of Thailand signed on the same day as the Formal Agreement contained clauses under which the government of Thailand agreed to:
- a) Sequestrate Allied banking and commercial concerns, and allow them to continue their business (Article 2 of the Annex).
- b) Reserve Japanese and other enemy property for the use of the Allies (Article 3).
- c) Cooperate in the arrest and trial of persons accused of war crimes or who had given active assistance to Japan (Article 4).
- d) Turn over to the Allied military authorities Allied nationals who were alleged to be deserters (Article 5).
- e) Negotiate an agreement giving judicial protection and immunity to the Allied forces in Thailand similar to such agreements made by the Allies with one another [Article 6(d) of the Annex].
- f) Control banking, business and other foreign commercial and financial transactions according to the wishes of the Allies for as long as this might be necessary for the conclusion of matters of military, economic and financial concern to the Allies arising out of their work in connection with the termination of the war with Japan [Article 8.]

Once it was agreed that the Heads of Agreement and Annex would be cancelled, England proposed that an exchange of notes be made which would deal with the above points as follows:

1. **Sequestration of Allied banking and commercial concerns.**

Actually this had already been mentioned in Article 4 of the Formal Agreement and in the Heads of Agreement 4(b). However, in Article 2 of the Annex the word "Allied" instead of "British" was used. England asked that the wording in the Annex be used. We did not see any drawback to this request, and therefore agreed to the change.

2. **Japanese and other enemy property.**

An exchange of notes was to be made stating that the Thai government would reserve Japanese and other enemy property for the use of the Allies after a deduction had been made for reasonable expenditures. The amount of this deduction, for expenses involved in the control and administration of the said properties, would be correctly certified and checked and an account rendered as already agreed to.

Thailand asked to be granted deductions for two categories of expenses, namely expenses incurred in the administration of the said properties, and secondly expenses incurred in the detention of Japanese soldiers and civilians.

England agreed to grant us a deduction of expenses for the first category, but objected to the second, claiming that every country incurred expenses for the detention of soldiers and enemy aliens. In the end we had to give in on this matter. However, we felt that the [new] arrangement was still somewhat more advantageous to us than the previous one, for the Annex had stated that we must reserve Japanese and other enemy property for the use of the Allies, but had not stipulated that we might receive deductions for expenses.[7]

3. **War criminals and deserters.**

In the draft exchange of notes on this matter it was set down that the Thai government would first arrest and send to trial those accused of having committed war crimes or who were alleged to have given active assistance to Japan; and secondly hand over Allied nationals alleged to be deserters to the Allied military authorities. In fact the first clause was taken more or less directly from Article 4 of the Annex to the Formal Agreement, which stated that the Thai government would "…cooperate in the apprehension and trial of persons accused of war crimes or notable for affording active assistance to Japan…"

The Thai government had already come to an understanding with England whereby if the [alleged] war criminals were Thai subjects they were to be brought before a Thai court of law. If, on the other hand, they were of other nationalities, then we would raise no objections to the Allies trying such individuals themselves. An agreement was come to because the wording of the [original] clause was somewhat ambiguous and could have been taken to mean that England could ask us to hand over war criminals even if they were Thai subjects. For this reason the government of M.R. Seni Pramoj had proposed to the National Assembly that we establish our own War Criminal Court to demonstrate that we had full rights of jurisdiction and sovereignty to try our own nationals.

One other point should be added here. On the same day that Nai Khuang Aphaiwong, the Prime Minister, handed in his resignation, on 23 or 24 March 1946, the War Criminal Court agreed to dismiss the cases [of those charged as war criminals][8] on the grounds that the War Criminal Court did not have the power to try persons retroactively.[9]

The first day that I received calls from foreign diplomatic representatives in my capacity as Minister of Foreign Affairs, on 26 March 1946, I was asked by the American Chargé d'Affaires, [Mr. Yost], why the cases concerning our war criminals had been dismissed. I replied that this was a matter for the Court to decide on, as it was independent in its actions. However, I asked the American Chargé for his opinion on the matter. He replied that this was indeed so [i.e. that the Court had the right to make its own decisions], and did not expand on the matter any further.

The British Minister did not discuss the matter with me, but consulted H.H. Prince Wanwaithayakon, Adviser to the Ministry of Foreign Affairs, about it. Once the Minister had left, Prince Wan told me that Mr. Thompson had asked him about the affair, and that he, Prince Wan, had replied by explaining that those charged with war crimes should be divided into two categories. The first were those guilty of acts of cruelty towards the Allies. Thailand had already given an undertaking to England and Australia that such people would be dealt with, and this had satisfied England somewhat. The second involved those guilty of political crimes. They had been released after having made clear their intentions to keep out of politics. The Minister had expressed satisfaction at this also.

Once the War Criminal Court had dismissed the cases of those charged as war criminals, there was no necessity left for it to remain. However, I learned that England wanted the article retained [in the Exchange of Notes] to intimidate those who had afforded help to Japan in general, even though the clause was no longer really effective.

As to Allied deserters, the question arose as to how a deserter was defined by law. England claimed that it would be narrow to define such persons only as those guilty of treachery. It was finally agreed that if the Allies wanted to deal with any of their nationals who were accused of being deserters, they should specify such persons by name and give the charges levied against them.

We at the Ministry of Foreign Affairs felt that both the clauses dealing with war criminals and those dealing with deserters had been taken from the Annex [Articles 4 and 5.]. We had already reached agreement over dealing with criminals of Thai nationality ourselves, and there was now no way to deal with such people any longer since the War Criminal Court had been dissolved. We therefore agreed to an exchange of notes on this subject, believing that we would not incur any disadvantages by doing so.

4. **Judicial protection for Allied troops in Thailand.**

The wording of the draft exchange of notes on this matter did not differ in any way from the wording in the Annex.

5. **Control of banking, business and other foreign transactions.**

The draft exchange of notes on this topic was also taken from Article 8 of the Annex, and did not involve either advantages or disadvantages for us.

6. **Allied property.**

[In Article 1 of the Annex attached to the Heads of Agreement] the Thai government agreed to take responsibility for safeguarding and restoring unimpaired the properties, rights and interests of the Allies, and to pay compensation for any damage or destruction thereto. Negotiations and discussions on this subject continued to be held by successive governments, for we felt that the use of the words "properties of the Allies" laid us open for any country to make claims on us. We felt that talks should be held and agreement reached with the specific country which might have cause to raise charges against us, and not because the country making the demands was using the umbrella term "Allies". Eventually it was agreed that when the government made an announcement in the National Assembly regarding the Formal Agreement, it should also take the opportunity to inform the Assembly of this matter.

It was also felt that beyond this it would be sufficient for a statement to be made by the Department of Public Relations stating that "the government of Thailand agrees to accept responsibility for the safeguarding and restoring in good condition the properties, rights and other interests in Thailand of any country or nationals of that country which was at a state of war with Thailand on or after 7th December 1941, so that reasonable compensation could be paid for any loss or damage sustained thereto, according to procedures which will be negotiated between the Thai government and the government concerned." We at the Ministry of Foreign Affairs put this proposal before the Cabinet, which in turn approved it.

7. **Interpretation of Article 3 of the Military Agreement.**

As already described in the chapter 10, Article 3 of the military agreement signed in Kandy, Ceylon on 8 September 1945 stated that we would maintain and allow Allied military officers the use of Thailand's naval, military and air forces, including harbors, airports, buildings, provisions, means of communication, weapons and every kind of equipment of that particular force which would be specifically listed. Further we would also allow them the use of ground facilities, buildings and warehouses as required by the Allied military authorities for the billeting of their soldiers and for the storage of their equipment. We would also agree to other requests that the Supreme Commander of the Allied Forces might consider necessary to make for the benefit of the Allied forces.

This statement was also incorporated into the Annex as Article 6, so that when the Heads of Agreement were cancelled England proposed that the Prime Minister send a letter to the Ministry of Defense confirming our continued acceptance of these points, and ending with the words that "this would continue as long as it was necessary for the Allied military authorities to handle several matters until the Japanese troops were completely evacuated from Thailand." This clause fixed a shorter and more definite time period than that given in the Annex, where it was only stated that this would continue "as long as might be necessary for the conclusion of all matters of military concern to the Allies arising out of the settlement of the war with Japan…"

As the Allied troops were about to withdraw from Thailand at the time this matter was under consideration,[10] we felt that it should not be too difficult to continue to provide the facilities that were required of us. The tasks that had lain ahead when this agreement had been signed [originally] at Kandy had now almost been completed. We at the Ministry of Foreign Affairs therefore felt that the British proposal could be accepted, and if the Cabinet so approved, then the Ministry of Foreign Affairs would hold consultations with the Ministry of Defense on the subject.

8. Thailand's obligations after World War II.

England informed us that it was ready to give us an undertaking in writing that once we were ready to come to an understanding on each of the above mentioned topics Thailand would not be subject to further obligations other than those laid down in the Formal Agreement and the Exchange of Notes on the above matters. The Heads of Agreement and Annex could then be cancelled.

The Cabinet warmly approved of the arrangements suggested by the Ministry of Foreign Affairs, and gave instructions that negotiations be conducted for an agreement with England along the principles outlined. Although we were, thus, ready to negotiate, England, surprisingly, kept silent on the subject. I pressed the issue several times, but was always told that the British government was consulting the various ministries and departments concerned, even though discussions had been going on for a long time on these matters. Four months after the decision had been taken by the Cabinet, or at about the end of January 1947, the British Minister came and informed me that he had received instructions to cancel the Heads of Agreement as already discussed, and would later bring the draft of the various exchanges of notes to the Ministry of Foreign Affairs for further consideration. However, before we had been able to hold further discussions, I resigned from my positions as Deputy Prime Minister and Minister of Foreign Affairs in early February 1947. The Exchange of Notes was carried through in March 1947 between Rear Admiral Thawan Thamrongnawasawat, the Prime Minister and subsequent Minister of Foreign Affairs, and the British Ambassador.

TREATY WITH AUSTRALIA

As has already been mentioned in chapter 10, on the same day that the government of Thailand signed the Formal Agreement with England, the Thai representative also exchanged notes with the Australian representative [entering into a preliminary agreement] for the termination of the state of war between the two countries, and arranging for the prompt conclusion of a final treaty for such termination.

Negotiations [leading to a final treaty] continued from January through March 1946. Just as an agreement was about to be signed, however, the government of Nai Khuang Aphaiwong, with M.R. Seni Pramoj as Minister of Foreign Affairs, resigned, and Nai Pridi Banomyong was appointed Prime Minister instead, with myself replacing M.R. Seni Pramoj as Minister of Foreign Affairs.

On 3 April 1946 I signed a treaty with representatives of the government of Australia. This had fifteen heads of agreement, the contents of which were similar to the twenty-four clauses of the Formal Agreement made with England on 1 January 1946. However, there was no clause requiring us to hand over rice supplies, nor was any mention made of the Kra Isthmus. We had to agree to make good the damage done to Australian properties in Thailand [during the war], and to pay damages or compensation to Australian nationals for any losses they had suffered during the war in our country.[11]

16
Thailand's Application for Membership in the United Nations

Thailand's application for membership in the United Nations was a major issue and one of the most important diplomatic concerns to affect Thailand after the Second World War. It is therefore a matter which all those studying Thai diplomacy should know about to some extent.

Nai Konthi Suphamongkhon, the Director-General of the Department of the United Nations,[1] has written about this subject in the souvenir issue of the magazine *Sranrom* of 10 February 1952. In it he notes that after the First World War ended in 1918, Thailand, as a nation which had cooperated with the Allies during the war, became one of the first members of the League of Nations set up under the peace treaty between the Allies and Germany. From that time onwards Thailand carried out its responsibilities as a member of the League with integrity and loyalty, never thinking in terms of receiving any return benefits from that organization.

During the Second World War which just ended in 1945 the Allies set up an international organization named the United Nations Organization[2] to replace the former League of Nations. Because of our circumstances at that time [i.e. because Japan had occupied the country], Thailand was unable to play any part in the United Nations Organization during this period even though it tried to do so from the beginning.[3] We therefore had to apply for membership in this new world organization all over again.

Article 4 of the Charter of the United Nations states that membership in the United Nations is open to all peace-loving nations that accept the obligations contained in the charter and which in the judgment of the organization are able and willing to carry out these obligations. There was no doubt as to the suitability of Thailand for membership on the basis of the above criteria, for Thailand had long shown her love of peace, and was both ready and able to carry out the obligations of the United Nations' Charter. The policy and attitude of Thailand during the existence of the League of Nations further provided ample proof of Thailand's qualifications for membership.

However, according to Article 4, paragraph 2 of the Charter, the procedure for admitting a new member was that this be effected by a decision of the General

Assembly on the recommendation of the Security Council. In other words any country seeking membership in the United Nations had first to receive the approval of the Security Council. This meant that the country in question had to receive supporting votes from at least seven countries out of the eleven making up the Security Council. Furthermore this supporting vote had to include the votes of the five major Powers, namely the United States, the United Kingdom, the U.S.S.R., China, and France.[4]

After the war came to an end, [Nai Konthi continued], there were rumors that France might stand in the way of Thailand's application for membership in the United Nations because the French were displeased with our regaining territories in Indochina through the Peace Treaty signed in Tokyo on 9 May 1941. When Thailand was first invited to a meeting of the [United Nations] Food and Agriculture Organization (F.A.O.) in Washington in May 1946, the government of His Majesty the King of Thailand therefore instructed the Thai delegate attending this meeting[5] to sound out the views and observe peoples' reaction to the idea of Thailand being admitted to the United Nations. The government would then be in a position to give the matter further consideration.

Once the meeting of the F.A.O. in Washington was over, the Thai delegate assigned to this task continued on to New York, where he contacted officials of the United Nations ranging from the Secretary General himself to representatives of countries that were members of the Security Council. The majority of these were willing to give us support, but some feared that France might object and use her veto power during the stage when the application had to pass through the Security Council, for border incidents had meanwhile broken out with French Indochina. However, no one knew for sure whether France would in fact exercise its veto power when Thailand came to seek entrance to the United Nations. Representatives from a number of countries hoped that France would not take such a step.

Countries currently seeking membership in the United Nations had to send in their applications to the Security Council before 5 August 1946 in order to reach the general meeting in time for the second part of the first session, which was due to open on 3 September. At the end of July the government of His Majesty the King of Thailand therefore instructed the Thai Chargé d'Affaires [in Washington], Luang Ditthakanphakdi,[6] together with the Thai delegate, to hand in Thailand's official application for membership of the United Nations to the Secretariat. This the Thai representative duly did on 3 August.

During this same period, eight other countries in addition to Thailand applied for United Nations' membership. They were Albania, Mongolia, Afghanistan, Transjordan, Ireland, Portugal, Iceland and Sweden.

The Security Council first sent these applications to the Committee on the Admission of New Members for consideration. This Committee met to discuss these applications fourteen times between 31 July and 30 August. In principle, if the Committee had any doubts or queries, or wished to obtain information from the applicant-nation, it could consult the representatives of that particular country. In the case of Thailand, no request whatsoever was made to the Thai representative for information or clarification, which showed that the Committee as a whole held no doubts about Thailand's attitude and intentions. Only the French representative made a statement [i.e. voiced reservations about Thailand's application.] During the Committee's meeting on 13 August, he stated that France still considered that a state of war existed between Thailand and his country, and that until we returned the territories gained under the Tokyo Peace Treaty to Indochina, France would not be able to support Thailand's admission to the United Nations.

This announcement by the French representative caused the representatives of Australia and the Netherlands to hesitate somewhat. The representative of the U.S.S.R. also announced that he likewise would not be able to support Thailand's application, as Thailand did not as yet have diplomatic relations with the U.S.S.R. Once these objections had been raised, the Thai representative, who had not been given an opportunity to make an official statement before the Committee, asked to talk with the delegates from the countries represented on it in order to clarify our position.

As far as the U.S.S.R. was concerned, the Thai representative pointed out that an exchange of notes to establish diplomatic relations had in fact been made a long time ago.[7] However, the sending of a Thai diplomatic representative to the U.S.S.R. had had to be postponed because of the war in Europe. The Russian representative then expressed the view that the government of His Majesty the King of Thailand should announce its disapproval of the anti-Russian attitudes that had been expressed by previous [Thai] regimes.

As for the French allegations, the Thai representative emphatically denied that Thailand was at a state of war with France. Not only had no declaration of war ever been made between the two parties, but during the entire Second World War and well after it had ended Thailand had cooperated with France. There had been constant attempts to end the frontier problems with Indochina by peaceful means, as could be seen from the fact that the government of His Majesty the King of Thailand had agreed to send a special delegation under H.H. Prince Wanwaithayakon to open negotiations with France in Washington on the subject.[8] When France had proposed that the case be sent to the World Court for adjudication, the government of His Majesty the King of Thailand had readily accepted the proposal. The confusion and unrest that had been taking place in Indochina had been brought about by Indochina's own doing, and Thailand had had no connection with it in any way whatsoever—in fact the Thai government had even instructed its border officials to be particularly careful to avoid any clashes with the French.

On 26 August 1946 the French alleged that they had evidence to show that the Thai government was partly responsible for the unrest in Siemreap, and they were therefore withdrawing their proposal that the territorial conflict be brought before the World Court. They also emphasized that unless Thailand first came to an agreement on the territorial problem, France would veto its application for membership in the United Nations.

On 28 August the Security Council decided to consider the applications for membership [in the United Nations]. The situation was a rather delicate one for Thailand. A full meeting of the Thai delegation assigned to negotiate on the dispute with France was therefore held on the 17th. Debates and discussions were held on every detail, and it was unanimously agreed by the meeting that France should not be allowed to confuse Thailand's application for membership in the United Nations with the territorial dispute over Indochina. It was decided that if there was no other way, it would be better to ask the Security Council to postpone consideration of Thailand's application temporarily rather than take the risk of it being vetoed by France.

The United States government, which had supported Thailand throughout, put forward an alternative suggestion that the Security Council recommend to a general meeting that the application for membership by the nine countries [seeking admission to the United Nations] should be considered together, for the United States believed this might result in the consent of the U.S.S.R., since some of the applicant countries were supported by the U.S.S.R. just as others were supported by the Western bloc. The United States government thought that a compromise might thus be reached. However, it was concerned that if France was determined to oppose Thailand's application, then the plan of having all nine countries admitted together might run into difficulties.

This last factor [i.e. United States' concern] went a long way towards Thailand's deciding to ask the Security Council to postpone consideration of Thailand's application. If a French veto of Thailand could be avoided, then it was hoped that the other eight countries would be accepted as members of the United Nations in accordance with the wishes of the United States government.

The Thai representative handling our application for membership in the United Nations left Washington by plane on the night of the 27th, and arrived in New York at 1:00 a.m. on the morning of the 28th. At 9:30 a.m. that same day he made a call on the United Nations Secretary General, who had not yet learned whether or not France definitely intended to exercise the veto. The

Thai representative told the Secretary General that Thailand's wish in seeking membership in the United Nations was based on good and honest intentions aimed at the goal of international cooperation. Thailand had no desire to cause difficulties within the United Nations organization, and if, therefore, a sacrifice on our part would help to avoid a veto being exercised in the Security Council and thus save new applicants from being debarred from admission, then Thailand was ready to ask the Security Council to postpone consideration of its application for membership.

Once this news reached Bangkok, the government came under severe questioning in the National Assembly, demonstrating that our application for a seat in the United Nations had received wide public attention, and was not merely a party issue. Despite the questioning it was pointed out, nevertheless, that the United Nations Secretary General had praised Thailand for the wise steps it had taken over this matter.

The Security Council took two days to consider the admission of the [remaining] eight applicants. The result was that Afghanistan, Iceland and Sweden received ten votes of approval from the Security Council with no objections, while Ireland received nine votes, with the U.S.S.R. objecting. Transjordan and Portugal received eight supporting votes, with Poland and the U.S.S.R. objecting, while Albania and Mongolia received five and six supporting votes respectively. The Australian representative abstained from voting throughout. It turned out, then, that three countries were turned down by the Security Council because they were vetoed by the U.S.S.R., while two additional countries failed as candidates because they did not receive the seven votes required by the United Nations' constitution. The attempt by the United States government to have all eight applicants accepted as members thus failed.

Once the United Nations General Assembly received the recommendations for admission of the new members, it agreed to accept Afghanistan, Iceland and Sweden as members, but asked the Security Council to reconsider the applications of the remaining countries, including that of Thailand, thereby implying that it did not fully agree with the decision of the Security Council [over rejection of these applications].

On 17 November 1946 negotiations between Thailand and France [regarding the territories under dispute between them] were concluded with the signing by representatives of the two countries of an agreement to terminate the conflict in Indochina.[9] The French now changed their attitude from one of obstructing Thailand from being admitted to the United Nations to one of support, so that the only obstacle now remaining in our path, therefore, was the attitude of the U.S.S.R.

CHAPTER 16

On 28 November Thailand asked the Security Council to reconsider Thailand's application again. H.H. Prince Wanwaithayakon arrived in New York on 3 December to try to come to an understanding with the Russian representative. After several days of negotiations the representative of the U.S.S.R. ultimately agreed to withdraw Russian opposition in the Security Council.

Finally, at a meeting held on the last day of that session of the General Assembly of the United Nations on 15 December 1946 Thailand was accepted as a new member of the United Nations. Ours was considered a special case, with the full membership of the General Assembly of the United Nations studying the recommendations and reports of the Security Council without these first having to be filtered through the Political [and Security] Committee of the General Assembly as was the usual procedure.

What Nai Konthi Suphamongkhon has written above is a brief account of events, to which I would like to add the following words. After the Second World War ended, Thailand was in a difficult position, as we had declared war on the United States and England. The United States never acknowledged our declaration of war, but England did so. Thailand therefore felt that if the world was to recognize us as an independent country, we should seek to become a member of the United Nations. We had long been a member of the international family of nations [i.e. as a past member of the League of Nations], and recognized that we would derive great benefits from being accepted into the United Nations [and thereby restored to the world community.]

It was not easy to be admitted as a member of the United Nations, however. The Charter of the organization laid down several conditions for admission, including the requirement that the applicant-country announce its intentions to abide by the obligations of the Charter. The most critical issue, though, was that the Security Council had to recommend and undertake to the General Assembly that the applicant nation was a suitable candidate for admission to the organization. Furthermore, this recommendation had to be made by all five [permanent] members of the Security Council, namely the Republic of China, France, the U.S.S.R., the United Kingdom, and the United States. If any one of the five raised an objection, then no recommendation to accept the applicant-country as a member could be made. We had therefore to adopt policies that would enable us to receive the unanimous approval of all five nations before we could become a member.

There was no problem with the United States, as America had supported us on the matter right from the beginning. England asked only that the Formal Agreement be signed before she could give us her support. France raised the issue of the return of the territories [in Indochina that were under dispute], while China asked for an agreement guaranteeing the rights of the Chinese in

Thailand so as to place them in a similar position to subjects of other nations that enjoyed diplomatic relations with our country. The U.S.S.R. stated that until diplomatic relations had been established between us they could not vote for us. I will discuss all these matters later. Here I will discuss only our actual application for membership, that is our handing in of an official application, and [the events leading up to] our being admitted to the United Nations.

It so happened that in May 1946 I was Minister of Foreign Affairs. I consulted the American Chargé d'Affaires, Mr. Yost, [about the possibility of our being admitted to the United Nations], and was advised that as a first step it would be a wise move if the Thai government showed interest in attending an international meeting [of a United Nations agency] by sending a representative to the meeting of the F.A.O. which was about to be held in Washington. The government thereupon appointed Nai Konthi Suphamongkhon to be the country's representative to that meeting. The government also permitted me to write a letter to the United Nations' Secretary General, Mr. Lie, regarding the possibility of Thailand's being admitted as a member of the United Nations.

This letter, which was [later] delivered [to Mr. Lie] by Nai Konthi, ran to the effect that as the latter was to be in Washington for the F.A.O. meeting, I was therefore taking this opportunity to appoint him my personal representative to call on the Secretary General. I first congratulated the Secretary General on his appointment, letting him know that we in Thailand were delighted about it, as it demonstrated the important role of small countries in the [United Nations] Organization. Thailand had been a faithful member of the League of Nations. In fact it had been among its founding members, and had always held great confidence in that body. It was true that the League had ultimately met with failure, but this had not in any way lessened our belief that this new organization [i.e. the United Nations] was essential to the maintenance of world peace and stability.

In January 1945, at a time when Japanese troops were still occupying Thailand, and right after secret contacts had been made with the Allies, the Thai Regent had sent a delegation to the United States to seek Allied support for the establishment of a Thai government-in-exile to be led by M.R. Seni Pramoj, the Thai Minister Plenipotentiary in Washington at that time. We had hoped that [such a government-in-exile] would be able to join the United Nations Organization which was then in process of being established. However, we had not been successful in this, as there had been many obstacles in the way of such a course, particularly in regard to security within Thailand itself, since at that time Japanese forces still occupied our country.

Now, however, the United Nations had opened up opportunities for countries to apply for membership in that organization. I was therefore asking Nai

Konthi Suphamongkhon, the bearer of this letter, to look into the possibility of Thailand's applying for such membership. I would be very grateful if the Secretary General could advise Nai Konthi on this matter, and I was confident that with the valuable help of the Secretary General, Thailand would be admitted as a member of the organization. I also wished to emphasize once again that Thailand and its people were ready to enter into the full responsibilities and obligations of such membership as defined in the Charter of the organization.

The following month, in June 1946, Nai Konthi Suphamongkhon sent a cable from Washington stating that he had contacted our Chargé d'Affaires, Luang Ditthakanphakdi, and had asked the latter to introduce him to senior State Department officials to ask for their help on the matter. He himself would be going to New York to get in touch with the United Nations Secretary General according to my instructions, and would report on the results of their discussions later. In the meantime he asked that we prepare an application form [for admission to the United Nations] and send it by cable to the Chargé d'Affaires in Washington so that this could be forwarded to the United Nations Secretary General. (Later the British Minister and the United States Chargé d'Affaires came to tell me discreetly that this application should not be sent yet but that we should first arrive at an agreement with France over the territorial dispute). Nai Konthi also reported that the United States government did not support our earlier acquisitions of land from France, and that the United States was upholding a policy of demanding a return to the *status quo ante*.

The Thai government finally sent in its official application on 21 July 1946. As this was an important document, I am therefore giving it here in full in translated form as follows:

The Ministry of Foreign Affairs,
Bangkok.
21 July 1946.

H.E. Trygve Lie,
Secretary General of the United Nations Organization,
United States of America.

Your Excellency,

In my last letter dated 20 May 1946 I pledged in the name of the people and government of Thailand our firm confidence in an international organization as the basis for guaranteeing the peace and stability of the world, as well as our country's readiness to accept to the full any responsibility or obligation laid down in the Charter of the United Nations. At the same time I also inquired about the possibility of Thailand joining the members of this organization.

Now that the government and people of Thailand are doing everything within their power to uphold those high ideals which form the basis and foundation of such an international organization, and will not overlook any opportunity in any circumstances to demonstrate their willingness to cooperate with other democratic countries in upholding peace and promoting the prosperity of the people of the entire world, I feel that this is the right occasion to declare Thailand's sincere wish to join in the upholding of these high ideals which have led to the establishment of this international organization.

In this official request that Thailand be permitted to join the United Nations, I am deeply honored to be able to pledge that my government and my Thai fellow citizens are all of one accord in solemnly agreeing to abide by and carry out all the obligations defined in the Charter of the organization. I am hopeful that given this sincerity on our part in making this promise, and that given our firm determination to play a part in the common goals towards which the United Nations Organization is concentrating all its efforts, our request will be considered with sympathy.

It is hoped that with the help of Your Excellency, and with the understanding of the members of the United Nations, our application for membership in this organization will be well received and successful, thus fulfilling the firm wishes of the government and people of Thailand.

I would like to take this opportunity to pay my respects to Your Excellency.

Direk Jayanama
Foreign Minister.

On 8 August of the same year, Nai Konthi reported that our application had been sent in, and that it was necessary that a representative be appointed to clarify any points to the Security Council [that might be necessary]. The Council of Ministers appointed Nai Konthi to this position, with instructions that if any problem should arise, he was to consult closely with the delegation which was [then] in Washington carrying out negotiations over the territorial dispute with France. This delegation was chaired by H.R.H. Prince Wanwaithayakon, Nai Khuang Aphaiwong was its Vice-Chairman, and the remaining members of the delegation consisted of persons ranging from representatives of various political parties to official representatives such as Nai Thanat Khoman,[10] as already mentioned previously.

On 14 August a radio broadcast from San Francisco announced that France would object to Thailand's application for membership in the United Nations, as it regarded itself as still being at war with Thailand. It added that the U.S.S.R. would also raise objections on the grounds that Thailand did not have diplomatic relations with it.

Upon receipt of this news, I sent a cable instructing Nai Konthi Suphamongkhon to call on Mr. Lie, the United Nations Secretary General, to clarify the matter with him. Nai Konthi replied that he had already discussed the question with Mr. Lie, pointing out that in regard to the subject of our diplomatic relations with Russia, it had already been agreed during the war that an exchange of diplomatic representatives should take place. Insofar as the French allegation that Thailand and France were still at war was concerned, Nai Konthi had told Mr. Lie that such in fact was not the case, for a Peace Treaty had already been signed in 1941,[11] while both countries were presently carrying out negotiations in Washington for the adjustment of their overall relations. The Secretary General had expressed his understanding and sympathy and had said that only recently during his visits to France and Russia he had explained matters in order to help Thailand. Nai Konthi reported he had also held discussions with representatives of the U.S.S.R. regarding their objections. It had been admitted at these meetings that even though the two countries had not yet exchanged diplomatic relations, this had nevertheless been agreed on. However, it had also been pointed out that the Thai government had not as yet carried out the condition proposed by the Russian Minister to the Thai Minister to Stockholm, namely that Thailand make an announcement expressing regret for its formerly anti-Russian policy.

I also invited the American Minister, Mr. Edwin Stanton, over to inform him about the situation as well as to ask for his advice. We saw each other almost every day at that time. In addition I sent a cable to H.R.H. Prince Wanwaithayakon giving him detailed information so that he could advise Nai

Konthi in the event of the latter seeking his advice. On 30 August Nai Konthi sent me a telegram to say that he had consulted the head of the Thai delegation [i.e. Prince Wan] and that they were of one accord in feeling that France would definitely exercise her power of veto if we did not first return the territories [under dispute]. They therefore felt that submission of our application should be postponed for the time being. I replied expressing my approval and my thanks to the head and members of the delegation, and asked Nai Konthi to continue in close consultation with the former and to send me regular reports of developments over the matter. I also sent a cable to Prince Wan giving him and the delegation in general as well as Nai Konthi authority to use their own judgment in situations when there was insufficient time to consult the government for its decision.

On 6 November I sent a cable to H.R.H. Prince Wanwaithayakon, as head of the delegation, saying that I had heard that the Security Council was about to consider the applications of six countries, including Thailand, once again. I would therefore like him to find out whether it was not time to ask the Security Council to reconsider our application following our request for postponement of such. I stressed that we needed to be sure first, however, that this would not be met with opposition from France or from the U.S.S.R.

H.R.H. Prince Wanwaithayakon replied that the French representative was in the process of consulting his government about the question.

On 3 December I sent a cable to the head of the Thai delegation to inform him that I had received a message from Nai Atthakitti kamchon,[12] the Thai Minister to Stockholm, stating that the Russian government had agreed to establish diplomatic relations with Thailand on condition that Thailand announce that it intended to carry out a friendly policy with Russia and that it regretted the hostile attitude former Thai governments had shown towards the U.S.S.R. Only then would the Russian government withdraw its objections [to Thailand's application for membership in the United Nations]. Our government did not object to the conditions put forward, but asked that a revision be made regarding having to denounce preceding governments, as we could not do this. Nai Atthakitti kamchon was therefore instructed to negotiate for a revision of terms. The U.S.S.R. agreed to this, and ultimately raised no objections to Thailand's being admitted as the fifty-fifth member of the United Nations on 15 December 1946.

As we only had very short notice [of our acceptance as a member of the United Nations], I was unable to attend the meeting of the General Assembly at which this took place. The government therefore decided to appoint H.R.H. Prince Wanwaithayakon as the Thai representative to sign for Thailand accepting the obligations laid down in the Charter of the United Nations.[13]

In conclusion, students may be interested in knowing in detail Thailand's reasons for wanting to join the United Nations. As I was responsible for the foreign affairs of our country at the time we applied for membership, I would like to outline these reasons below.

Firstly, there was the question of Thailand maintaining its sovereignty. Right after the war certain Western nations were insisting that we should be treated as a defeated power. Our government at that time also saw two possible sources of danger to us, one coming from the imperialist countries, which might bear grudges against us, and the other coming from the countries of the Communist bloc. It is true that the United States proved a good friend to us, but we could not be sure which side America would take in the event of having to make a choice between its European friends and ourselves as an oriental friend once real political pressures were placed on us. We therefore felt we should not place all our hopes on the United States. Instead we believed we should look to the United Nations as an organization possessing the greatest force capable of maintaining peace and security, and as one treating small countries like ourselves with justice. We might say, then, that the most important reason for our wanting to join the United Nations was the security of Thailand. The United States also considered that this [i.e. joining the United Nations] was a wise policy for us to adopt.

Secondly, we wanted to show that Thailand was one of the long-established nations of the world. As I have already mentioned, Thailand was among the original members of the League of Nations. We wanted to emphasize to the world at large that we had been independent for a long time. Being admitted to the United Nations would amount to a guarantee and recognition of Thailand's sovereignty by members of this world organization. It should be noted that of all the countries regarded by the West (with the exception of the United States) as having been on the side of the Axis, Thailand was the first country to be accepted as a member of the United Nations.

Thirdly, Thailand hoped for economic, social and cultural aid from the United Nations. As its Charter clearly showed, the United Nations was prepared to provide economic, social and cultural aid to under-developed countries. It would therefore be of great benefit to us if we were accepted as a member of the organization, while we in turn would be able to be of reasonable help to other less developed countries.

Lastly, we wished to demonstrate to the world that we wanted to cooperate in maintaining world peace and stability.

MY RESIGNATION

On 4 February 1947 I tendered my resignation as Deputy Prime Minister and Minister of Foreign Affairs to Rear Admiral Thawan Thamrongnawasawat, the Prime Minister, asking him to convey this [message on my behalf] to His Majesty the King. In my letter of resignation I stated briefly my reason for resigning, namely that as most of the major diplomatic problems [that had faced Thailand in the immediate post-war period], including work on the Formal Agreement, had now been completed, it was time that I resigned.

As twenty years have now passed since the time I resigned, a number of people have asked me to give an account of what my true reasons were for having done so. My reasons briefly were that I was not consulted on many of the issues which were dealt with by the government, even though I was Deputy Prime Minister. I raised objections [about the way in which some of these issues were handled], as I felt they involved actions that the people might not approve of. However, the Prime Minister told me it was necessary to do such things in order to please certain members of the National Assembly or a particular group of politicians, since they were supporting the government. I felt that if this were the case, I would have to shoulder responsibility for these actions even though I had not agreed to them. I therefore decided to resign.

Press Reports

[Press reports of this time show that Nai Direk's unexpected resignation created a major stir.[14] According to one report] he was generally considered one of Thailand's most experienced politicians in the field of foreign affairs, and his direction of Thailand's foreign policy during the early post-war period had met with success on many fronts. He was responsible not only for obtaining revisions to the Formal Agreement that improved the position of Thailand's economy, and for conducting negotiations which led to the ultimate cancellation of the Heads of Agreement, but also for handling the delicate negotiations whereby Thailand was successfully admitted to membership in the United Nations. His resignation was, therefore, regarded as a deep loss in Thai political circles.

Nai Direk denied that there had been any conflict between him and any members of the Council of Ministers as regards government policy, and claimed that his decision to resign was purely a personal one. When asked as to who should take over the post of Minister of Foreign Affairs in his stead, Nai Direk suggested that the Prime Minister fill this position. Reporters also asked Nai Direk if he would re-join the government if Nai Pridi Banomyong returned to power, but Nai Direk merely asserted that in his opinion Nai Pridi did not intend to re-enter politics on his return to Thailand.¹⁵ Reporters also asked him whether the true reason for his resignation was that the government was under heavy attack in both the National Assembly and the press, and that he had therefore resigned to safeguard his reputation. Nai Direk refused to be drawn on the subject, but did at one point during such questionings state that "the Prime Minister should be sympathized with. In my personal opinion the principles espoused by the present government are good, but there are shortcomings in practice that should be reformed."

Another reason Nai Direk gave for his resignation was that he planned to continue his writings, and to finish his work *Diplomacy* that he had begun four years earlier. He also wished to complete his lectures on "History of Government" for Thammasat University.

Nonetheless Nai Direk's resignation aroused considerable speculation. In an article in *Phim* of 6 February 1947 Noi Inthanon wrote that Nai Direk was "one of the few Ministers in the present government who stand outside the strong waves of criticism from the press and people and is among the few Ministers who receive the sincere affection, faith and trust of the people and press, even from those of the Opposition." The reason for his resignation was thus definitely not because of harsh public criticism of him personally, the reporter continued. It was possible, however, that Nai Direk was resigning because the position of the present government was not to his satisfaction and he, with his sense of responsibility, was not happy with the situation.

Eventually I was relieved of my duties on 7 February 1947. However, I still retained my position as Member of Parliament for the 5th District of Bangkok.¹⁶ About a month later, in early March 1947, Rear Admiral Thawan Thamrongnawasawat, the Prime Minister, invited me over to see him. He told me that the government had agreed to raise the status of our legations in both Washington and London to that of embassies. H.R.H. Prince Wanwaithayakon had already accepted the appointment of Ambassador to Washington, and the Prime Minister was now asking me to become Ambassador to London, where he felt I could be of service to the nation. There were still matters outstanding concerning the Formal Agreement that required further negotiations, in addition to other connected problems which I was already conversant with, while I was, furthermore, already well known to the English.

I told the Prime Minister I would have to think the matter over first, as there were many considerations involved. After the meeting I weighed the pros and cons of whether or not I should accept the offer. The arguments against accepting it were that once I had relinquished a political post, I felt I should not go back and get involved in governmental affairs again. Moreover I was a Member of Parliament, and my electorate would have cause to complain that it had wasted its time electing me if I only stayed in my position for a few months. The arguments in favor of my accepting the offer were that I was well-versed on the Formal Agreement, and so could serve the nation well in this regard, and that being appointed an ambassador does not necessarily indicate agreement or not with the policies of one's government. And even though I was a Member of Parliament, it could be arranged for me to resign from this post if I had to. There had been examples of such being done in a number of places. Besides, if I stayed on in Bangkok, I would not really be of much use to the nation, for I had only to go and listen to debates in the National Assembly and to cast my vote [on various issues]. This in itself placed me in an awkward position, for if I was to oppose certain policies strongly in the course of the debates, it would be alleged that I was ambitious and striving for power.

After consultations with certain close friends, I went to see the Prime Minister and told him that I was willing to accept his offer in principle, but found it rather awkward with regard to my election as a Member of Parliament, and that also I feared that the present Thai Minister in London[17] might think I had been angling for his position. The Prime Minister replied that steps had already been taken to cover the latter. The Thai Minister in London had graduated from France, and was thus well-versed in French affairs, so he would be transferred to Paris, where he could be of service to the nation. As to the question of my position as a Member of Parliament, if I had to resign, then the government would undertake to look after the welfare of the people in my district to the best of its ability, so they would be looked after as well as if I had remained in Bangkok. Despite these arguments, we had several discussions on the matter, and in the end, so as to have it put on record that I had not in any way worked at obtaining the appointment, written notes on the subject were exchanged between the Prime Minister and myself.[18] The Prime Minister's note stated that he had requested that I serve the nation by negotiating for the freeing of our country from the obligations placed on us by the Formal Agreement, and by asking England to show mercy and not put too much pressure on us. At the same time the government would help look after the welfare of the people in my electorate just as if I was still a Member of Parliament for that district. Once the government gave me the above undertaking, I wrote thanking the government and accepting its offer that I be appointed Ambassador to England.

On 1st July [June?—Ed.] 1947 a Royal Decree was passed appointing me Ambassador to the Court of St. James. A few days later I was received by Prince Krom Khun Chainatnarenthon,[19] Chairman of the Committee of the Regents of the Realm, and left Bangkok for London.

17
Negotiations with England Regarding the Formal Agreement[1]

Before I left for England Rear Admiral Thawan Thamrongnawasawat, the Prime Minister, told me that the most important aspect of our policy with England was to obtain the annulment of the Formal Agreement at the earliest opportunity so that our relations with England could return to their normal pre-war state. We would then be able to carry out the rehabilitation of our country without having to worry about indefinite obligations to England. The government, [he told me], was in the process of drafting a memorandum to the British Ambassador in Bangkok calling for the annulment of the Formal Agreement and briefly outlining our reasons for this request. Once this memorandum had been delivered, Mr. William Doll, the government's Advisor on Financial Affairs, would be sent to England to help on technical aspects of the negotiations. I was told to use my own judgment as to the political reasons I put forward for the annulment of the Agreement, as I was already well-versed in this matter. As to negotiations on other matters in general, the Prime Minister told me to use my own judgment and act in whatever way would best prevent our nation from incurring any disadvantages. In addition to these instructions, the Prime Minister also asked me to attend the meeting of the United Nations General Assembly, as this was the first year (1947) that Thailand was to be represented as a member of that organization.

I arrived in England at the end of June 1947, and on 9 July 1947 was received in audience by H.M. King George VI and presented him with my Letters of Credential. His Majesty showed me great kindness, and enquired about the overall situation in Thailand. He was well informed about me, possibly because he had been informed of my life history by officials beforehand. The Thai Embassy officials I presented to His Majesty that day were Luang Phinit-akson,[2] Advisor to the Embassy; Colonel Prince Chitchanok Kridakon,[3] Military and Air Force Assistant Attaché; Luang At-phisankit,[4] Financial Attaché; Luang Phattharawathi,[5] First Secretary; Luang Chamnong-ditthakan,[6] Second Secretary, and Nai Klin Thephatsadin Na Ayutthaya,[7] Second Secretary. After presenting my Letters of Credential, I issued a communiqué which is given below. I then followed British procedure by signing the visiting books to pay my

Fig. 18. Members of the Royal Thai Embassy and their wives, London, July 1947.

respects at Buckingham Palace and at the Palace of Queen Mary, and also left visiting cards for various important persons at the Court, for the Prime Minister, and for the Speakers of the House of Lords and House of Commons.

The communiqué that I issued after having presented my Letters of Credential to the King was reported in the press as follows:

> ...Today at 11:30 a.m. the Thai Ambassador was received by H.M. King George VI and presented his credentials to His Majesty.
>
> On this auspicious day the Thai Ambassador took the opportunity to express to the British public his profound appreciation of the initiative taken by the British government in elevating the status of the diplomatic missions of both countries to that of embassies. He believed that this was a clear indication of the importance that the British government attached to the role which his country was occupying at the present moment, at a time when great changes were taking place in Asia and elsewhere.
>
> Thailand had long been bound by close and cordial ties of friendship with Great Britain, and the government and people of Thailand were ever mindful of the cooperation and assistance extended by Great Britain to their country. It could be said that during the last twelve months or more, since the re-establishment of Anglo-Thai relations, the two governments had worked together in a most cordial atmosphere and had achieved much towards solving various outstanding problems

of mutual interest and concern. Nor would Thailand ever forget the unstinted aid given by Great Britain to the Thai resistance movement or the generous way it had treated Thailand by resuming friendly relations with her [after the war.]

British assistance was not lacking in the present task of rehabilitating the economy of Thailand. The wise counsel of British advisors and experts and the commercial activities of British businessmen, together with other forms of cooperation, had greatly contributed to the modern progress of Thailand.

With grateful appreciation for this manifold and generous assistance, the government and people of Thailand were firmly determined to render closer not only the ties of friendship but also the economic and cultural relations between the two countries. It was to the achievement of this purpose that the Ambassador would devote himself wholeheartedly as the first Thai Ambassador to the Court of St. James.

On 22 July I paid a visit to Mr. Bevin, the Secretary of State for Foreign Affairs. We had a general conversation on the subject of the long-standing relationship between Thailand and England. During the course of this he mentioned that the British government sympathized with us over past events, for these had been unavoidable. As for future actions Thailand would, however, have to speed up her rice production to help out with the severe food shortages currently being faced by the world. Thailand could contribute greatly to the easing of this situation as she was a rice-producing country. I replied that we were doing the best we could for the moment, and that the project for constructing a dam at Chai Nat was a part of this policy.[8] I also expressed the belief that Thailand would currently be able to export about thirty thousand tons of rice a month. We also discussed the world situation in general, and the Foreign Secretary told me I could contact him at any time if I had any problems. I also called on other senior Foreign Office officials, as well as on other members of the diplomatic corps, as is the normal practice.

NEGOTIATIONS TO INCREASE THE PRICE OF RICE[9]

The Foreign Office officials I met with the most frequently were those with whom I held regular discussions in the line of duty. The first of these was Mr. Maberly Dening,[10] an Assistant Under-Secretary in the Foreign Office in charge of the Far Eastern Department.

I had met Mr. Dening before during the war, when I led a secret delegation to hold talks in Kandy, Ceylon. At that time he was Political Advisor to Admiral Lord Louis Mountbatten, Supreme Allied Commander, South-East Asia

Command, as has already been mentioned. After the war it was this same Mr. Dening who conducted negotiations with us on behalf of the British government, and who signed the Formal Agreement with us as discussed in chapter 10. Apart from Mr. Dening, I also dealt with another Foreign Office official, a Mr. Richard Ellen,[11] the deputy head of the Far Eastern Department.

On 5 August 1947, not quite one month after I had presented my credentials, the government sent me instructions reminding me of our Exchange of Notes with the British Minister in Bangkok of 1 May 1946 whereby England had agreed to revise the Formal Agreement by buying rice from us instead of taking it free of charge. Thailand was to provide 1.2 million tons of rice within a period of twelve months from the date the agreement was signed, while the British government would agree to pay us £12.14.0 for each ton of rice sent. If at the end of this twelve-month period Thailand had not been able to meet its obligations by sending the total amount of rice agreed upon, then it would have to provide the remaining amount regardless free of charge. To encourage the flow of rice, England was ready to pay an additional premium of £3-0-0 per ton over and above the agreed price of £12-14-0 on rice sent up to the end of May, and an extra £1-10-0 per ton for rice sent between the end of May and 15 June 1946.

This agreement was going to be expiring shortly, on 31 August 1947. Even this arrangement had not been a very satisfactory one from our point of view, as the price paid for our rice was still low in comparison to that set by Indochina and Burma, despite the fact that the quality of our rice was superior.

Because of the low price being paid, rice was constantly being smuggled out of the country. The British government was well aware of this problem, and had instructed the British Ambassador in Bangkok to propose to the Thai government that if we agreed to continue sending the normal rice allocations to the Rice Commission, at least throughout the year 1947, as well as maintaining the same price [including export duties] throughout that same period, then the British government for its part would be willing to cancel the arrangement for payment of fines that had been agreed upon on 3 May 1946.

The Thai government was ready to accept England's first proposal, that is to continue to send rice as agreed, but asked that the British government show fairness by reconsidering the price we were being paid for it. Burma was able to sell her rice at a price of £35-0-0 per ton, for example, while Thailand received only £12-10-0 per ton. The government gave me instructions to try to obtain at least the same price for our rice as that paid to Burma, starting from 1 September 1947 onwards. In other words, once the former agreement expired, a new agreement should be drawn up and come into effect immediately [incorporating this change]. I was told to find every possible political and foreign policy as well as economic reason to back up our arguments.

The Thai government had meanwhile told the British government that Thailand would cooperate fully in producing and exporting as much rice as possible according to the agreement, since it recognized that the world was running low on food supplies. However, the price set for this rice was an important factor in obtaining increased production, in insuring its rapid transportation and in preventing rice smuggling, since once a reasonable price had been set for our rice it would no longer be profitable to smuggle it abroad. I was informed that the government had already explained these issues to the British Ambassador as well the American Ambassador. In the meantime, as the British knew me well, I was asked to do my best to obtain their sympathy and to report promptly to the Thai government on the results of my negotiations.

I straightaway got in touch with Mr. Dening, Assistant Under-Secretary at the Foreign Office and head of the Far Eastern department there, and presented him with detailed reasons for our seeking an increase in the price of rice. I urged the British government to consider the matter promptly, as the current agreement was due to expire on 31 August 1947. Mr. Dening explained that the British government sympathized with us, but that the government could not take any action on its own, since consultations would first have to take place within the various ministries and departments concerned.

Two or three days later, the Thai government sent me word that Lord Killearn,[12] the British Special Commissioner for South-East Asia, had been in Bangkok, where he had stated that the world would be facing severe food shortages within the next six months, and that he saw no way to solve this predicament other than by having rice-producing countries such as Thailand cooperate fully in easing this situation. He said that with regard to the price of rice, he had heard that the British Ambassador had already written to the British government expressing support for our proposal [regarding an increase in the price to be paid for Thai rice.] Lord Killearn had stressed that the price factor was a minor point: what was important was that the maximum possible amount of rice be obtained.

The people of Bangkok did not seem to know much about the problem of world food shortages, [Lord Killearn had claimed]. This, he thought, was probably because ours was a land of abundance. Right after the war the British government had set up a committee to make a survey of the world food situation, and a White Paper had been published on the subject in April 1946. Its contents gave real cause for concern. The White Paper had pointed out that the main cause of the food shortages was the war, which had lasted for six years, and which had disrupted normal patterns of work and living. Abnormal weather conditions had further aggravated the situation. Normally Europe (excluding the U.S.S.R.) was able to produce fifty-nine million tons of wheat and rye per year, but in 1945 it had only been able to produce thirty-one million tons, while livestock, which could provide a further source of food supplies, had died in great quantities.

Other areas outside Europe such as India, China, and northern and southern Africa had suffered a similar fate. Whereas before the war they had only imported two and a half million tons of foodstuffs per year, when the war ended they needed up to ten million tons. Before the war Thailand and Burma had been able to produce 8.4 million tons of rice per year, but after the war this figure had dropped to 4.9 million tons. The region suffering the worst hardships and which presented the most urgent problem was India, for it had suffered not only a drought but outright famine, while its population had been increasing at a rate of five million people per annum. India had formerly been able to depend on Burma for foodstuffs, but as Burma had also suffered from the war it was no longer in a position to provide much help.

The White Paper had also stated that one of the reasons why Asia faced extreme rice shortages was that Japan had occupied the three rice producing countries of Burma, Thailand and Indochina [during the war]. Before the war these countries had exported some six million tons of rice [annually], but it was feared that now they would not be able to produce enough to even feed themselves. However, it was hoped that Thailand could help out with one and a half million tons of rice[13] for the year 1946. Only a very small amount, which could not as yet be estimated, would be forthcoming from Burma, and only two hundred thousand tons of rice could be expected from Korea and Taiwan, although prior to the war they had been able to export 1.7 million tons annually. China and Japan had also suffered heavy damages, while the rice-producing areas of India had actually been diminished.

The White Paper had concluded by saying that the British government had already taken all necessary steps to initiate appropriate measures for increasing the production of food and ensuring its distribution to deficit areas, such as placing controls over the purchase of wheat, prohibiting the export of rice, encouraging the acceleration of production, signing an agreement with Thailand whereby the latter would provide the maximum amount of rice possible [for distribution to deficit areas], and appointing him [Lord Killearn] to Singapore [as Special Commissioner for South-East Asia to coordinate this economic machinery throughout the area].

One can see from Lord Killearn's speech that the entire Thai population can be considered as having helped feed a large number of the world's inhabitants through its role in helping ease the rice shortage problem.

Meanwhile I continued to hold regular meetings from time to time with British Foreign Office officials to learn about the British government's attitude towards our proposals [regarding an increase in the price of rice.] The Thai government stressed that it wished me to press the British government to make a new agreement right away, as the current session of the National Assembly would be ending on 15 August and the government would like to be able to inform the Assembly before the session ended that the old agreement had expired and that we had made a new agreement incorporating a better price [for our rice].

During this period Mr. William Doll, Advisor to the Ministry of Finance, happened to come to England on personal business. The government sent me a message to say that if I wished I could keep Mr. Doll to help me in England. I accepted this offer gladly, for Mr. Doll had worked with me both before and again after the war, when I was assigned to the Ministry of Finance. We arranged that he would contact the ministries and government departments concerned in his personal capacity, and not as an official of the Thai government. He was to explain Thailand's economic situation carefully, and to emphasize the friendly relations that had existed between Thailand and England in the past. Coming from an Englishman, it was felt that his arguments would be the more convincing. I would also carry out negotiations and explain our situation in the name of the Thai government. The reasons I would give or the undertakings I might make would in turn carry weight since the government had granted me the authority to carry out such negotiations. This dual approach proved very effective, as can be seen from the outcome described below.

On 13 August 1947 I gave a dinner party for Sir Orme Sargent, the Permanent Undersecretary of State for Foreign Affairs and other senior Foreign Office officials at Claridges hotel. The dinner was held in a friendly atmosphere. After the dinner, Luang Phinit-akson, the Embassy Advisor, reported that a senior Foreign Office official who was at the party had told him that the Foreign Office was very sympathetic to Thailand's request for an increase in the price for her rice, but that officials of other ministries such as the Ministry of Food and Ministry of Finance had expressed reluctance, saying we had not been sending them the required amount of rice and that the figure for August would only amount to twenty thousand tons. Rice smuggling had also been continuing, although it was believed that this was because of the low salaries paid to junior officials in the Thai Civil Service. If Thailand could send more rice, our proposals would be more likely to be viewed with favor. Luang Phinit had explained that the Thai government was already considering increasing the salaries of civil servants to cope with the increased cost of living. He maintained that Thailand could not, however, be held solely responsible for the rice smuggling. If authorities in Malaya had instituted strict controls, the smuggling of rice into their country would not have been so easy.

CHAPTER 17

I felt rather ill at ease when I received these reports, and because I could not get hold of definite statistics [regarding our rice deliveries] I sent a cable to the Thai government right away asking it to forward me the necessary facts and figures. The government promptly replied back that the allegation that we had been sending only a small amount of rice was not true, for by the end of August (the month under discussion), we would have sent altogether 300,000 tons of rice in accordance with our agreement, and that by the end of December 1947 we would have sent altogether 420,000 tons, which would fall only a few thousand tons below the amount agreed on. As for the month of August, 6,339.70 tons had already been sent between 1 and 8 August, and we would be able to send a total amount of 30,000 tons by the end of the month. Figures for the amount of rice sent since the beginning of the year (1947) were as follows: January: 46,831.05 [tons]; February: 20,530.02 [tons]; March: 33,837.11 [tons]; April: 58,054.75 [tons]; May: 52,257.13 [tons]; June: 23,913.92 [tons]; and July: 32,312.00 [tons]. We were already carrying out strict measures to combat rice smuggling, but the Malayan authorities would also have to introduce similarly strict controls, for the two governments would have to cooperate very closely with one another if such controls were to be effective.

It was pointed out that in fact the main problem was rather one of price, for once the price for our rice fell too far below rates on the world market, opportunists could easily be persuaded to smuggle rice and sell it outside the country instead of selling it to the government, since they could obtain much higher profits by so doing. I was therefore instructed to absolutely insist that we obtain a price for our rice at least equivalent to that paid for Burmese rice, and was told that I must try to obtain England's understanding on this, as it was a matter of great importance to our country.

Once I had received these facts and figures, I asked Mr. Doll to get in touch with senior officials at the Ministries of Food and Finance, while I myself went to explain matters to several senior Foreign Office officials. I produced the figures on our rice exports so that England, on seeing these official statistics, would have no further doubts about the way we were keeping up on our rice deliveries. I also proposed that in regard to our fight against rice smuggling, the British government issue strict orders to its officials in Malaya concerning the matter, and ask that the latter get in touch with members of the Thai government in Bangkok so that we could coordinate our strategy.

I pointed out that the price paid for our rice was an important factor in the situation, for as the British authorities well recognized, the price currently being offered [for our rice], which was kept down to a point where the rice was almost being given away free, encouraged smuggling. Even with the best will in the world it would be difficult to prevent smuggling if there was too much temptation to engage in it. Besides, it was highly unjust to keep the price of our rice down well below that of Burma, particularly when the quality of our rice was the best in the world, as everyone knew.

The British government had itself conceded, I reminded those I talked with, that the purchase of our rice was not a political move but a commercial transaction. I further mentioned that if negotiations to increase the price for our rice failed, the government in Thailand might have to resign (the government had told me this). I did not believe that any new government would be able to accept a rice price lower than that paid for Burmese rice. If this proved to be the case, England would then either have to resort to the fines arrangement, or take the rice free of charge, which would make the situation even worse. The Thai would feel great hostility to England, and England in turn would not receive the rice it was seeking. I added that if Thailand publicly announced that our feelings towards England had turned hostile because of the pressures the latter was placing on us [i.e. by refusing to pay us a higher price for our rice], this would be heeded by world opinion. Besides, senior British officials (I was thinking of Lord Killearn) had already said that the question of price was not important; what was important, rather, was to obtain the rice. I also outlined the [overall political and economic] situation in Thailand, pointing out that neighboring countries were all facing various difficulties, while Thailand was still a peaceful as well as a peace-loving country. If it was forced to undergo great economic and financial hardships, our country might suffer disorders that would make us an easy prey to doctrines hateful to our principles. In short, not only Thailand but England would suffer [if it continued to take a hard line over this issue.] The food situation, which was already critical, would deteriorate even further, as farmers would not want to cultivate their land if they could not get a good enough price for their rice to make a living from it. Already farmers were in pitiable straits.

On 28 August 1947, three days before the rice agreement of 3 May 1946 was due to expire, the Foreign Office informed me that the British government had agreed to give us the same price for our rice as that paid for rice in Burma, on the understanding that the Thai government continue its controls over rice exports. Further, the British government had already informed the British Ambassador in Bangkok of this. I expressed my deep gratitude for the understanding [shown by the British government on this matter], and sent a cable to inform the Thai government of the position that same day.

At the beginning of the following month, on 3 September 1947, the Thai government sent me a cable acknowledging receipt of my cable above, and stating that the British Ambassador in Bangkok had also handed a memorandum to the government on 1 September on this matter. The memorandum had stated that the British and Indian governments had given sympathetic consideration to Thailand's request for an increase in the price for rice, and had agreed to give us the same price as for Burmese rice, which amounted to £33-6-8 per ton. The British government asked that as a return gesture for this compromise by the British and Indian governments, the Thai government undertake to have this agreement ratified by the National Assembly, and maintain the same price for rice sold within the country, as well as continuing to control rice exports until the end of 1948. Once such an undertaking had been received, the British government would cancel the conditions concerning the payment of fines that had been laid down in the previous rice agreement between Thailand and England.

The Thai government replied thanking the British government and expressing its deep appreciation of such gestures of friendship on the part of the governments of Britain and India. It had put the matter before the National Assembly promptly, and had received the Assembly's approval of the actions taken. The British Ambassador had in turn expressed his satisfaction at the government's reply.

The cable continued that the Prime Minister, Rear Admiral Thawan Thamrongnawasawat, and the Minister of Foreign Affairs, Luang Atthakittikamchon,[14] wished to express their thanks to both Mr. Doll and myself as well as to every official who had played a part in these negotiations, for this was an issue of great importance to the nation and one that affected the well-being of our country. I was therefore instructed to convey thanks, in the name of the government of His Majesty the King of Thailand, to every British official who had shown us support and understanding over the matter.

In short the new agreement raised the price for our rice from £12-14-0 under the old agreement to £33-6-0 per ton. We therefore received an additional £20-0-0 or so (or 1,200 Baht) more per ton, so that for one million tons of rice we now received an additional sum of 1,200 million Baht.

The person who helped the most over this matter was Mr. Doll, the Financial Advisor. I would like to take this opportunity here to thank him. He cooperated with me throughout, and when he returned to Bangkok, even sent me a long letter [saying how much he had enjoyed working with me].[15]

NEGOTIATIONS TO REVISE OR ANNUL THE FORMAL AGREEMENT

On 7 September 1947, seven days after the rice agreement was signed, Luang Atthakittikamchon, the Minister of Foreign Affairs, sent me a telegram to say that as was already known the government had been contemplating proposing the revision or annulment of the Formal Agreement. It had now been decided to formally present this proposal. A memorandum on the subject had been handed to the British Ambassador and to the Indian Chargé d'Affaires on 6 September and I would be given detailed information on the matter and told of the government's views on this subject when we met in New York.[16]

Seven days later I left for the meeting of the United Nations Assembly in New York. While there, Luang Atthakittikamchon told me the various reasons we had put forward for proposing the revision or annulment of the Formal Agreement. The question of payment of damages to England and Australia was still outstanding, with no definite amount having been fixed for this as yet. Once payment for this had been agreed on, then negotiations for revision or cancellation of the Formal Agreement would become easier.

Our officials had already calculated the amount they considered payable as compensation. But they kept this a secret, as we wanted to know how much England would demand first. Luang Atthakitti told me that the government was sending a Mr. Reeve,[17] the Advisor to the Ministry of Finance, who was well-versed in the details of the various lists of damages that had been drawn up, to help me with the facts and figures needed in the course of the negotiations. Matters of policy would, however, be left to my judgment. The results of our negotiations with Britain were to be reported on to the government.

I had been in New York for only three weeks when I received government instructions to return to London and initiate negotiations immediately. I arrived in London on 7 October and made an appointment to see Mr. Dening, Assistant Under-Secretary of Foreign Affairs, on 13 October 1947 for preliminary approaches on the matter.

So that the reader may have a rough idea of the arguments we put forward in favor of revision of the Formal Agreement, I would like to give the following brief account of the reasons given me by the government, as well as my own views on this subject.

In the memorandum which our government handed to England and India, the three following reasons were given for our request that the Formal Agreement be revised or annulled:

(1) The Formal Agreement had been signed to bring to an end the state of war then existing between Thailand and Great Britain and India. It was now, however, nearly two years since friendly relations had been resumed [between the signatories], [i.e.] since 1 January 1946, [the date of the signing of the Agreement.]

(2) The Formal Agreement had been signed because at that time Thailand had not yet been admitted to the United Nations Organization, and hence was not then bound by any kind of [international] obligations.

Now that Thailand had become a member of that organization, and had thereby undertaken to fulfill the obligations incurred in being a member in good standing of that body, there was no longer any necessity for these obligations to be underwritten by the Formal Agreement.

(3) Most of the conditions and clauses of the Formal Agreement had already been carried out and were by now outdated, as a long time had elapsed since the signing of the Agreement.

The detailed arguments [taken article by article] for revising the Formal Agreement were as follows:

Foreword
The Foreword to the Formal Agreement had been drawn up before Thailand had been admitted to the United Nations, and the obligations entailed under the Foreword it now carried out as a member of that organization. There was therefore no longer any need to keep the Foreword.

Article 1, Articles 2 (a) and (b), Article 4 and Article 5
Regarding Thailand's consent to repudiate all measures pertaining to the declaration of war [Article 1] and regarding the Thai government's consent to declare as void Thailand's acquisition of British territories, as well as to withdraw Thai officials from these territories, and its agreement to sequestrate British banking and commercial concerns and to pay interest on any remaining debts and pensions [Articles 2 (a) and (b), 4 and 5]: these agreements had all been carried out by the Thai government.

Article 2 (c), (d) and (e) and Article 3
Regarding the restoration of all property taken from these territories, compensation for loss or damage to property, rights and interests in these territories arising out of the occupation of these territories by Thailand, as well as the redemption in pounds sterling out of former sterling reserves of current Thai notes collected by the British authorities in British territory occupied by Thailand since 7 December 1941: the Thai government felt that these were great responsibilities for us to shoulder, particularly as the above articles disregarded whether such damage had been caused by Thailand, Japan or even the Allies, and insisted that Thailand bear sole responsibility for such. Moreover Thai monetary reserves were still frozen by England. Article 3, in particular, placed even heavier obligations on us than had been placed on other Axis powers such as Italy. The Thai government felt that Thailand should not be held to account for any obligations other than those it had incurred directly, so that any damages that had not

been caused by Thailand should be paid out of Japanese war claims, while our payment for damages and compensation should be settled in a lump sum.

[In regard to Article 3], I had already looked into it and had found that even the peace agreement the Allies signed with Italy in February 1947 was not as severe as Article 3 of the [Formal] Agreement with Thailand, for we had had to agree to assume responsibility for safeguarding, maintaining and restoring unimpaired British property, rights and interests of all kinds in Thailand and to pay compensation for losses or damage sustained. According to an exchange of notes regarding the understanding of this Article, it was agreed that England could demand payment for such compensation in pounds sterling, while the agreement with Italy had only specified payment of two-thirds compensation for damages, and had stated that this could be paid off in Lire.[18]

Articles 6 and 7

I would like to provide some additional explanation in regard to Article 6. According to this article, Thailand had to admit that the war with Japan had provided ample proof of the importance of Thailand to the defense of Malaya, Burma, India and Indochina as well as to the stability of the region; and secondly, Thailand had to agree to cooperate fully in international security arrangements relating to this area. England had insisted on including this condition in the Formal Agreement because it had learned its lesson in the Second World War [i.e. it had come to appreciate the strategic importance of Thailand to the control of this region all too well.] As Thailand could not rightly be termed either defeated or victorious in the war, England had insisted on our entering into this agreement. Its basic concern in this regard was strategic. It has been said that whoever holds the Straits of Malacca and Singapore holds virtual power over the shipping routes of this part of the world, for the shipping route through the Malacca Straits is one of the world's major avenues of commercial communication between the West and the East. It is true that an alternative route exists further south via the Sunda Straits between Sumatra and Java, but this involves a rather long detour, while moreover the Sunda Straits at that time (1946) were controlled by the Netherlands.

During the war Japan's command of the two Straits enabled her to control a long stretch of sea route. Its occupation of Thailand provided Japan with additional benefits, strategically as well as economically. Even after the war, when Japan had been defeated, England was concerned about stability in the region. It saw a new threat arising there in the form of Communism, for the Chinese Communist Party was strengthening its forces and engaging in a major civil war with the Nationalists.

We sympathized with England's position, but at the same time we felt uncomfortable with it, for ours is an independent country, and we chafed at the existence of agreements placing restrictions on us. Moreover, by having been admitted to the United Nations and having thereby agreed to carry out the obligations incumbent on members of that organization, we had in fact accepted greater responsibilities and obligations than those in the Formal Agreement itself.

Article 7 concerned the agreement that no canal would be cut across Thai territory linking the Indian Ocean and the Gulf of Thailand without prior consent being obtained from the government of the United Kingdom. As regards this issue, we felt that any Thai government would have to give serious consideration to the strategic effects of any such construction, and that this would not be carried out if it involved possibly dangerous side effects. Furthermore, for the same reasons as those given above, the Thai government felt that as we had already been accepted as a member of the United Nations, the [continued] existence of this agreement would amount to a restriction of our independence and sovereignty.

Articles 8, 9, 10 and 11

These four articles concerned commercial and economic cooperation in accordance with an agreement that had been made in 1937,[19] before the start of the war. These conditions thus merely reaffirmed those principles which we had already been carrying out according to the previous agreement.

Article 12

This article concerned Thailand's agreement to cooperate in international arrangements on rubber and tin conforming to the principles of the United Nations or its Economic and Social Council. This clause had been inserted because at the time Thailand had not yet become a member of the United Nations. Now that she had been admitted to that organization, there was no further need for this agreement.

Article 13

By this article we agreed to prohibit any exports of rice, tin, rubber and teak except at the recommendation of the Combined Boards in Washington. This restriction was only valid until 1 September 1947. As this date had now passed, Article 13 therefore no longer had effect.

Articles 14 and 15

This concerned our agreement to provide free rice, in accordance with procedures to be recommended by a committee about to be established. This agreement was to last until 1 September 1947 only, and as its terms had already been cancelled and a new agreement drawn up at the beginning of May 1946 as already described, while a new rice price had been agreed upon equivalent to that paid for Burmese rice, these two articles were therefore no longer valid.

Article 16
By this clause the Thai government had agreed to accord to the civil air services of the British Commonwealth treatment in regard to the establishment, maintenance and operation of regular air services not less favorable than that accorded to Imperial Airways by the notes exchanged at Bangkok on 3 December 1937. This agreement had already been carried out, and the Thai government now stood ready for further negotiations.

Article 17
By this the Thai government had undertaken to enter into an agreement for the mutual upkeep of war graves. The Thai government had already shown charitable attitudes and gestures of goodwill in this regard, so that now only an agreement on the subject was pending.

Articles 18 and 19
These involved the carrying out of previous agreements made before the war. This had also been taken care of.

Article 20
Under this article the Thai government agreed to carry out the obligations of any international organization that England was a member of during the war until Thailand should itself be accepted as a member of such organization. In fact Thailand had sought to join these organizations from the start, and had already carried out these obligations and duties. However, we were reluctant to allow [the continued existence of] this clause because it suggested that we did not have full sovereignty. The Thai government therefore wished to see this clause abolished.

Article 21
This involved the termination of the state of war between Thailand and the United Kingdom. Once diplomatic relations between the two countries had been resumed, this article automatically lapsed.

Article 22
This involved agreement by England and India to pledge their support for Thailand's application for membership in the United Nations. As we had already

been accepted as a member of the United Nations in December 1946, this clause had now been superseded.

On 13 October 1947 I had a lengthy discussion with Mr. Dening regarding Thailand's proposals for revision or annulment of the Formal Agreement. I gave him our views on each clause of the agreement as outlined above, and concluded by saying that he must surely share my opinion that the Formal Agreement was now outdated, since Thailand had either carried out the conditions of almost every Article, or else the circumstances [under which these Articles had originally been drawn up] had changed.

I told Mr. Dening that should the Formal Agreement be revised or annulled, the Thai would never forget the gesture [on the part of the British], for as long as the Formal Agreement continued in effect, it amounted more or less to the entire Thai population being held guilty [of having allied with Japan during the war]—a matter that would always remain in their memory. I pointed out that he had been the person who had [originally] signed the [Formal] Agreement on behalf of his government. The Thai government would therefore appreciate it if he could be the one to arrange for revision of its obligations.

Mr. Dening replied that my explanations were perfectly sound, but that there was still a major problem outstanding, namely the payment of debts, and the fixing of a specific sum in this regard. The British government had had to shoulder great responsibilities for protecting the interests of British subjects who had been involved in the war. Close consultations and study would therefore have to be conducted between the ministries and departments concerned, as well as with the Indian government. He also pointed out that even though Australia was a member of the British Commonwealth, it was nevertheless an independent country, so that Thailand had had to sign a separate Agreement with Australia in Singapore similar to the Formal Agreement signed with England. Thailand should therefore also hand Australia a memorandum concerning the revision of the Formal Agreement similar to that which the Thai government had presented to England. I agreed to this, but pointed out that Australia would nevertheless probably follow the example of England over the matter.

I immediately reported on the situation to the Thai government, which in turn delivered a note similar [to that which had been handed to the British] to the Australian Chargé d'Affaires in Bangkok, Mr. Eastman. At the same time I also tried to contact other senior Foreign Office officials to explain our position to them.

At the same time Mr. Reeve, the Financial Advisor whom the government had sent to help me on the technical aspects of our negotiations, reported that he had already contacted officials directly concerned with the question of payment of compensation, and had learned that the British Foreign Office was sympathetic towards Thailand, and even felt that a lump sum should be fixed once and for all as the amount Thailand should pay as compensation lest the matter continue indefinitely. The Foreign Office had, however, to consult other ministries concerned, some of which might disagree with this position, as loss of benefits for British subjects was involved. Debates might also have to be held in the House of Commons on the issue. Nonetheless it was felt that the opinion of the Foreign Office would carry weight and be heeded by the majority. An inter-ministries meeting was expected to take place on 21 October. The views of this meeting would then have to be put before a committee of advisors to the Council of Ministers and then forwarded to the Prime Minister, who might bring the matter up at a Council of Ministers meeting before sending it back to the Foreign Office. Once a definite policy had been decided upon, Australia, India, Malaya and Burma would have to be consulted and their reactions obtained. After all this official negotiations could finally be opened with me. According to British Foreign Office estimates these would not take place until mid-November at the earliest.

On 22 October 1947 Lord Nathan of Churt,[20] the Minister of Civil Aviation, a man whom I had known previously and who had just come back from a trip to Thailand, invited me to lunch at the House of Lords. He asked me to convey his thanks to our government for the warm hospitality it had shown him during his stay in Bangkok. During his stay in our country Mr. Doll, the Financial Advisor to our government, had sought his help on several matters including the revision of the Formal Agreement, payment of compensation for war damages, and the gold problem with Japan [i.e. the question of the release of Thai gold reserves being held in Japan.] Lord Nathan said he had only been given a summarized account of these matters, however, and asked if I could therefore enlighten him with further details.

I saw this as a good opportunity, and told him about the negotiations which were in process on the Formal Agreement. Lord Nathan said he well understood the matter, and would give us his support, as Thailand was seeking only what was just. He also asked that I make him a record of the facts for his personal use, as there were a number of technical points involved which he might forget.

I readily agreed to do this, and told him that the British government was currently consulting the various ministries concerned about our payment for war damages. The Thai government would like to see a fixed sum settled quickly, and have the British government handle the claims itself. Prompt agreement on this question was desirable if our relations [with England] were to proceed smoothly, for if the matter was left pending it would not be in the interests of mutual goodwill and understanding, as the Thai would believe that England still bore us a grudge. Thailand had already been accepted as a member of the

United Nations, and intended to carry out all of its obligations [under the Formal Agreement] with integrity even when these might be unfair. I pointed out to Lord Nathan that as he must already know well by now, Thailand felt that the obligations it had incurred under that agreement were harsh, and that England had interpreted the agreement unjustly. This had affected the economy of our country, I continued, and might well affect the longstanding friendly relations between Thailand and England. Thailand had been obliged to assume even greater obligations than had been placed on Italy, as could be seen by comparing the Formal Agreement with the peace treaty Italy had signed with the Allies.

Even though Thailand may have declared war on England, this declaration, I maintained, had been made out of necessity. In fact, I pointed out, it had even turned out to be of service to England, for once we had allied with Japan, the latter had been forced to grant us the right to deal with Allied nationals in our country ourselves. The Japanese had not dared to interfere with Allied citizens detained in our land, and all Allied nationals interned in Thai camps had reported that they received every possible assistance from Thailand. In addition the Free Thai movement both within and without the country had helped the Allies in innumerable ways, as mentioned in detail in the reports of the British Force 136 and the American O.S.S. (Office of Strategic Services).

Lord Nathan was already well informed about Thailand's help as regards the rice question. The increase in price for Thai rice to the equivalent of that paid for Burmese rice was one inducement that should help prevent merchants from smuggling rice out of the country. Even so, I pointed out, the government of Thailand had already suffered considerably over the [rice] question. If I remember rightly, Thailand had already provided at least 150,000 tons of free rice. In addition part of our sterling reserves was still being held by the British government, even though it claimed the money had been confiscated for the time being as [guarantee for] payment of compensation that had not as yet been agreed upon. I pointed out that freezing our reserves had inevitably affected the reserve currency situation in Thailand. These actions [i.e. the continued withholding of Thailand's sterling reserves] had notably weakened Thailand, for we did not have enough foreign currency to buy the goods and materials necessary for the rehabilitation and development of our country. The Thai government had, therefore, I told Lord Nathan, proposed that the British government dissolve its Joint Committee for the Study of Payment of Compensation and decide once and for all on a lump sum payable as compensation.

I had some further information on the gold question, as I had been in the Finance Ministry right after the war and had studied the matter somewhat. In addition, before leaving for England I had foreseen that I might be asked to negotiate for the reserves held by England. When I went to the United States for the meeting of the United Nations General Assembly, Luang Atthakittikamchon, the Minister of Foreign Affairs, who was also in New York, had told me, however, that negotiations on this matter were under way with the American government and I should therefore postpone taking up this matter with England for the time being until instructed to do so, for fear of arousing the displeasure of the United States.

I could therefore only tell Lord Nathan that our government was presently considering the question of our frozen currency reserves, but that as I had not received any instructions on the subject I could only inform him briefly about it. Our gold stocks in Japan could be divided into two categories, one of which had been definitely earmarked during the war as the property of Thailand. Thailand therefore had every right to recover this gold, and even though in the eyes of the Allies it did not amount to a large sum, for Thailand it could do a great deal to help stabilize our economy, as ours was a poor country. If Thailand could rehabilitate itself economically, I continued, there was no doubt, moreover, but that England would derive indirect benefits from this. Lord Nathan expressed great satisfaction with our discussion, and emphasized again that once official talks had been opened with the British government, I should visit him again together with the afore-mentioned note [i.e. the record of the details he had asked for.] In the meantime, he would follow the matter insofar as he could. I expressed my deep gratitude for this expression of goodwill on his part.

In the meantime, our government sent me regular reminders that negotiations should be carried out promptly. Two days after my discussions with Lord Nathan, or on 24 October 1947 I made a call on the Rt. Hon. J.A. Beasley, the Australian High Commissioner to London.[21] He gave me a cordial welcome, and started off showing his goodwill by saying that he was ready to support any requests I might make of him. I told him I had asked to see him to discuss the final peace agreement between Thailand and Australia. I asked him to look upon my visit at this stage as a preliminary one at which we could exchange opinions and open the way for further meetings between us later on.

The High Commissioner agreed to this. I therefore went on to say that in April 1946 Thailand and Australia had signed a final peace agreement with one another similar to that which Thailand had signed with Great Britain and India. The Thai government, after having considered this subject, felt that most of the conditions of that Formal Agreement had already been carried out by Thailand, or had become unnecessary now that Thailand had been admitted to the United Nations, as it had thereby undertaken obligations exceeding even those of the Formal Agreement itself.

There was one remaining problem to be dealt with, however, namely the question of payment of compensation. The Thai government felt that if the procedure laid down in the Formal Agreement [for dealing with this matter] had to be followed, a great deal of time would be wasted, as every issue would have to pass through the Committee [the Joint Committee to Study the Payment of Compensation] for its consideration. This would not be in the interest of the parties concerned. The party due the payment would lose valuable time and miss the opportunity of having the money available immediately for investment.

As long as Thailand was kept in the dark as to the amount of money it must pay, it would be in an uncertain situation. Thailand had suffered great losses during the war. Any allegations made by certain Allied powers to the contrary were definitely not true. Further, comparisons could not be made [with other nations that had suffered damages in the war], I contended. Rather the real situation of the particular country should be taken into account. I gave as example that if a millionaire who owned ten million Baht lost five to six million Baht he would not suffer any real hardship, whereas if a poor man who possessed only one hundred Baht lost twenty to thirty of them, he would suffer greatly.

I reiterated, then, that as long as Thailand did not know the exact amount of compensation it needed to pay, work towards rehabilitation of the country would run into difficulties. Not only that, I continued, but if the Formal Agreement was compared with the agreement the Allies had made with Italy, one could see that the obligations imposed on Italy were much lighter than those that had been placed on us. I fully realized that the [Italian] situation had differed somewhat from ours, but I was also confident that Australia was well aware that the government and people of Thailand had treated Allied subjects who had been interned in our country kindly. In addition the Thai resistance movement both within and outside the country had cooperated with the Allies. For these reasons, then, the Thai government had handed notes to the respective governments of England, India and Australia asking that the Formal Agreement be terminated, and that a lump sum be fixed for the payment of compensation so that this question could be dealt with once and for all.

I told the Australian High Commissioner that the purpose of my visit that day was to inform him of these facts before official talks were opened. I also let him know that the British government, from what I had heard, was already in process of consulting the various ministries and departments concerned about the subject, and that once this had been accomplished, I would be invited by the Foreign Office to open negotiations.

The Australian High Commissioner thanked me for giving him this information, and told me that only two to three days earlier the Australian government had let him know that Thailand had handed a memorandum to the Australian Consul-General in Bangkok. However, he had not yet been told the details of this. The High Commissioner told me he knew that the main problem would be over Australian mines in Thailand,[22] and that he had heard over the radio that Australian mining experts would be leaving for Bangkok within the next two weeks to estimate the damages [that had been caused to Australian mining interests during the war]. I suggested that it would be a good idea if negotiations could be carried out simultaneously with Australia and with England, and mentioned that British officials had also suggested this idea.

The High Commissioner agreed to report to his government on the subject, but added that as he had not yet received any instructions on the matter, he could not therefore venture any opinion on it. His personal point of view was, however, in accordance with mine in regarding most of the conditions of the Formal Agreement as outdated. I then told him that once he received instructions from his government I was ready to confer with him at any time.

During my trip to New York I had, I went on to tell him, met Dr. [H. V.] Evatt, the Australian Minister of Foreign Affairs, every day, and the latter had openly shown his goodwill towards and understanding of Thailand's situation. I would therefore like to request that the High Commissioner send him a report on Thailand's views and feelings also. I had discussed the overall situation of Thailand after the war with Dr. Evatt, [I continued], and had told him that Thailand would be an important force for the Free World, whereas the situation in countries neighboring ours was somewhat disturbed. In addition to being the most stable country in the Far East, Thailand was also a nation with a sense of gratitude and one that showed goodwill to all nations. The High Commissioner replied that he was well aware of this, and could guarantee that Australian policy towards Thailand would continue to be one of friendship and goodwill as it had been since [the end of] the war. He then agreed to make a report to the Australian government supporting my statements and opinions.

Eleven days later I gave a dinner in honor of Mr. [Ernest] Bevin, the British Secretary of State for Foreign Affairs, and his wife at the Thai Embassy. Among my guests that day were the Australian High Commissioner and his wife; Sir Anthony and Lady Meyer; Mr. Arago, the Brazilian Ambassador and Dean of the diplomatic community, and his wife; Mr. Norman Young, an Assistant-Secretary to the Treasury; Mr. Reeve, our Financial Advisor, and various other persons. Mr. Bevin and his wife had shown great warmth to us. During the dinner, the former's secretary came to whisper discreetly that it was time for him to go and cast his vote in the House of Commons, so he asked to be excused for half an hour before returning to the dinner. That evening I asked the British Foreign Secretary to help Thailand over the question of termination or revision of the Formal Agreement, to which he immediately replied that there would be no problem whatsoever on this,[23] while the Australian High Commissioner gave me a similar undertaking. The following day I sent a cable to our government reporting on these replies that I had received from the British Foreign Secretary and the Australian High Commissioner.

On 7 November 1947 Mr. Reeve, Advisor to our Ministry of Finance, told me he had heard that the British Foreign Office had already held a meeting [regarding our payment of compensation] with the ministries concerned, and that a definite sum had been fixed for Thailand's payment of damages, although he did not know what the exact sum was. The British government was also in the process of consulting with various Commonwealth governments, and the Foreign Office would be arranging a meeting soon to allow various companies which had suffered during the war to put forward their claims for damages and to present the extent of the damages they had sustained.

As for the revision of the Formal Agreement, Mr. Reeve said he had heard that this might be carried out through an exchange of notes referring to such an agreement rather than by having to draw up a completely new document. He did not know for sure whether the British government would be holding a meeting to discuss this in London or in Bangkok. There was also another point which I had asked Mr. Reeve to discuss in private with Foreign Office officials following instructions I had received from my government. This was that Thailand felt it to be excessive that the British should insist that we repair their properties before handing them back. We felt that once the damage had been paid for, the British should carry out their own repairs. Mr. Reeve told me that the Foreign Office considered our arguments reasonable, but had asked for time to study the matter first. I sent a cable to the Thai government reporting on this additional information.

The following day, or on 8 November 1947, I received a telegram from Luang Wisutwiratchathet, the Under-Secretary of State for the Ministry of Foreign Affairs, informing me that a coup d'état had taken place in Thailand.[24] Two to three days later, Phraya Siwisanwacha,[25] who had been appointed Minister of Foreign Affairs in the new government of Nai Khuang Aphaiwong, sent me a telegram regarding the formation of the new government.

England's reaction was one of fear lest Field Marshal Phibun Songkhram [the leader of the coup], should carry out a policy of cooperation with the Axis as had been the case during the war. Mr. Dening invited me to see him and told me that the governments of Great Britain, the United States and Nationalist China had consulted with one another and had decided unanimously that they would not recognize the new government of Thailand until they had been satisfied that it would be run in accordance with democratic principles, and that the country would be granted a constitution and enjoy general elections. In the meantime, the British government agreed to continue to recognize me as the Ambassador of His Majesty the King, or in other words, I was to represent the head of the country but not the Thai government, which placed me in a very awkward position.

I sent a report of this decision to Bangkok, and decided that under the circumstances I must resign. I felt that I had been sent to England because the government wished me to carry out political negotiations with that country. Once our government had been dissolved as the result of a coup d'état I should resign so that the new government would have a free hand and not have to face any embarrassment in the event of my transfer or the termination of my appointment. However, as the British government had not yet recognized the new government, but had chosen to recognize me as the Ambassador of His Majesty the King, I felt obliged to continue to serve the head of our nation as well as our country until such time as the British government should recognize the new regime, for otherwise our country would not be represented in England.

For the time being I therefore continued with my work as usual, and sent political reports on general events to Phraya Siwisanwacha, the new Minister of Foreign Affairs. Meanwhile the British government still treated me in the normal way, sending me invitations to such functions as the Lord Mayor's dinner, which is a big annual celebration in London, to receptions held for the diplomatic community in the event of any new diplomatic appointment, to the wedding of H.R.H. Princess Elizabeth to the Duke of Edinburgh, to the twenty-fifth wedding anniversary of H.M. King George VI and H.M. Queen Elizabeth, and so on and so forth.

As for our negotiations with Britain, in view of the British government's reaction and attitude [towards the new regime], the Thai government recalled Mr. Reeve, the Advisor to the Ministry of Finance, to Bangkok. Thus the negotiations came to a halt for the time being. Some months later, however, on 5 March 1948, following the election of Nai Khuang Aphaiwong through properly conducted general elections,[26] the governments of Great Britain, the United States and Nationalist China announced their recognition of the new Thai government. The British Foreign Office informed me of this about six days in advance of the announcement. I thereupon sent a telegram reporting on this to the government, as well as writing a letter to Phraya Siwisanwacha requesting that I be relieved of my post so as to leave the government untroubled by any embarrassment regarding my position.

On 15 March 1948 Phraya Siwisanwacha sent me a cable to say that the government had received my letter of resignation with great dismay, as it had not entertained any thought of ousting me from the position, and had hoped I would continue to serve the nation. However, on learning of the various reasons I had put forward [for resigning], the government fully appreciated my feelings and situation, and had agreed to accept my resignation.

Fig. 19. A dinner given at the Savoy Hotel by the British government in honor of the author before he left England.

The actual date on which I would resign was left to my discretion, although the government asked that I handle certain financial matters before returning [to Bangkok], and stated it would be sending Mr. Doll, the Financial Advisor, to assist me, the details on which would be sent later. The telegram continued that the government hoped that I would, then, be willing to continue to serve the country for an additional two to three months, and ended by expressing the government's thanks for my having continued to carry out my duties as Ambassador, particularly from the time of the crisis [i.e. the coup] up to the present moment.

I replied that I was willing to help in any way I could, and that I would have time to do so, as I did not plan to leave London until May 1948. Twenty days later Nai Khuang Aphaiwong was forced to resign[27] after his government had been recognized by the British government for only thirty days. Phraya Siwisanwacha sent me a telegram saying that Mr. Doll would not be sent now after all, as the government had been forced to resign, but thanking me once again for my assistance.

In conclusion, I took up my duties in England on 9 July 1947, the day on which I presented my credentials, and was relieved of my post when I returned to Bangkok on 1 July 1948. Thus I served for altogether not quite one year as Ambassador to the Court of St. James, but enjoyed only five months of any effective official negotiations. I would like to thank my colleagues who worked with me during this period, for they assisted me willingly throughout, and united behind me for the honor of their country.

As for the British government representatives [I dealt with], even though I had only a short time in which to carry out negotiations with them, they were nevertheless most generous in their hospitality and provided me with all the facilities I required, whether in regard to official talks or in our general contacts.

When it was definitely settled that I would be going back home, the British government kindly gave a farewell dinner for me at the Savoy Hotel on 27 May 1948. I say that the British government gave me this dinner because the invitation card read that it was given on behalf of "His Majesty's Government of the United Kingdom of Great Britain and Northern Ireland." Mr. Christopher Mayhew[28] was host on behalf of the government at the dinner. The B.B.C. reported on the function as follows:

> The British government held a dinner on Thursday, 27th May at the Savoy Hotel, London, in honor of the retiring Thai Ambassador, His Excellency Nai Direk Jayanama and Madame Jayanama. Mr. Christopher Mayhew, M.P., Parliamentary Undersecretary of State for Foreign Affairs, presided at the dinner, and the guests included other well known figures in British parliamentary and diplomatic life.

In a speech of farewell to Their Excellencies, Mr. Mayhew expressed his deep regret at the departure from England of Nai and Madame Direk, whom, he said, had made numerous friends in private as well as in official circles and would be greatly missed. Mr. Mayhew referred to the Ambassador's distinguished career in the service of his country and warmly praised the understanding of the British people and institutions shown by Nai Direk, as well as his unremitting efforts to further the traditional friendship between the Thai and British peoples. He said he was sure that the Ambassador, as an acute observer, would have appreciated that the economic difficulties confronting Great Britain at the present time were the result of no inherent weakness, either material or moral, but of the tremendous expenditure of effort made in the cause of freedom during the late war. He was confident that the Ambassador had sensed the strength and unity of our people, based on a common tradition of democratic liberty. Great Britain valued greatly the common ties linking her with Thailand. Mr. Mayhew concluded by expressing his hope that Their Excellencies had enjoyed their time in London and would retain as warm a recollection of Great Britain as the British people would certainly retain of them.

His Excellency the Thai Ambassador, in a reply of great charm and distinction which deeply moved his fellow guests, thanked Mr. Mayhew for his appreciation of the services he had been able to render in enabling Thailand to be better known and understood. He expressed his warm affection for Great Britain and for all the many friends whom he had known here. He said that his stay in England would remain a permanently happy memory, and that he and Madame Direk deeply regretted their departure.

Thus it turned out that negotiations for the revision of the Formal Agreement had to be postponed temporarily. Later, however, during the government of Field Marshal Phibun Songkhram,[29] an exchange of notes was carried out regarding certain revisions. On 4 May and 8 November 1950 and on 3 January 1951, the government of Field Marshal Phibun Songkhram agreed to pay off the remaining sum that had been pending since the time I was Ambassador in London. The amount of money then paid by the government was £5,224,220.[30] Even after such payment had been made, it was another three years, however, before an exchange of notes terminating the Formal Agreement was finally carried out on 14 January 1954.[31]

During the return trip of my family and myself aboard the "Wilhelm Ruys" I received a radio message midway in the Indian Ocean from Mr. Malcolm MacDonald,[32] then Commissioner General [for the United Kingdom] in Southeast Asia, inviting my family and myself to be his guests at Government House at Bukit Serene[33] while the ship anchored at Singapore and we were awaiting our passage for the remaining part of our trip to Bangkok. I accepted his invitation with great appreciation, and during our two day stay with him we received the warmest hospitality and every comfort, for which I should like to take the opportunity to thank him here again.

I arrived in Bangkok on 1 July 1948 and was relieved of my duties as Ambassador that day. My work in so far as negotiations with the Allies was concerned thus ended on that day.

Appendixes

LIST OF APPENDIXES

1. Pacte de Non-Agression entre la République Française et la Thaïlande [Signed in Bangkok on 12 June 1940, with attached letters].
2. Treaty of Non-Aggression between Great Britain and Northern Ireland and Thailand. [Signed in Bangkok on 12 June 1940.]
3. Treaty between Japan and Thailand concerning the continuance of friendly relations between the two countries and the mutual respect of each other's territorial integrity. [Signed in Tokyo on 12 June 1940.]
4. Convention de Paix entre la France et la Thaïlande. [Signed in Tokyo on 9 May 1941, and related documents.]
5. Formal Agreement for the termination of the state of war between Siam and Great Britain and India, and Exchange of Notes between the Siamese Government and Australia with a view to terminating the state of war. [Signed at Singapore on 1 January 1946.]
6. Communiqué, Heads of Agreement and Annex [attached to the Formal Agreement above].
7. Treaty of Amity between the Kingdom of Siam and the Republic of China. [Signed in Bangkok on 23 January 1946, with attached letters.]
8. Final Peace Agreement between the Government of Siam and the Government of Australia. [Signed in Bangkok on 3 April 1946, with attached letters.]
9. Agreement to end the conflict between Siam and France. [Signed in Washington on 17 November 1946, with related documents.]
10. Rapport de la Commission de Conciliation Franco-Siamoise. [Signed in Washington on 27 June 1947.]
11. Report of findings and opinion of the Committee to Investigate the Expenditures out of the National Revenue by the Free Thai movement both within and outside the Kingdom.

EDITOR'S NOTE REGARDING THE APPENDIXES

In the Thai edition of *Thailand and World War II* only appendixes numbers 5, 6, 7 and 8 (see list of contents) appear in English as well as Thai. The remainder appear in Thai only. In these latter cases, whenever possible, the Editor has referred the reader to an official Western-language text of the document in question. Only the letters attached to appendix 1, the Proclamation at the beginning of appendix 9, and appendix 11 are given in translation, since no official Western-language version for these materials exists.

Whenever Western-language sources such as the United Nations' *Treaty Series* documents or *British and Foreign State Papers* are cited, in each such case the original document has been checked against these alternative sources in order to ensure complete correspondence of text, and any points of divergence have been noted.

The spellings of peoples' names and the names of places have been left as they appear in the original texts, even where those spellings do not follow a consistent system. The only exception to this principle occurs with documents that have been translated directly from the Thai (see above.) In those cases the editor has rendered all names in accordance with the system followed throughout the main text of this book (see Editor's Introduction to the Revised Edition at the beginning of this book).

As is the case throughout the main body of the text, all material in square brackets represents changes made by the editor.

APPENDIX I

PACTE DE NON-AGRESSION ENTRE LA RÉPUBLIQUE FRANÇAISE ET LA THAÏLANDE

Le Président de la République Française et Sa Majesté le Roi de la Thaïlande

Animés du désir d'assurer la Paix et convaincus qu'il est de l'intérêt des deux Hautes Parties Contractantes d'améliorer et de développer les relations entre les deux pays:

Attentifs aux engagements internationaux qu'ils ont précédemment assumés et dont ils déclarent qu'ils ne font pas obstacle au développement pacifique de leurs relations mutuelles et ne sont pas en contradiction avec le présent Traité,

Désireux de confirmer et de préciser, en ce qui concerne leurs relations mutuelles, le Pacte Général de Renonciation à la Guerre du 27 Août 1928.

Ont résolu de conclure un Traité à cet effet et ont désigné pour leurs Plénipotentiaires, savoir:

Le Président de la République Française;

Son Excellence Monsieur P.P. Lépissier, Officier de la Légion d'Honneur, Envoyé Extraordinaire et Ministre Plénipotentiaire du Gouvernement de la République à Bangkok;

Sa Majesté le Roi de la Thaïlande;

Son Excellence Le Major Général Luang Pibulasonggram, Grand Cordon de la Couronne de Thaïlande, Président du Conseil des Ministres et Ministre des Affaires Etrangères;

Lesquels, après avoir échangé leurs pouvoirs reconnus en bonne et due forme, sont convenus des dispositions suivantes:

Article 1

Chacune des Hautes Parties Contractantes s'engage à ne recourir en aucun cas à la guerre ou à tout acte de violence ou d'agression contre l'autre, soit isolément soit conjointement avec une ou plusieurs tierces Puissances et à respecter l'intégrité territoriale de l'autre Partie Contractante.

Article 2

Si l'une des Hautes Parties Contractantes est l'objet d'un acte de guerre ou d'agression de la part d'une ou plusieurs tierces Puissances, l'autre Haute

Partie Contractante s'engage à ne prêter ni directement ni indirectement aide ou assistance à l'agresseur ou aux agresseurs pendant la durée du présent Traité.

Si l'une des Hautes Parties Contractantes se livre à un acte de guerre ou d'agression contre une tierce Puissance l'autre Haute Partie Contractante pourra dénoncer le présent Traité sans délai de préavis.

Article 3

Les engagements énoncés aux articles 1 et 2 ne peuvent en aucune façon limiter ou modifier les droits et obligations découlant pour chacune des Hautes Parties Contractantes des accords conclus par Elle avant l'entrée en vigueur du présent Traité, chaque Partie déclarant d'ailleurs par les présentes n'être liée par aucun accord comportant l'obligation pour Elle de participer à un acte de guerre ou d'agression entrepris par un Etat tiers contre l'autre Partie.

Article 4

Rien dans le présent Traité ne sera considéré comme affectant les droits et obligations des Hautes Parties Contractantes d'après le Pacte de la Société des Nations.

Article 5

Chacune des Hautes Parties Contractantes s'engage à respecter à tous égards la souveraineté ou l'autorité de l'autre Partie Contractante sur ses territoires. Elle n'interviendra en aucune manière dans les affaires intérieures desdits territoires et s'abstiendra de toute action tendant à susciter ou favoriser une agitation, propagande ou tentative d'intervention ayant pour but de porter atteinte à son intégrité territoriale ou de transformer par la force le régime politique de tout ou partie de ses territoires.

Article 6

Le présent Traité, dont les textes français et thaï feront également foi, sera ratifié et les ratifications seront échangées à Bangkok dans le plus bref délai possible. Il entrera en vigueur à la date de l'échange des ratifications et restera en vigueur jusqu'à l'expiration d'une année à partir du jour où l'une des Hautes Parties Contractantes aura notifié à l'autre son intention d'y mettre fin. Cette notification ne pourra, en tout cas, être faite avant l'expiration d'un délai de cinq années à compter du jour de l'entrée en vigueur du présent Traité.

En foi de quoi, les Plénipotentiaires ont signé le présent Traité et y ont apposé leur sceau.

Fait en double à Bangkok, le douzième jour du mois de juin de la mil neuf cent quarantième année de l'ère chrétienne, correspondant au douzième jour du troisième mois de la deux mille quatre cent quatre-vingt-troisième année de l'ère bouddhique.

Paul Lépissier
Pibulasongkram

[Source: Thai Foreign Ministry Archives.]

APPENDIX I

[Letters attached to above Treaty of Non-Aggression between the Kingdom of Thailand and the Republic of France].

Ministry of Foreign Affairs,
Bangkok.
12th June 1940.

Confidential and secret.
Your Excellency,

I would like to confirm with Your Excellency the following principles in relation to the Agreement which we have made:

With regard to the good relations which have been maintained peacefully for a long period between Thailand and France, and as each of the two countries wishes to maintain such relations in a good state for ever, the two governments therefore agree to end any administrative complications existing between Thailand and Indochina for the sake of goodwill and friendship so that relations between the two countries may now be based on mutual trust and co-operation in every respect.

To this end the two governments have therefore agreed to solve the complications concerning the river Mekong by accepting as the frontier line in this river that water channel along which Thailand could navigate her shipping with ease in all seasons. Thus any territory, regardless of form, to the right of this line would be considered the property of Thailand, while any territories to the left of this line would likewise be considered the territory of France.

To define and determine such frontier line, the two governments would appoint representatives to be given due power and authority, and the agreement made between these same representatives would become effective within a period of one year from the date this note has been exchanged.

Further it is understood that the French delegation would be under the direction of a senior official having ambassadorial status so that such delegation would have full power to negotiate over any remaining administrative problems.

However, it should be emphasized once again that such arrangements would come into effect only after the exchange of ratifications of the Non-Aggression Treaty has been carried out.

With my deep respects to your Excellency,

                              (Signed) *Pibul Songkhram*
                              Minister of Foreign Affairs

His Excellency Monsieur P. P. Lépissier,
Minister of the Republic of France. Bangkok.

[Source: Direct translation from the Thai edition of this work.]

APPENDIX I

> The French Legation in Thailand.
> Bangkok,
> 12th June 1940.

77/40/A
Confidential and secret.
Your Excellency,

I would like to confirm with Your Excellency the following principles in relation to the Agreement which we have made:

With regard to the good relations which have been maintained peacefully for a long period between Thailand and France, and as each of the two countries wishes to maintain such relations in a good state for ever, the two governments therefore agree to end any administrative complications existing between Thailand and Indochina for the sake of goodwill and friendship so that relations between the two countries may now be based on mutual trust and co-operation in every respect.

To this end the two governments have therefore agreed to solve the complications concerning the river Mekong by accepting as the frontier line in this river that water channel along which Thailand could navigate her shipping with ease in all seasons. Thus any territory, regardless of form, to the right of this line would be considered the property of Thailand, while any territories to the left of this line would likewise be considered the territory of France.

To define and determine such a frontier line, the two governments would appoint representatives to be given due power and authority, and the agreement made between these same representatives would become effective within a period of one year from the date this note has been exchanged.

Further, it is understood that the French delegation would be under the direction of a senior official having ambassadorial status so that such delegation would have full power to negotiate over any remaining administrative problems.

However, it should be emphasized once again that such arrangements would come into effect only after the exchange of ratifications of the Non-Aggression Treaty has been carried out.

With my deep respects to your Excellency,

(Signed) *Paul Lépissier*

His Excellency the Prime Minister and Minister of Foreign Affairs, Bangkok.

[Source: Direct translation from the Thai edition of this work.]

APPENDIX 2

TREATY OF NON-AGGRESSION BETWEEN GREAT BRITAIN AND NORTHERN IRELAND AND THAILAND

His Majesty the King of Great Britain, Ireland and the British Dominions beyond the Seas, Emperor of India (hereinafter referred to as His Majesty the King and Emperor) and His Majesty the King of Thailand, animated by the desire to ensure peace and convinced that it is in the interest of the two High Contracting Parties to improve and develop the relations between the two countries:

Bearing in mind the international engagements which they have previously undertaken, and which they declare do not constitute an obstacle to the pacific development of their mutual relations and are not in contradiction with the present Treaty:

Desiring to confirm and, as regards their mutual relations, to give effect to the General Pact for the Renunciation of War of the 27th August 1928;

Have resolved to conclude a Treaty to this end and have designated as their Plenipotentiaries:

His Majesty the King of Great Britain, Ireland and the British Dominions beyond the Seas, Emperor of India:

For the United Kingdom of Great Britain and Northern Ireland:

Sir Josiah Crosby, K.B.E., C.I.E., His Majesty's Envoy Extraordinary and Minister Plenipotentiary at Bangkok;

His Majesty the King of Thailand:

Major-General Luang Pibulasonggram, His Majesty's President of the Council of Ministers and Minister of Foreign Affairs;

Who, after having communicated to each other their full powers, found in good and due form, have agreed as follows:

Article 1

Each High Contracting Party undertakes not to resort in any case either to war or to any act of violence or of aggression against the other, either alone, or in concert with one, or more than one, third Power, and to respect the territorial integrity of the other High Contracting Party.

Article 2

If one of the High Contracting Parties is the object of an act of war or of aggression on the part of one, or more than one, third Power the other High Contracting Party undertakes not to give, either directly or indirectly, aid or assistance to the aggressor or aggressors for the duration of the present Treaty.

If one of the High Contracting Parties commits an act of war or of aggression against a third Power, the other High Contracting Party shall have the right to terminate the present Treaty immediately without notice.

Article 3

The engagements set out in Articles 1 and 2 shall not in any way limit or modify the rights and obligations of either of the High Contracting Parties as a result of agreements concluded by him before the entry into force of the present Treaty, and each High Contracting Party hereby declares that he is not bound by any agreement which carries with it an obligation to participate in an act of war or of aggression committed by a third Power against the other Party.

Article 4

Nothing in the present Treaty shall be held to affect in any way the rights and obligations of the High Contracting Parties under the Covenant of the League of Nations.

Article 5

Each High Contracting Party undertakes to respect in every way the sovereignty or authority of the other High Contracting Party over his territories; he shall not intervene in any way in the internal affairs of such territories and shall abstain from any action calculated to give rise to or assist any agitation, propaganda or attempted intervention aimed against the integrity of any such territory or which has for its purpose the changing by force of the form of government of any such territory.

Article 6

The present Treaty, of which the English and Thai texts are equally valid, shall be ratified and the ratifications shall be exchanged at Bangkok as soon as possible. It shall come into force on the date of the exchange of ratifications and shall remain in force for one year from the day on which either of the High Contracting Parties notifies the other of his intention to terminate the Treaty. This notification shall not in any case be made before the expiration of a period of five years after the date on which the present Treaty enters into force.

IN WITNESS WHEREOF the above-named Plenipotentiaries have signed the present Treaty and have affixed thereto their seals.

DONE in duplicate at Bangkok this twelfth day of the third month in the two thousand four hundred and eighty-third year of the Buddhist Era, corresponding to the twelfth day of June in the nineteen hundred and fortieth year of the Christian era.

J. Crosby
Pibulasonggram

[Source: Thai Foreign Ministry Archives. Text also available in League of Nations, *Treaty Series*, CCIII, 1940–1941, no. 4782, 422–23, the text of which corresponds exactly with that given above. The exchange of ratifications of the above treaty took place at Bangkok on 31 August 1940 [ibid., 422, fn.1.]

APPENDIX 3

TREATY BETWEEN THAILAND AND JAPAN CONCERNING THE CONTINUANCE OF FRIENDLY RELATIONS BETWEEN THE TWO COUNTRIES AND THE MUTUAL RESPECT OF EACH OTHER'S TERRITORIAL INTEGRITY

His Majesty the King of Thailand and His Majesty the Emperor of Japan,

Being equally animated by the earnest desire of reaffirming and further strengthening the traditional bonds of friendship between Thailand and Japan, and

Being convinced that the peace and the stability of East Asia is the common concern of the two States,

Have resolved to conclude a treaty, and for that purpose have named as their Plenipotentiaries, that is to say:

His Majesty the King of Thailand:

Phya Sri Sena, Knight Grand Cross of the Most Noble Order of the Crown of Thailand, His Majesty's Envoy Extraordinary and Minister Plenipotentiary at the Court of His Majesty the Emperor of Japan;

His Majesty the Emperor of Japan:

Hachiro Arita, Zyosanmi, Grand Cordon of the Imperial Order of the Rising Sun, His Imperial Majesty's Minister for Foreign Affairs;

Who, after having communicated to each other their respective full powers, found to be in good and due form, have agreed upon the following articles:

Article 1

The High Contracting Parties shall mutually respect each other's territorial integrity and hereby reaffirm the constant peace and the perpetual friendship existing between them.

Article 2

The High Contracting Parties shall mutually maintain friendly contact in order to exchange information, and to consult one another, on any question of common interest that may arise.

Article 3
In the event of one of the High Contracting Parties suffering an attack from any third Power or Powers, the other Party undertakes not to give aid or assistance to the said Power or Powers against the Party attacked.

Article 4
The present Treaty shall be ratified and the ratifications thereof shall be exchanged at Bangkok as soon as possible.

Article 5
The present Treaty shall come into effect on the date of the exchange of ratifications and shall remain in force for five years from that date.

In case neither of the High Contracting Parties shall have given notice to the other six months before the expiration of the said period of five years of its intention to terminate the Treaty, it shall continue operative until the expiration of one year from the date on which either Party shall have given such notice.

IN WITNESS WHEREOF the respective Plenipotentiaries have signed the present Treaty and have hereunto affixed their seals.

DONE in duplicate, at Tokyo, this twelfth day of the third month in the two thousand four hundred and eighty-third year of the Buddhist Era, corresponding to the twelfth day of the sixth month in the fifteenth year of Showa, and the twelfth day of June in the nineteen hundred and fortieth year of the Christian Era.

Phya Sri Sena
Hachiro Arita

[Source: Thai Foreign Ministry Archives. Text also available in League of Nations, *Treaty Series*, op. cit, CCIV, 1941–1943, no. 4791, 132–33, the text of which corresponds exactly with that given above. The exchange of ratifications of the above treaty took place at Bangkok on 23 December 1940 [ibid., 132, fn.1].

APPENDIX 4

CONVENTION DE PAIX ENTRE LA FRANCE ET LA THAÏLANDE

Le Chef de l'Etat Français et Sa Majesté le Roi de la Thaïlande,

Ayant accepté la médiation du Gouvernement du Japon en vue d'apporter un règlement final au conflit armé survenu à la frontière de l'Indochine Française et de la Thaïlande,

Reconnaissant la nécessité de procéder au rajustement de la frontière actuelle de l'Indochine Française et de la Thaïlande, en vue de prévenir le retour de conflits à cette frontière, et de s'entendre sur les moyens de maintenir la tranquillité dans la zone frontière,

Désireux de rétablir pleinement les traditionnelles relations d'amitié entre la France et la Thaïlande,

Ont décidé, à cet effet, de conclure une Convention et ont nommé pour leurs Plénipotentiaires, savoir:

Le chef de l'Etat Francais:

    M. Charles Arsène-Henry, Ambassadeur Extraordinaire et Plénipotentiaire de la France au Japon;

    M. René Robin, Gouverneur Général Honoraire des Colonies; et

Sa Majesté le Roi de la Thaïlande:

    Son Altesse le Prince Varnvaidyakara, Conseiller de la Présidence du Conseil et du Ministère des Affaires Etrangères;

    Phya Sri Sena, Envoyé Extraordinaire et Ministre Plénipotentiaire de S.M. le Roi de la Thaïlande au Japon;

    M. le Colonel Phra Silpa Sastrakom, Chef de l'Etat Major Général de la Thaïlande;

    Nai Vanich Panananda, Directeur du Département du Commerce;

Lesquels, après s'être communiqué leurs pleins pouvoirs, trouvés en bonne et due forme, sont convenus des articles suivants:

Article 1

Les relations amicales sont rétablies entre la France et la Thaïlande sur la base fondamentale du Traité d'Amitié, de Commerce et de Navigation du 7 décembre 1937.

En conséquence, des négociations diplomatiques directes seront engagées dans le plus bref délai à Bangkok pour la liquidation de toutes les questions pendantes résultant du conflit.

Article 2

La frontière entre l'Indochine Française et la Thaïlande sera rajustée ainsi qu'il suit;

En partant du nord, la frontière suivra le fleuve Mékong depuis le point de jonction des frontières de l'Indochine Française, de la Thaïlande et de la Birmanie, jusqu'au point où le Mékong couple le parallèle du quinzième grade. (Carte du Service Géographique de l'Indochine-Echelle de 1:500,000).

Dans toute cette partie, la frontière sera constituée par la ligne médiane du chenal de navigation principal. Toute-fois, il est expressément convenu que l'île de Khong restera territoire de l'Indochine Française, tandis que l'île de Khone sera attribuée à la Thaïlande.

La frontière suivra ensuite, vers l'ouest, le parallèle du quinzième grade puis, vers le sud, le méridien qui passe par le point d'aboutissement au Grand Lac de la limite actuelle des provinces de Siemréap et de Battambang (embouchure du Stung Kombot).

Dans toute cette partie, la Commission de délimitation prévue à l'article 4 s'efforcera, s'il y a lieu, de rattacher la frontière à des lignes naturelles ou à des limites administratives, voisines du trace défini ci-dessus, de manière à éviter, dans la mesure du possible, des difficultés pratiques ultérieures.

Sur le Grand Lac, la frontière sera constituée par un arc de cercle de vingt kilomètres de rayon joignant le point d'aboutissement au Grand Lac de la limite actuelle des provinces de Siemréap et de Battambang (embouchure du Stung Kombot) au point d'aboutissement au Grand Lac de la limite actuelle des provinces de Battambang et de Pursat (embouchure du Stung Dontri).

Dans toute l'étendue du Grand Lac, la navigation et la pêche seront libres pour les ressortissants des deux Hautes Parties Contractantes, sous réserve du respect des installations fixes de pêcherie établies le long du rivage. Il est entendu que, dans cet esprit, les Hautes Parties Contractantes élaboreront, dans le plus bref délai, une réglementation commune de la police, de la navigation et de la pêche sur les eaux du Grand Lac.

A partir de l'embouchure du Stung Dontri, la nouvelle frontière suivra, en direction du sud-ouest, l'actuelle limite des provinces de Battambang et de Pursat, jusqu'au point de rencontre de cette limite avec la frontière actuelle de l'Indochine Française et de la Thaïlande (Khao Koup) qu'elle suivra ensuite sans modification jusqu'à la mer.

Article 3

Les territoires compris entre la frontière actuelle de l'Indochine Française et de la Thaïlande et la nouvelle ligne frontière définie à l'article 2, seront évacués et transférés conformément aux modalités prévues au protocole annexé à la présente Convention (Annexe I).

Article 4

Les travaux de délimitation de la frontière de l'Indochine Française et de la Thaïlande, telle qu'elle est définie à l'article 2, seront effectués, tant en ce qui concerne la partie terrestre que la partie fluviale de cette frontière, par une Commission de délimitation qui sera constituée dans la semaine suivant la mise en vigueur de la présente Convention et qui achèvera ses travaux dans le délai d'un an.

La constitution et le fonctionnement de la dite Commission font l'objet du Protocole annexé à la présente Convention (Annexe II).

Article 5

Les territoires cédés seront incorporés à la Thaïlande sous les conditions suivantes:

1. Ils seront démilitarisés dans toute leur étendue, à l'exception des territoires limitrophes du Mékong, faisant antérieurement partie du Laos français.
2. En ce qui concerne l'entrée, l'établissement et les entreprises, les ressortissants français (citoyens, sujets et protégés français) jouiront, dans toute l'étendue de ces territoires, d'un traitement absolument égal à celui qui sera accordé aux nationaux de la Thaïlande.

    Il est entendu que, en ce qui concerne les ressortissants français, les droits acquis résultant des concessions, affermages et permis obtenus à la date du 11 mars 1941, seront respectés sur toute l'étendue des territoires cédés.
3. Le Gouvernement de la Thaïlande assurera plein respect aux tombeaux royaux qui se trouvent sur la rive droite du Mékong en face de Luang Prabang et donnera toutes facilités à la Famille Royale de Luang Prabang et aux fonctionnaires de la Cour, pour la conservation et la visite de ces tombeaux.

Article 6

Dans les conditions prévues au Protocole annexé à la présente Convention (Annexe III), les principes suivants seront appliqués à la zone démilitarisée établie en vertu du point 1. de l'article précédent:

1. Dans la zone démilitarisée, la Thaïlande ne pourra entretenir d'autre forces armées que les forces de police nécessaires au maintien de la sûreté et de l'ordre public.

    Néanmoins, la Thaïlande se réserve le droit de renforcer momentanément ses forces de police dans la mesure où des opérations de police extraordinaires le rendraient nécessaire. Elle se réserve également la faculté d'effectuer sur son territoire, à travers la zone démilitarisée, les transports de troupes et de matériel qu'exigeraient des opérations de police dans les circonscriptions voisines ou des opérations militaires contre de tierces Puissances.

    Enfin, dans la zone démilitarisée, la Thaïlande sera autorisée à faire stationner en tout temps, des aéronefs militaires non armés.

2. Il ne pourra exister dans la zone démilitarisée ni places fortes, ni établissements militaires, ni aérodromes à l'usage exclusif de l'armée, ni dépôts d'armes, de munitions ou de materiél de guerre, à l'exception des dépôts de materiél courant et de combustible nécessaires aux aéronefs militaires non armés.

    Les divers casernements des forces de police pourront comporter l'organization défensive normalement nécessaire à leur securité.

Article 7

Les Hautes Parties Contractantes sont d'accord pour supprimer les zones démilitarisés existant de part et d'autre du Mékong sur la partie du course de ce fleuve où il forme la frontière entre le Laos Français et la Thaïlande.

Article 8

Dès que le transfert de la souveraineté sur les territoires cédés à la Thaïlande sera définitif, la nationalité de la Thaïlande sera acquise de plein droit par les ressortissants français établis sur ces territoires.

Toutefois, dans l'année qui suivra le transfert définitif de la souveraineté, les ressortissants français auront la faculté d'opter pour la nationalité française.

Cette option s'exercera de la manière suivante:

1. En ce qui concerne les citoyens français, par une declaration faite devant l'autorité administrative compétente.
2. En ce qui concerne les sujets et protégés français, par un transfert de domicile en territoire français.

Aucun obstacle ne sera apporté par la Thaïlande, quelle qu'en soit la raison, à l'évacuation ou au retour éventuel de ces sujets et protégés français. En particulier, ils pourront, avant leur départ, disposer librement de leurs biens mobiliers et immobiliers. Ils auront la faculté d'emporter avec eux ou de faire transporter, en franchise douanière, leurs biens mobiliers de toute nature, bétail, produits agricoles, monnaies ou billets de banque. En tout état de cause, ils pourront conserver, sur les territoires incorporés à la Thaïlande, la propriété de leurs biens immobiliers.

Article 9

La France et la Thaïlande sont d'accord pour renoncer définitivement à toute prétention d'ordre financier, d'Etat à Etat, résultant du transfert de territoires prévu à l'article 2, moyennant le paiement, par la Thaïlande à la France, d'une somme de six millions de piastres indochinoises. Le paiement de cette somme sera reparti, par tranches égales, sur six années à compter de la mise en vigueur de la présente Convention.

Pour assurer l'application du paragraphe précédent, ainsi que pour régler toutes questions monétaires et de transfert de valeurs que peuvent poser les cessions de territoires faisant l'objet de la présente Convention, les administrations compétentes de l'Indochine Française et de la Thaïlande entreront négociations dans le plus bref délai.

Article 10

Tout conflit pouvant surgir entre les deux Hautes Parties Contractantes au sujet de l'interprétation ou de l'application des dispositions de la présente Convention sera resolu amiablement par la voie diplomatique.

Si le conflit ne peut être ainsi résolu, il sera soumis à la médiation du Gouvernement de Japon.

Article 11

Toutes dispositions des Traités, Conventions et Accords existant entre la France et la Thaïlande, qui ne sont pas incompatibles avec les dispositions de la présente Convention, sont et demeurent maintenues en vigueur.

Article 12

La présente Convention sera ratifiée et les ratifications en seront échangées à Tokyo dans des deux mois suivant la date de sa signature. Le Gouvernement Français pourra, le cas échéant, substituer à son instrument de ratification une notification écrite de ratification; dans ce cas, le Gouvernement Français enverra son instrument de ratification au Gouvernement de la Thaïlande aussitôt que faire et pourra.

La présente Convention entrera en vigueur le jour de l'échange des ratifications.

En foi de quoi, les Plénipotentiaires respectifs ont signé la présente Convention et y ont apposé leurs cachets.

Fait en triple exemplaire, en langues française, japonaise et thaïe, à Tokyo, le neuf mai mil neuf cent quarante et un, correspondant au neuvième jour du cinquième mois de la seizième année de Showa, et au neuvième jour du cinquième mois de la deux mille quatre cent quatre-vingt-quatrième année de l'ère bouddhique.

Charles Arsène Henry
René Robin
Varnvaidyakara
Srisena
Group Captain Silpasastrakom
Vanich Panananda

[Source: Thai Foreign Ministry Archives. Text also available (with minor editorial differences) in *British and Foreign State Papers*, 1940–1942, London, H.M.S.O., 1952, vol. 144, 805–09. The exchange of ratifications of the above Convention took place at Tokyo on July 5, 1941 (ibid, 805)].

Annexe 1

Protocole Concernant les Modalités d'Evacuation et de Transfert des Territoires

Le Gouvernement Français et le Gouvernement de la Thaïlande conviennent de ce qui suit:

I. Transfert des biens publics immobiliers.

Le Gouvernement Français remettra au Gouvernement de la Thaïlande, dans les vingt jours qui suivront l'échange des ratifications, l'état des biens publics immobiliers se trouvant dans les territoires cédés, ainsi que la liste des délégués français chargés des opérations de transfert.

Le Gouvernement de la Thaïlande remettra au Gouvernement Français, dans le même délai, la liste des personnes chargées de prendre possession desdits biens immobiliers. Les délégués des deux Gouvernements seront repartis en cinq groupes correspondant aux régions de Paklay, Bassac, Kompong Thom, Siemréap et Battambang.

Les délégués de la Thaïlande se présenteront à une date qui sera fixée d'un commun accord, à Paklay, Bassac, Cheom Ksan, Samrong et Poipet, où ils seront reçus par les délégués français.

II. Transfert des archives.

Les archives communales et provinciales, les archives des tribunaux et autres organes d'Etat, ainsi que les plans cadastraux déposés dans les territoires cédés, seront transférés aux autorités de la Thaïlande. En ce qui concerne les plans, registres et autres documents cadastraux déposés hors de ces territoires, des copies certifées en seront remises au Gouvernement de la Thaïlande.

Le transfert sera achevé dans les deux mois qui suivront l'échange des ratifications.

III. Evacuation des territoires.

Les territoires faisant l'objet du présent Protocole seront évacués par les unités militaires françaises et occupés par les forces de police ou par les unités militaires de la Thaïlande conformément aux principes suivants:

a) Les unités militaires françaises, stationnées entre la frontière actuelle et la nouvelle ligne de frontière, se mettront en marche le vingtième jour qui suivra l'échange de ratifications, et devront se trouver, au plus tard, sept jours après, en deçà de la nouvelle ligne de frontière. Elles seront précédées par les gendarmes, la police et les autorités administratives françaises (à l'exception de celles qui participeront aux travaux de transfert stipulés aux parties I et II ci-dessus), se trouvant dans les territoires susmentionnés.

b) Les forces de police ou les unités militaires que le Gouvernement de la Thaïlande aurait l'intention d'envoyer dans les territoires susmentionnés se mettront en marche le lendemain du jour où les unités françaises auront commencé l'évacuation et pourront arriver, au plus tôt, sept jours après, à la nouvelle ligne de frontière. Elles pourront être suivies des autorités administratives de la Thaïlande appelées à stationner dans les territoires susmentionnés.

c) Les forces de police ou les unités militaires de la Thaïlande règleront leur marche de manière à maintenir une distance constante avec les unités françaises.

d) Les unités militaires de la Thaïlande qui se trouveraient dans la zone démilitarisée mentionée à l'article 5 de la Convention, seront évacuées dans le délai d'un mois à compter du transfert des territoires.

IV. Mesures pratiques.

Les Gouvernements des deux Parties prendront toutes mesures pratiques nécessaires pour que les operations d'évacuation et de transfert prévues au présent Protocole s'effectuent en bon ordre et sans incidents:

a) Les unités militaires évacuées ne pourront laisser en arrière ni forces militaires irrégulières, ni individus munis d'armes à feu. De même, les forces de police

ou les unités militaires occupantes ne pourront se faire précéder ni par des forces militaires irrégulières, ni par des individus munis d'armes à feu.
b) Les deux Gouvernements donneront respectivement à leurs unités militaires et de police l'ordre formel de s'abstenir de tout acte de pillage.

Le présent Protocole sera ratifié par la France et la Thaïlande en même temps que la Convention.

Le présent Protocole entrera en vigueur en même temps que la Convention.

En foi de quoi, les soussignés, dûment autorisés par leurs Gouvernements respectifs, ont signé le présent Protocole et y ont apposé leurs cachets.

Fait en triple exemplaire, en langues française, japonaise et thaï, à Tokyo, le neuf mai mil neuf cent quarante et un, correspondant au neuvième jour du cinquième mois de la seizième année de Showa, et au neuvième jour du cinquième mois de la deux mille quatre cent quatre-vingt-quatrième année de l'ère bouddhique.

Charles Arsène Henry
René Robin
Varnvaidyakara
Srisena
Group Captain Silpasastrakom
Vanich Panananda

Annexe 2

Protocole Relatif à la Constitution et au Fonctionnement de la Commission de Délimitation

Les Gouvernements de la France, du Japon et de la Thaïlande conviennent de ce qui suit, en ce qui concerne la Commission de délimitation prévue à l'article 4 de la Convention de Paix entre la France et la Thaïlande:

I. Composition.

Les Gouvernements des trois Parties désigneront respectivement cinq délégués et cinq délégués adjoints.

Les délégués de chacune des Parties pourront se faire accompagner des experts et secrétaires qu'ils jugeront nécessaires.

En cas d'empêchement, les délégués adjoints pourront remplacer les délégués dans leurs fonctions.

Les fonctions de Président de la Commission seront confiées à l'un des délégués japonais.

II. Attributions.

La Commission procédera sur place à la délimitation de la frontière terrestre et fluviale ainsi qu'il est prévu à l'article 4 de la Convention.

Elle établira une carte de cette frontière et procédera à la pose de bornes de délimitation aux points juges nécessaires.

III. Fonctionnement.

Le Gouvernement Français et le Gouvernement de la Thaïlande accorderont aux membres de la Commission toutes facilités nécessaires pour l'accomplissement de leur mission.

Les appointements et les frais de déplacement des membres de la Commission seront à la charge de leurs Gouvernements respectifs.

Les frais de travaux de la Commission seront partages par moitié entre le Gouvernement Français et le Gouvernement de la Thaïlande.

Il est prévu que la Commission pourra établir un règlement intérieur relatif à son fonctionnement.

Le présent Protocole sera ratifié par la France et la Thaïlande en meme temps que la Convention. En ce qui concerne le Japon, il sera approuvé par son Gouvernement.

Le présent Protocole entrera en vigueur en même temps que la Convention.

En foi de quoi, les soussignés, dûment autorisés par leurs Gouvernements respectifs, ont signé le présent Protocole et y ont apposé leurs cachets.

Fait en triple exemplaire, en langues française, japonaise et thaïe, à Tokyo, le neuf mai mil neuf cent quarante et un, correspondant au neuvième jour du cinquième mois de la seizième année de Showa, et au neuvième jour du cinquième mois de la deux mille quatre cent quatre-vingt-quatrième année de l'ère bouddhique.

Charles Arsène Henry
René Robin
Matsuoka Yasuke* (in Japanese)
Matsumiya Hajime* (in Japanese)
Varnvaidyakara
Srisena
Group Captain Silpasastrakom
Vanich Panananda

* [The names of the two Japanese signatories to this Protocol are not given in the version of this document cited in the Thai edition of this book. However, they are recorded both in the Thai Foreign Ministry Archives' source and in the *British and Foreign State Papers* source cited below.]

Annexe 3

Protocole Relatif à L'exécution des Dispositions Concernant la Zone Démilitarisée

Les Gouvernements de la France, du Japon et de la Thaïlande conviennent de ce qui suit, au sujet de l'exécution des dispositions concernant la zone démilitarisée et prévues aux articles 5 et 6 de la Convention de Paix entre la France et la Thaïlande.

I.   Pendant toute la durée de son fonctionnement, la Commission de délimitation instituée par l'article 4 de la Convention sera chargée de veiller à l'exécution des disposition prévues par le point 1. de l'article 5 et par l'article 4 de la Convention.

La même Commission soumettra à l'approbation du Gouvernement de la Thaïlande des dispositions ayant pour objet:
   a) de fixer la nature, l'effectif et l'armement des forces de police de la Thaïlande dans la zone démilitarisée;
   b) de déterminer les conditions dans lesquelles la Thaïlande pourra user des facultés qui lui sont accordées en vertu du deuxième alinéa du point 1. de l'article 6;
   c) enfin, de définir de régime particulier de la navigation aérienne dans la zone démilitarisée.

Elle pourra en outre proposer aux deux Gouvernements intéressés toutes mesures qu'elle jugera nécessaires pour assurer l'exécution des dispositions prévues.

II.   A compter de la dissolution de la Commission de délimitation les attributions définies ci-dessus seront exercées, le cas échéant, par une Commission mixte, composée de trois membres pour chacune des Parties, et qui se réunira à la demande de l'un des Gouvernements intéressés.

Les fonctions de Président de cette Commission seront confiées à l'un des délégués japonais.

Le présent Protocole sera ratifié par la France et la Thaïlande en meme temps que la Convention. En ce qui concerne le Japon, il sera approuvé par son Gouvernement.

Le présent Protocole entrera en vigueur en même temps que la Convention.

En foi de quoi, les soussignés, dûment autorisés par leurs Gouvernements respectifs, ont signé le présent Protocole et y ont apposé leurs cachets.

Fait en triple exemplaire, en langues française, japonaise et thaïe, à Tokyo, le neuf mai mil neuf cent quarante et un, correspondant au neuvième jour du cinquième mois de la seizième année de Showa, et au neuvième jour du cinquième mois de la deux mille quatre cent quatre-vingt-quatrième année de l'ère bouddhique.

> Charles Arsène Henry
> René Robin
> Matsuoka Yasuke* (in Japanese)
> Matsumiya Hajime* (in Japanese)
> Varnvaidyakara
> Srisena
> Group Captain Silpasastrakom
> Vanich Panananda

[Again, the Japanese names are not given in the Thai edition of this book, but are given in the sources cited below.]

[Source: All three Annexes are taken from the Thai Foreign Ministry Archives. Texts are also available in *British and Foreign State Papers*, op. cit., 1940–1942, vol. 144, 810–12 (Annexe I); 802–03 (Annexe II), and 803–04 (Annexe III). The texts correspond exactly to those quoted above except for minor editorial differences, together with one textual difference in Annexe II, Article 1. In the Thai Foreign Ministry Archives' text this reads: "Les Gouvernements des trois parties désigneront respectivement cinq délégués et cinq délégués adjoints". The *British and Foreign State Papers* version reads: "Les Gouvernements des trois parties désigneront respectivement cinq délégués adjoints...."]

APPENDIX 4

[Exchanges of Notes between Prince Wan Waithayakorn and Monsieur Charles Arsène Henry]

(Prince Wan Waithayakorn à Monsieur Charles Arsène Henry)

Traduction.   Royal Thai Legation,
                               Tokio [sic].
                               Le 9 mai 2484 (A.D.1941).

Monsieur l'Ambassadeur,

J'ai l'honneur de confirmer à Votre Excellence l'accord verbal déjà intervenu entre nous, et aux termes duquel il sera recommandé à la Commission de délimitation de la nouvelle frontière de tenir compte, en s'inspirant des stipulations de l'article 2, paragraphe 5 de la Convention de Paix, du désir du Gouvernement Française de conserver le temple de Banteai-Srei, comme faisant partie du groupe d'Angkor.

Il est entendu que la Commission de délimitation devra, le cas échéant, prévoir, dans le tracé de la nouvelle frontière, une compensation territoriale d'égale superficie en faveur de la Thaïlande.

Je saisis cette occasion, Monsieur l'Ambassadeur, pour renouveler à Votre Excellence les assurances de ma très haute considération.

                    Signé: *Varnvaidya*

Son Excellence Monsieur Charles Arsène-Henry, Ambassadeur Extraordinaire et Plénipotentiaire de la France au Japon, Tokyo.

(Monsieur Charles Arsène Henry au Prince Varnvaidyakara)

> Ambassade de la République Française
> au Japon, Tokyo.
> Le 9 mai 1941.

Monseigneur,

J'ai l'honneur de confirmer à Votre Altesse l'accord verbal déjà intervenu entre nous, et aux termes duquel il sera recommandé à la Commission de délimitation de la nouvelle frontière de tenir compte, en s'inspirant des stipulations de l'article 2, paragraphe 5, de la Convention de Paix, du désir du Gouvernement Français de conserver le temple de Banteai-Srei comme faisant partie du groupe d' Angkor.

Il est entendu que la Commission de délimitation devra, le cas échéant, prévoir, dans le tracé de la nouvelle frontière, une compensation territoriale d'égale superficie en faveur de la Thaïlande.

Je saisis cette occasion, Monseigneur, pour renouveler à Votre Altesse les assurances de ma très haute considération.

> Signé: *Charles Arsène Henry*

à Son Altesse le Prince Varnvaidyakara,
Conseiller de la Présidence du Conseil et du Ministère des Affaires Etrangères,
Premier Plénipotentiaire de Sa Majesté le Roi de la Thaïlande, Tokyo.

(Prince Varnvaidyakara à Monsieur Charles Arsène Henry)

Traduction. Royal Thai Legation
Tokio [sic.]
Le 9 mai 2484 (A.D. 1941)

Monsieur l'Ambassadeur,

J'ai l'honneur de confirmer à Votre Excellence l'accord verbal déjà intervenu entre nous, et aux termes duquel l'égalité de traitement, en ce qui concerne l'entrée, l'établissement et les entreprises, prévue par l'article 5, paragraphe 2, de la Convention que nous venons de signer, doit s'interpréter comme une égalité de traitement à tous égards, sons les deux exceptions suivantes:
1. Les ressortissants français ne bénéficieront pas de l'égalité de traitement en ce qui concerne l'acquisition des immeubles du domaine public. Ils seront soumis à ce sujet aux dispositions du traité d'Amitié, de Commerce et de Navigation du 7 décembre 1937 et de ses annexes.
2. Les ressortissants francais qui n'étaient pas domiciliés dans les territoires cédés au moment du transfert de souveraineté et qui entreront dans les territoires cédés seront soumis aux dispositions de la Loi d'immigration de la Thaïlande.

Je saisis cette occasion, Monsieur l'Ambassadeur, pour renouveler à Votre Excellence, les assurances de ma très haute considération.

Signé: *Varnvaidya*

Son Excellence Monsieur Charles Arsène-Henry,
Ambassadeur Extraordinaire et Plénipotentiaire de la France au Japon, Tokyo.

(Monsieur Charles Arsène Henry au Prince Varnvaidyakara)

> Ambassade de la République
> Française au Japon. Tokyo
> Le 9 mai 1941.

Monseigneur,

J'ai l'honneur de confirmer à Votre Altesse l'accord verbal déjà intervenu entre nous, et aux termes duquel l'égalité de traitement, en ce qui concerne l'entrée, l'établissement et les entreprises, prévue par l'article 5, paragraphe 3, de la Convention que nous venons de signer, doit s'interpréter comme une égalité de traitement à tous égards, sous les deux exceptions suivantes:

1. Les ressortissants français ne bénéficieront pas de l'égalité de traitement en ce qui concerne l'acquisition des immeubles du domaine public. Ils seront soumis à ce sujet aux dispositions du traité d'Amitié, de Commerce et de Navigation du 7 décembre 1937 et de ses annexes.
2. Les ressortissants français qui n'étaient pas domiciliés dans les territoires cédés au moment du transfert de souveraineté et qui entreront dans les territoires cédés seront soumis aux dispositions de la Loi d'immigration de la Thaïlande.

Je saisis cette occasion, Monseigneur, pour renouveler à Votre Altesse les assurances de ma très haute considération.

> Signé: *Charles Arsène Henry*

à Son Altesse le Prince Varnvaidyakara
Conseiller de la Présidence du Conseil et du Ministere des Affaires Etrangères,
Premier Plénipotentiaire de Sa Majesté le Roi de la Thaïlande, Tokyo.

[Source for Exchanges of Notes: Thai Foreign Ministry Archives.]

Communiqué on Protocol Between Thailand and Japan Concerning Guarantee and Political Understanding

This announcement is made by Royal Command, that as in the Protocol between Thailand and Japan concerning the Guarantee and Political Understanding signed in Tokyo on May 9, 1941, Article 3 states that this document will become operative on the day ratifications have been exchanged, and as the letters of ratification have now been exchanged in Tokyo on July 5, 1941, this Protocol therefore comes into force from this day onwards.

Announced as of July 5, 1941 in the eighth year of the present reign.

> By command of His Majesty,
> *Pibulsongkram*
> *Prime Minister*

[Source: Direct translation from the Thai edition of this work.]

Protocole entre la Thaïlande et le Japon Concernant la Garantie et L'Entente Politique

Translation.

Le Gouvernement de la Thaïlande et le Gouvernement du Japon, également désireux de maintenir la paix en Asie Orientale,

S'inspirant de l'esprit pacifique et amical qui a présidé à l'établissement du traité du 12 juin 1940, et également animés du désir sincère de persister dans cette voie,

Soucieux d'assurer la stabilisation des relations amicales qui viennent d'être rétablies entre la Thaïlande et la France,

Sont convenus de ce qui suit:

1. Le Gouvernement du Japon garantit au Gouvernement de la Thaïlande le caractère définitif et irrévocable du règlement du conflit entre la Thaïlande et la France, tel qu'il résulte, à la suite de la médiation du Gouvernement du Japon, de la Convention de Paix entre la Thaïlande et la France du 9 mai 1941 et des documents y annexés.
2. Le Gouvernement de la Thaïlande accepte la garantie susmentionnée du Gouvernement du Japon. Il s'emploiera au maintien de la paix en Asie Orientale, et en particulier à l'établissement de rapports amicaux de bon voisinage, ainsi qu'au développement des relations économiques étroites entre la Thaïlande et le Japon.

Le Gouvernement de la Thaïlande déclare en outre qu'il n'entend contracter aucun accord ou entente avec une tierce Puissance, prévoyant une coopération politique, économique ou militaire de nature à l'opposer directement ou indirectement au Japon.

3. Le présent Protocole sera ratifié et les ratifications en seront échangées à Tokyo dans les deux mois suivant la date de sa signature.

Le présent Protocole entrera en vigueur le jour de l'échange des ratifications.

En foi de quoi, les soussignés, dûment autorisés par leurs Gouvernements respectifs, ont signé le présent Protocole et y ont apposé leurs cachets.

Fait en double exemplaire, en langues thaïe et japonaise, à Tokyo, le neuvième jour du cinquième mois de la deux mille quatre cent quatre-vingt-quatrième année de l'ère bouddhique, correspondant au neuvième jour du cinquième mois de la seizième année de Showa.

Varnvaidyakara
Srisena
Group Captain Silpasastrakom
Vanich Panananda
Matsuoka Yosuke (in Japanese)
Matsumiya Hajime (in Japanese)

[Source: Thai Foreign Ministry Archives. Text also available in *British and Foreign State Papers*, op. cit., 1940–1942, vol. 144, 840–41. Text accords exactly with the above except for minor editorial differences. The above treaty was ratified at Tokyo on 5 July 1941 (ibid, 840.)]

APPENDIX 5

FORMAL AGREEMENT FOR THE TERMINATION OF THE STATE OF WAR BETWEEN SIAM AND GREAT BRITAIN AND INDIA, AND EXCHANGE OF NOTES BETWEEN THE SIAMESE GOVERNMENT AND AUSTRALIA WITH A VIEW TO TERMINATING THE STATE OF WAR, SIGNED AT SINGAPORE ON 1ST JANUARY 1946

Communiqué

Following the declaration of war on Great Britain by the Siamese Government at that time, Great Britain has considered that a state of war arose between the two countries as from that moment.

Normally speaking, in order to terminate a state of war, the victorious power usually imposes a peace treaty upon the defeated nation, and it is only upon the signing of the peace treaty that the state of war is terminated. Siam has fallen into such a situation, but in view of the resistance movement organised by the Siamese both inside and outside the country acting in co-operation against the enemy of the Allies and of the manifestation of the will to co-operate with the United Nations, as well as of the fact that the Government responsible for bringing about the state of war had already fallen, Great Britain generously decided to adopt a novel method, that is to say, instead of making Siam conclude a treaty of peace, Great Britain merely required Siam to accept certain terms relating to the restitution of the property which had suffered damage during the war and to the co-operation of Siam in the economic rehabilitation and in ensuring international security as well as promoting world peace in order to prevent war in the future.

The terms required of Siam by Great Britain were the subject of an agreement signed between the representatives of the two countries at Singapore on 1st January B.E. 2489. Upon the signing of this agreement the state of war between Great Britain and Siam is terminated and the friendly relations between the two countries which happily existed formerly and have unfortunately been interrupted are now restored as heretofore.

Whatever legislative measures which may have to be taken in order to comply with the terms of the agreement will be submitted to the Assembly as soon as possible.

From the agreement between Siam and Great Britain it hopefully appears that Great Britain has put forward only such claims as should be put forward and that she will show sympathy and accommodation in the application of the agreement. Great Britain has already manifested its friendly disposition by proposing to assist in financial and monetary matters with a view to the rapid economic recovery of Siam, by agreeing to regard the state of war as terminated and to proceed at once to the resumption of friendly relations with Siam and to exchange diplomatic representatives, and by undertaking to support Siam's candidature for membership of the United Nations. Such goodwill is evidence of her good intentions both now and in the future.

> Office of the Presidency of the
> Council of Ministers,
> 1st January 2489 [A.D. 1946].

[Source: Thai Foreign Ministry. Given in Thai and English in the Thai edition of this book, and copied directly from it.]

Formal Agreement for the Termination of the State of War between Siam and Great Britain and India, Signed at Singapore on 1st January 1946

WHEREAS by a Proclamation made in Bangkok on 16th August 1945 the Regent of Siam did, in the name of His Majesty the King of Siam, proclaim the declaration of war made by Siam on 25th January 1942, against the United Kingdom to be null and void in that it was made contrary to the will of the Siamese people and in violation of the constitution and laws of Siam, and

WHEREAS the proclamation of 16th August 1945 aforesaid was the same day unanimously approved by the National Assembly of Siam, and

WHEREAS the Siamese Government has repudiated the Alliance entered into by Siam with Japan on 21st December 1941, together with all other Treaties, Pacts or Agreements concluded between Siam and Japan, and

WHEREAS the Siamese Government is anxious to play its full part in mitigating the effects of the war, particularly in regard to such measures as may be designed to assist in the restoration of international security and general economic welfare, and

WHEREAS the Government of the United Kingdom and the Government of India, in consideration of the acts of repudiation already carried out by the Siamese Government, and not unmindful of the services rendered by the resistance movement in Siam during the war with Japan, desire to bring the state of war to an immediate end.

NOW THEREFORE the Government of the United Kingdom and the Government of India on the one hand and the Siamese Government on the other, being desirous of renewing the relations of close friendship which existed before the war, have resolved to conclude an agreement for these purposes and have accordingly appointed as their plenipotentiaries:

Government of the United Kingdom of Great Britain and Northern Ireland:
Mr. M.E. Dening, C.M.G., O.B.E.
Government of India:
Mr. M.S. Aney
Siamese Government:
His Serene Highness Prince Viwatchai Chaiyant
Lieutenant-General Phya Abhai Songgram
Nai Serm Vinicchayakul

WHO, having communicated their full powers, found in good and due form, have agreed as follows:

Restitution and Readjustment

Article 1

The Siamese Government agrees to repudiate all measures pursuant to the above-mentioned declaration of war made on 25th January 1942, and to take the necessary legislative and administrative measures to give effect to that repudiation.

Article 2

The Siamese Government declares as null and void all purported acquisitions of British territory made by Siam later than 7th December 1941, as well as all titles, rights, properties and interests acquired in such territory since that date either by the Siamese State or by Siamese subjects. The Siamese Government agrees to take the necessary legislative measures to give effect to the foregoing declaration and in particular

(a) to repeal and declare null and void *ab initio* all legislative and administrative measures relating to the purported annexation by, or incorporation in, Siam of British territories effected after 7th December 1941.

(b) to withdraw as may be required by the competent civil or military authority all Siamese military personnel from all such British territories and all Siamese official and nationals who entered these territories after their purported annexation by, or incorporation in Siam.

(c) to restore all property taken away from these territories, including currency except to the extent to which it can be established that fair value has been given in exchange.

(d) to compensate loss or damage to property, rights and interests in these territories arising out of the occupation of these territories by Siam.

(e) to redeem in sterling out of former sterling reserves current Siamese notes collected by the British authorities in British territory occupied by Siam since 7th December 1941.

Article 3

The Siamese Government agrees to assume responsibility for safeguarding, maintaining and restoring unimpaired, British property, rights and interests of all kinds in Siam and for payment of compensation for losses or damage sustained. The term "property, rights and interests" shall include *inter alia* the official property of the Government of the United Kingdom and of the Government of India, property whose ownership has been transferred since the outbreak of war, pensions granted to British nationals, stocks of tin, teak and other commodities, shipping and wharves, and tin, teak and other leases and concessions granted to British firms and individuals prior to 7th December 1941 and still valid at that date.

Article 4

The Siamese Government agrees to desequestrate British banking and commercial concerns and permit them to resume business.

Article 5

The Siamese Government agrees to accept liability, with the addition of interest, at an appropriate percentage, in respect of payment in arrears, for the service of loans and for payment of pensions in full since the date when regular payments ceased.

Security

Article 6

The Siamese Government recognises that the course of events in the war with Japan demonstrates the importance of Siam to the defence of Malaya, Burma, India and Indo-China and the security of the Indian Ocean and South-West Pacific areas, and the Siamese Government agrees to collaborate fully in all international security arrangements approved by the United Nations Organisation or its Security Council which may be pertinent to Siam and especially such international security arrangements as may relate to those countries or areas.

Article 7
The Siamese Government undertakes that no canal linking the Indian Ocean and the Gulf of Siam shall be cut across Siamese territory without the prior concurrence of the Government of the United Kingdom.

Commercial and Economic Collaboration

Article 8
The Siamese Government agrees to take all possible measures to re-establish import and export trade between Siam on the one hand and neighbouring British territories on the other, and to adopt and maintain a good-neighbourly policy in regard to coastal shipping.

Article 9
The Siamese Government undertakes to negotiate with the Government of the United Kingdom as soon as practicable a new Treaty of Establishment, Commerce and Navigation and a Consular Convention based on the reciprocal application of the principles in Article Eleven below.

Article 10
The Siamese Government undertakes to negotiate with the Government of India as soon as practicable a new Treaty of Commerce and Navigation based on the reciprocal application of the principles in the following Article.

Article 11
(1) Pending the conclusion of the Treaties and Convention referred to in Articles Nine and Ten above and subject to paragraph (2) of this Article, the Siamese Government undertakes to observe the provisions of the Treaty of Commerce and Navigation signed at Bangkok on 23rd November 1937, and further undertakes, except where the Treaty specifically authorises such action, not to enforce any measures excluding British commercial or industrial interests or British professional men on grounds of nationality from participation in Siamese economy and trade, or any measures requiring them to maintain stocks or reserves in excess of normal commercial, shipping, industrial or business practice.

(2) The above-mentioned undertakings of the Siamese Government (a) shall be subject to such exceptions, if any, as may at any time be agreed to between the Government of the United Kingdom or the Government of India, as the case may be, and the Siamese Government; (b) shall, unless

prolonged by agreement, lapse if the Treaties and Conventions referred to in Articles Nine and Ten have not been concluded within a period of three years from the coming into force of this agreement.
(3) Nothing in this Article shall be deemed to preclude the grant of equally favourable treatment to nationals and enterprises of any or all other United Nations.

Article 12
The Siamese Government undertakes to participate in any general international arrangement regarding tin or rubber which conforms with such principles regarding commodity arrangements as may be agreed by the United Nations Organisation or its Economic and Social Council.

Article 13
Until a date or dates not later than 1st September 1947, the Siamese Government undertakes to prohibit, except in accordance with the recommendations of the Combined Boards in Washington, or any successor body, and in the case of rice, under the direction of a special organisation to be set up for the purpose, any exports of rice, tin, rubber and teak and to regulate trade in and stimulate production of these commodities.

Article 14
The Siamese Government undertakes to make available free of cost at Bangkok to an organisation to be indicated by the Government of the United Kingdom and as quickly as may be compatible with the retention of supplies adequate for Siamese internal needs, a quantity of rice equal to the accumulated surplus of rice at present existing in Siam, subject to a maximum of one and a half million tons, or if so agreed the equivalent quantity of paddy or loonzain [partially husked rice—Ed.]. It is agreed that the exact amount of rice to be made available under this Article shall be determined by the organisation above-mentioned and that the rice, paddy or loonzain delivered under this Article shall conform to the agreed standards of quality to be determined by the same authorities.

Article 15
Until a date not later than 1st September 1947, the Siamese Government agrees to make available to the rice organisation mentioned in Article Thirteen and Article Fourteen all rice surplus to the internal needs of Siam. Such rice, with the exception of rice delivered free in accordance with the undertaking given in Article Fourteen, will be supplied in such manner as the special or-

ganisation mentioned in Article Thirteen and Article Fourteen shall indicate, and at prices fixed in agreement with it, having regard to the controlled prices of rice in other Asiatic rice-exporting areas.

Civil Aviation

Article 16

The Siamese Government shall accord to the civil air services of the British Commonwealth of Nations, by means of agreements to be negotiated with the Governments of members of the British Commonwealth of Nations, treatment in regard to the establishment, maintenance and operation of regular air services not less favourable than that accorded to Imperial Airways by the notes exchanged at Bangkok on 3rd December 1937.

War Graves

Article 17

The Siamese Government undertakes to enter into an agreement with the Government of the United Kingdom and the Government of India for the mutual upkeep of war graves, with a view to the permanent establishment and future care of British and Indian war graves and of Siamese war graves in their respective territories.

Miscellaneous

Article 18

The Siamese Government agrees to regard as in force such bilateral treaties between the United Kingdom and Siam and India and Siam as may respectively be specified by the Government of the United Kingdom and the Government of India, subject to any modifications the Government of the United Kingdom or the Government of India may indicate, and to regard as abrogated any such treaties not so specified.

Article 19

The Siamese Government agrees to regard as being in force between the United Kingdom and Siam and between India and Siam all multilateral treaties, conventions or agreements concluded prior to 7th December 1941, (a) to which Siam and the United Kingdom or India, as the case may be, were then and still are parties; (b) to which the United Kingdom or India, as the case may be, was then and still is a party, but to which Siam has not become a party, and which shall be notified to the Siamese Government by the Government of the United Kingdom or the Government of India. On the receipt of such notification the Siamese Government shall immediately take the necessary steps in accordance with the provisions of any such treaty, convention or agreement to which Siam is not a contracting party, to accede thereto, or if accession is not possible, shall give effect to the provisions thereof in respect of the United Kingdom or India, as the case may be, by such legislative or administrative means as may be appropriate. The Siamese Government agrees also to accept any modifications thereto which may have come into effect in accordance with the terms of such instruments since that date.

Article 20
Pending admission to any international organisation set up since 7th December 1941, being an organisation of which the United Kingdom or India is a member, the Siamese Government agrees to carry out any obligations arising out of, or in connection with, any such organisation or the instruments constituting it, as may at any time be specified by the Government of the United Kingdom or the Government of India, as the case may be.

Article 21
In consideration of the above undertakings made by the Siamese Government, the Government of the United Kingdom and the Government of India agree to regard the state of war as terminated and to proceed at once to the resumption of friendly relations with Siam and to exchange diplomatic representatives.

Article 22
The Government of the United Kingdom and the Government of India also undertake to support Siam's candidature for membership in the United Nations.

Definitions and Date of Entry into Force of Agreement

Article 23
It is agreed by the contracting parties that the term "British" in this agreement
    (1) when applied to physical persons shall mean all subjects of His Majesty the King of Great Britain, Ireland and the British Dominions beyond the seas, Emperor of India, and all persons under His Majesty's protection;

(2) when applied to territory shall mean any territory under His Majesty's sovereignty, suzerainty, protection or mandate, as the case may be;
(3) when applied to legal persons, shall mean all legal persons deriving their status as such from the law in force in any such territory; and
(4) when applied to property, rights or interests shall mean the property, rights or interests of persons specified under (1) or (3) above, as the case may be.

Article 24

This agreement shall enter into force as from today's date.

IN WITNESS WHEREOF the undersigned have signed the present agreement and have fixed thereto their seals.

DONE in triplicate at Singapore this first day of January in the nineteen hundred and forty-sixth year of the Christian Era, corresponding to the two thousand four hundred and eighty-ninth year of the Buddhist Era, in the English language.

Great Britain and Northern Ireland
    M.E. Dening
India
    M.S. Aney

(This signature is appended in agreement with His Majesty's Representative for the exercise of the functions of the Crown in its relations with Indian States.)

Siam
    Wiwat
    Phya Abhai Songgram, Lieut.-Gen.
    S. Vinicchayakul

[Source: Thai Foreign Ministry. Given in Thai and English in the Thai edition of this book, and copied directly from it. Text also available in United Nations *Treaty Series*, I, 1375, vol. 99, 132–46. The text cited above accords with this last exactly. See also Great Britain, Parliament, House of Commons, Sessional Papers, *Treaty Series* no. 10 (1951), British Command Paper (Cmd. 8140), 8–13. The text cited above accords with this source except for a few minor points of editorial difference.]

Communiqué

Following the declaration of war on Great Britain by the Siamese Government at that time, Australia declared war on Siam on 2nd March B.E. 2485, and considers that a state of war has existed between the two countries as from that date.

With a view to terminating the state of war with Australia, the representatives of His Majesty's Government have been engaged in negotiations at Singapore and have reached a preliminary agreement in certain respects by an Exchange of Notes, which will lead to the termination of the state of war.

Steps have already been taken by His Majesty's Government who are [sic] ready to act in accordance with the Royal Proclamation of Peace of 16th August B.E. 2488, that is, they have undertaken to compensate any losses or damage sustained by the Australian Government and Australian citizens; they have afforded succour and assistance to Australian prisoners of war interned in Siam; and they are ready to lend their co-operation in accordance with the resolutions of the United Nations; they are also prepared to collaborate in the apprehension of war criminals and the upkeep of the graves of Australians who lost their lives in the war. Such actions are an indication of the good disposition of Siam.

In the near future, the representatives of His Majesty's Government and the representative of the Australian Government will conclude a treaty for the termination of the state of war. Upon the signing of that treaty, the friendly relations between Siam and Australia will be happily restored as heretofore.

The Australian Government, through its representative, has expressed the greatest satisfaction in the success of these negotiations and is desirous of restoring the good friendly relations with Siam, which is an independent country appreciative of the principles of the United Nations. It can therefore be hoped that Australia will be a good friend of Siam in the future.

> Office of the Presidency of the
> Council of Ministers,
> 1st January 2489 [A.D. 1946].

[Source: Thai Foreign Ministry. Given in Thai and English in the Thai edition of this book, and copied directly from it.]

APPENDIX 5

[Exchange of Letters between Colonel A. J. Eastman and
Prince Wiwatthanachai Chaiyan.]

(Colonel A. J. Eastman to Prince Wiwatthanachai Chaiyan)

> Commonwealth of Australia,
> Singapore.
> 1st January 1946.

Your Serene Highness,

With reference to our discussions at Government House, Singapore, on 11th, 15th, 19th and 31st December 1945, and to the verbal agreement reached between us on the last mentioned date, I have the honour to request, on behalf of the Government of Commonwealth of Australia, that you forward to me a letter signed by yourself and the other plenipotentiary members of your delegation confirming the undertaking of the Government of Siam that it will:

(1) take promptly all action necessary for the complete repudiation of the declaration of war made against Great Britain on 25th January 1942, the Alliance with Japan made on 21st December 1941 and all measures operating to the detriment of Great Britain, Australia and their Allies;

(2) when called upon to do so at any time before 14th March 1946, conclude a treaty with the Government of the Commonwealth of Australia

   (a) certifying that the Government of Siam has taken all action necessary for the complete repudiation of the declaration of war, the Alliance and the measures referred to in Clause 1 above and

   (b) obliging the Government of Siam:
      (i) to assume responsibility for the maintenance and good upkeep of all Australian war graves in Siam;
      (ii) to assume responsibility for complying with the directions of the Commonwealth of Australia with respect to the well-being and interests of all Australian residents detained or interned in Siam since 8th December 1941.
      (iii) to undertake full assistance in the apprehension and punishment of persons guilty of war crimes against Australians;
      (iv) to assume responsibility for compensating the Government of the Commonwealth of Australia and Australian citizens for all losses and damage sustained by them directly or indirectly since 8th December 1941 in Siam or as a result of Siamese activity outside Siam;

(v) to undertake measures of regional, political and economic co-operation consistent with the principles of the United Nations Charter and designed to ensure the security of South East Asia and the South West Pacific area; and

(vi) to carry out such of the obligations specified in the Formal Agreement entered into this day between the Government of the United Kingdom and the Government of India on the one hand and the Government of Siam on the other (a copy of which is attached to this letter and initialled by me) as the Government of the Commonwealth of Australia considers to be applicable in principle to Australian policy and interests and requires the Government of Siam to undertake.

Such treaty to oblige the Government of the Commonwealth of Australia to terminate the state of war existing between Australia and Siam.

I have the honour to confirm that, upon the completion of the action mentioned in Clause 1 above and upon the coming into force of the treaty mentioned in Clause 2, the Government of the Commonwealth of Australia will be prepared to terminate the state of war existing between it and the Government of Siam.

I avail myself of this opportunity to express to Your Serene Highness the assurance of my high consideration.

>A. J. Eastman
>Plenipotentiary to the Government of the Commonwealth of Australia for the conclusion of arrangements relative to the termination of the state of war with Siam.

His Serene Highness Prince Wiwatthanachai Chaiyan,
Head of the Siamese Delegation,
Singapore.

APPENDIX 5

(Prince Wiwatthanachai Chaiyan to Colonel A. J. Eastman)

Singapore,
1st January 1946

Sir,

We have the honour to acknowledge your letter of 1st January 1946, and to state that we are instructed by His Majesty's Government to undertake on its behalf that it will:

(1) take promptly all action necessary for the complete repudiation of the declaration of war made against Great Britain on 25th January 1942, the Alliance with Japan made on 21st December 1941 and all measures operating to the detriment of Great Britain, Australia and their Allies;
(2) when called upon to do so at any time before 14th March 1946, conclude a treaty with the Government of the Commonwealth of Australia;
   (a) certifying that the Government of Siam has taken all action necessary for the complete repudiation of the declaration of war, the Alliance and the measures referred to in Clause (1) above, and
   (b) obliging the Government of Siam:
       (i) to assume responsibility for the maintenance and good upkeep of all Australian war graves in Siam;
       (ii) to assume responsibility for complying with the directions of the Government of the Commonwealth of Australia with respect to the well-being and interests of all Australian residents detained or interned in Siam since 8th December 1941;
       (iii) to undertake full assistance in the apprehension and punishment of persons guilty of war crimes against Australians;
       (iv) to assume responsibility for compensating the Government of the Commonwealth of Australia and Australian citizens for all losses and damage sustained by them directly or indirectly since 8th December 1941 in Siam or as a result of Siamese activity outside Siam;
       (v) to undertake measures of regional political and economic co-operation consistent with the principles of the United Nations Charter and designed to ensure the security of South East Asia and the South-West Pacific area; and
       (vi) to carry out such of the obligations specified in the Formal Agreement entered into this day between the Government of the United Kingdom and the Government of India on the one hand

and the Government of Siam on the other, (a copy of which is attached to this letter and initialled by us) as the Government of the Commonwealth of Australia considers to be applicable in principle to Australian policy and interests and requires the Government of Siam to undertake.

Such treaty to oblige the Government of the Commonwealth of Australia to terminate the state of war existing between Australia and Siam;

In this connection we have the honour to confirm that His Majesty's Government has already taken all necessary action to repudiate the declaration of war and the alliance referred to in Clause (1) and all other treaties, pacts and agreements between Siam and Japan; and that in the interval between the date of this letter and the conclusion of the Treaty mentioned in Clause (2), His Majesty's Government will take immediate steps, as far as possible, to put into effect the terms set out in that Clause and in all respects to act in accordance with their spirit.

His Majesty's Government notes that, upon completion of the action mentioned in Clause (1) above and upon the coming into force of the treaty mentioned in Clause (2), the Government of the Commonwealth of Australia will be prepared to terminate the state of war existing between it and His Majesty's Government.

We avail ourselves of this opportunity to express to you the assurance of our high consideration.

Wiwat
Phya Abhai Songgram
S. Vinicchayakul

Plenipotentiaries to the Government of Siam for the conclusion of arrangements relative to the termination of the state of war between Australia and Siam.

Colonel A. J. Eastman,
Plenipotentiary to the Government of the Commonwealth of Australia.

[Source: Thai Foreign Ministry. Text given in Thai and English in the Thai edition of this book and copied directly from it.]

APPENDIX 6

COMMUNIQUÉ, HEADS OF AGREEMENT AND ANNEX
[Attached to the Formal Agreement.]

[Letter from Mr. Dening to Prince Wiwatthanachai Chaiyan.]

Singapore,
1st January 1946

Your Serene Highness,

Following upon the satisfactory conclusion of our conversations, I have the honour to attach hereto a copy of the Heads of Agreement and Annex which set out the terms on which the Government of the United Kingdom and the Government of India are prepared to liquidate the state of war with Siam. I shall be glad to learn from you that the Siamese Government is prepared to sign without delay a formal agreement or agreements embodying the provisions set out in the attached documents, and that pending such signature the Siamese Government will in all respects act in accordance with these provisions.

For your information I would add that the term "British" in the Heads of Agreement will, in the Formal agreement or agreements, be so defined as to include all British subjects and protected persons, all territories under the sovereignty, suzerain protection or mandate of H.M. the King-Emperor, and all undertakings duly constituted in accordance with the law of any such territories.

I avail myself of this opportunity to express to you the assurance of my high consideration.

M. E. Dening

His Serene Highness Prince Wiwatthanachai Chaiyan.

[Source: Given in English in the Thai edition (marked "copy") and copied directly from this. Also available in Great Britain, Parliament, House of Commons, *Sessional Papers*, op. cit., Treaty Series no. 10 (1951), Command Paper (Cmd 8140), 2-3. The text cited above corresponds exactly with this. It should be noted, however, that in the British *Sessional Papers'* source the letter is preceded by an exchange of letters between Mr. Dening and Prince Wiwatthanachai Chaiyan in which the British Government had it placed on record that it did not recognize the acquisition by Thailand "of any territories acquired later than 11th December 1940," and that this non-recognition included "all the territory purported to have been ceded by the Vichy Government on 9th May 1941." This exchange of letters is not given in the Thai edition of this book.]

Heads of Agreement

The attitude of the Government of the United Kingdom and the Government of India towards Siam will depend on the degree of her co-operation in matters arising out of the termination of hostilities against Japan and on her readiness (a) to make restitution to the United Kingdom and India and their Allies for the injury done to them in consequence of Siam's association with Japan and (b) to ensure security and good neighbourly relations for the future.

The particular steps which the Government of the United Kingdom and the Government of India would expect the Siamese Government to take as a condition of recognising it and of agreeing to terminate the state of war are as follows:

A. Measures of Repudiation.
1. Repudiate the declaration of war made on the 25th January 1942 (which brought about a state of war between the United Kingdom and India on the one hand and Siam on the other) together with all measures pursuant to that declaration which may operate to the prejudice of the United Kingdom, India and their Allies.
2. Repudiate the Alliance entered into by Siam with Japan on 21st December 1941, and all other treaties, pacts or agreements concluded between Siam and Japan.
3. Recognise as null and void all acquisitions of British territory made by Siam later than 7th December 1941, and all titles, rights, properties and interests acquired in such territory since that date by the Siamese State or Siamese subjects.

B. Measures of Restitution and Re-adjustment.
1. Take the necessary legislative and administrative measures to give effect to Section A above, including in particular:
    (a) Repeal all legislative and administrative measures relating to the purported annexation by, or incorporation in, Siam of British territories effected after 7th December 1941.

(b) Withdraw as may be required by the competent civil or military authority all Siamese military personnel from all such territories; and all Siamese officials and nationals who entered these territories after their annexation by, or incorporation in, Siam.

(c) Restore all property taken away from these territories including currency except to the extent to which it could be established that fair value had been given in exchange.

(d) Compensate loss or damage to property, rights and interests in these territories arising out of the occupation of these territories by Siam.

(e) Redeem in sterling, out of former sterling reserves, current Siamese notes collected by the British authorities in British territory occupied by Siam since 7th December 1941.

2. (a) Take all possible steps to ensure the prompt succour and relief of all British prisoners of war and internees held in Siam or in any territories purported to have been annexed by or incorporated in Siam, and at Siamese expense provide them with adequate food, clothing, medical and hygienic services, and transportation, in consultation with the Allied military authorities.

(b) Undertake to enter into an agreement with the Government of the United Kingdom and the Government of India for the mutual upkeep of war graves.

3. Assume responsibility for safeguarding, maintaining and restoring unimpaired, British property, rights and interests of all kinds in Siam and for payment of compensation for losses or damage sustained. The term "property, rights and interests" to include, inter alia, the official property of the Government of the United Kingdom and the Government of India, property whose ownership has been transferred since the outbreak of war, pensions granted to British nationals, stocks of tin, teak and other commodities, shipping and wharves, and tin, teak and other leases and concessions granted to British firms and individuals prior to 7th December 1941, and still valid at that date.

4. Desequestrate British banking and commercial concerns and permit them to resume business.

5. Accept liability, with the addition of interest at an appropriate percentage in respect of payments in arrears, for the service of the loans and for the payment of pensions in full since the date when regular payments ceased.

6. Undertake to conclude as and when required, with the Supreme Allied Commander, South-East Asia Command, or in such other manner

as may be satisfactory to His Majesty's Government, an agreement or agreements to cover all or any of the matters specified in the Annex to this document.

C. Measures for Post-War Strategic Co-operation.
1. Recognise that the course of events in the war with Japan demonstrates the importance of Siam to the defence of Malaya, Burma, India and Indo-China and the security of the Indian Ocean and South-West Pacific areas, and agree to collaborate fully in all international security arrangements approved by the United Nations Organisation or its Security Council which may be pertinent to Siam, and especially such international security arrangements as may relate to those countries or areas.
2. Undertake that no canal linking the Indian Ocean and the Gulf of Siam shall be cut across Siamese territory without the prior concurrence of the Government of the United Kingdom.

D. Measures for Post-War Economic Co-operation.
1. Agree to take all possible measures to re-establish import and export trade between Siam on the one hand, and neighbouring British territories on the other, and to adopt and maintain a good neighbourly policy in regard to coastal shipping.
2. Undertake to negotiate with the Government of the United Kingdom as soon as practicable a new Treaty of Establishment, Commerce and Navigation and a Consular Convention based on the reciprocal application of the principles in Clause 4 below.
3. Undertake to negotiate with the Government of India as soon as practicable a new Treaty of Commerce and Navigation based on the reciprocal application of the principles in the following clause.
4. Pending the conclusion of the Treaties and Convention referred to in Clauses 2 and 3 above undertake to observe the provisions of the Treaty of Commerce and Navigation signed at Bangkok on 23rd November 1937, and except in regard to matters where the Treaty specifically provides to the contrary subject to such exceptions, if any, as may be agreed between the Government of the United Kingdom or the Government of India and the Siamese Government, not to enforce measures excluding British commercial or industrial interests or British professional men on grounds of nationality from participation in Siamese economy and trade or requiring them to maintain stocks or reserves in excess of normal commercial shipping industrial or business practice, provided that if the Treaties and Convention have not been concluded within a period of three years this

undertaking shall lapse unless it is prolonged by agreement. Nothing in this clause shall be deemed to preclude the grant of equally favourable treatment to nationals and enterprises of any or all of the United Nations.
5. Undertake to negotiate a Civil Aviation Agreement in respect of all British Commonwealth Civil Air Services not less favourable than the Agreement of 1937 with respect to Imperial Airways.
6. Undertake to participate in any general international arrangement regarding tin and rubber which conforms with such principles regarding commodity arrangements as may be agreed by the United Nations Organisation or its Economic and Social Council.

E. **Regularisation of Siamese Position in Relation to Bilateral and Multilateral treaties and Her Membership of International Organisations.**
1. Agree to regard as in force such bilateral treaties between the United Kingdom and Siam and India and Siam as may respectively be specified by the Government of the United Kingdom or the Government of India, subject to any modifications the Government of the United Kingdom or the Government of India may indicate and to regard as abrogated any such treaties not so specified.
2. Agree to regard as in force between the United Kingdom and Siam and India and Siam any multilateral treaties, conventions or agreements concluded prior to 7th December 1941, (a) to which Siam and the United Kingdom or India, as the case may be, were then parties, and (b) to which Siam was not then a party and which may be specified in a list to be furnished to the Siamese Government. Agree also to accept any modifications thereto which may have come into effect in accordance with the terms of such instruments since that date.
3. Pending admission to any international organisation set up since 7th December 1941, being an organisation of which the United Kingdom or India is a member, agree to carry out any obligations arising out of, or in connection with any such organisation or the instrument constituting it, as may at any time be specified by the Government of the United Kingdom or the Government of India as the case may be.

Annex

Points to be Covered in an Agreement or Agreements with the Supreme Allied Commander or in Such Other Manner as may be Satisfactory to the Government of the United Kingdom and the Government of India

The Siamese Government shall agree:

1. To assume responsibility for safeguarding, maintaining and restoring unimpaired Allied property, rights and interests of all kinds in Siam and for payment of compensation for losses or damage sustained.
2. To desequestrate Allied banking and commercial concerns and permit them to resume business.
3. To hold all Japanese and other enemy property at the disposal of the Allies.
4. To co-operate in the apprehension and trial of persons accused of war crimes or notable for affording active assistance to Japan.
5. To hand over to the Allied Military Authorities all alleged renegades of Allied nationality.
6. For so long as may be necessary for the conclusion of all matters of military concern to the Allies arising out of the settlement of the war with Japan:
    (a) to place at the disposal of the Allied military authorities ports and free traffic facilities in and over Siamese territory, as required.
    (b) to provide free of cost all other supplies and services for use in Siam and all Siamese currency that may be required by the Allied military authorities.
    (c) to meet administrative requirements of Allied forces in Siam in respect of labour, use of industrial and transport enterprises, means of communication, power, fuel and other materials as requested by the competent Allied military authority in pursuance of his task.
    (d) to negotiate an agreement granting judicial and other immunities for Allied forces in Siam similar to such agreements as have already been concluded by the Allies with one another.

7. To place Siamese merchant vessels primarily to meet the civil requirements of Siam under the direction of the competent Allied military authority until 2nd March 1946, or until such earlier date as may be fixed for the cessation of the Allied pooling arrangements.
8. To control banks and businesses, foreign exchange and foreign commercial and financial transactions as required by the Allies for so long as may be necessary for the conclusion of matters of military, economic

and financial concern to the Allies arising out of the settlement of the war with Japan.

9. Until a date or dates not later than 1st September 1947, to undertake to prohibit, except in accordance with the recommendations of the Combined Boards or any successor body, and in the case of rice under the direction of a special organisation to be set up for the purpose, any exports of rice, tin, rubber and teak, and to regulate trade in and stimulate production of these commodities.

10. (a) To make available free of cost at Bangkok to an organisation to be indicated by the Government of the United Kingdom and as quickly as may be compatible with the retention of supplies adequate for Siamese internal needs, a quantity of rice equal to the accumulated surplus of rice at present existing in Siam, subject to a maximum of one and a half million tons, the exact amount to be determined by the authorities appointed for the purpose of taking delivery of the rice. The rice should conform to the agreed standards of quality to be determined by the authorities appointed for the purpose of taking delivery of the rice. Equivalent quantities of paddy and loonzain [partially dehusked rice] may be accepted if so agreed in lieu of milled rice.

(b) Until a date not later than 1st September 1947, to make available to the rice organisations mentioned in Clauses 9 and 10 (a) all rice surplus to the internal needs of Siam, such rice with the exception of rice delivered free in accordance with Clause 10 (a) to be supplied in such a manner as the special organisation mentioned in Clause 9 shall indicate and at prices fixed in agreement with it having regard to the controlled prices of rice in other Asiatic rice-exporting areas.

[Prince Wiwatthanachai Chaiyan to Mr. Dening]

Singapore,
1st January 1946

Sir,

I have the honour to acknowledge your communication of today's date enclosing a copy of the Heads of Agreement and Annex which set out the terms on which the Government of the United Kingdom and the Government of India are prepared to liquidate the state of war with Siam.

In reply I have the honour to state, under instructions from His Majesty's Government, that they are prepared to sign without delay a Formal Agreement or agreements as indicated in your communication, and that pending such signature His Majesty's Government will in all respects act in accordance with these provisions.

They also take note that the term "British" in the Heads of Agreement will, in the Formal Agreement or Agreements, be so defined as to include all British subjects and protected persons, all territories under the sovereignty, suzerain protection or mandate of His Britannic Majesty the King-Emperor, and all undertakings duly constituted in accordance with the laws of any such territory.

I avail myself of this opportunity to express to you the assurance of my high consideration.

Wiwat

M. E. Dening, Esq., C.M.G., O.B.E.

[Source: The Heads of Agreement, Annex and letter from Prince Wiwatthanachai Chaiyan to Mr. Dening are given in English in the Thai edition (all three marked "copy") and copied directly therefrom. Also available in Great Britain, Parliament, House of Commons, *Sessional Papers*, op. cit., Treaty Series no. 10 (1951), Command Paper (Cmd. 8140), 3-7. The texts cited above correspond with the British *Sessional Papers'* source exactly.]

APPENDIX 7

TREATY OF AMITY BETWEEN THE KINGDOM OF SIAM AND THE REPUBLIC OF CHINA

The Kingdom of Siam and the Republic of China, being equally desirous of establishing friendly relations between the two countries and further promoting the mutual interests of their peoples, have decided to conclude a Treaty of Amity, based on the principles of equality and mutual respect of sovereignty, and have, for this purpose, appointed as their Plenipotentiaries:

His Majesty the King of Siam:
    His Excellency Mom Rachawong Seni Pramoj, President of the Council of Ministers and Minister of Foreign Affairs;

His Excellency the President of the National Government of the Republic of China:
    His Excellency Monsieur Li Tieh-tseng, Ambassador Extraordinary and Plenipotentiary to Iran;

Who, having communicated to each other their full powers, found in good and due form, have agreed upon the following Articles:

Article 1
There shall be perpetual peace and everlasting amity between the Kingdom of Siam and the Republic of China as well as between their peoples.

Article 2
The High Contracting Parties shall have the right reciprocally to send duly accredited diplomatic representatives, who shall enjoy, in the country to the Government of which they are accredited, all the rights, privileges, immunities and exemptions generally recognised by public international law.

Article 3
Each of the High Contracting Parties shall have the right to send Consuls-General, Consuls, Vice-Consuls and Consular Agents to the localities within the territories of the other which shall be determined by common accord. Such consular officers shall exercise the functions and enjoy the treatment generally recognised by international practice. Prior to their assumption of office, they

shall obtain from the Government of the country to which they are sent, exequaturs which are subject to withdrawal by the said Government.

The High Contracting Parties shall not appoint persons engaged in industry or commerce as their consular officers.

Article 4

The nationals of each of the High Contracting Parties shall be at liberty to enter or leave the territory of the other under the same conditions as the nationals of any third country, in accordance with the laws and regulations of the country applied to all aliens.

Article 5

The nationals of each of the High Contracting Parties shall receive in the territory of the other, the most constant protection and security for their persons and property, and shall enjoy in this respect the same rights and privileges as the nationals of the other High Contracting Party, subject to their compliance with the same laws and regulations.

The nationals of each of the High Contracting Parties shall receive in the territories of the other in regard to all legal proceedings and in matters relating to the administration of justice and the levying of taxes and requirements on connection therewith treatment not less favourable than that accorded to nationals of the other High Contracting Party.

Article 6

The nationals of each of the High Contracting Parties shall have the right to travel, to reside, to carry on all kinds of professions and occupations, to engage in industries and trade and, subject to reciprocity, to acquire, inherit, possess, lease, occupy and dispose of any kind of movable and immovable property, throughout the whole extent of the territories of the other, under the same conditions as the nationals of any third country, in accordance with the laws and regulations of the country.

They shall also have the liberty to establish schools for the education of their children, and shall enjoy the freedom of assembly and association, of publication, of worship and religion, in accordance with the laws and regulations of the country.

Article 7

Other relations between the two High Contracting Parties shall be based on the principles of international law.

Article 8

The High Contracting Parties agree to conclude as soon as possible a Treaty of Commerce and Navigation.

Article 9

The present Treaty is drawn up in duplicate in the Siamese, Chinese and English languages. In case of any divergence of interpretation the English text shall be authoritative.

Article 10

The present Treaty shall be ratified as soon as possible by the High Contracting Parties in accordance with their respective constitutional requirements, and shall enter into force on the day on which the exchange of the ratifications takes place. It shall remain in force continuously thereafter. Twelve months' notice of termination may, however, be given by either High Contracting Party after the lapse of ten years. The instruments of ratifications shall be exchanged at Chungking or Nanking.

In faith whereof, the above-mentioned Plenipotentiaries have signed the present Treaty and have affixed thereto their seals.

DONE at Bangkok this twenty-third day of the first month of the two thousand four hundred and eighty-ninth year of the Buddhist Era, corresponding to the twenty-third day of the first month of the thirty-fifth year of the Republic of China and the twenty-third day of January of the one thousand nine hundred and forty-sixth year of the Christian Era.

M.R. Seni Pramoj
Li Tieh-tseng

[Source: Thai Foreign Ministry, as given in the Thai edition of this book. Text also available in *British and Foreign State Papers*, op. cit., 1946, London, H.M.S.O., 1953, 683-85. Text accords exactly with the above except for minor editorial differences. The treaty was ratified at Chungking on 28 March 1946 (ibid., 683).]

APPENDIX 7

(M.R. Seni Pramoj to Monsieur Li Tieh-tseng)

Ministry of Foreign Affairs,
Saranrom Palace,
23rd January 1946

Monsieur l'Ambassadeur,

With reference to the Treaty of Amity signed this day between Siam and China, I have the honour to confirm on behalf of the Siamese Government, the understanding reached between us as follows:-

1. The stipulations contained in the said Treaty do not in any way affect, supersede or modify any of the laws and regulations with regard to naturalisation, immigration and public order which are in force or which may be enacted in the territories of either High Contracting Party, provided they do not constitute measures of discrimination particularly directed against the nationals of the other party.
2. In regard to land ownership, the rights already acquired by nationals of either High Contracting Party in the territory of the other, in accordance with the laws and regulations in such territory, at the coming into force of this Treaty shall be respected. In the event of expropriation, an indemnity will be paid, not less favourable than that paid to the nationals of the other party or the nationals of any other country.

I avail myself of this opportunity, Monsieur l'Ambassadeur, to renew to Your Excellency the assurance of my highest consideration.

M.R. Seni Pramoj
President of the Council of Ministers and
Minister of Foreign Affairs

His Excellency Monsieur Li Tieh-tseng,
Chief of Chinese Mission to Siam,
Bangkok

APPENDIX 7

(Monsieur Li Tieh-tseng to M.R. Seni Pramoj)

Bangkok,
23rd January 1946

Monsieur le Président,

With reference to the Treaty of Amity signed this day between China and Siam, I have the honour to confirm, on behalf of the Chinese Government, the understanding reached between us as follows:-

1. The stipulations contained in the said Treaty do not in any way affect, supersede or modify any of the laws and regulations with regard to naturalisation, immigration and public order which are in force or which may be enacted in the territories of either High Contracting Party, provided they do not constitute measures of discrimination particularly directed against the nationals of the other party.
2. In regard to land ownership, the rights already acquired by nationals of either High Contracting Party in the territory of the other, in accordance with the laws and regulations in such territory, at the coming into force of this Treaty shall be respected. In the event of expropriation, an indemnity will be paid, not less favourable than that paid to the nationals of the other party or the nationals of any other country.

I avail myself of this opportunity, Monsieur le Président, to renew to Your Excellency the assurance of my highest consideration.

Li Tieh-tseng
Chief of Chinese Mission to Siam

His Excellency Mom Rachawong Seni Pramoj,
President of the Council of Ministers and Minister of Foreign Affairs,
Bangkok

[Source: Thai Foreign Ministry, as given in the Thai edition of this book. Also available in *British and Foreign State Papers*, op. cit., 1946, 685–86. The text of these two letters accords with that cited above except for minor editorial differences.]

APPENDIX 8

FINAL PEACE AGREEMENT BETWEEN THE GOVERNMENT OF SIAM AND THE GOVERNMENT OF AUSTRALIA

WHEREAS by a proclamation made in Bangkok on 16th August 1945, the Regent of Siam did, in the name of His Majesty the King of Siam, proclaim the declaration of war made by Siam on 25th January 1942, against the United Kingdom to be null and void in that it was made contrary to the will of the Siamese people and in violation of the Constitution and laws of Siam, and

WHEREAS the proclamation of 16th August 1945 aforesaid was the same day unanimously approved by the National Assembly of Siam, and

WHEREAS the Government of Siam have [sic] repudiated the alliance entered into by Siam with Japan on 21st December 1941, together with all other Treaties, Pacts, or Agreements concluded between Siam and Japan, and

WHEREAS in pursuance of the Formal Agreement of 1st January 1946, between the Government of the United Kingdom and the Government of India on the one hand and the Government of Siam on the other, the state of war existing between the United Kingdom and Siam and between India and Siam has been terminated, and

WHEREAS a state of war between Australia and Siam exists in pursuance of a proclamation by the Governor-General of Australia of 2nd March 1942, and

WHEREAS the Government of Australia, taking into account the acts of repudiation already effected by the Government of Siam and the services rendered by the resistance movement in Siam during the war with Japan, and in pursuance of the assurances contained in letters of agreement exchanged at Singapore on 1st January 1946, by the plenipotentiaries of Australia and Siam, desires to bring to an immediate end the state of war between Australia and Siam,

NOW, THEREFORE, the Government of Australia on the one hand and the Government of Siam on the other, being desirous of re-establishing on a just and equitable basis peace between their respective countries, have resolved to conclude an agreement for these purposes and have accordingly appointed as their plenipotentiaries:

Government of Australia:
    Mr. Frank Keith Officer, O.B.E., M.C.,
    an Envoy Extraordinary and Minister Plenipotentiary:

Government of Siam:
  Nai Direck Jayanama, Order of the White Elephant,
  First Class and Order of the Siamese Crown, First Class,
  Minister of Foreign Affairs;

WHO, having communicated their full powers, found in good and due form, have agreed as follows:-

Article 1
The Government of Siam agrees to repudiate all measures pursuant to the above-mentioned declaration of war operating to the detriment of Australia and her allies and to take all necessary legislative and administrative measures to give effect to such repudiation.

Article 2
The Government of Siam undertakes to enter into arrangements acceptable to the Government of Australia for the upkeep of Australian war graves and for the establishment and future care of Australian war cemeteries in Siam.

Article 3
The Government of Siam undertakes to render every assistance in the apprehension of persons in its jurisdiction reasonably suspected of having committed war crimes against Australians.

Article 4
(a) The Government of Siam agrees to assume responsibility for safeguarding, maintaining and restoring unimpaired the property rights and interests of all kinds in Siam of the Government of Australia and of Australians, whether held by them individually or as members of firms, partnerships or companies, whether incorporated or unincorporated, and for the payment to the Government of Australia of such compensation for loss or damage suffered in respect thereof as appears reasonable and adequate to the Government of Australia or to a Board, Committee or Commission approved by the Government of Australia;

(b) The term "property, rights and interests" shall include *inter alia* the official property of the Government of Australia, property whose ownership has been transferred since 8th December 1941, all stocks of tin and other commodities and all leases and concessions granted to Australian firms or individuals prior to 8th December 1941, and still valid at that date.

Article 5
The Government of Siam:
(a) declares as null and void all titles, rights and interests acquired since 8th December 1941, in territories outside Siam by the Government of Siam or by their subjects in and to property, including currency, of the Government of Australia or of Australians whether held by them individually or as members of firms, partnerships or companies, whether incorporated or unincorporated, except to the extent to which it can be established that fair value has been given in exchange;
(b) shall restore all such property removed from these territories; and
(c) shall pay to the Government of Australia for loss or damage occasioned by Siamese activity to Australian property rights and interests in these territories such compensation as appears reasonable and adequate to the Government of Australia or to a Board, Committee or Commission approved by the Government of Australia.

Article 6
The Government of Siam agrees to desequestrate Australian commercial, mining and other concerns and to permit them to resume business.

Article 7
The Government of Siam undertakes to accept responsibility for the payment in full of all pensions due by them to Australians, payment to include interest at an appropriate rate on all arrears.

Article 8
The Government of Siam undertakes to pay to Australians detained or interned by the Government of Siam or its agents or subjects, compensation which appears reasonable and adequate to the Government of Australia or to a Board, Committee or Commission approved by the Government of Australia, for any loss or injury sustained by them as a result of their detention or internment, and to the dependents of any such Australians whose death was occasioned by the acts of the Government of Siam or their agents or subjects.

Article 9
The Government of Siam, recognising the importance of Siam to the defence, security and well-being of South-East Asia, the Indian Ocean area and Australia, New Zealand and the South-West Pacific area generally, agrees to participate, if requested to do so, in measures of regional, political and economic co-opera-

tion consistent with the principles of the United Nations Charter and relating to the countries or areas specified.

Article 10

(1) The Government of Siam undertakes to negotiate with the Government of Australia, if requested to do so, a Treaty of Establishment, Commerce and Navigation and a Consular Agreement upon a basis of reciprocity. In such treaty and agreement Australians will be given rights and treatment not less favourable than those given to subjects and citizens of any other country.

(2) Pending completion of such Treaty of Establishment, Commerce and Navigation and such Consular Agreement, the Government of Siam will:

   (a) accord to Australian commercial, industrial and maritime interests treatment not less favourable than that accorded to similar interests of any other country; and

   (b) accord to any Australian Consular Representatives who may be appointed to reside in Siam, rights, privileges and immunities not less favourable than those accorded to similar representatives of any other country.

Article 11

With a view to the more effective promotion of the interests of Australia and Siam the Government of Siam undertakes, pending the negotiation of the Treaty referred to in Article 10 (1) to inform and when so requested to confer with the Government of Australia regarding any proposed international arrangements relating to tin, rubber, oil or other commodities, and undertakes not to complete such arrangements unless the Government of Australia has been given an opportunity to become a party thereto.

Article 12

The Government of Siam shall accord to the civil air services of Australia treatment in regard to the establishment, maintenance and operation of regular air services not less favourable than that accorded to Imperial Airways by the Notes exchanged at Bangkok on 3rd December 1937.

Article 13

The Government of Siam and the Government of Australia acknowledge that the rights conferred and the duties imposed upon them or their subjects under treaties, agreements and conventions by which the two Governments were bound immediately prior to 8th December 1941, shall continue with the same force and effect as obtained immediately prior to that date, and the rights so conferred and the duties so imposed shall be observed and maintained until new treaties, agreements and conventions are negotiated and agreed upon by the two Governments.

Article 14
In consideration of the above undertakings made by the Government of Siam, the Government of Australia agrees to take immediately such steps as may be necessary to terminate the state of war existing between Australia and Siam and to proceed at once to the resumption of friendly relations with Siam.

Article 15
This agreement shall enter into force as from today's date.

IN WITNESS thereto the undersigned have signed the present agreement and have affixed thereto their seals.

DONE in duplicate in the English and Siamese languages at Bangkok this third day of April in the one thousand nine hundred and forty-sixth year of the Christian Era, corresponding to the two thousand four hundred and eighty-ninth year of the Buddhist Era.

Direck Jayanama
Keith Officer

(Nai Direck Jayanama to Monsieur Keith Officer)

>Ministry of Foreign Affairs,
>Saranrom Palace.
>3rd April 1946

Monsieur le Ministre,

With reference to the Final Peace Agreement between the Government of Siam and the Government of Australia, signed this day, I have the honour to state the understanding of the Government of Siam as follows:

A. Article 4, Article 5 and Article 8.

The procedure to be adopted for the assessment of Australian claims for compensation will be analogous to that adopted for the assessment of the United Kingdom claims.

B. Article 11.
1. This Article has no object other than the more effective promotion of the interest of Australia and Siam: it is not intended in any way to impair the sovereign rights of Siam.
2. It has been accepted by the Government of Siam in the expectation that the negotiation of the treaty therein referred to will take place within three years.
3. The term "international arrangements" refers to multilateral arrangements between Governments.
4. The term "other commodities" refers to "other principal products of Siam", that is to say, rice and teak.
5. On being informed by the Government of Siam of any proposed international arrangement under this Article, the Government of Australia will notify the Government of Siam with the least possible delay whether they are interested or not.

In case they are interested, the Government of Siam will inform the other Governments concerned accordingly, to the end that an opportunity may be given to the Government of Australia to become a party to the proposed international arrangement in question.

In the event, however, of the other Governments concerned not agreeing thereto, the Government of Siam will be deemed to have discharged its obligation under this Article and may then proceed with the completion of the proposed international arrangement in question.

I avail myself of this opportunity, Monsieur le Ministre, to express to you the assurance of my highest consideration.

Direck Jayanama
Minister of Foreign Affairs

Monsieur Frank Keith Officer, O.B.E., M.C.,
Envoy Extraordinary and Minister Plenipotentiary of Australia,
Bangkok.

(Monsieur Keith Officer to Nai Direck Jayanama)

Bangkok,
3rd April 1946

Your Excellency,

With reference to the Final Peace Agreement between the Government of Siam and the Government of Australia, signed this day, I have the honour to note the understanding of the Government of Siam as follows:-

A. Article 4, Article 5 and Article 8.

The procedure to be adopted for the assessment of Australian claims for compensation will be analogous to that adopted for the assessment of the United Kingdom claims.

B. Article 11.
1. This Article has no object other than the more effective promotion of the interests of Australia and Siam: it is not intended in any way to impair the sovereign rights of Siam.
2. It has been accepted by the Government of Siam in the expectation that the negotiation of the treaty therein referred to will take place within three years.
3. The term "international arrangements" refers to multilateral arrangements between Governments.
4. The term "other commodities" refers to "other principal products of Siam", that is to say, rice and teak.
5. On being informed by the Government of Siam of any proposed international arrangement under this Article, the Government of Australia will notify the Government of Siam with the least possible delay whether they are interested or not.

In case they are interested, the Government of Siam will inform the other Governments concerned accordingly, to the end that an opportunity may be given to the Government of Australia to become a party to the proposed international arrangement in question.

In the event, however, of the other Governments concerned not agreeing thereto, the Government of Siam will be deemed to have discharged its obligation under this Article and may then proceed with the completion of the proposed international arrangement in question.

APPENDIX 8

I avail myself of this opportunity to express to Your Excellency the assurance of my highest consideration.

Keith Officer

His Excellency Nai Direck Jayanama, Order of the White Elephant, First Class; Order of the Siamese Crown, First Class; Minister of Foreign Affairs

APPENDIX 8

(Nai Direck Jayanama to Monsieur Keith Officer)

> Ministry of Foreign Affairs,
> Saranrom Palace.
> 3rd April 1946

Monsieur le Ministre,

With reference to the Final Peace Agreement signed this day between the Government of Siam and the Government of Australia, which is drawn up in the English and Siamese languages, I have the honour to inform you that, in case of any divergence of interpretation, the English text shall be authoritative.

I avail myself of this opportunity, Monsieur le Ministre, to express to you the assurance of my highest consideration.

> *Direck Jayanama*
> Minister of Foreign Affairs

Monsieur Frank Keith Officer, O.B.E., M.C.,
Envoy Extraordinary and Minister Plenipotentiary of Australia,
Bangkok

APPENDIX 8

(Monsieur Keith Officer to Nai Direck Jayanama.)

Bangkok,
3rd April 1946.

Your Excellency,

With reference to the Final Peace Agreement signed this day between the Government of Siam and the Government of Australia, which is drawn up in the English and Siamese languages, I have the honour to note your assurance that, in case of any divergence of interpretation, the English text shall be authoritative.

I avail myself of this opportunity to express to Your Excellency the assurance of my highest consideration.

Keith Officer

His Excellency Nai Direck Jayanama, Order of the White Elephant,
First Class; Order of the Siamese Crown, First Class.
Minister of Foreign Affairs.

[Source: Thai Foreign Ministry, as given in the Thai edition of this book. Also available in *British and Foreign State Papers*, op. cit., 1946, 553–59. Text accords exactly with that cited above except for minor editorial differences. However, the *British and Foreign State Papers*' version also includes, on p. 552, the Proclamation signed by the Australian Minister for External Affairs, N. J. O. Makin, at Bangkok on 3rd April 1946 declaring the state of war between Australia and Siam to be terminated. This Proclamation precedes the Final Peace Agreement between Siam and Australia. It is not included in the Thai edition.]

APPENDIX 9

AGREEMENT TO END THE CONFLICT BETWEEN THAILAND AND FRANCE

Proclamation for the Enforcement of Agreement Made Between the Government of Thailand and the Government of France

This Proclamation is made by Royal Command for the information of all that in the Agreement made to end the conflict between Siam and France signed in Washington on 17th November 1946 it is stated in Article 5 that such Agreement is effective from the day the Agreement is signed. The Protocol attached to the above Agreement signed on 17th November 1946 also contains a clause at the end that such would enter into force from the day the Protocol is signed.

The Agreement and Protocol attached are now therefore effective and valid as from 17th November 1946 onwards.

In addition to the Protocol, other documents which were also agreed to are:

1. An exchange of letters on negotiations to settle the monetary questions and questions relating to the transfer of securities connected with the Settlement Agreement.
2. An exchange of letters on the establishment of a Thai Consulate in Phratabong [Battambang].
3. An exchange of letters on an agreement concerning frontier control.
4. An exchange of letters on the nationality and property of inhabitants of the transferred territories.

This Proclamation is made on 9th December 1946 in the first year of the present reign.

By Royal Command

Rear-Admiral T. Thamrongnawasawat,
Prime Minister.

[Source: Translated directly from the Thai given in the Thai edition.]

Accord de Règlement Franco-Siamois signé à Washington, le 17 novembre 1946

Le Gouvernement Provisoire de la République Française et le Gouvernement Siamois,

Agissant conformément à l'idéal des Nations Unies et dans l'intérêt de la paix du monde;

Considérant les points de vue exprimés par les Gouvernements Américain et Britannique;

Désireux de rétablir les relations de paix et d'amitié traditionelles entre leurs deux pays,

Ont nommé à cet effet leurs plénipotentiaires:

Le Président du Gouvernement Provisoire de la République Française:

> S.E.M. Henri Bonnet, Ambassadeur Extraordinaire et Plénipotentiaire de France aux Etats-Unis d'Amérique, Officier de l'Ordre National de la Légion d'Honneur;
>
> S.E.M. Guillaume Georges-Picot, Ambassadeur Extraordinaire et Plénipotentiare de France aux Etats-Unis du Venezuela, Chevalier de l'Ordre National de la Légion d'Honneur;

Sa Majesté le Roi de Siam:

> Son Altesse Royale le Prince Wan Waithayakon, Sénateur, Chevalier de l'Ordre de la Maison Royale de Chakri, Grand Croix Spécial de l'Ordre de l'Eléphant Blanc;
>
> S.E.M. Khuang Apaivongse, Membre de la Chambre des Représentants, Grand Croix Spécial de l'Ordre de l'Eléphant Blanc.

Lesquels, après s'être communiqué leurs pleins pouvoirs trouves en bonne et due forme, sont convenus des dispositions suivantes:

Article 1

La Convention de Tokyo du 9 mai 1941, précédemment répudiée par le Gouvernement français, est annulée et le *statu quo* antérieur à cette convention est rétabli. En conséquence les territoires indochinois objets de cette convention seront transférés aux autorités françaises dans les conditions indiquées au protocole conclu à cet effet.

Article 2

Aussitôt après la signature du présent accord, les relations diplomatiques seront rétablies et les rapports entre les deux pays se trouveront de nouveau régis par le Traité du 7 décembre 1937 et par l'Arrangement commercial et douanier du

9 décembre 1937. Les Parties Contractantes communiqueront le présent accord au Conseil de Sécurité et le Siam retirera la plainte qu'il a introduite auprès de lui. La France ne s'opposera plus à l'entrée du Siam aux Nations Unies.

Article 3

Aussitôt après la signature du présent accord, la France et le Siam constitueront par application de l'Article 21 du Traité franco-siamoix du 7 décembre 1937 une Commission de Conciliation composée de deux représentants des Parties et de trois neutres, conformément à l'Acte Général de Genève du 26 septembre 1928 pour le règlement pacifique des différends internationaux qui règle la constitution et le fonctionnement de la Commission. La Commission commencera ses travaux aussitôt que possible après que le transfert des territoires visés au 2e paragraphe de l'Article1 aura été effectué. Elle sera chargé d'examiner les arguments ethniques, géographiques et économiques des parties en faveur de la révision ou de la confirmation des clauses du Traité du 3 octobre 1893, de la Convention du 13 février 1904 et du Traité du 23 mars 1907, maintenues en vigueur par l'Article 22 du Traité du 7 décembre 1937.

Article 4

Dès le rétablissement des relations diplomatiques, des négociations seront ouvertes pour le règlement de toutes les questions pendantes entre les deux pays.

Les question financières connexes au présent Accord de Règlement, y compris les sommes à verser en compensation des dommages subis, seront soumises à la Commission de Conciliation, au cas où les deux Parties n'arriveraient pas à un accord direct dans un délai de trois mois.

Le présent accord entrera en vigueur dès sa signature.

EN FOI DE QUOI les Plénipotentiaires ont signé le présent accord et y ont apposé leurs cachets.

FAIT en double exemplaire, en français et en siamois, à Washington, le dix-sept novembre mil neuf cent quarante-six, correspondant au dix-septième jour du onzième mois de la deux mille quatre cent quatre-vingt-neuvième année de l'ère bouddhique.

Pour la République Française: Pour le Royaume de Siam:
Henri Bonnet   *Wan Waithayakorn*
G. Georges-Picot   *Khuang Apaivongse*

[Source: United Nations, *Treaty Series*, 1959, no 4943, 68–72. Given in Thai only in the Thai edition of this book.]

Protocole sur les Modalités D'evacuation et de Transfert des Territoires Visés à L'article 1 de L'accord de Règlement Conclu en Date de ce Jour

Le Gouvernement Français et le Gouvernement Siamois conviennent de ce qui suit:

1. Transfert des biens publics immobiliers

Le Gouvernement siamois remettra à la Commission mixte franco-siamoise d'Etat-Major dont la création est prévue à la partie 4-A, dans les vingt jours qui suivront la signature de 1'Accord de Règlement franco-siamois, la liste des biens publics immobiliers se trouvant dans les territoires interéssés, ainsi que la liste des délégués chargés des opérations de transfert.

Le Gouvernement français remettra à cette Commission, dans le même délai, la liste des personnes chargées de recevoir les dits biens immobiliers. Les délégués des deux Parties seront repartis en groupes par les soins de la Commission et se réuniront dans des lieux et à des dates qui seront fixés par la Commission.

2. Transfert des archives

Les archives communales et provinciales, ainsi que les archives des tribunaux et autres organismes d'Etat seront transférées aux autorités françaises, ainsi que les plans cadastraux déposés dans les territoires interéssés. En ce qui concerne les plans, registres et autres documents cadastraux déposés hors de ces territoires, des copies certifiées en seront remises au Gouvernement français.

Le transfert sera achevé dans les deux mois qui suivront la signature de l'Accord de Règlement franco-siamois.

3. Evacuation des territoires

Les territoires faisant l'objet du présent protocole seront évacués par les forces siamoises qui s'y trouvent et occupés par les forces françaises, conformément aux principes suivants:

A. Les forces siamoises stationnées entre la frontière actuelle et l'ancienne frontière (cf. Article 22 du Traité de 1937) se mettront en marche le vingtième jour qui suivra la signature de 1ûAccord de Règlement, et devront se trouver, au plus tard sept jours après, en deçà de l'ancienne ligne de frontière (cf. Article 22 du Traité de 1937). Elles seront précédées par les gendarmes, la police et les autorités administratives siamoises se trouvant dans les territoires susmentionnés, à l'exception de celles qui participeront aux travaux de transfert stipulés aux parties 1 et 2 ci-dessus, et de celles qui seraient nécessaires pour assurer le maintien de l'ordre. Les forces destinées à la garde des voies de communications et notamment des ouvrages d'art devront également être maintenues dans ces territoires jusqu'à leur relève par les forces françaises.

B. Les forces que le Gouvernement français aurait l'intention d'envoyer dans les territoires susmentionnés se mettront en marche le lendemain du jour où les forces siamoises auront commencé l'évacuation et pourront arriver au plus tôt sept jours après à l'ancienne ligne de frontière (cf. Article 22 du Traité de 1937). Elles pourront être suivies des autorités administratives françaises appelées à stationner dans les territoires susmentionnés.

C. Les forces françaises régleront leur marche de manière à maintenir une distance constante avec les forces siamoises.

4. Mesures pratiques

Les Gouvernements des deux Parties prendront toutes mesures nécessaires pour que les opérations d'évacuation et de transfert prévues au présent protocole s'effectuent en bon ordre et sans incident. Le Gouvernement siamois restera responsable du maintien de l'ordre dans chaque circonscription administrative jusqu'au passage effectif de ses pouvoirs.

A. Une Commission mixte franco-siamoise d'Etat-Major, comprenant, du côté français, une délégation composée d'un Colonel président, de onze officiers d'Etat-Major et de quatre fonctionnaires du Haut-Commissariat et des Administrations cambodgiennes et laotiennes, et, du côté siamois, d'une délégation ayant une composition analogue, sera créée et entrera en fonctions le jour de la signature de l'Accord de Règlement. Ses fonctions cesseront aussitôt que le transfert des territoires aura été effectué.

La Commission sera chargée de veiller sur place à la bonne exécution du présent protocole et de régler toutes les questions complémentaires. Elle résidera en principe à Battambang et elle pourra détacher des sous-commissions en tous lieux où elle le jugera nécessaire, notamment à Sisophon, Moung, Kralank et Bassac. Elle pourra avoir auprès d'elle des observateurs neutres, notamment des officiers anglais et américains.

B. Les forces évacuées ne pourront laisser en arrière ni forces militaires irrégulières, ni individus munis d'armes à feu, sous réserve des dispositions spéciales prévues à la partie 3-A in fine. De même les forces occupantes ne pourront se faire précéder ni par une force militaire irrégulière, ni par des individus munis d'armes à feu.

C. Les deux Gouvernements donneront respectivement à leurs unités militaires et de police l'ordre formel de s'abstenir de tout acte de pillage.

Le présent protocole entrera en vigueur dès sa signature.

EN FOI DE QUOI les soussignés, dûment autorisés par leurs Gouvernements respectifs, ont signé le présent protocole et y ont apposé leurs cachets.

FAIT en double exemplaire en français et en siamois à Washington, le dix-sept novembre mil neuf cent quarante-six, correspondant au dix-septième jour du onzième mois de la deux mille quatre cent quatre-vingt-neuvième année de l'ère bouddhique.

Pour la République Française: Pour le Royaume de Siam:
Henri Bonnet   *Wan Waithayakorn*
G. Georges-Picot   *Khuang Apaivongse*

[Source: Given in Thai only in the Thai original. For an English-language version, see United Nations, *Treaty Series*, 1959, no. 4943, 72–6.]

Échange de Lettres

I

>Ambassade de France aux Etats-Unis,
>Washington,
>le 17 novembre 1946.

Monseigneur,

J'ai l'honneur de confirmer à Votre Altesse l'accord verbal déjà intervenu entre nous aux termes duquel des négociations s'ouvriront dans le plus bref délai, pour régler les questions monétaires et de transfert de valeurs connexes à l'Accord de Règlement signé en date de ce jour.

Je saisis cette occasion pour renouveler à Votre Altesse l'assurance de ma très haute considération.

>*Henri Bonnet*

S.A.R. le Prince Wan Waithayakorn,
Chef de la Délégation siamoise

II

>Légation siamoise, Washington, D.C.,
>le 17 novembre 1946.

Monsieur l'Ambassadeur,

(Voir lettre I)

>*Wan Waithayakorn*

Son Excellence Monsieur Henri Bonnet,
Ambassadeur de France aux Etats-Unis d'Amérique,
Chef de la Délégation française.

III

> Ambassade de France aux Etats-Unis,
> Washington,
> le 17 novembre 1946.

Monseigneur,

J'ai l'honneur de confirmer à Votre Altesse l'accord verbal déjà intervenu entre nous aux termes duquel les ordres les plus strictes seront donnés et les mesures nécessaires seront prises pour éviter le retour d'incidents de frontière, notamment par la conclusion, dans le plus bref délai d'un accord sur la Police de la frontière.

Je saisis cette occasion pour renouveler à Votre Altesse l'assurance de ma très haute considération.

> *Henri Bonnet*

S.A.R. le Prince Wan Waithayakorn,
Chef de la Délégation siamoise.

IV

> Légation siamoise, Washington, D.C.,
> le 17 novembre 1946.

Monsieur l'Ambassadeur,

(Voir lettre III)

> *Wan Waithayakorn*

Son Excellence Monsieur Henri Bonnet,
Ambassadeur de France aux Etats-Unis d'Amérique,
Chef de la Délégation française.

V

                              Ambassade de France aux Etats-Unis,
Washington,
le 17 novembre 1946.

Monseigneur,

J'ai l'honneur de confirmer à Votre Altesse l'accord verbal déjà intervenu entre nous en ce qui concerne les habitants des territoires visés à l'Article 1 de l'Accord de Règlement signé en date de ce jour, ainsi que les biens de ces habitants situés dans ces territoires, dans les termes suivants:

1) Les habitants qui ont acquis la nationalité siamoise en vertu de la Convention du 9 mai 1941, seront réintégrés de plein droit dans leur nationalité antérieure dès que le transfert des territoires susmentionnés aura été effectué. Les habitants qui possèdent la nationalité siamoise d'origine où qui l'ont acquise conformément à la loi conservent cette nationalité.

2) Aucun obstacle ne sera apporté au départ de ceux d'entre ces derniers qui désireraient quitter ces territoires. Ils pourront en particulier avant leur départ disposer librement de leurs biens meubles et immeubles. Ils auront la faculté d'emporter avec eux ou de faire transporter en franchise douanière leurs biens mobiliers de toute nature, bestiaux, produits agricoles, monnaie ou billets de banque siamois. Ils pourront conserver la propriété de leurs biens immobiliers.

Je saisis cette occasion pour renouveler à Votre Altesse l'assurance de ma très haute considération.

Henri Bonnet

S.A.R. le Prince Wan Waithayakorn,
Chef de la Délégation siamoise.

VI

> Legation siamoise, Washington, D.C.,
> le 17 novembre 1946.

Monsieur l'Ambassadeur,

(Voir lettre V)

Wan Waithayakorn

Son Excellence Monsieur Henri Bonnet,
Ambassadeur de France aux Etats-Unis d'Amérique,
Chef de la Délégation française.

VII

> Légation siamoise, Washington, D.C.,
> le 17 novembre 1946.

Monsieur l'Ambassadeur,

En procédant à la signature de l'Accord de Règlement franco-siamois, j'ai l'honneur de faire savoir à Votre Excellence que le Gouvernement siamois a conclu, le 1 mai 1946, avec le Gouvernement britannique, un accord aux termes duquel il doit fournir aux Nations Unies, dans le délai d'un an, 1,200,000 tonnes de riz. Dans le calcul de ce montant figurent 200,000 tonnes provenant de la production des territoires visés à l'article 1 de l'Accord de Règlement.

Je serais donc reconnaissant à Votre Excellence de bien vouloir demander au Gouvernement français d'intervenir auprès du Gouvernement britannique afin que le montant total de riz dont il s'agit soit proportionnellement réduit par suite du transfert des territoires susmentionnés.

Je saisis cette occasion pour renouveler à Votre Excellence l'assurance de ma très haute considération.

Wan Waithayakorn

Son Excellence Monsieur Henri Bonnet,
Ambassadeur de France aux Etats-Unis d'Amérique,
Chef de la Délégation française.

VIII

Ambassade de France aux Etats-Unis,
Washington,
le 17 novembre 1946.

Monseigneur,

J'ai l'honneur d'accuser réception à Votre Altesse de Sa lettre de ce jour rédigée comme suit:

(Voir lettre VII)

Le Gouvernement français a pris note de cette demande et est disposé à prendre contact à ce sujet avec les autorités britanniques compétentes, étant entendu au aucune exportation de riz des territoires dont il s'agit vers le Siam ne sera effectuée à partir de ce jour.

Je saisis cette occasion pour renouveler à Votre Altesse l'assurance de ma très haute considération.

Henri Bonnet

S.A.R. le Prince Wan Waithayakorn,
Chef de la Délégation siamoise.

IX

Légation siamoise, Washington, D.C.,
le 17 novembre 1946.

Monsieur l'Ambassadeur,

J'ai l'honneur de porter à la connaissance de Votre Excellence qu'en considération des intérêts siamois dans les territoires visés par l'Accord de Règlement signé en date de ce jour, ainsi que de l'importance des échanges commerciaux du Siam avec ces territoires, mon Gouvernement attacherait un grand prix à l'établissement d'un Consulat a Battambang.

Je suis donc chargé d'en transmettre la demande au Gouvernement français et je me permets de recourir à l'obligeante entremise de Votre Excellence à cet effet.

Je saisis cette occasion pour renouveler à Votre Excellence l'assurance de ma très haute considération.

Wan Waithayakon

Son Excellence Monsieur Henri Bonnet,
Ambassadeur de France aux Etats-Unis d'Amérique,
Chef de la Délégation française.

X

Ambassade de France aux Etats-Unis,
Washington,
le 17 novembre 1946.

Monseigneur,

J'ai l'honneur d'accuser réception à Votre Altesse de Sa lettre de ce jour rédigée comme suit:

(Voir lettre IX)

Le Gouvernement français est prêt, au moment ou seront rétablies les relations consulaires entre les deux pays, à examiner cette demande dans un esprit favorable, conformément a l'Article 16 du Traité de 1937.

Je saisis cette occasion pour renouveler à Votre Altesse l'assurance de ma très haute considération.

Henri Bonnet

S.A.R. le Prince Wan Waithayakorn,
Chef de la Délégation siamoise.

XI

Ambassade de France aux Etats-Unis,
Washington,
le 17 novembre 1946.

Monseigneur,

J'ai l'honneur de faire savoir à Votre Altesse que, n'ayant pas eu la possibilité de faire vérifier la concordance des textes français et siamois de l'Accord de Règlement et du Protocole sur les modalités d'évacuation et de transfert des territoires visés à l'article 1 dudit Accord, nous signons les textes siamois sous réserve d'une modification éventuelle après examen de ces textes par les services compétents du Ministère des Affaires Etrangères.

Je saisis cette occasion pour renouveler à Votre Altesse l'assurance de ma très haute considération.

Henri Bonnet

S.A.R. le Prince Wan Waithayakorn,
Chef de la Délégation siamoise.

XII

Légation siamoise, Washington, D.C.,
le 17 novembre 1946.

Monsieur l'Ambassadeur,

J'ai l'honneur d'accuser réception de la lettre de Votre Excellence en date de ce jour rédigée comme suit:

(Voir lettre XI)

J'ai pris acte de ces réserves au nom de mon Gouvernement et je saisis cette occasion pour renouveler à Votre Excellence l'assurance de ma très haute considération.

Wan Waithayakorn

Son Excellence Monsieur Henri Bonnet,
Ambassadeur de France aux Etats-Unis d'Amérique,
Chef de la Délégation française.

[Source: The official text of the letters cited above is given in Thai only in the Thai edition. The above has been taken from United Nations, *Treaty Series*, 1959, no. 4943, 78–88. It does not accord fully with what appears in the Thai edition. In the latter a) the letters from Prince Wan Waithayakorn are given before the responses from M. Henri Bonnet; b) letters nos. VII, VIII, XI and XII do not appear in the Thai edition; c) the United Nations' source provides a declaration by M. Henri Bonnet whereby the French government, on signing the Settlement Agreement, resumed possession of the Indochinese territories under consideration on behalf of the Cambodian and Lao Governments (ibid, 76); and d) the United Nations' source gives a final exchange of letters whereby it was agreed that the question of sums payable as compensation for damages should be submitted to the Conciliation Commission within a period of three months beginning from 14 December 1946 (ibid, 90–92). This exchange does not appear in the Thai edition.]

APPENDIX 10

RAPPORT DE LA COMMISSION DE CONCILIATION FRANCO-SIAMOISE, WASHINGTON, 27 JUIN 1947

Première Partie

Préambule

1. Une Commission spéciale de Conciliation franco-siamoise a été constituée par les Gouvernements français et siamois à la suite de la signature à Washington par les représentants des Gouvernements de la République française et du Royaume du Siam de l'accord de règlement franco-siamois du 17 novembre 1946, conformément aux dispositions de cet accord.

2. La composition et le fonctionnement de la Commission sont régis par l'article 3 de l'accord en question, article dont le texte est le suivant:

Article 3: Aussitôt après la signature du présent accord, la France et le Siam constitueront, par application de l'article 21 du traité franco-siamois du 7 décembre 1937, une commission de conciliation composée des deux représentants des parties et de trois neutres conformément à l'Acte Général de Genève du 26 septembre 1928 pour le règlement pacifique des différends internationaux qui règle la constitution et le fonctionnement de la Commission. La Commission commencera ses travaux aussitôt que possible après que le transfert des territoires visés au deuxième paragraphe de l'article 1 aura été effectué. Elle sera chargée d'examiner les arguments ethniques, géographiques et économiques des parties en faveur de la révision ou de la confirmation des clauses du traité du 3 octobre 1893, de la convention du 13 février 1904 et du traité du 23 mars 1907 maintenues en vigueur par l'article 22 du traité du 7 décembre 1937".

3. Les attributions de la Commission sont déterminées par l'article 3 de l'accord du 17 novembre 1946 et par le chapitre premier de l'Acte Général de Genève.

4. Le siège de la Commission a été fixé à Washington par les deux gouvernements. Ils se sont mis d'accord sur le choix des trois Commissaires suivants:

M. Victor Andrés *Bélaúnde*, Ambassadeur, membre du Comité Consultatif des Affaires Etrangères du Pérou, Président de l'Université

Catholique de Lima, membre de la Cour Internationale d'Arbitrage de la Haye.

M. William *Phillips*, ancien Ambassadeur des Etats-Unis à Rome, ancien Sous-Secrétaire d'Etat.

Sir Horace *Seymour*, ancien Ambassadeur du Royaume-Uni en Chine.

Chacun des deux gouvernements a, de plus, désigné un commissaire choisi parmi ses nationaux, à savoir:

Le Gouvernement siamois:

S.A. le Prince *Wan Waithayakorn*, Ambassadeur du Siam aux Etats-Unis.

Le Gouvernement français:

M. Paul-Emile *Naggiar*, Ambassadeur de France en mission, anciennement Ambassadeur en Chine et en U.R.S.S., Délégué à la Commission de l'Extrême-Orient à Washington.

Chacun des deux gouvernements a également désigné son agent auprès de la Commission, à savoir:

Le Siam:

S.A. le Prince *Sakol Varavarn*, anciennement Conseiller du Ministère de l'Intérieur;

Nai *Tieng Sirikhanda*, Député, agent suppléant du Gouvernement siamois.

La France:

M. Francis *Lacoste*, Ministre Plénipotentiaire, Conseiller de l'Ambassade de France à Washington;

M. Jean *Burnay*, Conseiller d'Etat, Conseiller et suppléant de l'agent du Gouvernement français.

5. Les Gouvernements français et siamois se sont mis d'accord pour offrir la présidence de la Commission à M. William Phillips, qui a accepté cette offre.

6. La Commission a tenu, à date du 5 mai, de nombreuses séances plénières en présence des agents et des experts des deux parties, dans une suite de bureaux mis gracieusement à sa disposition par les autorités américaines.

Au cours des deux premières séances, diverses questions d'ordre ont été résolues: constitution de la présidence; désignation de M. Bélaúnde comme rapporteur; lecture d'une lettre en date du 5 mai 1947, par laquelle l'agent du Gouvernement siamois faisait connaître au Président son intention de déposer incessamment les arguments ethniques, géographiques et économiques de son Gouvernement en faveur d'une révision des clauses des traités franco-siamois mentionnés dans l'article 3 de l'accord du 17 novembre 1946, clauses relatives à la frontière entre le Siam et l'Indochine, maintenues en vigueur par l'article 22 du traité franco-siamois du 7 décembre 1937; lecture d'une lettre en date du 5 mai 1947, par laquelle l'agent du Gouvernement français faisait, de son côté, connaître au Président qu'il se tenait à sa disposition pour présenter et développer les arguments de son Gouvernement au sujet de ces mêmes clauses dès qu'il aurait reçu notification d'une requête siamoise.

7. Parmi les autres questions d'ordre réglées au cours des deux premières séances, il y a lieu de mentionner en outre les suivantes: les langues française et anglaise ont été reconnues les deux seules langues de travail de la Commission conformément aux règlements des Nations Unies; un communiqué du 5 mai a fait connaître à la presse la réunion de la Commission; conformément à l'article 10 de l'Acte Général de Genève, il a été décidé que les travaux de la Commission ne seraient pas publics; les deux gouvernements ont notifié par lettre du 9 mai la constitution de la Commission au Secrétaire Général des Nations Unies.

8. Le 12 mai, l'agent siamois a formellement déposé au nom de son Gouvernement sa requête devant la Commission ainsi que la carte annexée et la Commission a commencé l'examen des questions à elle soumises.

L'agent du Gouvernement français a répondu par un mémoire du 22 mai auquel l'agent du Gouvernement siamois a fait une réplique le 29 mai. A cette réplique, l'agent du Gouvernement français a opposé la siamois en date du 7 juin.

La Commission a entendu les agents des deux gouvernements dans leurs explications verbales et leurs réponses aux questions qui leur ont été posées, soit sous forme verbale au cours des séances, soit sur questionnaires écrits auxquels ils ont pu faire réponse verbale à loisir.

Elle a, de même, entendu les exposés faits devant elle par tes experts des deux parties en diverses matières ethniques, géographiques et économiques, et les réponses que ces experts ont faites aux diverses questions qui leur ont été posées.

La Commission a pris note, en outre, de l'accord des agents des deux gouvernements sur le fait que le statut juridique de la frontière entre le Siam et l'Indochine repose sur l'article premier de l'accord de règlement franco-siamois du 17 novembre 1946.

9. Les arguments présentés par l'agent du Gouvernement siamois en faveur d'une modification à l'avantage du Siam de la frontière entre l'Indochine et le Siam, et les arguments présentés par l'agent du Gouvernement français en faveur du maintien du *statu quo* antérieur à la convention du 9 mai 1941, annulée par l'accord franco-siamois du 17 novembre 1946, ayant été largement exposés par les représentants des deux parties, la tâche de ces derniers à cet égard s'est trouvée ainsi entièrement remplie.

10. Les chapitres suivants de ce rapport contiennent un résumé des principaux arguments développés devant la Commission ainsi que les conclusions de la Commission à leur égard.

En représentant les revendications de Son Gouvernement, l'agent siamois a mis en cause la révision de presque toute la frontière entre le Siam et l'Indochine. Par suite, il sera nécessaire d'examiner ces revendications une par une et dans l'ordre suivant:

Territoires de la rive gauche du Mékong
Luang Prabang rive droite (Lan Chang)
Mékong frontière
Bassac rive droite (Champasak)
Battambang.

Partie II

Territoires de la Rive Gauche du Mékong

1. Par une requête du 12 mai, l'agent du Gouvernement siamois a demandé la révision des clauses du traité franco-siamois du 3 octobre 1893 relatives à la renonciation par le Siam à ses prétentions sur l'ensemble des territoires de la rive gauche du Mékong et sur les îles du fleuve.

2. Il a fait valoir qu'au point de vue "racial," les habitants des territoires revendiqués par son Gouvernement sont de même origine que ceux de la rive droite du Mékong, que ces territoires forment une unité géographique séparée de l'Annam par la chaîne annamitique et que l'interdépendance entre ces deux groupes de territoires au point de vue de la production et de la distribution des principales commodités en fait une unité économique.

3. L'agent français a fait la critique des arguments ethniques, économiques et géographiques développés par l'agent siamois. Sans soulever à leur propos une exception formelle de non recevabilité, il n'en a pas moins posé à la Commission une question préalable, celle de l'admissibilité devant elle d'une requête ayant pour objet le transfert à une autre Etat d'une unité politique établie.

L'agent français affirme que c'est bien la nature de la requête siamoise car elle réclame, dit-il, sur le Laos tout entier et même au-delà des droits comportant la cession au Siam de parties constitutives de l'Indochine dont la structure politique serait par la même détruite.

4. La Commission constate que la carte déposée par l'agent siamois à l'appui de sa requête illustre de façon graphique la revendication siamoise et démontre que son étendue géographique comprend l'ensemble des territoires

de la rive gauche du Mékong jusqu'au Tonkin, soit plus du tiers du territoires de l'Indochine.

5. L'article 3 de l'Accord du règlement franco-siamois de 1946, mentionnant le traité du 3 octobre 1893 parmi ceux au sujet desquels la Commission a reçu son mandat d'examen, il importe que celle-ci élucide la question préalable soulevée par l'agent français.

6. La Commission considère que, du point de vue de sa compétence une requête en faveur de la révision des traités franco-siamois aux termes de l'article 3 de l'accord franco-siamois de 1946 peut être valablement portée devant elle si cette requête se réfère à des ajustements ou à des changements du tracé de la frontière même s'ils affectent des territoires non organisés en unité politique constituée, mais non si elle implique des transferts d'unités politiques constituées.

7. Il est vrai que la marge d'initiative d'une Commission de Conciliation est plus large que celle reconnue à un Tribunal arbitral ou à une Cour de Justice. Cette faculté dont la Commission pourrait se prévaloir ne peut être exercée cependant que dans les limites du domaine propre des controverses internationales. Or une question ne prend pas le caractère de controverse internationale pour avoir fait l'objet d'une requête, mais en raison de la nature intrinsèque de la question posée.

Il est évident que le transfert d'une unité politique constituée (modus vivendi franco-laotien du 27 août 1946) est l'objet de la requête siamoise relative au traité de 1893. Cet objet n'est pas du domaine des controverses internationales et échappe donc de ce fait à la compétence de la Commission.

8. Quoi qu'il en soit, la Commission estime que, même si elle était compétent quant à l'examen des revendications siamoises sur l'ensemble des territoires de la rive gauche du Mékong, l'élucidation des arguments ethniques, géographiques et économiques ne l'autoriserait pas à appuyer la requête siamoise ni la révision des clauses du traité de 1893 relatives à ces territoires. Cette conclusion résulte de l'examen fait par elle de ces arguments, examen qui figure à la partie III B de ce rapport.

Partie III

A. Luang Prabang Rive droite (Lan Chang)

1. L'agent siamois fait remarquer que la cession du territoire de Luang Prabang rive droite (Lan Chang) à la France résulte de la convention franco-siamoise du 13 février 1904. Ce territoire a une superficie de 15,000 kilomètres carrés.

Il appuie sa demande de révision des clauses de cette convention sur des arguments ethniques, géographiques et économiques.

Il assure que la plupart des habitants de Lan Chang appartiennent à la race Siamois et ne peuvent être distingués de leurs voisins du Nord-Est du Siam et que leur langage et leur culture sont similaires.

Il prétend qu'au point de vue géographique la cession de ce territoire à la France a projeté une enclave française dans le territoire du Siam et réduit la valeur du Mékong comme voie de grande communication internationale, parce que le passage dans cette section du Mékong qui, autrefois, était de droit, est aujourd'hui de tolérance.

Il ajoute que la frontière actuelle oppose un obstacle au courant commercial normal entre communes. Elle affecte de même, dit-il, celui des marches plus importants vers le sud et l'ouest et vers leur exutoire naturel. Le port de Bangkok, avec lequel les voies de communication sont plus courtes et meilleures que celles se dirigeant vers Saigon.

Enfin, il maintient qu'il y a toute raison de croire que l'état d'isolement dans lequel se trouve actuellement cette région ferait place bientôt a une plus grande activité commerciale comme suite à un développement des routes et à une augmentation en valeur et en volume de ses exportations.

Il conclut que les voies d'accès entre le Siam et Luang Prabang (Lan Chang) sont de beaucoup plus faciles que celles qui le relient à l'Indochine et que, par conséquent, la frontière actuelle constitue un obstacle à son développement futur.

2. L'agent français attire l'attention sur le fait que le tracé de la frontière occidentale de Luang Prabang (Lan Chang) définie par le traité de 1904 a été soigneusement délimité; que cette frontière est formée par une chaîne de montagnes continue qui, s'élevant à plus de 2,000 mètres en certains points, descend rarement à moins de 700 mètres; que cette chaîne forme la ligne de partage des eaux entre le bassin de la Ménam et celui du Mékong et qu'il s'agit d'une frontière qui, dans cette section comme dans les autres, depuis près d'un demi-siècle, a été paisible.

Il déclare que 80,000 habitants vivent sur la rive droite du Mékong (Lan Chang) et 22,000 sur la rive gauche (Luang Prabang).

Il fait remarquer que les territoires de la rive droite du Mékong (Lan Chang) forment justement avec ceux de la rive gauche une de ces unités ethniques et géographiques dont l'agent siamois recommande, dans sa requête, la constitution et le maintien ailleurs.

En outre, il signale, comme un fait bien établi, que la plus grande partie des exportations de Luang Prabang rive droite (Lan Chang) descend par le Mékong ou par la route vers Saigon.

Il rappelle, enfin, à la Commission que, par son article 4, le traité de 1904, maintenu en vigueur par l'article 4 de la convention franco-siamoise de 1926, garantit la liberté de navigation aux bateaux siamois dans la partie du Mékong qui traverse Luang Prabang, mais qu'en fait l'activité de cette navigation est peu importante dans ces secteurs de la rivière.

3. La Commission a examiné avec le plus grand soin les revendications du Siam sur Luang Prabang rive droite (Lan Chang) ainsi que les déclarations de l'agent français à l'encontre de ces revendications. Un accord entre les deux agents au sujet d'une révision de la frontière dans cette section ne lui a pas paru possible, puisque l'agent français a rejeté dans sa totalité la requête siamoise au sujet de Lan Chang.

En ce qui la concerne, la Commission est arrivée à la conclusion que les arguments ethniques mis en avant par l'agent siamois en ce qui concerne l'analogie de langage, d'origine et de culture des habitants de chaque côté de la frontière actuelle ne suffisent pas, en eux-mêmes, à justifier une modification de cette frontière en faveur du Siam.

L'examen de la situation économique ne paraît pas non plus à la Commission pouvoir comporter de conclusion favorable à cette modification, car le territoire des deux rives du Mékong constitue, en fait, dans cette région, une unité économique comportant des échanges intercommunaux constants à travers la rivière.

Au point de vue géographique, la Commission estime que la ligne de partage des eaux entre le Mékong et la Ménam est une frontière appropriée et naturelle, bien établie et clairement définie. Des forêts épaisses s'étendent de chaque côté de la ligne de faîte de la chaîne de montagnes et celle-ci n'est franchissable que par deux chemins de charrettes. Il en résulte qu'actuellement l'activité commerciale ne peut qu'être réduite entre habitants à l'est et à l'ouest de la frontière.

Aucun inconvénient particulier ne paraît résulter pour les habitants du Siam de l'emplacement actuel du tracé de la frontière et la même remarque est applicable aux habitants de Luang Prabang rive droite (Lan Chang).

En conclusion, sur aucun des arguments ethniques, économiques ou géographiques avancés, la Commission estime être en mesure d'appuyer les revendications siamoises sur Luang Prabang rive droite (Lan Chang) et sa demande de révision de la frontière.

B. Mékong Frontières

1. Dans cette section, les arguments exposés par la requête siamoise ont pour but de démontrer que les deux rives du Mékong forment une unité naturelle au point de vue ethnique, géographique et économique, que cette unité est anéantie par la frontière fluviale et qu'elle doit être rétablie au profit du Siam. A

l'appui de cette thèse, l'agent siamois soutient que les communications sont plus aisées entre cette région et Bangkok qu'entre elle et Saigon et il voit la preuve de l'existence de son unité naturelle dans le fait que les deux gouvernements ont créé la Haute Commission permanente franco-siamoise du Mékong.

2. L'agent français conteste, dans sa réponse, l'exactitude et la pertinence des arguments ethniques, géographiques et économiques de l'agent siamois. Il fait valoir qu'en matière ethnique il n'y a pas identité entre habitants des deux rives, mais seulement certains caractères communs qui les apparentent aux groupes parlant des langues d'origine thaï et que quelques-unes s'appartiennent à des groupes différents, entre autres, aux groupes Moï. Il dit qu'une route excellente relie la rive gauche à Saigon et que les échanges commerciaux entre les deux rives sont ceux qui se forment normalement entre des frontaliers. Il ajoute que le bassin du Mékong, comme tout bassin fluvial, pourrait, à ce titre, paraître constituer une unité géographique, mais que cela ne justifier pas la prétention de l'agent siamois de vouloir transformer au profit du Siam une unité géographique en une unité politique. Il suffit, dit-il, d'appliquer la thèse siamoise à d'autres bassins fluviaux pour mesurer le bouleversement que provoquerait une pareille doctrine dans les relations internationales, la plupart des grands bassins fluviaux, analogues à celui du Mékong, n'étant pas intégrés dans une seule unité politique.

3. Ayant pesé avec soin tant la requête siamoise que les réponses et répliques des parties, et en se référant aux considérations exposées dans la partie II du rapport, la Commission considère que les arguments avancés ne justifient pas, dans cette section du Mékong, le transfert de territoires demandés.

4. L'examen de la situation de droit et de fait, dans cette section, a permis cependant à la Commission de constater l'existence du régime suivant:

a) le tracé de la frontière, tel qu'il résulte des traités franco-siamois et de la délimitation faite sur place, est fixé au *thalweg* du Mékong là où ce fleuve coule en un bras unique; ce même tracé est fixé au *thalweg* du bras le plus proche de la rive siamoise là où le fleuve coule en plusieurs bras et, dans ce cas, les îles font partie de la rive française quand celles ne sont jamais recouvertes par les hautes eaux.

b) de chaque côté du tracé de la frontière, la convention franco-siamoise de 1926 a établi une zone démilitarisée de 25 kilomètres de large qui coïncide avec une zone franche de droits de douane également de 25 kilomètres de large établie en 1937 sous sa forme actuelle.

c) la même convention de 1926 a créé la Haute Commission permanente franco-siamoise du Mékong dans laquelle siègent des représentants de l'Indochine et du Siam. Cette Haute Commission possède des attributions, les unes de surveillance, les autres d'élaboration et de proposition dans des matières diverses du plus grand intérêt pour la vie des populations des deux rives, telles que: pêcheries, police frontière, délimitation du tracé, navigation fluviale, énergie électrique, navigation aérienne, etc....

5. La Commission estime que le régime ainsi établi dans cette région et auquel préside la Haute Commission répond, quant à son principe, aux intérêts des habitants mais qu'il pourrait être plus efficacement appliqué et plus complètement développé par les deux gouvernements.

6. L'agent français a déclaré, dans sa réponse du 22 mai, que, sous certaines conditions, son Gouvernement était disposé à donner au Siam un accès à un chenal navigable en eau profonde, sous réserve de la question de souveraineté. La Commission estime que, pour des raisons techniques et dans un but de conciliation, il y aurait avantage à fixer le tracé de la frontière au principal chenal navigable par une délimitation nouvelle qui serait confiée à la Haute Commission permanente franco-siamoise du Mékong, après conclusion d'un accord à ce sujet par les deux gouvernements.

7. En outre, l'aire géographique de la compétence de cette Commission, actuellement limitée au Mékong frontière, pourrait être utilement étendue à cette partie du Mékong qui ne coïncide pas avec la frontière et, dans ce cas, ses attributions également étendues en s'inspirant des dispositions des deux Conventions de Barcelone du 20 avril 1921 qui établissent le statut de la liberté du transit et celui du régime des voies navigables d'intérêt international.

C. Bassac Rive droite (Champasak)

1. La revendication mise en avant par l'agent siamois se réfère au transfert au Siam du territoire de Bassac (Champasak) situé à l'ouest de Mékong et au nord de la rivière Se Lam Pao. La superficie de ce territoire est d'environ 6,000 kilomètres carrés. Cette province a été cédée par le Siam à la France par la convention du 13 février 1904.

2. A l'appui de cette revendication, l'agent siamois a fait valoir que la presque totalité de la population de ce territoire appartient au même groupe ethnique (Lao) que celui du nord-est du Siam et que la frontière sépare des habitants de même origine, langage et culture.

Le tracé de la frontière suit le sommet d'un escarpement qui se dresse à pic sur sa face orientale (Indochine) et s'incline en pente douce sur sa face occidentale (Siam). L'agent siamois décrit là essentiellement une frontière de montagne qui, au sens strictement géographique de mot, peut être considérée comme l'idéal le plus proche de l'impénétrabilité et de la permanence.

Il prétend, cependant, que les considérations géographiques ne sont pas les seules importantes et que les meilleurs débouchés pour le district, déjà relié par la route au terminus des chemins de fer siamois à Oubone [Ubon], sont à travers le territoire siamois vers le port de Bangkok. Il ajoute que ces communications pourraient être améliorées pour obtenir des moyens d'accès plus avantageux que le Mékong et le réseau routier de l'Indochine française. Par exemple, si la frontière était déplacée vers le Mékong les chemins de fer siamois pourraient être étendus jusqu'à ce fleuve et la ville de Bassac amenée à deux jours de voyage de Bangkok. Le volume du trafic marchandises transportées en 1946 par la route entre Pimun au Siam et Chongmek à la frontière est évalué par lui à 10,000 tonnes. A son avis, si le territoire était cédé au Siam, l'amélioration des moyens de communication signifierait un commerce plus actif et un niveau de vie plus élevé dans cette région relativement isolée.

3. L'agent français reconnaît que la population parle un langage du groupe des langues thaï, bien que ce langage, Lao, soit différent du Siamois. Il fait remarquer que ce fait ne justifie pas un transfert du territoire au Siam.

Il signale que le tracé de la frontière n'a pas été fixe au hasard, mais qu'il suit la ligne de faite de la chaîne de montagnes qui sépare le bassin de la Semun de celui du Mékong.

Il fait remarquer que le régime dans cette section, comme dans les autres, est libéral et que les échanges intercommunaux de part et d'autre de la frontière ne sont soumis pratiquement à aucune restriction.

Il remarque, de plus, que le Gouvernement siamois n'a pas démontré que la population, d'un côté ou de l'autre de la frontière, souffre de façon quelconque de l'existence de cette frontière. De plus, il n'existe aucune minorité siamoise dans le territoire en question.

4. Pour ce qui est des communications, l'agent français a fourni des renseignements sur les liaisons entre le Bassac et les régions situées à l'est et au sud, les plus importantes étant le fleuve Mékong et la grande route fédérale no. 13 ainsi que deux routes vers la côte d'Annam.

Il a insisté sur le fait que les parties du Bassac traversées par le Mékong constituent une unité économique étroite et que le transfert au Siam du territoire revendiqué causerait un grave dommage aux habitants des deux rives du fleuve, sans qu'aucun avantage correspondant pour les intéressés puisse justifier la revendication de transférer sous la souveraineté siamoise un territoire qui fait partie intégrante de l'Etat du Laos.

5. D'après les chiffres fournis à la Commission par l'agent français, la population du territoire de Bassac rive droite s'élève à environ 50,000 (un tiers de la population de la province de Bassac). La production de riz est d'environ 30,000 tonnes, sur lesquelles 17,000 sont exportées vers la rive gauche et 3,000 au Siam.

6. La Commission considère que la frontière actuelle, formée comme elle est part des repères naturels bien marqués et facilement reconnaissables est une bonne frontière au point de vue géographique.

Elle est de plus d'avis qu'au point de vue de la composition ethnique de sa population. Le Bassac (Champasak) ne souffre en rien de son présent statut comme partie intégrante du Laos et que, à ce même point de vue, il ne souffrirait pas non plus si le territoire revendiqué était transféré au Siam.

C'est avec la rive gauche du Mékong plutôt qu'avec le Siam que se font actuellement les rapports économiques et, dans l'hypothèse où un changement de souveraineté sur une partie de ce territoire serait décidé par les deux gouvernements, de sûres garanties seraient à prévoir pour éviter que les deux parties du Bassac ne souffrent de l'interruption des échanges commerciaux à travers le fleuve.

7. La Commission estime, cependant, que les circonstances décrites ci-dessus ne l'autorisent pas à appuyer, en vertu d'arguments ethniques, économiques ni géographiques, les revendications siamoises sur le Bassac rive droite (Champasak) ni sa demande de révision de la frontière à ce sujet.

D. Battambang

1. La revendication du Gouvernement siamois a pour objet le transfert du Siam le l'actuelle province de Battambang. La superficie en est de 20,335 kilomètres carrés et la population est évaluée à 271,000. La province, partie actuelle de l'Etat du Cambodge, a été cédée par le Siam à la France en vertu du traité franco-siamois du 23 mars 1907.

2. A l'appui de sa revendication, l'agent siamois déclare que la population était à l'origine de souche Mon Khmer, mais que les habitants des deux côtés de la frontière se sont étroitement alliés à la suite de mélanges fort anciens et d'intimes relations économiques et culturelles. Il assure que les rapports naturels géographiques et économiques de la province sont avec les territoires siamois du nord et avec Bangkok, plutôt qu'avec l'Indochine.

Par exemple, Bangkok, situé à 35 kilomètres du golfe du Siam, offrirait un meilleur débouché que Phnom Penh avec lequel Battambang est relié par la route et par le rail mais qui se trouve à 350 kilomètres de la mer et qui ne peut pas recevoir de navire calant plus de 4 mètres. D'autre part, Battambang est également relié par la route et le rail à Bangkok, port dont la capacité est bien plus grande que celle de Phnom Penh et qui est en cours d'amélioration. D'autres liaisons routières avec le Siam pourraient être développées et offriraient à l'avenir de meilleures opportunités que les routes du sud. La frontière actuelle, de l'avis du Gouvernement siamois, empêche le futur développement de la province en limitant ses meilleurs moyens d'accès.

3. Du côté français, on assure que la démarcation ethnique entre Siamois et Cambodgiens passe, en fait, au nord et à l'ouest de la frontière actuelle et que la nouvelle frontière revendiquée par le Gouvernement siamois ne se conformerait à aucune donnée naturelle et qu'elle traverserait un territoire habité par des populations cambodgiennes.

L'agent français signale que la chaîne de montagne Dang Rek que suit la présente frontière, de même que les forêts qui en recouvrent au sud-ouest la masse terminale, fournissent une frontière naturelle (et la seul possible) entre les territoires de l'ouest où la majorité de la population est siamoise et le pays à l'est et au sud-est habité par les Cambodgiens.

4. En ce qui concerne les communications, l'agent français a montré que le territoire de Battambang est relié non seulement par la route et le rail à Phnom Penh mais aussi à Saigon par des voies d'eau ininterrompues et deux routes. Il déclare que les liaisons économiques de Battambang, ainsi que cédés du reste du Cambodge, ont toujours été et doivent nécessairement être orientées vers le sud-est vers Saigon pour ce qui est du trafic maritime, grâce au réseau des voies d'eau naturelles.

5. La province constitue un important centre rizicole. D'après l'agent français, les exportations de riz, avant 1941, atteignaient une quantité variable allant de 235,000 à 150,000 tonnes suivant l'importance de la récolte. L'exportation de poissons sèches, produit des remarquables pêcheries du grand lac, s'élevait à 35,000 tonnes environ dont quelques 2,000 tonnes allaient au Siam.

6. Pour autant qu'il s'agisse de considérations ethniques, la Commission estime que la justification d'un transfert sous la souveraineté siamoise d'un territoire dont la population n'est pas siamoise n'a pas été établie. La frontière principalement formée par la chaîne montagneuse du Dang Rek satisfait la Commission. Elle lui paraît correspondre aux exigences ethniques et géographiques mieux qu'aucune frontière suggérée.

Au point de vue économique, la Commission considère que, si les communications avec le Siam pourraient être sans aucun doute développées à l'avantage de tous les intéressés, il n'en est pas moins vrai que le courant naturel du commerce de Battambang suit les voies d'eau existantes et les autres voies de communication routières et ferroviaires vers le sud et l'est.

Dans ces conditions, la Commission exprime l'opinion que séparer la province de Battambang du reste du Cambodge serait au désavantage des habitants de la province et à celui des autres habitants de l'Etat, sans qu'aucun avantage suffisant soit à envisager en compensation.

7. La Commission n'est donc pas en mesure d'appuyer la revendication siamoise de transfert au Siam de la province de Battambang ni la demande de révision de la frontière à ce sujet.

8. En raison de l'importance du rôle que les pêcheries du grand lac jouent comme réservoir de produits alimentaires pour les territoires adjacents, la Commission recommande que des mesures soient prises, d'accord entre les deux parties, en vue d'assurer au marche siamois un approvisionnement régulier et suffisant de poissons préparés.

Partie IV

Commission Consultative Internationale

Au cours de l'élucidation qu'elle a faite des arguments soumis à son examen par l'article 3 de l'accord de règlement franco-siamois du 17 novembre 1946, la Commission a pu se rendre compte qu'il existe entre les divers pays de la péninsule indochinoise d'importantes questions techniques d'intérêt commun.

A titre d'exemple, on peut citer les sujets suivants:

Agriculture: Amélioration des récoltes et statistiques, maladies des animaux et des plantes, nouvelles techniques agricoles, une politique du riz, etc.

Irrigation
Santé publique
Pêcheries
Communications
Recherches scientifiques
Archéologie
Relations culturelles

La Commission recommande que les Gouvernements français et siamois se mettent d'accord pour prendre l'initiative de promouvoir la réunion d'une conférence de représentants des gouvernements voisins intéressés en vue d'examiner les conditions d'établissement, à titre permanent, d'une commission consultative internationale chargée d'étudier ces questions ou d'autres questions techniques analogues.

En raison de la position géographique centrale du Siam, le siège de cette commission consultative technique pourrait être avantageusement placé à Bangkok.

Partie V

Résumé des Recommandations

Les recommandations de la Commission, telles qu'elles résultent des parties précédentes de ce rapport, peuvent être résumées brièvement comme suit :

1. La Commission n'appuie pas les revendications siamoises sur Luang Prabang rive droite (Lan Chang) et les clauses de la convention du 13 février 1904 au sujet de la frontière entre le Siam et l'Indochine dans le secteur de Luang Prabang rive droite (Lan Chang) ne devraient pas être révisées (partie III A paragraphe 9).

2. La Commission n'appuie pas les revendications siamoises sur les territoires de la rive gauche du Mékong et les clauses du traité du 3 octobre 1893 ne devraient pas être révisées (partie II paragraphe 8). Le tracé de la frontière fluviale tel qu'il est défini par les traités et tel qu'il résulte de la démarcation faite sur place devrait être modifié, cependant, de façon à le mettre au principal chenal navigable (partie III B paragraphe 6).

3. L'aire géographique de la compétence de la Haute Commission du Mékong devrait être étendue ainsi que ses fonctions (partie III B paragraphe 7).

4. La Commission n'appuie pas les revendications siamoises sur le territoire de Bassac rive droite (Champasak) et les clauses de la convention du 13 février 1904 au sujet de la frontière entre le Siam et l'Indochine ne devraient par conséquent pas être révisées (partie III C paragraphe 7).

5. La Commission n'appuie pas les revendications siamoises sur la province de Battambang et les clauses du traité du 23 mars 1907 au sujet de la frontière entre le Siam et l'Indochine ne devraient pas être révisées (partie III D paragraphe 7).

6. En ce qui concerne les pêcheries dans le grand lac, la Commission recommande un arrangement entre les parties en vue d'assurer un approvisionnement adéquat de poissons au Siam (partie III D paragraphe 8).

7. La Commission recommande que les Gouvernements français et siamois entrent en négociation dans le but d'établir à Bangkok une commission consultative internationale chargée d'étudier des questions techniques d'intérêt commun aux pays de la péninsule indochinoise (partie IV).

Conclusion

La Commission désire souligner qu'agissant dans la limite de ses attributions, elle a borné son examen et ses délibérations aux arguments ethniques, géographiques et économiques, à l'exclusion des considérations politiques et historiques. Leurs dossiers respectifs ont été plaidés devant la Commission par les deux agents, parlant au nom de leurs Gouvernements.

Bien que la Commission n'ait pas jugé possible d'appuyer les revendications territoriales du Siam, elle n'en a pas moins fait certaines recommandations qui seraient à l'avantage des populations intéressées si les deux Gouvernements les acceptaient. La Commission estime que le simple transfert de territoires d'un côté à l'autre de la frontière sans le contentement des habitants ne comporterait pas en soi d'avantage pour les habitants des districts frontaliers dont le bonheur et le bien-être véritables dépendent de libres échanges avec leurs voisins de l'autre côté de la frontière. Les zones de 25 kilomètres (libres de douanes et démilitarisées) qui existent déjà de chaque côté de la frontière fluviale favorisent ces échanges communaux et stimulent le maintien de rapports amicaux entre les habitants du bassin fluvial.

Dans ces conditions et grâce à la mise en application par les deux Gouvernements de ses recommandations la Commission espère vivement que la bonne entente et la coopération se développeront dans les relations des deux parties, contribuant ainsi à la paix et à la prospérité si nécessaires non seulement pour l'avenir du Siam et de l'Indochine mais aussi pour celui de toute la péninsule.

Deux annexes jointes.

Fait à Washington, le 27 juin 1947. Pour la Commission:
Le Président,
William Phillips.

Liste des documents remis pas les agents des Gouvernements Français et Siamois à la Commission de Conciliation Franco-Siamoise

1. Traduction française de la lettre en date du 5 mai adressée au Président de la Commission de Conciliation franco-siamoise par l'agent du Gouvernement siamois.
2. Lettre en date du 5 mai adressée au Président de la Commission de Conciliation franco-siamoise par l'agent du Gouvernement français.
3. Traduction française de la requête en date du 12 mai présentée à la Commission de Conciliation franco-siamoise par l'agent du Gouvernement siamois.
4. Carte de l'Indochine annexée au document précité. (Photostat). (*Voir production VI bis*).

5. Lettre en date du 22 mai adressée au Président de la Commission de Conciliation franco-siamoise par l'agent du Gouvernement français.

6. "Observations" du 22 mai de l'agent du Gouvernement français sur la requête déposée le 12 mai 1947 par l'agent du Gouvernement siamois auprès de la Commission de Conciliation franco-siamoise.

7. Note annexé au mémoire du 22 mai présenté par l'agent du Gouvernement français en réponse à la requête déposée le 12 mai 1947 par l'agent du Gouvernement siamois.

8. Traduction française du mémoire ampliatif et de la réplique, en date du 29 mai, présentés à la Commission de Conciliation franco-siamoise par l'agent du Gouvernement siamois.

9. Lettre en date du 7 juin adressée au Président de la Commission de Conciliation franco-siamoise par l'agent du Gouvernement français.

10. "Observations et conclusions" du 7 juin de l'agent du Gouvernement français sur la requête présentée à la Commission de Conciliation franco-siamoise le 12 mai 1947 par l'agent du Gouvernement siamois et développée dans son mémoire en duplique du 29 mai 1947.

11. Annexe I aux "Observations et Conclusions" de l'agent du Gouvernement français en date du 7 juin 1947.

12. Annexe II aux "Observations et Conclusions" de l'agent du Gouvernement français en date du 7 juin 1947.

Traduction

No. 1/2490   Ambassade
5 mai 1947

A l'Honorable le Président de la Commission de Conciliation
Washington, D.C.

Monsieur le Président,

J'ai l'honneur de me référer à l'article 3 de l'accord de règlement franco-siamois signé à Washington le 17 novembre 1946 qui a prévu la constitution d'une commission de conciliation pour examiner les arguments ethniques, géographiques et économiques en faveur d'une révision ou de la confirmation des clauses du traité du 3 octobre 1893, de la convention du 13 février 1904 et du traité du 23 mars 1907 qui ont été maintenues en vigueur par le traité du 7 décembre 1937, et d'inviter la Commission de Conciliation à prendre toutes les mesures nécessaires en vue d'arriver à une solution amiable des sujets en question suivant les dispositions de l'accord franco-siamois et en conformité avec l'Acte Général de Genève du 26 septembre 1928 pour Le Règlement Pacifique des Différends Internationaux.

C'est le désir du Gouvernement Royal siamois que les frontières entre le Siam et l'Indochine établies au moyen des clauses des traités ci-dessus mentionnés soient révisées, et, à cette fin, des arguments ethniques, géographiques et économiques seront soumis avec le vif espoir que la Commission leur accordera une bienveillante attention.

J'ai l'honneur d'être, Monsieur le Président, votre obéissant serviteur.

(Signé) *Sakol Varavarn*,
Agent du Gouvernement royal siamois.

Washington, le 5 mai 1947

Monsieur le Président,

La Commission de Conciliation franco-siamoise prévue à l'article 3 de l'accord de règlement franco-siamois du 17 novembre 1946 étant désormais constituée, j'ai l'honneur de vous faire savoir, en qualité d'agent du Gouvernement français, que je me tiendrai à la disposition de la Commission pour présenter et développer devant elle les arguments de mon Gouvernement en faveur de la confirmation ou d'une révision des clauses du traité du 3 octobre 1893, de la convention du 13 février 1904 et du traité du 23 mars 1907, maintenues en vigueur par l'article 22 du traité du 7 décembre 1917, dès que mon Gouvernement aura, conformément aux dispositions de l'article 7 paragraphes 2 et 3 de l'Acte Général de Genève du 26 octobre [septembre?—Ed.] 1928, reçu notification d'une requête siamoise, et que la Commission aura entende les arguments du Gouvernement siamois à l'appui de cette requête.

(Signé) *Francis Lacoste*

Son Excellence Monsieur William Phillips,
Ambassadeur des Etats-Unis,
Président de la Commission de Conciliation franco-siamoise,
Washington, D.C.

P.S. Je joins à la présente communication, pour votre commodité et celle des autres commissaires, cinq exemplaires du texte de l'accord de règlement franco-siamois du 17 novembre 1946 et la partie de l'Accord Général de Genève du 26 octobre 1928 qui a trait à la procédure de conciliation.

Pour copie certifiée conforme
L'Agent du Gouvernement français
Francis Lacoste.

Traduit de l'anglais
No. 2/2490

Ambassade du Siam
Washington,
le 12 mai 1947

A l'honorable Président de la Commission de Conciliation,
Washington, D.C.

Monsieur le Président,

1. Comme suite à ma lettre No. 1/2490 en date du 5 mai 1947 par laquelle une demande de conciliation était déposée au nom de Gouvernement Royal siamois conformément à l'article 7 de l'Acte Général du 26 septembre 1928, j'ai maintenant l'honneur de présenter à la Commission les résumés sommaires suivants des principales dispositions du Traité de 1893, de la Convention de 1904 et du Traité de 1907 et les raisons ethniques, géographiques et économiques, sur lesquels sont fondées des propositions de révision des frontières établies par les dispositions des traités:

Traité du 3 octobre 1893

2. Le traité stipulait que:
    (1) Le Siam renonce à toutes prétentions sur les territoires de la rive gauche du Mékong et sur toutes les îles du fleuve.
    (2) Une zone de 25 kilomètres sur la rive droite du Mékong devait être démilitarisée.

3. Une annexe du traité disposait qu'en attendant l'exécution du traité, y compris la complète évacuation et la pacification de la rive gauche du Mékong et la démilitarisation de la zone de 25 kilomètres, les troupes françaises continueraient à occuper Chantaboun, ville stratégique sur le Golfe du Siam.

4. Racialement, la majorité des habitants des deux côtés du Mékong sont d'origine identique. Le déplacement des frontières en 1893 qui sépara les populations de cette zone en deux groupes politiques n'a pas eu d'effet sur leur inclination naturelle à être étroitement associées.

5. Géographiquement, les régions des deux rives du Mékong constituent ensemble une unité naturelle évidente à l'influence profonde non seulement sur la vie des habitants mais sur les activités administratives et autres qui rendent nécessaires des mesures de coopération étroite comme en témoigne la création d'un "Régime du Mékong" commun au moyen d'arrangements spéciaux de police, navigation, pêche, commerce et douanes.

6. Du point de vue économique, l'interdépendance des habitants des rives Est et Ouest du Mékong pour la production, la distribution et la consommation montre clairement que le bassin de la rivière est également une seule unité économique et pour son approvisionnement régulier en produits essentiels tels que le riz, le sel, et les salaisons, la population de la rive gauche dépende de celle de la rive droite. Une autre considération importante est qu'il est plus facile d'accéder naturellement à ces territoires de la rive droite du Mékong que n'importe quelle autre direction, les lignes de communication des centres principaux des territoires cédés étant non seulement plus développées et plus courtes vers Bangkok que vers Saigon mais encore plus capables d'amélioration dans l'avenir.

7. Comme la frontière établie par le traité désavantage non seulement le Siam mais la zone cédée à l'Indochine, les prétentions sur les territoires de la rive gauche et sur les îles du Mékong auxquelles le Siam fut obligé de renoncer ne vertu du premier article du traité devraient être établies.

Convention du 13 février 1904

8. De 1893 à 1904, les Français continuèrent à occuper Chantaboun. En conséquence, la Convention du 13 février 1904 fut négociée entre la France et le Siam. Ceci aboutit à la cession à la France de deux territoires siamois importants, tous deux sur la rive droite du Mékong, à savoir:

9. a) la Province de Lan Chang (Luang Prabang) au Nord; b) la Province de Champasak (Bassac) à l'Est.

Les considérations sur l'unité ethnique, géographique et économique de bassin du Mékong exposées dans le cas du Traité de 1893 portent autant de poids sinon plus quand on les applique à ces deux provinces.

Lan Chang (Luang Prabang)

La plupart des habitants de cette province appartiennent à la race thaïe et ne peuvent être distingués de leurs voisins du Siam du Nord-Est.

10. Géographiquement, la cession de ce territoire à la France a projeté une enclave française dans le territoire siamois et a réduit la valeur du fleuve comme voie d'eau internationale.

11. Economiquement, la nouvelle frontière a créé une barrière pour le commerce intercommunautaire normal et a gêné matériellement la commodité

d'accès de cette province vers les marchés plus importants du Sud et de l'Ouest et vers son débouché naturel, le port de Bangkok, avec lequel les lignes de communication sont plus courtes et meilleures que celles menant à Saigon.

12. Il est par conséquent proposé que la frontière existante soit écartée et que la province de Lan Chang fasse partie du Siam.

Champasak (Bassac)

13. Dans cette province, la grande majorité des habitants sont de race thaïe.

14. Ici, comme c'est fréquemment le cas, la géographie détermine l'accessibilité qui à son tour affecte l'économie d'une région. Les communications vers le Nord-Est rencontrent les montagnes qui limitent le débit du trafic.

Les routes les plus praticables sont:

15. (a) Sud, par voie d'eau du Mékong qui, cependant, même dans son cours inférieur est obstrué de récifs, chutes et autres obstacles rendant obligatoires à plusieurs endroits des transbordements de vapeurs à pirogues et vice-versa. La circulation par cette voie n'est donc pas susceptible d'être beaucoup augmentée;

    (b) Nord, par route menant du Mékong, en face de Paksé à Varin (Ubon) et de là par chemin de fer à Bangkok via d'importants centres commerciaux. La circulation peut se faire en remontant la rivière de Kong à Paksé et est suppléé par une route assez bonne parallèle à la rivière sur la rive gauche du Mékong.

16. Comme l'avenir économique de cette région dépend du développement de ses communications qui peut mieux se faire en améliorant la route du Nord via Varin (Ubon) vers Bangkok et en enlevant la barrière frontalière. Le territoire de Champasak qui se trouve au Nord de la rivière Se Lam Pao devrait de nouveau faire partie du territoire siamois.

Traité du 23 mars 1907

17. Trois ans après Convention de 1904, les Français s'étant retirés de Chantaboun en 1905 mais occupant le territoire siamois de Trat (Krat) à environ 50 kilomètres au Sud-Est, le Traité du 23 mars 1907 (avec Protocole annexe) fut conclu aux termes duquel le Siam cédait à la France les territoires de Battambang, Siemreap et Sisophon et recouvrait de la France les territoires de Trat (Krat) et Dan Sai (une petite projection à la pointe la plus au Sud de la province de Lan Chang (Luang Prabang) et les îles, y compris Koh Kut, au Sud de Laem Ling.

18. Racialement, bien que la majorité de la population des provinces cédées soit d'origine Mon Khmer, les liens entre les peuples séparés par la frontière actuelle sont très serrés à la suite d'une fusion raciale datant d'il y a de nom-

breux siècles. Religion et culture communes et l'assimilation due à des relations sociales et économiques étroites ont développé une intimité que la frontière séparante ne peut faire disparaître. Les habitants d'un côté de la frontière sont alliés racialement à leurs voisins de l'autre côté.

19. Géographiquement et économiquement ces provinces sont étroitement reliées aux territoires situés au nord de la frontière actuelle.

Battambang, le plus au sud des villes et centres commerciaux de ces provinces, est situé entre le port siamois de Bangkok et le port indochinois de Phnom Penh et est relié aux deux par fer et par route. Cependant, le port de Phnom Penh est à 350 kilomètres de la mer et a une capacité inférieure à celle du port de Bangkok qui est seulement à 35 kilomètres du golfe du Siam, et qui subit actuellement des améliorations qui augmenteront matériellement sa capacité. Les autres villes et centres commerciaux sont au moins autant désavantages, en étant séparés par la frontière de 1907 de leur débouché économique et commercial naturel, Bangkok.

20. Pour les raisons ci-dessus il est proposé que la province de Battambang soit restituée au Siam.

21. Les propositions de révision de frontière sont par conséquent pour le Traité de 1893, le rétablissement des prétentions siamoises sur la rive gauche du Mékong: pour la Convention de 1904, la rétrocession des provinces de Lan Chang et de Champasak au Nord de la rivière de Se Lam Pao et pour le Traité de 1907, la restitution de la province de Battambang.

22. En présentant les propositions ci-dessus, je désire expliquer ce que le Gouvernement Royal avait à l'esprit en les arrêtant. Pour mon Gouvernement, le but et l'objet de l'instance en conciliation est de mettre une fois pour toutes les relations entre la France et le Siam sur un pied de stabilité permanente et d'amitié sans réserve, assurant par là une paix durable et des rapports de bon voisinage dans l'Asie du Sud-Est en plein accord avec les principes énoncés dans la Charte des Nations Unies. Dans ce but, il a été tenu compte des sentiments de populations intéressées.

23. Les propositions ci-dessus représentent le sentiment qui subsiste chez le peuple siamois à la suite des différents transferts de territoire du passé. Ils constituent un exposé franc et sincère des vues que le Gouvernement Royal siamois désire soumettre à la Commission dans un but de conciliation avec les vues du Gouvernement français.

24. En se servant de cette procédure de conciliation internationale, le Gouvernement Royal siamois espère réellement que la présente requête exposée au nom du peuple siamois sera considérée par le Gouvernement français dans un esprit de bienveillance généreuse.

Pensant qu'ils pourront être utiles à la Commission, je me permets de lui adresser sous pli séparé cinq exemplaires d'une brève chronologie des événements qui ont précédé la conclusion des trois pactes et trois copies d'une carte montrant les différents transferts de territoire.

J'ai l'honneur d'être, Monsieur,
votre obéissant serviteur

(Signé) *Sakol Varavarn*,
Agent du Gouvernement royal siamois.

N.B. Le numérotage des paragraphes dans la marge a été ajouté par l'agent français pour faciliter la lecture de sa réponse en date du 22 mai.

Chronologie

La chronologie suivante des événements qui ont précédé le Traité du 3 octobre 1893, la Convention du 13 février 1904 et le Traité du 23 mars 1907 qui doivent être considérés par le Commission, peut être utile:

1863 Traité entre le Siam et la Cambodge, dont l'article 1 dit que "le Cambodge est un vassal de l'Etat du Siam"

1867 Traité entre la France et le Siam dont les dispositions principales étaient:
1. reconnaissance du protectorat français sur le Cambodge
2. annulation du traité entre le Siam et le Cambodge (1863)
3. les Provinces de Battambang et Siemreap reconnues comme territoire siamois.
4. droits de navigation non restreints accordés aux Français sur les parties du Mékong et du Grand Lac qui bordent le territoire siamois

1886 Convention (non ratifiée) entre le Siam et la France pour l'encouragement du Commerce entre l'Annam et la province siamoise de Luang Prabang. La France demande la permission d'établir un vice-consulat à Luang Prabang

1886–1887 Des bandes de bandits chinois (Chin-Haw) pillent les deux provinces de Sip Song Chu Thai et Luang Prabang, pendant ceci des troupes françaises pénètrent dans l'ancienne province et un arrangement fut conclu aux termes duquel les troupes siamoises occupaient Hua-Pan pendant que les troupes françaises occupaient Sip Song Chu Thai

1887–1893 Incidents de frontière

1893 Les français envoient deux bateaux de guerre à Bangkok. Chantaboun est occupé par les Français. Afin de résoudre pacifiquement une situation de plus en plus difficile le Traité du 3 Octobre 1893 est conclus.

Monsieur le Président,

Le Prince Sakol, Agent du Gouvernement siamois devant la Commission constituée en vertu de l'article 3 de l'Accord de règlement franco-siamois du 17 novembre 1946, m'a communiqué, conformément aux dispositions du paragraphe 3 de l'article 7 de l'Acte Général de Genève de 1928, le texte de la requête qu'il vous a remise le 12 mai. Cette requête fait suite à la lettre par laquelle il vous avait fait part, à la date du 5 mai, de son intention de présenter, au nom de son Gouvernement, certains arguments en faveur de la révision des clauses du traité du 3 octobre 1893, de la convention du 13 février 1904 et du traité du 23 mars 1907 maintenues en vigueur par l'article 22 du traité du 7 décembre 1937.

Me référant à la lettre que je vous ai, de mon côté, remise le 5 mai, j'ai l'honneur de vous faire tenir ci-joint, pour être soumises à la Commission, les observations que je présente, au nom du Gouvernement français sur la requête du Gouvernement siamois.

Ces observations sont groupées en un mémoire de discussion d'ensemble, auquel j'ai joint en annexe un examen point par point de la requête siamoise.

Vous trouverez ci-joint, pour votre commodité et celle des autres membres de la Commission, cinq exemplaires de ce mémoire, et cinq exemplaires de l'annexe ainsi que des traductions en anglais, en cinq exemplaires également, de chacun de ces deux documents. Enfin, cinq exemplaires du mémoire siamois dont les paragraphes ont été numérotés pour faciliter les références sont joints à cet envoi.

Veuillez agréer, Monsieur le Président, les assurances de ma très haute considération.

Washington, le 22 mai 1947

                                          (Signé) *Francis Lacoste*,
                                          Pour copie certifiée conforme
                                          L'Agent du Gouvernement français,
                                          Francis Lacoste

Son Excellence Monsieur William Phillips
Ancien Ambassadeur des Etats-Unis,
Président de la Commission de Conciliation franco-siamoise,
1718 Eighteenth Street N.W.,
Washington, D.C.

Observations de L'agent du Gouvernement Français sur le Mémoire Déposé le 12 Mai 1947 par L'agent du Gouvernement Siamois Auprès de la Commission de Conciliation Instituée en Vertu de L'accord de Règlement Franco-Siamois du 17 Novembre 1946.

1. Le trait essentiel de la requête présentée à la Commission le 12 mai au nom du Gouvernement siamois est qu'elle tend à un bouleversement total de la structure politique de la péninsule indochinoise. Elle propose, en effet, en reprenant des prétentions antérieures à 1893, de constituer au bénéfice du Siam, sur certains territoires du Cambodge, sur tout le territoire du Laos, et au delà, des droits indéfinis, dont l'effet serait de faire peser une menace permanente sur la paix et la prospérité de l'Asie du Sud-Est; elle propose aussi l'annexion au Siam de parties massives du territoire du Cambodge et du Laos, régions constitutives de l'entité même de ces deux pays, sans lesquelles ils seraient mutilés et défigurés.

2. En regard de cette politique destructive et dangereuse, dont il analysera d'abord les traits essentiels, puis discutera les arguments dans leur ensemble (cette discussion faisant d'autre part—cf. note annexe—l'objet d'un examen critique point par point), le présent mémoire soumettra à la Commission, sous réserve de certaines revendications du Cambodge et du Laos, les arguments du Gouvernement français en faveur du maintien du statu quo rétabli par l'article premier de l'Accord de règlement franco-siamois du 17 novembre 1946.

3. Sur cette base, qui lui paraît conforme à la fois à la situation ethnique et économique, à la géographie, au bon droit, et au véritable intérêt des parties, le Gouvernement français souhaite vivement que la Commission puisse trouver, dans le respect des droits de chacun des Etats intéressés, la voie d'une amélioration durable et féconde des rapports internationaux dans la péninsule indochinoise. A cette oeuvre, il est prêt à donner tout son concours.

I

4. Il importe tout d'abord de faire une remarque essentielle: la requête siamoise ne fait aucune mention de l'Accord de règlement du 17 novembre 1946, dont l'article 3 définit l'objet que la France et le Siam ont convenu de soumettre à l'examen de la Commission. Cet article charge la Commission "d'examiner les arguments ethniques, géographiques et économiques des parties en faveur de la révision ou de la confirmation des clauses du traité du 3 octobre 1893, de la convention du 13 février 1904 et du traité du 23 mars 1907 maintenues en vigueur par l'article 22 du traité du 7 décembre 1937." Or, tout le développement de la requête est consacré à un résumé, à une discussion critique, et à des demandes de révision, des clauses territoriales du traité de 1893, de la convention de 1904 et du traité de 1907, *considérés indépendamment du traité du 7 décembre 1937.*

Celui-ci n'est, en fait, pas plus mentionné que l'Accord de règlement de 1946 lui-même. Le mémoire du 12 mai a pu ainsi introduire dans la présente instance des considérations de caractère historique que l'Accord de règlement n'a pas admises, alors que, depuis le 17 novembre 1946, le traité de 1937 régit à nouveau les rapports des deux pays. Il est et demeure la loi des Parties.

5. Le mémoire du 12 mai formule successivement, à propos de chacun des traités de 1893, 1904 et 1907, des propositions qui n'aboutiraient qu'à détruire ce qu'ils avaient consacré, qui a été confirmé par le traité de 1925 au moment de leur annulation; et confirme une deuxième fois par le traité de 1937 dans son article 22.

6. Le paragraphe 7 de la requête siamoise déclare que "Comme la frontière établie par le Traité de 1893 désavantage non seulement le Siam mais la région cédée a l'Indochine, les prétentions sur les territoires de la rive gauche du Mékong et sur les îles du fleuve auxquelles le Siam a été obligé de renoncer par l'article premier du ce traité doivent être rétablies." Le mémoire substitue ainsi à l'expression employée par le traité de 1893, qui parle de "renonciation à des prétentions sur la rive gauche du Mékong", une expression, "région cédée", qui pourrait faire croire que le Siam a "cédé" a la France des territoires sur lesquels il avait des droits fermes. Une équivoque de même nature avait déjà été produite par le paragraphe 4, qui parle d'un "déplacement de frontières". Or il n'y a jamais eu dans ces pays d'autre établissement du Siam qu'une occupation militaire sporadique, qui n'a duré qu'un bref espace de temps. Il n'y donc jamais eu ni "déplacement de frontière", ni "cession" de territoire à la France. Il y a simplement eu, comme le dit le traité lui même, "renonciation à des prétentions" récentes et jamais validement affirmées; et il n'y a par conséquent jamais eu de "droits".

7. Ceci dit, même à supposer que soit valide l'affirmation suivant laquelle le Siam et le Laos souffrent de "désavantages" du fait de la frontière établie par le traité de 1893 (ce point est examiné au paragraphe 7 de la note annexe), on ne voit pas en quoi le rétablissement des "prétentions" du Siam sur ces régions porterait remède à ces "désavantages."

8. Mais, ce qui est plus important, le premier effet de la "résurrection" de ces prétentions serait d'abolir le traité de 1893, et par voie de conséquence, de faire revivre les difficultés auxquelles il avait mis fin et de faire renaître la politique de spoliation dont le Cambodge et le Laos avaient jusqu'alors été les victimes. Il en résulterait pour le Laos un danger mortel, et pour l'Annam et le Cambodge, une menace permanente et un très grave préjudice. Le moins que l'on puisse dire est que la "résurrection" de ces prétentions ne ferait que créer et entretenir dans la péninsule indochinoise un état d'incertitude dangereux pour la paix et désastreux pour sa prospérité.

Premières conclusions

9. J'ai donc l'honneur de suggérer à la Commission, comme premières conclusions, de rejeter comme non fondés, dangereux, et d'ailleurs non recevables en tant qu'ils reposent sur des considérations historiques, les arguments de la requête siamoise qui viennent d'être discutés.

II

10. L'argumentation ethnique, géographique et économique du mémoire siamois appelle les observations générales suivantes.

Arguments ethniques

11. La plupart de ces arguments présentent cette caractéristique qu'ils paraissent se fonder sur un principe raciste, suivant lequel le Siam aurait un droit naturel à s'annexer tous les territoires circonvoisins du sien où se trouvent des populations de race "thaï".

12. Le racisme a suffisamment fait ses preuves dans l'histoire récente du monde, notamment par celle de ses applications qui a pris le nom de pangermanisme, pour qu'il ne soit pas besoin d'insister sur les dangers qu'il présente, et donc sur l'impossibilité pour une commission de conciliation internationale de retenir des arguments fondés sur une telle doctrine.

Arguments géographiques

13. La requête siamoise expose en substance que le bassin du Mékong forme une unité naturelle, à laquelle doit correspondre, au profit du Siam, une unité politique.

14. Il suffit de transposer ces développements au cas de bassins fluviaux comme par exemple ceux du Rhin et du Danube en Europe, du Putumayo et du Rio Uruguay en Amérique du Sud, ou du Saint Laurent et du Rio Grande en Amérique du Nord, pour mesurer la puissance d'anarchie du précédent qui serait créé si l'on devait accueillir des arguments de cette sorte. Leur application généralisée poserait des problèmes immenses et insolubles, et entraînerait un bouleversement des frontières politiques pour ainsi dire universel. Aucune demande de révision de frontière ne pourrait reposer sur une telle argumentation.

Arguments économiques

15. La plupart des arguments invoqués par la requête siamoise se fondent sur le principe implicite que les régions de production et les régions de consommation des mêmes denrées devraient se trouver réunies à l'intérieur d'une même entité politique.

16. Or il n'y a pas de raison pour que l'union des régions de production et des régions de consommation appartenant à deux États souverains se fasse au profit de l'un plutôt que de l'autre. Le Laos et le Cambodge pourraient, par conséquent, revendiquer à tout aussi juste titre les territoires siamois.

17. La généralisation de ce principe, tout comme celle du principe géographique examine plus haut, provoquerait partout dans le monde une incertitude insoluble en droit quant au choix des états qui devraient en être les bénéficiaires, et en tout cas un bouleversement général.

18. Ce n'est pas sur un principe d'autarcie générateur d'appétits territoriaux dangereux pour la paix que les Nations Unies envisagent de régler les problèmes économiques résultant de l'existence des frontières. Le Gouvernement français estime pour sa part que c'est bien plutôt dans l'assouplissement de celles-ci par des arrangements appropriés qu'il convient de chercher la solution de ces problèmes.

Deuxièmes conclusions

19. En conclusion des développements qui précédent, et sur la base des observations complémentaires contenues dans l'annexe au présent mémoire, j'ai l'honneur de suggérer à la Commission, comme deuxièmes conclusions, de rejeter comme non fondés ou sans portée les arguments ethniques, géographiques et économiques proposés par la requête siamoise.

III

20. Les paragraphes précédents et la note annexe exposent les raisons pour lesquelles le Gouvernement français estime que les arguments du Gouvernement siamois sont dans forces.

21. Le statut territorial en vigueur, fondé sur des traités solennellement confirmés à trois reprises, a été célébré comme un monument de la sagesse du Roi Chulalongkorn, de son Conseiller américain Stroebel et des négociateurs français. Il mérite sa réputation. La frontière que les traités ont tracée a été minutieusement délimitée sur le terrain, et pendant près d'un demi-siècle elle a été une frontière paisible. Si cette paix a été troublée, c'est du seul fait du Japon et de la Thaïlande, à une époque toute récente, dans les conditions que la Commission connaît. Aucune autre frontière ne pourrait offrir aux relations franco-siamoises cette base éprouvée. En revanche, toute amputation du territoire du Cambodge et du Laos attenterait à leur intégrité nationale, dont la défense incombe à la France, et compromettrait gravement leur économie.

22. Enfin, et indépendamment de toutes autres considérations, la Commission se souviendra que ces états et leur population ont été durement éprouvés, économiquement aussi bien que moralement, par la guerre d'agression japonaise

et par les transferts successifs dont certaines parties de leurs territoires viennent d'être l'objet en l'espace de six ans, en sorte que de nouveaux changements affectant ces populations ne peuvent moralement être considérés comme possibles.

Dernières conclusions

23. J'ai donc l'honneur, en conséquence de toute l'argumentation qui précéde, de suggérer à la Commission, comme dernières conclusions, de reconnaître la valeur des arguments exposés ci-dessus et dans la note annexe en faveur de la frontière existante.

24. Le Gouvernement français croit fermement que le respect de traités et la stabilité des frontières sont la condition des relations de bon voisinage. Jusqu'à la veille des événements qui ont conduit à la perte des provinces qui viennent d'être rendues au Cambodge et au Laos, il a donné la preuve, notamment en ce qui concerne l'assouplissement de la frontière du Mékong, de la sincérité de l'esprit de coopération qui l'inspirait. Il est prêt à rechercher dans ce même esprit des aménagements susceptibles de promouvoir, dans le respect des droits de ses associés, l'établissement, entre les états intéressés, d'un régime de paix et de prospérité.

Pour copie certifiée conforme
L' Agent du Gouvernement français
Francis Lacoste

NOTE ANNEXE

Au Mémoire Présenté par L'agent du Gouvernement Français en Réponse au Mémoire Déposé le 12 mai 1947 par L'agent du Gouvernement Siamois

N.B. Les numéros ci-dessous correspondent à ceux qui ont été ajoutés dans la marge de l'exemplaire ci-joint du mémoire siamois.

1. a) La requête siamois omet de mentionner, parmi les références qu'elle cite, le traité du 7 décembre 1937 et le traité du 17 novembre 1946, et d'en tenir compte dans toute la suite de son développement. Les conséquences de cette omission sont examinées dans la partie II du mémoire français.

   b) La requête siamoise se présente elle-même comme un mémoire sommaire. Toutes réserves sont donc faites sur la recevabilité d'arguments nouveaux qui seraient éventuellement présentés dans un mémoire ampliatif.

2. Conséquence de l'omission signalée au point 1-a). Cf. partie II du mémoire français.

3. Même remarque. Cf. également partie II du mémoire français.

4. Indépendamment des considérations de moralité et d'opportunité internationales développées dans la partie II du mémoire français, il convient de noter que l'application de tels arguments dans le cas de la race "thaï" se heurte à des objections graves.

Tout d'abord, il faut rappeler que la notion de "race" est, scientifiquement, l'une des plus controversées et des plus incertaines. D'autre part, l'Accord de Règlement ne parle pas d'arguments "raciaux" mais "ethniques", ce qui met en jeu des facteurs différents. Il y a donc lieu de faire toutes réserves sur la substitution d'un terme à l'autre.

Ceci dit, l'aire d'extension des populations de langue thaï déborde les limites du Siam non seulement au Laos, mais aussi au Nord-Ouest, en Birmanie, sur les plateaux Shan; au Nord, en Chine méridionale (d'où les Thaï sont originaires) jusqu'au Yang Tse; au Nord-Est sur les confins sino-tonkinois, et peut-être jusque dans l'île de Hai Nan. Admettre les arguments "raciaux" du Siam en faveur d'une révision des frontières du Laos serait donc ouvrir la porte à d'autres revendications: d'abord de la part du Siam lui-même (on ne peut oublier qu'il a, pendant la guerre, occupé les Etats Shan peu après avoir occupé une partie du Laos et du Cambodge); et, aussi bien, de la part d'autres états possédant à l'intérieur de leurs frontières des groupes importants parlant des langues thaï.

D'autre part, le Laos est peuplé, partout où le relief s'élève et s'accident, de groupes humains bien différents des Thaï (Kha d'origine indonésienne, Méo et Man).

Enfin, les Laotiens, bien qu'appartenant au groupe des populations de langue thaï, se différencient de la masse de la population de langue thaï du Siam par maintes particularités qui s'expriment dans le dialecte, l'écriture, le costume, le droit, et en diverses coutumes. A cet égard, les Thaï du Siam septentrional et oriental constituent, sous le nom le Laotiens du Nord et de Laotiens de l'Ouest, des groupements qui s'apparentent beaucoup plus étroitement aux habitants du Laos qu'au reste de la population du Siam. La limite ethnique qui sépare les Siamois des populations laotiennes passe à peu près par la ligne de partage des eaux entre le Mékong et le Ménam, et laisse à l'est tout le plateau de Korat, qui s'appelle aussi le "Laos siamois."

On pourrait donc soutenir que, s'il devait y avoir déplacement de frontière, il serait plus logique que ceux des territoires du Siam qui sont peuplés de Laotiens soient rattachés à la seule entité laotienne autonome, c'est-à-dire au Royaume du Laos; plutôt que de voir les territoires de cet état passer sous une administration siamoise.

Pour en terminer avec les observations générales sur l'argumentation ethnique présentée à la Commission de Conciliation par le mémorandum du 12 mai, il reste à remarquer que c'est il y a huit ans seulement que le Siam a substitué à ce nom, dans la nomenclature internationale, le nom racial artificiel de "Thaïlande," au moment où le parti militaire a lancé le pays dans la politique pan-thaï. A la fin de la guerre en Extrême-Orient, le Siam a repris son nom traditionnel dans l'usage international.

Pour ce qui est de l'expression "déplacement de frontière," substituée à l'expression qu'employait le traité de 1893, c'est-à-dire: "renonciation à toute prétention sur la rive gauche du Mékong," cf. partie I du mémoire français.

5. Indépendamment des considérations générales développées dans la partie II du mémoire français, il faut noter qu'en l'espèce l'application du principe de l'unité politique des bassins fluviaux au cas du Mékong peut tout aussi bien conduire à la formation d'un grand Laos au bénéfice du Royaume laotien. Le paragraphe 5 reconnaît d'ailleurs qu'il existe un organisme, la "Haute Commission permanente franco-siamoise du Mékong," chargé de résoudre les difficultés que présente l'administration de cette longue frontière fluviale. Il suffirait de donner à cet organisme, qui a toujours bien fonctionné, les moyens appropriés, pour qu'il rende dans l'avenir de nouveaux services.

6. Cf. partie II du mémoire français. En ce qui concerne l'union des zones de transit et des zones de production ou de consommation, ce principe ne vaut pas mieux que celui de l'union des pays d'économie complémentaire ou prétendument tels. Le cas des Pays-Bas est un exemple frappant.

7. Cf. partie II du mémoire français.

La requête siamoise fait état du désir de voir revivre les prétentions du Siam antérieures à 1893 sur les territoires de la rive gauche du Mékong et sur les îles, mais ne présente aucun argument en faveur de la modification du régime du Mékong lui-même. Il faut rappeler ici les faits suivants:

Le Gouvernement français, dès avant 1939, avait fait connaître sa position et son intention de négocier aux fins d'ouvrir au Siam l'accès à un chenal en eau profonde. Cependant, il n'a jamais été question de céder au Siam toutes les îles du fleuve indistinctement. D'autre part, lorsqu'il a été, pour la dernière fois, c'est-à-dire en 1940, discuté du régime du Mékong au cours d'une négociation conduite dans l'esprit du traité de 1937, il avait été convenu que la France était prête à négocier sur cette question contre la conclusion d'un traité de non-agression lequel d'ailleures fut bien signé, le 12 juin 1940.

On sait ce qui est advenu depuis, alors que le traité de non-agression stipulait pour la troisième fois la confirmation des frontières et le respect mutuel du statu quo. Le Gouvernement français reste néanmoins fidèle à sa politique de 1904 et il est prêt à entrer de nouveau en négociations à ce sujet.

8. Conséquence de l'omission signalée au paragraphe 1. Cf. partie II du mémoire français.

9. Ce paragraphe, qui concerne le Luang Prabang, affirme que la population est en majorité thaï de part et d'autre de la frontière. Voir, sur la valeur de cet argument, la partie II du mémoire français.

10. Ce paragraphe déclare que le traité de 1904 "a projeté une enclave française en territoire siamois." Il convient de faire observer d'abord que le terme d'"enclave" (parfois employé aussi à propos de la province de Bassac), est impropre dans les deux cas: il ne peut s'appliquer qu'à un territoire entièrement entouré de territoires relevant d'une autre souveraineté.

Le fait capital est que le traité de 1904 a donné au Laos, au Nord-Ouest, une frontière qui mérite vraiment le nom de frontière naturelle, car elle est formée par une chaîne de montagnes continue, qui dépasse par endroits 2,000 mètres d'altitude, dont les cols s'abaissent rarement au-dessous de 700 mètres, et qui constitue la ligne de partage des eaux entre le Mékong et le Ménam. Cette frontière a été établie avec le plus grand soin par la Commission de délimitation instituée à la suite de la conclusion du traité de 1904, et elle est déjà le résultat d'une concession au détriment du Laos. Cette commission, en effet, n'a pas voulu retenir les revendications des souverains de Luang Prabang sur certaines hautes vallées situées à l'ouest de la ligne de crête, dans la région dont le chef lieu est Nan; et elle a d'autre part recommandé l'abandon au Siam de la pointe de Dan Sai, abandon auquel le Gouvernement français a effectivement consenti. Si le tracé de cette frontière est jamais remis en question, le Laos ne manquera pas d'invoquer ces droits anciens.

Il faut noter d'autre part qu'après avoir invoqué, au paragraphe 5, à l'appui de sa proposition de révision de la frontière établie par le traité de 1893, un principe suivant lequel les bassins fluviaux devraient constituer autant d'unités politiques, le mémoire siamois propose, dans le paragraphe 10, une grave entorse à ce même principe. En effet, il fait appel, pour justifier sa proposition de révision de la frontière établie par le traité de 1904, à un principe exactement opposé, suivant lequel l'unité de bassin du Mékong devrait être rompue dans le royaume de Luang Prabang, et la partie de ce royaume située en rive droite rattachée au Siam, "afin de donner au Mékong toute sa valeur comme voie d'eau internationale."

Les territoires de la rive droite constituent avec ceux de la rive gauche une de ces unités géographiques dont la requête siamoise recommande ailleurs la constitution. Mais celle-ci, à la différence de celle du Moyen Mékong, à laquelle la requête siamoise voudrait donner une existence politique au profit du Siam, au prix d'un bouleversement des traités, a été, elle, solennellement confirmée dans ses frontières par ces mêmes traités.

Il y a lieu de noter enfin que l'article 4 de la Convention de 1904 maintenu en vigueur par l'article 4 de la Convention de 1926 garantit aux bateaux siamois la liberté de la navigation sur la partie du Mékong qui traverse le territoire du Luang Prabang.

11. Cet argument économique est sans portée. Cf. partie II du mémoire français.

A noter que la région de Luang Prabang est reliée par route à la Cochinchine et aux ports de la côte d'Annam.

12. La requête siamoise demande que la province de Luang Prabang fasse partie du Siam, alors qu'elle n'en a jamais fait partie auparavant, et qu'en 1904 le Siam a renoncé à une simple prérogative de suzeraineté sur les territoires de la rive droite du Mékong comme faisant partie du royaume du Luang Prabang.

13. La grande majorité des habitants de Bassac parle en effet une langue thaïe, mais ceci n'implique pas la nécessité du rattachement au Siam de ce territoire laotien. Au demeurant, la langue parlée dans le Bassac est la langue laotienne, qui est différente du siamois.

14. Ce paragraphe déclare que, "comme c'est souvent le cas, la géographie détermine l'accessibilité, qui a son tour affecte la vie économique de la région," et poursuit par l'examen des facilités de communications dont jouit cette région, en fonction non seulement des éléments naturels, mais des facteurs créés de main d'homme, routes et chemins de fer.

Indépendamment de cet aspect de la question, qui est dûment examiné plus loin, il importe d'appliquer également au cas du Bassac les critères géographiques que la requête siamoise invoque ailleurs. Or, cette méthode montre que, dans cette région non plus, la frontière n'a pas été fixée au hasard, ni arbitrairement, mais, qu'elle passe par la ligne de crête du chaînon montagneux qui prolonge au Nord-Est, en direction de Paksé, la forte barrière naturelle constituée par la chaîne des Dang Rek, orientée Est-Ouest, qui borde au sud le plateau de Korat, et sépare le Siam du Cambodge. Ce chaînon constitue, comme les Dang Rek, la ligne de partage des eaux entre le bassin de la Samoun, qui est la grande artère fluviale du Laos siamois, et le Mékong. Pour la deuxième phrase de ce paragraphe, cf. discussion du point 15 ci-dessous.

15. Il est exact qu'il y a des montagnes au nord-est de la province; il est également exact que cette province est en communication avec le sud par la voie du Mékong, et qu'un transbordement est nécessaire au niveau des chutes de Khon. Une partie de ces transbordements se fait au moyen de pirogues et d'allèges, mais il existe une courte voie ferrée qui contourne les rapides. D'autre part, dire que le rendement de cette voie d'eau ne peut pas être amélioré est une affirmation sans preuve. Mais surtout, la requête siamoise omet de dire qu'il existe une route (la "Route fédérale No. 13") qui prolonge vers le sud jusqu'à Saigon la route dont il est parlé au sous-paragraphe b.

D'après ce sous-paragraphe, les voies de transit vers le nord et vers le Siam sont telles que, du point de vue des transports, il y aurait avantage à rattacher le Bassac, jusqu'au Se Lam Pao, au Siam, mais, de l'aveu même de la requête, il faudrait également transborder les marchandises à Pakse et à Oubon. D'autre part, le mémoire signale que la voie d'eau est doublée de ce qu'il appelle "une route assez bonne" sur la rive gauche. Cette route, dont il reconnaît les mérites quand elle conduit vers le nord, est la même dont il a omis de signaler la section sud. En réalité, la route fédérale No.13 qui relie Luang Prabang à Saigon, dessert Paksé et le Bassac. En outre, deux bretelles, également routes fédérales, la relient elle même aux ports de la côte d'Annam (Thakhekh à Vinh, et Savannakhet à Quang Tri).

16. Cf. partie II du mémoire français.

Il est remarquable que la requête siamoise invoque l'utilisation d'une route sur la rive gauche du Mékong comme argument en faveur du rattachement au Siam des territoires de la rive droite.

17. Cet article est hors du sujet.

18. Si les populations des territoires siamois contigus au Cambodge sont, comme le déclare le paragraphe 18, "racialement alliées" à celles du Cambodge lui-même, ce n'est pas, comme il le prétend, le résultat de fusions entre races différentes, mais la conséquence du fait que la frontière politique passe, en cette région, pour des motifs d'ordre purement géographique indiqués au paragraphe 19 ci-dessous, sensiblement à l'est de la limite ethnique. Si, comme le propose la requête du Gouvernement siamois, l'on faisait coïncider la frontière politique entre le Siam et ce qui resterait du Cambodge à la limite Sud et Est de la province de Battambang, cette frontière séparerait encore des populations khmères, tandis que si on voulait la faire coïncider avec la limite ethnique, il faudrait la déplacer considérablement vers le Nord et l'Ouest, donc au détriment du Siam.

19. Le paragraphe 19 se borne à affirmer que "géographiquement et économiquement, ces provinces sont étroitement liées aux territoires situés au nord de la frontière actuelle," mais omet d'articuler aucune démonstration de cette assertion en ce qui concerne son aspect géographique. En réalité, la structure géographique de cette région impose, comme il est indiqué au précédent paragraphe, une frontière naturelle évidente, qui est la chaîne des Dang Rek, ligne de partage des eaux entre le Semoun au Nord et le bassin constitué par le Mékong inférieur et son vaste réservoir du Grand Lac (la Tonlé Sap) au sud.

Si l'on abandonnait la ligne des Dang Rek, on ne trouverait, au sud, aucune frontière géographique satisfaisante. L'expérience a d'ailleurs été faite: lorsque le Gouvernement thaïlandais a voulu, en 1941, avec l'assistance du Gouvernement japonais, reporter la frontière politique au sud, afin de donner à la Thaïlande une partie du territoire cambodgien, il a dû, à défaut d'une frontière naturelle, fixer artificiellement la nouvelle frontière politique au 15ème grade, frontière aussi indifférente à la géographie physique qu'elle l'était à la géographie humaine, et au fait qu'entre les Dang Rek, au Nord, et elle, il n'y avait que des populations cambodgiennes et Mon Khmer, mais aucunes populations siamoises.

Bien que la requête siamoise omette de discuter les caractéristiques géographiques de la frontière du Cambodge à l'ouest, il paraît utile de les décrire: à la chaîne des Dang Rek succède, au sud-ouest, après la trouée de Poipet, un immense massif forestier, entièrement désert, qui constitue une véritable séparation naturelle entre les régions peuplées en majorité de Siamois à l'ouest et les pays de populations cambodgiennes à l'est et au sud-est. La seule observation que l'on puisse faire à ce sujet est que le tracé de la frontière à travers cette forêt inhabitée se trouve de 25 à 50 kilomètres à l'est de la ligne de partage des eaux entre les bassins du Ménam et du Mékong, en sorte que si l'on voulait appliquer ici le principe de l'unité des bassins fluviaux invoqué par la requête siamoise dans son paragraphe 5, c'est au détriment des territoires du Siam que cette frontière devrait être déplacée. Au sud de la forêt, le massif du Khao Kuop (1265 mètres) achève de fermer à l'ouest le pays cambodgien de Battambang.

La frontière de 1907 a laissé au Siam une bande littorale de territoire extraordinairement mince, large de quelques centaines de mètres seulement, mais longue de 40 kilomètres, dans le dessein évident de laisser au Siam quelques villages côtiers habités par de pêcheurs. Si des arguments de pure géographie étaient invoqués pour motiver ici une modification du tracé de la frontière, c'est manifestement au profit du Cambodge que cette modification devrait de faire.

Enfin, le paragraphe 19 fait observer que le port de Phnom Penh est à 350 kilomètres de la mer, et que sa capacité est inférieure à celle du port de Bangkok, situé à 35 kilomètres seulement du golfe du Siam. Mais le port de Phnom Penh, qui d'ailleurs reçoit des navires de 4,000 à 5,000 tonnes, n'est pas seul à assurer le trafic de la région de Battambang: cette région est également reliée par une voie d'eau continue, par deux routes, et, sur une partie de la distance, par la voie ferrée de Battambang à Phnom Penh, avec le port de Saigon. Or celui-ci reçoit des navires de 30,000 tonnes.

20. Il résulte de la discussion du paragraphe 19 ci-dessus que la conclusion inscrite au paragraphe 20 est sans fondement et entièrement inacceptable.

21. Récapitulation des propositions de révision formulées dans le mémoire siamois, auxquelles il a été répondu dans les paragraphes précédents.

22. Dans ce paragraphe le Gouvernement siamois indique qu'en élaborant ses propositions, il a considéré que le "but de la procédure de conciliation qui vient de s'engager était de placer les relations entre la France et le Siam, une fois pour toutes, sur un pied de stabilité permanente et d'amitié sans réserve afin d'assurer

une paix durable et des rapports de bon voisinage dans l'Asie sud-orientale en plein accord avec les principes énoncés dans la Charte des Nations Unies." Les sentiments et les désirs du Gouvernement français lui-même, en abordant la présente instance, ne sauraient être plus heureusement définis. Mais il semble y avoir quelque ironie à demander au Gouvernement français de consentir, pour prix de la réalisation de désirs aussi légitimes et aussi respectables, l'annulation des dispositions essentielles du traité conclu il y a six mois, en vertu duquel cette procédure de conciliation a été instituée; de forcer le Cambodge et le Laos, victimes de l'agression de 1941, à abandonner à nouveau les territoires qui viennent à peine de leur être rendus; et de laisser ressusciter, sur ce qui resterait du territoire de ces deux Etats, des prétentions que le mémoire du 12 mai ne tente même pas de justifier, et qui ne se fonderaient en réalité que sur des incursions militaires.

23. Le paragraphe 24 déclare que les propositions de la requête siamoise répondent au sentiment qui subsiste chez le peuple siamois à la suite des divers transferts de territoire du passé. La réalité, c'est que les revendications ne sont pas nées spontanément dans l'opinion, mais que l'état de l'opinion a été artificiellement créé, à une époque toute récente, dont le début coïncide avec les premiers efforts, en 1937, du parti militaire siamois pour prendre le pouvoir. Aussitôt après la défaite des armées françaises en Europe ces efforts, conjugués avec ceux du Japon, ont conduit à la guerre de 1940-1941 et à l'occupation par le Siam de territoires cambodgiens et laotiens.

Pour juger de l'état de l'opinion siamoise jusqu'à la veille même du triomphe des doctrines pan-thaï du parti militaire, il suffit de constater que jusqu'en 1940 aucun gouvernement siamois n'a formulé de réclamations contre l'ordre territorial définitivement établi en 1907.

Les deux déclarations suivantes sont édifiantes:

1. A la séance de clôture des négociations de l'arrangement commercial et douanier entre la France et le Siam, en octobre 1937, Luang Pradit (Nai Pridi Phanomyong) rendait hommage à l'esprit amical et compréhensif dans lequel la France et l'Indochine ont répondu aux demandes siamoises de révision des traités. Il ajoutait que l'arrangement commercial et douanier qui venait d'être négocié était bien l'expression de l'esprit de bon voisinage qui devait continuer à caractériser les relations des deux pays.

2. Au moment de la ratification du traité du 7 décembre 1937, le janvier 1939, le Ministre des Affaires Etrangères du Siam, Chao Phraya Srithammathibet, confirmait les dispositions de son prédécesseur en télégraphiant à son collègue français:

…permettez-moi d'exprimer à Votre Excellence, au nom du Gouvernement, ma vive appréciation de l'esprit amical que le Gouvernement français a témoigné pendant tout le cours des négociations. Je n'oublie point que le France a été la première des Puissances à entamer les négociations à Bangkok et que l'approbation des accords conclus a reçu le vote unanime des Chambres. Le nouveau traité j'en suis persuadé, servira à renforcer les rapports d'amitié qui unissent déjà si heureusement nos deux pays…

Ce n'est pas là le ton de ministres qui ont des revendications à faire valoir. Il fait contraste avec le ton de la requête actuelle du Gouvernement siamois.

Le pacte de non-agression franco-siamois signé le 12 juin 1940 et ratifié par le Siam le 5 août suivant confirmait à nouveau dans son article 1 l'engagement des Parties de "respecter leur intégrité territoriale." De plus, celles-ci s'interdisaient expressément par l'article 5 toute action tendant à susciter ou favoriser une agitation propagande ou tentative d'intervention ayant pour but de porter atteinte à leur intégrité territoriale.

Sans retracer ici l'histoire décevante des années qui ont suivi, il y a lieu de rappeler que c'est quelques semaines seulement après la ratification de ce pacte par le Siam que celui-ci renversait sa politique officielle et présentait ses premières exigences.

C'est en effet dans un aide-mémoire adressé à la France le 17 septembre 1940 qu'apparaît pour la première fois l'idée dangereuse d'une sorte d'hypothèque sur le Laos et le Cambodge qui s'exprime dans la requête du 12 mai 1947—l'aide-mémoire du 17 septembre 1940 demandait la délimitation du Mékong frontière en suivant le chenal en eau profonde et l'adoption du Mékong comme frontière du nord au sud jusqu'à la frontière du Cambodge, c'est-à-dire l'annexion par la Thaïlande des territoires situés sur la rive droite du Mékong en face de Luang Prabang et de Paksé (province de Bassac rive droite). Le document se terminait par la phrase suivante: "Le Gouvernement de Sa Majesté serait également reconnaissant au Gouvernement français de bien vouloir lui donner, sous forme de lettre, l'assurance qu'en cas de changement de souveraineté française, la France rétrocéderait à la Thaïlande les territoires du Laos et du Cambodge".

C'est donc de l'existence même de ces deux pays qu'il s'agit. Or, dans toute cette affaire, la France intervient pour défendre les intérêts du Laos et du Cambodge. Elle ne peut abandonner ses associés, et doit rester d'autant plus effectivement à leurs côtés qu'ils sont l'objet de menaces plus précises.

On voit bien, d'autre part, comment les demandes siamoises forment un ensemble indivisible. Toute concession accordée sur un point engagerait en réalité tout l'ensemble.

C'est pourquoi il paraît nécessaire que la Commission écarte, avec l'autorité qui s'attache à son caractère international, les arguments de la requête siamoise. C'est en effet à cette condition seulement que les relations de bon voisinage que la France et ses associés souhaitent entretenir avec le Siam pourront se développer.

N.B. La chronologie annexée au mémoire siamois ne fait dans le mémoire français l'objet d'aucune discussion, ce document étant sans pertinence aux termes de l'article 3 de l'Accord de règlement du 17 novembre 1946.

Pour copie certifiée conforme
L'Agent du Gouvernement français
Francis Lacoste

Traduit de l'anglais
No. 3/2490

Ambassade Royale du Siam,
Washington, D.C.
29 mai 1947

L'Honorable Président de la Commission de Conciliation
Washington D.C.

Monsieur le Président,

J'ai l'honneur de me référer à ma lettre No. 2/2490 du 12 mai 1947 qui présentait un résumé sommaire des arguments ethniques, géographiques et économiques sur lesquels sont fondées des propositions de révision des frontières de 1883, 1904 et de soumettre à la Commission pour examen additionnel, les observations ci-jointes, sur la lettre, les observations et la note annexe que l'Agent du Gouvernement français vous a présentées le 22 mai 1947, ainsi que des considérations ampliatives sur les aspects ethniques, géographiques et économiques des frontières de 1893, 1904 et 1907.

J'ai l'honneur d'être, Monsieur le Président, votre obéissant serviteur.

(Signé) Prince Sakol Varavarn,
Agent du Gouvernement
Royal siamois

Traduit de l'anglais
29 mai 1947

Observations de L'agent du Gouvernement Siamois sur la Note, les Observations et L'annexe Présentée le 22 Mai 1947 par L'agent du Gouvernement Français

I

1. Les observations présentées par l'Agent du Gouvernement français sont caractérisées par le fait qu'elles sont principalement fondées sur des allégations politiques. Dans de nombreux cas, l'Agent français a réfuté les arguments contenus dans la note de l'Agent siamois, non pas en se fondant sur des raisons ethniques, géographiques ou économiques conformément a l'Accord de règlement du 17 novembre 1946, mais au moyen d'allusions politiques explicites ou implicites que ne semblent pas pertinentes. Il n'entre pas cependant dans les intentions de l'agent siamois de rétorquer par ces arguments tendancieux. Seules, les explications et défenses nécessaires seront soumises afin d'éviter des malentendus.

II

2. L'Agent français affirme dans le point 1 de ses observations que la requête siamoise tendrait à bouleverser la structure politique actuelle en Indochine et constituerait une menace permanente pour la paix et la prospérité de l'Asie du Sud-Est. Sans entrer dans une discussion sur la nature de la soi-disant structure politique," il est nécessaire de remarquer que cette sorte d'argument ne semble pas compatible avec les termes de l'Accord de règlement du 17 novembre 1946, article 3 qui stipule expressément que la Commission de Conciliation "est chargée d'examiner les arguments ethniques, géographiques et économiques des parties en faveur de la *révision ou de la confirmation des* clauses des traités du 3 octobre 1893, etc....

En ce qui concerne les soi-disant mutilation et démembrement du Laos et du Cambodge suggérés par l'Agent français comme devant survenir dans le cas où la requête siamoise serait approuvée par la Commission, on devrait garder présent à l'esprit que la requête actuelle du Siam constitue seulement une part des sacrifices de ce pays pour la paix.

3. En fait, le souci principal du Siam est la paix et la stabilité et comme la requête soumise à la Commission par l'Agent siamois n'est fondée que sur des considérations ethniques, économiques et géographiques, en stricte conformité avec les termes de l'Accord de règlement, cette requête ne produire aucun des effets prévus au point 2 des observations françaises.

De plus, les réserves faites par l'Agent du Gouvernement français concernant les "revendications" du Cambodge et du Laos ne semblent également pas pertinentes. Comme l'Accord de règlement de 1946 n'est intervenu qu'entre le Siam et la France, des revendications faites au nom des tiers, qui pourraient ne pas profiter de leur satisfaction, sont inadmissibles. Cet argument n'implique pas, cependant, que le Gouvernement siamois a des objections à savoir des rapports directs avec le Laos et le Cambodge libres et indépendants. Au contraire, le Gouvernement siamois est prêt à les accueillir dans la Famille des Nations.

Le Gouvernement siamois, pour sa part, n'est pas moins désireux que quiconque de voir une amélioration constructive et durable des relations internationales dans la partie du monde qui le concerne le plus. Il est cependant d'avis qu'un tel état de choses ne peut être atteint à moins que les véritables intérêts des peuples concernes ne soient pris en considération et que compte soit tenu de leur opinion exprimée librement et équitablement. Sur de telles bases le Gouvernement siamois donnerait de tout son coeur son appui total.

III

4. L'Agent français au point 4 de ses observations dit que la note siamoise n'a pas fait mention de l'Accord de règlement de 1946 ni du Traité de 1937, ceci semble être le résultat d'un malentendu. En fait, la note du 12 mai de l'Agent siamois au Président de la Commission de Conciliation fait suite à sa lettre du 5 mai, dans laquelle il s'était déjà référé au Traité de 1937 ainsi qu'à l'Accord de règlement de 1946. De plus, la note siamoise ne s'est occupée que des clauses des traités qui furent maintenues en vigueur par le Traité de 1937, afin de permettre à la Commission d'examiner en ordre convenable les arguments ethniques, géographiques et économiques visés à l'article 3 de l'Accord de règlement de 1946.

5. L'affirmation contenue dans le point 5 des observations françaises, d'après laquelle les propositions comprises dans la note siamoise auraient pour résultat la destruction de tout ce qui avait été achevé et avait été ensuite confirmé par les traités successifs entre le Siam et la France, semble ignorer les termes de l'Accord de 1946 qui a établi la Commission de Conciliation dans le but de reconsidérer la situation résultant des clauses des Traités de 1893, 1904 et 1907? Il est donc évident qu'en concluant l'Accord en question, les parties en cause reconnurent explicitement la nécessite d'un tel ré-examen.

6. Le point 6 des observations françaises discute les droits du Siam sur les territoires de la rive gauche du Mékong et prétend qu'en fait, ces droits n'existaient pas avant la conclusion du Traité de 1893.

Néanmoins, malgré cette objection, bien des documents et faits contemporains au traité mentionné plus haut, tels que le témoignage contenu dans le Livre Bleu publié par le British Foreign Office,[1] une carte française intitulée "Carte pour suivre l'expédition du Tonkin," faite à Paris en 1884 (E. Andriveau-Goujon, Editeur, 4 rue du Bac),[2] et spécialement une requête adressée par le Gouvernement français au Gouvernement siamois pour la nomination d'un Vice-Consul français à Luang Prabang, prouvent de façon concluante la réalité des droits du Siam sur ces territoires. D'un autre côté, bien que le Traité de 1893 n'ait seulement mentionné que le Siam renonçait à ses prétentions ou "claims" sur les territoires de la rive gauche, la simple existence d'une pareille clause montre clairement que le Gouvernement français à cette époque admettait implicitement les véritables liens politiques qui liaient le Siam à ces territoires.

Le point 12 de l'appendice français prétend aussi que la province de Luang Prabang n'avait jamais fait partie du Siam et qu'en 1904 le Siam a renoncé à une simple prérogative de suzeraineté sur les territoires de la rive droite du Mékong comme formant partie du royaume de Luang Prabang. A cet égard, l'Agent siamois ne désire pas se lancer dans une argumentation purement historique; la carte française citée plus haut et la citation suivante d'une lettre envoyée par le Comte de Rosebery au Comte de Dufferin en date du 2 septembre 1893 devrait suffire à justifier la requête siamois:

> …Il était au moins certain qui l'Etat de Luang Prabang avait pendant une période de plus de 70 ans reconnu la suzeraineté siamoise, et que pendant plusieurs années il avait été en pratique contrôlé par un Commissaire siamois. Le Gouvernement français avait, de plus, reconnu lui-même la souveraineté du Siam sur Luang Prabang par la signature de la Convention du 7 mai 1886 qui prévoit la nomination d'un Vice-Consul français là, et par la demande qu'il a adressée ensuite au Gouvernement siamois en vue d'obtenir l'exequatur pour le fonctionnaire qui fut nommé…[3]

Comme ce document émane d'une source autorisée, il devrait être considéré comme suffisant pour neutraliser l'effet de l'affirmation française.

7. Il ressort des considérations précédentes, que si un changement était fait conformément à la requête siamoise, les habitants des territoires concernés, qui réclament la réalisation de leurs aspirations, partageraient avec les populations du Siam qui leur sont apparentées une totale liberté politique, sociale et économique et jouiraient d'une vie libre et démocratique dans laquelle chacun, quels que soient sa croyance, son rang, son dialecte ou sa religion peut exercer les mêmes droits et recevoir la même protection et par là prendre une part complète dans le Gouvernement de son pays. Un autre avantage qui résulterait de la révision du Traité de 1893 est que seraient de nouveau réunis les membres de familles qui vivaient autrefois des deux côtés du Mékong en communautés étroitement associées mais qui ont été séparés en 1893 en contravention de raisons ethniques, géographiques et économiques et même de principes d'humanité, par une rivière qui jusque là était leur centre de vie commun. C'est par la réalisation d'aspirations aussi légitimes et par le retour de fleuve à sa fonction antérieure de source non limitée de vie et de liberté au lieu de son emploi actuel comme

barrière séparant des familles et des communautés, que la paix, la prospérité et le bonheur reviendront enfin à ces territoires. Aucun rapport écrit ou oral sur les relations intimes des habitants des deux rives du Mékong ne peut représenter les liens uniques qui existent entre eux. Pour les comprendre, il faut les voir et si la Commission décide de vérifier elle-même la vérité sur place, l'agent siamois fera tout son possible pour assurer leur bienvenue.

8. La description contenue dans le point 8 des observations de l'Agent français des conséquences qui résulteraient de l'annulation du Traité de 1893, semble sortie du domaine des considérations d'ordre ethnique, géographique et économique. Il suffit de suggérer un examen complet des conditions actuelles des populations sur les côtés français et siamois de la frontière. Quant au "danger mortel" qui menacerait le Laos s'il s'était réuni au Siam, on croit qu'après tous les importants faits ethniques, géographiques et économiques déposés devant la Commission, on verra qu'il est imaginaire. "Dans de larges parties de l'Indochine" écrit Bruno Lasker dans *Peuples de l'Asie du Sud-Est* (page 69),

> ...les populations n'ont pas de quoi se nourrir et pourtant, alors que les entreprises dominées par du capital étranger—la culture du caoutchouc et les mines de charbon par exemple—se sont développées par bonds rapides, la production du riz et aussi celles de toutes les plantes nourricières indigènes est restée en arrière de l'augmentation de la population.

Il semble de plus que l'affirmation française visée ci-dessus n'est étayée par aucun fait ou opinion équitablement exprimée de la part des peuples intéressés. Au contraire, l'Agent siamois est fermement convaincu que si l'on donnait aux populations du Laos, du Cambodge et de l'Annam l'occasion de le faire par un referendum, les véritables sentiments et dispositions seraient révélés. La Commission aurait alors la preuve absolue qu'au lieu de faire des objections à ce que leurs compatriotes ou voisins atteignaient l'indépendance et la liberté, les peuples du Cambodge et de l'Annam appuieraient de coeur. Bruno Lasker a dit ceci à la page 222 de son même livre: "Les patriotes indochinois attendent, sans doute prêts à se servir de l'échec des français, à exercer leur protection, pour réclamer après la guerre le statut de nation".

En raison de ce qui précède, l'agent siamois réaffirme que la requête qu'il a soumise à la Commission ne tend en aucune façon à créer ou à maintenir un état d'incertitude dangereux dans la péninsule indochinoise. Au contraire, si la frontière était révisée comme il est suggéré dans la note du 12 mai, la paix et la prospérité seraient sur le point d'être atteintes dans cette partie du monde.

9. Contre la première conclusion de l'Agent français contenue dans le point 9 de ces remarques, l'Agent siamois fait remarquer que dans sa note du 12 mai,

il n'a soumis à l'examen de la Commission aucun autre argument que ceux mentionnés à l'article 3 de l'Accord de règlement de 1946, à savoir: les arguments ethniques, géographiques et économiques. De plus, comme ils sont fondés sur des témoignages dignes de confiance et qu'ils ne tendent à aucun autre objet que la paix et la stabilité, ils ne pourraient être sans fondement et dangereux. L'Agent siamois a, par conséquent, l'honneur de recommander l'adoption par la Commission de la requête siamoise.

IV

10. La réfutation sur le terrain ethnique contenue dans les assertions françaises a, de l'avis de l'Agent siamois, manqué son but et est sans rapport avec les dispositions de l'Accord de règlement. En fait, les considérations ethniques contenues dans la note siamoise sont aussi loin du racisme que la revendication de droits antérieurs du Siam est loin d'aucune forme d'expansionnisme. En fait, dans les arguments présentés par l'Agent siamois, aucune allusion d'aucune sorte n'a été faite à une forme de supériorité de la race thaï ni à aucun autre élément de doctrine raciste, et étant donné que le Siam n'a pas l'intention de dominer les peuples dans les territoires concernes mais de leur donner le bénéfice de la liberté démocratique ainsi que d'autres droits ainsi qu'il a été exposé dans les paragraphes précédents, on ne peut lui attribuer aucune ambition expansionniste. A cet égard, une citation de Bruno Lasker *Peuples de l'Asie du Sud-Est* (page 207) peut être utile. Il dit:

> …seules quelques personnes sophistiquées, avec une éducation moderne, pourraient être racistes, car les différentes branches des souches indigènes ont été séparées et exposées à de nombreuses expériences historiques différentes. Chaque branche a eu à s'adapter aux demandes de son environnement géographique qui ne pouvait manquer de mettre sa marque sur leur façon de vivre, sur la sélection naturelle et ainsi éventuellement sur les caractéristiques physiques également. Ils furent écartes de plus les uns des autres par des possibilité différentes d'interménage avec d'autres groupes raciaux. Et ils oublièrent leurs ancêtres communs.

Il semble y avoir, d'autre part, quelque malentendu dans les observations françaises sur la signification des mots "ethnique" et "racial" employés dans la note siamoise. Pour corriger ce malentendu, l'Agent siamois demande la permission de se référer au dictionnaire de l'Académie française par lequel le terme "ethnique" est défini ainsi qu'il suit: "ethnique:—qui tient à la race".

En ce qui concerne l'argument contenu dans le point 4 de l'appendice français, une partie tombe dans le cadre des paragraphes précédents et n'a pas besoin d'être revue davantage. En ce qui concerne les allusions d'une nature politique indiquant que la "révision de la frontière du Laos ouvrirait les portes à d'autres revendications de la part du Siam ainsi que de la part d'autres pays possédant à l'intérieur de leurs frontières d'importants groupes parlant la langue thaï," l'Agent siamois désire faire observer que le mémoire français a complètement oublié le fait qu'il existe entre la France et le Siam un Accord de règlement conclu en 1946 dont l'article 3 mentionne clairement la possibilité de révision des Traités de 1893, 1904 et 1907. Il n'existe par de pareil document international en ce qui concerne les autres parties auxquelles il est fait allusion dans le document français.

L'appendice français a aussi fait remarquer les différences existant entre les Laotiens et la masse de la population du Siam, aussi bien que l'existence dans le Siam du Nord d'habitants qui sont plus apparentés à ceux du Laos qu'à ceux du reste de la population du pays et par raisonnement logique, a suggéré que si un transfert devait avoir lieu, les territoires siamois qui sont habités par des Laotiens devraient être rattachés au "Royaume français du Laos" plutôt qu'au territoire laotien du Siam.

A cet égard, il convient de remarquer qu'il y a très peu de pays, s'il y en a, qui peuvent se vanter d'avoir une population homogène. Il est à peine besoin de citer le cas de la France elle-même dont le provincialisme fait la joie des touristes qui, quand ils traversent le pays d'Alsace en Bretagne et d'île de France en Provence, ne sont jamais fatigués d'admirer les changements locaux, les costumes, dialectes, usages, aussi bien que de bien d'autres caractéristiques.

Pour ce qui est du Siam, les arguments français ne mettent pas en question l'identité d'origine raciale ou ethnique de sa population mais insiste seulement sur les variations de langue et de traits culturels qui peuvent être remarquées dans tout pays.

En ce qui concerne la suggestion que dans le cas d'un transfert, le territoire siamois habité par les Laotiens devrait être logiquement rattaché au "Royaume du Laos" plutôt que l'alternative contraire, l'Agent siamois regrette d'avoir à faire remarquer le danger d'une pareille implication, à laquelle il fait allusion non seulement au point 4 de l'appendice français, mais aussi également, dans d'autres paragraphes du même document. Le Laos et Le Cambodge étant pour le moment inclus dans le cadre politique français des revendications éventuelles faites par la France, même pour leur compte, ne peuvent signifier, la résurrection de la période d'expansion dont les Traités de 1893, 1904 et 1907 portent la marque et dont les victimes furent le Laos et le Cambodge.

De plus, le paragraphe de l'appendice français mentionné plus haut parle du "Royaume du Laos." Des éclaircissements supplémentaires seraient nécessaires sur cette appellation avec laquelle même des personnes qui devraient être bien au courant des affaires d'Indochine, ne semblent pas être familières. En 1893, le Siam perdit au profit de la France, le territoire de la rive gauche du Mékong, y compris le territoire de Luang Prabang, qui ne possédait qu'une juridiction limitée. En 1904, le Siam eut à nouveau à céder à la France les provinces de Lan Chang et Champasak (ou Bassac); la première fut ajoutée au Royaume de Luang Prabang. A cette époque et même plus tard, la juridiction du Royaume de Luang Prabang était limitée et ne s'étendit jamais à tout le territoire du Laos. A la fin de la guerre du Pacifique et après la capitulation des forces japonaises, un mouvement appelé le Lao Libres fut constitué et aida l'armée chinoise à désarmer des troupes japonaises. Plus tard, quand les autorités françaises reprirent le contrôle du Laos, elles commencèrent à établir ce qui est appelé dans les remarques françaises le "Royaume du Laos".

La remarque concernant le nom de "Thailand" qui, selon le document français a correspondu à la période pendant laquelle le soi-disant parti militaire s'est lancé dans une politique pan-thäi, ne mène à aucune conclusion définitive; au contraire, elle fait ressortir bien plus clairement le fait que les Siamois ont toujours, depuis un temps immémorial, et même jusqu'au moment présent, appelé leur pays "Muang Thai" [ou?—Ed.] de "Pratet Thai" qui veut dire "le pays des Thai." Comme d'autre part, les circonstances qui ont amené le retour de l'appellation "Siam" n'ont aucun rapport avec les termes établis par l'Accord de règlement. L'Agent siamois s'abstient d'une digression sur ce sujet.

Arguments géographiques

10. En ce qui concerne les arguments géographiques présentés par l'Agent français, il est nécessaire de bien faire remarquer que le Gouvernement siamois n'a jamais eu le désir de suggérer une généralisation du régime propose pour la rivière Mékong. Il se rend trop bien compte du fait que toute rivière par sa nature géographique, ses conditions locales économiques et autres devrait recevoir un régime approprié s'il doit être tenu compte du bien-être des populations. Dans le cas particulier du Mékong, la différence de régime rend son emploi par les habitants locaux exagérément difficile, incommode et même dangereux. Pour appuyer cette affirmation, on peut citer les lignes suivantes extraites d'un livre par un auteur français, A. Agard, intitulé *L'Indochine orientale*:

> Les relations directes de Vientiane avec le Sud trahissent en quelque sorte l'influence française en permettant d'écouler vers le Siam un important trafic de produits animaux (boeufs, buffles, éléphants, chevaux, peaux, de produits forestiers (teck) et d'en recevoir des produits manufacturés (étoffes, pacotilles, pétrole) échappant à tout contrôle par le fait de la contrebande...

Les difficultés résultant de la diversité des régimes existent probablement sur d'autres frontières, mais dans le cas du Mékong, elles sont très accentuées.

Cette rivière était jusqu'en 1904 un cours d'eau interne, servant la communauté riveraine qui formait une unité géographique, économique aussi bien que sociale. Avec son nouveau rôle de frontière, elle divise les familles et sépare les parents qui vivaient ensemble autrefois et tend à créer de nouvelles barrières à la vie en commun antérieure.

En ce qui concerne la référence faite par l'Agent français dans ses observations au sujet de différentes rivières en Europe, observations au sujet de différentes rivières en Europe et en Amérique au Nord et du Sud, on ne peut nier que la diversité des régimes a amené des difficultés importantes, spécialement dans le cas du Danube, du Rhin et du Rio Grande, difficultés pour les quelles les Commissions qui ont été établies à cet effet ont à peine pu trouver des solutions. De plus, si aucun changement pour le mieux n'a été adopté dans ces cas, ce fut à cause d'obstacles qui n'existent pas dans le cas du Mékong. Cette rivière, comme il a été expliqué expressément plus haut, n'a connu aucun autre régime que celui d'une rivière interne jusqu'au moment où la domination française s'est étendue sur les territoires de la rive gauche. Les difficultés qui de sont élevées depuis cette époque sont les conséquences de sa fonction artificielle.

Il résulte de ce qui précède que la réfutation présentée par l'Agent français contre les arguments sommaires soumis par l'Agent siamois, est loin d'atteindre son objet, parce qu'elle est fondée sur une supposition qui n'a jamais été exprimée ou appliquée par la note siamoise, et parce qu'elle a recours à des insinuations politiques qui ne sont pas supportées par les faits, étant donné que cette même rivière avait servi un groupe ethnique qui peut être considéré comme une unité.

Les points 18 et 19 de l'appendice français, bien qu'ayant trait à une matière technique, révèlent des idées expansionnistes dangereuses et le Siam a eu l'expérience pénible d'efforts de ce genre pour trouver une frontière techniquement, d'abord en 1867, puis en 1893, puis de nouveau dans les Traités de 1904 et 1907—tous tendant à des frontières meilleures. Dans ces recherches successives, de bonnes frontières ne pouvaient être trouvées qu'en entrant plus avant dans le terrain siamois.

L'allusion à la période de 1941 a, d'un autre côté, peu de rapport avec le sujet. L'Agent siamois indiquera seulement que si une soi-disant "frontière artificielle" fit l'objet d'un accord entre les Gouvernements français et siamois à cette époque, ce fut à cause du fait que le Gouvernement siamois consentit à ne pas inclure Angkor Wat dans les territoires rétrocédés par respect pour les sentiments des Cambodgiens et par déférence pour les efforts archéologiques des savants français.

Arguments économiques

11. Les raisons sommaires avancées par l'Agent siamois dans sa note du 12 mai indiquent simplement la nature complémentaire des occupations économiques des habitants du bassin du Mékong. L'Agent siamois maintient qu'une association aussi rapprochée justifie le terme d'unité économique. Cette caractéristique n'est pas entendue pour une application générale. Dans certains cas, quand les circonstances sont favorables, les régions intéressées peuvent faire partie d'accords spéciaux par lesquels un régime économique commun est adopté. Ceci fut le cas de la Belgique et du Luxembourg.

D'un autre côté, en proposant cet argument économique, l'Agent siamois ne pensait à aucun principe d'autarchie qui, selon les observations françaises stimule les appétits territoriaux. Les événements au contraire ont montré que le Siam a souffert de diminutions territoriales et en toute justice d'esprit on ne peut pas l'accuser d'avoir convoité, de mémoire d'homme, des territoires qui ne lui avaient jamais appartenu. Si la présente requête a été faite, c'est parce qu'elle peut trouver sa justification dans l'Accord de 1946 dont les termes on été observes strictement.

12. En conséquence, l'Agent siamois se permet de suggérer que les arguments réfutant la note du 12 mai tels qu'ils sont présentés par l'Agent français soient rejetés à cause des allusion politiques qui y sont incluses et de présentation erronée donnée aux intentions et au but de la requête siamoise et aussi parce qu'il ne conviendrait pas de les admettre sur le terrain ethnique, géographique et économique ainsi que la note du 12 mai et les présentes remarques le démontrent clairement. On espère donc que les propositions siamoises seront approuvées par la Commission, non seulement pour la raison qu'elles sont fondées sur des arguments de fait strictement pertinents en ce qui concerne les termes de l'Accord de 1946, mais aussi parce qu'elles sont inspirées par le sincère désir d'assurer la stabilité de cette partie du monde et par le haut but de donner de l'expression au principe de liberté et de démocratie qui a été jusqu'à présent dénié aux peuples des territoires en question.

13. Si l'Agent siamois se joint volontiers à l'agent français pour louer la sagesse montrée par Sa Majesté le regretté roi Chulalongkorn et son Conseiller américain, en exécutant la délicate et dangereuse mission d'instituer le présent statut territorial, il désire faire aussi remarquer qu'une telle sagesse n'a pas été acquise sans sacrifices de sa part, sacrifices dont les peuples de l'Indochine, avec le peuple siamois, peuvent avec raison lui être reconnaissants à cause des vies sauvées et des destructions évitées qui auraient été les conséquences d'un conflit. Cette sagesse peut apparaître encore plus profonde et plus humaine si l'on se rappelle que chaque fois que la paix et la tranquillité en Indochine ont

été menacées, le Siam par ses sacrifices renouvelés a épargné à cette partie du monde le sang répandu et la destruction.

Dans différents passages des observations françaises et de l'appendice, il est fait mention des relations du Siam avec le Japon avec la regrettable tendance de faire porter la seule responsabilité sur le Siam. L'Agent siamois ne désire pas entreprendre une discussion sur la substance de ses remarques sur lesquelles il laisse à la Commission le soin de porter un jugement pour savoir si elles sont légitimes ou compatibles avec les termes de l'Accord de règlement. Il se bornera seulement à donner des informations détaillées ayant en vue de compléter l'image dont le sommaire précédent n'était qu'une esquisse.

14. En rapport avec les observations contenues dans les paragraphes précédents, l'Agent siamois désire assurer la Commission qu'aucune mauvaise intention quelle qu'elle soit n'est entretenue envers la France dont la grandeur immortelle aussi bien que le haut sens de générosité, d'humanité est universellement connu. Si cependant certaines objections aux affirmations de l'agent français ont dû être faites et certains faits mis en avant, ce n'était pas dans un esprit d'agressivité. Ces remarques sont inspirées seulement par le désir d'éviter des malentendus et par la ferme croyance du Siam en ses droits. Le Siam et son peuple sont bien connus comme aimant la paix. A cause de leur amour de la paix ils ont consenti à des sacrifices comme peu de pays l'ont jamais fait pendant leur longue vie. Le Siam et le Gouvernement Siamois croient fermement dans la paix et les règlements amiables et pour cette raison même, ils on accepté de soumettre leurs doléances à la Commission de Conciliation dont le haut but a déjà gagné le respect confiant des parties.

Ils sont également attachés aux principes des droits humains, à la liberté et gouvernement de soi qui, à leur avis, s'ils sont reconnus, apporteront non seulement la paix et la stabilité, mais une civilisation plus grande se rappelant la vérité profonde que seulement un pays en avant vers la démocratie peut assurer l'harmonie sociale. "Un bon Gouvernement" n'est pratiquement pas possible à l'intérieur du cadre du "colonialisme."

Le Gouvernement siamois espère par conséquence que les délibérations de ce corps international hautement responsable rendront une justice prévoyante qui apportera non seulement une solution aux difficultés existant actuellement entre le Siam et la France, mai contribuera matériellement à la cause de la paix du monde par leur décision finale.

Annexes

À la Requête (no. vi)

Traduit de l'anglais

29 mai 1947

Amplification des Aspects Ethniques, Géographiques et Économiques des Frontières Franco-Siamoises

1893
Aspect ethnique

La plupart des habitants des rives gauches et droites du Mékong appartiennent au même groupe ethnique, appelé "Lao," un peuple d'origine thaï. Non seulement ils ont des caractéristiques physiques, linguistiques et culturelles identiques mais ont, dans d'innombrables cas, des liens de véritable parenté. En fait, la population du bassin central de la rivière peut être considérée comme une unité ethnique.

Le Mékong comme frontière a ainsi divisé un peuple d'origine, langue et culture identiques en groupes politiques séparés, et quoique la frontière ait duré plus d'un demi-siècle, les caractéristiques ethniques et la sympathie mutuelles des habitants des régions d'écoulement des eaux de l'Est et de l'Ouest sont restées inchangées à tous égards. Leur désir d'association plus rapprochée subsiste et est devenu récemment plus impératif. "Derrière la division extérieure des peuples en tant que groupes conscients de leur nationalité, il y a un vaste champ d'expériences, d'intérêts, de désirs communs qu'aucune manipulation de frontières politiques et de constitutions à la table de la paix ne pourra indéfiniment maintenir séparées." (*Peuple de l'Asie du Sud-Est* par Bruno Lasker, 1945).

Aspect géographique

L'aspect prédominant de n'importe quelle carte physique de la péninsule Indochinoise est le bassin de la rivière Mékong qui s'étend des collines du Siam Central, à l'Ouest, à la chaîne de montagnes le long de la mer de Chine, à l'Est. Un voyageur survolant par avion le bassin est frappé vivement par le caractère uniforme de toute cette zone, par le fait que la rivière et ses affluents sont des dessins incidentels du passage et par le fait que le bassin du Mékong est une seule unité géographique. Cette impression est vraiment une réalité qui a une profonde influence sur la vie des peuples habitant le bassin et sur toutes leurs activités sociales et économiques. Dans les conditions politiques existantes, cette unité nécessite des mesures administratives telles que la création d'un "Régime du Mékong" commun dans des arrangements spéciaux de police, santé, navigation, pêche, commerce et douanes. Certaines complications inhérentes à ces arrangements fournissent une preuve de plus que de tels expédients artificiels sont souvent insuffisants pour restreindre la force et la tendance de la nature.

Ce que Lord Curzon à dire dans les *"Frontières"* peut être intéressant:

> Maintenant nous arrivons à l'importante catégorie des rivières. En tant que créations de la nature, en opposition aux créations de l'homme, aucunes frontières ne sont plus naturelles. Mais dans un autre sens, c'est-à-dire dans celui qui est en accord avec les habitudes naturelles de l'homme, *les rivières ne sont pas des divisions naturelles*, parce que des populations de même race peuvent souvent habiter sur les deux rives.… Tant des peuples du Laos habitaient à cheval sur le Mékong que les Français trouvèrent bientôt que c'était *une frontière impossible*.… En fait, l'enseignement de l'histoire est que les rivières unissent plutôt qu'elles ne séparent. Des raisons stratégiques ont presque toujours été responsables de leur transformation en *frontières*…

Les conditions d'accessibilité imposées par la frontière de 1893 sur les territoires de la rive gauche du Mékong dépendent, d'une part, de la nature de la rivière elle-même et, d'autre part, du caractère de l'arrière-pays de chaque côté. C'est un fait bien connu que bien que le Mékong soit une des rivières les plus longues du monde, il n'est pas utilisable par les bâtiments de mer excepte dans son cours inférieur. C'est pourtant le seul débouché naturel du Laos. La navigation par de petits bateaux dans le cours supérieur, spécialement aux abords du courant à la latitude Nord 200 [20°00′?—Ed.], est précaire à cause des rapides et des bancs. Le moyen fleuve ne permet pas la navigation continue, étant interrompu par des hauts fonds et des chutes qui nécessitent le transbordement des passagers et des marchandises de vapeurs à pirogues et vice-versa. Dans ces conditions les transports sont lents et coûteux. De Saigon il faut 32 à 44 jours pour atteindre Luang Prabang et de 16 à 20 jours pour atteindre Vientiane. En dépit de beaucoup d'efforts et de dépenses pour son amélioration, les obstacles naturels font du Mékong un débouché peu efficace pour la commerce de ces régions. Aussi ce débouché peut-il être compare au goulot étroit d'une bouteille large qui étouffe tout son continu.

Les territoires du Nord, sur la rive gauche du Mékong, sont presque entièrement couverts de montagnes et de terres hautes, et bien qu'ils puissent être atteints en partant des côtes du Tonkin et d'Annam, les communications directes par route ne se sont pas jusqu'ici montrées praticables ou valant la peine au Nord de la latitude 1905 [19°05′?—Ed.]. Depuis la latitude Nord de sens vers le Sud la chaîne de montagnes, qui s'étend presque parallèlement à la mer sur la côte Est, a formé un obstacle naturel séparant l'Annam du Nord de ces territoires.

L'arrière-pays sur la rive droite du Mékong bien que généralement montagneux dans le Nord est cependant d'un autre caractère, depuis plus haut que la latitude N. 1805 [18°05′?—Ed.] il s'aplit en pays ouvert. Entre les latitudes 180 [18°00′?—Ed.] et 150 [15°00′?—Ed.]la rive droite du Mékong est constituée par le plateau du Siam du Nord-Est.

On peut facilement voir par la nature physique et la forme de la zone sur la rive gauche du Mékong que n'importe quel projet encore à l'examen—de construction de ligne de chemin de fer venant longitudinalement du Sud à travers ces territoires rencontrera des déconvenues financières pendant longtemps, en raison de l'étendue limitée de terres fertiles et exploitables de chaque côté de la ligne. Par conséquence, sans compter sur la rive droite, seulement des accès par route de l'Est et du Sud sont possibles. Trois toutes ont jusqu'ici été établies à travers les montagnes. Un chemin de fer de 180 kilomètres de long de Tan-Ap à Thaket sur le Mékong a été commencé il y a une vingtaine d'années; mais apparemment il n'a pu être continue puisqu'il n'existe actuellement à sa place qu'une route de plus. De Pak Hin Boun vers le Sud la route du Mékong est également supplée par une route qui suit la rivière jusqu'à Saigon.

On montrera sous une autre rubrique que ces régions ne sont pas économiquement accessibles de l'Est au Sud par la rivière ou par les montagnes.

D'autre part, l'accès par l'Ouest n'est pas seulement favorable mais est capable de développement presque illimité. Longtemps avant l'existence de cette frontière, l'expérience a montré que ces territoires pouvaient être atteints sans difficulté de la rive Ouest. Cette condition naturelle, et le *"Laos touristique"*, un livre publié en 1925, se référant au Haut-Mékong, admet à la page 270,

> les moyens de communication vers la Laos sont extrêmement précaires et le Siam seul peut offrir un débouché certain aux produits de la région.

Il continue en disant à la page 278,

> c'est donc jusqu'à nouvel ordre par le Siam que l'on peut surtout essayer de développer économiquement le pays.

Actuellement, des voies d'accès de l'Ouest vers le Laos sont possibles le long de la plupart des parties de la frontière du Nord au Sud.

1. De Chieng Rai et Chieng Saen, reliés avec le chemin de fer d'Etat du Nord à Lampang par une route empierrée, un flot régulier de commodités, à la

fois produites localement et importées, est descendu le long du Mékong pour être distribué en route vers Luang Prabang. Un autre centre frontalier sur le Mékong est Chieng Kong, un point de formation des trains de teck. Une certaine quantité de sticklaque et de produits de la jungle entre également au Siam à ces points.

La supériorité de cette route du Nord vers Luang Prabang est démontrée par le fait que pendant des périodes de disette, de larges envois de riz ont été, à la demande expresse des autorités franco-indochinoises, acheminés par cette route, parce que plus pratique et plus rapide. La possibilité de transporter le courrier français par cette route a également été examinée.

2. Nan et Prae, reliés par route avec le chemin de fer d'Etat siamois, aussi bien qu'Utradit et Pichay, sur la ligne elle-même, sont des centres pour le commerce de caravane à travers la Lan Chang vers le Mékong.

3. Le terminus de chemin de fer à Udorn (Mak Khaeng) est relié par route avec Nong Khai et Ta Boa sur le Mékong, en face de Vientiane.

4. Entre Nong Khai et l'estuaire de la Nam Mun, au-dessus de la latitude 150 [15°00'?—Ed.] les centres riverains de Ta Uten, Nakorn-Pnom, Tat Pnom, Mukdaharn et Komarat sont reliés par route et sont en puissance des points de débouché pour le commerce.

5. Le terminus de chemin de fer à Varin (en face d'Ubon) sur le Nam Mun est relié par route à travers Pimun avec le Mékong à Muang Kao en face de Paksé.

Le rapport ci-dessus a montré qu'il existe bien des débouchés possibles vers l'Ouest, et que leur développement futur, s'il n'est pas gêné par des restrictions frontalières, sera plus favorable que ceux de l'Est et de l'Ouest.

On peut conclure par conséquent que la frontière de 1893 a imposé une condition limitative sous laquelle un accès géographique plus favorable a été remplacé par un accès moins favorable.

Les conditions de la frontière en ce qui concerne les îles du Mékong sont si évidemment inéquitables et anormales qu'il n'est pas nécessaire de faire le développement là-dessus. Le principe de les distribuer suivant le critère du chenal navigable (thalweg) est d'acceptation générale.

Aspect économique

Comme le bassin du Mékong est une unité géographique, il s'ensuit que c'est aussi une entité économique. Les habitants des deux rives sont interdépendants pour la production, la distribution et la consommation. Ceux de la rive droite procurent des produits essentiels comme le riz, le sel et les salaisons en échange du sticklaque et des produits de la jungle de la rive gauche.

Cet échange peut être considéré comme égalisé dans une certaine mesure par des produits manufacturés mais qui ne profitent pas directement aux habitants indigènes puisque la plupart des intermédiaires sont étrangers. Dans les circonstances présentes la source d'économies pour placement en capital humain sur la rive gauche doit dépendre des efforts et sacrifices de la part des populations des deux rives. Le Mékong dans son cours supérieur et moyen n'a généralement pas plus d'un kilomètre de large, il existe naturellement en temps normal une quantité considérable d'échanges sociaux et commerciaux entre les habitants des deux rives qu'il n'est pas facile de contrôler effectivement. Dans les circonstances actuelles, la réglementation de telles associations spontanées équivaut presque à la suppression d'un droit humain élémentaire.

L'aspect économique de la frontière est le plus conditionné par les traits géographiques qui commandent, ainsi qu'il a été démontré, la question des possibilités relatives d'accès.

On a vu sous la rubrique précédente que le Mékong est un débouché insuffisant et que le développement ferroviaire de la rive droite n'a pas jusqu'ici était praticable. Le transport par route et par air n'est économique que pour les passagers et les produits de valeur relativement élevée. Les routes vers l'Est et le Sud sont utiles principalement pour le transport de produits manufacturés importés et peut difficilement contribuer à une balance des comptes favorable pour le Laos à son stade actuel d'économie agricole.

Cet aspect économique particulier de la frontière est considéré de plus, premièrement, du point de vue du bien-être économique interne des populations qu'elle sépare et, deuxièmement, du point de vue des relations commerciales extérieures.

Les deux études de l'économie rurale entreprises au Siam en 1930–31 et en 1934–35 en coopération avec l'Université Harvard, avec l'aide d'experts américains, ont démontré avec évidence que le progrès de l'économie rurale dépend dans une large mesure du développement des communications qui offre différents moyens d'augmenter le revenu familial. L'accès facile des centres commerciaux stimule une demande croissante des produits qui ne peuvent être obtenus localement, et ceci agit comme stimulant à un effort plus grand.

Il fut trouvé, surtout au cours de la première de ces études, qu'en général la population rurale dans le Siam du Nord-Est se suffisait en gros à elle-même et avait une économie agricole, que le riz et les autres denrées étaient cultivés pour la consommation personnelle et que peu de produits agricoles ou autres étaient vendus.

Comme la population des territoires de l'Est du Mékong est apparentée étroitement, ethniquement, géographiquement et économiquement à la population du Nord-Est du Siam, il y a de bonnes raisons de croire que leur situation économique est comparable.

Dans le Siam du Nord, habité également par des gens appartenant à la même branche ethnique, où le rail et les transports par route étaient beaucoup mieux développés, les rapports sur les études faites montrent que le foyer rural moyen tirait de ses profits commerciaux 1/5 à 1/4 de ses gains annuels, alors que dans le Nord-Est le revenu commercial était faible. A peu près 40% du riz produit dans le Nord était à vendre, mais seulement la moitié de ce pourcentage était à vendre dans le Nord-Est.

Sur les bases théoriques on peut tenir que les gens sont plus heureux si on les laisse dans un état de développement si peu commercialisé. Il n'en reste pas moins que la commercialisation est l'état du monde aujourd'hui, et que ses progrès sont inévitables. Le Gouvernement Siamois ne peut donc qu'exécuter avec des sacrifices considérables, des projets étendus d'extension ferroviaire et routière dans le Nord-Est.

Un fonds de routes a été créé, et en dix ans (1933–1944) la longueur totale des routes empierrées ouvertes à la circulation a progressivement passé de 90 à 1,750 Kms. Les routes achevées dans le Siam du Nord-Est totalisent maintenant 1,828 Kms. avec 520 Kms. en construction et 340 Kms. déjà levés.

Il est remarquable qu'avant même le commencement de ces activités il y a eu beaucoup de commentaires dans la presse indochinoise sur le développement des transports au Siam, en général sous le titre "Développement du Laos". Il est aussi significatif qu'un livre sur la géographie économique, publié en 1935, poussant à un plus grand développement des communications au Laos, contient la phrase "ouvrir le Laos à la vie moderne et l'arracher à l'attraction économique du Siam." Pour de telles raisons, il a été considéré prudent que la branche supérieure du chemin de fer Nord-Est ne soit pas étendue au-delà d'Udorn, bien que ceci aurait été à l'avantage de son économie, et le terminus n'est relié que par route avec Nong Khai sur la frontière du Mékong.

Les problèmes économiques plus importants du Nord-Est peuvent être résumés dans quelques phrases. Au moment des études il y avait sous-peuplement dans beaucoup de secteurs. Les cultures commerciales autres que le riz, telles que le coton, tabac, arachide et fourrage n'étaient pas développées. L'industrie de la soie et l'élevage pouvaient être considérablement développés. Surtout les facilités de transport étaient encore insuffisantes. Faisant un rapport sur cette question, le Professeur Carl C. Zimmerman écrivait:

> Il suffit d'insister sur le fait qu'avec l'extension des communications cette région se développera probablement plus par rapport à sa condition actuelle qu'aucune autre partie du Siam.

Sans doute une corrélation analogue existe dans les territoires situés de l'autre côté du Mékong, et le développement envisagé dans la citation ci-dessus aura sans aucun doute pour résultat l'élévation du standard de vie des populations.

Il y a tout lieu de croire, qu'avec de meilleurs communications, la condition actuelle d'isolement relatif de ces territoires sera vite remplacée par une plus grande activité commerciale dont le résultat sera l'augmentation progressive de la quantité et de la valeur du surplus exportable avec lesquels plus de bien importés peuvent être achetés. Ceci est en effet le cas dans le Siam du Nord-Est et le changement de condition est presque révolutionnaire pour un observateur qui n'a pas visité la région pendant plusieurs années.

Comme l'accès à ces territoires est plus facile de l'Ouest que de l'Est ou du Sud, leurs routes commerciales devraient normalement converger vers Bangkok. L'amélioration de ce port fluvial en développement et de ses abords est en cours en ce moment et son achèvement ne réduira pas non seulement directement le coût des transports mais augmentera indirectement la production et l'activité commerciale des zones qu'il peut atteindre en procurant l'accès à des marchés étrangers plus étendus et en augmentant le rayon d'action et la quantité des commodités d'exportation de ces régions.

Il est conclu, en conséquence, qu'à la fois du point de vue du bien-être interne et de celui du commerce extérieur, la frontière de 1893 est dommageable en ce qui concerne le progrès économique.

1904

Les considérations d'unité ethnique, géographique et économique de Bassin du Mékong décrites dans le cas du Traité de 3 Octobre 1893 sont applicables peut-être à un degré encore plus grand aux territoires de ces deux provinces sur la rive droite du Mékong.

Aspect ethnique

Presque toute la province de Lan Chang appartient au même groupe ethnique que la population du Siam du Nord-Est, et la plupart des arguments mis en avant en ce qui concerne la frontière du Mékong s'appliquent avec une égale force spécialement à la partie Sud de la frontière de ce territoire.

Aspect géographique

Par le Traité franco-siamois de 1893, la frontière Nord-Est du Siam a suivi constamment le cours du Mékong depuis l'embouchure du Nan Ruak au Nord jusqu'à un point plus bas que Stung-Treng dans le Sud.

La Convention de 1904 a projeté des territoires français à travers le Mékong vers l'Ouest faisant une encoche profonde dans la section Nord du territoire siamois.

Cette projection de territoire français a également entraîné l'annexion de la section Nord du Mékong depuis au-dessus de la latitude Nord 200 [20°00′?—Ed.] jusqu'à environ la latitude 180 [18°00′?—Ed.]. Malgré toute disposition contraire, cette annexion a diminué la valeur de la rivière comme route internationale de communications parce que le passage le long de la section annexée qui était un droit devient maintenant une tolérance.

Cependant, le trait le plus caractéristique de la partie Nord de la frontière est la limite qu'elle impose au territoire de Luang Prabang en ce qui concerne le développement des communications des côtés Nord-Ouest et Sud de ce territoire. Ceci est un grand désavantage en vue du fait que l'accès du territoire de l'Est et du Sud est pour des raisons géographiques limité dans ses possibilités.

Les communications avec le Sud au moyen du Mékong sont lentes et coûteuses. De Saigon il faut de 32 à 40 jours pour atteindre Luang Prabang et de 16 à 20 jours pour atteindre Vientiane. En dépit de beaucoup d'efforts et de dépenses pour des améliorations, des obstacles naturels comme rapides, récifs ou chutes font que le Mékong est un débouché insuffisant pour le commerce de ce territoire.

Le débouché vers la côte Est par la route de Vinh qui traverse sur presque 300 kms des pays montagneux ne peut être économique, spécialement pour le transport des denrées volumineuses de petite valeur qui sont produites localement dans ce territoire. Les facilités d'accès ne sont guère améliorées par la combinaison de routes plus courtes vers l'Est et de transport fluvial.

On peut comparer les conditions de transport sur le cours supérieur et moyen du Mékong jusqu'à Luang Prabang situé à 2,111 kms de la Mer de Chine par le fleuve. Ces deux parties du fleuve sont loin d'être des routes commerciales idéales parce que le cours supérieur est difficile à naviguer par de petits bateaux alors que le cours moyen, bien que plus large, est coupé par des rapides et des récifs. L'expérience a cependant décidé en faveur de la route remontante comme étant plus pratique et gagnant du temps. Entre Chieng Saen et Luang Prabang il faut, suivant les saisons, de 11 à 17 jours en remontant le courant mais seulement 6 à 7 jours en descendant. Cet avantage est prouvé par le fait que dans les époques de disette de gros envois de riz ont été transportés à Luang Prabang, de Chieng Saen à la demande expresse des autorités indochinoises. La possibilité de transporter le courrier français par cette route a également fait l'objet de négociations parce que le courrier ordinaire d'Europe mettait de 35 à 40 jours pour Houei-Sai, ville principale du Haut Laos, mais de 75 à 80 jours par Saigon et le Mékong.

Les villes siamoises de Nan, Prae, Utradit et Pichay ont été des débouchés pour le commerce des caravanes avec Lan Chang depuis des temps anciens. Les deux dernières sont sur le chemin de fer alors que les deux premières sont reliées par route avec la voie ferrée.

En dehors des routes commerciales existantes, la meilleure ligne de communication avec Lan Chang sont le prolongement de la route de Khon Kaen à Loei actuellement en construction à travers la frontière du Sud jusqu'à Paklay et même plus au Nord et la prolongation de la route de Nan jusqu'à Luang Prabang. Mais leur prolongement est peu probable tant que la frontière présente demeure.

On peut conclure par conséquent que les possibilités d'accès du Lan Chang partant du territoire siamois sont considérablement plus grandes que les possibilités d'accès partant du territoire de l'Indochine française et que la frontière de 1904 est un élément préventif du futur développement de la meilleure alternative.

La section de la frontière qui a exclu du Siam la province originale de Champasak (Bassac) est définie dans l'article premier de la Convention. Sa définition, depuis le début sur la rive gauche du Grand Lac jusqu'à son point de jonction avec la ligne de partage des eaux le long de la chaîne de montagnes des Dang Rek n'est pas pertinente à la présente instance, étant donné qu'elle a été remplacée par la frontière postérieure de 1907. La section discutée présentement commence au point mentionné de jonction avec la chaîne des Dang Rek et suit la ligne de partage des eaux d'autres chaînes courant dans une direction Nord-Est et finit au-dessous de l'estuaire du Nam Mun sur le Mékong.

En établissant cette frontière, la Convention de 1904, comme dans le Nord, affecte une autre section du Mékong au territoire de l'Indochine française enlevant à celle-ci la possibilité de servir comme route internationale de communication.

Cette frontière est essentiellement une frontière de montagnes et dans un sens géographique étroit, peut être considérée comme approchant les idéaux de permanence et d'exclusivité. L'aspect géographique cependant devrait comprendre une vue plus large. L'exclusivité et la possibilité de se satisfaire à soi-même devant donner place tôt ou tard aux nécessités du commerce international. Dans le cadre dont il s'agit, l'existence de la route à travers la partie Nord de cette frontière qui relie Paksé avec le terminus du chemin de fer siamois à Varin en face de Oubone est la meilleure preuve de cette nécessité. Sous cet angle plus large de géographie, la frontière peut être considérée comme ayant imposé au territoire exclu par elle du Siam une limite à ses possibilités d'accès sous laquelle les débouchés insuffisants vers le Nord-Est et le Sud sont préférés au débouché meilleur vers l'Ouest au détriment des populations de ce territoire.

Bien que les routes à travers les montagnes de Vinh et Tan Ap à Thakkek et de Quang Tri à Savannaket soient reliées avec Paksé, il est douteux que des transports de denrées volumineuses par ces longues routes à travers un pays difficile soient économiques. Le Mékong par conséquent reste une voie de sortie commerciale relativement meilleure pour Champasak. Il fut estimé par une autorité française reconnue en 1935 que quelque 4,000 tonnes de marchandises sont transportées de où vers le Laos par an au moyen du fleuve et que le maximum annuel ne pourrait jamais excéder de 20 à 25,000 tonnes (A. Agard, *Régions naturelles et géographie économique*, p. 271) en raison de la nature de la rivière, qui même dans son cours moyen est obstruée par des chutes, des récifs et des passages étroits comme par exemple les sections de Kratié Khong, Phna Kred et Kamott, qui obligent à des transbordements de vapeurs à pirogues et vice versa. Il fut estimé que sa capacité existante et future ne suffirait pas aux besoins économiques du Laos.

D'un autre côté, le terminus du chemin de fer d'Etat Siamois à Varin (Oubone) déjà relie avec Champasak par route à travers Pimun vers le Mékong à Muang Kao en face de Paksé offre une voie de transit économique et directe vers la mer par Bangkok. Cette voie de sortie convient au transport des marchandises de toute nature. Les marchandises transportées par camions et charrettes entre Pimun et la frontière à Chong Mek se sont élevées à environ 10,000 tonnes au cours de l'année dernière. Le port de Bangkok et ses abords sont en cours d'amélioration suivant un projet recommandé par les experts de la Société des Nations. Son achèvement contribuera indirectement au progrès de toutes les zones qu'il touche.

En l'absence de cette frontière, la ligne de chemin de fer peut être étendue et la ville de Champasak (Bassac) sur le Mékong sera ainsi à deux jours de Bangkok à comparer avec les 8 ou 9 jours qui sont nécessaires généralement entre cette rivière et Saigon par la voie fluviale.

Le prolongement de la route de Varin à Det Udom à travers la montagne est une possibilité future qui ne sera pas réalisable tant que la frontière ne sera pas déplacée. Cependant, ce débouché est insignifiant compare à celui offert par le rail. Quand il y a une porte, on préfère généralement s'en servir pour entrer dans une maison plutôt que de grimper par une fenêtre. Il y a bien entendu le Mékong et ses affluents du cours moyen, le Mun et le Chi comme débouchés supplémentaires vers l'Ouest, dans la direction du Siam du Nord-Est.

Aspect économique
L'aspect économique de la frontière de 1904 dépend dans une large mesure des conditions géographiques comprenant les questions de possibilités d'accès relatif. Les deux provinces séparées du Siam par la frontière peuvent être considérées ensemble à la fois du point de vue du bien-être intérieur économique et de celui du développement commercial extérieur.

En considérant le bien-être économique de la population, il doit être entendu qu'en raison du manque d'informations quantitatives, les arguments mis en avant dans la présente discussion ne peuvent être basés que sur des suppositions puisque les deux études sur l'économie rurale entreprises en 1930–31 et en 1934–35 ne comprenaient pas les deux provinces en question. On trouva dans le Siam du Nord-Est qu'en général la population rurale se suffisait à elle-même presque partout et que son économie était agricole. Comme cette population est liée de près avec la population de Lan Chang et de Champasak, il est très probable que leurs conditions économiques sont similaires. Les rapports faits à la suite de l'étude montrent que dans le Siam du Nord habité également par les populations appartenant à la même branche ethnique ou les communications étaient mieux développées, le revenu des foyers ruraux était pour 1/5 à 1/4 tiré du commerce alors que dans le Nord-Est le revenu tiré du commerce était relativement faible. A peu près 40% du riz cultive dans le Nord était à vendre, alors que seulement 20% environ du riz cultivé dans le Nord [Nord-Est?—Ed.] était vendu. La corrélation entre le progrès économique et les communications était clairement démontrée et il est maintenu qu'une telle corrélation existe également à Lan Chang et Champasak en vue de l'état présent de leur développement économique.

Si les communications améliorées sont données à ces deux provinces, leur condition actuelle d'isolement relatif sera sans doute remplacée par une activité commerciale plus grande tendant à augmenter la quantité et la variété de leurs produits. Ceci leur apportera les produits importés qui sont nécessaires pour leur bien-être matériel aussi bien que des moyens de plus grands progrès. L'effet économique du développement routier dans le Siam du Nord-Est doit être vu pour être cru et l'affirmation que ce n'est rien moins qu'un miracle n'apparaîtra pas alors exagérée.

Il est conclu en conséquence que du point de vue du bien-être interne et du commerce extérieur, la frontière de 1904 en gênant l'amélioration des communications empêche le progrès économique.

1907
Aspect ethnique
Bien que la majorité de la population des trois provinces ait été originellement de souche Mon Khmer il ne faut pas perdre de vue que les liens entre eux et les Siamois ne sont pas seulement le résultat d'une fusion ethnique d'il y a plusieurs siècles mais d'une assimilation plus récente due à des relations intimes sociales et économiques qui ont été poussées encore par le fait de la religion et de la culture communes.

Une autre considération importante, d'une nature plus pratique, est qu'une partie considérable de la population des provinces du Siam bordant cette frontière, spécialement sur ses côtés Nord-Ouest et Nord-Est est composée de personnes appartenant au même groupe ethnique et ne peut être distinguée de ceux qui habitent de l'autre côté de la frontière, sauf en ce que le nombre de ceux qui parlent à la fois le cambodgien et le siamois est beaucoup plus grand dans le territoire siamois actuel. Ceci est dû sans doute au fait que la séparation politique pendant les dernières 40 années a fait une différence dans leurs possibilités d'éducation. L'éducation élémentaire est obligatoire au Siam et seulement ceux appartenant à la génération plus âgée peuvent vraisemblablement rester ignorants de la langue siamoise.

Un grave défaut de la partie du Sud de la frontière au point de vue ethnique est qu'en spécifiant l'exclusion de tout le bassin du Klong Koh Pao (Ko Po) du territoire siamois, on a séparé une communauté à peu près purement thaï (siamoise) de ses voisins de la province de Krat.

Aspects géographiques et économiques

On se propose de discuter les aspects géographiques et économiques de la frontière de 1907 dans le même chapitre, étant donné qu'il semble que les deux aspects soient pratiquement inséparables, la distinction entre la géographie, la géographie économique et l'économie n'étant que d'intérêt théorique.

La définition de la section de la frontière excluant les provinces de Battambang, Sisophon et Siemreap du Siam est contenue dans la section 1 du protocole concernant la délimitation des frontières annexées au Traité du 23 mars 1907.

D'un point de vue strictement géographique, une définition comme celle de la ligne frontière entre Phnom Penh et Namsai qui spécifie qu'elle "suit" d'abord dans une direction Nord-Ouest et ensuite Nord "la frontière actuelle" entre la province de Battambang d'une part et la province de Chantaboon et Krat d'autre part..." est historique plutôt que géographique et par conséquent éphémère. De nouveau, d'un point sur la rivière Sisophon, 10kms en-dessous Aran "la description d'une ligne 'droite' d'un point dans les Dang Rek à mi-chemin entre les passes… étant entendu que cette ligne sera dessinée de façon à laisser dans le territoire siamois la route directe entre Aran et Chong Takoh" est apparemment contradictoire avec elle-même. Le résultat est tout plutôt qu'une ligne droite sur la carte de la frontière.

Mais ces fautes sont peu de chose comparées avec les traits géographico-économiques de la frontière. Pour comprendre ces traits, il est nécessaire de comparer les routes de transit Sud et Ouest de ces territoires.

C'est une vérité banale que le moyen de transport le moins cher spécialement pour les denrées non périssables de faible valeur est la voie d'eau. Le moyen suivant dans l'ordre de l'économie est le transport par rail. Le transport routier n'est économique que pour les passagers et les marchandises légères de plus grande valeur sur des distances relativement plus courtes. En prenant la ville de Pratabong comme critérium, on se propose de passer en revue différentes facilités de transport partant de ces points.

Le Grand Lac relie par rivière avec Pratabong n'est navigable toute l'année que jusqu'à Snoc Trou, ce passage n'étant navigable qu'à peu près 5 mois par an. Au-delà de ce point il y a le libre passage vers Phnom Penh et vers la mer.

Un chemin de fer va de Pratabong à Phnom Penh, et [sic] port fluvial assez bien équipé situé à 350 kms de la mer de Chine. Ce port peut recevoir des bâtiments tirant jusqu'à 12 pieds. Le trafic par mer de ce port est généralement côtier.

Bien qu'une route relie Pratabong à Phnom Penh et Saigon, une distance totale de 532 kms, il a été déjà démontré que le transport par route n'est pas économique spécialement pour les longues distances.

La capacité du port de Phnom Penh est par conséquent le facteur principal déterminant des routes de transit vers le Sud.

Tournons-nous maintenant vers l'Ouest :

Le chemin de fer d'Etat siamois reliant Bangkok avec la frontière de Aranyapratet (Aranh) depuis 1927 a après un délai de plusieurs années été réuni avec Pratabong. Cette ville est aussi reliée par route avec Bangkok.

Le port de Bangkok est situé à 35 kms de la mer, une distance 10 fois moindre que celle entre la mer et Phnom Penh. Bien que sa capacité présente comme port soit déjà plus grande que celle de Phnom Penh, il est en plein développement suivant un plan dressé par un comité d'experts de la Société des Nations. Quand il sera terminé, il sera accessible aux bâtiments tirant jusqu'à 28 pieds contre 12 pieds dans le cas de Phnom Penh. Plus tard des vaisseaux tirant 31 et même 33 pieds pourront y être abrités. Ce programme d'améliorations est destiné non seulement amener une simple réduction du prix des transports mais à encourager le développement des activités économiques de toutes les zones qu'il atteint en obtenant l'accès des marchés étrangers plus étendus et en augmentant la portée et la quantité des biens exportés de ces régions.

En plus de la voie ferrée par Bangkok, des débouchés plus courts vers Chantaburi et ensuite vers Krat, sont clairement indiqués quand on examine une carte routière de la côte Est du golfe du Siam. En modernisant la section de cette route qui était une ancienne grande route khmer entre Pailin et le premier de ces ports de mer, la distance entre Pratabong et la mer sera réduite à seulement 175 kms au lieu de 500-600 kms par les routes du Sud.

Une bonne carte montrera aussi qu'il y a plusieurs débouchés possibles à travers la chaîne des Dang Rek qu'on pourrait développer. Jusqu'à très récemment, deux routes étaient en construction. On espérait que le trafic primitif actuel de poisson des Grands Lacs échangé contre le sel du Nord pourrait par ces routes devenir un commerce organisé.

On peut voir par conséquent que les voies de communication vers l'Ouest et le Nord ont des possibilités de développement futur plus grandes que les routes vers le Sud mais que leur plein développement et leur utilisation seront peu probables aussi longtemps que la frontière restera dans sa position récente.

Il reste seulement maintenant la question du bien-être économique intérieur à discuter et l'on verra que c'est un résultat indirect des possibilités d'accès et du commerce extérieur.

Les études sur l'économie rurale pratiquée au Siam en 1930-31 et en 1934-35 ont montré que le progrès de l'économie rurale dépend dans une très grande mesure des communications qui offrent différentes façons d'accroître le revenu familial par lequel un standard de vie plus élevé peut être obtenu. Le transport rural et spécialement le développement des routes rurales reliées au centre où il y a des marchés dépend également du revenu provincial et communal qui est tiré des différentes sources centrales et locales. Celles-ci dépendent alors à leur tour de la prospérité relevant à la fois du commerce intérieur et extérieur.

Il est par conséquent conclu que la frontière de 1907, en limitant le développement futur des moyens routiers des meilleures routes est une gêne pour le développement économique futur des territoires exclus par elle du Siam.

Monsieur le Président,

L'Agent du Gouvernement siamois devant la Commission de Conciliation franco-siamoise m'a communiqué le mémoire ampliatif de sa requête du 12 mai qu'il vous a remise le 29 de ce même mois et qui constitue en même temps sa réplique à mes observations du 22.

Comme suite a ces dernières, j'ai l'honneur de vous adresser ci-joint, pour être soumis à la Commission, un mémoire d'observations générales sur l'ensemble de la requête du Gouvernement siamois, ainsi que les conclusions que je dépose, au sujet de cette requête, au nom du Gouvernement français.

Une notice rappelant les circonstances qui ont conduit à la conclusion de l'Accord de règlement du 17 novembre 1946, et une étude contenant l'examen point par point des considérations développées dans le mémoire siamois du 29 mai, sont annexées à ce mémoire.

Pour la commodité de la Commission, ces documents sont remis en cinq exemplaires, et des traductions en anglais y sont jointes.

Veuillez agréer, Monsieur le Président, les assurances de ma très haute considération.

Washington, le 7 juin 1947.

(Signé) *Francis Lacoste*
Pour copie certifiée conforme
L'Agent du Gouvernement français
Francis Lacoste.

Son Excellence
Monsieur William Phillips,
Ancien Ambassadeur des Etats-Unis,
Président de la Commission de Conciliation franco-siamoise,
1718 Eighteenth Street N.W.,
Washington, D.C.

7 juin 1947

Observations et Conclusions de L'agent du Gouvernement Français sur la Requête Présentée à la Commission de Conciliation Franco-Siamoise le 12 mai 1947 par L'agent du Gouvernement Siamois et Développée Dans Son Mémoire en Duplique du 29 mai 1947

L'Agent du Gouvernement siamois a remis à la Commission, le 29 mai, à l'appui de l'argumentation sommaire sur laquelle reposaient les conclusions de sa requête du 12 mai, un mémoire ampliatif auquel sont annexées des "observations" sur la réplique française du 22 mai. Il ne semble, toutefois, se trouver dans le mémoire et dans les observations de l'Agent du Gouvernement siamois, hormis certaines imputations, d'ailleurs sans fondement, à l'adresse du Gouvernement français, aucun argument nouveau en substance, en sorte que le mémoire français du 22 mai et la note détaillée à ce mémoire, se trouvent avoir déjà répondu à l'essentiel des deux documents siamois du 29 mai.

Il a cependant paru opportun, pour achever d'éclairer la Commission, de lui soumettre:

10. une notice (annexe I) rappelant les circonstances qui ont abouti à la conclusion de l'Accord de règlement du 17 novembre 1946, en vertu duquel la Commission a été réunie;

20. une étude (annexe II) ou sont systématiquement rappelées ou analysées, à propos de chaque point du nouveau mémoire siamois, les réponses déjà faites aux arguments qu'il réitère;

30. un résumé, sous forme de synthèse (c'est l'objet du présent mémoire), de l'essentiel de l'argumentation déjà développée en réplique aux prétentions avancées par le Gouvernement du Siam;

40. des conclusions, qui sont inscrites à la fin du présent mémoire et qui sont, au nom du Gouvernement français, proposées à la Commission pour adoption.

Observations

I

1. Le second mémoire siamois déclare dans son point 5 que "L'accord de 1946... a constitué la Commission de Conciliation pour reconsidérer la situation résultant des clauses des Traités de 1893, 1904 et 1907. Il est donc évident, poursuit-il, qu'en concluant cet accord, les Parties intéressées ont explicitement reconnu la nécessité d'une telle reconsidération".

2. En réalité, le Gouvernement français n'a pas cessé de déclarer que les territoires qui lui avaient été arrachés en 1941 par la force, et en violation des traités de frontière solennellement conclus, confirmes et garantis, devaient lui

être rendus, et que cette restitution devait être définitive. Cette restitution a été consacrée par l'article 1 de l'Accord de règlement du 17 novembre 1946.

3. C'est par une mesure d'extrême bonne volonté, d'un caractère exceptionnel, et dont il existe sans doute peu d'exemples dans l'histoire du droit international, que le Gouvernement français a accepté, par l'article 3 de ce même accord, de soumettre à une Commission constituée par une application *ad hoc* de l'article 21 de son traité d'amitié de 1937 avec le Siam, les arguments que ce dernier voudrait articuler en faveur d'une révision.

4. En acceptant de faire entendre par une Commission de Conciliation des arguments qu'il ne connaissait pas, à l'appui de prétentions dont il ignorait l'étendue, le Gouvernement français a conscience d'avoir fait à la paix et à l'amitié une concession d'autant plus digne d'être appréciée qu'elle succédait au plus grave préjudice: une agression soudaine, au mépris d'engagements anciens tout fraîchement renouvelés, survenant où les événements que l'on sait l'avaient place dans une position difficile, et aboutissant au démembrement de populations et de territoires appartenant à des États que, depuis plus d'un demi-siècle, la France protège et relève.

5. Mais, en consentant à l'inclusion de l'article 3 dans l'accord de 1946, il n'a nullement admis, quant à lui, la nécessité ou l'opportunité d'une révision de la frontière. L'article 3 portant mention de l'éventualité d'une révision *ou de la confirmation* des clauses des traités auxquels il se réfère, il a entendu donner au Gouvernement siamois l'occasion de soumettre ses arguments, alors informulés, à une instance internationale qui pût décider impartialement de leur bien-fondé; et il s'est réservé, pour sa part, de faire reconnaître par cette instance la force de son droit, et le bien-fondé de sa propre conviction que les clauses des traités visées par l'article 3 doivent être *confirmées*.

6. Encore le Gouvernement français, en donnant son accord à la constitution d'une commission internationale par application de l'article 21, a-t-il délibérément négligé le fait qu'aux termes de cet article, qui reflète lui-même les dispositions de l'Acte Général de Genève de 1928 (article I), seules des "questions litigieuses" pourraient être soumises à une telle commission. Or, aucun litige, au sens propre du terme, n'existait entre lui et le Gouvernement siamois.

7. D'autre part, ces questions litigieuses n'auraient du pouvoir être soumises à une telle commission qu'après échec de toutes tentatives de "solution par voie diplomatique"—alors qu'aucune tentative de ce genre n'avait été faite, et que d'ailleurs les relations diplomatiques, interrompues par l'agression de 1941, n'étaient même pas encore rétablies entre les deux Gouvernements.

8. Ces deux considérations donnent une valeur supplémentaire à l'effort de conciliation que le Gouvernement français a ainsi fait, dans le désir de voir se rétablir une bonne entente propre à faciliter la reprise de rapports de bon voisinage entre l'Union française et le Siam.

9. Il convient enfin d'observer que, s'il était reproché au Gouvernement français de manquer à ses engagements aux termes de l'article 3, du fait qu'il n'accepté pas la révision de la frontière en cause, on pourrait, par l'emploi du même argument spécieux, reprocher au Gouvernement siamois de manquer à ses propres engagements aux termes du même article, parce qu'il refuse de plaider, d'accord avec le Gouvernement français, la thèse de la confirmation de traités du reste en vigueur, et dont la validité n'est contestée par aucune des Parties.

II

1. Le mémoire siamois du 29 mai donne à entendre, dans son paragraphe 5, que le seul fait de l'inscription de l'article 3 dans l'Accord de règlement du 17 novembre 1946 supposait l'existence d'une situation telle qu'une révision du *statu quo* territorial fixé par le traité de 1937 s'imposât.

2. C'est, en effet, uniquement de ce point de vue que le Siam aurait pu justifier valablement sa demande de modification des clauses de traités maintenues en vigueur par le traité de 1937.

3. Or, ni la requête du Gouvernement siamois, ni le mémoire ampliatif qui a entrepris d'en développer l'argumentation et de la justifier, n'ont même tenté de faire apparaître l'existence, aux confins du Siam, du Laos et du Cambodge, d'une situation ethniquement, géographiquement ou économiquement intolérable pour le Siam, de nature à rendre indispensables l'adoption des mesures extraordinaires, ainsi que les sacrifices qui résulteraient inévitablement de ces mesures pour les populations intéressées ainsi que pour le Cambodge, le Laos et la France elle-même.

4. La raison pour laquelle cette démonstration n'a été ni faite ni même essayée, c'est qu'elle n'est pas faisable, parce qu'une telle situation n'existe pas.

III

1. A supposer même que le Gouvernement siamois eût quelque motif valable de plaider le rattachement de territoires laotiens et cambodgiens au sien propre, il aurait convenu qu'il fît au moins la preuve que cette modification n'entraînerait, soit pour les territoires transférés, soit pour ceux dont ils seraient détachés, aucun dommage considérable. Or, les deux mémoires des 12 et 29 mai n'ont fait aucune tentative pour effectuer cette démonstration, et, à vrai dire, ils ne laissent apparaître aucune préoccupation de cette sorte.

2. En revanche, la démonstration été faite, du côté français, que, pour les uns et les autres de ces territoires, les modifications proposées entraîneraient les plus graves conséquences.

IV

1. Enfin, ce n'est pas, comme le prétend le second mémoire siamois en son premier paragraphe, "par des allusions politiques directes ou indirectes, sans rapport avec le sujet" que le premier mémoire français (22 mai) et son annexe ont réfuté les arguments ethniques, géographiques et économiques alignés par le mémoire siamois du 12 mai. Le premier mémoire français a employé des arguments de même sorte. Et c'est toujours dans les limites fixées par l'article 3 de l'Accord de règlement que l'annexe au présent mémoire reprend un a un les arguments du second mémoire siamois. Si, par moments, des considérations politiques se trouvent introduites dans cette discussion, c'est en raison des conséquences politiques inévitables impliquées par les prétentions du Gouvernement siamois.

2. Le premier mémoire français, remis à la Commission le 22 mai, exprime en effet la surprise que le Gouvernement français a éprouvée en prenant connaissance des demandes de révision formulées par le Gouvernement siamois.

3. Comme le second mémoire (29 mai) paraît trouver naturelles des prétentions dont il ne retranche rien, mais qu'il maintient au contraire dans leur entier avec une insistance accrue, il semble opportun de revenir sur le caractère, exorbitant du droit international, qui marque ces prétentions: ainsi que l'observation en a déjà été faite, ces prétentions tendent à la suppression totale de l'Etat du Laos; et à tout le moins, en un premier temps, à une mutilation de cet Etat qui mettrait en danger son existence même, tandis que le Cambodge souffrirait une amputation d'une gravité comparable. Or, le Laos et le Cambodge sont des entités politiques douées d'une vie propre, et dont la personnalité a, au regard du droit international, un droit absolu au respect.

4. Cette considération paraît au Gouvernement français avoir une importance capitale, et l'attention de la Commission est tout particulièrement attirée sur elle.

V

1. Les explications verbales données au cours des séances de la Commission en réponse au questionnaire que celle-ci a présenté aux agents, ont fait apparaître qu'aucun des motifs de caractère ethnique, géographique ou économique, invoqués par le Siam, ne pouvait, pris à part ou ensemble, justifier les revendications présentées au nom du Gouvernement siamois aux dépens du Laos et du Cambodge.

2. D'autre part, ainsi qu'il a été déjà dit, la généralisation de modifications qui ne reposeraient que sur de tels principes entraînerait un bouleversement politique général. Des situations analogues à celles que signalent les mémoires siamois existent en d'autres parties du monde, et sont heureusement réglées depuis des siècles par des traités dont l'application est assurée par une longue expérience, consacrée par le droit international.

3. Mais qui plus est, si les arguments qu'invoquent les mémoires siamois devaient être objectivement appliqués aux frontières qu'ils critiquent, ce n'est qu'à l'encontre du Siam qu'ils pourraient jouer :

4. *Ethniquement*, la ligne de démarcation entre Siamois et Laotiens passe à l'ouest de la frontière actuelle entre le Siam et le Laos; entre Siamois et Khmers, elle passe au nord et à l'ouest de la frontière actuelle entre le Siam et le Cambodge.

5. *Géographiquement*, la ligne de partage des eaux entre le Ménam et le Mékong passe à l'ouest de la frontière entre le Siam d'une part, le Laos et le Cambodge de l'autre, sans parler du tracé anormal de la frontière cambodgienne le long du golfe du Siam, à quelques centaines de mètres du littoral. En conséquence, le Laos et le Cambodge estiment tous les deux qu'un grave préjudice leur est causé du fait que des populations authentiquement et indiscutablement laotiennes et cambodgiennes sont séparées d'eux par le tracé actuel de la frontière, en sorte que si jamais une modification du tracé de la frontière devait être faite, ce serait, en bonne logique, au profit du Laos et du Cambodge que cette modification devrait être effectuée.

6. *Economiquement*, enfin, la démonstration a été faite verbalement en séance, et se trouve confirmée par écrit dans la note annexe au présent mémoire, que le Siam d'une part, le Laos et le Cambodge de l'autre, pays de ressources analogues, ne sont nullement complémentaires ni interdépendants.

7. En effet, sauf dans une zone extrêmement limitée, et qui se trouve amplement couverte par la zone de franchise douanière qui borde le Mékong frontière, il n'existe d'interdépendance entre régions situées de part et d'autre du Mékong que dans les provinces de Luang Prabang et de Bassac: dans les deux cas, les parties situées en rive droite, et qui sont d'ailleurs limitées à l'ouest par des accidents géographiques importants, apportent une contribution essentielle à la subsistance de la population des territoires montagneux de la rive gauche.

8. Ainsi, d'une part, le régime en vigueur tout au long de cette frontière, fluviale ou terrestre, est d'un libéralisme tel que pratiquement aucune entrave n'est apportée à ces "échanges intercommunautaires" qui font l'objet des préoccupations des deux mémoires siamois. Et, d'autre part, le Laos voit ses débouchés propres à travers le reste de l'Indochine en croissance continue depuis une période qui n'a été interrompue par la guerre, tandis que la vie économique de la Province de Battambang, comme celle de tout le Cambodge, a été de tout temps, et sera demain plus qu'aujourd'hui naturellement et nécessairement orienté vers le Sud-Est et vers les pays d'outre-mer par Saigon.

9. Au demeurant, toute amélioration des moyens de transport internationaux doit normalement se traduire par des arrangements commerciaux et douaniers d'un type qui est devenu banal dans le monde entier entre états voisins

civilisés. La France et ses associés s'attendent donc à trouver le Siam prêt à les admettre au bénéfice des facilités de communications actuelles ou nouvelles qui seraient susceptibles d'avantager leur commerce, de même qu'ils sont prêts, pour leur part, à lui accorder la réciprocité.

Aucun déplacement de frontière n'est, dans la péninsule indochinoise plus que dans les autres parties du monde, nécessaire à cette fin.

Conclusions

1. Au vu de ces considérations, le Gouvernement français ne peut que persister à juger que les arguments avancés dans la requête siamoise du 12 mai, ainsi que dans le mémoire ampliatif et dans les "observations" du 29 mai, en faveur de la révision du statu quo, sont non fondés, non pertinents et non susceptibles d'être retenus par la Commission; tandis que ceux qu'il a déjà fait valoir en faveur du maintien du statu quo gardent, même après lecture des documents siamois du 22 mai, une force intacte.

2. Bien que le tracé actuel de la frontière ne donne pas satisfaction au légitime désir du Laos et du Cambodge de voir réunis à eux des éléments de population très importants qu'ils considèrent a bon droit comme des parties détachées des communautés qui relèvent de leur autorité, et bien qu'il ne leur donne pas non plus les limites géographiques naturelles qui devraient normalement définir à l'ouest leurs territoires, le Gouvernement français estime que le maintien d'une frontière certaine et paisible depuis 1907 (sauf l'agression de 1941) est désirable et nécessaire.

3. En conséquence, étant donné qu'il est hors de constatation que l'Accord de règlement du 17 novembre 1946 constitue la base juridique du statut des frontières entre le Siam et l'Indochine, et que ce même instrument diplomatique gouverne le statut de la Commission elle-même, je propose, au nom du Gouvernement français, à la Commission de Conciliation, d'adopter les conclusions suivantes:

1. a) En signant l'Accord de Règlement du 17 novembre 1946, en particulier l'article 3, le Gouvernement français, auquel était, du reste, expressément réservé, comme au Gouvernement siamois, le droit de présenter des arguments en faveur de la confirmation, n'a nullement reconnu qu'il fût *nécessaire* de remettre en question les clauses territoriales des traités de 1893, 1904 et 1907, confirmées par le traité de 1937.
   b) Dans ces conditions, l'Agent du Gouvernement siamois n'est pas fondé à arguer d'un préjugé en faveur de la révision.
2. a) Pour que les arguments présentés par l'Agent du Gouvernement siamois en faveur de la révision fussent recevables à l'encontre de traités solennellement conclus, confirmés et garantis, il aurait fallu

que ces arguments démontrent que le Siam subit, à raison du *statu quo*, un préjudice non pas quelconque mais intolérable.

b) Or, aucun des arguments ethniques, géographiques et économiques présentés par l'Agent du Gouvernement siamois n'est de nature à prouver que le Siam subit, à raison du *statu quo*, un préjudice.

3. a) En effet, les mémoires présentés par l'Agent du Gouvernement siamois n'ont pas prouvé que les populations de la rive droite souffrent d'une manière sérieuse de l'existence d'une frontière politique entre elles et les populations de la rive gauche du Mékong parce qu'elles se trouvent de ce fait séparées de populations parlant un dialecte voisin ou ayant des coutumes semblables.

b) Ils n'ont pas plus apporté cette démonstration en ce qui concerne le Luang Prabang rive droite et le Bassac rive droite.

c) Ils n'ont pas démontré non plus que les populations de la rive droite du Mékong et des régions à l'ouest des provinces de Luang Prabang et de Bassac fussent empêchées par l'existence de la frontière politique d'entretenir des rapports économiques et sociaux avec les populations qui habitent de l'autre côté de la frontière.

d) Les mémoires siamois n'ont fait état d'aucune minorité siamoise dans les territoires auxquels prétend le Siam; et en fait il n'en existe aucune.

4. D'une manière générale, la frontière est, au point de vue géographique, certaine, marquée par des accidents de terrains soigneusement choisis et repérés à la suite de travaux de délimitation accomplis contradictoirement par des experts des deux pays.

5. Les mémoires présentés par l'Agent du Gouvernement siamois n'ont pas démontré que le Siam souffre dans son économie de l'existence de cette frontière politique en ce sens que l'existence de la frontière politique ait pour effet de paralyser ou de ruiner son commerce.

6. Les inconvénients qui peuvent résulter de la frontière sont ceux qui résultent normalement en tous lieux de l'existence d'une frontière, et il n'y a là aucun argument qui puisse prévaloir contre des traités définitifs, solennellement confirmés par le Siam et contre une frontière garantie par lui.

7. a) L'Agent du Gouvernement siamois n'a pas montré que les changements qu'il suggère n'auraient causé aucun préjudice sérieux aux populations et aux territoires en cause.

b) Il a tenté, en revanche, de démontrer qu'il ne résulterait de ses propositions que des avantages désirables pour des territoires non siamois,

plaidant ainsi, contrairement aux principes généraux du droit, un dossier qui n'est pas celui du pays dont il est le porte-parole.
8. En revanche, l'Agent du Gouvernement français a montré qu'il résulterait des propositions siamoises un préjudice intolérable pour les territoires et les entités politiques, personnes du droit international, qui sont en jeu.
9. a) En effet, les mémoires de l'Agent siamois tendent a l'anéantissement de l'Etat laotien par annexion au Siam de la totalité de son territoire, et au moins à l'amputation et à la défiguration du Cambodge et du Laos, entités politiques constituées, personnes du droit international, auxquelles des provinces entières seraient arrachées aux fins d'annexion au Siam.
   b) Indépendamment de tous autres arguments déjà invoqués, les territoires de Luang Prabang rive droite est une partie importante de la province de Luang Prabang, qui est le centre politique de Laos.
   c) Le Bassac rive droite constitue une partie importante de la province du Bassac, que l'on ne pourrait arracher au Laos sans créer des perturbations graves.
   d) Ce serait porter un préjudice injustifiable à ces provinces et au Laos que de suivre le Siam dans des prétentions non fondées, au mépris d'un traité de frontière dont la force et la valeur ont été démontrées.
   e) Les mêmes raisons valent pour la province de Battambang, partie intégrante du Cambodge, dont la vie est tout entière tournée vers Phnom Penh, le Mékong et la mer de Chine.
10. a) En résumé, ce que l'Agent siamois demande à la Commission, c'est, pour satisfaire les *convenances* du Siam, de préférer à une situation territoriale bien établie, confirmée et garantie par des traités solennels, des bouleversements territoriaux très gravement préjudiciables, et dans une large mesure moralement et matériellement intolérables pour l'autre partie.
    b) Enfin, en demandant la restauration sur la rive gauche du Mékong de ses prétentions d'avant 1893, le Siam prétend créer une situation dont le droit international public ne connaît pas d'autre exemple, et qui, en constituant une sorte d'hypothèque sur l'avenir du Laos et du Cambodge, ne pourrait avoir d'autre effet que d'instituer dans ces régions un état d'insécurité de nature à compromettre la prospérité et la paix dans cette partie du monde.

Conclusion finale. Pour tous ces motifs, l'argumentation siamoise en faveur de la révision est rejetée, et le bien-fondé de l'argumentation française en faveur de la confirmation des clauses des traités visées à l'article 3 de l'Accord de règlement franco-siamois du 17 novembre 1946 est reconnu.

> Pour copie certifiée conforme
> L'Agent du Gouvernement français
> *Francis Lacoste.*

Annexe 1

Aux "Observations et Conclusions" de L'agent du Gouvernement Français en Date du 7 Juin 1947
Notice Sur des Circonstances Qui Ont Conduit à la Conclusion de L'accord de Règlement Franco-Siamois du 17 Novembre 1946

7 juin 1947

1. En annulant la Convention de Tokio du 9 mai 1941, dès longtemps répudiée par la France, l'Accord de règlement du 17 novembre 1946 a, dans son article 1, rendu toute sa force au traité du 7 décembre 1937, qui reste la loi des parties.

2. Dans son article 3, l'Accord de règlement stipule qu' "aussitôt après la signature du présent accord, la France et le Siam constitueront, par application de l'article 21 du traité franco-siamois du 7 décembre 1937, une commission de conciliation composée de deux représentants des parties et de trois neutres conformément à l'Acte Général de Genève du 26 septembre 1928 pour le règlement pacifique des différends internationaux qui règle la constitution et le fonctionnement de la Commission. La commission commencera ses travaux aussitôt que possible après que le transfert des territoires visés au dernier paragraphe de l'article 1 aura été effectué. Elle sera chargée d'examiner les arguments ethniques, géographiques et économiques des parties en faveur de la révision ou de la confirmation des clauses du traité du 3 octobre 1893, de la convention du 13 février 1904 et du traité du 23 mars 1937.

3. C'est donc le statut territorial établi par l'article 22 du traité du 6 décembre 1937 qui se trouve être, dans des circonstances tout exceptionnelles, l'objet des débats qui se déroulent devant la Commission.

4. L'objet de la présente notice est d'étudier ce statut territorial en lui-même et d'en décrire le fonctionnement depuis son entrée en vigueur.

I—Le Statut de la Frontière Entre le Siam et L'Indochine et Son Fonctionnement

1. L'article 22 du traité de 1937 a confirmé le règlement de 1907, déclaré définitif dès le principe dans le préambule du traité de 1907, est confirmé par l'article 2 du traité du 14 février 1925. Ce dernier texte stipulait en outre que les deux Hautes Parties Contractantes *se garantissaient* mutuellement le statut territorial qu'elles venaient de confirmer, c'est-à-dire qu'elles *s'interdisaient de le constater*. Cette garantie est répétée dans l'article 22 du traité de 1937, auquel l'article premier de la Convention de 1946 a rendu toute sa force. Le traité de frontières de 1937 n'a donc fait que confirmer et garantir une fois de plus une situation vieille de 30 ans, qui n'avait jamais donné lieu à aucune contestation de la part du Gouvernement siamois.

2. La frontière établie en 1907 avait un double mérite; elle était *certaine*, ayant donné lieu à une délimitation extrêmement soigneuse et complète; elle était aussi ce qu'on peut appeler une frontière *paisible*. Jusqu'aux incidents de 1940–41, elle est restée une frontière sans histoire.

3. D'autre part, le Gouvernement français s'était rendu aux représentations du Gouvernement siamois en ce qui concerne la seule partie du tracé de la frontière qui eut soulevé, non des difficultés entre les Parties, mais des problèmes: la frontière du Mékong. La définition de la frontière fluviale entre l'Indochine et le Siam, le long du Mékong, résulte de l'article 3 de la Convention du 25 août 1926; le système ainsi défini était compliqué, et de nature à rendre difficile une bonne administration. A certains égards, il avait déjà été porté remède à la situation qui résultait de ce tracé par les travaux de la Haute Commission du Mékong. D'ailleurs, sauf en ce qui concerne le tracé de la frontière elle-même, le régime auquel les Hautes Parties Contractantes avaient abouti assurait entre elles une juste réciprocité. (Convention de 1926 article 5 et suivant).

4. Au cours des années 1939 et 1940, les deux Gouvernements s'entendirent pour donner une force concrète aux idées qui s'étaient fait jour au cours des conversations antérieures à ce sujet. Le Gouvernement français et le Gouvernement siamois s'entendirent sur une formule de délimitation de la frontière du Mékong agréé par les deux parties dès le mois de mars 1940, et qui a été définitivement acceptée dans les lettres échangées le 12 juin 1940 lors de la conclusion du Pacte de non-agression. Dans la première phrase de cette négociation, le Gouvernement français avait reçu du Gouvernement siamois une communication selon laquelle la modification adoptée d'un commun accord de la frontière fluviale du Mékong au profit du Siam n'affectait en aucune manière le principe général, acquis depuis 1907, de l'intangibilité des frontières.

5. En liaison avec cette négociation, les deux Gouvernements avaient négocié un Pacte de non-agression que la Commission connaît. Par son article premier,

chacune des Hautes Parties Contractantes s'engageait à respecter à tous égards la souveraineté ou l'autorité de l'autre Partie Contractante sur ses territoires. Chacune des Hautes Parties Contractantes s'interdisait d'intervenir en aucune manière dans les affaires intérieures desdits territoires, et elles s'engageaient à s'abstenir de toute action tendant à susciter ou favoriser une agitation, propagande ou tentative d'intervention ayant pour but de porter atteinte à l'intégrité territoriale de l'autre Partie, ou de transformer par la force le régime politique de tout ou partie des territoires de celle-ci.

6. Ce traité était signé le 12 juin 1940, et ratifié par l'Assemblée siamoise le 4 août. Cependant, les démarches françaises pour obtenir l'échange de ratifications restaient sans résultat, et, le 9 septembre, le Ministre de France à Bangkok apprenait par une communication du Premier Ministre siamois que cette formalité était considérée comme inopportune.

II—Le Siam et le Traité de 1937 de 1940 [sic] à 1946

1. Le 17 septembre 1940, la Légation de Thaïlande en France adressait aux autorités de Vichy un aide-mémoire selon lequel le Gouvernement siamois proposait qu'avant de mettre le pacte en vigueur un accord fût conclu touchant les questions qui avaient fait l'objet de négociations officielles:
    I. —délimitation du Mékong frontière en suivant le chenal en eau profonde, et règlement de toutes les questions administratives pendantes, ainsi qu'il avait été prévu dans l'échange de lettres en date du 12 juin 1940.
    II. —adoption du Mékong comme frontière entre les deux pays, du Nord au Sud, jusqu'à la frontière du Cambodge, impliquant la rétrocession à la Thaïlande des territoires situés sur la rive droite du Mékong en face de Luang Prabang et de Paksé.

2. Le Gouvernement siamois demandait en outre au Gouvernement français de bien vouloir lui donner, sous forme de lettre, l'assurance qu'au cas de changement de la souveraineté française, la France *"rétrocéderait à la Thaïlande les territoires du Laos du Cambodge."*

3. Le Gouvernement siamois invoquait pour toute justification *"les circonstances."*

4. Le 18 septembre, un aide-mémoire français était remis à la Légation de Thaïlande:

> Le Gouvernement français, disait-il, ne peut apprécier les motifs du Gouvernement siamois. Pour répondre au désir du Président du Conseil de Thaïlande exprimé par une lettre adressée au Ministre de France le 8 juillet 1940, le Gouvernement français a accepté que la Commission mixte chargée de régler diverses

questions relatives au Mékong se réunisse en même temps que serait ratifié le pacte de non-agression. Le Gouvernement français demeure pour sa part disposé à se conformer à cette prévision. La demande de rétrocession des territoires situés sur la rive droite du Mékong est irrecevable.

5. Le 30 septembre, la Légation de Thaïlande revenait à la charge. Elle répétait ses prétentions en les assortissant d'un essai de justification. Toutefois, elle renonçait pour le moment à sa demande d'assurance relative aux territoires du Cambodge et du Laos.

6. Le 2 octobre, le Gouvernement français répondait à la Légation de Thaïlande en repoussant ces prétentions. L'aide-mémoire français s'exprimait ainsi:

> Le Gouvernement français a étudié la situation tendant à faire inscrire au programme des travaux de la Commission mixte la question des territoires situés sur la rive droite du Mékong. Après un attentif examen, il doit constater l'impossibilité de répondre sur ce point aux vues du Gouvernement thaïlandais. L'inscription de cette question au programme des travaux ne serait possible en effet que si le Gouvernement français pouvait admettre le principe d'une cession desdits territoires. Or, tel ne saurait être le cas. Le Gouvernement français, pour sa part, a constamment marqué qu'il tenait pour définitive la frontière actuelle. Il rappelle au surplus que le Gouvernement thaïlandais, loin de contester cette manière de voir, a pris l'initiative de faire préciser dans le préambule du traité du 23 mars 1907 qu'il s'agissait dans l'espèce d'un règlement final, ce terme étant destiné à traduire la ferme volonté des Hautes Parties Contractantes de renoncer pour l'avenir à présenter de nouvelles revendications. Tout récemment encore, les deux Gouvernements ont eu l'occasion de confirmer ces positions. Si le Gouvernement français en juin dernier, dans un souci de relations de bon voisinage, et dans un sentiment de large compréhension des intérêts thaïlandais, a consenti à soumettre certaines questions relatives aux îles du Mékong à un examen particulier, il ne l'a fait, compte tenu de la lettre et de l'esprit de l'accord solennellement conclu en 1907, que sur l'assurance formelle donnée par le Président du Conseil de Thaïlande au Ministre de France à Bangkok que le Gouvernement thaïlandais ne se proposait pas de s'en prévaloir pour présenter d'autres revendication d'ordre territorial.

7. La position juridique du Gouvernement français était encore plus forte que la rédaction concise et modérée de son aide-mémoire du 2 octobre ne le laissait paraître. Non seulement dans les traités successifs de 1925 et 1937 les Hautes Parties Contractantes avaient confirmé le règlement de frontière de 1907, déclare définitif dès le principe, mais encore elles s'étaient garanti mutuel-

lement leurs frontières, s'interdisant par là de les contester. Il ne pouvait donc être question de l'application dans la circonstance de l'article 21 du traité de 1937, puisque aucune question litigieuse au sens de cet article ne pouvait être soulevée à propos de la frontière. Le refus catégorique du Gouvernement français était parfaitement fondé.

8. On connaît les événements qui ont suivi et qui ont abouti à la conclusion, sous l'oeil du Japon, de la Convention de paix de Tokio [sic]. Il suffira d'observer que, même à Tokio [sic], le Siam n'a obtenu qu'une partie de ce qu'il demandait, et que ses prétentions d'aujourd'hui excèdent de beaucoup ce qu'il a réussi à obtenir alors, au mépris de traités solennellement confirmés à plusieurs reprises, et de stipulations par lesquelles il garantissait le statu quo territorial.

9. La convention de Tokio, répudiée par le Gouvernement français, a été annulée par l'article premier de l'Accord de Règlement du 17 novembre 1946, et le statu quo ante, rétabli.

Pour copie certifiée conforme
L' Agent du Gouvernement français
Francis Lacoste.

Annexe 2

Aux "Observations et Conclusions" de L'agent du Gouvernement Français en Date du 7 Juin 1947
Réponse Point Par Point au Mémoire de L'agent du Gouvernement Siamois du 29 Mai et à Son Annexe

7 juin 1947

N. B. Le plus grand nombre des arguments contenus dans le deuxième mémoire de l'Agent du Gouvernement siamois et dans l'annexe à ce mémoire ont déjà été mentionnés dans le premier mémoire siamois en date du 12 mai. Ils ont déjà fait l'objet de réponses dans le mémoire français du 22 mai et dans son annexe, ainsi que dans le mémoire du 7 juin.

Il a donc paru inutile de les réfuter à nouveau, et le présent document se borne dans tous les cas de ce genre, à renvoyer, par simple référence, aux réponses déjà faites.

I—Réponse au Mémoire du 29 Mai

I-1   Réponse déjà donnée dans le mémoire du 7 juin section IV paragraphe I.

II-2   Réponse déjà donnée dans le mémoire du 7 juin section I et section IV.

II-3   Réponse déjà donnée dans l'annexe au mémoire du 22 mai page 2ème paragraphe et dans le mémoire du 7 juin (conclusion no. 9-a). En ce qui concerne le deuxième et le troisième paragraphe, voir ci-dessous III-8.

III-4   Le fait que la requête siamoise du 12 mai n'ait pas fait mention de l'Accord de règlement de 1946 ni du traité de 1937 n'a pas été relevé comme simple omission matérielle. En réalité, la requête du 12 mai n'a pas tenu compte de l'incidence de ces deux textes sur la définition de l'objet soumis à l'examen de la Commission: il ne s'agissait pas de reprendre le statut de la frontière aux dates successives de 1893, 1904 et 1907, ce qui donnait un caractère historique à la présentation des arguments siamois. La requête siamoise aurait dû se borner à considérer le statut de la frontière sous l'angle ethnique, géographique et économique, tel qu'il existe actuellement en vertu du traité de 1937. La remarque faite dans le mémoire du 7 juin, section I paragraphe 4, est maintenue.

III-5   Réponse déjà donnée dans le mémoire du 7 juin section I et par l'annexe I à ce mémoire.

III-6   La remarque faite dans le mémoire du 22 mai paragraphe 6 est maintenue. Aucun argument ne peut être tiré d'une erreur commise à cette époque faute d'avoir pu connaître les éléments réels d'une situation politique locale particulièrement troublée.

III-7   Toute comparaison, explicite ou implicite, entre le régime intérieur du Siam et celui des pays de l'Indochine française est étrangère à l'objet de la présente instance. Cf. ci-dessous III-8 et mémoire du 7 juin section III-1 et 2. Pour la suite du développement, cf. mémoire du 7 juin section IV-8.

III-8   Tout développement sur l'organisation politique des Parties, aussi bien du Siam que de la France ou des Etats qui sont associés, est irrecevable aux termes de l'article 3 de l'accord de règlement du 17 novembre 1946. D'autre part, le mémoire du 29 mai paraît croire que le "danger mortel" signalé par le mémoire français du 22 mai aurait un caractère alimentaire. Il s'agit du danger qui menacerait l'Etat du Laos, en tant qu'entité politique, personne du droit international, si les revendications formulées dans la requête siamoise du 12 mai étaient satisfaites. Les remarques des paragraphes 1 et 8 du mémoire du 22 mai trouvent confirmation de leur bien-fondé dans le mémoire siamois du 29 mai et sont maintenues.

III-9   La position affirmée dans le paragraphe 9 du mémoire du 22 mai est maintenue.

IV-10   Le fait que la requête siamoise n'ait pas expressément soutenu la supériorité de la "race" thaï n'enlève pas leur caractère raciste à des prétentions qui tendent à l'annexion au Siam de territoires pour la raison que ceux-ci seraient habités par des éléments "racialement" apparentés. (Cf. paragraphes 4, 9 et 13 de la requête siamoise du 12 mai).

IV-10, page 9. Le mémoire siamois dénonce l' "expansionnisme" du Gouvernement français, parce que ce page 9 dernier à rappelé l'existence de groupes importants de populations cambodgiennes et laotiennes au delà des frontières du Cambodge et du Laos. Une simple référence aux conclusions formulées dans les deux mémoires français fait justice de cette accusation.

Il est rappelé, en revanche, que les prétentions de la requête siamoise, si elles étaient satisfaites, vaudraient au Siam une "expansion" de quelque 270,000 kilomètres carrés, occupés par quelque 1,500,000 habitants. (Cf. III-8 ci-dessus, dernier paragraphe.)

IV-10 Réponse déjà donnée par le mémoire du 7 juin, section V-8 et 9 par exposé verbal en séance de la Commission le 4 juin.

La remarque du mémoire du 22 mai paragraphe 14 est maintenue. (Cf. remarque ci-dessus IV-10.)

Les "avances" successives des frontières du Cambodge et du Laos ont rendu à ces deux pays des territoires qui leur avaient été enlevés.

IV-11 Réponse déjà donnée par mémoire du 7 juin Section V paragraphe 6 et dans l'exposé oral en séance du 4 juin (cf. minutes de cette séance) au cours duquel il a été indiqué que les économies siamoise et laotienne n'étaient pas complémentaires. C'est d'ailleurs ce que l'annexe au mémoire siamois du 29 mai (page-1er paragraphe et page-2ème alinéa) constate elle-même en termes exprès.

12   La position affirmée dans les conclusions des mémoires français des 22 mai et 7 juin est maintenue.

Pour le dernier paragraphe, cf. III-8.

13   Réponse déjà donnée: cf. ci-dessus observation sur IV-10.

II—Réponse à L'annexe au Mémoire du 19 Mai

Cette annexe est consacrée essentiellement au développement de l'idée que les frontières orientales du Siam doivent être reportées vers l'Est afin de donner au réseau de voies de communication siamois une sphère d'activité plus vaste.

En ce qui concerne les avantages que ces voies de communication seraient susceptibles d'apporter aux régions voisines du Laos et du Cambodge, il a déjà été répondu: 1) que ces deux pays jouissent par eux-mêmes de voies de communication suffisantes pour écouler leurs produits vers leurs débouchés les plus rénumérateurs et assurer leur ravitaillement dans des conditions économiques normales (mémoire du 7 juin, section V paragraphe 8 et exposé oral en séance de commission du 4 juin); 2) que la France et ses associés s'attendent à trouver le Siam prêt à les admettre au bénéfice de communications actuelles ou nouvelles susceptibles d'avantager leur commerce, sans qu'il soit pour autant nécessaire de déplacer la frontière (mémoire du 7 juin, section V paragraphe 9).

Aspect ethnique 1893, 1904, 1907.
Réponse a déjà été donnée par l'annexe au mémoire du 22 mai (paragraphes 4 et 18) et par le mémoire du 7 juin (section V paragraphes 3 et 4).

Aspect géographique
Aucun argument spécifiquement géographique n'est invoqué dans ce document. Ceux qu'il énonce sont de caractère en réalité économique, et se confondent avec ceux qui sont traités au paragraphe ci-dessus.

Il faut en déduire qu'aucun argument de caractère proprement géographique ne pouvait être articulé en faveur d'une révision de la frontière actuelle. Les remarques de l'annexe au mémoire du 22 mai (paragraphes 5, 10, 15, 19) et de l'exposé oral fait en séance de la Commission le 4 juin sont intégralement maintenus.

Aspect économique
Indépendamment de l'observation préliminaire essentielle faite au début du présent chapitre, les points suivants paraissent devoir être relevés:

Les indications qui ont été fournies à la Commission sur les travaux de la Haute Commission permanente franco-siamoise du Mékong ont montré que cet organisme était parfaitement apte à rendre les meilleurs services, si un sincère esprit de collaboration animait ses membres. L'oeuvre qu'elle élaborée est déjà considérable, et le Gouvernement français a entériné, en leur temps, les arrangements conclus, d'accord entre les parties, sous son égide. La mise en application de certains de ces règlements a été considérablement retardée: l'imputation de ces retards ne saurait être mise au compte du Gouvernement français.

Il n'y a aucune raison d'ordre géographique qui puisse empêcher l'établissement d'une ligne de chemin de fer le long du Mékong. La route fédérale no. 13, qui ne traverse aucune dénivellation importante, puisqu'aussi bien elle longe une voie d'eau navigable, peut être doublée par une voie ferrée.

La citation est tirée d'un ouvrage de vulgarisation à l'usage des touristes publié il y a 22 ans.

Réponse déjà donnée dans l'annexe au mémoire du 22 mai (paragraphe 7) et dans la partie I de l'annexe I du mémoire du 7 juin paragraphes 3 et 4.

Contrairement aux assertions du mémoire siamois, la passe de Snoc-Trou n'interdit pas l'accès des Grands Lacs pendant 7 mois par an. Il est, en revanche, exact qu'à l'époque des plus basses eaux, de mars a juin, seules les embarcations d'un tirant d'eau réduit peuvent franchir cette passe. Mais le trafic ainsi assuré est suffisamment actif pour permettre, notamment, la sortie continue en toute saison de la production de poisson sec des Grands Lacs.

Il résulte des observations qui précèdent qu'aucun argument nouveau, pertinent ou fondé, ne se trouve dans le mémoire du 29 mai ou dans son annexe, et l'agent du Gouvernement français ne peut en conséquence que maintenir les conclusions de ses mémoires des 22 mai et 7 juin.

> Pour copie certifiée conforme
> L'Agent du Gouvernement français
> (Signé) *Francis Lacoste.*
> Pour copie conforme
> L'Agent du Royaume du Cambodge
> (Signé)

[Source: International Court of Justice. Pleadings, oral arguments, documents. *Case concerning the temple of Preah Vihear (Cambodia and Thailand).* Vol. I. Application–Pleadings, 1962, annexe 6, 21–92. In the Thai edition of this book the documents given under appendix 10 are given in Thai only. The text presented here accords with the Thai except in one section, namely that entitled "Amplifications des aspects ethniques, géographiques et économiques des frontières franco-siamoises," where there are several points of divergence.]

APPENDIX II

REPORT OF FINDINGS AND OPINION OF THE COMMITTEE TO INVESTIGATE THE EXPENDITURES OUT OF NATIONAL REVENUE BY THE FREE THAI MOVEMENT BOTH WITHIN AND OUTSIDE THE KINGDOM

As this Committee has been assigned the task of investigating the expenditures paid for out of the national revenue by the Free Thai movement both within and outside the country, it would first like to define the meaning of "national revenue" in this case, and has invited the proposer of this motion to clarify the phrase. Mr. Bunchuai Atthakon has explained to the Committee that there is no evidence to indicate that anyone has been guilty of embezzlement, but that there are unseemly rumors going around, possibly implying that certain people who were in the movement had made use of the money they received from the Free Thai headquarters for their own personal benefit. No allegations have been made regarding other property such as military equipment, however. His Excellency [Nai] Pridi Banomyong has explained that the military equipment [made available to the Free Thai] was provided by the Allies, not by the [Thai] nation, and that this equipment may be handed over to Thailand. It is, then, understood that the Free Thai movement did not receive any military equipment belonging to the nation. This subject does not therefore fall within the sphere of this Committee's consideration.

The amount of various monies the Free Thai received and spent on their work both within and outside the country will be reported on further here in accordance with the motion passed on this matter. This motion initially called for the investigation of internal expenditures [only], but M.R. Seni Pramoj proposed that it be extended to cover expenditures for work outside the country as well.

The Committee has already studied the various documents presented, and according to Document "D", page 2, income and expenditure for 1942 was as follows: Thai money in the U.S.A. deposited with the National City Bank of New York amounted to $2,730,478.61, of which the following was withdrawn: (1) $657,092.39 paid to the Thai legation in Washington; (2) $411,557.95 for the Free Thai working through the O.S.S., and (3) $63,124.18 paid to the O.S.S. for gold delivered [to Thailand] to cover the expenses [of the Free Thai] in Thailand.[1]

The present investigation is not directly concerned with amount (1), or the $657,092.39 paid to the Thai legation, since this was for expenses incurred by the Thai legation in Washington in the course of its duties, as reported on page

4 of the same Document "D". This states that this sum was spent for payment of legation officials' salaries; legation expenses; expenses for supervision of students; pocket money and fees for government and private students; the salary of Mr. [Frederick] Dolbeare; the cost of the return fare to Thailand of the family of M.R. Seni Pramoj; pensions for Dr. Ellis and Phraya Nithet Wiratchakit; salary and travel expenses for Mr. Lecount; expenses connected with the Free Thai in England; expenses for Free Thai officials' uniforms in the U.S.A.[2] and advances for those sent out of Thailand [on missions.]

Even though this approximately $600,000 is not the main subject under discussion, nevertheless it can be divided here into three categories, namely (a) expenses for the Free Thai movement in England, amounting to $34,747.00; (b) payment of Free Thai officials' uniforms in the U.S.A., amounting to $13,451.44, and (c) advances for those sent out of Thailand [on missions], amounting to $63,417.55. Points (a) and (b) raise no problem, as Luang Ditthakan, the official in charge of handling these financial matters, has signed a guarantee certifying these as the correct amounts paid, while (c) represents an advance of monies which the legation may claim back, and should not therefore be connected with the work of this Committee.

Sum (2), paid via the O.S.S. for the use of the Free Thai movement, and amounting to $411,557.95, must be understood as payment for the Free Thai overseas, and refers principally to the Free Thai operating from the United States, as part of sum (1) had already been set aside for the use of the Free Thai in England [see above]. Page 4 of Document 14 states that Mr. Mani Sanasen will collate the accounts and send them in to the legation in the United States for its perusal, and that he will send in any monies which might still be remaining.

A detailed breakdown of sum (2) is given in Document "B", part 2. This states that the O.S.S. received $500,000 and spent this on the following items: the [running] expenses and pocket money used during operations; the cost of equipment; construction of headquarters building in China; costs of transportation; and daily expenses at sea, leaving $88,442.05 which has already been returned to the Government account. The expenditure for these categories has already been signed for by Major James H.W. Thompson in a letter of 17th April 1946 in which he states that the O.S.S. had already paid these amounts, while the Thai Chargé d'Affaires in Washington, Luang Ditthakan, has signed his name guaranteeing that the sums reported in Document "D" page 2 had been paid, and also signing an acknowledgement that the O.S.S. had already paid the remaining $88,442.05 into the Thai government's account with the National City Bank of New York on 24 March 1946. These amounts of money together with the sum of money returned add up to $500,000, the amount that the O.S.S. received.

On the basis of evidence received, the Committee finds, then, that the sum of $500,000 which the O.S.S. received for the expenditure of the Free Thai outside the country was properly spent, and that the sum left over has been correctly returned to the Thai government. Expenses totaled $411,577.95, and the sum returned came to $88,442.05. These two amounts added together make a total of $500,000, the amount that the O.S.S. received in the beginning.

Now we come to sum (3), which covers expenditures incurred by the Free Thai movement for its work within Thailand, amounting to $63,124.18. This sum was used [by the O.S.S.] to purchase gold [which was then sent into Thailand] for the expenses of resistance work within the kingdom. The first lot sent was worth $49,957.06, while a bill for $128.62 was incurred for expenses connected with this arrangement [see below—Ed.], while the expenses of sending Mr. Thawin Udon to China[3] amounted to $13,038.50, making a total of $63,124.18. Once this sum is subtracted from the total of $500,000 designated for the use of the Free Thai movement within the country $436,875.82 is left. Details of expenses between 17 April 1945 and 19 November 1945 are given in the O.S.S. accounts under the section entitled "Thai currency account," and also in Document "D," page 7.

The Committee finds that $49,957.06 was received by the Free Thai headquarters in this country, as is made clear in Document "A," which consists of a letter dated 17 April 1946 from Mr. Charles W. Yost [then United States Chargé d'Affaires to Thailand] to Mr. Direk Jayanama, the Thai Foreign Minister, confirming that gold sent in by the O.S.S. to Bangkok for the expenses of the Free Thai movement in the spring of 1945 was worth $49,957.06. In addition to this Document "A," a detailed account of the sums paid from this amount was sent in on 17 April 1946 by the American legation, and signed by Major James H.W. Thompson, to His Excellency [Nai] Pridi Banomyong, marked by the Committee as "B" in Document 3. This stated that the gold delivered in Bangkok and valued at $49,957.06 had been signed for by Mr. Wichit Lulitanon of the Free Thai movement's headquarters within the country and Mr. Thawi Tawethikun, acknowledging receipt of such from Major Wester[4] on 7 April 1945, and marked by Mr. Direk in evidence as "correctly certified today. D.J. 9th April 1946." The gold in this lot weighed about fifty kilograms, which is worth $49,957.06 American dollars, which is only fifty cents below the sum reported in the letter of the American legation and in the report of the Thai legation in Washington. The Committee has enquired about this from Mr. Wichit Lulitanon and was told that the deliverer of the gold at the time had no attached inventory with him, and the accounting and calculation was carried out hurriedly in a secret hide-out used by the Free Thai movement. The Committee found that only a very small error was made, amounting to fifty cents, as appears in Document "C".

APPENDIX II

Mr. Wichit Lulitanon arranged for the banks to sell the gold, and after deduction of bank fees, an amount of 1,460,184.84 Baht was received as stated in Document "C," page 2. According to Document "L", the Free Thai movement headquarters spent this sum on the following:

		Baht
1.	Expenses for sending people abroad	184,605.00
2.	Expenses of the Uttaradit - Sukhothai unit	20,000.00
3.	Expenses of the Bang Kapi unit	20,000.00
4.	Expenses of the Loei unit	36,000.00
5.	Expenses of the Kanchanaburi unit	3,500.00
6.	Expenses of the Nakhon Si Thammarat–Phetchaburi unit	42,100.00
7.	Expenses of the Chaiyaphum unit	5,000.00
8.	Expenses of the Hua Hin - Pran Buri unit	1,000.00
9.	Expenses of the Ranong unit	80,000.00
10.	Expenses of the Sakon Nakhon–Nakhon Phanom–Nong Khai–Mahasarakham–Udon–Ubon unit	165,200.00
11.	Expenses for intelligence agents	47,000.00
12.	Expenses for water transportation	168,253.30
13.	Expenses for the British camp	158,292.10
14.	Expenses for the American camp	165,510.00
15.	Expenses for the transmission of secret radio messages	211,127.00
16.	Expenses for the China line	57,197.51
17.	Expenses for fuel	30,800.00
18.	Miscellaneous: reception, transport, pocket money, vehicle repairs	124,599.93
	Total	1,410,184.84[5]

Thus the sum of $49,957.06 American dollars was all spent according to Document "L" which Mr. Wichit Lulitanon signed guaranteeing the expenditures incurred by the Free Thai movement [within the country].

The other amount specified in the letter of the American legation Document "B," as $128.62 for operating expenses, is supported by the report of the Thai legation in Washington, marked "D," page 5, which states that this $128.62 represented expenses incurred for that transaction (meaning the purchase of gold for the Free Thai movement in Thailand). Page 7 of this same Document also gives the details of this sum as being $72.08 for the molding of the gold bullion, and $56.54 for the cost of transport in the United States, these two amounts added together coming to $128.62. These documents are certified by the authorities concerned, so that payment of this amount can be regarded as having been carried out correctly.

The further sum of $13,038.50 specified in Document "B" as item 4, was spent for gold sent to Mr. Thawin Udon. Document "D," or the report of the Thai legation in Washington, states on page 6 that the gold delivered to Mr. Thawin Udon was worth the total sum of $13,038.50. Page 7 of the same document gives the following details, namely that on 30 August 1945, gold worth $11,783.54 was sent to Mr. Thawin Udon and that gold worth $1,255.96 was sent him on 5th October 1945, making a total of $13,038.50. These two documents are signed and certified by the authorities concerned, so that such payment can be accepted as having been properly made for the work of the Free Thai movement.

Once these three items are added together, namely the sums for the purchase of gold for the Free Thai headquarters in Thailand, amounting to $49,957.06; for the expenses incurred in that arrangement, amounting to $128.62; and for gold delivered to Mr. Thawin Udon worth $13,038.50; this, together with the amount which the O.S.S. returned to the Thai government account as stated on page 7 of Document "D" amounting to $436,875.82, gives a total of $500,000.00, or the same amount as that set aside for the use of the Free Thai movement within the country paid through the O.S.S. Thus it can be concluded that the expenditure of the Free Thai within the country met by dollars frozen in the United States [part of which were released] are all accounted for, and that there are no sums missing. The $436,875.82 returned was stated on page 3 of Document "D" as having been returned to the Thai government account on 31 December 1945.

In conclusion, then, the sum that M.R. Seni Pramoj paid to the O.S.S. in two lots of $500,000 each out of government money confiscated by the United States and totaling one million dollars in all, is correctly accounted for, and there are no sums which have not been considered by the financial authorities concerned.

According to the first item of Document "I" of the Budget for the People's Assistance, or what later became known as the Peace Budget, 8,867,989.87 Baht were used out of national revenue for resistance work against the Japanese up till 10 August 1945. According to Document "M" this money was all spent, the breakdown being as follows:

		Baht
1.	Military units	300,000.00
2.	Police units	2,000,000.00
3.	Chon Buri unit	567,450.00
4.	Kanchanaburi unit	528,000.00
5.	Suphan Buri unit	217,500.00

6.	Prachin–Chachoengsao unit	39,217.16
7.	Ang Thong–Ayutthaya unit	350,465.00
8.	Headquarters	42,000.00
9.	Ubon unit	53,000.00
10.	Interior office units	536,441.87
11.	Sukhothai-Uttaradit unit	120,000.00
12.	Communication units	233,000.00
13.	Krathum Baen unit	25,310.50
14.	Phrae unit	6,117.72
15.	Foreign units	109,287.97
16.	Sakon Nakhon unit	52,000.00
17.	The Northeast units	100,000.00
18.	Korat [Nakhon Ratchasima] unit	50,000.00
19.	Fuel and transport	3,548,199.65
	Total	**8,867,989.87**

Expenses for the above items have been signed for and certified by the financial officer of the Office of the Secretariat to the Council of Ministers, Mr. Arun Prasanthong, who stated that such expenses were properly incurred by the Free Thai movement. Thus the sum of 8,867,989.87 Baht used from the People's Assistance Budget according to item (1) thereof was properly incurred.

Item (2) of Document "I," or the Budget for the People's Assistance, states that expenses met by the Peace Budget amounted to 15,088,996.20 Baht. This Document "I" specifies nine items amounting to 737,439.91 Baht incurred for expenses of the Free Thai movement after the Japanese surrender. These, which have been certified by the financial officer of the Office of the Secretariat to the Council of Ministers as having been correctly incurred in the work of the Free Thai movement, are as follows:

		Baht
1.	Kanchanaburi unit	488.10
2.	Prachin-Chachoengsao unit	61,260.49
3.	Ang Thong-Ayutthaya unit	28,752.39
4.	Krathum Baen unit	1,650.00
5.	Ubon unit	8,485.00
6.	Sakon Nakhon unit	190,000.00
7.	Nakhon–Pathom unit	10,000.00
8.	Public relations and reception unit	323,139.23
9.	Fuel and transport unit	113,664.70
	Total	**737,439.91**

In addition, Document "J" lists expenses incurred by the Free Thai movement which have not yet been paid for, including for cash paid out, such as the claims of Group Captain Kat Kengradomying listing 144,660 Baht spent by certain persons working for the Free Thai movement. As this sum has not been paid, it is the responsibility of the leader of the Free Thai movement to consider reasonable compensation for such people.

The Committee would also like to point out that a secret organization such as this [the Free Thai movement] cannot be expected to keep detailed accounts and receipts like the ordinary accounts kept by companies or other organizations during peace time. Those conducting these enquiries should be satisfied when they see that these sums were used in special circumstances necessary for the success of the movement. For example, the Committee feels that the construction of military barracks, air bases, camps, headquarters, etc. was carried out in difficult circumstances with admirable efficiency, and demonstrates that the amount of money spent was worth the work it accomplished. General Jex,[6] in particular, has commented that the air bases built by the Free Thai can generally be said to have cost very little, which is to the credit of those responsible for having built such.

It is also inevitable that there should be what General Jex has referred to as unaccountable expenditures, such as money given to those parachuted into hostile territory. In fact it is necessary that under such secret and dangerous situations great caution should be exercised for the safety of those within the movement. Identities had to be kept secret and code names such as "Ruth" for the leader of the Free Thai movement used. Special documents such as checks, invoices, receipts, orders, etc. could not therefore disclose the names of senders or receivers lest these reveal the identification of such persons and thereby threaten their lives and safety should such documents get picked up by the enemy. Secret codes had to be used to prevent such fearful consequences in the event of slip-ups.

Such precautions were not peculiar to Thailand alone. Similar circumstances pertained in other countries which carried out similar undertakings and enterprises. Major Thompson has told this Committee that members of the Resistance movement in France also had to keep matters secret to engender trust and confidence and avoid any misunderstandings. Major Macdonald has also explained that in the case of Thailand, the O.S.S. did not express any wish to be informed of details concerning the expenditures incurred (by members of the Free Thai movement). General Jex, head of British Force 136, has referred to the general instructions which laid down that no documents, receipts or names of persons were to be kept, and that matters [involving the work of the movement] were to be kept absolutely secret lest such lead to arrests that might involve the destruction of the network. In fact, for the sake of security the Free Thai movement was requested by Force 136 to destroy every kind of document which could lead to a dangerous situation, just as while in practice particular assignments were known, their details were kept secret.

The Committee feels that given these circumstances, it is impossible and would be out of line to demand details of the items specified above.

It seems that the cause of the doubts [leading to these enquiries] stemmed [principally] from a misunderstanding over the $500,000 in the United States which had been set aside for the use of Free Thai movement [within Thailand]. It appears that originally M.R. Seni Pramoj had planned to send [all] this sum to the Free Thai movement in Thailand, but that later only $63,124.18 was sent to Asia. The rest of the sum remained in the United States, but has not by any means disappeared. This has been clearly disclosed by investigations. Prior to these [being held, however], there was confusion with regard to both intention and facts, so that certain persons suspected that part of this sum had gone astray somewhere.

It should be noted that such misunderstandings, even though they are not put forward out of malice but are pure misunderstandings, can nevertheless easily lead to rumors once politics are mixed with financial matters. The Committee has found, after investigating the documents and accounts placed before it, that such rumors are definitely unfounded, and that the sums can be accounted for. Those putting forward before the Committee the motion [that irregularities took place] do not have any evidence or facts to support such rumors or on which to base suspicions that there has been embezzlement of national revenue, expenditures on matters other than the work of the Free Thai movement, or slips and shortcomings in regard to such expenditures, etc.

The Free Thai movement, or what is also known as the underground movement has, for its part, its own justification. By law this movement was considered as offering aid to the enemy. Hence those who worked for the movement were subject to the death penalty in accordance with Article 110 of the Criminal Law. Those who worked for the movement thus risked their lives during a time of great national crisis because of their determination to maintain the independence of their country, and their desire to clear Thailand from being classed as a defeated power and to see their country's independence preserved in name in the peace treaty.

In Document "C," the United States Acting Secretary of State guaranteed to the leader of the Free Thai movement that Thailand's independence would be respected, while in Document "R" Mr. H.R. Bird [the British representative in Bangkok after the war—Ed.] stated that the results of the resistance activities carried out against the Japanese by the Free Thai movement had led the British government to impose only the lightest requirements [on Thailand] under the [Formal] Agreement. Had such an agreement been drawn up with the Field Marshal Phibun Songkhram government, the conditions imposed would have been many times more severe, as Thailand would have been accounted an enemy in the same way as Germany and Japan.

In Document "Z", which gives Mr. Bevin's statement of 20 August 1945, he mentions in regard to the Free Thai movement that the British government recognized the help and activities of the Free Thai movement in the resistance against Japan, but whether such work could eradicate the Thai government's declaration of war against England and its acquisition of British territory from the hands of the Japanese would depend on Thailand's future actions in regard to the reception of British troops in Thailand.

Document "P" gives Mr.Yost's reply to the [Thai] Foreign Minister on 17 September 1945, stating that the government of the United States would always remember the work of the Free Thai movement, and expressing his thanks and praise to the Free Thai for the help they had shown the Allies.

Document "T" is a statement by Mr. Harrington on the Free Thai movement stating that the latter had contributed greatly to confirming the belief of the United States that Thailand was its friend, leading the United States to be willing to give financial aid for the development of the country.

The [above] documents show that the Free Thai movement thus successfully revised the situation into which the country had been placed as a consequence of the war. The people of Thailand should be grateful for the work of its members, and if there is any way in which the country can express its appreciation for those who risked their lives to save the country, such actions would be most fitting and suitable.

Thepwithun
Nalaratsuwat
Wikromratthanasuphat
Nitisat (Phaisan)
Phichan Bunyong

[Source: Translated directly from the Thai edition.]

NOTES

Chapter 1

1. Later raised to Field Marshal. From this point on, to avoid confusion, the name and status of the person concerned will be given as it was at the time of the event being described.

    [Phibun Songkhram was a Colonel from the time this book opens until 14 July 1939, when he was made a Major General. He became a Field Marshal on 28 August 1941.]
2. Later dropped his title and became known as Nai Pridi Banomyong.
3. Nai Thawi Bunyaket took over this position from me in 1939.
4. *Royal Gazette*, 20 December 1938, vol. 44, 210. Later on changes were made in the Council as members resigned, or as it was re-structured. For details see Manun Borisut, *Rueang khana ratthamontri (Concerning the Council of Ministers)*, Bangkok, cremation volume for Nai Kasoem Siphayak, distributed by the Council of Ministers, [n.d.], 134–36.
5. On 14 July 1939, Chaophraya Sithammathibet resigned as Minister of Foreign Affairs. He was replaced by Major-General Luang Phibun Songkhram, while I was appointed Deputy Minister of Foreign Affairs.
6. On 22 August 1941, Colonel Luang Chawengsaksongkhram was appointed Minister of the Interior. I replaced Major-General Phibun Songkhram, the Prime Minister, as Minister of Foreign Affairs. This left Luang Phibun Songkhram in one position only, namely that of Prime Minister. Many other ministerial positions were also changed. See Manun Borisut, op. cit.
7. Later, on 10 April 1939, Luang Naruebetmanit was appointed by Royal Decree as Deputy Minister of Finance, while Colonel Luang Phromyothi became Deputy Minister of Defense.
8. On 19 August 1941, Lieutenant-General Luang Phromyothi replaced Major-General Luang Phibun Songkhram as Minister of Defense.
9. On 31 October 1941, Luang Wichitwathakan, Minister without portfolio, was appointed Deputy Minister of Foreign Affairs.
10. *Royal Gazette*, op. cit., 17 July 1939, vol. 56, 647.
11. Ibid., 22 August 1941, vol. 58, 1069.
12. [The last paragraphs of this chapter, while still containing the material of the Thai original, have been rearranged in the English edition.]

Chapter 2

1 [In the Thai original the author follows the opening paragraph with an overall discussion of colonialism. Since much of this material is known to Western readers, this section has been omitted in the English edition.]
2 [Heading added by the editor to parallel the author's later headings for this chapter.]
3 [Reign dates added on the first occasion a ruler is mentioned.]
4 [Highest rank of the Thai nobility at that time.]
5 [An island off the southwest coast of Thailand.]
6 [Including an attempt to convert King Narai himself.]
7 [Then the capital of Siam.]
8 [A section on the Bowring treaty follows in the Thai edition. This has been condensed in the English edition and inserted in the subsequent section on Thailand's relations with England.]
9 [Except for Battambang, Siemreap and Sisophon.]
10 [A region in northwestern Vietnam inhabited by Tai-speaking people.]
11 Regarding the loss of Thai territories to France, see the author's *Kanthut*, I, 331–420. [In the Thai edition the author lists the territories taken over from Thailand by France. In this edition the names and dates on which those territories were taken over have been incorporated into the text.]

   [A useful map showing the territories taken over by France between 1867–1907 is given in Thailand, Public Relations Department, *Comment des territoires de la Thailande ont été enlevés par la France*, Bangkok, 1941, Preface. The map can also be seen in Pensri (Suvanij) Duke, *Les relations entre la France et la Thailande (Thailand) au xixème siècle d'après les Archives des Affaires Etrangères*, Bangkok, Chalermnit, 1962, 61.]
12 [The honorific name he was given by the Thai.]
13 See Francis Bowes Sayre (Phraya Kalayanamaitri), Glad Adventure, New York, Macmillan, 1957, 104–23 and Prince Narathip-phongpraphan's *Prawat kanthut khong Thai* (*History of Thai Diplomacy*), 54–7.
14 For details see *Kantham sonthisanya mai khong Thai* (*The Making of New Treaties for Thailand*), which the Ministry of Foreign Affairs edited, and which was published and distributed by the Public Relations Department for the Royal ceremony celebrating the new treaties on 24 June 1939.
15 [In the Thai original the section on the role of the Mekong as a boundary line appears at the end of the chapter. Here it has been condensed to avoid undue repetition and inserted at the end of the section on Thailand's relations with France.]
16 *Kanthut*, op. cit., 356–60.
17 [A river in northeast Thailand that flows east into the Mekong above Pakse.]
18 [1622?]
19 [The Dutch had first arrived in Siam in 1602.]
20 [Port in Tenasserim on the Bay of Bengal. At that time Mergui was under Thai suzerainty.]

21 [See Prince Narathip [Phongpraphan], *Prawat Kanthut khong Thai*, op. cit.]
22 [In other words the Bowring treaty established the principle of extraterritoriality for British subjects. The treaty stipulated that a British consul was to reside at Bangkok and exercise all civil and criminal jurisdiction over British subjects in the country.]
23 [By the Treaty of Yandabo of 24 February 1826, which brought the first Anglo-Burmese war to a close, Britain acquired certain territories within and bordering on present-day Burma. They included Assam, Manipur, Arakan and Tenasserim, thus bringing the British right up to Thailand's southwestern border.]
24 [The Thai original contains considerable detail on the history of that war. This has been omitted here.]
25 [Born in 1866, Prince Damrong, a son of King Rama IV, was the first Minister of Education under King Rama V and the founder of the modern Ministry of the Interior. He is also renowned as a scholar and historian.]
26 On this subject see Prince Damrong, *Khati khon farang khao ma mueang Thai* (Account of Western Entrance into Thailand), [The Siam Society Journal, 1926, 20, No. 2.]
27 [At that time the Thai representative to the League of Nations.] Later became Deputy Foreign Minister and ambassador to a number of countries. Now retired.
28 Mr. [Yosuke] Matsuoka, later Minister of Foreign Affairs, and the arbitrator in the dispute between ourselves and France in 1941. After the war he was arraigned before the War Crimes Tribunal and died in prison.
29 See Seiji Hishida, *Japan among the Great Powers: [A Survey of her International Relations]*, London, Longmans Green & Co., 1940, 316–22.
30 [The deep water channel in a river that remains navigable throughout the year.]
31 For the full text of these treaties, see appendixes 1, 2 and 3 at the end of this book.
32 [In fact this stipulation was not written into the text of the Non-Aggression Treaty between Thailand and France, but was incorporated in an exchange of secret and confidential letters attached to the Treaty and signed by Major-General Luang Phibun Songkhram and Mr. Paul Lépissier (See appendix 1)].

Chapter 3

1 [The title of this chapter in the Thai edition is "Peace Agreement between Thailand and France." This has been altered in the English edition to more accurately reflect the chapter's contents.]
2 [Referring to French acquisition of Thai-controlled territory in the past. He was now asking the Thai to overlook these actions and to extend sympathy to France in her present plight.]
3 [The Japanese were determined to cut off all war supplies being shipped in by the Allies to the Chungking government of Chiang Kai-shek via the Haiphong-Kunming railway.]
4 [Fort Bayard lay in what was then the French-leased zone of Kwangchouwan. This was attached administratively to the Indochinese Union.]

5 [The Governor-General of French Indochina, General Georges Catroux. The French government was not happy with Catroux' handling of the situation, and on 20 July 1940 replaced him as Governor-General of Indochina with Vice-Admiral Jean Decoux.]
6 Later signed the Tokyo peace treaty of 9 May 1941 with us [ending our border dispute with French Indochina].
7 The same Mr. Matsuoka mentioned in chapter 2 in connection with the League of Nations' refusal to recognize Manchukuo in February 1933. Later the mediator in our dispute with France, he signed his name to the 9 May 1941 peace treaty.
8 Ironically this agreement did not provide for the respect of existing boundaries. At the time Thailand did not know the details of the agreement other than that France had granted Japan special military rights in Indochina.

[For the text of this agreement see International Military Tribunal, Far East, Tokyo, 1946–8; *Record of Proceedings, Exhibits, Judgments, Preliminary Interrogations, Miscellaneous Documents*, 3 October 1946, 6936–39.]
9 *The Memoirs of Cordell Hull*, [London, Hodder & Stoughton, 1948] I, 904–07.
10 [Final details were not worked out until 22 September, when France agreed to the possible transfer of a maximum of 25,000 Japanese soldiers through Tongking to Yunnan. At the same time provisions were made providing for the establishment of three Japanese airfields in Tongking, with a garrison of not more than 6,000 troops (F. C. Jones, *Japan's New Order in East Asia: Its Rise and Fall 1937–45*, Royal Institute of International Affairs and the Institute of Pacific Relations, London, Oxford University Press, 1954, 227–30)].
11 See appendix 1.
12 [Implying that the islands in the river would not be visible.]
13 [Sir Josiah Crosby originally came to Bangkok in 1904 as a Student Interpreter in the British Consular Service. Apart from eleven years spent in what was then known as Java and two in French Indochina, he spent his entire official career in Thailand (see Josiah Crosby, *Siam: The Crossroads*, London, Hollis & Carter, 1945, introduction, 1).]
14 See later section in this chapter for the views which the British government communicated to the United States government on this matter.

Admiral Decoux, the Governor-General of Indochina, wrote after the war that the British Minister to Bangkok had been prepared to sacrifice Indochina for England's own purposes. [See Jean Decoux, *A la barre de l'Indochine: histoire de mon gouvernement général 1940–1945*, Paris, Plon, (1949).]
15 For the meaning of this New Order in Asia see *Kanthut*, op. cit., I, 708–12.
16 The new American Minister, Mr. Grant, had just arrived.
17 See Francis Bowes Sayre, *Glad Adventure*, op. cit., 95–127.
18 [Namely for the islands in the Mekong that emerged when the water level was low, and that would be restored to Thailand if the *thalweg* became the official boundary line.]
19 The members of the French delegation chosen to conduct negotiations over the demarcation of the Mekong frontier line were:

NOTES TO CHAPTER 3

1. M. Lépissier, French Minister to Thailand, Chairman.
2. M. Mantovani, Director-General of the Political Affairs Department of Indochina.
3. M. Gassier, Director-General of the Indochinese Public Works Department.
4. M. Nadeau, Chief of Police of Indochina.
5. A representative of the Résident Supérieur of Laos.
6. M. Lecoutre, Chief of the Customs and Revenue Department of Indochina.

The members of the Thai delegation comprised:
1. Major-General Luang Phibun Songkhram, Minister of Foreign Affairs, Chairman.
2. Nai Direk Jayanama, Deputy Minister of Foreign Affairs.
3. Major-General Chawengsaksongkhram, Deputy Minister of the Interior. Now dead.
4. H.R.H. Prince Wanwaithayakon, Advisor to the Ministry of Foreign Affairs.
5. Colonel Phraya Aphaisongkhram, Advisor to the National Defense Council and Chief of Staff. Later rose to the rank of Lieutenant-General. Now dead.
6. Phraya Sunthonphiphit, Under-Secretary of State for the Ministry of the Interior. Later Minister of the Interior.
7. Luang Sitthisayamkan, Under-Secretary of State for the Ministry of Foreign Affairs. Now dead.
8. Captain Phra Riamwiratchaphak, R.N., Chief of Protocol for the Ministry of Foreign Affairs, and Chief Commissioner of the Thai Committee for the Mekong.
9. Colonel Phra Saraphaisaritsadikan of the Ministry of Defense. Later raised to the rank of Lieutenant-General. Now dead.
10. Phra Anurakphubet, Head of the Foreign Affairs Section of the Ministry of the Interior.

[In the Thai edition the above names are listed in the main body of the text. Here they have been presented as endnotes to avoid breaking up the main body of the text. The order in which the Thai and French committees have been presented has also been reversed so as to present them in chronological sequence.]

20 Now dead.
21 See appendix 1.
22 See *Record* [*of Proceedings…etc.*] *of the International Military Tribunal*, Far East, Tokyo, 1946–8, 6931–32.
23 We signed the non-aggression treaty with France about ten days before France surrendered to Germany.
24 My lecture on "State boundaries" appeared in a publication of the Public Relations Department issued on 27 November 1940, 37–45.
25 Because these negotiations were very important, I requested that Captain Phra Riamwiratchaphak, then Director-General of the Protocol Department, come and serve as interpreter and take notes at them.
26 A Thai official was sent to investigate the situation. He and a French doctor performed an autopsy on the body at Nong Khai on the Thai side of the border where the body had been

taken. We also sent an official to Vientiane to carry out an investigation on the French side of the border. The provincial Governor issued a report on the Thai investigations and sent this to the French with a request for compensation for the family of the dead man (see announcement of the Department of Public Relations issued on 10 October 1940).

27 Announced by the Department of Public Relations on 11 October 1940.
28 See the letters of exchange attached to the treaty of mutual non-aggression between France and Thailand signed on 12 June 1940 and given in appendix 1.
29 [The speech, quoted in full in the Thai edition, has been condensed here to eliminate repetitive material.]
30 Department of Public Relations press release of 20 October 1940.
31 After the war he became French Ambassador to Poland and French representative to the United Nations. After retiring from government service in 1956 he traveled to Taipei as the guest of Chiang Kai-shek. On his way he stopped over in Bangkok and visited me, and thanked me for my fair treatment during the [1940–41] border dispute.
32 Regarding the United States' delay in sending the planes we had ordered, and its holding them in the Philippines, see the next chapter.
33 [Approximately one hundred and fifty miles east of Bangkok on the Cambodian border.]
34 [In order to clarify the somewhat confusing description given in the Thai edition of the geographical extent of Thai military operations during the fighting with French Indochina, the next three paragraphs have been altered. A small amount of material taken from M. Sivaram, *Mekong Clash and Far East Crisis: a survey of the Thailand-Indochina conflict and the Japanese mediation…*, Bangkok, printed by Thanom Punnahitanan at the Thai Commercial Press, 1941, 79 *et seq.* has also been added.]
35 F. C. Jones, *Japan's New Order in East Asia*, [op. cit.], 234.
36 [Ibid.]
37 [Ibid, 10–11.]
38 In fact the British had not yet made any announcement on this subject. It was only conversations between England and France that had been revealed (ibid, 236.)
39 See Decoux, *A la barre de l'Indochine*, [op. cit]. In this book it is stated that Japan first offered to mediate the dispute on 28 November 1940.

[According to F. C. Jones, op. cit., 235–36, Japan first considered mediating the Thai-Indochinese border dispute at two meetings of the inner Cabinet held on 5 and 21 November 1940. On 28 November Mr. Matsuoka proposed to the Vichy government a "peaceful arbitration" of the dispute.]
40 [The agreement of 30 August 1940 whereby the French recognized Japan's vital political and economic interests in the Far East.]
41 *Foreign Relations of the United States*, 1941, op. cit., V, 34–36.
42 [The proposal was formally accepted by the Thai government on 25 January 1941.]
43 *Foreign Relations of the United States*, 1941, [V], 44–45.

44 [The following paragraphs up to the one opening with the sentence: "I would like to add just a little about this conflict between Thailand and France..." have been altered in the English edition of this work. In the Thai edition the author gives first the list of the Thai delegates who helped negotiate the truce agreement of 31 January 1941 and the peace agreement of 11 March 1941 respectively; then the text of a speech to the nation by Prince Wanwaithayakon following the signing of the peace agreement; next the text of the official joint communiqué broadcast by Thawi Tawethikun on the same date; and finally the full text of a speech to the nation on the Thailand-Indochina border dispute by the Prime Minister on 9 June 1941. The subject matter of the speeches overlaps, resulting in considerable repetition. Moreover the Prime Minister, in his speech of 9 June 1941, goes over the entire history of the border dispute between Thailand and Indochina, thereby including much material that has already been described earlier in this chapter. The speeches have therefore been condensed into a continuous narrative, and all material that is strictly repetitive excluded. In addition the names of delegates negotiating the peace treaty have been presented in the form of endnotes instead of being listed in the main body of the text, to avoid breaking up the narrative.

One final alteration has been made. In the Thai edition the geographical parameters of the territory regained from the French through the preliminary peace agreement of 11 March 1941 are given in great detail. These details have been condensed, as a full description of the territory acquired, including any changes made between 11 March and 9 May 1941, the date of the signing of the final agreement, is given in appendix 4.]

45 Members of the Thai delegation sent to help negotiate the truce were:
  1. Group Captain Phra Sinlapasatstrakhom, chief of the delegation.
  2. Luang Sitthisayamkan.
  3. Captain Luang Samdaengphitchachot, R.N.
  4. Group Captain Luang Thewaritphanluek.
  5. Nai Wanit Pananon.
  6. Major Net Khemayothin.
  7. Nai Thawi Tawethikun, Secretary.

46 ["Natori" refers to a class of Japanese war vessel, namely a light cruiser.]

47 Members of the Thai delegation sent to help negotiate the peace agreement were:
  1. H.R.H. Prince Wanwaithayakon, chief of the delegation.
  2. Phraya Sisena, Thai Minister to Tokyo.
  3. Group Captain Phra Sinlapasatstrakhom.
  4. Colonel Luang Wichitsongkhram.
  5. Nai Wanit Pananon.
  6. Colonel Luang Wirayotha, Thai military attaché to Tokyo.
  7. Captain Luang Samdaengphitchachot, R.N.
  8. Group Captain Luang Thewaritphanluek.
  9. Commander Luang Sombunyutthawicha, Thai naval attaché to Tokyo.
  10. Nai Thawi Tawethikun.

11. Major Luang Sathityutthakan.
12. Major Net Khemayothin.
13. Major Phao Siyanon.

Members of the delegation's secretarial staff were:
1. Nai Thawi Tawethikun.
2. Luang Phinit-akson.
3. M.C. Wongsanuwat Thewakun.
4. Phra Nararatchamnong.
5. Nai Arun Wichitranon.
6. Nai Chai Suwannathat.

48 In the final agreement of 9 May 1941 it was specified that the territories ceded to Thailand should be demilitarized only in Cambodia (see M. Sivaram, op. cit., 179).]
49 [The 9 May 1941 final agreement also decreed that Khone Island should become Thai territory and Khong Island remain French territory. This, according to M. Sivaram, op. cit., 178, was to avoid any complications that might arise from joint administration. France also gave Thailand the small sector on the right bank of the Mekong opposite Stoeng Treng that had been reserved to France under the preliminary agreement of 11 March 1941 (ibid.)].
50 Document put out by the Department of Public Relations on 11 March 1941.
51 See appendix 4.
52 Report of the Special Meeting [of the National Assembly], 2nd series, III, 9 June 1941
53 [The text of this newspaper article is given in full in the Thai edition.]
54 Replaced Mr. Grant as American Minister to Thailand in September 1941.

Chapter 4

1 See *Kanthut*, op. cit., I, 636–65.
2 Mr. Grant, the American Minister to Bangkok, reporting on the mediation negotiations in Tokyo, states that even by then there was "…already evidence of Japanese encroachments in the Thai economic field, rice, tin and rubber figuring in the deals…" (*Foreign Relations of the United States*, op. cit, 1941, V, 150).
3 [On 9 October 1940 the Chief of the Division of Far Eastern Affairs of the United States State Department informed the Thai Minister in Washington, M.R. Seni Pramoj, that in view of the needs of the United States national defense program, the United States government had been obliged to take steps towards requisitioning for its own defense needs ten North American dive bomber airplanes destined for Thailand that were now sitting in Manila. The Thai government would, of course, receive fair compensation for these planes (*Foreign Relations of the United States*, op. cit., 1940, V, 176–77.) This caused considerable bitterness in Thailand. Compensation was not in fact paid until December 1941 (ibid., 1941, V, 280, fn. 72).]

4   [On 25 and 26 July 1941 respectively.]
5   [The Yokohama Specie Bank first opened a branch in Bangkok in July 1936.]
6   At that time, namely in July 1941, Nai Pridi Banomyong was the Minister of Finance, and M.C. Wiwatthanachai Chaiyan, who was later raised to the royal rank of Phraongchao in 1950, was Advisor to the Ministry.
7   [The agreement was finally concluded on 26 August 1941.]
8   [In September 1941.]
9   [Three paragraphs existing in the Thai edition but considered by the editor to be repetitive have been omitted here.]
10 *Foreign Relations of the United States*, op. cit, 1941, V, 136–37. At that time Thailand was not in the hands of Japan, but much weight was being given to the reports of Mr. Grant.
11 [See n. 3.]
12 This report had great influence in swaying the government of the United States, as we shall see subsequently (see *Foreign Relations of the United States*, op. cit, 1941, V, 146–47).
13 [At this date still Major-General.]
14 [The final agreement over the territorial dispute between Thailand and French Indochina.]
15 *Foreign Relations of the United States*, op. cit., 1941, V, 148–49.
16 [Following the passing of the Liquid Fuel Act of March 1939.]
17 See *Foreign Relations of the United States*, op. cit., 1941, V, 150–54.
18 [Weeks later?—Ed. See Mr. Grant's telegram of 24 May 1941 to the Secretary of State mentioning that the British would be supplying Thailand with two boatloads of fuel products "within the next few weeks" (ibid., 58)].
19 [48,000 tons being Thailand's estimated total rubber production for 1941 (ibid.,188).]
20 Ibid, 195–96.
21 Ibid, 205–06.
22 This meeting took place at the end of July 1941, about four and a half months before Japan declared war.

Chapter 5

1   *Foreign Relations of the United States*, 1941, [op. cit.], V, 411.
2   Now Lord Avon.
3   *Foreign Relations of the United States*, [op. cit.], V, 236–37.
4   [On 12 September 1941.]
5   [This section has been moved from a little further on in the Thai original.]
6   Now dead.
7   Then head of the Finance Division of the Ministry of Foreign Affairs. Now dead.
8   Later became Police-General. Now dead.
9   [These letters are given in full in the Thai original.]
10 [In August 1941.]

11 Now Lieutenant-General Prayun Phamonmontri.
12 Later Deputy Head of the Office of the Prime Minister. Now dead.
13 *Foreign Relations of the United States*, op. cit., 1941, V, 284.
14 The ideas of Mr. Peck, the new American Minister, were exactly the same as those I had put forward to Mr. Grant, the former American Minister, on 27 July 1941. However, Mr. Grant had not agreed with them (see above text and also *Foreign Relations of the United States*, 1941, [op. cit.], V, 235 and 306–09.
15 Now a Privy Councilor.
16 Even though Japan had raised its legation to embassy status and had appointed Mr. Tsubokami as its new Ambassador to Thailand, Mr. Futami still remained as Minister.
17 *Foreign Relations of the United States*, 1941, [op. cit.], V, 367.
18 Ibid, 370.
19 Ibid, 371–72.
20 Ibid, 378–80.
21 See Cordell Hull's *Memoirs*, [op. cit.], II, 1018–19.
22 United States Congress Joint Committee on the Investigation of the Pearl Harbor Attack, *Report*... [Washington, United States Government Publication Office, 1946], 403.
23 Ibid, 403–04. See also [Winston] Churchill, *The Second World War*, Boston, Houghton Mifflin, 1951, [vol. 3: The Grand Alliance], 534.
24 Ibid, 404.
25 Testimony of General Tojo given before the International Military Tribunal, Far East, Tokyo, in *Records of Proceedings*..., op. cit., 36401.
26 A coastal town in Kelantan, at the northernmost tip of the east coast of peninsular Malaya, just south of the Thai border.
27 Report of the Joint Committee on the Investigation of the Pearl Harbor Attack, [op. cit.], 405.

   [In other words forcing the British to enter Thai territory further north, approaching it from the west coast of the Malayan peninsula instead of from the east. Padang Besar, a coastal town in Perlis, the northernmost state on the west side of the peninsula, borders Satun and Songkhla provinces in Thailand.
28 Ibid, 439.
29 Ibid, 429–30.
30 Now dead.
31 [I.e. Malaya and Burma.]
32 After the war Ambassador Tsubokami, who carried on these negotiations with me, gave testimony before the International Military Tribunal in Tokyo to which I shall refer later.
33 [On 11 September 1941 (see *Foreign Relations of the United States*, op. cit., 1943, III, 1121.)
34 [Towns on the eastern side of the Thai peninsula.]
35 [Inland in the far south of the Thai peninsula.]
36 [Southwest of Bangkok.]

37 For details, see subsequent text.
38 See the testimony of Ambassador Tsubokami given on 18 April 1946 in the Preliminary Interrogations of the International Military Tribunal in Tokyo.

Chapter 6

1 Sir Josiah Crosby, the British Minister, wrote of my appointment that "Nai Direck, whom the Japanese had once denounced as a tool of the British Foreign Office, was obliged to surrender his portfolio and was compelled by Luang Phibun to take up immediately afterwards the post of Ambassador in Tokyo, where his activities would, of course, be under Japanese supervision" (Sir Josiah Crosby, *Siam: The Crossroads*, [op. cit.], 107). This work was written during the war, at the beginning of 1945.
2 In diplomatic practice, before appointing a diplomatic representative, the government sending that representative must first receive the consent (*agrément*) of the government to which the representative is to be sent.
3 Nai Pridi had resigned as Minister of Finance and been promoted to membership in the Regency Council.
4 I was really referring to Field Marshal Phibun Songkhram.
5 Now dead.
6 Now Minister of Foreign Affairs.
7 Now Ambassador to Bonn.
8 Now dead.
9 Now dead.
10 Now Second Secretary at the Embassy in Bonn.

Chapter 7

1 [In keeping with the family's wishes to condense the text in the English edition, the second chapter of part 2 in the Thai original, entitled "General situation in Japan before the War," which covers historical and political events in Japan up to 1939, has been omitted. There are therefore only four chapters in part 2 instead of five; the numbering of the chapters has been re-arranged accordingly.]
2 Later sentenced to life imprisonment by the International Military Tribunal in Tokyo.
3 Formerly Ambassador to Germany and Russia, Togo was Foreign Minister when his government declared war on England and the United States. He was sentenced to twenty years' imprisonment by the International Military Tribunal, and died in 1950.
4 Committed *hara kiri* when Japan surrendered.
5 Died during the hearings before the International Military Tribunal.
6 Sentenced to life imprisonment by the International Military Tribunal.
7 Committed suicide when Japan surrendered.

8 Head of the special diplomatic mission that visited Thailand during the war [in mid–July 1942]. After the war he was sentenced to death by the International Military Tribunal.
9 Completed his studies at Harvard, and became Finance Minister in the Prince Konoye government of 1938.
10 This pact was signed on 25 [21?] December 1941, as mentioned earlier. I first learned of it on 13 January 1942.
11 Later raised to the rank of Vice-Admiral.
12 Later made Ambassador to Djakarta. Now retired.
13 Now Minister of Foreign Affairs.
14 Now Ambassador to Bonn.
15 Now dead.
16 [Two paragraphs describing the trip to the palace have been omitted here in the English edition.]
17 [The different sections of this chapter have been re-arranged in order to present them in chronological sequence. The headings, such as Thailand's declaration of war, Thailand's seeking to join the Axis' alliance etc., do not therefore follow the order in which they appear in the Thai text.]
18 [Crosby, op. cit., 136 points out that since the Japanese were making use of Bangkok and other places in Thailand as bases for conducting hostilities against British territories, the British had been carrying out bombing raids on Thai territory].
19 Concerning the Axis see *Kanthut*, [op. cit.], I, 584–98.
20 Ibid, 684–707.
21 [The following couple of paragraphs has been altered and includes some material taken from Jones, *op. cit.*, to round out the picture of Wang Ching-wei's background.]
22 See *Kanthut*, [op. cit.], I, 705.
23 Prince Konoye was not a prince of the royal line, but had inherited his title from his ancestors. When the war ended he was afraid of being captured and arraigned as a war criminal, and committed suicide.
24 In 1931 Japan invaded Manchuria. The following year they established the puppet regime of Manchukuo there under Pu Yi, the last Emperor of the Manchu (Ch'ing) dynasty of China.
25 See *Kanthut*, [op. cit.], I, 589–98.
26 [Succeeded Prince Konoye.]
27 Sentenced to death by the International Military Tribunal.
28 Mr. Togo was arraigned as a war criminal before the International Military Tribunal in Tokyo and sentenced to twenty years in jail, where he died.
29 [Thai forces took part with those of Japan in the invasion of the Shan States of Burma that took place between the end of March and the end of May 1942].
30 At that time Chungking was the capital of the Chiang Kai-shek government.
   [In December 1941, when the Japanese first entered Burma, General Chiang Kai-shek, concerned lest the Burma Road along which lend-lease supplies were reaching China from

Rangoon should be cut, offered Chinese troops to assist in the defense of Burma. When the Thai joined Japanese forces entering parts of Burma, Thailand therefore found itself fighting not only against British and Burmese forces but also those of Nationalist China.]

31 See Victor Purcell, *The Chinese in South-East Asia*, [op. cit.], 190.
32 At the time Field Marshal Luang Phibun Songkhram was our Prime Minister and Minister of Foreign Affairs and Luang Wichitwathakan the Deputy Minister of Foreign Affairs. The latter was raised to be Minister of Foreign Affairs on 19 June 1942.
33 Later promoted to General.
34 This topic is discussed later in this chapter.
35 [Succeeded Mr. Togo.]
36 [The section that follows is a considerably condensed version of what appears in the Thai original. Passages giving detailed accounts of Japanese cultural customs such as the tea ceremony have been omitted altogether.]
37 The Deputy Minister of the Ministry of Foreign Affairs at the time was named Nishi. He resigned at the same time as Mr. Togo. After the war he became Ambassador to London. At that time there were two Advisors to the Ministry of Foreign Affairs, namely Naotake Sato, who later became Ambassador and Minister of Foreign Affairs, and Mr. Kawagoe, who later became Ambassador to China.
38 [General Tojo held this position until 17 September 1942, when Mr. Masayuki Tani was appointed Foreign Minister.]
39 It is the normal diplomatic custom in all countries including Thailand that when a new Minister of Foreign Affairs assumes his duties, he has appointments with all the ambassadors and chargés d'affaires in order to meet each of them personally.
40 [Now Taiwan.]
41 This section about the author attending General Tojo's speech at the Japanese Diet appears in the form of a footnote in the Thai edition.]
42 [The editor has omitted a subsequent section in the Thai original on the overall development of the war situation in Europe and Asia during the period covered in this chapter. Instead this has been incorporated into the chronology of the war given at the beginning of part 2.]

Chapter 8

1 Later promoted to Major-General. Died in 1962.
2 [During the war Field Marshal Phibun Songkhram decided to set up a second capital at Phetchabun, a town some 450 kilometers north-northeast of Bangkok. At the same time he proposed the establishment of a holy Buddhist city, or Buddhaburi, in the vicinity of Saraburi, a town about 120 kilometers northeast of Bangkok and south of Phetchabun. Phibun's schemes proved highly unpopular. Many laborers lost their lives building roads and construction projects in malaria-infested Phetchabun. By then it was also becoming clear that the tide of war was turning against Japan. A number of Thai began to feel that a change of government was

advisable if Thailand was not to be held accountable once a post-war settlement was drawn up. Accordingly in July 1944 bills calling for the establishment of a second capital at Phetchabun and for the setting up of a Buddhist territory were rejected by the National Assembly, forcing Phibun to resign.]

3 [The full translation for this department was "the Allied Coordination Department." However, according to Prince Wanwaithayakorn, the term "Allied" was not liked, and the department was therefore always referred to as "the Coordination Department."]

4 [Two new headings entitled "Financial relations with Japan" and "The resignations of General Tojo and Field Marshal Phibun Songkhram" have been added to this chapter to tally with the author's final heading of "Thailand's relations with Germany and Italy."]

5 [The following paragraph in the original has been transferred to the end of this section to better fit into the chronological framework.]

6 In [April] that year [1942] the Thai government was forced to devalue the Baht to make one Baht equal one Yen (see part 3, chapter 3 [now chapter 12]).

7 Today holds the royal rank of Krommamuen Narathip-phongpraphan.

8 Later raised to the royal rank of Phraongchao. Died in 1960.

9 [See n. 2.]

10 [As the following chapters describe, the author now joined the Free Thai movement and served in the underground until the end of the war.]

11 See Manun Borisut, *Khana ratthamontri*, op. cit., 146–48.

12 After I took up my appointment in Bonn [the author was later appointed Ambassador to Bonn], I met Dr. Wendler again, and we had dinner together several times.

13 [On 25 July 1943.]

14 [On 8 September 1943 Italy surrendered to the Allies, and on 13 October declared war on Germany, its former ally. Mr. Crolla's position at this period was, therefore, ambiguous.]

15 [The section on the war situation in Europe and Asia during the period covered by this chapter that follows in the Thai original has been omitted, and the dates of major events given in this section incorporated into the chronology at the beginning of part 2.]

Chapter 9

1 [The title in the Thai edition reads: "Events between August 1944 and August 1945, the month the war ended." This has been changed in the English edition to accord more closely with the contents of this chapter.]

2 Several authors have written about the resistance movement against Japan that grew up at this time. They include General Net Khemayothin, *Chiwit naiphon* (*Life of a General*); *Ngan tai din* [(*khong phon-ek Yothi*) (*The Underground Work* [*of Phon-ek Yothi*])], Bangkok, distributed by Kasem Bannakit, 1967, 3 vols.); Nicol Smith and Blake Clark, *Into Thailand: Underground Kingdom*, [New York, Bobbs-Merrill, 1945], which has been translated [into Thai] by General Witsakun; John Coast, *Some Aspects of Thai Politics*, op. cit.; a lecture by M.R. Seni Pramoj,

"Kanpatthibatngan khong Seri Thai nai Saharat America" ("Work of the Free Thai movement in America"), which appears in General Net Khemayothin's book *Ngan tai din*, [op. cit.], 753–806; and a lecture by Dr. Puey Ungphakorn, "Concerning the relations between the United States and Thailand during the Second World War," and the annex "Temporary Soldier," which appears in the same volume, 845–97; and the chapters by Dr. Puey Ungphakorn, Nai Thawi Bunyaket, and Phra Phisansukhumwit (Prasop Sukhum) which appear at the end of part 2 of this book.

3 [By the end of July 1944 Pridi had become the sole Regent on what had originally been a three-man Regency Council. Phraya Phichayenyothin died on 21 July 1943, and Prince Adithaya, President of the Council, resigned on 31 July 1944.]

4 [Attended military staff college in France and England. Member of the Thai delegation that visited Tokyo between February to May 1941 to help negotiate the ceasefire and treaty with the French over Thailand's former territories in French Indochina.]

5 *Ngan Tai Din*, [op. cit.], 744–49.

6 [Son of Prince Svasti and brother of Queen Rambhai. Educated in England and commissioned in the British army.]

7 Concerning the post-war consequences of the activities of the Thai at this time, see part 3, chapters 1, 2 and 3 [now chapters 10, 11, and 12].

8 The report of this Committee is given in appendix 11. It had as its chairman Phraya Thepwithun, former Minister of Justice and Chief Justice of the Supreme Court, and as legal consultants Phraya Nalaratchasuwat, former Minister of Justice and Justice of the Supreme Court, Phraya Wikromratanasuphat, Chief Justice of the Supreme Court, Phraya Nitisatphaisan, former Minister of Justice, and Nai Pichan Bunyong.

9 *Ngan tai din*, [op cit.], chapter 42. [Several paragraphs from this speech have been omitted here as repetitive.]

10 [Commander of Japan's 39th Army, stationed in Bangkok.]

11 At that time he had not yet received his doctorate.

12 Now a full General.

13 Now Ambassador to Bonn. [Also a former member of the embassy staff whom the author had chosen to accompany him when he was appointed Ambassador to Japan in January 1942.]

14 [In February 1945 Konthi Suphamongkhon and Sanguan Tularak arrived in Washington to propose the establishment of a Thai government-in-exile and the obtaining of recognition from the Allied governments. (See *Foreign Relations of the United States*, op. cit., 1945, VI, 1252 and 1252 fn. 38.]

15 Today his name is Phatthanaphong Rinthakun and he is Assistant Manager of the Thailand Cement Company.

16 Today a Special Grade Civil Servant in the Department of Science, Ministry of Economics.

17 [A coastal town just southwest of Bangkok.]

18 [An island off the west coast of peninsular Thailand.]

19 Later Assistant Under Secretary of State in the British Foreign Office at the time I was Ambassador to London [July 1947–July 1948]. He was later knighted and appointed [British] Ambassador to Tokyo. Now retired from government service.

At the time I was Ambassador to London Mr. Dening was the British representative at the negotiations concerning the price to be paid for the rice demanded from Thailand [as reparations] under the terms of the Formal Agreement of 1 January 1946 [see chapter 10] and the carrying out of the terms of that agreement. He was most cooperative, about which I will speak again later in part 3.

20 [In October 1945.]

21 [As early as August 1943 Cordell Hull, the United States Secretary of State, in describing the attitude of the United States towards Thailand, had said that the United States recognized Thailand as an independent state which was currently under the military occupation of Japan, and that the United States looked forward to the re-establishment of Thailand's independence as soon as possible (see *Foreign Relations of the United States*, op. cit., 1943, III, 1118–19.]

22 [In other words American and British requests that Thailand not make any moves for the time being that would create an open conflict with the Japanese were responsible for preventing a premature uprising in which many Thai might have lost their lives.]

23 Record of the Proceedings of the National Assembly, no. 29/2488 (Ordinary), 2nd session, 3rd sitting, Thursday 11 October B.E. 2488, 15.32 hours. [During the war Thai parliamentary proceedings were classified as "Ordinary", "Extraordinary" or "Secret". This affected what could or could not be released to the public.]

24 [*Foreign Relations of the United States*, op. cit., 1943, China, 13–14, 23–24 and 36–37]. M.R. Seni Pramoj played on China's fear that Britain might move into Thailand at the end of the war and extracted an agreement from General Chiang Kai-shek to recognize Thailand's independence once the war ended.

25 [On 16 August 1945, two days after the Japanese surrender, Pridi Banomyong, the Regent, issued a proclamation stating that Thailand's declaration of war against the United States and Britain of 25 July 1942 was null and void (see chapter 10.)]

26 [For the text of Secretary of State James F. Byrnes' statement on relations between the United States and Thailand see the United States Department of State Bulletin, 19 August 1945. The relevant passage reads that "…during the past four years we have regarded Thailand not as an enemy but as a country to be liberated from the enemy."]

27 [Mr. Bevin had stated that before England would be willing to bring the state of war between Thailand and Britain to a close, Thailand would have to provide all necessary help for British forces entering Thailand to disarm the Japanese; provide compensation for war damages; and lastly cooperate economically and financially with Britain.]

28 Record of the Proceedings of the National Assembly, no. 29/2488 (Ordinary), 2nd session, 3rd sitting, Thursday, 11 October, B.E. 2488, 15.50 hours.

29 Before the war he had been a barrister in Bangkok. He knew Thai well and was a friend of the Thai. Now dead.

30 [The section on the progress of the war in Europe and Asia which follows in the Thai edition has been omitted here, and the relevant data incorporated into the chronology at the beginning of part 2.]
31 [Refers to the statue of the Emerald Buddha in the temple of the same name in the Royal Palace grounds. Regarded as Thailand's divine guardian and the palladium of the kingdom.]

Article by Thawi Bunyaket

1 [South of Bangkok, at the mouth of the Chao Phraya River.]
2 [At some places Thailand had no regular military forces. Police, military school cadets and even boy scouts fought the Japanese with whatever weapons they had to hand.]
3 [Battambang province in what is now Cambodia. One of the areas in Indochina that was returned to Thai jurisdiction under the peace agreement of 9 May 1941 between France and Thailand.]
4 [All locations on the east side of peninsular Thailand.]
5 [An island off the east coast of peninsular Thailand.]
6 [At the mouth of the Chao Phraya River.]
7 [In 1935 King Prajadhipok (King Rama VII) abdicated. His successor, King Ananda Mahidol, was only ten years old at the time. A Regency Council was therefore established to rule the country until such time as the king came of age. It consisted of three members, namely H.H. Prince Aditaya, Chaophraya Phichayenyothin, and Pridi himself.]
8 [A few days after the Japanese invaded Thailand, Direk tried to resign as Foreign Minister (see chapter 5). Shortly thereafter Field Marshal Phibun Songkhram took over the post of Minister of Foreign Affairs, making Direk Deputy Foreign Minister. On Direk's appointment as Ambassador to Tokyo Luang Wichitwathakan was made Deputy Foreign Minister in Direk's stead.]
9 [The Yen/Baht parity agreement was signed on 22 April 1942.]
10 [On 25 July 1943.]
11 [For accounts of this and subsequent efforts to contact the Allies through Chungking, see Nicol Smith and Blake Clark, op. cit., 91–2.]
12 [For full details see "Political Memoirs of Nai Thawi Bunyaket" in Jayanta K. Ray, *Portraits of Thai Politics*, op. cit., 92–100.]
13 [At that time Ceylon was administratively still part of British India.]
14 [Locations in central and west central Thailand.]
15 [A Thai administrative division below the provincial level. Usually translated as "district."]
16 [In Phetchaburi province, southeast of Bangkok and north of Hua Hin.]
17 [A coastal town southeast of Bangkok.]
18 [Then on the outskirts of Bangkok.]
19 [The royal grounds near the Grand Palace in Bangkok.]
20 [A town east of Bangkok.]

21 [By the end of the war Pridi Banomyong had become sole Regent (see chapter 9, n. 3).]
22 [For an analysis of Britain's guarded and negative reaction, see chapter 10.]

Article by Puey Ungphakorn

1 This article was written for Professor Direk Jayanama of the Political Science Department faculty of Thammasat University, to be incorporated into his book, which was written for the information and use of future students.

   Section 3 of this article was printed in the cremation volume for Colonel San Yutthawong (my brother-in-law) on 19 July 1953.

2 [Chairman of the Bank of Thailand 1959–71 and Rector of Thammasat University 1975–October 1976.]

3 [A high-ranking member of the Thai royal family.]

4 [Widow of former King Prajadhipok (King Rama VII), who died in exile in England in May 1941.]

5 [The Pioneer Corps provided labor support to the army wherever in the globe they were called upon to do so. During the war there was practically no task that was not performed by Pioneers. The Corps handled all kinds and types of stores and ammunition, built camps, airfields and fortifications, cleared rubble and demolished roadblocks, built roads, railways and bridges, loaded and unloaded ships, trains and planes, constructed aircraft pens against enemy bombing and a host of other jobs.]

6 [The following paragraph has been omitted in the English edition, as it repeated information already provided by the author.]

7 On 29 June 1942 all American legation staff and all non-official American citizens in Bangkok, with the exception of four American women missionaries, who elected to remain in Thailand, were embarked on the Thai vessel *Valaya*. They were transferred to the Japanese exchange vessel *Asama Maru* near Saigon on 3 July, and landed at Lourenço Marques (Mozambique) on 22 July (*Foreign Relations of the United States*, op. cit., 1942, I, 934). Here they were exchanged for Thai citizens returning to Thailand.

8 After the war Nai Mani worked for a United Nations agency until he retired, and has since been living in Switzerland. [This biographical note, which appears in the text in the Thai edition, has been presented as an endnote here.]

9 Towards the end of the war [actually in November 1946—Ed.] the Pioneer Corps, [in recognition of its services], was granted the title of "Royal Pioneer Corps" [by King George VI.]

10 We had just been moved from Denby in North Wales, where we had slept in tents and garages, to Bradford, Yorkshire, where we were sleeping in what had formerly been a secondary school.

11 [As has been mentioned previously, before the United Nations Organization was formally established in 1945 it was common practice to refer to the Allied powers as the "United Nations".]

12 [For more on this see Thawi Bunyaket's article.]

13 [Archaeological sites in north central Thailand.]

14 [A low mud bank surrounding a rice-field.]
15 [The Thai word for village.]
16 [In central Thailand.]
17 [In western Thailand, on the river Ping.]
18 [At the confluence of the Nan, Ping, Wang, and Yom rivers that flow from the north into the Chao Phraya River that exits into the Gulf of Thailand below Bangkok.]
19 [The message which Puey was carrying from Lord Louis Mountbatten, Supreme Commander of the Allied Forces in South-East Asia, to the Thai Regent, Pridi Banomyong.]
20 [A Thai drama form.]
21 [A long strip of cloth worn by men and used as a waist cloth and for a wide variety of other purposes.]
22 [North of Chai Nat, on the Chao Phraya River.]
23 [One of the decrees passed by the Phibun Songkhram government during the war years stated that all Thai must wear hats when in public places. Daeng and Di were clearly unaware of this edict. By not wearing hats they rendered themselves conspicuous, leading to their getting arrested.]
24 [The ordination hall of a temple.]
25 [The meeting hall of a temple compound.]
26 [A local plant.]
27 [A settlement on the Chao Phraya River, a little over 100 kilometers north of Bangkok.]
28 [On the northern outskirts of Bangkok.]
29 [Pier in Bangkok near the Grand Palace.]
30 [About 58 kilometers west of Bangkok.]
31 [Referring to Isan, or the northeastern provinces of Thailand.]
32 [A Pali phrase meaning "Not telling a falsehood". One of the five Buddhist precepts adhered to by devout Buddhists. *Ukotsan* was an annual publication of the boys of Assumption College, Bangkok.]
33 For further details see General Net, *Ngan Tai Din*, op. cit., chapters 7–9 and 17–19.
34 [A town in the far south of Thailand.]
35 [Himself a leading member of the Free Thai movement (see the preceding chapter by Thawi Bunyaket).]
36 [Bangkok suburb where the Don Mueang airport is located today.]
37 [See chapter 12.]
38 [See chapter 10 for details on the two missions.]
39 [In November 1941 Field Marshal Phibun sent a military mission under Luang Suranarong to Singapore to discuss the question of what aid the British could supply to Thailand in the event of the latter being invaded by Japan.]

Article by Phra Phisansukhumwit

1 [By this time it was clear that the Allies would win the war, and that the defeat of Japan was merely a matter of time. In view of having declared war on the United States, Britain and Australia, Thailand was now beginning to turn its attention to the treatment it might receive from the Allies once the war came to an end.]
2 [At the time Prasop Sukhum was Director-General of the Highway Department.]
3 [Tensions between the Japanese and Thai were running very high by this time, particularly in Bangkok. The Allies feared that some incident might provoke the Japanese into having to take action and possibly taking over the administration of the country in the way that they had done in French Indochina in March 1945.]
4 [Commanding General of the United States Forces in the India-Burma theater.]
5 [The famous commander of "Merrill's marauders" who had led forces behind the Japanese lines in Burma and thrown the Japanese into confusion by attacking them from behind.]
6 [A town in eastern Thailand on the border with Cambodia.]
7 [The author of this article had just graduated in engineering from the Massachusetts Institute of Technology (Nicol Smith, op. cit., 205).]
8 [After Thailand declared war on the United States and Britain, it recalled all Thai citizens living abroad. Some returned to Thailand; others opted to remain overseas (see Puey Ungphakorn article, n. 7).
9 [By the middle of 1945 Pridi Banomyong, as leader of the Free Thai movement, was pressing for an armed uprising against the Japanese. However, as mentioned earlier, this was strongly discouraged by the Allies, who were not yet ready to synchronize their support for such a revolt.]
10 [See n. 8 above.]
11 [Here the author is referring to the border dispute of the latter part of 1940 and early part of 1941 between Thailand and French Indochina.]
12 [See chapter 3.]
13 [En route to Chungking. See Thawi Bunyaket's article, n. 11.]
14 [From hardships suffered en route.]
15 [The First Quebec Conference of August 1943. At this conference, which was attended by Churchill and Roosevelt, Mountbatten was appointed Supreme Allied Commander for South-East Asia.]
16 [Prior to World War II it had been the practice for a number of Thai ministries to employ Foreign Advisors. The British had served as Advisors to the Thai Finance Department for many years.]
17 [With the exception of Pridi Banomyong (see Thawi Bunyaket's article).]
18 [Editor and author of a number of works, including *My Boyhood in Thailand*, New York, The Day Company, (circa 1940). Kumut lived in the United States from 1938–1939. When he returned to Thailand in 1941 he became editor of a government publication that criticized certain aspects of the Phibun Songkhram regime. He was jailed in December 1941, pardoned

two years later, joined the underground, and was sent to the United States by Pridi Banomyong to carry secret information to Washington (Nicol Smith, op. cit, 205–06).]
19 [For details see chapter 6.]
20 [The Twenty-one Proposals were first put forward to Thai representatives in September 1945. By the time they appeared in the American press in December they had gone through several revisions in the course of negotiations between Britain and the United States. When the news broke in the American press, public reaction was strong, as it was not understood that United States' attempts to obtain a reduction of the requirements contained in the proposals had already been underway for some while.]
21 [Military Attaché to the Thai legation in Washington, and head of the Free Thai unit which operated from southern China in conjunction with the O.S.S. during the war.]
22 [See n. 18.]
23 [A member of the Free Thai unit that worked under Colonel Khap Kunchon out of South China. Son of an English police officer formerly living in Bangkok and a Thai mother (Nicol Smith, op. cit., 18).]
24 [See n. 20.]
25 [On 27 November 1944.]
26 [Article 14 of the Agreement of 1 January 1946 between Britain and Thailand stipulated that Thailand should provide 1,500,000 tons of rice free of charge, to be distributed to deficit areas in the Far East and Southeast Asia.]
27 [Dr. Sayre had been responsible for securing the abrogation of the unequal treaties with several nations that had placed restrictions on Thailand's sovereignty and imposed unilateral legal and economic disadvantages on her (see chapter 2, and Sayre, op. cit.).]

Chapter 10

1 [The chapter heading in the Thai edition reads: "Negotiations between Thailand and Britain, France and China: Thailand's financial situation". In fact this chapter deals only with Thailand's relations with Britain and Australia. The other topics are discussed in subsequent chapters. In the English edition the title of this chapter has been adjusted accordingly.]
2 [A representative from outside the country could not be accused by the Allies of having cooperated with the Japanese.]
3 [When Japan surrendered on 14 August 1945, Allied military responsibilities in Southeast Asia were divided between the United States, China and Britain. Disarming the Japanese in Thailand fell under the sphere of South-East Asia Command, headed by Admiral Lord Louis Mountbatten. British and American troops entered Thailand soon after Japan's capitulation, and on 2 September 1945, under the terms of General Order no. 1, Japanese forces in Thailand were called upon to surrender to the Supreme Allied Commander, South-East Asia (Lord Louis Mountbatten).]

NOTES TO CHAPTER 10

4   [? King Ananda did not return to Thailand until December 1945.]
5   [See n. 4.]
6   Came into office on 1 September 1945 and resigned on 17 September 1945 (see *Royal Gazette*, vol. 62, part 47, 509–11).
7   Came into office on 17 September 1945 and resigned on 31 January 1946 following the holding of general elections (*Royal Gazette*, vol. 62, part 52, 557).
8   [For an account of Thailand's negotiations with France and China, see chapters 11 and 14.]
9   [The author is referring to the activities of the Free Thai movement.]
10 [Appointed on 3 July 1945.]
11 See Keesing's publication [*Keesing's Contemporary Archives*], 1945, 7371 and 7379; also 1946, 1535.
12 See reports of the meeting of the National Assembly, January 1946.
13 [The headquarters of South-East Asia Command.]
14 [Britain was concerned about the world shortage of these commodities that had come about as a result of the war.]
15 [The Combined Boards were set up by the Allies in January 1942 to encourage the production and facilitate the procurement of essential supplies and raw materials needed by them for the war effort in view of the Axis powers having captured important sources of Allied raw materials. The term "Combined Boards" came to refer to four civilian agencies, namely the Combined Raw Materials Board, the Combined Shipping Adjustment Board, the Combined Food Board and the Combined Production and Resources Board.]
16 [In charge of distributing rice supplies in accordance with allocations determined upon by the Combined Food Boards.]
17 [In other words although this treaty would have been drawn up in the name of the Allies, it would be administered primarily by the British.]
18 The government of Nai Thawi Bunyaket. At the time he was both Prime Minister and Minister of Foreign Affairs.
19 [The United States maintained representatives at Kandy who kept the United States informed of the negotiations between Thailand and Britain. While America was prepared to have the British negotiate as to immediate military arrangements, it insisted that any negotiations of an overall political and economic nature be decided upon jointly by Britain and the United States (see *Foreign Relations of the United States*, op. cit., 1945, 1282–83 and 1304–06). Although the United States did not formally participate in the negotiations at Kandy, it made its views known to the British and led them to modify their original proposals.]
20 See reports of the meetings of the National Assembly of 6 September 1945.
21 See General Net Khemayothin, *Ngan tai din khong phon ek Yothi* (*Underground Work of Colonel Yothi*), op. cit., pp. 647–712.
22 Cordell Hull was Secretary of State of the United States from 4 March 1933 to 30 November 1944.
23 *The Memoirs of Cordell Hull*, New York, Macmillan, 1948, II, 1587–88.

24 [? See n. 4.]
25 [Held on 6 January 1946.]
26 The Formal Agreement [full title: The Formal Agreement for the Termination of the State of War between Thailand and Great Britain and India.] See appendix 5.
27 [The Treaty of Amity between the Kingdom of Thailand and the Republic of China.] See appendix 7.
28 Later promoted to Phraongchao. He died in 1960.
29 Now dead.
30 Currently Minister of Finance.
31 Now Lieutenant-General. Formerly Ambassador to Japan and to Ethiopia.
32 Now dead.
33 Currently Ambassador to Bonn.
34 Director of the National Bank.
35 Presently Secretary of the National Development Board.
36 [During earlier meetings at Kandy which took place at the beginning of September 1945 Thailand had agreed to make a free gift of rice to the Allies amounting to 20,000 tons monthly for one year (*Foreign Relations of the United States*, op. cit., 1945, 1342).]
37 [The office of the Political Advisor to South-East Asia Command was moved from Kandy to Singapore on 23 November 1945.]
38 After diplomatic relations between Britain and Thailand were later resumed following the signing of the Formal Agreement [on 1 January 1946]. Mr. Bird became British Chargé d'Affaires in January 1942. He died a few months later in Bangkok.
39 [As Political Advisor to the Supreme Allied Commander, South-East Asia Command, Mr. Dening was also involved in negotiations between Britain and the Netherlands regarding responsibility for maintaining law and order in what were then known as the Netherlands East Indies during the immediate post-war period. He therefore had to make visits to Java. The British were implying that Thailand had been deliberately dragging out the negotiations in order to play for time.]
40 [The young King Ananda Mahidol (King Rama VIII), then aged twenty years, returned to Thailand from his studies in Switzerland in December 1945.]
41 [On 12 September 1945 Charles W. Yost was designated Chargé d'Affaires at Bangkok, but until such time as formal diplomatic relations were reopened between the United States and Thailand he was given the temporary assignment of Political Advisor to the Commanding General of the United States Armed Forces in the India-Burma Theater (also the Deputy Supreme Allied Commander of South-East Asia Command). Following the signing of the Formal Agreement for the Termination of the State of War between Thailand and Great Britain and India on 1 January 1946, the United States and Thailand reopened diplomatic relations, and on 5 January 1946 Mr. Yost presented his credentials and assumed the functions of United States Chargé d'Affaires.]

42 [Mr. Dening had told Prince Wiwat that he must report back with the Thai government's decision by 15 December.]
43 [On 15 December 1945 Mr. Yost recommended to United States Secretary of State Byrnes that in order to relieve the Thai of the onus of refusing to sign the treaty at the last moment, the State Department should apprise the British that the Thai were delaying pursuant to the United States' recommendation.]
44 [The United States' recommendation that Thailand should not sign the agreement while British-American discussions were still proceeding reached Prince Wiwat in Singapore on 17 December 1945, just in time to stop the signing of the treaty.]
45 [In the proposed exchange of letters Thailand wished to have Britain state publicly that the terms Thailand was agreeing to were the minimum terms the British would accept, and that these were not subject to further negotiation.]
46 [The United States was, like Britain itself, anxious to see the termination of the state of war between Thailand and Britain. It would therefore have been dissatisfied had agreement broken down over Thai insistence that Britain publicly declare its demands were not negotiable.]
47 See appendix 5.
48 [The numbers listed, and their ordering, do not correspond with those in the articles of the treaty itself, as the author was listing only the main provisions of the Agreement. For full text see appendix 5 at the end of this book.]
49 See Formal Agreement, Article 14.
50 For details on the Formal Agreement, the Heads of Agreement and Annex, see reports of the National Assembly, January 1946.
51 [Again the list shown gives only the main points of the Heads of Agreement and Annex. For the full text of these documents see appendix 6.]
52 [This section actually covered the regularization of Thailand's position in relation to bilateral and multilateral treaties and its membership in international organizations.]
53 [In fact the text of this article reads that Thailand should safeguard the property etc. of the Allies, not just of the British.]
54 Announcement of the Office of the Prime Minister, 1 January 1946.
55 Crosby, op. cit., 9–10.
56 Ibid, 136–43.
57 Ibid, 144–45.
58 Ibid, 146–47.
59 Ibid, 150–64.
60 A final Peace Agreement between the government of Australia and that of Thailand was signed on 3 April 1946. For details see part 3, chapter 6 [now chapter 15] and the text of the agreement in the appendix [appendix 5].

Chapter 11

1. According to the Population Survey carried out in 1947, two years after the war ended, 750,000 people out of a total population of 17,442,687 people [in Thailand] were Chinese. However, in other works it has been calculated that the Chinese population at the time was probably one million.
2. [A literary and historical term used to refer to the Indo-Chinese peninsula, or that area today comprising mainland Southeast Asia.]
3. See the lecture "Laksana kanpokhrong prathet Thai tae boran" ["Characteristics of Ancient Thai Administration"] by Prince Damrong Rajanubhab; [H.G.] Quaritch Wales, *Ancient Thai Government and Administration*, [London, Bernard Quaritch, 1934], 43–56; and Wiwatthana kankotmai Thai [Evolution of Thai Law] by the author.
4. [In the latter part of the Ch'ing dynasty Kiangnan referred to the two present-day provinces of Kiangsu and Anhwei combined.]
5. [In 1913–14 the Thai government promulgated the first Nationality Act. This claimed as Thai every person born on Thai territory. The only exception made was for those registered by their parents with the legations or embassies of countries with which Thailand had treaty relations as nationals of that power. As Thailand did not have treaty relations with China, this option was not open to the Chinese.]
6. [An Ayutthayan period Thai king who ruled during the fifteenth century A.D.]
7. [In pre-modern times Thai society was divided into two main classes. At the apex of society stood the king, together with the royal aristocracy and in later times the bureaucratic nobility. Beneath this level came the masses of the people, who were divided into freemen and slaves. Freemen, who were chiefly agriculturalists, on reaching the age of eighteen, had to attach themselves to a patron, usually a noble or head of a department. He in turn was responsible for providing the services of a certain number of clients to specified government departments. These clients were known as *phrai som*. During the next two years, the patron of the *phrai som* would see that his client received instruction in the type of work he would be called upon to do for the government, and was entitled to a small amount of work from the client for himself. At the age of twenty, the *phrai som* would normally become a *phrai luang*, or retainer of the king, and was assigned to a particular nobleman acting as representative of a particular government department. The *phrai luang* were available for public service until they reached the age of sixty years, or until they had three sons in the royal service. It was through this system that corvée labor was provided to build public works in Thailand during the pre-modern era.]
8. [See n. 7.]
9. La Loubère, *A New Historical Relation of the Kingdom of Thailand*, London, [Theodore Horn], 1963, 53.
10. Sir John Bowring, *The Kingdom and People of Thailand* [with a Narrative of the Mission to that Country in 1855, London, John W. Parker and Sons, 1857, 2 vols.] 85–8.
11. W. A. Graham, *Siam* [London, Alexander Moring, 1924, 3rd edition], II, 96–7.

[Because no treaty was drawn up between Thailand and China, the Chinese were free to travel or settle anywhere in the kingdom. This was in contrast to the position of other aliens. Prior to the Bowring Treaty of 1855, Western nationals were forbidden to own houses or land, export rice, or travel in the interior, and even though the Bowring Treaty secured considerable commercial rights and other privileges for British nationals, and this was followed by similar treaties between Thailand and a number of other nations, foreign nationals still required passes to travel in the interior of Thailand.]

12 James C. Ingram, *Economic Change in Thailand Since 1850*, [Stanford, Stanford University Press, 1955], 19–20, and Quaritch Wales, op. cit., 204–08.

[The Bowring treaty of 1855 brought an end to royal trading monopolies, and enforced a 3 percent ceiling on import duties. The Thai government was thus suddenly faced with a marked loss of revenue. To overcome this deficit, it introduced new taxes, the farming out of which was taken over by the Chinese.]

13 [A passage in the Thai edition of this book, consisting of a proclamation by King Rama IV appointing a Chinese businessman to be a tax farmer, has been omitted here.]

14 Luang Wichitwathakan, "*Khambanyai prawatsat sethakit Thai* [*Lecture on Thai Economic History*"], Thammasat University, 1950. Also published by the Council of Ministers as a cremation volume for the author, 1962, 90–94.

15 [During the Ch'ing/Manchu dynasty.]

16 [This paragraph has been taken from an earlier section in the Thai edition and inserted here, as it fits more appropriately in this passage.]

17 [Should be 1911.]

18 Dr. Victor Purcell, *The Chinese in Southeast Asia* [London, Oxford University Press, 1951], 144–51.

19 [The *coup d'état* of 24 June 1932 whereby a group of young liberals and military officers overthrew the absolute monarchy and replaced it with a constitutional monarchy.]

20 [G. William] Skinner, *Chinese Society in Thailand*: [*An Analytical History*, Ithaca, New York, Cornell University Press], 227–33.

21 At the time the exchange rate stood at 1/10 Baht; today the rate is 1/60 Baht. Since the value of the Baht has decreased six times, the [present-day] equivalent of the sum would be 156 million Baht.

22 [W. A. M. Doll, a British national who was Financial Advisor to the Thai government from 1936 until the outbreak of World War II, and again in the immediate post-war period.]

23 [From the reign of King Rama V on, a number of foreign nationals were employed by the Thai government to serve as Advisors to different government departments.]

24 [1939? Mr. Doll did not take up his position as Financial Advisor to the Thai government until 1936 (see n. 22).]

25 [See *Report of the Financial Advisor in Connection with the Budget of the Kingdom of Thailand 1938–39*, 39–40.]

26 [This was an extension of the government's prohibited areas policy originally applied to the provinces of Lop Buri and Prachin Buri and the district of Sattahip in the province of Chon Buri in May 1941, and extended in September 1941 to three areas in northeast Thailand.]
27 [A decree of June 1942 reserved twenty-seven different occupations for Thai nationals only.]
28 [A Chinese quarter in Bangkok.]
29 [See chapter 6 for a discussion of American and British attitudes toward Thailand in the immediate post-war period.]
30 [Mr. Li Tieh-cheng, who arrived in Bangkok on 6 September 1945, was the head of a Chinese mission sent to negotiate a treaty with Thailand. He later became the first Chinese Ambassador to Thailand.]
31 [A section on the historical status of the Chinese in Thailand, seen as repetitious, has been omitted here.]
32 [Author of *China and Southeastern Asia*, Chungking and New York, Institute of Pacific Relations, 1945. At the time of writing Chen Su-ching was associated with the National Southwest Associated Universities (see Skinner, op. cit., 281–82 and 423.]
33 This was not true (see part 2, chapter 3 [now chapter 8] in connection with [Thailand's recognition] of the Wang Ching-wei regime). No exchange of diplomats took place.
34 Skinner, op. cit., 281–82.
35 The text of the treaty is given in the appendixes [appendix 7].
36 Skinner, op. cit., 283–84.

Chapter 12

1 [The author had been a Minister without portfolio in the Ministry of Finance in 1938, but as he points out in chapter 1, he only held this position for a few months before being transferred to the Ministry of Foreign Affairs. As Minister of Foreign Affairs between November 1943 and July 1944, however, he was called upon to try to gain sympathy from the Japanese for Thailand's financial plight, necessitating the command of background knowledge of Thailand's financial affairs during the war period demonstrated in chapter 8.]
2 At the time he had not yet been raised to the rank of Phraongchao.
3 [The cooperative movement in Thailand was a government-sponsored institution, and cooperatives were financed almost exclusively out of funds supplied by the central government.]
4 [In other words, now that the war was over the expenses, both direct and indirect incurred as a result of the Japanese occupation, would come to an end.]
5 See proposal 20 of the "Twenty-one Proposals."
6 At the time he had not yet received the title Krommamuen.
7 Now dead.
8 Former Minister of Finance.
9 Later became Krommamuen Nakhonsawansakphinit. Now dead.
10 At the time Deputy Minister of Finance.

11 At the time acting Minister of Economics. Now dead.
12 At the time Minister of Industry. Now dead.
13 At the time Minister without portfolio. Now dead.
14 Former Minister without portfolio.
15 At present Deputy Under-Secretary of the Office of the Prime Minister.
16 Advisor to the Legislative Committee. Now dead.
17 A National Assembly representative. Now dead.
18 At present Under-Secretary to the Minister of Finance.
19 Nai Wichit Lulitanon.
20 M.C. Wiwatthanachai.
21 Former Under-Secretary of the Ministry of Finance. Now dead.
22 Former head of the Comptroller-General's Department.
23 Luang Sathianchotisan.
24 [A Thai language newspaper. The article, given in full in the original, has been condensed here.]
25 [A unit of measurement of weight of gold as well as the name of a unit of currency.]
26 [Conference of Allied nations held in Bretton Woods, New Hampshire in July 1944 to promote international monetary cooperation and rebuild the world economy once the war was concluded.]
27 *Royal Gazette*, vol. 62, 6 February 1946 and Manun Borisut, *Khana ratthamontri*, op. cit.,155–56.

Chapter 13

1 *Royal Gazette*, 1946, vol. 63, part 16, 270 and Manun Borisut, *Khana ratthamontri*, op. cit., 156–58.
2 [On 9 June 1946 King Ananda was found shot in bed under mysterious circumstances which have never been fully clarified. The day after the King's death Pridi Banomyong resigned as Prime Minister, since the king who had appointed him to his position was now no longer living. However, the Regency Council, headed by Prince Rangsit of Chai Nat, acting for the new king, Bhumipol Adulyadej, who was then still a minor, re-confirmed Pridi in his position, and the latter continued as head of the government until August, when Rear Admiral Luang Thamrongnawasawat was voted in as Prime Minister. As Direk later makes clear, Pridi's term of office thus extended for a couple of months beyond the date of 9 June 1946 cited in the Cabinet list given here.]
3 *Royal Gazette*, 1946, vol. 63, part 56, p. 3 and Manun Borisut, *Khana ratthamontri*, op. cit, 161–63.
4 [The government of Admiral Thamrongnawasawat came under increasing criticism for failing to stabilize the cost of living and eliminate corruption, and in May 1947 was faced with a censure motion. The government withstood the motion, and on 30 May Admiral Thamrong was reelected Prime Minister, remaining in office until 8 November 1947, when a group of

army officers led by Field Marshal Phibun Songkhram seized power. Although the majority of Cabinet members remained the same under the first and second Thamrong governments, there were a number of changes, the most significant being the replacement of the author as Foreign Minister by Atthakit Banomyong, the half-brother of Pridi Banomyong, following Direk's resignation in February 1947.]

5 Later knighted and appointed British Ambassador to Thailand.
6 [It was not until March 1947 that the British and American diplomatic missions in Thailand were raised from legation to embassy status.]
7 See the Formal Agreement in the appendixes [appendix 5]. Article 14 dealt with the question of Thailand having to provide one and a half million tons of rice free of charge.]
8 [A reduction in the amount of rice originally demanded.]
9 [As has already been described in chapter 10, in the immediate post-war period Britain, as head of South-East Asia Command, was concerned about the severe rice shortages that were being suffered throughout much of South and Southeast Asia as a consequence of World War II. During the first few months after the war, South-East Asia Command distributed supplies of rice to the area in accordance with allocations made by the Combined Food Board in Washington, D.C. However, in March 1946 the British government appointed a Special Commissioner in Southeast Asia whose duties were to encourage increased rice production and to initiate appropriate measures for distributing food supplies to deficit areas, and generally to coordinate the economic machinery of Southeast Asia in regard to food production and distribution. It was through the office of this Special Commissioner that the negotiations which resulted in the revision of the Formal Agreement were conducted.]
10 [The office of the Special Commissioner in South-East Asia was in Singapore.]
11 [In other words it was currently controlled not by the Thai government but by Chinese merchants.]
12 [Rather than make a free gift of rice to the British, much of the rice was smuggled out of the country (usually to Hong Kong or Malaya) where the prevailing shortages made it possible for merchants to sell rice at huge profits.]
13 See exchange of letters between the Thai Minister of Foreign Affairs and the British Minister dated 3 May 1946.
14 See part 3, chapter 1 [now chapter 10].
15 For negotiations leading to the Formal Agreement see part 3, chapter 1 [now chapter 10].
16 [In fact Allied forces entered Thailand right after the end of the war, several months before the signing of the Formal Agreement. See chapter 10, n. 3.]
17 Report of the meeting of the National Assembly no. 13/1946 [13/2489], (Special), Thursday, 31 October 1946, 17.
18 See part 3, chapter 5 [now chapter 14].
19 [A bridge in Bangkok that was bombed by the Allies during the war.]
20 For Thailand's application for membership in the United Nations see part 3, chapter 6 [now chapter 15].

21 [Knighted in 1949.]
22 Sir Geoffrey Thompson, *Front-line Diplomat*, [London, Hutchinson, 1959], 191.
23 [In May 1947 after the status of the legation was raised to that of an embassy in March of that year. Mr. Stanton presented his Credentials on 4 July 1946.]
24 [As of the time of writing. Mr. Stanton died in 1968.]
25 Edwin Stanton, *Brief Authority*: [*Excursions of a Common Man in an Uncommon World*, New York, Harper, 1956], 183–84.
26 In my note on this discussion, I do not have any record of alluding to this date. I only stated that the land which we acquired in 1940 was land that the French had taken from us by force and which was returned in accordance with the treaty [i.e. the treaty between Thailand and France of 9 May 1941.]
27 For negotiations with the French regarding Thailand joining the United Nations see part 3, chapter 5 [now chapter 14].
28 See the earlier part of this chapter for a discussion of arrangements for a tripartite rice agreement.
29 [The Combined Thailand Rice Commission, established in March 1946. This body, set up to help Thailand meet its rice export commitments, had British, American, Indian, Australian, and Chinese as well as Thai members on its board, and continued in operation for approximately a year and a half.]
30 The reasons for the insufficient amount of rice delivered, as I explained, included not only the lack of rolling stock but also the railway tracks, [i.e. the damage caused to these tracks during the war, making it difficult to transport the rice demanded]; the [low] price being offered for the rice, resulting in rice smuggling; and many other factors. For details see earlier sections [of this chapter] regarding our negotiations over the rice problem, and part 3, chapter 8 [now chapter 17] regarding our petition for an increase in the price to be paid for our rice.
31 Stanton, *Brief Authority*, [op. cit.], 183–84.

Chapter 14

1 The Report of this Commission is given in detail at the end of this book as appendix 10.
 [The Conciliation Commission, established under the terms of the Franco-Thai Agreement of 17 November 1946 terminating the Indochina dispute, was to examine the ethnic, geographic and economic claims of the two parties for a revision of the frontier, and to settle questions of compensation.]
2 [On 17 November 1946 a Franco-Thai agreement was signed in Washington setting up a Conciliation Commission to consider the question of whether the Franco-Thai agreements of 1893, 1904 and 1907 involving the seizure by France of large areas of territory formerly belonging to Thailand should be revised or confirmed. It was the report of this Commission that was issued on 27 June 1947.]
3 [The author was appointed Ambassador to the Court of St. James in June 1947.]

4 [See chapter 10, n. 38.]
5 The government of Nai Khuang Aphaiwong, which remained in office after the war ended until 1 September 1945.
6 [The Peace Proclamation put forward by the Regent, Pridi Banomyong, in the name of the King on 16 August 1945 stating that the declaration of war made by Thailand against Britain and the United States in January 1942 was now to be regarded as null and void.]
7 [M.R. Seni Pramoj took office on 17 September 1945 following his return from Washington.]
8 See the first chapter of this part [now chapter 10].
9 Later served as French Ambassador to Thailand, from 1960 to the present day [i.e. the time of writing].
10 See the second chapter of part 1 concerning this treaty.
11 [The treaty and annex referred to is that of the original draft of the proposed Formal Agreement. This was modified substantially before reaching its final form (see chapter 10).]
12 [A Buddha image housed in Wat Phra Kaeo (temple of the Emerald Buddha) in Bangkok. A sacred image regarded as the palladium of the Kingdom of Thailand.]
13 See third chapter of part 1.
14 [Since the Emerald Buddha was regarded as the palladium of Thailand, no self-respecting Thai government could possibly consider handing it over to any other nation.]
15 At that time M.R. Seni Pramoj was both Prime Minister and Minister of Foreign Affairs.
16 [Mr. Maberly Esler Dening.]
17 [The British equivalent of the O.S.S.]
18 Abbreviation for the Office of Strategic Services, which was under the direction of General Donovan. The General was later (in 1954 [1953—Ed.]) appointed American Ambassador to Thailand. Now dead. The General was a very capable person who carried out clever maneuvers and was always on the winning side.
19 [Mr. Dening was presumably suggesting that these additional provisions could touch on the question of the dispute between France and Thailand.]
20 At that time French High Commissioner for Indochina.
21 Mr. Dening's dispatch is quoted in the Reports of the Meeting of the National Assembly of 17 June 1946.
22 Now Ambassador to the Hague.
23 See the Reports of the Meeting of the National Assembly of 17 June 1946, [op. cit.].
24 Subsequently Deputy Minister of Foreign Affairs. His last post was as Ambassador to Sweden. Now retired.
25 Later Minister of Industry. Currently Ambassador to Paris.
26 These principles had already been agreed to with the signing of the Non-Aggression Treaty [between Thailand and France on 12 June 1940]. (See part 1, chapter 2.)
27 [Principal town of a northeastern Thai province bearing the same name.]
28 [A town on the Lao side of the Mekong opposite Nakhon Phanom.]

29 [A small town on the Lao side of the river upstream from Thakhaek.]
30 [French rule in Laos was overthrown by the Japanese in March 1945, but once the Japanese surrendered at the end of World War II, the French set out to reinstate their authority over the area. Although they succeeded in doing so without difficulty in Champassac in southern Laos, once they started moving further north they were confronted by supporters of the Lao Issara (Free Lao) movement, which sought independence from France. This movement not only had the backing of the Viet Minh, but also the tacit support of the Chinese Kuomintang forces that occupied northern Laos from mid-September 1945 to May 1946.

In March 1946 the French moved north to Thakhaek, which was being held by the Lao Issara, openly supported by Viet Minh agents. After heavy fighting the French took the town and proceeded northward in their reoccupation, entering Vientiane on 24 April 1946 and from there proceeding towards Luang Prabang. Meanwhile the Lao Issara government and the majority of its supporters, including many of the 30,000 Vietnamese who had formerly been residents of Laos, fled to Thailand. It was this group of refugees that the French claimed were crossing the border from Thailand back into Laos and conducting raids against the French.]
31 [See ns. 29 and 30.]
32 [In other words no Thai were involved, and where Thai had crossed the Mekong it had only been to carry goods across for trading purposes.]
33 [French nationals who also fled to Thailand during the guerrilla skirmishes between the Lao Issara and the returning French occupation forces.]
34 Former President of the United States of America. He had recently visited Thailand [in his role as Chairman of the Famine Emergency Committee. This committee, sponsored by the United States government and inaugurated in Washington on 1 March 1946 had been established to help meet the world food crisis.]
35 [Lord Killearn had been appointed Special Commissioner for South-East Asia on 16 March 1946. His role in revising those clauses of the Formal Agreement dealing with Thailand's rice payments has already been described in chapter 13.]
36 Now holding the rank of Krommamuen Narathip-phongpraphan.
37 As far as I remember these were Luang Wisutwiratchathet, Lieutenant Colonel Prince Subha Svasti, Nai Thanat Khoman as a reserve delegate and secretary, Nai Konthi Suphamongkhon, Luang Ditthakanphakdi, Prince Dilakrit Kritdakon, Nai Charun Itsarangkun Na Ayutthaya, Nai Suchit Hiranyapruek, Nai Dusit Buntham and Nai Chaphikon Setthabut.
38 [As the author subsequently explains, in September 1946 Khuang Aphaiwong and Thanat Khoman left the United States for Paris to sound out the views of the French government on ways of handling the dispute. At the same time Prince Subha Svasti was sent to London to ascertain the opinions of the British government on the matter.]
39 See details in the Report of the Meeting of the National Assembly dated 14 October 1946.
40 [In other words the French government was prepared to settle the dispute under the indirect umbrella of the United Nations to satisfy Thailand's wishes in this regard.]
41 [A member of the delegation. See n. 37 above.]

42 [The constitution of May 1946 established a bicameral legislature consisting of a popularly elected House of People's Representatives and an upper house or Senate. This was in contrast to the previous constitution of December 1932, which had a unicameral assembly.]
43 [For further details see chapter 16.]
44 [See "Draft of proposals to end the dispute between France and Thailand" given subsequently in this chapter as Supplementary Document no. 1.]
45 Regarding the 1941 agreement, see part 1, chapter 3.
46 [The Treaty of Friendship, Commerce and Navigation concluded at Bangkok on 7 December 1937 between France and Thailand.]
47 [The Commercial and Customs Agreement concerning Indochina signed at Bangkok on 9 December 1937.]
48 For text of the Agreement see appendix 9.
49 *Kanthut*, op. cit., I, 360-65.
50 Ibid.
51 Ibid, 356–420.
52 See the translation of the Commission's Report in the appendixes [appendix 10.]
53 This agreement involved our losing territories on the right bank of the Mekong opposite Luang Prabang and facing Phakse (see *Kanthut*, [op. cit.], I, 360–65).
54 [Part 3A, paragraph 3?—Ed.]
55 For the agreement whereby Thailand lost territories on the left bank of the Mekong see *Kanthut*, [op. cit.], I, 356–60.
56 This matter had already been agreed to by France when the Non-Aggression Treaty was signed in [June] 1940 (see part 1, chapter 2).
57 *Kanthut*, [op. cit.], I, 360–65.
58 [The Tonle Sap, or Great Lake of Cambodia.]
59 [Part 4?—Ed.]
60 Rear Admiral Thawan Thamrongnawasawat.
61 [The author.]

Chapter 15

1 [The chapter heading has been altered in the English edition to make it conform more closely to the contents of the chapter.]
2 The government of M.R. Seni Pramoj.
3 See the Exchange of Notes and Heads of Agreement [in appendixes 5 and 6].
4 [It should be noted that the actual details concerning British war claims were not worked out until January 1947. On 6 January 1947 Britain submitted a Memorandum to the Thai government outlining in detail the arrangements to be made in regard to such claims. This was accepted on behalf of the government of Thailand by the author, as Minister of Foreign

Affairs, on that same date (British Command Paper (Cmd. 8140), Treaty Series no. 10 (1951), 15–20).]

5 This sum had already been proposed to England by the governments of Nai Khuang Aphaiwong and Nai Pridi Banomyong, but no agreement had been reached on the subject thus far.

6 [On 8 May 1947 the British Embassy in Bangkok presented the Thai Foreign Ministry with an *aide-mémoire* suggesting that the Thai Prime Minister issue a memorandum stating that "in view of their cooperation in the task of the Allied military authorities in disarming and interning the Japanese forces in Thailand, the Thai government undertakes to provide free of cost Thai currency that may be required by the Allied military authorities in the pursuance of their task." On the same day the Thai Ministry of Foreign Affairs forwarded to the British Embassy in Bangkok a Memorandum issued by the Office of the Prime Minister containing the above words. Britain, for its part, agreed to deduct any moneys that might have been used for non-military purposes, with such amounts to be credited to the Thai government in pounds sterling. Further, it was stated that the total amount of Thai currency used by the Allied military authorities was expected "not to exceed 80 million Baht inclusive of amounts already made available" (British Command Paper (Cmd. 8140), op. cit., 22–3).]

7 [On 8 May 1947 Prime Minister Thawan Thamrongnawasawat, in his concurrent capacity as Minister for Foreign Affairs, formally agreed in writing that the Thai government would continue to hold all Japanese and other enemy property at the disposal of the Allies after the deduction of reasonable expenses properly vouched for incurred in the control and management of such property (ibid., 21).]

8 [At least thirteen Thai were charged as war criminals, the most important of whom was Luang Phibun Songkhram (Sawang Lanlua, *37 pi haeng kanpatiwat* [*37 years since the coup d'état*], Thonburi, Pho Sam Ton Press, 1969, 198)].

9 The War Criminal Court dismissed the cases brought to trial while England was proposing an exchange of notes on the matter.

10 The matter was discussed in the middle of October 1946. The Allied troops withdrew at the end of that month, as mentioned previously.

11 For the text of this [Final] Agreement [with Australia] see appendix 8 at the end of this book.

Chapter 16

1 Now Ambassador to Bonn.
2 [The term "United Nations" was first used in the joint declaration signed in Washington on 1 January 1942 by representatives of those nations fighting the Axis powers. From that time on this group set up increasingly extensive arrangements for military and economic cooperation, and meetings were held by the heads of the major powers concerned at which the question of a post-war peace organization received increasing attention. It was not until the Dumbarton Oaks meeting of 24 August 1944, however, that preparation of a draft constitution for a permanent

United Nations organization was begun. In April 1945 fifty nations sent delegates to the San Francisco Conference, where the remaining problems that needed to be taken care of before a charter could be formulated were worked out. The United Nations Charter was completed on 26 June 1945 and ratified on 24 October 1945.]

3 [In February 1945 the Regent, Pridi Banomyong, sent a delegation led by Sanguan Tularak and Suni Thaparaksa to Washington to try to establish a provisional free Thai government or government-in-exile. This delegation gave as one of its reasons for wishing to do so that it "desired such a government in order to publicly identify the Thai with the cause of the United Nations" (Memorandum by the Director of the Office of Far Eastern Affairs, Joseph W. Ballantine, to the Assistant Secretary of State, James Clement Dunn, of 22 February 1945, *Foreign Relations of the United States*, op. cit., 1945, 1252).]

4 [Article 23 of the Charter of the United Nations stated that the Security Council was to consist of eleven members of the United Nations, with the Republic of China, France, the U.S.S.R., Great Britain and the United States forming the permanent members of the Council. The remaining six members were non-permanent and elected for a two-year term. Article 27 stated that decisions on all issues other than procedural matters were to be made by an affirmative vote of seven members including the concurring votes of the permanent members.]

5 [Mr. Konthi Suphamongkhon.]

6 Now Ambassador to the Hague.

7 This agreement had been made between Colonel Phra Prasatphitthayayut, the Thai Minister to Berlin, and the Soviet Minister of Foreign Affairs in 1940, the year before the Germans attacked the U.S.S.R.

8 [See chapter 14.]

9 [Ibid.]

10 Now Minister of Foreign Affairs.

11 [See n. 8.]

12 Later appointed Minister of Foreign Affairs. Died in 1957.

13 United Nations *Yearbook*, 1946–1947, 419.

14 [The following is a précis by the editor of a large number of newspaper clippings which appeared in the press immediately after the announcement of the author's resignation, and which are quoted in full in the main body of the text in the Thai edition of this work. These reports have been greatly condensed here, as they contain considerable amounts of repetitive material.]

15 [In November 1946 Pridi Banomyong, in his capacity as "Senior Statesman" and former leader of the Free Thai movement, left Thailand for the United States and Europe on a goodwill tour.]

16 At that time Bangkok was divided into six electoral districts. The 5th district, where I ran for election, was composed of Amphoe Phra Khanong, Phra Pradaeng, Samut Prakan, Bang Bo and Amphoe Bang Phli.

17 Colonel Prince Nakkhatramongkhon Kittiyakon. Later raised to Phraongchao and made Krommamuen Chantaburisuranat.

18 Rear Admiral Thawan Thamrongnawasawat, as both Prime Minister and Minister of Foreign Affairs, wrote to me on 19 March 1947 and I replied with a letter of acceptance on 25 March 1947.
19 Later raised to the rank of Krom Phra, and at his death honored by His Majesty with the title of Somdet Krom Phraya.

Chapter 17

1 [The preliminary section of this chapter, which deals with the British political system, has been omitted from the English edition.]
2 Now Ambassador to Indonesia.
3 Later Lieutenant-General, and Ambassador to Japan and to Ethiopia. Now retired.
4 Later Comptroller-General. Now retired.
5 Later Ambassador to various countries. Now retired.
6 Now dead.
7 Presently Chargé d'Affaires in Ceylon.
8 [This project, part of a plan for irrigating the entire Central Plains, was originally put forward in a report by J. H. Van der Heide, a Dutch irrigation expert, in 1903. It was rejected by the Thai government as being too costly, and nothing further was done on the project until after World War II. Then, as part of the efforts to increase rice production, the Thai government submitted the Chao Phraya River Dam Project (of which a dam at Chai Nat was to be a part) to the FAO in 1946 (*Thailand Official Yearbook*, 1964, Bangkok, Government House Printing Office, 338). Again, the project ran up against the need for massive funding. It was submitted to the World Bank for negotiation of a loan in 1949, and in October 1950 the World Bank granted a loan of U.S. 18 million for the project. Work began on the dam in 1952, and was completed in 1956.]
9 [Sections on the Labour government and the economic situation in Britain immediately after the war that follow in the Thai edition have been omitted in the English version.]
10 Later knighted, and became British Ambassador to Japan. Now retired.
11 Later knighted and made British Ambassador to Burma. Now retired.
12 Formerly British Ambassador to Cairo. After the end of the war [in March 1946] he was appointed Special Commissioner for South-East Asia [with headquarters in] Singapore, with the duties of advising the British government on political problems affecting international relations in the region as well as of carrying out research on the food situation in the area. He died in 1964.
13 Estimate based on [Article 14] of the Formal Agreement.
14 [A second Thamrong government took office in June 1947. The new Foreign Minister was Atthakit Banomyong (Luang Atthakittikamchon), the half-brother of Pridi Banomyong.]
15 [Extracts from this letter are given in the Thai edition.]
16 The Minister of Foreign Affairs and I were both due to attend the meeting of the United Nations General Assembly in New York on 15 September.

17 Mr. D.W. Reeve was the Advisor to the Ministry of Finance. The government sent him to help me with negotiations regarding the amount payable to England as compensation under the terms of the Formal Agreement. Mr. Reeve was subordinate to Mr. Doll, who was the Financial Advisor to the government.
18 [See Article 78 of the Italian Peace Treaty of 10 February 1947.]
19 [The Treaty of Commerce and Navigation signed at Bangkok on 23 November 1937.]
20 Died in 1963.
21 I learned that he has since died. The Commonwealth countries refer to their diplomatic representatives sent to member countries of the Commonwealth as High Commissioners rather than Ambassadors.
22 Australia had more extensive mining interests in Thailand than any other nation at that time.
23 When Mr. Bevin died about ten years ago, I was asked by the *Standard* to write a commemorative article on him. I agreed to do this gladly, as he was a person who had shown great goodwill towards Thailand.
24 [On 8 November 1947 a group of army officers headed by Field Marshal Phibun Songkhram seized control of the government, set aside the 1946 Constitution and forced many civilian leaders, including Rear Admiral Thawan Thamrongnawasawat, the former Prime Minister, and Pridi Banomyong into hiding. Khuang Aphaiwong agreed to take over the post of Prime Minister in a caretaker government pending the holding of elections, but only after he had received a firm pledge that the military faction would not interfere in the administration of the government.]
25 Later Privy Councilor, and now Assistant to the Office of the Prime Minister.
26 [The general elections were held on 29 January 1948. Khuang was returned to office by a large majority. Towards the end of February he presented his program to the National Assembly and received an overwhelming vote of confidence. Shortly thereafter the governments of Britain, the United States and China officially recognized the Khuang regime.]
27 [On 6 April 1948 Khuang was forced out of office, and Field Marshal Phibun Songkhram took over the government.]
28 Later became Minister of Defense in the Labour government. He resigned from this position in February 1966.
29 [Field Marshal Phibun Songkhram remained Prime Minister from 6 April 1948 until September 1957, although several attempts were made to overthrow him during this time.]
30 [Great Britain. Treaty series no. 16 (1951). Exchange of notes… regarding the settlement of outstanding Commonwealth war claims against Thailand … London, H.M.S.O., Cmd. 8163.]
31 See the *Royal Gazette* (17 January 1950) [1954?—Ed.] and Exchange of Notes between Thailand and Great Britain; [also Great Britain, Treaty series no. 19 (1954), Cmd. 9090.]
32 Son of Mr. Ramsey MacDonald, the Labour Prime Minister of thirty years earlier, and former Minister of the Colonies. Presently High Commissioner to Kenya.
33 [In Johore.]

Appendix 10, Note Annexe

1. British Foreign Office Blue Book No. 1 (1894), *Corréspondance concernant les affaires du Siam*.
2. Document joint à l'original.
3. British Foreign Office Blue Book No. 1 (1894), op. cit., 151.

Appendix 11

1. [As is subsequently made clear, the O.S.S. used the money to buy gold in the U.S.A. This gold was then molded and sent in to Thailand through O.S.S. agents. It was then picked up in Thailand and exchanged through the banks for Baht, which were in turn used for the work of the Free Thai in Thailand.]
2. [As Dr. Puey Ungphakorn points out in his article "Temporary Soldier" given at the end of part 2, the Free Thai in the United States had a semi-autonomous position within the United States Army, and were permitted not only to have their own officers but to wear their own uniforms as well.]
3. [Thawin Udon was sent to China as an emissary of the Free Thai movement at the end of November 1944 (Nicol Smith, op. cit., 193).]
4. [Major John Wester had lived in Thailand for eighteen years before the war, became a member of the O.S.S., and was one of the first Americans to enter Japanese-occupied Thailand (ibid, 199).]
5. [In the immediately preceding paragraph the figure quoted was 1,460,184.84 Baht; one of these two figures is therefore probably a typing error.]
6. [Head of British Force 136 (see subsequent text).]

INDEX

Page numbers in italics refer to photos

A

Acheson, Dean, 195, 196
administration, ancient Thai, 227
Adun Adundetcharat, Luang, 3, 52, 74–78, 85–87, 117–118, 125, 134–140, 149, 178, 186, 205, 206, 207
aliens, restriction on, 233
Allied banking concerns, sequestration of, 293
Allied forces
   air strikes, 151
   entry into Thailand, 246
Allied prisoners of war, 158
Allied property, safeguarding of, 296
Allied troops, judicial protection of, 296
Allies, and International Military Tribunal, 112
Ambassador to Tokyo
   acceptance of appointment, 86
   duration of appointment, 89
   end of tenure, 114
Aoki, Minister, 14, 89, 102, 111, 113–114
Appreciation I, Free Thai group, 167
Appreciation II, Free Thai group, 167, 170, 176
Arakan, annexation of, 12
Aranyaprathet (District), 71, 187
   attack on, 40
Arita, Hachiro, 21
Asia, declaration of war, 63
Association for International Cultural Relations, 104

Atlantic Charter, 72
Atthakittikamchon, Luang, 309, 24–325, 333
Australia, separate agreement with, 330
Australian High Commissioner, 334
Austria-Hungary, treaty with, 13
Axis powers, 49, 90–94, 143
   signing of Triple Alliance, 139

B

Baht
   devaluation of, 243
   deterioration of status of, 244
   exchange rate to Pound Sterling, 248
   valuation of, 245, *245*
Baht loans, 120
balance of payments (1944), 243
Baldwin Locomotive Company, 200
Bangkok Rotary Club, 46
Bang Phu, Japanese landing in, 77
Bank Federation, 52
banking, control of, 296
banknotes
   circulation increase during World War II, 243
   decision to issue new ones, 248
Bank of Asia, 52
Bank of Japan, 53, 118, 242
Bank of Siam, 118. *See also* Bank of Thailand
Bank of Thailand, 242
   issue of treasury bonds, 239
Ban Phailin, 40
Bassac, Thai claims on, 288

Battambang, seizure by France, 8
Belgium
  fall of, 5
  treaty with, 13
Bennett, Director of Far Eastern Political Division of Foreign Office, 130, 131
Berlin, signing of Axis alliance agreement, 94
Berrigan, Darell, 194
Bevin, Secretary of State for Foreign Affairs, 130, 180, 209, 317, 335
bills
  creation of Buddhist territory, 121
  establishment of Phetchabun as capital, 121
Boriphanyutthakit, Phra, 5, 74
boundary, drawing of, 25
Bowring, Sir John, 12, 229
Bowring treaty, 8, 12, 13
Boxer War, 96
Bretton Woods, international treaty on currency, 249
Britain
  close cooperation with, 126
  control of oil supplies, 57
  displeasure at Thai declaration of war, 130
  release of frozen Thai assets, 258
  support for Thailand's U.N. membership, 224
  Twenty-one Proposals, 237
  withdrawal from Thailand, 259, 260
  See also England, Great Britain
British Force 136, 267, 332
  stationed at Kandy, 147
British guerilla trainers, 147
British policy, 56
British territories, annexation of, 222
Brunskill, Gerald, announcing British troop withdrawal, 259
Buckingham Palace, 316
Bunphop Phamponsing, 164
Burma, rice producing nation, 320
Burney, Henry, 12

Byrnes, United States Secretary of State, 130, 208–209

C

Cabinet of Seni Pramoj, resignation of, 250
Cabinet of Khuang Aphaiwong, 250
Cabinet of Pridi Banomyong, 253
Cabinet of Thawan Thamrongnawasawat, 254
Cambodia
  formerly within Thailand's jurisdiction, 8
  under French rule, 37
Cambridge, Thai students at, 158, 159
Ceylon, 127
Chainat, 174, 175
  construction of dam, 317
Chamnannitikaset, Luang, 5, 253
Champassac, 40
Chan Samittawet, 87, 89
Chantha Sintharako, killing by French police, 34
Chao Bang, 24
Chapman, John, 26, 64, 196
Charter of the United Nations, 307, 309
  Article 4, 299
Chatnakrop, Luang, 127
Chawengsaksongkhram, Luang, 5, 63, 253, 254
Chekiang, 227
Chen Su-ching, 234
Chiang Kai-shek, 96, 227
  displeasure at Thai recognition of Wang Ching-wei, 98
  German military advisors, 95
  non-interference with Thai independence, 131
Chiang Khan, 10
Chiang Mai, 233
Chiang Rai, 233
China, attack by Japan, 95
China Affairs Board (Japan), 109, 110
Chinese
  after World War II, 233, 234
  growing sense of nationalism, 230

Chinese (*continued*)
   limitations, 228
   population in Thailand, 99
   privileges, 228
   remittances out of Thailand, 232
   tax collectors, 229
   treatment under the Japanese, 233
Chinese House of Representatives, 230
Chinese Nationality Act, 230
Chonburi, Free Thai camp located at, 152
Chulalongkorn, King, 229. *See also* Rama V.
Chungking, 177
Churchill, Winston, 72, 115
   warning to Japan, 73
Civil Law Code, 9
Clarac, M., 266, 270, 271, 272
Cochin-China, occupation by France, 8
Colombo, 166
Combined Boards, 221, 328
Combined Food Board, 256
Committee of the Privy Council, 111
Committee on Revenue and Expenditure, 247
Committee to Consider and Draft the Budget for the year 1946, 247
communication systems, condition after war, 256
compensation, lump sum, 334
Compulsory Education Act, 231
concessions, for Japan from Thailand, 138
Conciliation Commission, 265, 283, 284, 287
Connally, Tom, 196
constitutional monarchy, 38
   change to, xxi, 8, 15, 231
Coordination Department, handling of queries regarding military cooperation with Japan, 118
cost of living index (1938 to 1944), 119
Coughlin, Colonel, significant items of information conveyed by, 184–185
Council of Ministers
   minor changes after treaty with Japan, 78

Council of Ministers (*continued*)
   under Luang Phibun Songhkram, 3
Craigie, Robert, 46
Crawfurd, John, 12, 227
Crosby, Sir Josiah, 16, 20, 26, 53, 54, 63, 66, 189, 224–225
   warning to Thailand, 28
Crolla, Italian Minister, 17, 122
Cultural Pact, 102–104
   Japan and Thailand, 102
currency
   importance of stability, 245
   state of, 244
   valuation, 245
   See also Baht
currency rate, 241, 244

D

Daonakon, damaged, 273
Damrong Rajanubhab, Prince, 13
d'Argenlieu, Admiral, 270, 271
de Chaumont, Chevalier, 7
declaration of war
   against Allies, 91
   explanation, 224, 225
   null and void, 152
Decoux, Admiral, 38, 41, 43, 131
de Gaulle, Charles, 145
Dening, Maberly, 127–128, 216–220, 267–268, 270, 282, 291, 317–319, 325, 330, 336
Denmark
   fall of, 5
   treaty with, 13
Detsahakon, Luang, 5
Det Sanitwong, Mom Luang, 119, 120, 122
Devawongse Varoprakarn, Prince, 14
Diplomatic Corps, Dean of, 46
Direk Jayanama, 5, 20, 68, 70, 71, 103, 124, 125, 132, 133, 136, 139, 141, 142, 151, 183, 206, 207, 253, 254, 338

INDEX

Direk Jayanama (*continued*)
  lectures for Thammasat University, 312
  letter regarding application to join U.N., 307
  presentation of Letters of Credential, 316
  resignation from Foreign Affairs, 123
  resignation of, 311–313
  return to Foreign Affairs, 117–122
  tenure as Ambassador to Japan, 90
Ditthakanphakdi, Luang, 194, 202, 271, 300, 306
Doll, William, 232, 247, 248, 315, 321–322, 324, 363
Dutch East Indies
  change in situation, 50
  source of raw material, 49

E

East India Company, 11
Eaton, Richard, 195
Eden, Anthony, 62, 69, 179–180, 214
Ekathotsarot, King, 14
embassy in Tokyo, choice of staff for, 87
Emerald Buddha, 266–268, 272
Emperor Komei, death of, 14
Emperor of Japan, 115
England
  aid offered by, 67
  alliance with France, 16
  declaration of war against, 143
  declaration of war against Japan, 70, 74
  early relations with, 11–13
  Free Thai movement in, 157
  general elections, 180
  military equipment from, 54
  non-agression pact with, 17, 21
  ratification of non-aggression treaty with, 29
  support for Thailand, 73
  territories in Burma and Malaya, 16
  treaty ceding parts of Malayan Peninsula, 13
  treaty with Japan, 14
Europe
  break out of World War II in, 16

Europe (*continued*)
  war in, 5
Evatt, H. V., 335
Exchange Agreement, Thailand-Australia, 226
Exchange of Notes, 318
exchange rate, 248

F

F.A.O., 300
Far East, maintenance of peace in, 45
Far East International Military Tribunal, 24
fighter planes
  need for, 65
  purchase of by Ministry of Defense, 66
financial situation, after World War II, 237, 247
fishing rights, ensuring sufficient supply, 288
Food and Agriculture Organization. *See* F.A.O.
food shortages, 319
foreign affairs, 253–263
Foreign Economic Administration, 200
foreign policy, change in, 85
foreign relations of the United States, 65
foreign transactions, control of, 296
Formal Agreement, 121, 222, 226, 255
  arguments for revision of articles, 326–329
  arrival of British troops, 259
  Exchange of Notes, 298, 318
  foreword, 326
  issue of termination of, 334
  Italy's peace treaty, 332
  negotiations over, 315–341
  negotiations to revise, 324–341
  postponement, 340
  reasons for revisions, 325–330
  request for revision, 256
  See also Heads of Agreement
Formosa (Taiwan), 110
Fort Bayard, 24
France
  aggression on Thai territories, 275

France (*continued*)
    alliance with England, 16
    bombardment of Thai territory, 39
    ceasefire agreement with, 44, 45
    continued violation of Thai territory, 38
    defeat by Germany, 42
    demand for return of territories, 269
    draft proposals to end dispute with, 283, 284
    historical relationship with, 33
    invasion by Germany, 23
    military aggression, 276
    military pact with, 24
    negotiations with, 265–289, 301
    non-aggression pact with, 17, 21
    non-aggression treaty with, 16
    peace agreement with, 45, 55
    problems with, 277, 278
    ratification of non-aggression treaty with, 31
    record of verbal statements of, 284
    relations with, 7–11
    request for agreement similar to Formal Agreement, 271
    surrender to Germany, 5, 23
    territorial demands from, 35
    territorial dispute with, 277, 278
    treaty with, 12
Franco-Thai trade and shipping agreement, 36
Free Thai, 123, 145
    activities in England, 160
    activities in United States, 201, 202
    cooperation with Thai army, 150
    establishment of, 157
    establishment of contacts abroad, 130
    leader, 147
    meetings in Thailand, 179
    members enlisted in army, 161
    members from United States, 176
    members not enlisted in army, 160
    members overseas, 148
    objectives in England, 162

Free Thai (*continued*)
    parachute drop of medical provisions, 151
    parade of fighters, 154
    Pridi Banamyong, 147
    service to country, 125
    training in guerilla warfare, 147, 165
    two groups, 149
    White Elephants, 167
Frontier line
    adjustment according to international law, 36
    drawing of, 25
frozen assets
    release by Britain, 258, 259
    release by United States, 261
fuel shortage, 56, 57
Fukien, 227
Futami, 53, 60, 61, 67

G

Garreau, M., 38, 39, 43, 46
geographical position, importance of, 224
Germany
    Axis coalition, 49
    defeat by USSR at Stalingrad, 144
    distrust of Japan, 94
    invasion of Poland, 5
    non-aggression treaty with Russia (1939), 49
    relations with, 122
    sale of weapons to China, 95
    sympathy for Thai territorial claims, 41
    treaty with, 13
    troops entering Paris, 23
Golden Peninsula, 227
Graham, W. A., 229
Grant, Minister, 31, 39, 47, 48, 54–55, 58–59, 63
    recall of, 62
Great Britain
    negotiations with, 255–257
    tripartite agreement with, 255
    See also Britain, England

Greater East Asia Co-Prosperity Sphere, 108, 111–112
  Japan's policy about, 103
  reasons behind, 106
Greece, resistance to German invasion, 54
guerilla warfare, training in, 147

H

Ha Giang, 24
Hainan, 227
Haiphong, 24
Heads of Agreement, 222, 291
  Allied military authorities currency needs, 292
  cancellation of, 292–298, 297
  cooperation with Allies, 293
  payment of compensation, 292
Henry, Charles Arsène, 24, 31, 43
Hiroshima, atomic bomb, 132
Holland
  fall of, 5
  See also Netherlands
House of Representatives, Foreign Affairs Committee, 192
Hull, Cordell, 28, 47, 54, 61, 69, 72, 196, 214
  memoirs of, 24
Hutchinson, Arthur, 192

I

Indochina
  Decoux, Admiral, 131
  deterioration of situation in, 27, 30
  French forces in, 24
  Japan's agreement with, 43
  maintenance of status quo, 28, 31
  military bases set up by Japan, 32
  presence of foreign troops, 33
  rice producing nation, 320
  territorial integrity of, 32
  threat from Japan, 42
  intelligence service, 149

International Emergency Food Commission, 262
International Military Tribunal, 31, 41, 112
  Hideki Tojo, 72
  Greater East Asia Ministry, 109
  Tsubokami, 78, 79
Isthmus of Kra, 72, 73, 221, 298
Italy
  Axis coalition, 49
  relations with, 122
  treaty with, 13

J

James I, King, 11
Japan
  agreement with Indochina, 43
  allies with Thailand, 85,
  announcement of surrender, 132
  assets frozen by US and British governments, 52
  attack on China, 95
  attacks on Hawaii and Philippines, 77
  Baht loan made to, 142
  concessions in China, 96
  cultural pact with Thailand, 102–104
  declaration of war, 61, 70
  declaration of war against England and United States, 74
  demand for closure of Chinese frontier, 23
  distrust of Germany, 94, 95
  drafts of plans if victorious, 112
  encroachment on Indochina, 5, 6
  financial relations with, 118–120
  granting of military concessions to, 141
  handing over of British-ruled territories, 113
  invasion of Thailand, 6
  life in, 89–115
  mediation by, 44
  military agreement with, 78
Japan (*continued*)

military defeats (1944), 120
naval expeditions, 137
negotiations with (December 1941), 73
relations with, 14, 15
request for loan from Thailand, 129
request for passage through Thailand, 77, 135
restriction of exports to, 50
restriction on products exported to, 50
restriction on oil purchases, 57
self-imposed isolation, 14
signing of treaty with United States, 14
threat in Southeast Asia, 42
treaties with European countries, 14
treaty with, 13, 15, 21
undertaking to respect independence and sovereignty of Thailand, 77
war on Asian front, 5
war with China, 49
withdrawal from League of Nations, 15
Japan-Thailand Association, 104
Japanese Greater East Asia Ministry, establishment of, 89
Japanese military
   disarmament, 155
   expenses in Thailand, 242
   fighting Thai military and police forces, 136
   landing in Kota Bahru, 77
   landings in Thailand, 77, 134
   passage through Thailand, 67, 70, 75
Japanese press, favoring alliance with Thailand, 90
Japanese property, use by Allies, 294
Japanese royal family, 115
Japanese troops
   disarmament of, 246
   finances available to, 243
Jesuits, French, 7
Joint Committee for the Study of Payment of Compensation, 332
judicial independence, treaties signed, 9

K

Kalayanamaitri (Kalaya), Phraya, 8, 29, 199
Kamchat Phalangkun, 145, 165
Kanchanaburi-Burma Railway Track, purchase by Thai government, 257, 258
Kanchana, 273
Kandy (Sri Lanka), 184, 266
   meeting at, 147
   negotiations after Japanese surrender, 180
   Riverdale Estate, 127
Katsongkhram, Luang, 5
Kedah, 13
   annexation by Thailand, 114
Kelantan, 13
   annexation by Thailand, 114
   Japanese landing on, 137
Kengtung, annexation by Thailand, 114
Khap Kunchon, Mom Luang, 195, 202
Khong Island, 8
Khuang Aphaiwong, 145, 265
   as Prime Minister of Thailand, 121
   resignation of, 339
Khuang Aphaiwong government
   duration of, 122
   threat of resignation, 129
Kiangnan, 227
Killearn, Lord, 274, 319, 323
Kings, *see individual names*
Koichi, 102–103, 120
Konthi Suphamongkhon, 87, 92, 127, 216, 299, 304, 305, 306, 308–309
Kosapan (Phraya Wisut), 8
Kota Bahru, 73
   Japanese attack on, 137
Kowit-aphaiwong, Luang, 3
Kri Dechatiwong, Mom Luang, 145, 253, 254
Kumut Chanrueng, 194, 195
Kuroda, Count, 104
Kwangtung, 227

L

Labour Party, England, 180
Lamphun, restriction on aliens, 233
Lan Chang, claims on, 287
Lang Son, 24
Laokay, 24
Laos
    return of, 32
    under French rule, 37
Laski, Professor, 180
League of Nations, 15, 299
Lepissier, M., 26
Letters of Credentials, presentation to Japanese Emperor, 89
liberation of Thailand, 125
Li Tieh-cheng, 234
Lower Burma, annexation by England, 12
Luang, *see individual names*
Luang Prabang, 34

M

MacDonald, Malcolm, 340
Manchukuo, 15
    puppet government in, 106
Mangkon Phromyothi, Luang, 5, 6
    reappointment as Deputy Minister of Defense, 78, 85
Mani Sanasen, 159, 160, 171
Martaban, annexation by England, 12
Mekong
    boundary line, 16
    boundary question, 10
    treatment as natural frontier line, 34
Merrill, Frank, 186, 190, 194
military agreement, signed in Kandy, 296
military equipment, need for, 65
military forces, insufficient to resist Japan, 76
mines, ownership of, 51
Ministry of Education
    establishment of curriculum, 231

Ministry of Education (*continued*)
    inspection of private schools, 232
Ministry of Foreign Affairs
    exercise of purely diplomatic matters, 105
Ministry of Greater East Asian Affairs, 104, 104–113
    official opening of, 111
    Thai displeasure with establishment of, 107
Mitobe, Professor, 18
Moffat, Abbot Low, 193, 194, 200
    discussion with, 197
Mongkut, King, *See* Rama IV, King.
Mountbatten, Lord Louis, 126, 127, 129, 141, 151, 185, 186, 190, 217, 266
    call for closer Allied cooperation, 126
    request for military delegation, 127
Muang Pan, annexation by Thailand, 114
Mun River, 11
Mussolini, 122, 144
Mutsuhito, Crown Prince, succession to the throne, 14

N

Nakamura, General, 132
    Commander-in-Chief in Thailand, 126
    last days of war, 132
Nakhon Phanom
    municipality of, 272
    French planes over, 40
Nakhon Si Thammarat
    fighting with Japanese, 136
    Japanese landing in, 77
Narai, King, 7
Naresuan, King, 14
Naruebetmanit, Luang, 5
Nathan of Churt, Lord, 331–333
National Assembly, frequent conflicts in, 144
National Assistance Loan (1940), 239, 240
National Bank of Japan, 118
National Loan (1942), 239, 240

national rehabilitation, importance of stable currency, 245
Nawawichit, Luang, 5, 121
Net Khemayothin, 123, 125
Netherland East Indies,
  threat from Japan, 42
  See also Indonesia
Netherlands
  treaty with Japan, 14
  treaty with, 13
  See also Holland
neutrality, readiness to maintain, 140
New Delhi, United States forces, 186
New Order, Asia, in, 26
newsletter, Free Thai movement, 159, 160
Nishihara, General, 24
Norway
  fall of, 5
  treaty with, 13

O
O'Neal, Emmet, 187–188, 191, 195
  Ambassador to the Philippines, 192
Office of Strategic Services 147, 184, 186, 332
  discussions with in Kandy, 184–187
Okabe, Viscount, 103
Ohashi, Chuichi, 31
oil, supply to Thailand, 56
Opium War, 13
O.S.S. *See* Office of Strategic Services
Ott, General, 113

P
Pakse, 34, 40
Palace of Queen Mary, 316
Pattani, 71
  fighting with Japanese, 136
  Japanese landing in, 77
Peace Proclamation, 152
  acceptance by United States, 153

Peace Treaty of 9 May (1941), 267, 287
  call for nullification of, 279
  view of United States, 282
peace treaty of Compiegne, 5
Pearl Harbor, attack on, 73, 189
Peck, Willys R., 48, 53, 62–65, 66, 67, 68–72
Perlis, 13
  annexation by Thailand, 114
Perry, Commodore, 14
Petain, Marshal, regime of, 270
Phahitthanukon, Phra, 30, 32
Phao Siyanon, 63
Phattharawathi, Luang, 15, 161, 315
Phaulkon, Constantine, 7
  protection of English traders, 11
Phibun Songkhram, Luang, 3, 6, 19, 20, 23, 30, 39, 46, 55, 63
  announcing signing of pact with France, 25
  protest against France, 33
  resignation of, 120
Philippines
  attack by Japan, 77
  delivery of planes to, 52
Phinit-akson, Luang, 321
Phisansukhumwit, Phra, 183–202
phoi kuan, 232
Phra Men Grounds, parade of Free Thai divisions, 155
Phratabong, 135
  Thai claims on, 288
  See also Battambang
Phrae, restriction on aliens, 233
phrai som, 227, 228
Phraram Hok Bridge, repair of, 260
Phromyothi, Luang. *See* Mangkon Phromyothi
Phu Kradueng, 179
Picot, Guillaume Georges, 280, 281
Pioneer Corps, 158, 163
Poland, 5
Poona, 164, 165, 166

Portugal, 13
post-war economic cooperation, 222
post-war strategic cooperation, 222
Prachuap Khiri Khan, 71
  fighting at, 136
  Japanese landing at, 77
Praditmanutham, Luang, 3, 28. *See also* Pridi Banomyong
Praeger, Otto, 196
Prasat Thong, King, reign of, 14
Prayun Phamonmontri, 5, 64
Pridi Banomyong, 3, 140–147, 146, 205, 311
  cabinet of, 253, 254
  finance minister, 53, 75–77, 136, 141–142, 146,
  leader of Free Thai, 123, 126, 146–147, 154, 165, 178, 185
  prime minister, 253–254, 256, 259, 269, 274–276, 289, 298
  professor, 179–180
  regent, 86, 123, 142, 152, 183, 208, 214, 218, 266
  See also Praditmanutham, Luang
Prince of Wales, 142, 143
Private Schools Act, 231
public debt, types, 240
Purcell, Dr., 230

R

Radio Saigon, 23
radio station, communication with United Nations, 164–178
Rama II, King, foreign relations during reign of, 11
Rama III, King
  trade pact with England during reign of, 12
  trade relations during reign of, 229
Rama IV, King
  Bowring treaty during reign of, 8, 12
  reduction of *corvée* obligations, 228
Rama V, King
  abolition of *corvée* obligations, 228

Rama VI, King, 230, 231
  compilation of legal code during reign of, 9
  missions to Japan, 14
rate of depreciation, currency, 245
rate of exchange, Baht and Yen, 243
Rawalpindi, parachuting practice venue, 167
raw material, purchase on open market, 60
Reed, Michael, 270
Regency Council, 142, 143, 191
remittance agencies, 232
Republic of China, 230
Repulse, 142, 143
Reserve Fund, 246
resistance movement, 125
restitution and readjustment, 222
revenue and expenditure
  for the years 1937 to 1944, 238, 239
  for the year 1945, 239
Riam Wiratchaphak, Phra, 20
rice
  donation of to specified organization, 221
  export to United Kingdom, 246
  negotiations over price increase, 317–324
  procedure to increase production, 255
  shortage in Asia, 320
  smuggling of, 322
Rice Commission, 318
Riverdale Estate, Kandy, 127
Roosevelt, President, 61, 72, 73, 214
Royal Dutch Shell, 57, 58
Royal Peace Proclamation, 266
Royal Thai Air Force, 33
rubber, 51
  allocations of, 58
  demand from Japan, 60
Russia
  treaty with Japan, 14
  treaty with, 13

S

Sala Sivaraksa, 87
Samahanhitakhadi, Khun, 5
Sangwonyutthakit, Luang, 5
Sangwon Suwanchip, 125, 152, 205, 206
Sanoe Tanbunyuen, 158, 159, 160
Sargent, Sir Orme, 321
Sarityutthasin, Luang, 5
Savoy Hotel, farewell dinner at, 338, 339
Sayre, Francis Bowes, Dr. *See* Kalayanamaitra, Phraya
Scholtz, Herman F., 18, 187, 188, 190, 191, 195
scorched earth policy, 135
Security Council, 221, 301, 302
Senanarong, Luang, 180, 210
Seni Pramoj, Mom Ratchawong, 47, 62, 64, 67, 151, 154, 188, 193, 198, 202, 223
  and the Free Thai movement, 123, 157, 159
  formal treaty with Britain, 215–219, 223
  formal treaty with China, 234–235
  government of, 205–208, 215–216
  signing of Treaty of Amity, 235
  statement after becoming Prime Minister, 130
Seriroengrit, Luang, 5
Shanghai, 96
Shoguns of Japan, contact with Thai monarchs, 14
Shonanto, 144
Siam City Bank, 52
Siam Commercial Bank, 52
Siemreap, 280, 302
  seizure by France, 8, 40
Sin Kamonnawin, 134
Singapore
  bombardment by air, 137
  Japanese bombardment, 77
  Shonanto, 144
Sinsongkhramchai, Luang, 3
Sipsong Chu Thai, ceding to France, 8
Sisena Sombatsiri, Phraya, 21, 48, 66, 121, 250

Sisophon, seizure by France, 8
Sithammathibet, Chaophraya, 3
  resignation of, 5
Siwisanwacha, Phraya, 15, 247, 250, 336, 337, 339
Songkhla, 71
  fighting with Japanese, 136
  Japanese landing in, 77
Soviet Union, allied front, 49
Spain, treaty with, 13
Standard Vacuum Oil Company, 57, 58
Stanton, Edwin, 261–263, 279, 308
  book entitled *Brief Authority*, 262
  duties as Minister to Bangkok, 276
  Minister to Bangkok, 261
Suan Kulab Palace, Prime Minister's Office, 74
Subha Svasti, Mom Chao, 256, 157, 162, 163, 165, 277, 281
submarine, life in, 166
Suchit Hiranyapruek, 277, 281
Sukhumnaipradit (Pradit Sukhum), Luang, 183, 187, 191
Sun Yat-sen, 95, 230
Supreme Commander of Allied Forces, 149
Suranarong, Luang, 181
Surat Thani, Japanese landing in, 77, 137
Sweden, treaty with, 13

T

Ta Kung Pao, 234
Tarutao Island, 127
taxation, immediately after war, 248
tax collectors, 229
temporary soldier, 157
Tenasserim, annexation by England, 12
Thai Charge d'Affaires, appointment of, 87
Thai citizens, in England, 158
Thai freemen, service of patrons, 229
Thai Information Service, 194, 195
Thai law, based on *jus soli*, 230
Thai Mai, 247

Thai monetary system, after war, 248
Thai Peace Proclamation, 130
Thailand
　Chinese population in, 99, 227
　informing U.S. of situation in, 186–198, 186–200
　membership to the United Nations, 221
　obligations after World War II, 297
　promise to help Japan in war, 79
　request to join Axis Powers, 91–95
　rice producing nation, 320
　territorial demands from France, 35
Thailand-Australia exchange agreement, 226
Thailand Committee of the Asia Society in New York, 261
Thailand-French Indochina borders, 287
Thammasat University, 178, 289
Thamrongnawasawat, Luang. See Thawan Thamrongnawasawat
Tha Phae, Japanese invasion of, 136
Thawan Thamrongnawasawat, 5, 265, 279, 286, 298, 311, 312, 315
　cabinet of, 254
Thalweg line, 30
Thalweg principle, 16
Thanat Khoman, 87, 89, 92, 127, 131, 277, 308
Thawi Bunyaket, 122, 125, 133–155, 151, 151, 155, 205, 215, 230, 253
　prime minister, 207–208, 237
Thawi Tawethikun, 45, 63, 89, 92, 206–207, 210, 247
　advisor to embassy, 87
Thiam Ladanon, 87
Thomas, Wilhelm, 17
Thompson, Geoffrey, 255, 256, 260, 269–271, 273, 274, 295
tin
　allocations of, 58
　exports, 51
　mines, 59

Togo, Shigenori, 89, 96
　resignation of, 104
　view on Thailand joining Axis powers, 93
Tojo, Hideki, 72
　cutting aid to Chungking government, 136
　explanation of Greater East Asia Ministry, 108
　meeting with Phibun Songkhram, 113, 114
　Prime Minister of Japan, 108
　resignation, 120–122
Trade and Shipping Act (United States), 15
Trailokanat, King, 228
transportation system, condition after the war, 256
Treasury, 238–241
Treasury bonds, 239
treaties
　complete judicial independence for Siam, 9
　ratification, 25
　regularization of Thailand's position in regard to, 222
Treaty of Amity between Thailand and China, 235
Trengganu, 13
　annexation by Thailand, 114
tripartite agreement, 255, 262
Triple Alliance, 71, 91, 94, 139
Tsubokami, Japanese Ambassador to Thailand, 48, 70, 74, 78–79
Tua Laphanukrom, 5
Twenty-one Proposals, 214, 216, 225, 246
　See also Formal Agreement

U

United Nations, 129, 130, 221
　application to be member of, 260
　Committee on the Admission of New Members, 301
　Thailand bringing dispute before, 276
　United Nations Relief and Rehabilitative Organization, 198, 199

United States
  aid to Thailand, 67
  application for membership, 299–313
  appointment of Minister to Bangkok, 261
  arms supply to Thailand, 64
  close cooperation with, 126
  control of oil supplies, 57
  cooperation with, 56
  declaration of war against, 143
  economic aid from, 59
  forces in New Delhi, 186
  Free Thai movement in, 157
  House of Representatives, 192
  Japan declaration of war against, 70, 74
  memorandum of intentions, 285
  negotiations with, 260–263
  release of frozen Thai assets, 261
  restriction on exports to Japan, 50
  seeking concessions from, 129
  soldiers stationed at Free Thai camps, 148
  supply of airplanes, 55
  tripartite agreement with, 255
Uthai Thani, 147, 172
Uttaradit, 233

V
Vichy government, 24, 34, 265, 270, 282

W
Wang Ching-wei
  follower of Sun Yat-sen, 95
  foreign policy views, 95
  official visit to Japan, 101
Wang Ching-wei government
  diplomatic representative from, 234
  recognition of, 95–102
  Thai recognition, 90, 98, 227
Wang Nam Khao, 172
Wanwaithayakon, Prince, 16, 44–45, 120, 136, 247, 277, 278, 279, 289, 295, 308–309

Wanwaithayakon, Prince (*continued*)
  appointment as Thai representative, 309
  discussion with Russia, 304
  head of special delegation to Washington, 286–287, 301, 312
War Criminal Court, 294
  dissolution of, 295
war criminals, arrest of, 294
war graves
  Australian, 226
  upkeep of, 221
Watthana (now Watthana Nakhon District), 71
Watthananakhon, 273
World Court, 279, 280, 302
Wat Sing, 172–174
Welles, Sumner, 42
Wendler, Dr., 122
Wetchayanrangsarit, Phra, 3
White, Samuel, Governor of Mergui, 11
"White Elephants"
  capture of, 177
  entry to Thailand, 165, 167
  Free Thai from England, 165
  further training, 164, 166
Wichit Lulitanon, 178, 202, 206, 207, 247, 253, 254
Wichitwathakan, Luang, 5, 64, 91, 94, 100, 102, 143, 229
  Thai Ambassador to Japan, 78, 98, 117
Wilat Osathanon, 142, 254
Wisutwirathchathet, Luang, 336
Wiwatthanachai Chaiyan, Mom Chao, 120, 181, 216–219, 237, 248, 266–270, 282, 291
World Court, jurisdiction of, 302
World War I, 8
World War II
  chronology, 2, 82, 83
  final months, 125, 126, 129

Y
Yamada Nagamasa, 14

Yamamoto, Deputy Minister of Foreign
    Affairs Ministry (Japan), 107–108
Yamashita, General, 144
Yaowarat Road, 233
Yokohama Specie Bank, 52, 118, 242
Yugoslavia, resistance to German invasion, 54
Yunnan, 165, 167, 228